AQUINAS'S ESCHATOLOGICAL ETHICS
AND THE VIRTUE OF TEMPERANCE

MATTHEW LEVERING

Aquinas's Eschatological Ethics and the Virtue of Temperance

University of Notre Dame Press
Notre Dame, Indiana

Copyright © 2019 by the University of Notre Dame
Notre Dame, Indiana 46556
undpress.nd.edu
All Rights Reserved

Published in the United States of America

Paperback edition published in 2025

Library of Congress Cataloging-in-Publication Data

Names: Levering, Matthew, 1971– author.
Title: Aquinas's eschatological ethics and the virtue of temperance /
Matthew Levering.
Description: Notre Dame, Indiana : University of Notre Dame Press, [2019] |
Includes bibliographical references and index.
Identifiers: LCCN 2019037190 (print) | LCCN 2019037191 (ebook) |
ISBN 9780268106331 (hardback) | ISBN 9780268106348 (paperback) |
ISBN 9780268106362 (pdf) | ISBN 9780268106355 (epub)
Subjects: LCSH: Thomas, Aquinas, Saint, 1225?-1274. | Christian ethics—
Catholic authors. | Temperance (Virtue) | Eschatology—History of
doctrines—Middle Ages, 600–1500.
Classification: LCC BJ255.T5 L48 2019 (print) | LCC BJ255.T5 (ebook) |
DDC 241/.042092—dc23
LC record available at https://lccn.loc.gov/2019037190
LC ebook record available at https://lccn.loc.gov/2019037191

GPSR Compliance Inquiries:
Lightning Source France,
1 Av. Johannes Gutenberg,
78310 Maurepas, France
compliance@lightningsource.fr
Phone: +33 1 30 49 23 42

To Reinhard Hütter

CONTENTS

Acknowledgments		ix
Introduction		1
ONE	Aquinas and the Ethics of the Inaugurated Kingdom	17
TWO	Shame and *Honestas*	31
THREE	Abstinence and Sobriety	51
FOUR	Chastity	79
FIVE	Clemency and Meekness	107
SIX	Humility	129
SEVEN	Studiousness	153
Conclusion		173
Notes		181
Bibliography		359
Index		407

ACKNOWLEDGMENTS

The immediate context for this book is the assault on Christian temperance that characterizes contemporary Western culture and that threatens the life of the Church. I say this not as someone who claims to be particularly temperate, but rather as a sinner who yearns for the true life that Jesus Christ offers all people. More proximately, the book has its foundations in an S.T.L. seminar titled "Aquinas on Temperance" that I offered at Mundelein Seminary in fall 2014. I thank the students in this class, including Fr. Matthew Alexander, Jack Bates, Fr. Conor Danstrom, Fr. Edward Looney, Fr. Scott Harter, Fr. Nick Parker, Fr. Adam Droll, and Chris Smith, for helping me to conceive of the structure of this book.

In the course of writing the book, I presented two of its chapters as public lectures and received valuable feedback and corrections. I presented "Aquinas on Studiousness" as the Aquinas Lecture at Christendom College in February 2017, and I thank John Cuddeback, James DeFrancis, and Michael Hahn, among others, for their gracious hospitality. Thanks to Michael Dauphinais and Roger Nutt, I presented part of what became chapter 4 (on chastity) as "Paul and Aquinas on Lust" to a Theology Graduate Programs Master Seminar at Ave Maria University in January 2017. Earlier, in October 2016, I presented a version of this same essay in Chicago to a conference entitled "Beauty, Order, and Mystery: The Christian Vision of Sexuality," sponsored by the Center for Pastor Theologians. The essay has appeared as "Thomas Aquinas on Sexual Ethics" in *Beauty, Order, and Mystery: A Christian Vision of Human Sexuality*, ed. Gerald Hiestand and Todd Wilson

(Downers Grove, IL: InterVarsity Press, 2017), 165–80. Sadly for all Christian theologians, during the period in which this book was under preparation, my friend and editorial colleague John Webster died. I wrote the chapter on humility with him in view, and this chapter has appeared in a slightly different version as "On Humility," *International Journal of Systematic Theology* 19 (2017): 462–90 in tribute to John. I thank my editorial colleague Martin Westerholm for his suggestions for revision of the essay.

Prior to the submission of the manuscript to the University of Notre Dame Press, versions of the full draft were painstakingly read by Daniel Lendman, a doctoral student at Ave Maria University; Matthew Traylor, a master's student at Trinity Evangelical Divinity School; and Jörgen Vijgen, a longtime friend and distinguished Belgian Thomist philosopher. I wish to thank these three scholars for making countless superb suggestions for improvement. Without their help, I can't imagine having been able to push the manuscript to a publishable state. At the University of Notre Dame Press, Stephen Little took an immediate interest in this manuscript, and I thank him for his generosity and professionalism. He secured two readers, both of whom allowed their identities to be revealed and gave me important corrections and encouragement: Patrick Clark of the University of Scranton and Bill Mattison of the University of Notre Dame. I really cannot thank them enough, not least for their leadership in the field of Catholic moral theology. Since that time, Bill and I have initiated an annual Pinckaers Symposium, which thus far has twice met at the University of Notre Dame, in May 2018 and May 2019.

I thank my colleagues at Mundelein Seminary, especially my dean, Fr. Thomas Baima; my rector, Fr. John Kartje; and Dr. Melanie Barrett, whose insight into moral theology has been a great help. I thank Jim and Molly Perry for graciously making possible the chair that I hold. David Augustine, a dear friend and doctoral student at Catholic University of America, did the bibliography for this book. Bob Banning, who copyedited the book, did an amazing job, correcting numerous infelicities. My research assistant Caitlyn Trader skillfully and quickly prepared the index. I thank my parents, brother, and in-laws for their love and support, as well as the Chicago-area friends who have encouraged my work over the past few years. To my wife, Joy, you are such a wonder; may God make you "exceedingly great" (2 Chr 1:1) in his kingdom. To my children, may God bless you and assist you in the path of temperance, which is the path of human flourishing for the sake of the kingdom of God.

This book is dedicated to a truly temperate friend, Reinhard Hütter, who has written well about the virtues and who embodies them. For a number of years, he coedited with me the quarterly journal *Nova et Vetera*. Working with him was a delight, as was having him here at Mundelein Seminary in the fall of 2015 as the visiting Paluch Chair. To know him is to admire him. More than anything, Reinhard is a man of Christ's Church. Of him it may be truly said: "You have declared this day concerning the LORD that he is your God, and that you will walk in his ways, and keep his statutes and his commandments and his ordinances, and will obey his voice" (Deut 26:17).

Introduction

This book argues that Aquinas's moral theology, and indeed the broader whole of Catholic and biblical ethics, can only rightly be understood as an ethics of the inaugurated kingdom of God—an eschatological ethics. I focus on the Christian virtue of temperance. The book approaches this virtue along the lines set forth by Aquinas, but in dialogue also with numerous contemporary biblical scholars and theologians. The purpose is to show that Christian morality, while firmly rooted in the created order (here I differ from contemporary "apocalyptic" theologians[1]), is the life befitting Christ's inaugurated kingdom.

I have chosen temperance partly because it is a deeply unpopular virtue today. Many books have been written in recent decades with the goal of undermining and dislodging the component parts of Christian temperance, especially with respect to chastity. By contrast, I hope to show that chastity and the other parts of Christian temperance are inseparable from the moral life of the inaugurated kingdom, as set forth in the New Testament and as elucidated systematically in Aquinas's theology. The book is therefore a constructive defense of the Christian virtue of chastity that makes its case on the grounds of what is required by the inaugurated kingdom of God according to the New Testament.

Some moral theologians place temperance in the dustbin of pagan ethics, supposedly no longer of much interest to theology, even if philosophers continue to rifle through the dustbin every now and again. For example, the moral theologian Bernard Häring tries to settle matters by stating: "The basic virtues or character of the disciples of

Christ cannot easily be expressed by the four cardinal virtues of Hellenistic philosophy. It is, rather, the eschatological virtues that characterize the patterns of his disciples."[2] This sharp opposition, I hope to show, is mistaken. Häring's neglect of temperance causes grave problems for his theology. As the New Testament makes clear, the component parts of Christian temperance are certainly eschatological virtues.

This can be seen in the Sermon on the Mount. In the obeying of the beatitudes and commandments of the Sermon, all depends upon the life-giving power of the risen and ascended Christ and his eschatological Spirit that has been poured out. The beatitudes are not merely ideals for a spiritual elite because, now that Christ has inaugurated the kingdom, "God dwells in the hearts of those living in his grace."[3] Is it practical to expect men to go many days without looking "at a woman lustfully" (Mt 5:28)? The answer has to do with the inaugurated eschatological kingdom. When practiced as part of the fullness of life in Christ by those who recognize themselves as sinners and "invoke the help of the Holy Spirit,"[4] Christ's beatitudes and commandments show themselves to be norms for human happiness that are not only profoundly desirable but also possible for God's family.[5] The commandments have direct application to temperance. Jesus teaches, "If you would enter life, keep the commandments" (Mt 19:17);[6] and he specifies, "You shall not kill, You shall not commit adultery, You shall not steal, You shall not bear false witness, Honor your father and mother, and, You shall love your neighbor as yourself" (Mt 19:17–19). When the Spirit dwells within us, we are transformed so as to be able to follow Jesus and to live Christian temperance along with the other eschatological virtues. In the Spirit, we experience that "love is the fulfilling of the law" (Rom 13:10).

What do I mean by the inaugurated kingdom? Through his teaching and preaching, his dying on the cross for the sins of the world, his rising from the dead and ascending in glory to the Father, and his pouring out his Spirit, Jesus Christ inaugurated the kingdom of God whose coming he proclaimed during his earthly ministry and for which he prepared the Twelve. In the Spirit, then, we discover what Christ means when he says that "whoever then relaxes one of the least of these commandments and teaches men so, shall be called least in the kingdom of heaven; but he who does them and teaches them shall be called great in the kingdom of heaven. For I tell you, unless your righteousness exceeds that of the scribes and Pharisees, you will never enter the kingdom of heaven" (Mt 5:19–20). Such exceeding righteousness can only be possible because the kingdom has been inaugurated.[7] Jesus understood himself to be "proclaiming the kingdom's coming and inculcating the kingdom life."[8] Now that the kingdom has been inaugurated, as the biblical scholar Richard Hays says, "The church community is God's eschatological beachhead, the place where the power of God has invaded the world."[9] This is so despite the weakness and fallenness that still plague Christians.

Christian ethics is sometimes thought to be merely an effort to find a merciful middle ground for troubled consciences faced by exacting laws.[10] Archbishop Charles Chaput has pointed out that "legalism is very much alive in the Church" today, even if not "the rigorist, 'conservative' legalism of the past."[11] When Catholic ethicists approach morality as a set of rules that can situationally be applied more or less strictly by individual conscience, the compassionate choice may inevitably seem to be "less strictly." In such a legalistic framework, the eschatological newness of the Christian moral life has not yet been grasped.[12] After all, as the moral theologian Stanley Hauerwas emphasizes, Christian ethics properly starts with "the community already formed by the story of the kingdom of God."[13]

Thomas Aquinas defines temperance as the virtue tasked with "withholding the appetite from those things which are most seductive to man" or withdrawing "man from things which seduce the appetite from obeying reason."[14] Not surprisingly, then, temperance is a notoriously difficult virtue to live out. Christians often fail in temperance, both among the laity and, as the recent scandals involving Catholic bishops and cardinals have made all too clear, among the clergy. Temperance is difficult in all cultures, but perhaps especially so today, in a culture driven by consumerist images and understandings of food and sex.[15] For some people today, therefore, discussion of the virtue of temperance can seem to exude the stultifying aroma of puritanical or hypocritical moralism that Western media and academic elites regularly pin upon Christianity.[16] In light of this painful situation of misunderstanding, which can be an impediment to faith, the present book focuses upon retrieving Christian temperance as intrinsic to the inaugurated kingdom.

Responding to contemporary critiques of Christian temperance, the Catholic theologian R. R. Reno has offered the following thought experiment: "Imagine a contemporary American college professor who takes up St Paul's Letter to the Romans for the first time. Reading the first chapter, she is outraged by the regressive and puritanical attitude toward sexual desire. . . . She thinks, not just of Roman Catholic sexual morality, which she regards as ridiculously outmoded, but of . . . Western moral thought."[17] Reno's imagined college professor perceives that Catholic theology of temperance accords with the teachings of the New Testament, but what she misses is that the New Testament reveals the outpouring of the Holy Spirit as the source of the renewal of our created human nature and the flourishing of the covenantal family of God. In Pope Francis's words, the Gospel offers "a life of wisdom, self-fulfillment, and enrichment" through "the fragrance of Christ's closeness and his personal gaze" and in "docility to the Spirit."[18] When we possess it, Christian temperance enables us not to be "ruled by the passions" but instead to be "gripped by the attraction of beatitude."[19] The theologian David Fagerberg sums up: "To live subject to the passions is to be unnatural and less real; it is asceticism that builds up reality"—so that each person, in Christ, can progress on his or her "journey to union with the Father."[20]

Yet, if one does not perceive what Pope Francis describes as "the goodness and beauty which shine forth in a life of fidelity to the Gospel,"[21] the contents of Christian temperance may appear to be a mere amalgam of Jewish and Greco-Roman customs and prejudices. For Americans aware of the history of the Prohibition era, furthermore, the virtue of temperance may sound like a repristination of the late-nineteenth- and early-twentieth-century "temperance movement" against alcohol.[22] This temperance movement exemplified what Archbishop Chaput calls "rigorist legalism," which is always "deadly to the life of faith" since it fails to give a real place to the redemptive work of Christ and the transforming power of his Spirit.[23] If Christian temperance were simply a set of rules that fit the prejudices of the ancient

Near East or the prejudices of early-twentieth-century America, then one would be quite right to assume, as many today do, that "Catholic moral theology can be more life-affirming to the degree that it cedes territory to our unfettered freedom."[24]

Fortunately, rather than being a mere set of rules, Christian temperance flows from the Holy Spirit's enabling the believer to "control [one's] own body in holiness and honor, not in the passion of lust like heathen who do not know God" (1 Thess 4:4–5) and "to live sober [σωφρόνως, *sōphronōs*: temperate], upright, and godly lives in this world, awaiting our blessed hope, the appearing of the glory of our great God and Savior Jesus Christ" (Tit 2:12–13).[25] The biblical scholar Timothy Gombis observes that for Paul, "those who obey God in Christ can do so only because of the divine empowerment enjoyed by all those who have been united to Christ by the Spirit."[26] An important instruction in this vein is found in 2 Timothy 1:7, which states, "God did not give us a spirit of timidity but a spirit of power and love and self-control [σωφρονισμός, *sōphronismos*]." This "self-control" or temperance comes to us through "our Savior Christ Jesus" and "the Holy Spirit who dwells within us" (2 Tim 1:10, 14). The theologian Hans Urs von Balthasar therefore remarks that for Christians—who are already (even if not yet fully) "eschatological beings"—"there is no 'neutral' form of existence, which is not affected or illumined by the mystery of absolute love."[27] Indeed, indebted to Wisdom 8:7, Aquinas explains that supernatural love "teaches us to be just, prudent, and virtuous in our acts. The Wisdom of God, through the theological virtue of charity, can be said to be the *cause* of the presence in us of moral virtues."[28]

To explore why the inaugurated kingdom requires and enables Christian temperance, despite the fact that Christians still fall into intemperance, is therefore a central purpose of the present book. As the moral theologians Patricia Lamoureux and Paul Wadell comment, "To leave behind the 'blindsight' of sin and fantasy for the beatitude of seeing God, we must enter the reign of God."[29] It is in the inaugurated "reign of God" that we begin to overcome the "'blindsight' of sin" and perceive why and how the virtues associated with temperance serve the flourishing and transformation of our created humanity. Looking anew upon our lives and upon the call of Christ to repent and believe, we discover (in Reno's words) that "Christian moral demands involve a formation of and not assault upon our finite, embodied realities, a humanizing project of self-correction and even self-perfection, not an inhumane endeavour that leads to self-mutilation."[30] Temperance belongs to God's gracious and ongoing healing and elevation of his people, called to be sanctified in Christ by the Holy Spirit.

The Plan of the Work

Aquinas tells us that the virtue of temperance "directly moderates the passions of the concupiscible which tend towards good," chiefly the "desires and pleasures of touch."[31] To put the same point in somewhat less technical language: "Temperance perfects the emotions to follow the intellect" in pursuing the bodily pleasures of food, drink, and sex.[32] In enumerating the various virtues that are "parts" of temperance, however, Aquinas observes that "any virtue that is effective of moderation in some matter or other, and restrains the appetite in its impulse towards something, may be reckoned a part of temperance."[33] Thus, the parts of temperance include not only the explicitly bodily virtues of abstinence, fasting, sobriety, chastity, and virginity but also the virtues of humility, clemency, meekness, and studiousness.[34] Aquinas divides these virtues into subjective parts, integral parts, and potential parts of temperance. Romanus Cessario explains, "For each of the cardinal virtues, the scholastic theologians identified three classifications of parts. These classifications help us to organize the variety of virtues that are clustered around the cardinal virtue."[35] The terms "subjective," "integral," and "potential" come from the three kinds of wholes. Specifically, the three parts function as follows: "Like the integral parts of an organic body, there are component parts of a virtue; whatever belongs essentially to the constitution of a virtue is called an *integral part*. Like the species contained in a genus, there are the specific types of a generic virtue; these are its *subjective parts*. Like the various active powers of a living substance," finally, the "virtues accessory or allied to the principal virtue" are its "*potential parts*."[36] In identifying the virtues that are parts of temperance, Aquinas draws especially upon the work of Albert the Great and upon the thirteenth-century theologian Philip the Chancellor, along with Stoic thinkers such as Cicero and Macrobius.[37]

The chapters of the present book illumine the "parts" of Christian temperance by examining them in light of the inaugurated kingdom of God.[38] Scripturally, I emphasize three dimensions of the promised kingdom of God that Christ inaugurated. Each of these dimensions is well known in contemporary New Testament scholarship, even if they do not exhaust what can be said about the kingdom of God. For the purposes of this book, I draw them particularly from the work of the biblical scholar N. T. Wright, though I am aware that other biblical scholars often disagree with him on the details even when they agree with him about the broad dimensions that I highlight.[39] These three dimensions are the eschatological renewal of the temple, the eschatological restoration of the people of God and their reigning in the world, and the eschatological forgiveness of sins and the outpouring of the Spirit. Jesus Christ accomplishes all this by his cross, resurrection, ascension, and sending of the Spirit. In connecting these dimensions of the inaugurated kingdom of God to the virtues associated with Christian temperance, my intention is to illumine temperance rather than to draw any strict correlations between specific virtues and specific dimensions of the inaugurated kingdom.

After an introductory chapter that expounds upon the grounds for reading Aquinas's moral theology in light of the inaugurated kingdom, chapter 2 treats the integral parts shame and *honestas*, which I link with the eschatological renewal of the temple. Paul's insistence that the bodies of believers are temples of the Holy Spirit means that, in the inaugurated kingdom, shame and *honestas* belong to the renewed temple in which God dwells.[40] As Lamoureux and Wadell comment, Aquinas "illustrates that shame is connected to self-respect, to a genuine love and appreciation for one's self. . . . Shame is a very valuable quality to have because it helps restrain us from pursuing some of our more destructive tendencies by alerting us to behavior that can cost us our integrity and reputation, as well as do great harm to others."[41] In a parallel way, *honestas* refers to the spiritual beauty and integrity of the virtuous person, who has found the source of true honor.[42]

Chapter 3 treats the subjective parts abstinence, fasting, and sobriety, which I connect heuristically with the ongoing eschatological restoration of God's people as the family of God. I make this connection in light of the biblical scholar Karl Olav Sandnes's study of Paul's condemnations of the fallen human tendency to make an idol of our own belly and body. Chapter 4 treats the final subjective part, sexual chastity, again drawing a link to the restoration of God's people and their reigning in the world. In light of the approaches of N. T. Wright and Margaret Farley, I argue that Aquinas develops a family-centered understanding of chastity that accords with the New Testament's authoritative teachings on sexual ethics and that appreciates the ways in which (in the philosopher Mary Keys's words) "moral virtue is at the nexus point of personal and common goods."[43]

The final three chapters show how the eschatological forgiveness of sins and outpouring of the Spirit fuel the potential parts of Christian temperance, namely those virtues that moderate our desire for nonbodily human goods. Chapter 5 shows that due to the forgiveness of sins and outpouring of the Spirit, Christ's true followers will be clement and meek rather than irrationally vengeful and angry. Chapter 6 treats humility, as opposed to the pride displayed by Adam and Eve. Indebted to the theologian John Webster, I argue that what is at stake is a proper understanding of creatureliness, in which our need for the forgiveness of sins and the outpouring of the Spirit becomes apparent. Chapter 7 treats studiousness. Indebted to the theologian Paul Griffiths, I explain that studiousness involves retraining our desire to know, so that we desire not a mere self-centered mastery of the things that we know, but rather a God-centered participatory intimacy with reality, rooted in wonder and praise.[44]

The Primacy of the Holy Spirit

The theologian Reinhard Hütter has observed that Aquinas insists upon "the primacy of the Holy Spirit . . . in the Christian life."[45] At the same time, as Hütter makes clear, Aquinas holds that created human reason, even in its fallen state, can know much about human nature and human flourishing, not least through natural law. It follows that the insights of pagan philosophers and the lessons of everyday experience with respect to our creaturely flourishing belong integrally to the study of Christian temperance. Rationally, we know that people who are shameless, gluttonous, lustful, irrationally angry, cruel, proud, and desirous for knowledge-as-domination may succeed in becoming rich and powerful, but such people cannot truly love others or relate well to others. When we are shameless, gluttonous, lustful, irrationally angry, cruel, proud, and desirous for knowledge-as-domination—when we are intemperate—our humanity is deformed and our families and societies suffer. In this light, Lamoureux and Wadell rightly remark that "temperance reflects a very honest and realistic assessment of our human nature. It counsels us to be honest about our weaknesses, honest about areas in our lives with which we continually struggle, and honest about how certain desires can be pursued in patently destructive ways."[46]

Christian temperance, then, is for Aquinas at one and the same time a reality of the inaugurated kingdom (intelligible to faith) and a wisdom about human flourishing (to some degree intelligible to fallen reason). This Thomistic perspective on the new creation in Christ fits with the approach found authoritatively in the New Testament. The biblical scholars Grant Macaskill and Jonathan Pennington have shown that in the New Testament, the wisdom traditions' reason-centered teachings on human flourishing and virtue are united with faith-centered "apocalyptic and eschatological traditions" and their "future-oriented eschatological hope."[47] With regard to the New Testament's eschatologically inflected portrait of human wisdom, Pennington observes: "It is precisely in the eschaton that the ultimate human flourishing will occur, as this can only come about when God restores his reign of justice, peace, and rest. This central biblical vision and idea is precisely the backdrop for the Beatitudes . . . : Jesus is offering a vision for a way of being in the world that will result in true flourishing."[48] Faith and reason, nature and grace, creation and eschatological restoration are all needed for Christian temperance to be understood and lived.

Although Aquinas does not explicitly mention the inaugurated kingdom in his treatise on temperance, in Aquinas's theology of temperance we find what Pennington (describing the Sermon on the Mount) calls "an eschatological wisdom teaching on virtue."[49] By inaugurating his kingdom, Jesus offers us the true peace that—so Aquinas observes—is found only "where the appetite is directed to what is truly good."[50] After the fall, the appetite tends toward lesser goods. Its restoration happens through the work of Christ and the Spirit. For this reason, as the theologian Bernard McGinn observes, in the *secunda-secundae pars* of the *Summa theologiae* (the part that includes the treatise on temperance) Aquinas "is targeting acts *insofar as they are salvific*, that is, those that proceed from grace as their primary cause, though also involving the human will as cooperating with God."[51]

An approach similar to mine has recently been advanced by the moral theologian William Mattison in his *The Sermon on the Mount and Moral Theology*, which draws together Aquinas's virtue ethics and the Sermon on the Mount. Mattison does not employ my book's heuristic device of correlating the virtues associated with temperance to the major elements of the inaugurated kingdom awaited by Israel. But he makes explicit the profound connections between Thomistic virtue ethics and the eschatological Sermon. He contends that "the convergence between the Sermon and the virtues" should enable us to perceive "a deeper wisdom about the beauty of Scripture and the way it draws us into contemplation of and relationship with the Author of Scripture who is Author of all."[52]

Among the topics that Aquinas includes in his theology of temperance, I do not discuss continence (which is not technically a virtue, though it serves to resist strong inappropriate desires) or modesty in outward movements and in dress.[53] Other than these exceptions, after a first chapter on the place of biblical reasoning and the grace of the Holy Spirit in Aquinas's moral theology, my chapters follow the order and content of Aquinas's treatise on temperance in the *Summa theologiae*. Throughout the book, I have in view the infused (specifically Christian) moral virtue of temperance. The infused moral virtues, however, are not intelligible without knowledge of human nature and of the acquired moral virtues, and so my book also has relevance for appreciating the acquired virtue of temperance.[54] As the theologian Frederick Christian Bauerschmidt states, "The way of life of the Christian must conform itself to the truth revealed in creation and redemption in order for it to be a training of a new humanity."[55]

A Pedagogy for Sinners

The importance of the virtue of temperance for vibrant Christian life should be evident, but it can be underlined by observing the place of temperance in God's pedagogy of his people.[56] In giving Israel the Decalogue, with its commandments against adultery and lust, God is aware that Israel—and all of humanity—suffers from a captivity to sin, a captivity from which God in Christ wills to rescue both Israel and the nations.[57] Now that the kingdom has been inaugurated by Christ and he has poured out the Spirit so that we can obey God's law of love, we can be confident that God will "cleanse us from all unrighteousness" (1 Jn 1:9) and that "every one who thus hopes in him [Christ] purifies himself as he is pure" (1 Jn 3:3).

Nonetheless, as is all too evident, Christians remain deeply prone to the various vices that undermine and destroy temperance. The Letter to the Hebrews therefore exhorts believers, "Lift your drooping hands and strengthen your weak knees, and make straight paths for your feet," and, "Strive . . . for the holiness without which no one will see the Lord" (Heb 12:12–14). But if the kingdom of God has been inaugurated and the Spirit poured out, why do its effects often seem so weak in us? The answer consists in the ongoing effects of original and personal sin, even after such sin has been forgiven. Put simply, believers can advance toward perfection, but believers can also easily fall back into intemperance, because the sanctifying grace of the Holy Spirit does not remove the weakness and sinful inclinations that are the effects of our prior sinful actions and of the lingering consequences of original sin.[58] The infusion of virtues does not mean that they are fully formed (or even properly received). Failure happens especially when we grow in pride and imagine that we can govern our passions without actively seeking God's gracious help.

The healing and elevation of our fallen nature constitutes "the mystery of the Kingdom of God" that Christ inaugurates, the mystery that is already fully present in Christ himself and in which we participate through the Spirit.[59] Despite our ongoing proneness to fall into intemperance, Christ's inauguration of his kingdom in the power of the Holy Spirit means that Christ, who is "the expiation for our sins" (1 Jn 2:2), truly offers us the ability to "keep his commandments" (1 Jn 2:3), even if we continue to fall and need continual conversion.[60] It is our need for the eschatological Spirit that Aquinas recognizes when he places his account of human nature and action within what John Webster calls a "Christological-eschatological frame."[61] As David Fagerberg puts it, we are truly called to "become the sacrificial city of God in our bodies."[62]

Christian Temperance and Greco-Roman Philosophy

It will be evident that Aquinas's understanding of Christian temperance has significant debts to Greco-Roman philosophical insights. When in faith one knows that God has inaugurated his eschatological kingdom, however, why should one bother any further with pagan thought? N. T. Wright sharply warns against such a viewpoint. He observes that in 1 Corinthians 13 and other similar texts, "What Paul is arguing for is a Christian form of the ancient pagan theory of virtue."[63] This does not mean that by comparison with Paul, the pagan philosophers are equally inspired or equally authoritative teachers for Christians. To suppose this would be to miss the point of the eschatological victory accomplished by Jesus Christ. But Wright correctly perceives that "if there is *no* overlap, *no* point of contact, then we are in a closed world."[64] As Wright asks rhetorically, "If we claim that Christian faith produces genuine humanness, must there not be many areas of massive overlap on which we can work toward agreement?"[65] In accord with this view, Aquinas's moral theology includes an account of human nature and action drawn constructively from numerous Greco-Roman philosophers.[66] As background to Aquinas's theology of temperance, therefore, let me here very briefly set forth some of the contributions of three particularly influential philosophers—Plato, Aristotle, and Cicero—to the elaboration of the virtue of temperance.[67]

In his *Republic*, Plato argues that humans have the ability to attain virtue and wisdom, but instead many people spend their lives entirely in the pursuit of material goods and pleasures: "With eyes ever bent upon the earth and heads bowed down over their tables they feast like cattle, grazing and copulating, ever greedy for more of these delights."[68] Plato is not here rejecting physical pleasures. On the contrary, he argues that "when the entire soul accepts the guidance of the wisdom-loving part," then the part of the soul that enjoys physical pleasures will be able to enjoy such pleasures in a virtuous manner.[69] But rationality must govern the pursuit and enjoyment of physical pleasure.

In this regard, Plato contrasts nobility with disgrace, noting that the latter follows from reason's being dominated by animal lust, whereas the former gives reason "complete domination over the entire man."[70] Plato (or Socrates) concludes this discussion by singing the praises of temperance—a "soberness of spirit"—on the grounds that only in this way can humans avoid handing their lives over to "brutish and irrational pleasure," which earlier has been described as "the pleasures of food, drink, and the rest."[71] Temperance orders and controls these desires, enabling the person to live according to what is higher rather than according to what is lower. The higher dimensions of the soul take up the lower desires, rather than negating such desires.[72]

In *Nicomachean Ethics*, Aristotle argues that temperance, as distinct from mere self-restraint or continence, not only restrains or dominates desires but actually ensures that we do not "have excessive or evil desires."[73] Our passions themselves become the subject of a virtue. Aristotle defines temperance as "the observance of the mean in relation to pleasures," and he contrasts temperance with profligacy.[74] He focuses on the pleasures of touch, specifically eating, drinking, and sex. Arguing that "it is bestial to revel in such pleasures, and to like them better than any others," he observes that overeaters are called "mad-bellies," whereas temperance ensures that the appetite is in harmony with reason, with the result that the temperate person "desires the right thing in the right way at the right time."[75] For Aristotle, as the philosopher Robert Roberts says, the virtue of temperance (or *sōphrosynē*) "belongs to an irrational part of the soul" that "is also rational" in the sense that it has an ability to obey reason."[76] Our concupiscible passions or desires can be guided by reason and themselves become virtuously reasonable.

Lastly, in *De officiis*, Cicero remarks that "man is the only animal that has a feeling for order, for propriety, for moderation in word and deed."[77] Cicero then compares our sense for external beauty with our sense for interior beauty: "No other animal has a sense of beauty, loveliness, harmony in the visible world; and Nature and Reason, extending the analogy of this from the world of sense to the world of spirit, find that beauty, consistency, order are far more to be maintained in thought and deed."[78] He concludes that thought and action characterized by beauty, consistency, and order establish "moral goodness" (*honestum*).[79] Observing that such moral goodness involves the four virtues of prudence, justice, courage, and temperance, he explains that temperance conserves "honestatem et decus" (beauty and grace), and he praises its contribution to "honestinaturam" (the beauty or moral goodness of human nature).[80]

For Cicero, all four cardinal virtues are needed for "moral goodness" (*honestum*).[81] But he notes that temperance belongs in a fundamental way to the distinction between humans and other animals, since other animals "have no thought except for sensual pleasure and this they are impelled by every instinct to seek; but man's mind is nurtured by study and meditation."[82] Since we are not mere animals, our "physical comforts and wants, therefore, should be ordered according to the demands of health and strength, not according to the call of pleasure."[83]

Hans Urs von Balthasar has pointed out that these four cardinal virtues can and should be taken up by Christian ethics, but not in a way that conceals the "folly" and "stumbling block" of the cross at the heart of the inaugurated kingdom (1 Cor 1:23). In this sense, Christian temperance will inevitably seem to be "foolishness" to those who rely upon "the wisdom of the world" (1 Cor 1:20, 25). Von Balthasar emphasizes that the cardinal virtues should not "be violated by Christianity, but rather elevated and thereby perfected. But they must be perfected in such a way that all four dimensions of virtue . . . are measured by a standard of judgment that lies beyond what can be achieved or even understood on the basis of the virtues themselves, and so which must appear 'foolish.'"[84] The measuring stick for the Christian cardinal virtues is human nature healed and perfected by the cross and resurrection of Jesus. Even so, it remains the case that "grace does not destroy nature, but perfects it."[85] Christian temperance involves a great deal that even fallen reason can understand, and it never contradicts rightly functioning reason. Aquinas gladly grants that there were pagans who, by comparison to many Christians, were "more devoted to leading a temperate life in the face of temptation."[86]

Temperance has sometimes been misunderstood as a lack of passion and as a diminishment of the human person. In fact, Christian temperance heals and perfects the *vitality* of human passionate life. As the theologian Albert Plé remarks, "For the virtue of temperance to exist, it is necessary not only for reason but also for the passion to be exercised freely and strongly."[87] Temperance exercises a moderating and chastising influence upon passions in the sense that, for fallen humans, the passions (such as anger[88]) tend otherwise to dominate a person's life, rather than being guided by reason. Plé comments that "in man, because of the unity of the person, it is of the nature of passions to call for the moderation of reason. This moderation, when perfect, is nothing else than an internal and dynamic modification of the passions which makes them participate of themselves in the reasonable order of the powers which are superior to them."[89] Andrew Pinsent observes in a similar vein that when we moderate our desires through the Christian virtue of temperance, "we mortify ourselves not to be empty, but to be filled superabundantly with a new life, fruitful in the Spirit."[90]

Without losing their vitality, therefore, temperate passions do not exceed rational bounds or lead the person to act in an irrational and destructive way, as unruly passions such as anger and lust too often do.[91] Aquinas's understanding of human nature involves a hylomorphic unity of body and soul, and thus of intimately united material and immaterial elements.[92] It follows that the temperate Christian enjoys wisely ordered rational and sense desires. This is the effect of the eschatological presence in the Christian of the healing and transformative Spirit. Summing up Aquinas's theology of the Christian life, the theologian Réginald Garrigou-Lagrange remarks, "Fundamentally, the same divine life exists as a germ or a seed in the Christian on earth and as a fully developed life in the saints in heaven," in accord with Jesus' teaching that "the kingdom of God is in the midst of you" (Lk 17:21).[93]

※ ※ ※

The psalmist proclaims, "I know my transgressions, and my sin is ever before me," and the psalmist begs for "a clean heart" and "a new and right spirit" (Ps 51:3, 10). The infused virtue of Christian temperance comes from "the redemption which is in Christ Jesus" (Rom 3:24), through whom "we have obtained access to this grace in which we stand" (Rom 5:2). In Christ's inaugurated kingdom, however, "we all make many mistakes" (Js 3:2), and we depend at all times upon the mercy of Christ.[94] This book is not an exercise in moral triumphalism. Although Christian ethics is rooted in the eschatological outpouring of the Spirit, it is so not least because we continue to need the Spirit's healing.

As redeemed and repentant sinners to whom Christ has given his Spirit, we know that intemperance is never far away. We have mercy upon our fellow sinners because we have been there too. Yet we know that true flourishing, both now and everlastingly, requires temperance. With renewed dependence upon the Spirit's gifting, let us "put away all filthiness and rank growth of wickedness and receive with meekness the implanted word," which has the power of salvation (Js 1:21). Let us even now follow the apostle Paul's injunction: "Do not yield your members to sin as instruments of wickedness, but yield yourselves to God as men who have been brought from death to life, and your members to God as instruments of righteousness" (Rom 6:13).

CHAPTER ONE

Aquinas and the Ethics of the Inaugurated Kingdom

In fruitful ways, many scholars have studied Aquinas's ethics without any explicit reference to its Christian context. For example, consider the moral theologian Herbert McCabe's *The Good Life: Ethics and the Pursuit of Happiness*, a collection of essays that argues persuasively for Aquinas's understanding of the human being and that does so almost exclusively in philosophical terms.[1] But the eschatological character of Aquinas's ethics—that is to say, its location within the inaugurated kingdom of Christ, marked by the indwelling Spirit—is nonetheless at the core of Aquinas's moral theology. As the philosophers Rebecca Konyndyk DeYoung, Colleen McCluskey, and Christina Van Dyke remark, "His Christian commitments infuse his moral thought, not only in its structure but in its very substance."[2]

Even so, Aquinas's theology of temperance has much to teach anyone, Christian or non-Christian, who is attentive to the needs and dynamisms of the human being. Aquinas deeply appreciates the intelligible structures of the created order, including the capacities and dynamisms of human nature. Diana Fritz Cates points out in this regard that "the rational and faithful ordering of human appetites is, in one form or another, as much a question for the modern reader as it was for people in Thomas's day. Innumerable human beings suffer directly and indirectly from painful, crippling, and even deadly addictions to food, alcohol, and dehumanizing sexual activities" as well as "other forms of desperate grasping."[3] Cates astutely observes that Aquinas seeks "to encourage readers to form better habits of being moved so that one can consistently experience the pull of desire in ways that contribute to, rather than diminish, the enjoyment of a decent human life."[4] But Cates also makes clear that for Aquinas, "a decent human life" has an eschatological horizon. Every human life has as its proper goal the consummated kingdom of God, and God even now offers every human being a share in the inaugurated kingdom. Thus, Cates comments that "reason and divine law require that persons desire, use, and enjoy" appetible things "in ways that protect and enhance the quality of human life and community under the reign of God."[5]

With respect to the "reign of God," Aquinas famously begins the second part of his *Summa theologiae*—the part devoted to ethics—with an analysis of beatitude. Indebted to Augustine, he finds that only the beatific vision of God can make humans happy. He therefore understands the beatitudes of the Sermon on the Mount in light of "subsistent Beatitude, the holy Trinity," who "communicates, in a participated mode, his own proper beatitude to spiritual creatures."[6] Rowan Williams's contention that "the heart of discipleship is bound up with the life of the Trinity" accords firmly with Aquinas's approach.[7] Aquinas gives much more attention than do most modern theologians to spelling out the constitutive elements of created human nature, while at the same time Aquinas's moral theology bears a richly Trinitarian imprint.[8]

The word "eschatological" evokes the last things, the final consummation that God will bring about when Christ comes to judge and renew the whole creation (may it happen soon!). But "eschatological" means more than this. Now that Christ has inaugurated his kingdom and poured out the Spirit upon his people, the "eschatological" age is already present in and through the Church of the Holy Spirit. Indeed, the kingdom is found in Christ himself. Believers look forward to the glorious day when Christ will come to consummate his kingdom and to incorporate all of his members "in every way into him who is the head" (Eph 4:15). As the "body of Christ" being built up by the Holy

Spirit, the Church on earth is the inaugurated kingdom, striving in repentance, faith, charity, and temperance (among other virtues) toward the fullness of "the kingdom of Christ and of God" (Eph 5:5).[9] *Pace* the Franciscan friar Joachim of Fiore, Aquinas recognizes that the age of the Holy Spirit is now.[10] Even in the midst of the world of sin, suffering, and death, we are already caught up in Christ's Spirit-filled "body, the church" (Col 1:18).

The purpose of this chapter is to build upon themes that the introduction of the book began to explore. I will proceed in three steps. First, using the work of N. T. Wright—who will remain an interlocutor throughout the book—I set forth the basic elements of Christ's inauguration of the kingdom and its consequences for temperate Christian living.[11] Second, drawing especially upon the work of Servais Pinckaers, I indicate how the scriptural world, with its proclamation of the new creation in Christ and the Spirit, undergirds Aquinas's moral theology. Third, I explore our graced transformation in Christ, despite our failures and sins. It is necessary to perceive that Christian temperance does not merely make us respectable citizens of earthly society, but rather pertains intrinsically to the ways in which "we are drawn by God into a life of beatitude."[12]

Christ's Inauguration of the Kingdom and the Virtue of Temperance: N. T. Wright's Perspective

In *Paul and the Faithfulness of God*, N. T. Wright describes the "Israel-shaped vocation" of the messianic community.[13] Wright makes three points about the Second Temple expectations of many Israelites. First, "Israel was called to be the people in whom . . . the life held out by Torah would become a reality—both in the sense of the 'life' of glad, loving obedience and the 'life' promised to Torah-keepers."[14] The eschatological forgiveness of sins and outpouring of the Spirit answers to this expectation. Second, "Israel was the people in whose midst the living God had deigned to dwell."[15] The eschatological renewal of the temple answers to this expectation. Third, "Israel was to be the people who inherited YHWH's sovereign rule over the world."[16] The eschatological restoration of God's people answers to this expectation. Paul believed that these things were now coming true through the crucified and risen Messiah and through the people the Messiah had gathered around himself by his cross, resurrection, ascension, and outpouring of the Spirit.

Wright explains that according to Paul, "in the Messiah Jesus, God has launched his project of bringing the human race together into a new unity."[17] God is accomplishing a "new Exodus" by which "the spirit enables all who are justified by faith to live as the biblical people of God" and "to *love* the one God from the heart."[18] The result is "the creation of the new-covenant people," who on their new exodus journey are "the new tabernacle" led by the indwelling Spirit.[19] Renewed temple, restored people, and fulfilled Torah (through the outpouring of the Spirit) all come together here. Paul insists, Wright says, that the "*Messiah-people do in fact keep Torah*," through "*a fuller range of ethical behaviour as a new form of Torah-keeping*. The spirit produces *agapē*, and this *agapē* is the fulfilling of the Torah."[20] Again, Paul holds that the inaugurated eschatological kingdom has three primary characteristics: the temple is being renewed (since God now dwells in his people), the people are being restored (through the ingathering of Jews and Gentiles in one family under Christ the King), and the Torah is being fulfilled (through the forgiveness of sins and the outpouring of the Spirit).

Wright holds that the original (and eschatological) purpose for which God created human beings consists in "'image-bearing,' reflecting the Creator's wise stewardship into the world and reflecting the praises of all creation back to its maker. Those who do so are the 'royal priesthood.'"[21] Sin, therefore, is more than doing bad things that go against God's commandments; it is breaking the "covenant of vocation" that we have received from God.[22] It follows that to claim that Jesus Christ has inaugurated his kingdom is to claim that "*a new way of being human* has been launched."[23] The risen Christ calls upon Christians to announce his victory over sin and death, by living it out in holiness and by celebrating it in the eucharistic liturgy. As sharers in the inaugurated kingdom through the grace of the Holy Spirit, Christians must conquer the idols of the world that still threaten to master us, including idolatrous power, money, and sex. Christians must make manifest, by our actions, that our bodies are the "temple of the Holy Spirit" (1 Cor 6:19).

Wright emphasizes that in a world marred by an explosion of sexual exploitation of children, sex trafficking, and the like, Christians must exhibit the restoration of God's holy people by practicing "marriage, virginity, abstinence, and self-control."[24] The widespread use of internet-channeled pornography has been strongly correlated with depression, intimacy problems and sexual dysfunction, lack of satisfaction with one's spouse or partner, and divorce.[25] As Wright observes, Christians must help the world to see that humans are not "defined by whatever longings and aspirations come out of our hearts," since in fact such longings are often fallen and defiling.[26] Through the forgiveness of sins and the outpouring of the Spirit, Christians have received the vocation to be royal priests of the inaugurated kingdom. When Christians fail in holiness (as Wright recognizes that we often do), the whole world suffers through our distortion of what Wright calls "the new play, the great drama in which the royal priesthood takes up its new duties," at the heart of which is true worship of the true God as the temple of Christ's body, filled with the Spirit.[27]

Scripture and Aquinas's Ethics

The Second Vatican Council's Dogmatic Constitution on Divine Revelation, *Dei Verbum*, urges that "the 'study of the sacred page' should be the very soul of sacred theology."[28] Likewise, the Council's Decree on Priestly Training, *Optatam Totius*, states, "Students should receive a most careful training in holy Scripture, which should be the soul, as it were, of all theology."[29] After urging that dogmatic theology be rooted in scripture and the fathers and be illumined scientifically with the aid of Thomas Aquinas, *Optatam Totius* has this to say: "In like manner the other theological subjects should be renewed through a more vivid contact with the Mystery of Christ and the history of salvation. Special care should be given to the perfecting of moral theology. Its scientific presentation should draw more fully on the teaching of holy Scripture and should throw light upon the exalted vocation of the faithful in Christ."[30]

Does Aquinas's "scientific presentation" of moral theology draw deeply upon Scripture? As evidence of Aquinas's biblical richness, it is noteworthy that in the *secunda pars*—the part of the *Summa theologiae* devoted to ethics—Aquinas quotes from more than half of all the chapters of the Old Testament alone, and from forty-three of its forty-six books.[31] Jean-Pierre Torrell rightly observes, "Far ahead of all other sources, philosophical or theological, the Word of God [scripture] remains for Thomas the Word of life, and he finds in it his primary inspiration and standard."[32]

Servais Pinckaers is the contemporary master of Aquinas's use of Scripture in moral theology. His *The Sources of Christian Ethics* begins with the passage from *Optatam Totius* that, as noted above, requires moral theology to "draw more fully on the teaching of holy Scripture." Strongly supporting this goal, Pinckaers states that "the chief task for today's moral theologians is to reopen the lines of communication between Christian ethics and the Word of God."[33] But as he points out repeatedly, simply to quote Scripture frequently, let alone simply to read the work of biblical scholars, cannot suffice for the renewal of moral theology. Instead, the theologian must penetrate to the heart of the moral life as revealed in Scripture. What is this heart? Pinckaers identifies it as our transformation by the Holy Spirit through faith in Christ.

According to Pinckaers, Paul "did not reject the desire for justice and wisdom but gave them a new source: no longer human virtue, but what might be called the virtue of God acting through Jesus Christ."[34] For Paul, Christian morality goes to the root of pride and replaces it with the humility of faith in the humble Lord and with docility to the Holy Spirit. Christian morality centers upon "personal union with Christ through faith and love," and "faith delivers us from the secret despair born of the knowledge of our weakness and faults" and "wins for us the gracious strength of the Spirit."[35] Thus, faith is not an abstract knowing but rather is "an active, operative, practical virtue" that, in baptism, incorporates us into Christ and makes us a new creation.[36] Paul's insistence upon the centrality of humility and chastity flows from his understanding of union with Christ, as does his emphasis on joy and peace.[37]

Pinckaers gives special attention to the Sermon on the Mount. He contrasts Albert Schweitzer's view that the Sermon is an impossible "interim legislation" with Augustine's placement of the Sermon—the Beatitudes—at the center of the Christian moral life.[38] Augustine connects the Sermon with Paul's view of life in the Spirit. Aquinas follows Augustine's path, not only in his understanding of the New Law of the Holy Spirit but also in his identification of beatitude as the goal of Christian life and in his connection of the Sermon's beatitudes with the virtues and with the gifts of the Holy Spirit enumerated in Isaiah 11.[39] For Aquinas, as for Augustine, "the Beatitudes are Christ's answer to the question of happiness and thus, together with the whole Sermon on the Mount, dominate Christian ethics."[40] Aquinas links temperance specifically with the gift of the Holy Spirit called the fear of the Lord.[41] This fear is not a cringing fear, rooted in lack of charity, but rather presupposes charity and enables our "withdrawal from certain things through reverence for God."[42] As Aquinas observes, "whoever has charity has all the gifts of the Holy Spirit, none of which can one possess without charity."[43]

For Pinckaers, the renewal of moral theology in accord with the intention of Vatican II means returning to the perspective of Augustine and Aquinas, precisely in "going back to the actual Word of God, the Gospel text inspired by the Holy Spirit in faith."[44] He urges us to reclaim the Sermon's starting point, eschatological happiness, as well as the Sermon's interior deepening of the precepts of the Decalogue and the way in which the Sermon brings together catechesis and theology. We need the full dimensions of the gospel, which include not only hope and longing for happiness and justice but also the testing of faith in the encounter with God.[45] To be attuned to this dynamic requires understanding that, as Jonathan Pennington observes, the message of the Sermon on the Mount "is born of two intersecting worlds, Second Temple Judaism and the Greco-Roman virtue tradition."[46] These worlds likewise intersect in Aquinas, through the combination of the New Testament and the writings of the pagan philosophers. In words that could apply to Aquinas's moral theology, Pennington remarks that in the Sermon we "find an eschatological, Christ-centered, kingdom-oriented piece of wisdom literature with roots in the Jewish Scriptures that invites hearers into human flourishing through faith-based virtue."[47]

In the inaugurated kingdom that Christ proclaims and Pentecost confirms, the eschatological dimension of the moral life is central. In this context, Aquinas connects the scriptural commandments and exhortations with a revised framework of pagan virtue ethics. Put simply, he works out the premises of the Sermon on the Mount. His moral theology is biblical and eschatological, and the divinely infused virtues, beginning with faith and including the infused moral virtue of temperance, stand at the center of his approach.[48] The gifts of the Holy Spirit are also central in this eschatological ethics. Yves Congar observes that Aquinas "makes room here for the *event* of the Holy Spirit," since "only God, in person, can give divine fullness to the exercise of the theological virtues, and only God can perfect the action of a child of God."[49] At the same time, God's grace makes us a "new creation" (Gal 6:15), rather than grace remaining merely extrinsic to our human capacities.[50]

Thus, charity does not play the role of directing otherwise autonomous natural moral virtues. As the moral theologian Jean Porter explains, for Aquinas "grace must be expressed directly through virtues appropriate to every faculty of the soul, which is to say, through infused versions of all the cardinal virtues."[51] In order to partake supernaturally in the divine life with our whole selves, Christians need the infused moral virtue of temperance and its associated gift of the Holy Spirit. Indeed, Aquinas notes that this gift of the Spirit—fear of the Lord—constitutes "the foundation . . . of the perfection of the other gifts, for 'the fear of the Lord is the beginning of wisdom' (Ps 111:10)."[52]

Transformation in Christ and the Weakness of Christians

The power of the New Law is the Spirit of Christ.[53] This emphasis on Christ and the Spirit, however, does not undermine the ways in which

Aquinas's moral theology depends upon truths about human nature and action identified by the Greco-Roman philosophers. Commitment to the transformative work of Christ and the Spirit upon fallen human nature goes hand in hand with recognizing that "moral theology requires a sound philosophical vision of human nature and society as well as of the general principles of ethical decision making."[54] Without an adequate account of human nature and its flourishing, governed by Scripture and drawing upon philosophical wisdom, it would be impossible to appreciate grace's healing and elevation of human nature.[55]

Christian norms regarding eating, drinking, sex, meekness, clemency, humility, and studiousness pertain to the transformation of fallen human nature that Christ has accomplished through his cross, resurrection, ascension, and pouring out of the Holy Spirit.[56] The virtues associated with temperance are not mere ideals that only an elite can be expected to attain, let alone a rule book that allows some Christians to lord it over others. Christ has in fact enabled all of us to live in this way through his Spirit, who renews, restores, and heals our fallen human nature.[57] As Robert Roberts states from a philosophical perspective, "Temperance is an important virtue because food, drink, and sex, if desired improperly, can be sources of disruption, corruption, misery, and ill being both to the intemperate or weak-willed person and to others in his or her social world; but if properly loved and pursued, they can be sources of joy and wellbeing."[58] This is even more the case when it comes to life in Christ.

Nonetheless, as noted above, it is evident that Christians often fail to live temperately, and private and public failures in temperance are painfully common among Christians. Sometimes this occurs through incontinence, in which we fail to resist the impulse of strong passions due to weakness.[59] Most seriously, those who bear the name Christian sometimes abandon temperance entirely; our will becomes habituated to choose (as good) a particular sinful action that separates us from Christ.[60] The answer to such failure is not to give up. Recommitting ourselves in repentance to the mercy of Christ, we should beg for and trust in the transformative power of Christ's grace for those who heed his call to "repent, and believe in the gospel" (Mk 1:15). Given our failures, the biblical scholar David deSilva describes the Church as "a sort of 'sinners anonymous'" in which none of us should conceal "the truth of our fallenness."[61] At the same time, as the biblical scholar John Barclay remarks, "Paul certainly expects that the *moral* incongruity at the start of the Christian life will be reduced over time, as the believers' slavery to righteousness draws them toward holiness."[62]

When we face moral failure, we need to be met with help from our fellow Christians that, as Pope Francis urges, is "sympathetic, realistic [and] concerned for individual cases."[63] We do not need mere condemnation. Even so, when we struggle with sins of intemperance, we have to be willing to hear the truth about our actions. Rather than defending our actions or retreating into a privatized conscience that functions as a de facto barricade to Christian moral teachings, we need to be open to healing grace and ask God to free us from intemperance. Together with those who love us, we must implore the grace of the Holy Spirit to accomplish anew "the restoration of God's image in us."[64] In *Evangelii Gaudium*, Pope Francis emphasizes that the work of "spiritual accompaniment must lead others ever closer to God, in whom we attain true freedom. . . . To accompany them would be counterproductive if it became a sort of therapy supporting their self-absorption and ceased to be a pilgrimage with Christ to the Father."[65] In such spiritual accompaniment, we do not assume the role of the guide; Christ is the guide, and we must conform our counsel to the word of Christ, who insists, "If you love me, you will keep my commandments" (Jn 14:15).

The Christian virtue of temperance belongs to God's plan for drawing us in Christ "into the abundant, Spirit-saturated life of *shalom* that characterizes the new creation."[66] The virtues associated with temperance are *social* virtues, fostering the happiness of the human being who "is by nature a political animal," created to live and flourish in the society of others.[67] For well-functioning families and communities—and for the flourishing of the inaugurated kingdom on its path to the consummation of all things—we need these virtues. They are what Rabbi Jonathan Sacks calls virtues of "character"; and, as he emphasizes, "Character is not marginal to the ethical life but of its essence."[68] Stanley Hauerwas makes this point in his *A Community of Character*, which, in its discussion of family and sex, critiques precisely the assumption "that such issues are purely private."[69] As Hauerwas pointedly says, "Nothing ... could be further from the truth."[70]

The transformative perfecting of our concupiscible appetites comes about through grace. Citing 1 Peter 1:4, Aquinas underscores that grace is a real "participation of the divine nature," and grace is always christologically grounded: Jesus "causes our salvation by grace."[71] United to Christ, believers receive the Spirit that he poured out upon the disciples at Pentecost. Christian temperance depends upon the reality that "the Holy Spirit is possessed by man, and dwells within him, in the very gift itself of sanctifying grace."[72] Understandably, as Gilles Emery has remarked, "readers of the *Summa* do not always perceive there the significance of the teaching on the Holy Spirit," because the method and structure of the *Summa theologiae* can prevent readers from appreciating how the doctrine of the Holy Spirit flows into Christology, the sacraments, and moral theology.[73] In the *secunda pars*, Aquinas explores how God is acting to draw human beings to everlasting beatitude by his gifts of law and grace. These transformative gifts reach all the way down, not only to our spiritual dynamisms but also to our bodily ones. Christian temperance comes about when our appetites "become virtuous, and their sensibilities expand in the euphoria of their transformation."[74]

Aquinas makes clear that the goal of the Christian moral life is the eschatological perfection of the human person by the Holy Spirit in the consummated body of Christ. Edgardo Colón-Emeric nicely describes what the indwelling Spirit accomplishes in each believer: "First, the theological virtues [faith, hope, charity] perfect the intellect and the will with respect to God. Second, the infused moral virtues perfect the intellect and the will with respect to means (things ordered) to God. Finally, the gifts of the Holy Spirit ... render the intellect and the will pliable to the guidance of the Holy Spirit."[75] The eschatological character of Christian ethics makes sense of the Holy Spirit's work through the sacraments to unite believers to the power of Christ's Pasch. Aquinas explains that "in the sacraments of the New Law, which are derived from Christ, grace is instrumentally caused by the sacraments, and principally by the power of the Holy Spirit working in the sacraments, according to Jn 3:5: 'Unless a man be born again of water and the Holy Spirit he cannot enter into the kingdom of God.'"⁷⁶ Although believers are still imperfect, Aquinas holds that the transformative power of Christ's Spirit is such that even now, believers can live according to "the justice of the kingdom."⁷⁷ It follows that, as Bauerschmidt says, "there ought to be no sharp delineation of the doctrinal and the moral," since what we believe about Christ and the Holy Spirit will shape "how we believe we should act."⁷⁸

Even if all that Aquinas had done was to defend the insights of the best pagan philosophy, this achievement would already pose a significant challenge to the current cultural dismissal of temperance. The Jewish thinker Solomon Schimmel has commented that "our culture teaches that pleasure and possessions *are* happiness," and many people today favor the quest to get as much physical pleasure and wealth as possible, at least if this can be done without harming one's health and social standing.⁷⁹ As a result, the virtues associated with temperance have been neglected and misunderstood in contemporary culture. For many people, "abstinence" from food now seems good only as part of dieting to avoid obesity. The word "chastity" can hardly be used in public. Sexuality is generally taken to be a purely individual matter, so long as no one is physically assaulted or abused. To call someone "meek" is an insult, since it is supposed that "meekness" characterizes only people who are subject to others' domination and that "humility" means dangerously low self-esteem. "Studiousness" has better standing, but only because it is seen as a path to power and wealth—precisely the opposite of the virtue as Aquinas understands it.⁸⁰

In this context, a renewed emphasis that Christ has indeed inaugurated the holy kingdom of God can help to show that Christian temperance is not only reasonable but also possible, good for us, and worth the sacrifices involved. The kingdom of God is eternal beatitude. Aquinas holds that the kingdom of God also is, in a certain sense, "the present Church," given that the present Church is ordered to eternal beatitude.⁸¹ He adds that the kingdom of God also is "Christ himself dwelling in us by grace," and this indwelling means that believers derive from Christ (as our Head) a "spiritual sense consisting in the knowledge of truth, and spiritual movement which results from the instinct of grace."[82] Jean Porter remarks that even some specialists in Aquinas's ethics can be inclined "to read Aquinas as if he not only baptized Aristotle, but is himself little more than Aristotle baptized."[83] But in fact, Aquinas's *Summa* always places the kingdom of God at the forefront.

As we will see in the chapters that follow, the eschatological renewal of the temple helps to make sense of temperance's integral parts of shame and *honestas*. When we realize that our bodies are God's temple, we regain an appreciation for the value of shame and for the beauty of bodily *honestas*. The eschatological restoration of God's people or family helps to reorient us to the centrality of the needs of family and community for our proper enjoyment of food, drink, and sex. As Matt Fradd puts it, we cannot "rip sex out of its obvious relational context, turn it into a commodity, and then expect individuals, families, and society to flourish."[84] The eschatological forgiveness of sins (and outpouring of the Spirit) helps to show that by the power of the Spirit, it is possible for us to overcome our pride and attain well-balanced humility, to overcome our anger and cruelty and attain well-balanced meekness and clemency, and to overcome our desire for dominative knowing and attain well-balanced wonder and praise.

By taking this approach to the Christian virtue of temperance, I hope to assist the work of contemporary virtue ethicists in making direct use of "the wealth and depth of material in the New Testament," as N. T. Wright urges be done.[85] Wright's emphasis upon Scripture's contribution to virtue ethics fits not only with Aquinas's theology but also with the admonitions of the Second Vatican Council. Indeed, the chapters that follow seek to unite *Optatam Totius*'s insistence that moral theology "should draw more fully on the teaching of holy Scripture and should throw light upon the exalted vocation of the faithful in Christ"[86] with *Lumen Gentium*'s teaching that the Church is "the kingdom of Christ already present in mystery" and that the Church is "the seed and the beginning of the kingdom."[87]

In the inaugurated kingdom of God, the beauty of temperance has become possible through the grace of the Holy Spirit. In Joseph Ratzinger's words, "returning to God in Jesus Christ is identical with a return to the manner of life of Jesus Christ."[88] This manner of life involves *honestas*, abstinence, chastity, meekness, clemency, humility, and studiousness. Let us live in faith that God, in Christ, has already begun to fulfill his promise: "I will give them one heart, and put a new spirit within them; I will take the stony heart out of their flesh and give them a heart of flesh, that they may walk in my statutes and keep my ordinances and obey them; and they shall be my people, and I will be their God" (Ezek 11:19–20).

CHAPTER TWO

Shame and *Honestas*

In the *secunda pars* of the *Summa theologiae*, Thomas Aquinas's treatise on temperance first addresses the "integral parts" of temperance, namely, the parts without which the virtue of temperance could not be present: shame and *honestas*. In this chapter, I suggest that the two integral parts of temperance illuminate how Christ's eschatological renewal of the temple takes shape in the Christian moral life.

As the biblical scholar Michael Gorman remarks, the ancient Mediterranean culture in which Paul lived "was a culture of *honor and shame*."[1] Christians had their own form of honor and shame.[2] After detailing his selfless service on behalf of the Corinthians, for example, Paul pauses to assure his flock that he is not trying to shame them (see 1 Cor 4:14). Gorman speaks of Paul's strong sense of "the honorable . . . behavior appropriate for believers."[3] Christians who exhibit honorable behavior do so by imitating Christ and thereby manifesting themselves to be filled with his Spirit, whereas Christians who act in contrary ways incur shame.[4] The New Testament teaches that Christians, in following Jesus, can expect to be *dishonored* by the surrounding culture while obtaining honor through the goodness or wickedness of their actions, above all their worship of God.[5] Jesus instructs his followers, "Blessed are you when men hate you, and when they exclude you and revile you, and cast out your name as evil, on account of the Son of man" (Lk 6:22).[6]

My focus in this chapter will be on how shame and honestas pertain to the eschatologically renewed temple that Jesus' followers are. Indebted especially to N. T. Wright and Nicholas Perrin, the first section of the chapter examines Second Temple Jewish expectations regarding the temple. Paul holds that these expectations have been fulfilled in Jesus Christ, who has reconfigured the temple around himself and has constituted his members as the renewed temple by sending the Spirit upon them. In the chapter's second section, I suggest that the eschatological renewal of the temple can shed light on shame and honestas as integral parts of temperance. As Cajetan Chereso describes Aquinas's perspective, "*Honestas* perfects temperance from above—as it were—while shamefacedness supports it from below, after the manner of a foundation. *Honestas* is temperance's royal crown of beauty; shamefacedness, the footstool for her feet."[7] Protected from intemperate disgrace by praiseworthy shame, believers who are the renewed "temple of the Holy Spirit" (1 Cor 6:19) display the spiritual beauty, clarity, and harmony constitutive of "the *honestas* of virtue."[8]

Biblical Background

Describing the need for the renewal of the temple that was felt by many strands of Second Temple Judaism, N. T. Wright begins with the standard Jewish understanding of the first temple. He summarizes this understanding: "The first Temple, built by Solomon, was the place where YHWH chose to dwell. He had formerly revealed his glory in the tabernacle set up in the wilderness; now he had done so in Solomon's Temple."[9] In the temple, "heaven and earth met" in a localized way.[10] According to Ezekiel, however, the divine glory or "shekinah" departed from the temple shortly prior to the destruction of the temple by the Babylonians.[11] In Ezekiel's prophetic visions, the "glory of the God of Israel," having dwelt in the temple since Solomon's time, leaves the temple and thereby abandons Israel, due to Israel's shameful idolatry. Ezekiel describes what he sees: "Then the cherubim lifted up their wings, with the wheels beside them; and the glory of the God of Israel was over them. And the glory of the LORD went up from the midst of the city, and stood upon the mountain which is on the east side of the city" (Ezek 11:22–23). The result is that Jerusalem itself, representative of the entire people of God, is abandoned.

Toward the end of the Book of Ezekiel, however, the Lord promises to rebuild the temple, this time in a perfect and supremely life-giving manner for the whole world. The Lord also promises to return to the temple. In prophetic visions, Ezekiel actually sees this return. Ezekiel describes it as follows: "And behold, the glory of the God of Israel came from the east. . . . As the glory of the LORD entered the temple by the gate facing east, the Spirit lifted me up, and brought me into the inner court; and behold, the glory of the LORD filled the temple" (Ezek 43:2, 4–5). Ezekiel makes explicit that this event will be the definitive reversal of God's abandonment of the temple in 587 BC, and he underscores its eschatological implications. He reports, "[God] said to me, 'Son of man, this [the temple] is the place of my throne and the place of the soles of my feet, where I will dwell in the midst of the people of Israel for ever. And the house of Israel shall no more defile my holy name" (Ezek 43:7). God will dwell with Israel, and Israel will be his holy people. God remarks about this new Jerusalem, "The name of the city henceforth shall be, The LORD is there" (Ezek 48:35).[12]

Recall that when the exiles returned from Babylon in the late sixth century BC under the leadership of Ezra and Nehemiah, they rebuilt the temple, and "many of the priests and Levites and heads of fathers' houses, old men who had seen the first house, wept with a loud voice when they saw the foundation of this house being laid, though many shouted for joy" (Ezra 3:12). Joseph Blenkinsopp points out that although we know little about the rebuilt sixth-century temple, "what we do know has nothing in common with Ezekiel's temple."[13] The rebuilding of the temple was not the eschatological renewal of the temple envisioned in symbolic terms by Ezekiel. Even when the temple and Jerusalem's walls had been rebuilt, Nehemiah still had to wrestle with the people over their lack of observance of the Sabbath and over the fact that many of them "had married women of Ashdod, Ammon, and Moab, and half of their children spoke the language of Ashdod, and they could not speak the language of Judah" (Neh 13:23–24).[14]

The reality behind Ezekiel's eschatological vision of the renewed temple had not yet arrived. God had not yet returned to the temple in the manner prophesied by Ezekiel. In the Second Temple period, those attuned to Ezekiel's prophecies awaited a royal son of David who would renew the temple: "I will set up over them one shepherd, my servant David, and he shall feed them: he shall feed them and be their shepherd" (Ezek 34:23). In Ezekiel 36, God foretells what he will do when this Davidic king appears: "I will vindicate the holiness of my great name, which has been profaned among the nations, and which you have profaned among them; and the nations will know that I am the Lord, says the Lord God, when through you I vindicate my holiness before their eyes" (Ezek 36:23). In this light, and with a variety of other texts in view, Wright describes the "longing for *the return of YHWH to Zion*," which would involve the eschatological and perfect "rebuilding of the Temple."[15]

Turning to Jesus' ministry, Wright states that through his "actions and words in the Temple," Jesus was making clear that "the time had come for the institution [the temple] to be transcended," since in fact "in his work *the Temple was being rebuilt*."[16] What does Wright mean by this? In *Jesus and the Victory of God*, Wright suggests that Jesus' words about the temple's coming destruction, his cleansing of the temple, and his Passover meal with the twelve disciples (symbolic of Israel) had the effect of forming "a strange but deliberate alternative to the Temple."[17] In *Paul and the Faithfulness of God*, building upon his fundamental thesis that Jesus understood himself to be enacting the salvific return of YHWH to Zion (and thus to the temple) for the sake of the restoration of Israel and the ingathering of the nations, Wright proposes that "when Paul speaks of the individual Christian, or the whole church, as the 'temple' in which the spirit 'dwells', such language from a second-temple Jew can only mean (a) that YHWH has returned to his Temple as he had promised and (b) that the mode of this long-awaited, glorious, tabernacling presence is the spirit."[18]

Wright then tests this proposal in light of 1 Corinthians 3:16–17 ("Do you not know that you are God's temple and that God's Spirit dwells in you? If any one destroys God's temple, God will destroy him. For God's temple is holy, and that temple you are"); 1 Corinthians 6:19 ("Do you not know that your body is a temple of the Holy Spirit within you, which you have from God?"); and 2 Corinthians 6:16 and 7:1 ("What agreement has the temple of God with idols? For we are the temple of the living God.... Since we have these promises, beloved, let us cleanse ourselves from every defilement of body and spirit, and make holiness perfect in the fear of God"). He concludes that, for Paul, Jesus has established the new temple, and the new temple is anywhere that Jesus' Spirit dwells: not only in the whole Church, but also in individual believers. Believers are therefore called to "sexual holiness," the lack of which "is to deface the divine Temple."[19]

Wright emphasizes that the status of believers as God's Spirit-filled temple involves renewing our interior beauty and holiness.[20] We must "cleanse ourselves from every defilement of body and spirit" (2 Cor 7:1) and "shun immorality" (1 Cor 6:18), so that we can "glorify God in [our] body" (1 Cor 6:20). We must seek to ensure that "those parts of the body which we think less honorable we invest with the greater honor" (1 Cor 12:23), not merely through external signs but through interior virtues. We must "abstain from every form of evil" (1 Thess 5:22), recognizing evil actions and shunning them. Thus, we cannot fall into the arrogance of refusing to worry about our intemperate actions (1 Cor 5:2). We cannot follow "dishonorable passions" and commit "shameless acts" (Rom 1:26–27). We cannot be God's renewed temple in Christ if we join with those whose "god is the belly" (food, drink, and sex) and who "glory in their shame" (Phil 3:19), or if we join with the man "who sows to his own flesh" and will "reap corruption" (Gal 6:8).

Indeed, the Letter of Jude warns that some persons, though in name followers of Christ, in fact are "ungodly persons who pervert the grace of our God into licentiousness," "are blemishes on [the] love feasts [of Jude's addressees], as they boldly carouse together, looking after themselves," and are like "wild waves of the sea, casting up the foam of their own shame" (Jude 4, 12–13). As God's renewed temple in Christ, we must reflect and embody the "beauty" of the temple of YHWH (Ps 96:6). Otherwise, in claiming to be members of Christ, we would hypocritically be "like whitewashed tombs, which outwardly appear beautiful, but within they are full of dead men's bones and all uncleanness" (Mt 23:27). As Wright says, arguing that true external beauty is a manifestation of interior beauty, "If the Temple in Jerusalem, the place where God's own glory was to dwell, was seen as the 'little world,' the microcosm where the world's beauty was to be concentrated, then part of the virtue of the royal priesthood, the new and living Temple, ought to be the cultivation and celebration of beauty at every level."[21]

Through the prophet Isaiah, God describes the false beauty of intemperate persons, who do not truly worship God and who thereby are defiling his people Israel: "Woe to the proud crown of the drunkards of Ephraim, and to the fading flower of its glorious beauty, which is on the head of the rich valley of those overcome with wine!" (Is 28:1). Believers need an interior beauty of the kind found in Christ, who "had no form or comeliness that we should look at him, and no beauty that we should desire him" (Is 53:2). Those who trust in external beauty and have no interior beauty fall under the condemnation that God assigns to the kingdom of Tyre in the prophecy of Ezekiel: "Your heart was proud because of your beauty; you corrupted your wisdom for the sake of your splendor.... All who know you among the peoples are appalled at you; you have come to a dreadful end" (Ezek 28:17, 19).

In *Jesus the Temple*, Nicholas Perrin argues that "Jesus ... saw himself as the human embodiment of the temple."[22] Perrin points out the central place that the temple played in Israel's identity and covenantal relationship with YHWH, and he observes with respect to the exodus that "the final goal of Israel's redemption was not merely freedom, but the opportunity to establish a proper temple and with it proper worship."[23] He comments that many Israelites in the Second Temple period expected the coming of "the divinely wrought eschatological temple that would prove to be the terminal goal of the Exodus and thus too, on analogy, the ultimate goal of all Yahweh's redeeming purposes."[24] According to this common Second Temple worldview, the onset of this eschatological temple would be marked by "apostasy within the temple" and by a profound tribulation, as well as by a "jubilee" liberating the poor.[25]

Perrin describes the variety of Second Temple messianic counter-temple movements, and he finds that "early Christianity saw itself as the community in which the eschatological temple was taking shape."[26] The Gospel of John, for instance, presents Jesus as the one who "fulfills the role of the eschatological temple-builder and indeed becomes the temple, the source of life, light, and truth—God's glory."[27] For Paul, too, Jesus has established the eschatological temple, and the Church is this renewed temple, though still suffering tribulation rather than planted in the new Jerusalem. The Church is the renewed temple insofar as the Church receives Christ's Spirit, since "where the Spirit settles, there one finds the temple."[28]

Perrin emphasizes that the central mark of the eschatological temple is benefaction to the poor, and indeed it is quite clear that almsgiving stands at the heart of the "kingdom practices" of Christianity.[29] Perrin further argues that in Jesus' exorcisms, healings, meals, and parables, we find evidence that Jesus "saw the messianic banquet (Isaiah 25) as something occurring in the present" and that, in fact, Jesus held that he was inaugurating—even if not yet consummating—"the new convergence of heaven and earth, the new temple."[30] According to Perrin, Jesus reconfigured the attainment of purity, the condition in which a person must be in order to worship God in his temple. Cultic purity, Perrin underlines, rests for Jesus largely upon treatment of the poor. But since the new temple is not only Jesus' risen body but also the bodies of his followers, the cultic purity of the renewed temple also requires the interior beauty of the person who does not make a "god" of his or her own "belly" (Phil 3:19) but who instead lives in the conviction that "the body is not meant for immorality, but for the Lord, and the Lord for the body" (1 Cor 6:13).[31] As Wright observes, "Royal priests are . . . to work at revealing the glory of God to the world. That is the task of the renewed Temple," a task that requires (among other virtues) "chastity" and "self-control."[32]

The renewed temple is the body of Christ (the Church), and the renewed temple is also the bodies of individual believers, since believers are indwelt by Christ's Holy Spirit—the Spirit or *shekinah* who filled Solomon's temple and who later left the temple, as depicted by Ezekiel. Recall that according to Aquinas, the "integral parts" of a virtue "are the conditions the concurrence of which are necessary for virtue."[33] Thus the "integral parts" of temperance are not the proper species of temperance (which has properly to do with food, drink, and sex), but rather are the conditions without which a person cannot be said to have virtue with regard to food, drink, or sex. These integral parts, Aquinas states, are "*shamefacedness*, whereby one recoils from the disgrace that is contrary to temperance, and *honesty*, whereby one loves the beauty of temperance."[34]

Insofar as our desire for bodily pleasures exhibits temperance, the renewed temple that is the bodies of believers will be filled with interior grace and beauty. Just as the temple needs to be pure in order to be a place of offering worship to God, so also our bodies need to be pure in order for us to "present [our] bodies as a living sacrifice, holy and acceptable to God, which is [our] spiritual worship" (Rom 12:1). Temperance is opposed to bodily disgrace or defilement: "Let us cleanse ourselves from every defilement of body and spirit" (2 Cor 7:1), from everything that "defiles a man" (Mt 15:18). This is why temperance must be characterized by interior beauty or moral goodness. As Aquinas states, "Beauty is a foremost attribute of temperance which above all hinders man from being defiled. In like manner honesty [honestas, moral goodness or beauty] is a special attribute of temperance: for Isidore says (*Etym.* x): 'An honest man is one who has no defilement, for honesty means an honorable state.'"[35] Biblically speaking, someone who possesses interior beauty or goodness (honestas) will not be enslaved to "dishonorable passions" and "shameless acts" (Rom 1:26–27). Such a person will indeed be "a temple of the Holy Spirit," manifesting the renewed temple by glorifying God in his or her body (1 Cor 6:19–20).

It follows that those who are seeking the renewed temple in the Messiah will find it where believers have interior purity. Because persons who embody the renewed temple are good, such persons have an interior beauty that is attractive to others. In Christ, they are royal and priestly images of God, able to offer the whole of creation in "spiritual worship" as God's embodied eschatological temple. As Wright sums up: "The early Christians believed that they were the true Temple of

God, filled with God's glorious presence by his Spirit and called to reveal that glory to the world."[36]

THOMAS AQUINAS ON SHAME AND *HONESTAS*

Shame

Thomas Aquinas's understanding of shame (*verecundia*) and honestas—temperance's "integral parts," without which a person could not be temperate—provides insight into the ways in which our bodies, as the renewed temple, glorify God. Let me first investigate Aquinas's theology of shame. Since to feel shame is connected with guilt, shame will not be experienced by believers whose bodies are perfectly temples of the Holy Spirit. Shame is not a perfection, but rather is a kind of fear or horror at the incursion of sin, so that we flee (in Cajetan Chereso's words) from "every occasion of contracting the disgrace and ugliness of intemperance."[37] Aquinas notes that John of Damascus defines shame as "fear of a base action."[38] Shame therefore is not a virtue, since it is not a perfection but rather is a response to the threat or presence of sin, whether one's own or that of someone else. Aquinas remarks that "anything that is inconsistent with perfection, though it be good, falls short of the notion of virtue."[39] Someone who is perfect, who does not need to fear sin in any way, will not possess shame.

Needless to say, however, such perfection does not characterize many people on earth. As an appropriate fear of something "disgraceful," shame is therefore "a praiseworthy passion," arising fundamentally from a "love of the beauty [or honestas] of temperance."[40] Paul commands all whose "bodies are members of Christ" to "shun immorality" (1 Cor 6:15, 18)—in other words, to fear the disgrace of sin by which we are separated from Christ. A person who possesses the "praiseworthy passion" of shame will desire to be God's temple perfectly, worshiping God with a pure heart, and therefore will fear the disgracing impact of sin. The sinner knows that he "sins against his own body" (1 Cor 6:18); and the repentant sinner—who is the "temple of the Holy Spirit," even if not yet perfectly—is rightly shamefaced when confronted with his past actions against his own body, which God created to be the temple of the Holy Spirit.

Aquinas distinguishes the praiseworthy shame that he has in view from the shame endured by the righteous at the hands of the wicked. He refers to the psalmist's plea to God, "For it is for thy sake that I have borne reproach, that shame has covered my face" (Ps 69:7).[41] Aquinas also distinguishes praiseworthy shame from the shame that people who undertake menial jobs may feel without having done anything disgraceful. Aquinas even recognizes that in some instances people feel too ashamed to dare to perform a virtuous action. Aquinas draws an example of this from Luke 9:26, where Jesus warns, "Whoever is ashamed of me and of my words, of him will the Son of man be ashamed when he comes in his glory and the glory of the Father and of the holy angels."[42] To be ashamed about Jesus' words—unwilling to defend and proclaim them—is far from a "praiseworthy passion." Aquinas also notes that sometimes people are very ashamed of small sins but boast in great sins, about which they feel no shame. He quotes Psalm 52:1, "Why do you boast, O mighty man, of mischief done against the godly?"[43]

Given that the term "shame" encompasses all these varied meanings and situations, is Aquinas right to associate shame with fear of a disgraceful action and to identify shame as an "integral part" of the virtue of temperance? In addressing this question, Aquinas draws upon John of Damascus, pairing him with Nemesius (whom he misidentifies as Gregory of Nyssa): "Damascene (*De Fide Orthod.* ii. 15) and Gregory of Nyssa say that 'shamefacedness is fear of doing a disgraceful deed or of a disgraceful deed done.'"[44] Affirming that this definition is correct, Aquinas adds that sins of intemperance—gluttony, drunkenness, adultery, and the like—are particularly likely to cause us public disgrace or embarrassment.[45] For this reason, praiseworthy shame especially fosters the virtue of temperance or at least strengthens continence. Shame does so by serving to make it more likely that we will refrain "from vicious acts through fear of reproach."[46] We see the presence of a salutary shame, even if too late, when persons try to hide their disgraceful acts from public knowledge.

Sadly, however, it is possible to become *shameless* when one is "steeped in sin."[47] With regard to shamelessness, Aquinas notes that "those who excel in wickedness are not ashamed," and he cites Jeremiah 3:3, where the Lord complains of idolatrous Israel: "You have a harlot's brow, you refuse to be ashamed."[48] Shameless persons are not made shamefaced by being found in disgraceful acts, because "instead of disapproving of their sins, they boast of them."[49] As Paul puts it, "They not only do them but approve of those who practice them" (Rom 1:32). Gabriele Taylor comments that "if someone has self-respect [a sense of one's true value] then under certain specifiable conditions he will be feeling shame. A person has no self-respect if he regards no circumstances as shame-producing."[50] If we felt no shame in the presence of God after committing sin, that would be terrible because it would indicate a failure in proper self-respect and would impede our ability to repent. If, however, in our shame we assume that God now does not care for us because we have committed such a disgraceful sin, then we have failed to recognize the basis for our standing before God, namely, God's unmerited mercy toward sinners in Jesus Christ.

Aquinas observes that fortunately, friendship and community generally work to increase our salutary shame or fear of reproach. Not surprisingly, we especially fear being reproached by wise people who know us well. When we are around strangers, we have less fear of reproach. But when we fear that people who are well known for wisdom in our community might discover our disgraceful sins, we then fear to commit such sins — and if we have committed such sins, we fear their discovery. It follows that shame operates best in the context of a community in which we are known and accountable and in which are present "wise and virtuous men [and women], by whom man is more desirous of being honored, and by whom he is brought to a greater sense of shame."[51] Such persons are those who, as Jesus says, have repented and sought God's "kingdom and his righteousness" (Mt 6:33), so that they are able to "see clearly to take the speck out of [their] brother's eye" (Mt 7:5). If our community is composed of people who share in our sin or in similar sins, however, they will either approve of our sin or at least will not be able to reproach us for it.[52]

Paul's struggles with the oft sinful Corinthians make clear that even though Christ has renewed the temple by reconstituting it around his own perfect worship, the temple is only *beginning* to be renewed. As the Church built up by the Holy Spirit, Jesus' followers "worship God in spirit, and glory in Christ Jesus" (Phil 3:3). The Spirit enables those who are in Christ to "worship the Father in spirit and truth" (Jn 4:23). Yet Jesus' followers on earth are still only members of the inaugurated kingdom, in which the "weeds" and "wheat" will "grow together until the harvest" (Mt 13:29–30). Given that believers' divided hearts are often very imperfectly temperate, shame continues to play a significant role in encouraging and fostering temperance. It is important, therefore, that the Church nourish intimate friendships among its members and that there are wise and faithful Christians among us, because as Aquinas says, "Persons connected with us make us more ashamed, since we are to be continually in their society" and "the attestation of those among whom we live is more cogent since they know more about our concerns in detail."[53] Of course, we also fear the reproach of those whose friendship or favor we seek, even if we do not yet know them personally.[54] I note how significant it is that Jesus calls us "friends" (Jn 15:15) and that in his messianic community we seek his friendship and favor, fearing his reproach and the shame of those to whom he will say, "Depart from me, you cursed" (Mt 25:41).

As noted above, Christians who perfectly possess temperance do not have shame, because those who are perfectly temperate "apprehend disgrace as impossible to themselves, or easy to avoid."[55] In more normal cases, however, temperate persons can err in a venial manner without losing temperance.[56] Discussing the fact that it is actually the "virtuous" who "are more inclined to be ashamed," Aquinas explains this by appeal to the divided hearts of most people.[57] He adds that "average men" may have no shame about some sins, even if they do have shame about other ones, because people often "have a certain love of good, and yet are not altogether free from evil."[58] This point makes clear why Christ and those who are most deeply united to him constantly call all people to the full holiness proper to God's eschatological temple.

Summing up the rationale for associating shame with temperance, Aquinas remarks that "shamefacedness is a part of temperance, not as though it entered into its essence, but as a disposition to it: wherefore Ambrose says (*De Offic.* i. 43) that 'shamefacedness lays the first foundation of temperance.'"[59] As a "disposition" or "first foundation," shame helps us to recoil from those actions that oppose temperance. By contrast, when we live according to the "lusts" (Rom 1:24) of our hearts and feel no shame, we have entered upon a phase of action in which our "senseless minds" have become "futile" and "darkened" (Rom 1:21). Aquinas emphasizes that we need to be "so disposed, that if there were anything disgraceful" in us, we "would be ashamed of it."[60] As Taylor observes, "shame is the emotion of self-protection" — protection from intemperate desires and activities.[61]

Honestas

The second "integral part" of temperance, without which temperance cannot function, is honestas. In deeming honestas to be a part of temperance, Aquinas follows Cicero and Ambrose.[62] Aquinas explains that honestas refers to "'an honorable state,' wherefore a thing may be said to be honest through being worthy of honor."[63] The possession of honestas means simply that a person is morally excellent or morally honorable. Since to be morally excellent or morally honorable requires possessing the virtues, a person who possesses honestas possesses virtue.[64] Aquinas also reflects upon Cicero's statement that something that is honestas is desired *for its own sake*. This fits with virtue, since we would want virtues "even if no further good accrued to us through them."[65]

But if to possess honestas is to possess virtue, why does Aquinas treat honestas as an integral part of temperance in particular? It would seem that if the word *honestas* is simply another way of describing moral goodness or moral virtue, honestas has no special relationship to temperance. Aquinas helps us to understand the special relationship of honestas to temperance by linking honestas to spiritual beauty. According to Isidore and Cicero, things that possess honestas are worthy of honor and are desirable for their own sake. On this basis, Aquinas asks whether all that is honestas is beautiful.[66] He gives three reasons why the answer might be no. First, what is honestas is desirable to the intellectual appetite, whereas what is beautiful is pleasing to sight. Second, what is honestas is honorable, whereas what is beautiful has "a certain clarity, which is characteristic of glory."[67] Third, what is honestas is virtue, whereas beautiful things need not be virtuous, as we can see from Ezekiel 16:15, where God says of idolatrous Israel: "But you trusted in your beauty, and played the harlot because of your renown."

In response to these objections to a link between honestas and beauty, Aquinas first sets forth the Vulgate text of 1 Corinthians 12:23–24, in which the term *honestas* is applied to our beautiful bodily parts.[68] The Vulgate text, however, differs significantly from modern translations, and so it is fortunate that Aquinas's argument does not rest solely upon 1 Corinthians 12. His argument builds upon Pseudo-Dionysius's explanation of why "beauty" is among the divine names or attributes. Given that beauty is present wherever we find "the concurrence of clarity and due proportion," God must be infinitely beautiful, because God is the cause of the clarity and harmonious proportion that we find in the universe (which, as God's effect, cannot possess a perfection lacking in an infinite mode to its divine cause).[69] Indebted to the Platonic thought mediated by Dionysius, Aquinas explains that there is a spiritual beauty analogous to physical beauty. Just as there is physical beauty in the clarity of color and well-proportioned limbs, so also there is spiritual beauty composed of spiritual clarity and proportion. Aquinas holds that right reason—reason conformed to divine wisdom as manifested in Christ and creation—provides the measure of the "clarity" and "proportion" of our actions.[70] When we act in a virtuous manner and possess virtue, we possess spiritual beauty. It follows that the person who possesses honestas will possess not only virtue but also spiritual beauty.[71]

This point easily applies to the renewal of the temple. The beauty of the temple as a place of worship fits with Ezra's joy over the Persian king's desire "to beautify [or glorify] the house of the Lord which is in Jerusalem" (Ezra 7:27) and with the Song of Songs' depiction of the beloved (or Israel) as "beautiful as Tirzah" (Song 6:4). It fits, furthermore, with Jesus' pointed description of some scribes and Pharisees—as corrupt as some later ecclesiastical elites have been—as "like whitewashed tombs, which outwardly appear beautiful" (Mt 23:27). To worship God with true righteousness rather than in "hypocrisy and iniquity" (Mt 23:28), we need renewal; only then will we be spiritually beautiful temples of the Holy Spirit. Although Aquinas does not here cite these passages, he is aware that Christ and his Spirit make this temple renewal possible for all people.

The connection that Aquinas makes between honestas and spiritual beauty is indebted to Dionysius, but the connection is also explicitly made by Augustine, as quoted by Aquinas: "By honesty [honestas] I mean intelligible beauty, which we properly designate as spiritual."[72] For Aquinas, the key point is that intemperance is spiritually ugly, since we destroy our own bodily temple through our intemperate actions. Honestas is honorable and desirable, whereas intemperance means to be enslaved to "dishonorable passions" (Rom 1:26) and to be caught up in "the dishonoring of [our] bodies" (Rom 1:24). The opposite of dishonored bodies is bodies that are honorable. Temperance, therefore, makes our bodies honorable and spiritually beautiful. When our bodily actions are temperate, they possess clarity and proportion as measured by reason, and our bodily actions thereby manifest spiritual or interior beauty and desirability. The temples of our bodies thereby possess their proper spiritual beauty as befits the eschatological indwelling of the Holy Spirit. Honestas from this perspective has a particular bond with temperance, even though every virtue pertains to honestas and interior beauty.[73]

Augustine helps Aquinas to distinguish honestas from what is simply useful or pleasant. In Augustine's taxonomy, the "honest" good is desired rationally for its own sake, whereas a "useful" good is an instrument for attaining other goods, and a "pleasant" good is desired by the senses.[74] Aquinas notes that "a thing is said to be honest, in so far as it has a certain beauty through being regulated by reason."[75] He adds that "an honest thing is naturally pleasing to man," because true virtue is always pleasing.[76] Since virtue also is useful in leading us to beatitude, true virtue stands as an honest, useful, and pleasant good.

Thus, temperance makes a person's bodily actions honest (honorable and spiritually beautiful), pleasing (perfecting the person's nature in accordance with reason), and useful (for attaining beatitude). I note that this would serve as an excellent description of the renewed temple and its "rational worship" (Rom 12:1). In the renewed temple, we find the fulfillment of the psalmist's affirmation, "The Lord is in his holy temple" (Ps 11:4) — a temple that God's enemies have not "defiled" (Ps 79:1).

Yet, if *honestas* is that which is honorable, it would seem that *honestas* pertains not to temperance but to courage and to justice, since those who are courageous and just receive the greatest honor.[77] As an objection, Aquinas gives the aged Israelite scribe Eleazar, who, rather than choosing to violate the Torah by eating pig's flesh, freely accepted torture and death. Surely such a courageous and just death is more honorable than being temperate.[78] In response, Aquinas grants that courage and justice are more honorable than temperance, but he holds that because temperance saves a person from particularly dishonorable vices, *honestas* (and honor) pertains especially to temperance. He explains that the opposite of the beautiful is the disgraceful and that what is most opposite to the rational vocation of human beings is irrational "animal lusts."[79] Since temperance wards off what is most opposed to reason — namely living "according to the flesh" rather than "according to the spirit" (Rom 8:5)[80] — it follows that *honestas*, with its honor and spiritual beauty, has a special relation to temperance. Intemperance destroys honor and spiritual beauty by turning rational beings (created for self-giving) into self-seeking slaves of bodily passions.

In his commentary on Romans, Aquinas describes "the mind that is set on the flesh" (Rom 8:7) as characteristic of a person who takes "as his goal a pleasure of the flesh" and consistently acts with this end or goal in view.[81] Such a person is the definition of an intemperate person, because the fundamental goal of rational creatures is interpersonal union with God and neighbor in Christ, not physical pleasures such as eating, drinking, or sex. Speaking about temperate persons, Paul makes clear that they are true temples. He tells the members of the Church in Rome, "But you are not in the flesh, you are in the Spirit, if the Spirit of God really dwells in you" (Rom 8:9). As Cajetan Chereso concludes, therefore, "When this lower appetite in man severs its bond with reason by clamoring after, and surfeiting itself with unreasonable animal pleasures, the integrity of man's nature is virtually destroyed, and man becomes only half a man.... Man is ugly when he is only half of what he should be."[82]

✽✽✽

In this chapter, I have suggested that Aquinas's reflections on the integral parts of temperance, shame and honestas, are illumined by the eschatological ethics of the inaugurated kingdom, and specifically by the renewal of the temple. Israel awaited the return of God to the temple and the permanent renewal of the temple as the place of true worship of God. Jesus accomplished this renewal of the temple, both in his own flesh and by sending his Spirit upon all believers to make them temples of God as the body of Christ. Thus, Paul proclaims that believers in Christ are the "temple of the Holy Spirit" (1 Cor 6:19), who should recoil from impurity and should glorify God in their bodies. The renewed temple is protected from impurity by a disposition to the "praiseworthy passion" of shame, and the renewed temple possesses spiritual beauty or honestas that is worthy of honor.

In his study of Aquinas on shame and honestas, Jean-Paul Bernard remarks that honestas involves "the elevation of the concupiscible appetite to the role of servant of reason."[83] For this to happen, our reason itself must be rightly ordered, so that it may rightly order our bodily desires. It makes sense, therefore, that throughout Scripture idolatry (the greatest distortion of human rationality) and intemperance (the greatest distortion of human bodiliness) are consistently brought together. This is because when we live under the rule of our bodily desires rather than under the rule of rightly ordered reason, we mistake our proper end, supposing our purpose in life to be bodily pleasure rather than union with God and neighbor in self-giving love. When we become enslaved to bodily desires, we can no longer govern our bodily desires in a manner that orders them toward our true ultimate end of self-giving love.

Josef Pieper points out that "it is quite particularly in the sphere of *temperantia* that the attitude toward creation and 'the world' is most incisively decided."[84] When we idolatrously worship the creature rather than the Creator, we imagine that our end is a creaturely one and therefore we do not appropriately govern our eating, drinking, and sexual actions. This leads not to happiness, but to its opposite. Given the contemporary culture of sexual "liberation" — which mirrors the pagan culture resisted by first-century Christians (and Jews) — Wright remarks that "as those of us who care pastorally, or in families, for people who have embraced the present habits of society will know, the bruises and wounds caused by those habits are deep, long-lasting, and life-decaying. The church is often called a killjoy for protesting against sexual license. But the real killing of joy comes with the grabbing of pleasure."[85]

At present, of course, although Christ has renewed the temple, his followers on earth remain sinners, and so we all have some painful experience of incontinence or intemperance. In this sense, we are all in the same boat and we "have no excuse" when we "judge another" (Rom 2:1). Through the grace of the Holy Spirit, however, Christ enables his repentant followers to partake in the perfect worship of the true temple, who is Christ himself. Christ enacted this perfect worship on the cross, and we participate in it most fully in the liturgy of the Eucharist, which is "the high point towards which the activity of the church is directed, and, simultaneously, the source from which all its power flows out."[86] As what G. K. Beale calls "the inaugurated latter-day temple," God's people "need to shine God's light in a dark world."[87] God's people need to shine with spiritual beauty, with honestas that displays the honor of virtue and that recoils from vice, by living "according to the spirit" rather than "according to the flesh." Shame plays an important role here, because as David deSilva says, "The promise of being honored in God's house reinforces the value of not yielding to the lusts of the body (2 Tim 2:20–22)," as does "the threat of disgrace before God."[88]

In a world where temperance is difficult and many of us at various times serve our own bellies (through intemperate eating, drinking, and sex) rather than God and neighbor (see Js 2:15), God's people should make manifest the Spirit-enabled temperance of the well-ordered renewed temple, a temperance that reflects the true fear of the Lord that characterizes those who are "poor in spirit" (Mt 5:3). As Jean-Paul Bernard observes, although temperance is the least of the four cardinal virtues, temperance "is an educative virtue, that is to say, it is the first crossing from the sensible domain to the intellectual."[89] In this movement, rising from fear of sin (shame) to love of interior beauty (honestas), we are enabled to "glorify God in [our] body" as "a temple of the Holy Spirit" (1 Cor 6:19–20) and to offer true "rational worship" on behalf of all creation (Rom 12:1). In Christ, we are enabled to "conduct ourselves becomingly as in the day, not in reveling and drunkenness, not in debauchery and licentiousness, not in quarreling and jealousy" (Rom 13:13). In this way, we recover the "inner order" that God willed for humans to enjoy from the beginning.[90]

CHAPTER THREE

Abstinence and Sobriety

In contemporary Western culture, the daily practices of eating and drinking are not an area of moral concern for most people. Even so, many people will have had experiences that confirm the view that "food-pleasures are designed to lead us into loving relationships with God and one another."¹ This chapter proposes that our normal practices of eating and drinking in fact necessarily involve a crucial moral concern. Namely, we eat and drink wrongly when we focus solely on ourselves and our bodily life rather than on the fundamental purpose of eating and drinking, which consists in nourishing the body in a manner that fosters loving and serving God and neighbor in thanksgiving for God's gifts.² The ordering of eating and drinking toward the service of God and neighbor, and away from mere self-satisfaction, is the key to the good eating and drinking that make manifest God's inaugurated kingdom in the world.³ Christians must undertake reasonable eating and drinking that ensures that we truly care for others, rather than being focused on self-centered pleasures or self-centered attitudes (including obsession with weight and health). As the Christian theologian Norman Wirzba puts it, we must ensure that our eating and drinking have in view "the needs of others and the responsibilities of maintaining life's memberships" through self-offering rather than "self-satisfaction."⁴

In this chapter, I suggest that Thomas Aquinas's theology of temperate eating and drinking—namely, abstinence, fasting, and sobriety—illumines the eschatological restoration of God's people accomplished by Jesus Christ. Certainly, good eating and drinking are not the ingathering of the twelve tribes and the inclusion of the gentiles (which are central elements of the restoration of God's people). But without good eating and drinking, the restored people or family of God would break down due to the focus on our own pleasure that marks bad eating and drinking. The importance of eating and drinking is such that, as the biblical scholar Robert Karris has pointed out, "in Luke's Gospel Jesus is either going to a meal, at a meal, or coming from a meal."[5] Imitating Jesus' example, we Christians must sustain our bodily life in a way that has in view the service of God and neighbor. In *Deus Caritas Est*, Pope Benedict XVI explains that "the Church as God's family must be a place where help is given and received, and at the same time, a place where people are also prepared to serve those outside her confines who are in need of help."[6]

The first section of this chapter will examine eating and drinking according to scripture, with particular attention to fasting and feasting. In this section, I am indebted especially to the biblical scholars Brant Pitre and Karl Olav Sandnes. Not surprisingly, eating and drinking were important in the cultural and religious life of Israel and among the first followers of Jesus.[7] Indeed, in 1 Corinthians 11, Paul teaches that if we do not eat and drink rightly, then we can hardly hope to celebrate the Eucharist rightly. Thus, it is no exaggeration to claim that the onset of the eschatological restoration of the people of God by Jesus Christ is manifested when his restored people or family eat and drink rightly. In the second section of the chapter, I explore Aquinas's teaching on abstinence, fasting, and sobriety, in light of the restored people or family of God. Aquinas can help us to perceive the concrete ways in which eschatological ethics requires that we train our desire for food and drink to "serve us in our relationships with others and God."[8]

Biblical Background

In *The New Testament and the People of God*, N. T. Wright describes the importance of the liturgical year for the people of Israel, their "festivals and fasts" that "summed up a good deal of the theology and national aspiration" of Israel and "celebrated it in great symbolic actions and liturgies."⁹ Not only communal eating but also periodic abstinence from certain foods was (and is) central to Israel's way of being God's people.¹⁰ Beyond the festivals and fasts, of course, the laws of the Torah reject certain foods entirely as unclean (see, for example, Lev 11). God's provision of the manna during the exodus provides a paradigmatic example of communal eating, and God commands that the people abstain from leaven during the feast of the Passover.¹¹ Another instance of significant communal eating appears when God called Moses, Aaron, Nadab, Abihu, and seventy elders to ratify the covenant stipulations in an ascent of Mount Sinai, where "they beheld God, and ate and drank" (Exod 24:11).

Fasting is occasionally a part of the exodus, though not in a regular way. After the disaster of Israel's idolatrous worship of the golden calf, Moses went up to meet God anew on Mount Sinai. During this time, Moses fasted: "And he was there with the Lord forty days and forty nights; he neither ate bread nor drank water" (Exod 34:28). Arguably, this fasting expresses the fact that "man does not live by bread alone, but . . . man lives by everything that proceeds out of the mouth of the Lord" (Deut 8:3). In Deuteronomy 8, Moses describes God's people as being disciplined by God during the exodus journey by means of a nonvoluntary fasting, followed by feasting (the manna). Moses tells the people, "[The LORD] humbled you and let you hunger and fed you with manna" (v. 3).¹²

By the time of the prophets, individual and communal fasting in repentant supplication of God had become a common practice. For example, Isaiah depicts an exchange between God and his people, in which the people refer to their fasting: "'Why have we fasted, and thou [God] seest it not? Why have we humbled ourselves, and thou takest no knowledge of it?' Behold [God replies], in the day of your fast you seek your own pleasure, and oppress all your workers" (Is 58:3). Similarly, during a drought, the Lord tells the prophet Jeremiah, "Do not pray for the welfare of this people. Though they fast, I will not hear their cry" (Jer 14:12).

When the people of Judea were exiled to Babylon in 587 BC, the Davidic kingship came to a seeming end; and even when the exiles in Babylon had largely returned to Judea, the consequences of the earlier exile of the northern ten tribes by the Assyrians endured. Wright argues that many Second Temple Jews found good reason in the prophetic books to hope for a future eschatological restoration of God's people. According to Wright, the liturgical cycle of feasts and fasts became especially important during this time as a reminder of the people's covenantal election and of the truthfulness of God's promises.[13]

As we might expect, feasting and fasting belong to the New Testament's testimony to the coming of this eschatological restoration or "redemption from exile." The Gospel of Matthew depicts Jesus as stating that he "came eating and drinking" and that he was accused of being "a glutton and a drunkard" (Mt 11:19). Jesus fasted regularly, as for instance during his temptation in the wilderness at the outset of his public ministry, when, like Moses, "he fasted forty days and forty nights" (Mt 4:2). But Jesus also feasted regularly, eating with "many tax collectors and sinners" (Mt 9:10). Asked why his disciples (unlike John's) were not fasting, Jesus replies by employing an eschatological image: "Can the wedding guests fast while the bridegroom is with them? As long as they have the bridegroom with them, they cannot fast. The days will come, when the bridegroom is taken away from them, and then they will fast in that day" (Mk 2:19–20). Jesus presents himself as the divine bridegroom who has come to accomplish the restoration of Israel, as foretold in Isaiah: "You [Israel] shall no more be termed Forsaken, and your land shall no more be termed Desolate; but you shall be called My delight is in her, and your land Married; for the Lord delights in you ... and as the bridegroom rejoices over the bride, so shall your God rejoice over you" (Is 62:4).[14] From this perspective, Jesus feasts as an explicit sign of the eschatological wedding banquet.

Strengthened by communion with him as the "living bread" (Jn 6:51), Jesus' followers share in his tribulation in anticipation of the final consummation of all things (see Mt 10:38–39; Lk 9:23–24; Jn 15:18–20). For this reason he expects his followers to fast. In his Sermon on the Mount, Jesus instructs his followers, "When you fast, do not look dismal, like the hypocrites, for they disfigure their faces that their fasting may be seen by men. Truly, I say to you, they have their reward. But when you fast, anoint your head and wash your face, that your fasting may not be seen by men but by your Father who is in secret; and your Father who sees in secret will reward you" (Mt 6:16–18). He also expects them to feast—and to do so inclusive of the poor. He teaches, "When you give a dinner or a banquet, do not invite your friends or your brothers or your kinsmen or rich neighbors, lest they also invite you in return, and you be repaid. But when you give a feast, invite the poor, the maimed, the lame, the blind, and you will be blessed, because they cannot repay you. You will be repaid at the resurrection of the just" (Lk 14:12–14).[15]

The preeminent example of New Testament feasting is the Last Supper. Brant Pitre has shown both that Jesus characteristically portrayed the eschatological "kingdom using the imagery of a banquet (Matt 22:1–14; Luke 14:15–24; Matt 26:29; Mark 14:25; Luke 22:15–18, 28–30; cf. Luke 12:35–40)," and that Jesus "connected the ingathering of the twelve tribes of Israel into the heavenly kingdom of God with his words and deeds at the Last Supper."[16] According to Pitre, the eating and drinking involved in the Last Supper (and in the disciples' re-enactment of the Last Supper in liturgical remembrance of Jesus) is the "mechanism" by which the restoration of Israel and the upbuilding of the eschatological kingdom is ongoing.[17] Pitre terms this the "eucharistic restoration of Israel," which unfolds "through the mission and ministry of his disciples after his death."[18] In the Last Supper, Jesus gives himself to his disciples as "the eschatological Passover lamb" and as the eschatological manna, food for the new exodus journey to the promised land of the heavenly new Jerusalem.[19] In this eucharistic restoration of Israel, eating and drinking play a central role as an efficacious sign of the new Passover that unites the restored people of God on their journey toward the true promised land.[20]

Lest the eating and drinking of the restored people of God be conceived of solely in sacramental terms, two points deserve further attention. First, Paul in 1 Corinthians 11 makes clear that Christians' eating and drinking of "the Lord's supper" (1 Cor 11:20) must ensure that the whole community has enough to eat and drink.[21] Part of "proclaim[ing] the Lord's death until he comes" (1 Cor 11:26) is that the eucharistic meal must not turn into an occasion for the manifestation of gluttony, privilege, or status. It must be grounded in generously sharing food and drink with each other. Paul warns the wayward Corinthians in the strongest possible terms: "When you meet together, it is not the Lord's supper that you eat. For in eating, each one goes ahead with his own meal, and one is hungry and another is drunk. What! Do you not have houses to eat and drink in? Or do you despise the church of God and humiliate those who have nothing?" (1 Cor 11:20–22). If generous love is not present, then the offending person has consumed "the Lord's supper" in "an unworthy manner" and is "guilty of profaning the body and blood of the Lord" (1 Cor 11:27), so much so that such a person "eats and drinks judgment upon himself" (1 Cor 11:29).

Paul describes this devastating "judgment" as resulting from a failure in "discerning the body" (1 Cor 11:29). The "body" here is the body of Christ, both his eucharistic body and his ecclesial body. As Paul goes on to say, "For just as the body is one and has many members, and all the members of the body, though many, are one body, so it is with Christ. For by one Spirit we were all baptized into one body—Jews or Greeks, slaves or free—and all were made to drink of one Spirit.... Now you are the body of Christ and individually members of it" (1 Cor 12:12–13, 27). The point is that if we are to eat and drink the new Passover meal rightly, we must rightly discern Christ's "body" by loving our neighbor and recognizing that "if one member suffers, all suffer together" (1 Cor 12:26). To do anything else is to "despise the church of God" and to eat and drink "judgment" through the profanation of Christ. Thus the restored people of God must eat and drink in a way that shares with others and is concerned with the welfare of others rather than gluttonously or drunkenly engaging in self-indulgence. As Wirzba puts it, "Coming to the Eucharistic table, eaters are encouraged to learn that they do not need to eat only to their own benefit and glory."[22]

Second, the restoration of God's people must cause a change in the priorities of believers with regard to eating and drinking. Put simply, we "live as enemies of the cross of God" when our "god is the belly" and our minds are "set on earthly things" (Phil 3:18–19). Paul complains about those who "do not serve our Lord Christ, but their own appetites" (Rom 16:18). To manifest the restoration of God's people requires certain habits of eating and drinking, not only vis-à-vis caring for other hungry and thirsty people but also with regard to our own appropriate abstinence and sobriety (as opposed to gluttony and drunkenness). Paul states that no one who is "greedy" or who is a "drunkard" (1 Cor 5:10–11) is truly a member of the restored people of God.

Karl Olav Sandnes explains that Paul has in view pagan banquets, which involved gorging on food, drunkenness, and sexual license (with female prostitutes and also homosexual coupling). Sandnes comments, "Banquets were occasions for eating and drinking accompanied by sexual interludes. . . . For Jewish and Christian writers, banquets of this kind were characteristic of paganism."[23] Among the Second Temple Jewish texts cited by Sandnes, Sirach belongs to the Catholic canon. Sandnes quotes the prayer of Sirach 23:4–5: "O Lord, Father and God of my life, do not give me haughty eyes, and remove from me evil desire. Let neither gluttony nor lust overcome me, and do not surrender me to a shameless soul."[24] Other Second Temple Jewish texts justify the Old Testament's food laws as serving to prevent gluttony, so that Jews might live in a way that is "compatible with the Jews' status of being divinely elected."[25] For Philo, Sandnes notes, "The pleasures, desires or lusts reside in the stomach. It is, therefore, at the centre of Philo's concerns to keep the belly under control."[26] Otherwise, Philo fears, the people of God will be dominated by bodily desires and will not be willing to contemplate or practice the things of God laid down in the Torah. The paradigmatic person governed by his belly is Esau, who sells his covenantal birthright to Jacob/Israel, and who is therefore the opposite of elect Israel.[27]

Paul adopts much of this perspective in his ethical injunctions for the people of God as eschatologically restored by Christ. For Paul, our eating and drinking are directly related to whether we will attain to the fullness of the consummated kingdom. As Sandnes observes, Paul in Philippians 3:19–21 sets before Christians two "options, a transformed and glorious body in the future or a present life according to the belly, which brings perdition."[28] On this view, believers who serve their own bellies and who "are unprepared to undertake a self-abnegating life according to the pattern set by Christ, have neglected their heavenly citizenship."[29] Their self-focused eating and drinking shows that they do not truly belong to the eschatological kingdom that Christ has inaugurated by undergoing the tribulation of the cross and over which the risen and ascended Christ reigns through his Spirit. Commenting on Philippians 3, Sandnes explains, "A true citizen of heaven follows the example of Christ; the example of self-loving belly-devotees leads to final destruction. The belly-devotees fail to participate in the suffering and will therefore also miss the future glory which the resurrected Christ embodies."[30]

Sharing in Christ's inaugurated kingdom, believers receive "a new agenda for their bodies" and a "new identity."[31] As members of the Church, we have been caught up by the Spirit into Christ's eschatological action of kingdom inauguration, and the indwelling Spirit is transforming our bodies; thus, who we have become "has consequences for what to do with the belly and the genitals."[32] Again, we display by the manner of our eating and drinking where our allegiances lie. Gluttony and drunkenness involve us in "belly-worship" and "enmity to Christ's cross" because we show that we are living according to our unruly and selfish passions rather than according to the Spirit of Christ.[33] The "bodily transformation" that is "under way" in those who are united to Christ characterizes the journey of the restored people of God on the new exodus to the heavenly Jerusalem.[34] Sandnes notes in this regard that the failures of God's people on the exodus had to do in significant part with failures of eating and drinking. He remarks, "The Exodus narrative is a story about how the demands of the belly overcame belief in God's providence" through the murmuring and idolatry of God's people.[35] Just as eating and drinking (and failures therein) were central to the first exodus, so also they are central to the new exodus of God's restored people. We show that we are God's restored people, worshiping him rightly and loving our neighbors, when our eating and drinking serve above all "for glorifying God."[36]

In *The Moral Vision of the New Testament*, Richard Hays asks: "How is the new community in which the kingdom of God is manifest related to the kingdoms of this world?"[37] One way of answering his question would be to look at the politics of eating and drinking. In the inaugurated kingdom of Christ, Christians are to live out the moderation in eating and drinking and fasting that God expected of Israel. They are not to live as nonbelievers do in the Wisdom of Solomon, where nonbelievers encourage each other, "[Let us] take our fill of costly wine" and live in "revelry," "because we were born by mere chance, and hereafter we shall be as though we had never been" (Wis 2:2, 7, 9). Such self-centered hedonism produces lack of concern for the poor, which quickly manifests itself in oppression of those whose neediness or whose accusations might disrupt the life of pleasure: "Let us oppress the righteous poor man; let us not spare the widow nor regard the gray hairs of the aged" (Wis 2:10). The fruits of hedonism become apparent in the devastating judgment that the Lord communicates through the prophet Amos: "Woe to those who lie upon beds of ivory, and stretch themselves upon their couches, and eat lambs from the flock, and calves from the midst of the stall; . . . who drink wine in bowls, and anoint themselves with the finest oils, but are not grieved over the ruin of Joseph! Therefore they shall now be the first of those to go into exile" (Amos 6:4–7).

It follows that the restored people of God must exhibit the care for others that God, through the prophets, insists must characterize his people. They must "practice hospitality" (Rom 12:13).[38] They will thereby show that the restoration of God's people, who worship God rather than worshiping "their own appetites" (Rom 16:18), has commenced. What Hays calls "the new community in which the kingdom of God is manifest" will worship God through hospitable eating and drinking.

What about fasting, however? Jesus speaks of the fasting of his disciples, but in books of contemporary Christian moral theology or New Testament ethics, fasting often goes unmentioned.[39] Granted that appropriate eating and drinking are important marks of the inaugurated kingdom, does the inaugurated kingdom need to include fasting? Certainly, periods of fasting characterized the lives of those who, prior to the coming of Jesus, prayed to be restored from exile. Ezra and the people who were returning from Babylonian exile gathered in a solemn assembly to celebrate a liturgical fast (Neh 9:1). Later, perceiving that the people were not obeying Torah, keeping Sabbath, or honoring the temple properly, Ezra spent a whole day "fasting" (Ezra 9:5). But in the period of the inaugurated kingdom, now that Christ has come, why does fasting need to persist?

In part, the answer is that fasting sometimes pertains to the mission of evangelization. Among the things that he has endured in service to God, Paul names hunger (2 Cor 6:5 and 11:27)—an enforced fasting, but one that he willingly endures in order to serve God. But more to the point is a comment that the biblical scholar Mary Healy makes about Mark 2:20: "Since Jesus will no longer be visibly present on earth, his disciples will rightly resume the [Jewish] practice of fasting, though on a different basis than before. From then on, fasting will be a way to prepare for and heighten the full joy of the messianic banquet in which we will one day share."[40] In the inaugurated but not yet consummated kingdom, fasting recalls us ever more deeply to the reality that—as Jesus says, quoting Deuteronomy 8:3—"man shall not live by bread alone, but by every word that proceeds from the mouth of God" (Mt 4:4). Fasting prepares us for the messianic banquet by heightening our yearning for it, a spiritual yearning of which bodily hunger is a sign, since only God can truly fill our deepest hunger. In this way, fasting enables us to share willingly in Christ's saving death. The Coptic monk Matta El-Maskeen (Matthew the Poor) observes that fasting's "essence is the intentional acceptance of death, that we may be counted fit to be mystically united in the flesh and blood of Christ."[41]

Fasting is presented by Jesus in the Gospel of Matthew as one of three central "kingdom practices," along with almsgiving and prayer.[42] Healy points out that, as with almsgiving, "Christian tradition has always closely linked fasting with charity to the poor."[43] This is because by freely fasting, believers become a sign of the restoration of Israel through solidarity with the poor and through concern that others besides ourselves are fed. As the prophets make clear, God wills for the restored Israel to care self-sacrificially for the poor—otherwise, as Paul says, we "despise the church and God and humiliate those who have nothing" (1 Cor 11:22). It follows that fasting, like the avoidance of gluttony and drunkenness, belongs to the eschatological ethics of followers of Christ. Wirzba rightly remarks, "The logic and the practice of sacrifice [understood as a participation in God's self-offering in Christ] leads to both feasting and fasting as two complementary and mutually correcting rhythms of a self-offering life."[44] Fasting, Wirzba explains, should be "understood as the restraining of personal desires that otherwise would seek to possess and consume the world.... People should fast so they do not degrade or hoard the good gifts of God."[45]

Thomas Aquinas on Temperance with Respect to Food and Drink

In this section, I explore how Aquinas contributes to the theology of the eating and drinking of the eschatologically restored people of God. Aquinas considers that abstinence and sobriety are "subjective parts" of temperance, which means that they belong to the proper species of temperance.[46] Christian abstinence does not mean abstaining from food, but rather it means eating rightly in particular circumstances, in accord with our vocation as God's eschatologically restored people or family in Christ. Fasting might therefore seem to be opposed to abstinence, since of course fasting involves abstaining even from appropriate bodily demands for food. One of Aquinas's tasks is to show how fasting fits with abstinence, especially (though not solely) for members of Christ. Aquinas also helps us to understand the vice opposed to abstinence, namely gluttony, as well as sobriety and its opposite, drunkenness. I will conclude this section with some brief reflections on alcoholism, which, as an addiction, cannot be accounted for simply in terms of intemperance.

Let us first recall that Aquinas holds that "temperance withdraws man from things which seduce the appetite from obeying reason," things that "are most seductive to man," namely the "greatest pleasures."[47] The greatest bodily pleasures are attached to those things that are necessary for bodily survival, both as an individual and as a species. Thus, temperance is principally about the things "which preserve the nature of the individual by means of meat and drink, and the nature of the species by the union of the sexes. Hence temperance is properly about pleasures of meat and drink and sexual pleasures."[48] Temperance moderates our desire for these pleasures, so that we do not get carried away beyond the rule of reason and end up living solely for these bodily pleasures, with little or no attention to their purpose or to the higher things for which we were created as rational animals. Aquinas describes temperance as the most "difficult" virtue, since "it is more difficult to control desires and pleasures of touch than to regulate external actions."[49]

Note that temperance, thus construed, does not seek to do away with bodily pleasure. On the contrary, as Rebecca Konyndyk DeYoung emphasizes, for Aquinas "the more natural and necessary the activity . . . the more pleasure God designed to accompany the activity. God did make food good. Eating and drinking are meant to give us pleasure."[50] Aquinas holds that pleasure both encourages us in undertaking good acts and adds a further good or end to the act, supervenient upon the primary good or end of the act.[51] The point, then, is not to exclude pleasure but to ensure that, in our fallen condition, we do not become irrationally and destructively wedded to seeking physical pleasure.[52] Aquinas criticizes those who are insensible to the pleasures of food, drink, and sex, while at the same time making clear that physical pleasure is not the greatest good and that we easily take pleasure in things that, morally speaking, we should not take pleasure in.[53]

Abstinence

Notwithstanding this overarching account of temperance, Aquinas recognizes that it may seem odd to associate eating and drinking with "virtue," let alone with the ethics of the inaugurated kingdom of God. In an objection, therefore, he quotes Romans 14:17, where Paul urges believers to recognize that "the kingdom of God does not mean food and drink but righteousness and peace and joy in the Holy Spirit."[54] If the "kingdom of God does not mean food and drink," does not this make clear that no virtue pertaining to eating or drinking belongs to the ethics of the inaugurated kingdom? In response to this concern, Aquinas grants that our use of food is, in a certain sense, not important to God. Persons who eat only a little are not thereby saints, nor are persons who eat a lot thereby sinners. Nor does God care whether we eat or do not eat certain foods. Instead, what is important to God is the intention with which we approach food. If we crave simply to satisfy our bodily appetites no matter whether this involves selfish self-centeredness, then we have separated ourselves from Christ's inaugurated kingdom. Aquinas concludes, therefore, that our use of and abstinence from food truly "belong to the kingdom of God, in so far as they are done reasonably through faith and love of God."[55]

Aquinas also raises the concern that the proper use of food pertains not to a virtue, but only to medicine's rules for bodily health. Especially today, the consumption of food tends to be seen in terms of health, and people who are overweight feel shame for lacking the self-control to be of a healthy weight—since virtuous eating is on this view "virtuous" only when it assists us in living longer and making fewer demands upon our health insurance.[56] If the proper use of food in fact belongs not to virtue but simply to the rules of bodily health, then it would be a stretch to believe that immoderate eating constitutes a sin rather than simply being bad for our health.

Aquinas replies by emphasizing the interior motivations of our eating. It is not a matter of what we eat or how much we eat, since evaluating those aspects of eating does indeed belong to the art of medicine rather than the art of virtue.[57] Instead, it is a matter of whether we allow our eating to be guided by reason, and thus not to be done in a self-centered or fundamentally pleasure-focused way (or, for that matter, in a way intentionally aimed at destroying our bodily health). Morally speaking, eating belongs to the manner in which human bodily life is meant to serve God and neighbor. When we eat in accord with membership in the people of God restored by Christ, we eat with enjoyment and pleasure, but with primary attention to strengthening our bodily life so that we can worship God properly and serve our neighbor as members of families and societies. By contrast, a selfish focus on satisfying ourselves through the pleasure of eating—a quest that in fact becomes an insatiable hunger—turns our minds and hearts away from both God and neighbor, so that we no longer care about what is reasonable or in accord with the true purposes that food serves.

Commenting on Aquinas's perspective, which is indebted to Augustine, Rebecca DeYoung remarks that "eating is a social act. How and what and why we eat should reflect what is appropriate given the needs of others in our family and our community."[58] According to Aquinas, the virtue of temperate eating or "abstinence" enables us to eat with regard not only for our own bodily life—let alone solely for the pleasure of eating—but also with proper regard for our neighbor's needs and for the work to which God has called us, including the work of worshiping God. The temperate eater will be able to put others first, as befits God's restored people. Aquinas notes that "right reason makes one abstain as one ought, i.e. with gladness of heart, and for the due end, i.e. for God's glory and not one's own."[59]

Even so, why should abstinence (temperate eating) be a virtue distinct from other forms of temperance? Aquinas quotes Paul's statement that "if we have food and clothing, with these we shall be content" (1 Tim 6:8).[60] But there is no distinct virtue regarding the use of clothing. Why then posit a distinct virtue regarding the use of food? Furthermore, why should "abstinence" differ from "chastity" (which regards sex), since it seems that temperate eating is just another way of chastening our bodily desire?

Aquinas answers that in fact we should identify a distinct virtue regarding the pleasures of food, because these pleasures are much stronger even than our desire for clothing. We need to be virtuously habituated with respect to the pleasures of food. As we know from experience, members of God's restored people will be tempted by "the onslaughts of gluttony" and will be tempted to focus on "pleasures of the table," given the central place of the desire for food within our bodily constitution.[61] If we give way to these temptations, we will end up serving our bellies rather than serving God and neighbor, and we will cling to our food rather than making sacrifices out of love for God or neighbor. On this basis, although Aquinas does not make this point, we can extend the meaning of Paul's argument in Romans 14 beyond its reference to Israel's food laws: "If your brother is being injured by what you eat, you are no longer walking in love" (Rom 14:15). We must walk "in love," and this requires temperate eating, so that we care about our neighbor's needs and care about service to God more than we care about satisfying our bodily desire for the pleasure of food.

Fasting

The biblical scholar Scot McKnight remarks, "A person who is totally open to God and responds to life's sacred moments with fasting can discover the life-giving presence of God and sometimes a palpable experience of God's presence."[62] By limiting our consumption of food below the amount that is in accord with reason, however, fasting seems to undermine the virtue of abstinence. Furthermore, Aquinas identifies other dangers of fasting: it can produce impatience (due to unmet hunger) and pride (when the fasting person focuses on his or her ability to fast rather than on God and neighbor).[63] Sandnes concludes his book by emphasizing the tendency for fasting to become inordinate: "If belly-worship is not necessarily a reference to quantity of food but to its obsession as well, what then about extreme asceticism? It may be that some of the Christian ascetic texts we have come across should fall under their own critique of gluttony, owing to their preoccupation with food."[64] Sensitive to such concerns about fasting, Aquinas wonders whether "fasting forsakes the mean of virtue, which in the virtue of abstinence takes account of the necessity of supplying the needs of nature."[65]

In response, citing the prophets and Augustine, Aquinas gives three reasons for the goodness of fasting during the period in which the restoration of God's people is still ongoing. Two of these reasons are negative: namely, fasting aids in sexual chastity by cooling off lust,[66] and fasting serves as part of penitential mourning for sins. With respect to negative (but good) reasons for fasting, the Quaker theologian Richard Foster remarks that "more than any other Discipline, fasting reveals the things that control us."[67] The third reason is positive, and it fits with Mary Healy's observation that in the inaugurated kingdom "fasting will be a way to prepare for and heighten the full joy of the messianic banquet in which we will one day share."[68] Aquinas's positive reason is that "we have recourse to fasting in order that the mind may arise more freely to the contemplation of heavenly things."[69] As the patristic scholar Margaret Miles puts it in light of Augustine's theology, fasting helps in "rebalancing the soul's weight of love" away from solely one's own body and toward God, and fasting thereby "makes the soul 'capacious.'"[70] For Aquinas, the prophet Daniel serves as an exemplar of fasting in a manner that strengthens the contemplative ascent to God or that opens us to God's revelatory descent. Fasting as an act of penitential mourning prepares repentant sinners for the consummated kingdom; and fasting to lift up our minds to God also prepares us for this consummation, because it removes us from our daily routine and reveals our hunger for divine realities.

Aquinas concludes that without overthrowing the virtue of abstinence, reason can rightly determine that it is "expedient, on account of some special motive, for a man to take less food than would be becoming to him under ordinary circumstances."[71] He points out that we can reasonably fast for purposes other than spiritual ones, as for instance when we fast "in order to avoid sickness."[72] Today we still sometimes fast for health reasons, including fasting prior to a medical test or surgery. Since we reasonably fast for bodily purposes, it is reasonable also occasionally to fast for spiritual purposes. Aquinas adds the clarification that fasting should not so restrict our eating that we suffer bodily to the point of becoming incapacitated. As a general rule, fasting should mean eating one full meal per day.[73] He also clarifies that since fasting aims to "bridle the concupiscences of the flesh," animal flesh and animal products are not appropriate for those who fast—although the exclusion of animal products (such as eggs and milk) is arguably not necessary, since for most people the simple exclusion of meat cuts sharply into the pleasure of eating.[74]

Because reasonable people will want to avoid sin, raise their minds to God, and do penance for past sins, it can even be said that fasting belongs to "natural law." Fasting also belongs to the Church's law, through the days of fasting (primarily in Advent and Lent) that the Church prescribes for the restored people of God who still are awaiting perfect restoration.[75] The Church's fasts are "of use in hindering the slavery of sin, which is opposed to spiritual freedom."[76] To those who would appeal to Christian freedom against the Church's requirement of communal fasting, Aquinas responds by quoting Galatians 5:13: "For you were called to freedom, brethren; only do not use your freedom as an opportunity for the flesh."[77] In the freedom enjoyed by the members of the inaugurated kingdom, fasting has a significant place, just as Jesus indicated when he identified fasting as one of the three "kingdom practices."

It is no wonder, then, that such scholars as Margaret Miles and Sarah Coakley have called for a "new asceticism."[78] As Miles approvingly observes with regard to fasting and other ascetic practices, "The immediate goals of asceticism . . . include self-understanding, overcoming of habituation and addiction, gathering and focusing of energy, ability to change our cultural conditioning, and intensification or expansion of consciousness."[79] These goals clearly serve the ongoing eschatological restoration of the people or family of God.[80]

However, does not Jesus' saying, "As long as they have the bridegroom with them, they cannot fast" (Mk 2:19; cf. Lk 5:34), overthrow his commandment to fast, since Jesus tells us that he is with us "always, to the close of the age" (Mt 28:20)?[81] In reply to this objection, Aquinas gladly affirms that Jesus is present even now, insofar as he indwells the righteous (see Jn 14:23). Since Jesus is present, Aquinas accepts that "the righteous are not bound by the commandment of the Church to fast," at least not bound in a strict sense.[82] The Church's commandment to fast is not binding in the sense of allowing no exceptions. If righteous persons have good reason not to fast during a period set aside for fasting by the Church, they may use their "own judgment in omitting to fulfil the precept."[83] Aquinas explains that "if one be under the necessity . . . of doing much work, either for one's bodily livelihood, or for some need of the spiritual life, and it be impossible at the same time to keep the fasts of the Church, one is not bound to fast."[84] He also states that the poor "who beg their food piecemeal" are exempt from observing the Church's fasts, "since they are unable at any one time to have a sufficiency of food."[85] The purpose of the Church's establishment of periods of fasting is to serve the spiritual growth of the restored people of God, not to burden them in unfruitful ways.

Aquinas reflects a bit more upon the various ways of interpreting Jesus' statement that "as long as they have the bridegroom with them, they cannot fast" (Mk 2:19). He gives three patristic interpretations, all rooted in the Vulgate's phrase "children of the bridegroom" ("wedding guests" in the RSV translation of Mk 2:19). First, John Chrysostom holds that the "children" are those who are imperfect in the spiritual life, as the disciples were during Jesus' public ministry. On this view, since the disciples were so imperfect, Jesus spared them "the harshness of fasting," and other beginners should also be spared.[86] Second, Bede argues that Jesus was speaking simply of the fasts of the Jewish liturgical cycle, which Jesus allowed his disciples to ignore in certain instances. Third, Augustine distinguished two kinds of fasting, one for the imperfect ("children"), who fast in order to avoid sin and do penance, and the other for the perfect, who fast in order to rejoice "in adhering to spiritual things."[87] Aquinas favors the third view. This position makes fasting necessary during earthly life even for those who have been fully configured to Christ, but the reason for their fasting will differ from the reason that persons who are less fully configured to Christ need to fast. As Wirzba remarks, "Fasting, in its most fundamental aspiration, is about developing a sacrificial, self-offering life."[88]

Aquinas is experientially aware that "those who are desirous of giving themselves up to contemplation and divine things need much to refrain from carnal things."[89] If our attention is glued to the latter, we will not be appropriately attentive to the former, as everyone knows who has thought longingly about Sunday lunch during Mass. Aquinas gives the example of the penitent fasting that Daniel undertook in preparation for his divinely given vision.[90] He explains that Daniel did not reject the pleasures of food and drink as such, but rather gave them up for a good purpose, namely that of "adapt[ing] himself to the heights of contemplation."[91] Fasting in service of contemplation characterizes the prophet who saw the great eschatological vision of conflict followed by restoration, with the promise that his people would be delivered—"every one whose name shall be found written in the book" (Dan 12:1).

Today, in the kingdom that Christ has inaugurated but not consummated, followers of Christ continue to seek "the heights of contemplation."[92] Aquinas observes in this regard that "contemplation may be delightful on the part of its object, in so far as one contemplates that which one loves; even as bodily vision gives pleasure, not only because to see is pleasurable in itself, but because one sees a person whom one loves."[93] For Aquinas, Mary of Bethany is a model of this contemplation. Just as Mary sat "at the Lord's feet and listened to his teaching" (Lk 10:39), so those who today contemplate the mysteries of the Lord must pray fervently and listen attentively to their beloved Lord.[94]

Aquinas appreciates that not all Christians need to devote their lives to contemplation. Moreover, even fasting for the purpose of contemplation does not require abstaining from all bodily pleasure, since contemplatives too must sustain their bodily life by eating and drinking. For believers who "are in duty bound to bodily occupations and carnal procreation," comparatively more eating and drinking is appropriate.[95] All believers, however, must live in the world with the primary awareness that the kingdom has been inaugurated.[96] As Paul exhorts, believers must "deal with the world as though they had no dealings with it. For the form of this world is passing away" (1 Cor 7:31). The affairs of this world can no longer be at the center of attention. Instead, we must first "seek the things that are above, where Christ is, seated at the right hand of God" (Col 3:1). In the inaugurated kingdom, "prayer and fasting" (Mk 9:29) have transformative power.

Gluttony

Gluttony and drunkenness are what Aquinas calls "childish" vices.[97] They strive to satisfy concupiscence—desire for physical pleasures—whereas in fact concupiscence becomes stronger and more insatiable the more we feed it. Aquinas explains that "concupiscence, if indulged, gathers strength," and he compares this process to a spoiled and irrational child who becomes even more self-willed when indulged.[98] He recognizes that once intemperate eating or drinking has arisen, the only solution consists in resisting and restraining it, just as one corrects a spoiled child. God's restored people must exhibit such mature temperance, since persons entrapped by gluttony and drunkenness damage not only their own bodily health but also the healthy functioning of their families and society. As the moral philosopher Robert Kruschwitz states, "Gluttony is essentially a deformation within the human self . . . yet this deformation always has social implications because its origin, in part, and destructive outworking are in distorted personal relationships and institutions of society."[99] Proverbs 23:19–21 warns firmly against gluttony: "Hear, my son, and be wise, and direct your mind in the way. Be not among the winebibbers, or among gluttonous eaters of meat; for the drunkard and the glutton will come to poverty."

Aquinas poses a problem, however, for those who wish to hold that gluttony is a sin. Jesus says, "Hear and understand: not what goes into the mouth defiles a man, but what comes out of the mouth, this defiles a man" (Mt 15:10–11).[100] If so, then Christians should not worry about "what goes into the mouth." In fact, of course, Jesus is not denying that there are sinful modes of eating, but he is responding to misunderstandings of the food laws of the Torah. Aquinas explains that in eating, we are tempted to ignore the order of reason, which requires that our eating be ordered toward bodily sustenance and, above all, toward the service of God and neighbor. In our fallen state, we are liable to crave the pleasures of eating over against the real but forgotten purposes of eating. Aquinas specifies the problem as "the inordinate desire of food."[101] As he points out, indebted to Gregory the Great, it is quite possible for our desire to eat (and to eat well) to go beyond the bounds of natural hunger and to take over the direction of our lives. It is easy to conceive of a person who "adheres to the pleasure of gluttony as his end, for the sake of which he contemns God, being ready to disobey God's commandments, in order to obtain those pleasures."[102] God's commandments include worshiping God and caring for one's neighbor, but care for God and neighbor goes by the wayside when our goals revolve around eating. Thus the question is whether our eating retains a reasonable ordering to (or care for) the proper nourishment of the body, the worship of God, and the service of our neighbor.

The most easily recognized forms of gluttony involve eating unnecessarily large amounts or eating hastily and greedily, with the result that mealtimes become periods of gorging ourselves rather than periods of nourishment and care for family and neighbors. But there are other, less recognizable forms of gluttony, including fastidious or "dainty" eating, where we refuse to eat anything but foods prepared in a specific way, as well as "sumptuous" eating, where we insist upon only the best food. Often without our recognizing it, these forms of gluttony blind us to food's real purposes and cause us to ignore God and neighbor, so focused do we become on our own high-maintenance eating.[103] As DeYoung comments, in order to perceive whether gluttony has become part of our lives, we need to ask whether we are eating "in a way that elevates our own satisfaction above other good things."[104]

Although Aquinas notes that "lust . . . is a greater vice than gluttony, and is about greater pleasures," he finds that gluttony can lead us seriously astray.[105] The sins of eating are by no means the gravest sins that we can commit, but they can still be mortal sins that separate us from God due to our focusing upon our own bodily pleasures to the detriment of caring for others and for God. Aquinas adds that "the sin of gluttony is diminished . . . on account of the necessity of taking food, and on account of the difficulty of proper discretion and moderation in such matters."[106] He emphasizes that the sin of gluttony can often be venial rather than mortal, as "when a man has too great a desire for the pleasures of the palate, yet would not for their sake do anything contrary to God's law."[107] As Kruschwitz observes in commenting upon Aquinas's position, "gluttonous actions" do not "typically" rise to the level of mortal sin, although we do commit mortal sin (separating ourselves from charity) when we purposefully "harm other people and the created order or ignore God's direction . . . in order to protect our preferred pleasures of eating and drinking."[108] Even though most sins of gluttony are venial, therefore, it remains the case that a gluttonous person can mortally sin by willfully neglecting his or her relationships with God and neighbor and becoming "preoccupied with only physical desires in an escalating and futile cycle of avoiding spiritual starvation by indulging ourselves physically."[109]

Indebted to Gregory the Great, Aquinas describes five "daughters of gluttony," that is, vices that result from the vice of gluttony.[110] The first consists in the dulling of the rational powers due to overeating.

When we live a life based on overeating, as today can easily be done in societies that are saturated by inexpensive fast food, we are likely to have less mental energy for thinking about and serving God and neighbor. The second is "unseemly joy" in the wonderful delight of eating — it is unseemly because it exaggerates the true place of eating among the human goods and relegates rational activity to a place below the joy of eating.[111] DeYoung explains that "this is why, traditionally, the glutton is portrayed as being more animal-like than human. Animals go straight for food without any thought for manners, conversation, health, or social commerce — that is, without any thought for the symbolic or social aspects of eating that make it fully human."[112] The third, fourth, and fifth vices are loquaciousness, scurrility, and uncleanness, by which Aquinas has in view the descent of the gluttonous person into an increasingly animal-like existence. When we are afflicted with gluttony, we may devote our lives to the pleasures of the table, which include the foolish talk, laughter, and sexual licentiousness that we associate with people who are heavy partiers. People who are known (in modern parlance) as "party animals" can make us laugh, but their lives are often separated from love of neighbor and love of God by what Catherine of Siena calls "sensual selfish love."[113]

Sobriety and Drunkenness

The virtue of abstinence, which deals with the pleasures of the table, includes drink in a certain way, when drink is understood as food or nourishment.[114] But a special virtue, "sobriety," is needed for the drinking of alcohol.[115] In taking up the topic of sobriety, Aquinas grounds himself in Sirach 31:27: "Wine is like life to men, if you drink it in moderation" (the Vulgate verse is translated, "Wine taken with sobriety equals life to men; if thou drink it moderately, thou shalt be sober").[116] The very next lines of Sirach 31 read: "What is life to a man who is without wine? It has been created to make men glad. Wine drunk in season and temperately is rejoicing of heart and gladness of soul" (Sir 31:27-28; see also Ps 104:14-15). Reasonable drinking, therefore, does not mean the avoidance of alcohol. But it does mean careful moderation in the use of alcohol, and in this regard Aquinas also has

Sirach 31 on his side. Sirach 31:29–30 states, "Wine drunk to excess is bitterness of soul, with provocation and stumbling. Drunkenness increases the anger of a fool to his injury, reducing his strength and adding wounds."[117] Sirach 31 approves of "merrymaking" (Sir 31:31), but rejects drunkenness. Aquinas does the same, remarking about alcohol that "the measured use thereof is most profitable, while immoderate excess therein is most harmful."[118]

The problem with the excessive drinking of alcohol is that it clouds human rationality, and therefore it is in itself an irrational action that leads to further irrational actions. Because of this problem, should we ban the drinking of wine? In an objection that favors banning alcohol, Aquinas cites Ecclesiastes 2:3 (Vulgate): "I thought in my heart to withdraw my flesh from wine, that I might turn my mind to wisdom."[119] Drinking alcohol can undermine the contemplation of God (and of neighbor in relation to God) for which humans were created. Aquinas adds that it is possible to interpret Romans 14:21 as excluding the drinking of alcohol: "It is right not to eat meat or drink wine or do anything that makes your brother stumble."

In response to arguments that favor banning alcohol, Aquinas quotes 1 Timothy 5:23, which instructs Timothy as follows: "No longer drink only water, but use a little wine for the sake of your stomach and your frequent ailments."[120] The point is that if Paul advocates the drinking of wine, then Christian communities need not ban wine. In Aquinas's view, this tolerance holds for all alcoholic drinks, since it is not the drinks themselves but rather the quantity or improper use that is the problem. On the other hand, recognizing that some people have a propensity toward drunkenness, Aquinas holds that in some cases it is indeed "unlawful" for a person to drink wine, as when a person "is easily the worse for taking wine" or when others might be "scandalized thereby."[121] Certainly, as Christopher Cook remarks, Christians will seek to avoid drunkenness not only on grounds that we share with non-Christians but also insofar as drunkenness can be "the result of a desire which exerts over an individual a power which competes with the call of God" and leads to "a life which is inappropriate to, or unready for, the kingdom of God."[122] Aquinas adds that contemplatives do not normally drink wine, since perfect wisdom requires the full use of reason.[123] He expects the Spirit-filled Church to include some persons who altogether avoid wine in order "that they may aim at perfection."[124]

Should we expect young people to exercise less sobriety, while the older and wiser members of the community should be expected to be more sober in their drinking habits? This is sometimes the way that the world works, but Aquinas thinks that it should not be so among believers. He cites 1 Timothy 3:11 and Titus 2:6, both of which urge young men and women to behave with sobriety.[125] Aquinas notes that "concupiscence of pleasure thrives in the young on account of the heat of youth," and too much wine further encourages sins of drunkenness and lust.[126] He notes that older persons should also display sobriety, and he quotes Titus 2:2 and 1 Timothy 3:2 in this regard. Otherwise, the leaders of the community will not be able to lead with wisdom, since "immoderate use of wine is a notable obstacle to the use of reason: wherefore sobriety is specially prescribed to the old, in whom reason should be vigorous in instructing others."[127] The whole Christian community should display a reason-governed use of alcohol, including "bishops and all ministers of the Church, who should fulfil their spiritual duties with a devout mind."[128]

Aquinas's concerns about drunkenness find a strong echo in Paul. Paul warns that members of God's inaugurated kingdom must "cast off the works of darkness and put on the armor of light; let us conduct ourselves becomingly as in the day, not in reveling and drunkenness" (Rom 13:12–13).[129] Aquinas cites this text, which is followed by Paul's manifesto for eschatological temperance: "Put on the Lord Jesus Christ, and make no provision for the flesh, to gratify its desires" (13:14). This means living in accord with Christ-like love of God and neighbor, rather than living for sensual pleasures.

In his discussion of drunkenness, Aquinas grants that sometimes persons can become drunk by mistake and without it being their fault, if they do not recognize how strong the wine is. He gives the example of Noah, who "planted a vineyard" and then, after drinking the wine, "became drunk" (Gen 9:20–21).[130] More usually, getting drunk is deliberate and constitutes a sin, which Aquinas shows by reference to the Church's canonical practice with regard to drunken clergy.[131] The "drunkenness" that Paul warns against in Romans 13:13 occurs when a person knows that the drink will make him or her drunk and chooses to drink it. Again, the problem with drunkenness consists in its obscuring of our use of reason, since it is by the use of reason that a person "performs virtuous deeds and avoids sin."[132] When we are drunk, we cannot govern ourselves toward charitable service of God and neighbor, and indeed drunk persons often inflict harm upon other people, including family members.

Aquinas does not suppose that deliberate drunkenness is the *worst* of sins, since, with Gregory the Great, he holds that "spiritual vices are greater than carnal vices."[133] But drunkenness, like other sins of bodily intemperance, is among the sins to which humankind "is most prone."[134] This means that we believers need to guard against drunkenness so as to retain our ability, as Paul says, to "put on the Lord Jesus Christ" and make him manifest in the world. We do not want to be like Lot, who, when drunk, unconsciously fell into the unspeakably terrible action of incest.[135]

Aquinas's treatment of drunkenness leaves room for further discussion of the problem of addiction to alcohol or the cognate problem of addiction to other mind-altering substances.[136] Although alcoholism obviously cannot be separated from the vice of drunkenness,[137] the ethicist Kent Dunnington (among others) has shown that even if a person's addiction to alcohol begins with an intemperate love of alcohol, the addiction soon goes beyond "sensory pleasure" and can stay with a person even despite "strong sensory *aversions*."[138] Dunnington shows that what attracts alcoholics to drinking are such goods as "the ability to communicate, being at ease with oneself, being unafraid and being part of the community."[139] It follows that addiction to alcohol or drugs cannot effectively be opposed or thwarted by shame, a fact that Christopher Cook attributes both to "neurochemistry" and to the underlying desire of addictive personalities "to be something other (or rather better) than that which they actually find themselves to be."[140]

Since alcoholism therefore cannot be solely addressed in terms of intemperance (which is directed by the quest for sensory pleasure), it is not surprising that Alcoholics Anonymous and other similar programs succeed by forming intentional communities of friendship and shared purpose.¹⁴¹ For Alcoholics Anonymous, much depends upon recognizing that we cannot escape the habituation of addiction by force of will, but must instead rely upon divine grace to overcome our captivity to sin (cf. Rom 7:23) and to restore us as the truly flourishing people of God—freed from choosing alcohol over real relationships—that we were created to be.¹⁴² This modern insight into addiction to alcohol goes beyond what Aquinas says about drunkenness, while being fully congruent with it.

* * *

In this chapter, I have argued that Aquinas's reflections on abstinence, fasting, and sobriety shed light on Christ's eschatological restoration of the people or family of God. Discussing God's giving of the manna to Israel, Ellen Davis argues that the giving of the manna has to do with whether Israel is willing to be distinctive as a "counterculture to Egypt" with regard to "the moral economy of eating."¹⁴³ On the exodus, despite being the family of God, Israel shows every sign of loving its own bodily needs and pleasures more than it loves God, even given the salvific actions of God on its behalf.

This situation is all too familiar in our own lives. As I have suggested in this chapter, we tend to value our own belly more than we value service to and love of God and neighbor. We easily focus on the enjoyment that we will take from our next meal or our next drink, rather than worshiping God or caring for the hungry neighbor. Aquinas is right to acknowledge the "greater force" and "impetuousness" of the natural desires for the pleasures of food and drink, since these belong to our self-preservation. These pleasures can quickly become selfish.¹⁴⁴ Fallen people such as ourselves, therefore, need the Messiah whom God sends "to restore the preserved of Israel" and who will be "a light to the nations, that [God's] salvation may reach to the end of the earth" (Is 49:6).

For Aquinas, then, "the moral economy of eating" has a central place among God's eschatologically restored people. God intends for his restored people to eat and drink in a rational way, to order their eating and drinking to the nourishment of bodily life and above all to the service and love of God and neighbor. The essayist Francine Prose points out that gluttony "may well be the most widespread" today of the seven deadly sins, at least among well-to-do Westerners.[145] Given this situation, if Christians are truly to be an eschatological people configured to Christ's cruciform love, we must work to ensure that we do not in fact love our own bellies more than we love God and neighbor. We cannot be among those persons who, despite claiming to be followers of Jesus, "do not serve our Lord Christ, but [our] own appetites" (Rom 16:18).

Learning to eat reasonably, healed by Christ's Spirit, therefore requires what Aquinas calls "abstinence." Abstinence means that we eat for the proper reasons, above all for the service of God and neighbor. Such eating will bring glory to God and will manifest his inaugurated kingdom of love, because we will care for God and neighbor—and thus for the poor—rather than simply for ourselves. Put succinctly, the abstinent person does not care for himself or herself in a way that undercuts attentiveness to God and the poor. Even when hungry, the abstinent person orients his or her eating toward the care of God's whole family. This means caring about all those who are hungry: "If a brother or sister is ill-clad and in lack of daily food, and one of you says to them, 'Go in peace, be warmed and filled,' without giving them the things needed for the body, what does it profit?" (Js 2:15–16). It is easy to see that neither gluttony, in which we focus on our bellies, nor drunkenness befits the manifestation of God's inaugurated kingdom in the world. Instead, such vices describe an animal-like and selfishly self-centered existence, whose focus is earthly life alone.

As we have seen, Aquinas also devotes a good deal of attention to fasting, which is one of the "kingdom practices" identified by Jesus as characteristic of the restored people of God. In his discussion of fasting, Aquinas's main purpose consists in showing that fasting is reasonable, rather than being an example of exaggerated asceticism. Fasting helps us to avoid and overcome sin, and it also helps us to raise our minds beyond our earthly sustenance to divine realities.

Liturgically, the feasts and fasts of Israel focus eating and drinking upon the people's covenantal relationship with the Lord. The Eucharist does the same for Christ's restored people or family on the new exodus. "Someday," as the biblical scholar Ben Witherington III says in his book on the Lord's Supper, "the currently invisible Host will show up, and we will see him face to face. It is a consummation devoutly to be wished. In the meantime, we must learn to be better dinner guests, waiting on one another, communing together with one eye on heaven and one on each other. We need to relearn how to make a meal of it rather than a mess of it."[146] In learning to be "better dinner guests," the eschatologically restored people of God need to eat and drink temperately, not only (as the Jewish thinker Leon Kass observes) in "the reverent ritual meal" but also in "feeding the stranger at our hearth; the well-mannered family supper; the convivial and witty dinner party."[147] May it be so.

CHAPTER FOUR

Chastity

Like many biblical scholars today, N. T. Wright considers that "Genesis 1 is in fact a 'temple'-vision, God making a heaven-and-earth house for himself in which he would place, at its heart and as the climax of creation itself, the humans who would be his image-bearers, his royal priesthood."[1] The task of these humans as God's images and royal priests is to give worship to God on behalf of the whole creation and to reflect God's "wise order into his world."[2] In Genesis 1, God's "wise order" attains its pinnacle when "God create[s] man in his own image" as "male and female," and God commands the man and woman to "be fruitful and multiply" (Gen 1:27–28). Genesis 2 describes the man's joy at the creation of woman and concludes—in a verse quoted by Jesus when he is asked about marriage and divorce—"Therefore a man leaves his father and his mother and cleaves to his wife, and they become one flesh" (Gen 2:24; Mt 19:5).[3] The wise order of God includes the "one flesh" union of man and woman for the purpose of bearing and raising children to be royal priests of creation who give praise to God in their actions. The "dominion" on earth that God grants to humans (Gen 1:28) is for the purpose of reflecting God's "wise order" for creaturely flourishing and making this order present in the world.

In this chapter, I ask what it means for humans to reflect God's "wise order into his world" specifically with regard to sexual desire and sexual actions. I argue that God's wise order for human sexuality requires the virtue of chastity. Chastity has a central place in the eschatological restoration of God's people and their reigning in the world as his royal and priestly images, as what Wright calls a "new family" that lives together in a "way that declare[s] to the world that Jesus, the crucified and risen one, [is] the world's true sovereign."[4] In contemporary culture, the term "chastity" often is taken to mean sexual repression and forced renunciation of sexual pleasure, as in the infamous "chastity belt." But in fact, as the theologian Dennis Okholm observes, the Christian virtue of chastity "is a social virtue that has to do with human relationships truly founded on love over against selfish desire or vainglorious manipulation."[5]

Not surprisingly, the fact that humans are male and female is highly important for understanding chaste use of our sexual organs. After all, human bodiliness as male and female possesses certain complementary natural purposes or ends that pertain to the flourishing of human beings, individually and communally.[6] Given our creation as male and female, our sexual constitution inscribes procreative and unitive ends for the purpose of the upbuilding of family life—and thereby the life of the restored family of God. Since sexual actions should express self-giving love for one's beloved, this uniquely embodied love should value the intrinsic spiritual and bodily ends of both sexual partners.[7] Ultimately, therefore, chaste sexual acts have much more meaning than today we tend to associate with sexual activity, which often is seen as being merely about using one's body in the pursuit of pleasure or in the fulfillment of the human need for intimacy.[8]

Due to our fallen condition, we can easily find ourselves desiring to engage in sexual acts that actually impede our true flourishing and prevent us from manifesting the inauguration of God's eschatologically restored people. The sociologist Mark Regnerus notes that contemporary culture has seen a rise in sex that does not involve or sustain strong relational commitments and that therefore will be ultimately unsatisfying for human beings.[9] When we are "aflame with passion" (1 Cor 7:9), we want the consummation of sexual pleasure without concern for much else, including the bonds of marriage and family.[10] But the misguided pursuit of sexual intimacy greatly harms persons, families, and communities. Although we sometimes hope that our sexual acts have no consequences outside the consenting participants, the fact is that when we fornicate, commit adultery, use pornography, and so forth, these actions undermine the stable bond that is needed for the flourishing of marital intimacy and for the raising of children by their own mother and father.[11]

By contrast, chaste sexual activity, in accordance with the intrinsic (even if normally unconscious) ends of embodied human sexuality, always includes an ordering to familial flourishing and thus to the affirmation of "a child's right to a family background," namely the right to be raised by one's mother and father.[12] As the philosopher Janet Smith comments, our "natural urge for sexual pleasure" is good—without it the intimate communion of man and woman would be greatly impoverished and the human race would have ceased to exist long ago—but we need chastity in order to appreciate that, as befits God's images who are called to reflect his wise order, "this urge must be put in service of the goods of the persons whom that urge affects."[13] In God's eschatologically restored people or family, we receive the grace of the Holy Spirit so that we may "embody the divine love that sent the Son into the world."[14]

My chapter proceeds in two steps. First, I examine the New Testament's teachings about sexual ethics. In recent years, Christian ethicists have relied less and less upon Scripture's teachings about sexual morality, which can appear to be culturally conditioned in a way that renders them devoid of authority for contemporary Christian practice. I survey two representative accounts of Scripture's authority over Christian moral life, namely those of N. T. Wright and the moral theologian Margaret Farley.[15] Wright argues that Scripture is authoritative (including for Christian ethics) because it teaches the transformative ways in which God wishes for us to live in union with Christ through the Spirit. According to Farley's book on Christian sexual ethics, by contrast, scripture essentially offers no authoritative teaching on sexual ethics. In her view, when scripture teaches about sexual ethics, it is usually either self-contradictory or just plain wrong. Aquinas's perspective accords with that of Wright. Aquinas understands scripture as communicating divine revelation about holiness of life, including commandments and instructions about the moral status of the particular kinds of acts by which we love—or fail to love—other persons "through the body" as temples of the Holy Spirit.[16]

Second, having identified the central importance of divine revelation and scriptural teaching for Christian theological understanding of chastity, I address Aquinas's discussion of chastity and the sins against chastity, with brief attention to his theology of virginity. Aquinas's theology of chastity makes manifest the eschatological restoration of God's family accomplished by Jesus Christ, who enables his followers to reflect God's wise order in their sexual actions. As the theologian Beth Felker Jones observes, "God's good intention is for sex to embody a one-flesh union. That union is supposed to be radical, permanent, and intimate. It's supposed to be about mutual fidelity and to affirm the goodness of bodies and of sexual difference."[17] Aquinas helps us to appreciate how and why this is so in the inaugurated kingdom of God, instructed by the "law of Christ" (Gal 6:2) and living out what Aquinas calls "the Gospel of the kingdom."[18]

Scripture and Sexual Ethics

The biblical scholar Joseph Atkinson remarks that for Israel sexuality is no "mere random copulation but the actual reproducing, nourishing, and transmitting of the divine image," and so "the family emerges as the instrument God has created by which His primary blessing in creation is realized."[19] Sexual lust is shown to cause great problems already in the book of Genesis. The insatiable lust of the men of Sodom, who desired to have sex with male strangers who were staying in Lot's house, helps to bring about God's vengeance upon the city (Gen 19). When "Shechem the son of Hamor the Hivite, the prince of the land" (34:2), raped Jacob's daughter Dinah, the result was that all the men of that land—including Shechem and Hamor—were slain by Jacob's sons. Jacob had to gather his family and flee to Bethel. When Joseph was a slave in the house of the Egyptian soldier Potiphar, the wife of Potiphar developed lust for Joseph because he was "handsome and good-looking" (39:6). Joseph repeatedly refused to have sex with her, and as a result she invented a story that got Joseph cast into prison and nearly killed. The Ten Commandments that God gives to Moses at Mount Sinai include prohibitions of both adultery and coveting someone else's wife (Exod 20:14, 17). Directly after forbidding the offering of a child by fire to the god Molech (the worst kind of idolatry), God commands Moses to forbid homosexual acts: "You shall not lie with a male as with a woman" (Lev 18:22). God likewise forbids incest and making one's daughter into a prostitute, "lest the land fall into harlotry and the land become full of wickedness" (19:29). Lest anyone think chastity unimportant, God assigns the punishment of death to adultery, homosexual acts, and incest (20:10–21).

In the book of Judges, furthermore, a man and his concubine are passing through Gibeah (in the land of Benjamin) when the men of the city seek to rape the man but settle for raping the concubine, leading to her death. The outrage caused by this action leads to a civil war (Judg 19–20). King David's decline begins when he commits adultery with Bathsheba, wife of his soldier Uriah the Hittite (2 Sam 11). To cover up this adultery David has Uriah killed, and a cycle of familial violence ensues, which includes the incestuous rape of David's daughter Tamar by his son Amnon. The result of this rape, in due time, is not only the death of Amnon but also a civil war led by Tamar's brother Absalom against his father, David (2 Sam 13-18). King Solomon outdoes all others in polygamy—which in due time is ruled out for Israel—and his excessive attention to his numerous wives eventually leads to his downfall (1 Kgs 11:1–8). Meanwhile, numerous married couples such as Hannah and Elkanah (1 Sam 1–2) receive praise and are blessed with children.

In Proverbs, we find grave warnings against lust. We read, "Should your springs be scattered abroad, streams of water in the streets? Let them be for yourself alone, and not for strangers with you. Let your fountain be blessed, and rejoice in the wife of your youth, a lovely hind, a graceful doe. Let her affection fill you at all times with delight, be infatuated always with her love" (Prov 5:16–19). Repeatedly, the recipient of the proverbs is urged to avoid "a harlot" and "an adulteress," on the grounds that committing adultery is like playing with fire: "Can a man carry fire in his bosom and his clothes not be burned? Or can one walk upon hot coals and his feet not be scorched? So is he who goes in to his neighbor's wife; none who touches her will go unpunished" (6:26-29).

Since over the course of time God reveals and clarifies core elements of sexual ethics to his people Israel, Paul retains much of "classic Jewish sexual ethics" in teaching the Gentiles about sexual ethics in Christ, even though Christ fills in the loophole in the Mosaic law's teaching on divorce and remarriage.[20] Paul teaches his churches to avoid "immorality, impurity, licentiousness, idolatry," and so on (Gal 5:19–20; cf. 2 Cor 12:21).[21] Paul warns against the "unnatural passions" of women having sexual relations with women and men having sexual relations with men (Rom 1:26–27). With sorrow, Paul finds himself having to inform Gentile Christians, who should be living in accord with the Spirit, "There is immorality among you, and of a kind that is not found even among pagans; for a man is living with his father's wife" (1 Cor 5:1). Paul even has to warn against sexual intercourse with prostitutes: "Shall I . . . take the members of Christ and make them members of a prostitute? Never! Do you not know that he who joins himself to a prostitute becomes one body with her?" (6:15–16). In condemning such behavior, which Greco-Roman culture assumed to be acceptable for men, Paul points out that whereas "every other sin which a man commits is outside the body," "the immoral man sins against his own body" (6:18). Such sin is particularly disastrous for Christians, whose bodies should "glorify God" (6:20). Commenting on 1 Corinthians 6:19–20, N. T. Wright remarks, "Those who already stand on resurrection ground, and must learn to live in this new world, need to be reminded that what they do with their bodies in the present matters."[22]

Indeed, Wright points out that "the common life of the church . . . seems to have functioned from the first in terms of an alternative family."[23] The restored people of God can be rightly described as the family of God (see Eph 3:15). Similarly, the theologian Joseph Hellerman highlights "the New Testament model of the church as a strong-group family."[24] This does not mean, of course, that standard families become unimportant. On the contrary, the New Testament makes clear that families, rooted in the husband and wife's sacramental signification of "Christ and the church" (5:32), are crucial for nourishing the friendship with Christ that encompasses all who love the Lord. Christian sexual ethics begins with the married couple and the unity of the family, whose flourishing serves the broader flourishing of the entire restored people or family of God.

Wright holds that Paul's eschatological ethics "reflects Paul's vision of the coming divine rule over the whole creation, and of humans being called to share in this rule," so that Christian moral life is about becoming "the sort of people through whom the one God will establish his sovereign rule, bringing his wise order into the world."[25] This means that Christ's eschatological family must image God with respect to sexuality in a manner that fosters the flourishing of human families and the whole family of God. Freed "from the dominion of darkness" and transferred "to the kingdom of his beloved Son" (Col 1:13), we are to overcome the vices of fallen sexual desire that have long undermined family life, namely "immorality" and "impurity" (3:5).[26]

Like the Decalogue, Jesus condemns adultery, and he also condemns looking "at a woman lustfully" (Mt 5:28). He goes so far as to say that the latter is tantamount to committing adultery in one's heart, and he even suggests that it will have the same consequences as adultery. He states, "If your right eye causes you to sin, pluck it out and throw it away; it is better that you lose one of your members than that your whole body be thrown into hell" (5:29). Obviously, these are not the words of a teacher who takes adultery or fornication or sexual lust lightly.

Positively, Jesus teaches the goodness of marriage (Mt 19:3–9), and Paul observes that "because of the temptation to immorality, each man should have his own wife and each woman her own husband. The husband should give to his wife her conjugal rights, and likewise the wife to her husband" (1 Cor 7:2–3). The letter to the Ephesians teaches that "husbands should love their wives as their own bodies" (Eph 5:28). Jesus speaks positively about the place of children (Mk 10:14), and Jesus interacts positively with numerous married people, as does Paul. Jesus removes the punishment of death for adultery (and, I assume, other sexual sins) on the grounds that sexual sins are so common: "Let him who is without sin among you be the first to throw a stone at her [a woman caught in adultery]" (Jn 8:7). Yet he does not remove the need for sincere repentance and conversion: "go and do not sin again" (8:11).[27] More examples of New Testament sexual ethics could be given, but these examples convey the central outlook.

Wright on Biblical Authority and Christian Ethics

Wright assumes that Christ has inaugurated the restoration of Israel, and he assumes that the New Testament, inspired by the Holy Spirit, communicates the sexual ethics that should be followed by the restored people of God on the new exodus journey to the consummated kingdom. For Wright, therefore, Paul's teaching on adultery, fornication, and homosexual acts should be taken as an authoritative communication of God's wisdom and will for Christian chastity.[28] In Wright's view, Paul's judgment on these matters is shaped by the fact that Paul has "a mind renewed by the Spirit."[29]

Wright's theology of biblical authority follows from his theology of Israel, Jesus, and the Holy Spirit. He argues that Jesus brings "God's fresh Kingdom-order to God's people and thence to the world. He is, in that sense as well as others, the Word made flesh. Who he was and is, and what he accomplished, are to be understood in the light of what scripture had said. He was, in himself, the 'true Israel,' formed by scripture, bringing the Kingdom to birth."[30] It follows that scripture is not merely a set of propositions which we should consult—though indeed we should consult scripture and obey its judgments. Rather, the authority of scripture in our Christian discipleship derives from the *living Jesus'* authority, since scripture testifies to Jesus, and the risen and ascended Jesus even today is enacting scripture's truth by the power of the Holy Spirit in the Church.[31]

Although it is sometimes supposed that the New Testament authors did not intend to be writing "scripture," Wright challenges this supposition. Certainly Paul understands himself to be "writing as one authorized, by the apostolic call he had received from Jesus Christ, and in the power of the Spirit, to bring life and order to the church by his words."[32] While Paul could not foresee the canon of scripture, he was consciously writing with the authoritative power and truth that, in Christ, scripture possesses. Guided by Christ and the Spirit, Paul and the other New Testament authors recognized that some aspects of scripture no longer apply to God's "renewed-Israel people, now transformed through Jesus and the Spirit into a multi-ethnic, non-geographically-based people charged with a mission to the whole world,"[33] but for Wright it is crucial to note that Paul did not merely pick and choose among biblical texts, rejecting uncomfortable verses. Rather, Paul read the whole of scripture through the lens of what Christ has accomplished. The whole of scripture continues to be authoritative for Paul, but in Christ, scripture is now authoritative within "a *renewed-Jewish* view of God, the world and humankind."[34]

For us today, scripture reveals the truth by which God is renewing his creation and inaugurating his kingdom. Only if this is so can Christians claim that "theology and Christian living" are in fact "rooted in God himself" rather than being rooted "in our own selves."[35] Scripture announces God's intentions for the life of the whole world and gives believers the mission of carrying out these intentions in Christ and his Spirit. Wright summarizes his perspective by stating that scripture "offers a picture of God's sovereign and saving plan for the entire cosmos, dramatically inaugurated by Jesus himself, and now to be implemented through the Spirit-led life of the church *precisely as the scripture-reading community.*"[36] Listening to and obeying God's Word in the Church, we submit "in faith to the lordship of the crucified and risen Jesus" and become "through baptism and membership in the body of Christ, a living, breathing anticipation of the final new creation itself."[37] Because the Holy Spirit about whom we read in Scripture is powerfully at work today, Wright concludes, "We recognize ourselves as the direct successors of the churches of Corinth, Ephesus and the rest, and we need to pay attention to what was said to them as though it was said to us."[38] In sum, when our minds are renewed by Christ and his Spirit as part of God's work of restoring his people, we will be able to understand and gladly obey Scripture's teachings, including Paul's teachings on sexual ethics.

Farley on Biblical Authority and Christian Ethics

By contrast, scripture has only a marginal place in Margaret Farley's *Just Love: A Framework for Christian Sexual Ethics*. She states, "The Bible is central to the received wisdom that Christians count on to illuminate their moral questions.... Yet when we turn to Scripture, to the Bible, for guidance in our sexual lives, the message is spare and often confusing."[39] As her fundamental exegetical principle, Farley holds that "the biblical witness ... claims to present truths that will heal us, make us whole; that will free us, not enslave us to what violates our very sense of truth and justice."[40] On this basis, she argues that the authority of biblical texts cannot be separated from our response to them, by which we evaluate whether or not the texts are healing and liberative. She points out that "even if one accepts the authority of a source on some apparently extrinsic basis (for example, that it is God's word, or that the voice of the faith community is determinative), this very acceptance must have meaning, must 'make sense' to the one who accepts it."[41] From this perspective, the truth of scripture can only be authoritative for us if this truth resonates clearly with us, that is to say, if it makes sense as good and just.[42] Responding to the objection that this view seems to relativize the Bible, making us the arbiters, she suggests that it does so only if we assume that the ultimate author of the Bible is not the same God as the Creator of our hearts and our minds. Surely, she says, the good Creator would not give us an authoritative scripture that does not speak to our true depths. When we find passages in the Bible about sexual ethics that in our view are not liberative or whole-making, such passages cannot be accepted. Given that she also understands Catholic tradition in this way, there are very few norms of sexual ethics that she receives as divinely revealed or as grounded in our created male-female constitution—leaving her free to construct the details of Christian sexual ethics afresh, with a free hand guided by contemporary experience (even if this experience arises from the matrix of our fallenness).[43]

Farley finds that due to the procreative and marital emphasis of Roman Stoicism, "the Greco-Roman legacy to Western sexual ethics held little of the freedom for sexuality that had characterized ancient Greece. The dominant themes carried through to later traditions were ones of skepticism and control."[44] She observes that the "profound tensions" in the Hebrew Bible's view of sexuality with respect to polygamy, concubinage, and divorce did not help matters, nor did Judaism's general focus on procreation and patriarchal marriage, and its ruling out of "masturbation, incest, adultery, male homosexuality."[45] In the "Christian Testament" of the Bible, moreover, Farley does not find "unanimity on more specific sexual rules."[46] Her view of the New Testament's "sexual rules" can be seen in her assessment of biblical teachings on homosexuality.[47] She argues that even if one wished to draw "moral prohibitions or permissions" from the New Testament, one would be prevented from doing so by the ambiguities and cultural specificity of its teachings. In light of disputes among biblical exegetes, she holds that the New Testament's "few texts that appear to refer to homosexuality offer problems of interpretation—whether because of ambiguity in the use of rhetorical devices and specific terms, or disparity between the meaning of same-sex relationships in the historical context of Paul (Rom. 1:26–27; 1 Cor. 6:9; 1 Tim. 1:10) and the meaning we assume for same-sex relationships today."[48]

For Farley, therefore, it is solely the broad values or principles of the New Testament that we need to hold on to, especially in the face of what she considers to be the later contamination of Christian sexual ethics by Augustine's highly negative and patriarchal "valuation of sex."[49] She enumerates a set of largely disembodied broad values that focus in particular on whether our internal attitude expresses love. Her list of values normative for Christian sexual ethics includes "do no unjust harm," "free consent of partners," "mutuality," "equality," "commitment," "fruitfulness," and "social justice."[50] In defining and elaborating upon these principles of sexual ethics in *Just Love*, Farley quotes scripture extremely rarely, and almost never in defense of her own views on sexual ethics.[51]

The difference between Wright and Farley can be reduced to whether the Second Vatican Council's Dogmatic Constitution on Divine Revelation, *Dei Verbum*, is correct that "by divine Revelation God wished to manifest and communicate both himself and the eternal decrees of his will concerning the salvation of mankind" and that the Gospel is "the source of all saving truth and moral discipline."⁵² For Wright, the sexual ethics or "moral discipline" taught in the New Testament is authoritative because God gives it to us for our salvation. Farley argues that in fact this sexual ethics is fundamentally unreasonable and repressive, and therefore God must have intended us to discover something different via the development of modern societies.

In exploring the content of chastity, therefore, it will be important to ask whether its content has not only biblical warrants but also reasonable ones, in the sense of conducing to the flourishing of the restored family of God. Together, biblical and philosophical foundations can ensure that, as the Second Vatican Council requires, Christian moral theology for God's eschatologically restored family draws deeply "on the teaching of holy Scripture" and "throw[s] light upon the exalted vocation of the faithful in Christ."⁵³

Aquinas's Sexual Ethics

Aquinas's theology of chastity is in tune with the sexual teachings of the New Testament. His questions on chastity, virginity, and the sins against chastity quote Scripture fifty-five times and receive as authoritative the scriptural teaching handed on in tradition. Marie-Dominique Chenu remarks that the "*Summa [theologiae]* is implanted in and fed with a continuous study of Scripture," and its purpose always is "to arrive at a better knowledge of the Word of God."⁵⁴ In Aquinas's view, the differences between the Old and New Testaments in sexual ethics are accounted for by Christ's teaching, extended by Paul under the guidance of the Holy Spirit. Wright's emphasis that God aims to build up a people "through whom . . . God will establish his sovereign rule, bringing his wise order into the world," fits nicely with Aquinas's understanding.⁵⁵ Like Wright, Aquinas holds that God knows the "wise order" of human flourishing, namely, the flourishing of God's royal images who possess (as rational animals) "a natural aptitude for understanding and loving God."⁵⁶ Indeed, for Aquinas,

God himself is the ultimate common good, and so our flourishing is always God-centered.[57]

Aquinas on Chastity

God created us as sexual creatures, as can already be seen in Adam's joy at seeing Eve and in the narrator's explanation, "Therefore a man leaves his father and his mother and cleaves to his wife, and they become one flesh" (Gen 2:24). In our fallen condition, however, sexual desire easily devolves into irrational lust. For this reason, says Aquinas, "*chastity* takes its name from the fact that reason *chastises* concupiscence, which, like a child, needs curbing."[58] Concupiscence needs curbing not because it is merely a created good that can be overly exuberant, but because it is a created good that is fallen and causes widespread harm. The curbing of lustful concupiscence therefore should not be imagined to be a function of asserting arbitrary limits or obeying repressive rules. It is rather a matter of living according to what is truly reasonable—most conducive to human flourishing—and not allowing lustful concupiscence to lead us away from God's wise order.[59] As Daniel Westberg comments with regard to sexual activity, "There are inherent purposes in human activities that need to be recognized and respected; we are not free simply to impose our individual desires and purposes as our culture trains us to."[60] In chastity, then, a person makes "moderate use of bodily members, in accordance with the judgment of his reason and the choice of his will."[61] Against individualistic notions of chastity, Albert Plé adds that "sexual desires and pleasures do not affect only the body; their virtuous ordering cannot be exercised without . . . reference to others."[62] To be able to order our sexual desire in this way rather than simply following "the lusts of [our] hearts" (Rom 1:24), we need to possess right reason, whose judgments about human action are attuned to God's wisdom and reliably ordered to the attainment of our true good.

Right reason discerns in particular circumstances the suitable path of action, in accord with our spiritual and bodily ends. Since this is so, some explanation of the oft misunderstood "procreative end" of sexual intercourse is needed. A teleological "end" describes that to which something is primarily ordered; it is a purpose that explains what a thing is primarily "for." In this sense, sexual organs are primarily for procreation: they are reproductive organs. The procreative end, however, does not mean that we always seek to procreate when we engage in sexual acts, nor does it require us to have children. Infertility does not negate the procreative end. The "end" is inscribed in our sexual organs whether or not we are able to produce sperm (in men) or to release an ovum and carry a baby to term (in women).

Given his understanding of the unity of body and soul, Aquinas holds that the bodily and spiritual "ends" of human sexual acts cannot rightly be cut off or separated from one another.[63] The human body is intrinsically informed by the soul and cannot be understood rightly except in relation to the soul. As a work of divine art, the human body is "most suited to such a form" (namely the rational soul) and "to such operations" (namely rational activity and communion).[64] Rather than being a "morally neutral playground" for providing "pleasure or enjoyment for the 'self,'"[65] the human body has rational ends inscribed within it that help reason to discern God's "eternal law" for human flourishing.[66]

In Aquinas's view, sexual acts that deliberately violate the bodily ordering to the procreative end are less than fully personal, because our body belongs integrally to our personhood. Sexual acts cause problems when they seek reductively to strip away one or both of the integral ends of human sexuality.[67] A morally good sexual act cannot be one that disjoins the integrally united body-soul ends of human sexuality. In this regard, the moral theologian Paulinus Odozor remarks that "African Christian ethics and Christian ethics share a belief in the connection between the unitive and the procreative aspects of human sexuality."[68] Yet Odozor recognizes that for many people today, it does not seem necessary to insist upon the intrinsic connection of sexual acts with the procreative end, given that some men and women prefer sexual acts (such as same-sex acts or masturbation) that are intrinsically nonprocreative in their use of their sexual organs, and these acts can be pleasurable and can join a couple in relational experiences. For many people, talk about the procreative end of reproductive organs seems to be beside the point and to be missing out on the range of expression open to human sexuality.[69]

Indebted to Aquinas, the philosopher J. Budziszewski suggests that people misunderstand reality when they reject the moral value of the procreative end. After all, the fact that human sexuality has unitive and procreative ends is a basic foundation of family life. In actual practice, we always depend upon the integral relationship of the two ends (procreative and unitive) for our flourishing as individuals and families. As Budziszewski states, "One is procreation—the bringing about and nurture of new life, the formation of families in which children have moms and dads. The other is union—the mutual and total self-giving [of the couple]. . . . These two meanings are so tightly stitched that we can start with either one and follow the threads to the other."[70] In upholding both ends, human sexual acts serve the personal bond of love between the man and the woman, preparing them to welcome a family.[71]

When we deliberately cut off sexual actions from their proper ordering to family life in which children are raised by their mother and father, this causes harm.[72] Today we sometimes suppose that private sexual acts are either not important morally or else are morally indeterminate, given the variety of personal contexts. But our sexual acts have consequences upon our relations with others and thereby upon ourselves as well.[73] Anything that fosters lust is a serious matter with respect to love of God and neighbor, even if, as John Grabowski observes, "some kinds of sexual acts at particular stages of personal development, such as masturbation by adolescents, may be more symptomatic of an immature sexuality in need of integration rather than being in themselves constitutive of one's moral character."[74] At present, in fact, adult masturbation and (correspondingly) pornography use are causing an increasing array of problems for individuals, families, and communities.[75] All of us, whether heterosexually or homosexually inclined, are part of the problem; but in God's restored people, through the grace of the Holy Spirit and the infused virtue of chastity, we can share in the solution.

Some people contend that pleasure itself is a directive "end" of human sexuality. Aquinas recognizes that pleasure accompanies sexual activity, but he finds that pleasure can never be among the deepest ends of sexual activity, which is directed toward much more (though generally not less) than pleasure. Yet it should go without saying that pleasure, both physical and emotional, is a large part of sexual activity. Affirming this dimension of human sexuality, Aquinas postulates that prior to the fall, sexual intercourse between Adam and Eve would "have been without lust" but not without sexual desire and sexual pleasure.[76] He holds that the "sensible delight" that characterizes sexual intercourse would "have been the greater in proportion to the greater purity of nature and the greater sensibility of the body."[77] Without exaggerating it, he appreciates the place of pleasure in sexual acts.

In accordance with Aquinas's perspective, Albert Plé observes that what is morally at issue "is not the intensity of pleasure, but the way (oblatory [self-giving] or narcissistic) in which the power to love is affected" by the pleasure.[78] Chastity does not aim to "suppress desires and pleasures of the senses,"[79] but instead it moderates sexual desire and calls us to abstain from sexual activities of certain kinds, with the goal of ensuring that the unitive and procreative ends are not hampered or cut off from each other. Ultimately, the goal is fostering stable families in which children are raised by their mother and father and in which the "one flesh" communion of the man and woman (Gen 2:24) can image the self-sacrificial and fruitful love of "Christ and the church" (Eph 5:32).[80]

Summing up the journey of chastity, Reinhard Hütter remarks that "uprooting the vice of lust means attending to the spiritual nature of its root cause," whose healing ultimately requires "sanctifying grace and the infused moral virtues."[81] Since chastity involves the way in which we think about, look at, and touch others, chastity also involves purity.[82] Living chastely in accord with graced right reason by the power of the Holy Spirit, we are enabled to reflect God's love as his royal images and share in his inaugurated reign as his restored people, his family called to "inherit the kingdom of God" (Gal 5:21).

Aquinas briefly discusses consecrated virginity in relation to chastity, and so I will briefly touch upon it here.[83] As Jesus indicates in the Gospel of Matthew, now that he has inaugurated the kingdom of God, some of his followers serve God as an anticipatory sign of the consummated kingdom in which there will not be marriage. After affirming the goodness of marriage among his followers in the present life, Jesus teaches that "there are eunuchs who have been so from birth, and there are eunuchs who have been made eunuchs by men, and there are eunuchs who have made themselves eunuchs for the sake of the kingdom of heaven. He who is able to receive this, let him receive it" (Mt 19:12).[84] This contrast among the three kinds of "eunuchs" distinguishes people who physically cannot have sexual intercourse from people who freely choose to give up marriage and sexual intercourse "for the sake of the kingdom of heaven"—in order to devote themselves to the service of God. David Fagerberg comments in this regard, "The only way to understand Christian celibacy is in an eschatological light. If the eighth day [the day of new creation] has not dawned, then Christian celibacy is false; if Christian celibacy is true, it is because the eighth day has truly dawned."[85] This does not mean that Christian marriage is noneschatological, but it means that celibacy points forward to the consummation of the kingdom in a way that instructs us uniquely about the God-centered joy of that kingdom.

According to Aquinas, eschatological beatitude consists primarily in beatific contemplation of God, which fits with Jesus' teaching that "in the resurrection they neither marry nor are given in marriage, but are like angels in heaven" (Mt 22:30).[86] Consecrated virgins anticipate this beatitude by abstaining from marriage and sexual intercourse in order to devote "themselves to the contemplation of divine things, for the beauty and welfare of the whole human race."[87] Given that "the form of this world is passing away," the decision of consecrated virgins to spend their lives in contemplation of God anticipates the condition of the consummated kingdom, in which "God [will] be everything to every one" (1 Cor 15:28, 31). While married Christians are an eschatological sign of the indissoluble union of Christ and his Church, therefore, consecrated virgins specially anticipate the focus on "the affairs of the Lord" (7:32) that will constitute the beatitude of the kingdom.

For the flourishing of God's restored people in the inaugurated kingdom, both states of life are needed.[88] Today, consecrated virginity is generally less respected than previously, in part because we mistakenly assume that all vocations must, in every respect, be equal. But Aquinas draws inspiration from Revelation 14:4, where the seer describes the blessedness of the 144,000 (a symbolic number of perfection) who in their earthly lives were "chaste" and virginal and who therefore were able to "follow the Lamb wherever he goes."[89]

The Vice of Lust

Strengthened by the Holy Spirit, some persons will "refrain from lustful pleasures chiefly through hope of the glory to come," but in the face of concrete temptation, this hope can lose its hold for Christians inclined toward lust.[90] The Christian can all too easily neglect "to control his [or her] own body in holiness and honor" and can succumb again to "the passion of lust like heathen who do not know God" (1 Thess 4:4–5). Aquinas therefore attends to the vice of lust (*luxuria*), in which we follow our sexual desire in ways that betray God's wise order, ignore his reign over his restored people, and fail to image his self-giving love.[91]

The term "lust" can be used to express disordered desires other than sexual ones, but Aquinas notes that it applies preeminently to disordered sexual desires.[92] Just as a fully human desiring of the pleasures of eating and drinking must have a proper relation to sustaining bodily life in order to be good, so also a fully human desiring of the pleasures of sex must have a proper relation to the procreative end.[93] In response to the objection that "everyone can lawfully make use of what is his" and so "there can be no sin in venereal acts," Aquinas quotes 1 Corinthians 6:20: "You were bought with a price. So glorify God in your body."[94] He comments that there is no autonomous possession of one's own body, neither within the kingdom of God (where the Spirit indwells the body) nor "outside" this kingdom, since the Creator God "is the Supreme Lord of our body."[95] Of course, God is not an arbitrary Supreme Lord, arbitrarily refusing to let us use our sexual organs in any way we like. Rather, God seeks our flourishing, which accords with our ordering in charity toward the common good.

Charitable sexual acts, with their concomitant pleasure, are reasonable and serve our personal good insofar as they also serve the common good of our families and communities.[96] By contrast, "lust consists essentially in exceeding the order and mode of reason in the matter of venereal acts," as when the full personal potentialities of our sexual organs are deliberately suppressed in a particular sexual act, thereby turning the sexual act into a less than fully personal reality ordered to an end (pleasure) that cannot by itself bear the weight of human sexuality.[97]

In an act of lust, the person enjoys satisfying the concupiscible appetite's desire for sexual pleasure, a desire generally motivated by the strength or "vehemence of the pleasure."[98] In lust, "sexual passions ... have a great power of anarchy and of destruction of the person."[99] Aquinas refers in this regard to Daniel's condemnation of the unjust judges of Israel who, impelled by their sexual desire for Susanna and for other young women, fell into crimes of lust. Condemning these unjust judges, Daniel says, "Beauty has deceived you and lust has perverted your heart" (Dan 13:56).[100] If we simply follow our sexual desire wherever it leads, we act in subpersonal ways: we become blind both to the good end of the act and to what should (and should not) be done in attaining the end of the act. The lustful person can also fall into a *"hatred of God,* by reason of His forbidding the desired pleasure," along with a disordered *"love of this world,* whose pleasures a man desires to enjoy," and a *"despair of a future world,* because through being held back by carnal pleasures he cares not to obtain spiritual pleasures, since they are distasteful to him."[101] Awash in the desire to gain sexual pleasure in ways that are not fully personal, we lose touch with the core of our relational identity toward God and our loved ones. We may believe that such sexual acts are good because consensual or private, but their lack of due order inevitably produces harmful effects — even though sinful sexual acts do not sum up anyone's life, which will display other positive deeds and fruits.[102]

In the task of identifying what sexual acts are not in accord with God's wise order for the flourishing of his eschatologically restored family, Aquinas's answers flow from both biblical revelation and rational discernment. Logically, he points out that a sexual act can fail to be in accord with right reason either because of the wrong circumstances or because of something bodily that does not accord with the intrinsic ordering of human sexuality toward the end of procreation and the raising of children. Aquinas's critique of fornication is especially instructive for perceiving his pattern of thought.[103] First, on biblical grounds, Aquinas rejects fornication because it "debars a man from God's kingdom," unless it is followed by repentance and conversion.[104] As Jesus says, "Out of the heart come evil thoughts, murder, adultery, fornication" (Mt 15:19).[105] Paul similarly observes that "the immoral man sins against his own body" by taking "the members of Christ" and making them "members of a prostitute" (1 Cor 6:15, 18).[106] If we listen to scripture, we will repudiate fornication, even when it seems harmless enough and we are tempted to fall into it.

Second, on the basis of rational discernment, Aquinas explains the sinfulness of fornication as being due to the fact that it undercuts the wise order of God's plan for the flourishing of God's people. It might seem that the fornicator (male or female) is simply using his or her body to obtain and give sexual pleasure, and therefore no harm is done.[107] But as Aquinas explains, fornication—and of course adultery as well—intrinsically undermines the stable bond that children need their mother and father to have.[108] The fornicating man and woman have made no binding promises to each other; their act is simply one of satisfying their desire for sexual pleasure or for intimacy. The result is that the eventual formation of the stable male-female unions that enable the flourishing of individuals, families, and societies is undermined by fornication, because the man and woman do not think it worthwhile to bind themselves to each other or to the raising of the child that may come into being from their action.[109] They have adopted an attitude toward sexual intercourse that considers the stability of their interpersonal union to be dispensable, when in fact such stability is indispensable where sex is involved.

For its part, adultery, which is condemned in the Decalogue (see Exod 20:14), violates the marital vow, jeopardizes the stability of the marriage(s), and results in children not knowing who their father is. With reference to Sirach 23:22–23, Aquinas explains that adultery on the part of a man (and thus also on the part of a woman) involves "a twofold offense against chastity and the good of human procreation. First, by accession to a woman who is not joined to him in marriage, which is contrary to the good of the upbringing of his own children. Secondly, by accession to a woman who is united to another in marriage, and thus he hinders the good of another's children."[110]

Aquinas's emphasis is on the damage that our disordered sexual acts do to the most vulnerable among us, namely children.[111] As Pope Francis observes in *Amoris Laetitia*, "Every child has a right to receive love from a mother and a father; both are necessary for a child's integral and harmonious development. As the Australian Bishops have observed, each of the spouses 'contributes in a distinct way to the upbringing of a child. Respecting a child's dignity means affirming his or her need and natural right to have a mother and a father.'"[112] This point is widely neglected today, but it can hardly be emphasized enough. Aquinas compares humans in this regard to other emotionally sensitive animals. He argues that God's creative order aims to ensure that where two parents are needed for raising the offspring, indeterminate fornication is avoided. In the case of dogs, where puppies grow up very quickly and "the female suffices for the offspring's upbringing," sexual union is naturally "indeterminate."[113] A female dog in heat often has sexual intercourse with more than one male dog, and this causes no problems. The example of dogs stands in for many other animals, as Aquinas recognizes. But a human child does not grow to maturity for many years, and the raising and educating of a human child to function well in the world is difficult. Aquinas remarks that "the upbringing of a human child requires not only the mother's care for his nourishment" but also "the care of his father as guide and guardian, and under whom he progresses in goods both internal and external."[114]

Since human children need both their mother and their father, the practice of fornication harms children by promoting familial instability and the absence of fathers. It is reasonable, then, that humans should direct themselves to individual and social flourishing by not acting upon sexual desire to fornicate, and by instead directing sexual desire to conditions of stable marriage in which the end of procreation (which includes raising the children) can be more suitably attained. As

John Rziha comments, "Humans are naturally inclined [though sin has somewhat corrupted this natural inclination] to procreate within a permanent, loving union that provides the proper environment for children to truly learn how to know and love God and others."[115]

As is well known, the institution of male-female marriage is widespread across cultures and times. Humans have recognized it to be valuable. Generally speaking, as Aquinas says, "human nature rebels against an indeterminate union of the sexes and demands that a man should be united to a determinate woman and should abide with her a long time or even for a whole lifetime."[116] Yet Aquinas also has no trouble admitting that "among the Gentiles, fornication was not considered unlawful."[117] He grants that his own rejection of fornication is rooted primarily in biblical revelation, which teaches us about God's wise order. Uninstructed by revelation, reason often does not suffice for discerning right and wrong in particular circumstances, given the "corruption of natural reason" caused by the fall.[118] Aquinas thinks that right reason can show that fornication is opposed to God's wise order for human flourishing, but he does not pretend that reason will be able to draw this conclusion easily in particular prudential circumstances, without the aid of divine revelation and the grace of the Holy Spirit. He would not be surprised at all by the prevalence of fornication in modern societies.

Recall that for Aquinas "man's reason is right, in so far as it is ruled by the Divine Will, the first and supreme rule"[119]—a rule in which human reason participates by natural law. But fallen humans have turned away from God, and so it is no wonder that we often fail to act reasonably in the way that best pertains to our flourishing. Furthermore, despite the inauguration of the kingdom of God and the beginning of the restoration of God's people through the Spirit, Christians often find chastity very difficult. With his typical realism, Aquinas states that "of all a Christian's conflicts, the most difficult combats are those of chastity; wherein the fight is a daily one, but victory rare."[120] Even in the first century, Paul was already bemoaning this frequent lack of victory in matters of chastity among the members of Christ's Church.

Studies show that a majority of Catholics today, at least in the United States, consider fornication to be morally fine, even though scripture condemns it and right reason (as Aquinas shows) rejects it. Where Aquinas and contemporary norms find solid agreement is in opposition to the violent sexual act that is rape.[121] Here it is evident that such an act does not serve human flourishing, since one of the participants is unwilling and suffers terrible assault. Rape also subverts the intrinsic rational ordering of sexual desire to the "end" of the procreation and raising of children, not because a child cannot be conceived during a rape, but because such violence attacks the very basis of the family in which the child would be raised. Likewise, although sexual relationships between very close relatives ("incest") are now legal in some European societies, most Christians and most societies today still agree with Aquinas that such relationships are wrong, despite the inroads being made (in a further confirmation of the harm caused by lust) by the increasing popularity of incest-themed pornography.[122] Aquinas notes that Leviticus 18 contains a number of commandments against incest. He reflects that "there is something essentially unbecoming and contrary to natural reason in sexual intercourse between persons related by blood, for instance between parents and children who are directly and immediately related to one another."[123] It is not reasonable to turn the family into a place of sexual relations, outside of those between husband and wife. Parents and children owe each other debts of love, but the kinds of love appropriate to close familial relations do not include sexual intercourse between parents and children or between other close relatives, for all sorts of obvious reasons connected with the flourishing of families.

For Aquinas, aware of the sad reality of sexual sin even in the ranks of consecrated Christians, there is also the problem of what happens when a person has sexual intercourse with a consecrated virgin. In this case, fornication and possibly seduction are present. But something even worse is also present, since the person has taken a vow of virginity in order to serve God. In such a case, the fornicator violates "something pertaining to the worship of God."[124] First, fornication with a virgin who has taken Christ as her spouse is akin to adultery.

Second, in such cases we find an instance of "sacrilege," the violation of what has been specially consecrated to God. Of course, baptism consecrates all Christians to God by union with "the new and living way which he [Jesus] opened for us ... through his flesh" (Heb 10:20), and so it is also the case that fornication among Christians always violates what belongs to Christ, even if not with the additional element of sacrilege.

Lastly, like the Old Testament and Paul, Aquinas does not think that homosexual acts belong to God's wise order for human flourishing.[125] As Wesley Hill, who himself is sexually attracted to his own sex, observes, "Same-sex sexual partnerships. . . . are outside the bounds of God's will for human flourishing. They cut against the grain of God's hallowing of male and female as the marital unit—a covenantal bond ordered toward the bearing and raising of children and, together with the corresponding Christian vocation of celibacy, signifying Christ's love for the church."[126] In the restored family of God, persons with homosexual desires either will not act upon their inclinations or, having acted upon them, will seek out God's mercy through repentance and the sacrament of reconciliation. Homosexual acts involve shared pleasure and relationship, and these goods are not negligible. Yet the way in which such acts employ the sexual organs contradicts the ordering of human sexuality toward the end of procreation and the raising of children and thereby makes for sinful acts. Again, sexual acts do not need to result in the conception of a child in order to be morally good. But the ordering of human sexuality to the procreative end is deep-seated and cannot be removed. The desire for family does not go away, often resulting in one of the partners conceiving a child by other means, thus preventing the child from being raised by his or her biological father or mother.

It is no wonder that after the fall, many of us (whether attracted to the opposite sex or to the same sex) experience ourselves to be rather disordered sexually. Today, seeking to be charitable and just toward persons with same-sex attractions who have long suffered abuse and vituperation that has ignored their human dignity and their gifts, we may be tempted to ignore the reality of what *Gaudium et Spes* calls marriage's "endowment with various values and purposes," including the value of the difference between the mother and the father in complementary service to their children.[127] But the truth that the Second Vatican Council was expressing is even more evident today.[128] The misuse of our bodies at a fundamental relational level—our attraction toward another person as an object of sexual desire and companionship—wounds the family of God that Christ has come to restore.

Aquinas classifies homosexual acts under lust, because the ordering of these acts deliberately separates sexual pleasure from the end of procreation and because "use of the right sex [namely male or female] is not observed."[129] Lest there be any misunderstanding, charitable persons agree that "those living a homosexual lifestyle have a natural and divine right to be loved by other humans, and virtuous people will love them by helping them to be truly happy."[130] At the same time, because human nature is created by God, our bodies are not things for us to use as we see fit. Aquinas appreciates that, in the words of Paulinus Odozor, "biological nature has moral significance" in the free actions of the human person.[131] The restored family of God can recognize that it matters greatly for the personal meaning of our sexual actions that as a biological fact our "sexual organs, whether fertile or infertile . . . are ordered to procreation."[132]

***

Ellen Davis has commented that "the Bible is all about the desire for what is good, and how that desire so easily gets derailed, squandered, poisoned, so it becomes destructive of what is good in oneself and others."[133] In this chapter, I have argued that this harmful result is what happens when sexual desire loses touch with the virtue of chastity. Christian attention to sexual morality can be dismissed as a misbegotten focus on "pelvic issues," as has been done by the theologian William Shea.[134] But in my view, this is a serious mistake. In fact, John Grabowski is right to perceive that chastity exhibits the "inbreaking of God's Kingdom and the invitation to discipleship in the area of sexuality and marriage," an invitation that requires obedience to the New Testament's authoritative teachings on sexual "sins that break down the Christian community."¹³⁵ In the inaugurated but not yet consummated kingdom, chastity requires constant recourse to the grace and gifts of the Holy Spirit, since at various points in our lives all of us will be strongly drawn toward unchaste actions. As the restored family of God, however, we Christians must present our "bodies as a living sacrifice, holy and acceptable to God" (Rom 12:1), and this means that we must "put on the Lord Jesus Christ, and make no provision for the flesh, to gratify its desires" (13:14).

Yet as everyone knows, the New Testament's understanding of the chastity of God's restored people has become deeply controversial in contemporary culture, both outside and within the Church—so much so that defending the Christian teaching on chastity can be deemed to be bigoted. With regard to the classical understanding of the contents of chastity and lust, Colleen McCluskey notes that "a significant part of the current secular literature argues that lust is the virtue and chastity the vice."¹³⁶ Expressing an increasingly common view, the theologian Joseph Selling bemoans the fact that "the official position of the RCC [Roman Catholic Church] became inexorably tied to the sex-reproduction connection."¹³⁷ Selling suggests that this inexorable tying occurred only with Pope Paul VI's 1968 encyclical *Humanae Vitae* and that this connection needs to be untied.¹³⁸ Like Farley, Selling thinks that in sexual matters "*attitude* has been shown to be more important than behaviour, at least in the New Testament. All the law and the prophets are contained in the double commandment to love God and love one's neighbour as oneself."¹³⁹ He is aware that "when a married person engages in a sexual relationship with someone other than their spouse, they bring on an entire set of repercussions."¹⁴⁰ But the key point for him is that these repercussions should never be analyzed in bodily terms, as though the central problem with adultery had to do with "the performance of physical actions."¹⁴¹ Once "physical actions" are not central to moral analysis of sexual matters, the biblical and Thomistic understanding of chastity makes little sense. Selling argues that Aquinas, too, focuses simply on intention.¹⁴² But as we have seen, Aquinas is not a dualist of this kind; he thinks that bodies and bodily ends are foundational for evaluation of human sexual acts.

Jesus commands his followers not to judge the interior moral condition of others and to "first take the log out of your own eye" before trying to deal with the speck in a neighbor's eye (Mt 7:5). Christian teachings on chastity are misunderstood when taken as a species of moral judgmentalism. We all are in the same boat, insofar as we all possess disordered sexual desires of one kind or another, and insofar as we can find ourselves acting upon such desires. Still, this is no reason to get rid of the teachings of revelation and reason that are for our good and that serve the good of families and communities. Despite the failings that we all suffer from, Paul's warning regarding the eschatological kingdom cannot be ignored: "Do not be deceived; neither the immoral, nor idolaters, nor adulterers, nor homosexuals, nor thieves, nor the greedy, nor drunkards, nor revilers, nor robbers will inherit the kingdom of God" (1 Cor 6:9–10).

With respect to the Christian virtue of temperance, we face choices between chaste and unchaste bodily actions, and the grace of the Holy Spirit makes it possible for all of us to make the right choices. Even when we have not "yet obtained the victory" over all unchaste desires in our lives,[143] there is always the opportunity to repent and, in faith, to live anew in the wondrous mercy of Christ. Thus Paul immediately goes on to say: "And such were some of you. But you were washed, you were sanctified, you were justified in the name of the Lord Jesus Christ and in the Spirit of our God" (1 Cor 6:11). Christian chastity pertains to our calling to be royal and priestly images of God in Christ and to reflect God's wise order in the world as God's restored people or family. Aquinas shows on biblical and philosophical grounds that God wills for chaste sexual desire to be operative in modes that accord with the divine artwork of the human body-soul constitution and build up stable human families in which the father and mother love each other selflessly and raise and educate their children in Christ. As the American agrarian Wendell Berry puts it, therefore, sex is not merely "between two people," but rather is inevitably—due to the intrinsic ends of human sexuality—"a bond between those two people and their forebears, their children, and their neighbors."[144] Or, in the words of the French philosopher Fabrice Hadjadj, "The passage of generations [through the mother's womb] . . . possesses the characteristic of being neither a contract nor a transaction. It accomplishes a *gift without reciprocity*."[145] In the restored people of God, Christian chastity enables us to live our sexuality in accord with the full truth of this intergenerational gifting.

CHAPTER FIVE

Clemency and Meekness

Clemency means moderation or leniency in punishing, and meekness means mildness or moderation in anger. Each of us knows how much we need these virtues and how important they are for a healthy culture. Cruelty and irrational anger cause so much harm in the world. In his encyclical *Lumen Fidei*, Pope Francis observes, "Faith's understanding is born when we receive the immense love of God, which transforms us inwardly and enables us to see reality with new eyes."[1] When we look at reality with the eyes of faith, we see a great deal of beauty, but we also see a great deal of sin and brokenness. The fact is that fallen human existence often has a rather grim character, much of it due to cruelty and irrational anger. In our daily lives, we perceive that cruelty is often met with more cruelty and that anger begets even more anger.

Scripture is well aware of this cycle and of our own participation in it through our intemperate desire for vengeance and our inordinate anger at those who have harmed us. Indeed, the biblical scholar John Barton has noted that "the whole Deuteronomistic History [Deuteronomy through Kings] might . . . be regarded as a confession of national sin," in which (for example) the growing idolatry under King Solomon led his son to tell the leaders of the ten northern tribes, "My father chastised you with whips, but I will chastise you with scorpions" (1 Kgs 12:11).[2] In Barton's view, however, God's own responses to his people's sins frequently violate clemency and meekness. The divine anger and punishment seem at times to go beyond what is reasonable. As an example, Barton comments that in the book of Isaiah, "when God is executing judgement, there is often a scandalous disproportion between deserts and punishment. Not only are the wrong people punished, but even the real culprits are often punished to an excessive extent."[3]

Barton takes at face value texts such as the divine smiting of the women of Jerusalem in Isaiah 3 and the divine command to kill all the inhabitants of Ai in Joshua 8. For my part, I do not see the need to take at face value all the specific commands or actions that the human authors attribute to God. Interpreting Scripture canonically, Augustine rightly observes that when shameful things are "spoken or actually performed either by the person of God or by men whose sanctity is commended to us," we should either take these things as figurative or interpret them in a manner guided by the fact that "no one is good but God alone" (Mk 10:17) and that "God is love" (1 Jn 4:8).[4]

When taken as a whole, the biblical testimony to God reveals God to be "meek" (Mt 5:4) and "gentle" (Mt 11:29), just as God commands his people to be.[5] As Bernard of Clairvaux points out, drawing upon Psalm 72:1, Psalm 85:5, and Isaiah 55:7, Scripture reveals over and over again "how good God is, how kind and gentle, how willing to pardon."[6] The biblical portraits of God's "anger" at sin express the fact that sin alienates us from God, rather than expressing any lack of love or any injustice on God's part.

But even if God can be justly provoked to "anger" or to the infliction of punishment due to the horrors of human sins against God and neighbor, can *human* anger or *human* desire for punishment ever be just? In his study of the ascetic tradition, Dennis Okholm notes that Gregory the Great, in condemning anger as unjust, "taught that anger propagates an army consisting of strifes, swelling of mind, insults, clamor, indignation, and blasphemies."[7] By contrast, Thomas Aquinas holds that humans can justly possess anger.[8] As William Mattison remarks, "Thomas claims anger can be reasonable in object and/or mode."[9] When we experience or witness an injustice, we have cause for righteous anger, and it is not wrong to desire that an evildoer be punished for the purpose of restoring the relational order of justice.[10] For Aquinas, the problem occurs when anger exceeds the bounds of reason. Okholm states that "anger's devolution into hatred wishes evil without measure and for its own sake. Further, anger turned to hatred is long-lasting."[11] Thus, Paul (quoting Ps 4) instructs his Ephesian flock, "Be angry but do not sin; do not let the sun go down on your anger, and give no opportunity to the devil. . . . Let all bitterness and wrath and anger and clamor and slander be put away from you, with all malice, and be kind to one another, tenderhearted, forgiving one another, as God in Christ forgave you" (Eph 4:26–27, 31–32; cf. Gal 5:20). To do otherwise, says Paul, would be to "grieve the Holy Spirit of God" (Eph 4:30).

Paul's proclamation of Christian freedom from "bitterness and wrath and anger and clamor and slander" is only possible due to the eschatological forgiveness of sins and outpouring of the Holy Spirit that gives God's people a "new heart" and "new spirit" (Ezek 36:26–27). Through the meek Jesus Christ, God takes away the sins of the world and enables those who receive Christ to be meek rather than being sinfully and irrationally angry. In the world's normal way of operating, those who do others an injury generally do not find the injured parties to be meek or clement.[12] For God's Spirit-filled people, by contrast, anger no longer need be ungoverned by reason, but instead can now be a reasonable anger that is responsive to evil actions such as the oppression of the poor while not carrying us overboard. In the Spirit, God's forgiven people can be "slow to anger," recognizing that all too often "the anger of man does not work the righteousness of God" (Js 1:20).

This chapter therefore examines in depth the virtues of meekness and clemency, which enable us to avoid irrational anger and cruelty. Meekness and clemency are "potential parts" of temperance, meaning that they apply the moderation that distinguishes temperance to a specific passion—in this case anger—whose object is not the proper object of temperance (in other words, not food, drink, or sex). The chapter's discussion of the place of meekness and clemency in Aquinas's eschatological ethics proceeds in two steps. First, I describe the biblical background for reflection on divine and human meekness and clemency, with attention to the eschatological forgiveness of sins and thus also in connection with divine mercy. Second, I explore Aquinas's account of meekness and clemency. I seek to illumine the ways in which the inaugurated kingdom makes it possible for believers' anger against injustices to be exercised in a meek and clement manner. Since "the fact is that much of our anger is distorted" and "out of control," this is a domain in which human beings urgently need the transformation wrought by the forgiveness of sins and the outpouring of the Holy Spirit.[13]

Biblical Background

In his *Jesus and the Forgiveness of Sins*, the biblical scholar Tobias Hägerland arrives at the conclusion that "Jesus' practice of announcing forgiveness seems to be an expression of his identity as the prophet through whom God was fulfilling Isaiah's prophecies about the eschatological restoration of Israel."[14] Hägerland's study focuses on assessing the historicity and meaning of Mark 2:1–12. More broadly, N. T. Wright notes that Israel anticipated an eschatological forgiveness of sins. Citing numerous prophetic texts and Second Temple nonbiblical Jewish texts, Wright sums up his reconstruction of the eschatological worldview that was widespread among Israelites during Jesus' time: "When Israel finally 'returned from exile,' and the Temple was (properly) rebuilt, and reinhabited by its proper occupant—this would be seen as comparable with the making of the covenant on Sinai. . . . It would be the real forgiveness of sins; Israel's god would pour out his holy spirit, so that she would be able to keep Torah properly, from the heart."[15] Without adopting Wright's overall schema, the biblical scholar James Dunn emphasizes that Jesus caused offense when he forgave sins not only outside the temple cult but also without reference to it. Jesus "usurped the role" that God had given to the temple and the sacrificial cult laid out in the Torah.[16]

Wright is certainly correct about the prophets' expectation of an eschatological forgiveness of sins. In Zechariah 8–13, for example, God promises not only his return to the temple but also Israel's renewed fidelity and righteousness. God promises to gather the scattered Israelites and to restore them to the land in a new exodus, through a day of terrible tribulation in which Israel will emerge victorious. This day will also involve bitter mourning and repentance over "him whom they have pierced" (Zech 12:10).[17] The eschatological day of the Lord will culminate in the complete forgiveness of sins. God promises through Zechariah, "On that day there shall be a fountain opened for the house of David and the inhabitants of Jerusalem to cleanse them from sin and uncleanness. And on that day, says the LORD of hosts, I will cut off the names of the idols from the land" (13:1–2).

Prophesying at the time of the Babylonian exile, Jeremiah also envisions an eschatological event in which God takes away Israel's sin and enables Israel to obey Torah perfectly. After informing Israel, "Your hurt is incurable, and your wound is grievous ... because your sins are flagrant" (Jer 30:12, 14), God promises through Jeremiah, "Behold, I will restore the fortunes of the tents of Jacob, and have compassion on his dwellings.... Again I will build you, and you shall be built, O virgin Israel!" (31:4). This restoration of Israel will include the regathering of the scattered people and the complete forgiveness of sins. Thus, God promises through Jeremiah, "Behold, the days are coming, says the Lord, when I will make a new covenant with the house of Israel and the house of Judah.... I will put my law within them, and I will write it upon their hearts.... I will forgive their iniquity, and I will remember their sin no more" (31:31, 33–34).[18]

In the prophecies of Isaiah, we find a similar connection of the eschatological restoration of Israel with the complete forgiveness of sins, so that the people of Israel will not only be free of the guilt of past sins but also be able to obey the Torah perfectly. Through Isaiah, God promises a day when finally "a king will reign in righteousness" and even "the mind of the rash will have good judgment" (Is 32:1, 4). This will happen when "the Spirit is poured upon us from on high," a time when "justice will dwell in the wilderness, and righteousness abide in the fruitful field" (32:15–16). At this time, God will exalt himself by conquering sin and restoring the land and people of Israel. Isaiah prophesies, "Your eyes will see the king in his beauty.... The people who dwell there will be forgiven their iniquity" (33:17, 24).

Indeed, as the book of Isaiah progresses, this affirmation that God will forgive Israel takes on an even clearer focus and specificity. God promises to "be glorified" in his "servant" Israel (49:3). This "servant" is all Israel, but the servant is also arguably a specific person, since God says to him, "It is too light a thing that you should be my servant to raise up the tribes of Jacob and to restore the preserved of Israel; I will give you as a light to the nations, that my salvation may reach to the end of the earth" (49:6). God promises that his "servant" will redeem the sinful people. Isaiah states in this regard, "All we like sheep have gone astray; we have turned every one to his own way; and the Lord has laid on him the iniquity of us all" (53:6). Since all Israel has sinned, it follows that the "servant" must be a holy representative of Israel who, by his righteousness, redeems all Israel. The servant does this not through power, but through weakness. Isaiah states, "Surely he has borne our griefs and carried our sorrows; yet we esteemed him stricken, smitten by God, and afflicted. But he was wounded for our transgressions, he was bruised for our iniquities; upon him was the chastisement that made us whole, and with his stripes we are healed" (53:4–5). In weakness, the servant brings about the forgiveness of the whole people: "He bore the sin of many, and made intercession for the transgressors" (53:12).[19]

The Gospel of Matthew proclaims that the servant who will accomplish the eschatological forgiveness of sins has come in Jesus of Nazareth. Thus, the angel of the Lord reassures Joseph about the provenance of Mary's child: "Joseph, son of David, do not fear to take Mary your wife, for that which is conceived in her is of the Holy Spirit; she will bear a son, and you shall call his name Jesus, for he will save his people from their sins" (1:20–21).[20] Jesus is the "king of the Jews" (2:2) and "God with us" (1:23). In his Sermon on the Mount, Jesus outlines the ethics of the kingdom that he has come to inaugurate. This kingdom will not only establish God's forgiveness of the sins of Israel but also be marked by people who themselves are meek and forgiving. Jesus teaches, "Blessed are the meek, for they shall inherit the earth. Blessed are those who hunger and thirst for righteousness, for they shall be satisfied. Blessed are the merciful, for they shall obtain mercy" (5:5–7). Jesus urges the necessity of reconciliation with those whom we have harmed, and he commands us to love our enemies and our persecutors.

In the Gospel of Matthew, Jesus connects his kingship with his meekness. He states, "All things have been delivered to me by my Father.... Take my yoke upon you, and learn from me; for I am gentle and lowly in heart" (11:27, 29). Certainly, he has power, but he uses this power to cleanse the people from evil. In this regard, in a controversy with the Pharisees, he points out, "If it is by the Spirit of God that I cast out demons, then the kingdom of God has come upon you" (12:28). He comes to cure sinners by his mercy; he is both the "physician" and the "bridegroom" (9:12, 15). The biblical scholars W. D. Davies and Dale Allison comment that "Moses was, for Judaism, the exemplar in meekness [see Num 12:3]," and they propose that the Gospel of Matthew, in presenting Jesus as the meek "king of the Jews," is intentionally identifying Jesus as the new Moses.[21]

Jesus commands Peter that, if someone sins against us, we must forgive that person not merely seven times, but "seventy times seven" (Mt 18:22). He instructs his disciples that the kingdom of God (or the "kingdom of heaven" [18:23]) is known by the presence of divine mercy, which those who wish to enter the kingdom must imitate. In a parable, he depicts God as a lord who forgives the enormous debt of his servant, and who then expects his servant to forgive the small debt that the servant is owed by a fellow servant. Jesus commands the hearers of the parable, "Forgive your brother from your heart" (18:35). In addition to requiring mercy, Jesus calls for his followers to serve each other rather than striving to dominate each other. The model for greatness through self-giving service is Jesus himself, since "the Son of man came not to be served but to serve, and to give his life as a ransom for many" (20:28).

Jesus' meekness is such that he insists that "every one who is angry with his brother shall be liable to judgment, whoever insults his brother shall be liable to the council, and whoever says, 'You fool!' shall be liable to the hell of fire" (Mt 5:22). Likewise, in his meekness Jesus counsels, "Do not resist one who is evil. But if any one strikes you on the right cheek, turn to him the other also" (5:39). A meek person can overcome sin. As Paul urges the Romans, "Do not be overcome by evil, but overcome evil with good" (Rom 12:21). Paul similarly entreats the Corinthians "by the meekness and gentleness of Christ" (2 Cor 10:1) to attend to Paul's authority, which he exercises in humility. The path of self-sacrificial love is necessarily meek rather than violent or vengeful, and it is through this path that God conquers sin.

No contemporary biblical scholar has paid more attention to this self-sacrificial path of meekness and forgiveness of sins than Michael Gorman. Gorman emphasizes that in the Roman empire, "to suffer crucifixion was to suffer the most shameful death possible."[22] The cross was an instrument of horrendous torture meant to secure peace. Politically speaking, such torture indicates a profound lack of peace, and it contributes to the lack of peace that it is supposed to reverse. But Jesus endured it as a path by which to transform our violence from within and thereby to bring about real peace. For Paul, the inaugurated kingdom is marked by Jesus' "status-renouncing, others-regarding love"; as Gorman remarks in light of Romans 15:7–13, "When this kind of loving community exists, the prophetically declared plan of God for humanity is achieved."[23]

Gorman links this cruciform love to the forgiveness of sin. With Ephesians 4–6 in view, he states that the center of the Christian way of life "is the experience of God's forgiveness, found in the self-sacrificing love of Christ and logically requiring a corresponding life of forgiveness and self-sacrificial love."[24] All our relationships must be suffused with charitable mercy and meekness. Gorman points to Paul's comment in 2 Corinthians 12:10: "For the sake of Christ, then, I am content with weaknesses, insults, hardships, persecutions, and calamities; for when I am weak, then I am strong."[25] Through what seems to be weakness, the divine power of love can show itself for what it is, namely a way of operating that stands opposed to all forms of oppression and that can transform such oppression through forgiveness. The "apocalyptic action" of Christ builds "communities of cruciformity," in which "meekness and humility" reveal the divine life-giving love that alone conquers death.[26]

We can see the connection between the forgiveness of sins and clemency when we examine the biblical accounts of God's punitive wrath against his sinful people. Although God does not have bodily passions and therefore does not have anger as we know it, God is just. When we turn away from God, we incur a just punishment of alienation from God, and this fact leads the Bible to describe God as angry with sinners. For example, in Deuteronomy, Moses frequently warns the people to avoid "doing what is evil in the sight of the Lord your God, so as to provoke him to anger" (Deut 4:25). Yet, in his anger, God shows clemency.[27] Moses rightly reassures the people, "The Lord your God is a merciful God; for he will not fail you or destroy you or forget the covenant with your fathers which he swore to them" (4:31).

The divine clemency sometimes appears as the fruit of interchanges between Moses and God, where God allows Moses to intercede for the people—just as Jesus, the incarnate Word, later intercedes for the people as the one Mediator through the power of his cross. For example, after the Israelites on the exodus crafted a golden calf and worshiped it, God "said to Moses, 'I have seen this people, and behold, it is a stiff-necked people; now therefore let me alone, that my wrath may burn hot against them and I may consume them; but of you I will make a great nation'" (Exod 32:9–10). Moses replies by begging God to remember his covenant with the people and his promises to Abraham, Isaac, and Jacob. In response to Moses' plea that God not act upon his "fierce wrath" (32:12), God changes his mind and shows clemency to the people, even though God does punish them.[28]

The prophets show the unity of the divine clemency and the divine mercy. Through the prophet Jeremiah, God complains, "[Jerusalem] has aroused my anger and wrath, from the day it was built to this day," and God therefore proclaims that he will justly abandon Jerusalem to the punitive power of the Babylonians, who will "set this city on fire, and burn it" (Jer 32:29, 31). But immediately after indicating the onslaught of this devastating punishment, God promises, "I will gather them from all the countries to which I drove them in my anger and my wrath and in great indignation; I will bring them back to this place, and I will make them dwell in safety. And they shall be my people, and I will be their God" (32:37–38). In punishing his sinful people, God consistently is shown moderating his just "anger" rather than unleashing absolute destruction. At the root of everything God does in punishing Israel is his merciful intention to forgive the sins of his people and make them righteous: "I will forgive their iniquity, and I will remember their sin no more" (31:34).

Similarly, consider Jesus' clemency, rooted in his mission of mercy. For example, when Peter rebukes Jesus for saying that he (Jesus) would have to suffer and die, Jesus rebukes him with evident anger: "Get behind me, Satan! You are a hindrance to me; for you are not on the side of God, but of men" (Mt 16:23). Jesus corrects Peter's worldliness by rebuking him, but Jesus does not abandon him. On the contrary, he shortly thereafter takes Peter "up a high mountain" and enables Peter to witness his transfiguration (17:1). Later, Jesus prophesies that Peter will abandon him, and when Peter does so — by denying three times that he knows Jesus — Peter feels the interior rebuke of guilt: he "went out and wept bitterly" (26:75). But in Jesus' mission of mercy, Jesus again renews his clemency to Peter.[29]

I suggest that clemency and meekness fit with what Wright describes as "the real forgiveness of sins" that Israel expected to occur in the eschatological age, when God would pour out the Spirit and enable the people of God "to keep Torah properly, from the heart."[30] Christians, living in the Spirit in the time of the eschatological forgiveness of sins, show that they have received the healing of the Spirit by being clement and meek, as Jesus himself was.

Aquinas on Clemency and Meekness as Virtues of the Inaugurated Kingdom

Aquinas takes his definition of "clemency" from the Roman philosopher Seneca: "Clemency is leniency of a superior towards an inferior."[31] Clemency moderates the punishment of evildoers, since otherwise, in our anger, we might often wish to "inflict a too severe punishment" upon them.[32] Clemency has to do, then, with the moderation of the passion of anger with respect to punishment, and this moderating influence is why Aquinas associates clemency with temperance. Aquinas notes that clemency and meekness both have to do with the anger that arises when someone unjustly harms us. Specifically, clemency has to do with moderating the external punishment that we seek to inflict, whereas meekness has to do with moderating our anger. These virtues do not overthrow justice or rule out punishment.[33] Instead, they ensure that we are not carried away by the passion of anger when someone has harmed us and deserves punishment.

Jesus is sometimes thought to have done away with all retributive punishment, but in fact he promises repeatedly that just punishment will be given to unrepentant sinners by God (see Lk 13:27–28 and many other instances).[34] Of course, the clemency and meekness that we find in Jesus are far more perfect than what we find in fallen humans, for Jesus' passions are not unruly or in need of restraint. Jesus' anger does not need restraining but is always virtuously temperate, fully under his rational control. Thus, Jesus stands far from "those who delight in a man's punishment for its own sake."[35] Jesus' clemency appears in how he treats his disciples: he rebukes and disciplines them (and thereby punishes them), but he never punishes them by dissolving their fellowship and sending them away, even after they abandon him to his persecutors.

In an objection, Aquinas quotes an Old Testament verse that seems to favor the view that clemency (along with meekness) is in fact the greatest virtue. This verse is Proverbs 20:28, which in the Vulgate reads "Roboratur clementia thronus eius," "His throne is strengthened by clemency."[36] Aquinas does not deny the greatness of clemency and meekness. Although the greatest virtue is charity, clemency and meekness "concur with charity ... towards the same effect, namely the mitigation of our neighbor's evils."[37] Although Aquinas does not say it explicitly here, Jesus' royal "throne is strengthened by clemency," which accords with the love for neighbor that Jesus exemplifies on the "throne" of the cross.

Aquinas finds much scriptural evidence for Jesus' meekness. The Vulgate version of Matthew 11:29, cited by Aquinas, describes Jesus as "mitis sum et humilis corde," "meek and humble of heart" (the RSV reads "gentle and lowly of heart").[38] Aquinas also refers to Matthew 5:5, where Jesus in the Sermon on the Mount states, "Blessed are the meek, for they shall inherit the earth."[39] In addition, Aquinas cites Old Testament passages that can easily be applied to Christ, such as Sirach 10:31, which in the Vulgate reads "Fili in mansuetudine serva animam tuam," "My son, keep your soul in meekness" (the corresponding verse in the RSV, Sirach 10:28, reads, "My son, glorify yourself with humility").[40] Aquinas also points out that in Sirach 1:27, we learn that the Lord "delights in fidelity and meekness."[41] Christ is meek because his anger is properly moderated; meekness removes "anger that urges to vengeance."[42] Rather than taking vengeance upon sinners or upon his oppressors, Christ freely suffers and dies for the forgiveness of their sins. Followers of Christ, too, must keep their souls "in meekness," in order to attain to the eschatological inheritance. We should keep in mind here that for Aquinas, many of the people of the Old Testament period (both Jews and Gentiles) in fact already belonged by faith and love to the Spirit-filled eschatological people of Christ, since the Holy Spirit has always been active in joining people to Christ, even before Christ's birth.[43]

Of course, meekness is important for all people, whether Christian or not. Aquinas explains that "anger, which is mitigated by meekness, is, on account of its impetuousness, a very great obstacle to man's free judgment of truth: wherefore meekness above all makes a man self-possessed."[44] Aquinas points out that Aristotle praises meekness in book 4 of his *Nicomachean Ethics*, and Seneca deems that "every good man is conspicuous for his clemency and meekness," since otherwise a person would be subject to irrational bursts of vengeful anger and excessive punishment.[45] The link between meekness (and clemency) and temperance is made by Seneca. It should be evident, however, that without the help of the eschatological Spirit, it is difficult to be consistently clement or meek. Aristotle and Seneca were cognizant of this difficulty.

In his reflections on clemency and meekness, Aquinas shows that he has the inaugurated kingdom in view by quoting not only Matthew 11:29 (as noted above) but also such biblical texts as James 1:21, which urges believers, "Receive with meekness the implanted word, which is able to save your souls." Prior to the verse quoted by Aquinas, James urges that believers be "slow to anger, for the anger of man does not work the righteousness of God" (Js 1:19–20). To belong to the inaugurated kingdom, we must be meek like Jesus and "slow to anger." Persons bursting forth with vengeful anger do not exhibit the forgiveness of sins or the Spirit's outpouring in the world. In a passage cited by Aquinas, Augustine refers both to Jesus' command in Matthew 5:39, "Resist not one who is evil," and to Paul's injunctions for the eschatological people of God, "Bless those who persecute you" and "overcome evil with good" (Rom 12:14, 21).[46] Paul makes clear that vengeful anger, untempered by meekness or clemency, has no place in the inaugurated kingdom: "Beloved, never avenge yourselves" (12:19).

Thus, if we find ourselves wishing that Jesus had come among us filled with violent wrath against sin and sinners, we need to pray for the virtue of clemency. In this regard, Aquinas observes that "a man who takes pleasure in the punishment of others is said to be of unsound mind . . . because he seems on this account to be devoid of the humane feeling which gives rise to clemency."[47] A clement person "recoils from anything that may be painful to another," and indeed there is "a certain roughness of soul in one who fears not to pain others."[48] Again, the clement person does not reject punishment per se. But in Aquinas's words, "Love makes one quick to mitigate punishment."[49] Indeed, after noting that "judgment is without mercy to one who has shown no mercy" (Js 2:13),[50] James immediately adds: "Yet mercy triumphs over judgment" (2:13). The clement God wills to forgive our sins. Even if we reject this forgiveness, preferring even hell to living in repentant love, God punishes "short of what is deserved."[51]

Aquinas is aware that it is "natural to man to desire vengeance for injuries done to him," and by "natural" he has in view not only fallen nature with its irrational anger but also graced human nature, which cries out for justice.[52] I note that we see this reasonable desire in the book of Revelation, where "under the altar the souls of those who had been slain for the word of God and for the witness they had borne . . . cried out with a loud voice, 'O Sovereign Lord, holy and true, how long before thou wilt judge and avenge our blood on those who dwell upon the earth?'" (Rev 6:9–10). Yet Aquinas points out that in our fallen condition on earth, irrational anger often adds fuel to this desire for vengeance, with terrible results. God's eschatological people therefore need meekness and clemency in order to make manifest to the world the forgiveness of sins. We need the Holy Spirit to turn us from irrational anger and commit us to true forgiveness, as followers of Christ.

The vices opposed to meekness and clemency are anger and cruelty, respectively. With respect to anger, Aquinas recognizes that Paul generally does not see it as fitting for Christians. In a passage cited approvingly by Aquinas, Paul commands the Ephesians, "Let all bitterness and wrath and anger and clamor and slander be put away from you, with all malice" (Eph 4:31)[53]—to which Paul adds that believers should instead be "forgiving one another, as God in Christ forgave" them (4:32). In his discussion of whether anger is a sin, Aquinas considers the argument that since anger is a natural and unavoidable passion, it cannot in fact be a sin.[54] He answers by making a distinction, one made also by Gregory the Great. Aquinas observes, "A passion of the sensitive appetite is good in so far as it is regulated by reason, whereas it is evil if it set the order of reason aside."[55] In Aquinas's view, therefore, Paul is warning against irrational anger, anger that exceeds the "order of reason" either by desiring something beyond what is just or by being "immoderately fierce," either internally or externally.[56]

We have all experienced the way in which even just anger, when it blazes fiercely, can cause unnecessary division and harm among people who should be friends. The community that bears witness to the eschatological forgiveness of sins, therefore, must keep itself from the counterwitness of immoderate anger, since immoderate anger fuels not reconciliation but hatred. Aquinas points out that although it is natural to get angry in certain circumstances, we have the ability to check or restrain the passion of anger so as to ensure that it remains governed by reason.[57] This limiting of *sinful* anger to that which goes beyond the bounds of reason, however, may seem to be only partially attuned to what scripture teaches. In this regard Aquinas cites Job 5:2, "Vexation [or anger] kills the fool," and Matthew 5:22, "Every one who is angry with his brother shall be liable to judgment"—so that even saying "You fool!" to one's brother causes one to be "liable to the hell of fire."[58] He also references the position of the Stoics, namely that all disturbing passions, including anger, are evil. Could it be that all anger, at least for fallen people, is sinful?

Due not least to Jesus' display of anger against the money changers in the temple, Aquinas responds that although "it is unlawful to desire vengeance considered as evil to the man who is to be punished," it is lawful to be angry within rational bounds when confronted with injustice, so as "to desire vengeance as a corrective of vice and for the good of justice."[59] We should not be misled by the word "vengeance," which now generally means irrational retribution. What Aquinas means is rational retributive punishment. Certainly, God has clearly told his people, "Vengeance is mine, and recompense" (Deut 32:35). But God has also made clear that "the authorities" are "ministers of God" who do "not bear the sword in vain" (Rom 13:4, 6). Thus God can and does "execute his wrath on the wrongdoer" through human authorities (13:4), for example through their power to incarcerate wrongdoers and to punish wrongdoers in other ways.[60] Even in the inaugurated kingdom of God, believers can be angry without sin, as Paul urges: "Be angry but do not sin" (Eph 4:26, citing Ps 4:4).[61] Believers can witness to the eschatological forgiveness of sins without thereby brushing under the rug the violations of justice that should make virtuous persons angry.

Why then does Jesus teach that "every one who is angry with his brother shall be liable to judgment"? Aquinas explains that anger against those who harm us can easily surpass rational bounds, if we allow it to do so—which happens regularly if we are not meek. When an angry person freely desires "unjust revenge" in a significant matter, Aquinas thinks that this situation always means that the angry person has sinned mortally and is thereby "liable to judgment."[62] But when an angry person has been overwhelmed by the movement of passion, or is unjustly angry over an insignificant matter, Aquinas suggests that the person's anger may be a venial sin. He gives the example of "pulling a child slightly by the hair" in anger about what the child has done, as has happened to some of the best parents.[63] With regard to anger that oversteps the bounds of reason through its sudden but brief fierceness, Aquinas holds that such anger is generally a venial sin. Fierce anger becomes a mortal sin when it produces hatred of God and neighbor, as manifested in blasphemy or in harming one's neighbor. Aquinas considers that Jesus' threefold distinction—anger that is "liable to judgment," "liable to the council," and "liable to the hell of fire" (Mt 5:22)—involves a movement from the internal passion of sinful anger (which is "liable to judgment") to external actions of increasing gravity.⁶⁴ Whenever anger is "liable to judgment," this means that one's internal anger already is in a state of mortal sin, and so it must have to do with a significant matter, as Jesus indicates in Matthew 5:21.

Since anger is an explosive passion, it can easily get out of hand if we do not moderate it through the virtue of meekness. Sinful anger "deprives man of his reason, whereby he is master of himself"; such anger makes people ruthless and cruel.⁶⁵ If we allow anger to flourish, it can consume us. Aquinas quotes Augustine's warning—indebted rhetorically to Matthew 7:3—that anger can easily begin as a venial "speck" and become a mortal "log" that completely blinds us.⁶⁶ Aquinas also reflects upon varieties of anger, from choleric wrath that blazes up suddenly and dies down quickly, to sullen ill-will that lasts a long time at a low heat, to bitter rancor that lies in wait until revenge can be obtained.⁶⁷ Anger is sinful when people "are angry too quickly and for any slight cause" and when "anger endures too long."⁶⁸ I note that the witness of the eschatological people of God to the forgiveness of sins and to the Spirit's outpouring cannot flourish when people allow anger to blaze up at any moment or to fester stubbornly. When we find ourselves succumbing to frequent bursts of anger or to festering anger, we need to recall Paul's warning against "bitterness and wrath and anger and clamor" (Eph 4:31) and to follow Paul's counsel "not [to] let the sun go down on [our] anger, and give no opportunity to the devil" (4:26–27). We must focus on being "imitators of God" (5:1) in his work of reconciliation in Christ and the Spirit.

What does Paul mean when he urges us to "give no opportunity to the devil" and to ensure that anger does not fester overnight? Without citing this biblical text, Aquinas gives us an idea of the kinds of "opportunity to the devil" that anger unfortunately provides. He notes that Gregory the Great identifies six "daughters" of anger: quarreling, swelling of the mind, contumely, clamor, indignation, and blasphemy. Anger produces indignation when, nursing our own dignity, we devalue the dignity of the person who has offended us. Anger produces swelling of the mind when we fill our mind with thoughts of revenge. Anger produces clamor when we respond with "disorderly and confused speech."⁶⁹ Anger produces contumely when we direct injurious words to our neighbor. Anger produces blasphemy when we direct injurious words to God. None of these accords with making manifest, in the community of believers and to the whole world, the eschatological forgiveness of sins and the outpouring of the Spirit.

Aquinas describes cruelty as the vice opposed to clemency. In distinguishing between clemency and mercy, Aquinas affirms their close relation. He states, "Mercy and clemency concur in this, that both shun and recoil from another's unhappiness, but in different ways. For it belongs to mercy to relieve another's unhappiness by a beneficent action, while it belongs to clemency to mitigate another's unhappiness by the cessation of punishment."[70] Cruelty involves excessive and irrational punishment, which is opposed to clemency. Aquinas notes that due to the "mutual likeness" of clemency and mercy, "cruelty is sometimes taken for mercilessness."[71] Cruelty indicates a hardness and bitterness of soul, whereas clemency indicates a "smoothness or sweetness of soul, whereby one is inclined to mitigate punishment."[72] Although Aquinas does not mention it here, I think of Paul's defense of his apostolic authority in his dealings with the recalcitrant Corinthians. Paul makes clear his desire to avoid punishing the community if possible, but he also makes clear that if necessary he will exercise his authority to punish. He exhibits this balance when he says, "I write this . . . in order that when I come I may not have to be severe in my use of the authority which the Lord has given me for building up and not for tearing down" (2 Cor 13:10). As a clement person, attentive to "the meekness and gentleness of Christ" (10:1), Paul is "inclined to mitigate punishment," if only the Corinthians will set their church in order. Hans Urs von Balthasar observes, "Threatening to use the authority of his office is not unchristian because that authority is not separate from Paul's love."[73]

Aquinas concludes his reflections by remarking that cruelty at least has in view the punishment of a real fault. Cruelty is not merely a thirst for blood or torture for its own sake. Cruelty differs, therefore, from what Aquinas calls "savagery or brutality," which is "comprised under bestiality" because it has no association whatsoever with reason.[74] Here Aquinas shows his awareness of how far sin can go in the human person—the tremendous depths of what Paul calls the "ungodliness and wickedness of men" (Rom 1:18). We sometimes take it for granted that people will not be irrationally angry or cruel. But Aquinas, like Paul, knows that the eschatological Spirit's actions of healing and elevating our passions are needed for Christians consistently to put away the "anger" and "wrath" in which we "once walked," and thereby to "put off the old nature with its practices and ... put on the new nature" (Col 3:7–10). With Paul, Christians can joyfully proclaim, "The law of the Spirit of life in Christ Jesus has set me free from the law of sin and death" (Rom 8:2), even if Christians must constantly be watchful not to fall back into sin (see 1 Cor 9:26–27).

※ ※ ※

In this chapter, I have argued that the eschatological forgiveness of sins and outpouring of the Spirit, which enable us to fulfill God's law by giving us "a new heart and a new spirit" (Ezek 18:31), empower us with meekness and clemency. The meek person will not become irrationally inflamed when hurt or insulted, and the clement person will not seek retribution beyond what reason mandates. Admittedly, this position may not sound radical enough for the inaugurated kingdom. Some great theologians and fathers of the Church have held that there can be no place whatsoever for anger among Christians, let alone for retribution. When Jesus states that the meek will inherit the earth, and when he calls upon his followers to imitate his gentleness or meekness of heart, does he intend to repudiate all forms of anger and retribution as unbefitting to the members of his inaugurated kingdom?

In my view, Aquinas rightly perceives that the answer is no. Jesus himself becomes angry when the Pharisees oppose his healing of a man with a withered hand on the Sabbath. Jesus "looked around at them with anger, grieved at their hardness of heart" (Mk 3:5).[75] Although this justified and rational anger may seem to conflict with Jesus' teaching in the Sermon on the Mount that "every one who is angry with his brother shall be liable to judgment" (Mt 5:22), in fact Jesus leaves room for righteous anger. In this vein, James can be angry about the injustices of the rich (see Js 5:1, 4). With regard to irrational anger (as well as greed), James condemns fighting and war: "What causes wars, and what causes fightings among you? Is it not your passions that are at war in your members?" (4:1–2).

Commenting on Matthew 5:4, "Blessed are the meek," Davies and Allison note that "the praise of mildness and gentleness was known in both the Greek and Jewish worlds."[76] But they argue that in Jesus' beatitude, the "meek" are not simply the "gentle" but the powerless; the meek "are not so much actively seeking to avoid hubris (an attitude) as they are, as a matter of fact, powerless in the eyes of the world (a condition)."[77] As we have seen, Aquinas connects meekness with gentleness, with a moderation of the anger that we feel when we are harmed unjustly.[78] Even so, the connection that Davies and Allison make between meekness and powerlessness is not so far from what Aquinas has in mind. Powerful people often become accustomed to getting their own way and to not being harmed. Poor and powerless people, by contrast, often become accustomed to absorbing unjust injury without being able to do anything about it. This does not necessarily make poor and powerless people meek, but it conduces to it by not inflaming their self-regard.[79]

It is clear that what is normally meant by "power" in the fallen world does not generally include "meekness" understood in the sense of "mildness and gentleness." A power that is truly meek, able to govern anger rationally, would be a power that, like Christ's, truly serves others. By contrast, as Rebecca Konyndyk DeYoung says, "The wrathful seek revenge, not due punishment; they protect their own honor and cause at all costs, instead of defending what is truly good or deserved."[80] Niccolò Machiavelli was correct when he judged that in the fallen world—oblivious to the forgiveness of sins and the outpouring of the Spirit—"if any man be grievously wronged, either by a state or by another individual, and satisfactory reparation be not made to him, if he lives in a republic he will revenge himself, even if it involves the ruin of the state, and if he lives under a prince, and be at all high-spirited, he will never rest until he have revenged himself in some way, though he may see that it will cause his own ruin."[81] Machiavelli therefore considers that cruelty, rather than clemency, necessarily pertains to holding on to power. Here I recall Jesus' words to his disciples,

"You know that the rulers of the Gentiles lord it over them, and their great men exercise authority over them. It shall not be so among you; but whoever would be great among you must be your servant" (Mt 20:25–26).

What an extraordinary difference it makes in the world when people are actually meek and clement, moderating their anger and punishment strictly within the bounds of reason. DeYoung gives the example of the meekness and clemency of Martin Luther King Jr., whose actions profoundly changed the United States for the better and whose "passion for justice was deeply rooted in his desire that all people learn to love one another and see others as God sees them."[82] As DeYoung notes, "King engaged in his project among a community of believers. He did not attempt to discern God's will all by himself or mete out God's judgment as an individual."[83] Through his speeches and actions against the terrible injustices of segregation and racial discrimination, King shed light upon something that Catherine of Siena likewise discerned in the fourteenth century, namely, that there are people "who are so bloated with the power in their hands that the standard they carry is injustice. They inflict their injustice on God and their neighbors and even on themselves."[84] Catherine remarks upon the power of gentleness and patience to defuse irrational anger. When we refuse to become angry in response to an irrationally angry person, the angry person often calms down and makes amends.[85] Quoting Proverbs 25:21–22, Paul urges, "'If your enemy is hungry, feed him; if he is thirsty, give him drink; for by so doing you will heap burning coals upon his head.' Do not be overcome by evil, but overcome evil with good" (Rom 12:20-21). Or as Proverbs 15:1 puts it succinctly, "A soft answer turns away wrath."

In the inaugurated kingdom, marked by the divine forgiveness of sins and the outpouring of the Spirit, Christ's meekness and clemency become a possible path for human beings united to him, even if at times we fail. This path requires "a change of heart, a reordering of priorities, a transformation of one's vision" through the Spirit's work and our cooperation with it, leading us toward "a deep trust in God to handle things" as opposed to the supposition that our security and status ultimately depend upon us.[86] Otherwise, as Michel de Montaigne notes, "There is no passion that so shakes the clarity of our judgment as anger."[87] Although Jesus makes clear that anger against injustice is appropriate and salutary, we see the destructive impact of irrational anger both in ourselves and in the world around us.[88] Invoking the divine mercy, therefore, let us rely upon Christ's eschatological forgiveness of sins and outpouring of the Spirit to enable us, having "put away all malice," to "grow up to salvation" and to live as those who "have tasted the kindness of the Lord" and who love his will (1 Pet 2:1–3).

CHAPTER SIX

Humility

In the inaugurated "kingdom of [God's] beloved Son" (Col 1:13), the Holy Spirit is poured out upon us for the "forgiveness of sins" (1:14). Christ's crucifixion, resurrection, and ascension to the right hand of the Father are the source of this eschatological outpouring. As N. T. Wright notes, for Paul "the cross is the victory through which the powers of the old age are brought low, enabling the new age to be ushered in at last."[1] Quoting Colossians 1:13–14 — "He has delivered us from the dominion of darkness and transferred us to the kingdom of his beloved Son, in whom we have redemption, the forgiveness of sins" — Wright suggests that this Pauline portrait of deliverance harkens back to the exodus and portrays God's action of freeing his people from the terrible slavery that sin produces. In order to overcome this slavery and to obey God's law, we need the eschatological Spirit. The biblical scholar Luke Timothy Johnson points out in this regard that "the Holy Spirit pervades the pages of the New Testament as the power of new life and personal presence and the transformation of human existence."[2]

In *Paul and the Faithfulness of God*, Wright specifies that Paul believes that the eschatological forgiveness of sins has occurred through "God's faithful covenant justice" in Christ.[3] Christ reverses Adam's primal sin (indeed the sin of the whole world), reflected in the primal sin that Israel committed during the exodus, namely the idolatrous worship of the golden calf.[4] For Paul, idolatrous pride is the root of lust, as in Romans 1:22–24: "Claiming to be wise, they became fools, and exchanged the glory of the immortal God for images resembling mortal man or birds or animals or reptiles. Therefore God gave them up in the lusts of their hearts to impurity, to the dishonoring of their bodies."[5] When Christ takes our death upon himself in obedience to God's will (which is sheer love), "we have peace with God through our Lord Jesus Christ" and we discover to our joy that "where sin increased, grace abounded all the more" (5:1, 20).

Given Paul's assertion of a connection between the sin of pride and the proper species of intemperance (namely lust), we can better understand why Thomas Aquinas includes the antidote to pride within his treatise on temperance. This antidote is humility. As the theologian Raniero Cantalamessa remarks, "There is a great affinity between humility and chastity, just as there is between pride and lust."[6] Properly speaking, temperance moderates vehement bodily desires for the preservation of life (eating, drinking, and sex). Temperance in its extended sense (its "potential parts") moderates, among other things, the desire for our own excellence.[7] Obviously, as the philosopher Gabriele Taylor observes, "being virtuously humble does not mean losing one's human dignity and self-respect."[8] Instead, the virtue of humility curtails the desire for excellence that otherwise may flower into sinful pride, in which we seek to claim what does not truly belong to us and even to claim for ourselves what belongs only to God.

With respect to humility's place among the virtues, the philosopher Alasdair MacIntyre comments that "Aristotle finds no place among the virtues either for humility or charity," whereas "Augustine and Gregory [the Great] assert that without humility and charity there can be no such virtue as justice."[9] The difference that makes all the difference, MacIntyre argues, "is Augustine's biblical understanding of the relationship of the soul to God, as created by God, required by God to obey his just law and destined for eternal life in society with him."[10] This destiny of eternal life depends upon Christ's forgiveness of sins and outpouring of the Spirit. Peter tells the devoutly Jewish onlookers who witness the miracle of Pentecost, "Repent, and be baptized every one of you in the name of Jesus Christ for the forgiveness of your sins; and you shall receive the gift of the Holy Spirit.

For the promise is to you and to your children and to all that are far off, every one whom the Lord our God calls to him" (Acts 2:38–39).[11] Christ's victory over sin and death reverses the exile described by God through the prophet Isaiah, and does so by embracing the path of humility that Israel's punishment of exile requires: "Therefore my people go into exile for want of knowledge [of God].... Man is bowed down, and men are brought low, and the eyes of the haughty are humbled" (Is 5:13, 15).

The biblical scholar Reinhard Feldmeier notes that in Greco-Roman literature prior to the New Testament, humility generally has "a negative meaning that lies, depending on the context, somewhere between sycophancy and pusillanimity, servility and shabbiness."[12] By contrast, Paul gives humility high praise: "Do nothing from selfishness or conceit, but in humility count others better than yourselves" (Phil 2:3). In the Sermon on the Mount, Jesus begins his Beatitudes by stating, "Blessed are the poor in spirit, for theirs is the kingdom of heaven" (Mt 5:3). It might seem, however, that by placing humility under temperance, the lowliest of the four cardinal virtues, Aquinas has failed to appreciate or convey the greatness of humility in the Christian narrative of creation and redemption. Jean Porter comments in this regard that "humility, which plays a secondary role in a doctrinal analysis of the virtues [as exemplified by Aquinas's approach], is regarded as a leading virtue within monastic and pastoral traditions."[13] Has Aquinas, by comparison with Paul, Augustine, and the monastic tradition, wrongly humbled humility?

In response to this concern, Servais Pinckaers has observed that the *Summa theologiae*'s question on humility needs to be read in light of "the two following questions on pride and Adam's sin, in which ... the fundamental importance of humility appears to better advantage."[14] In his discussion of pride, Aquinas argues that pride *should* be easy to avoid, since pride is completely irrational for a mortal and finite creature. Yet pride is actually highly difficult for fallen humans to avoid, and pride stimulates the growth of all the other vices in us. The problem consists in our rebellion against creatureliness; we simply do not want to be "subject to God and his rule."[15] We constantly wish to deny our creaturely dependence, as though there were "a good which is not from God" or as though grace were "given to men for their merits."[16] Humility is at the center of the moral life because it enables us to embrace our true creatureliness, our "subjection . . . to God."[17] The inaugurated kingdom of God belongs to the humble, because only the humble allow God to be King.

The embeddedness of humility within the lowly virtue of temperance, then, should instruct us about the importance of what is lowly. No contemporary theologian has recognized this importance more profoundly than John Webster. Lowly dependence upon God stands continually at the heart of his thinking. As he says of our stance before God, "Holy reason is mortified reason. . . . The Spirit of holiness reproves reason's idolatry, pride, vain curiosity and ambition."[18] Certainly, for Webster, only God is holy (cf. Mt 19:17). Yet "God's holiness . . . is a fellowship-creating holiness," because God's holiness is love.[19] God's holiness creates such fellowship, however, only among those who receive and embrace the Spirit's humbling. To be human properly is to be humble.

Although Aquinas's *Summa* gives a relatively low place to humility, this will mislead only those who do not look for God's power in what is lowly. The philosopher Julia Annas states that the person who is growing in the virtue of humility undergoes "revisions in her opinions of the respect due to other people" and "development of a different conception of the kind of life she aims at living, the kind of person she now aims to be."[20] This may sound easy, but in fact, as Réginald Garrigou-Lagrange has observed, "to reach this humility of mind and heart, a profound purification is needed," which only the Holy Spirit, poured out for the forgiveness of sins, can bring about.[21]

My exploration of the virtue of humility in this chapter turns first to two important essays by John Webster. Grounding himself in Colossians 1, Webster shows that Christ's inauguration of the kingdom of God through "the forgiveness of sins" (Col 1:14) depends upon the spiritual temperance that enables us to embrace our condition of creatureliness. Armed with Webster's account of human creatureliness, I then examine Aquinas's treatment of humility and pride. I propose that Aquinas's understanding of the humble person exemplifies the renewed relational creaturehood that Webster articulates.[22] After surveying Aquinas's discussion of humility, I set forth Aquinas's understanding of sinful pride and especially of the sin of Adam (and Eve). For Aquinas and Webster, the eschatological forgiveness of sins and outpouring of the Spirit are concretely manifested in the humble human creature, freed from the original sin of idolatrous pride.

JOHN WEBSTER: RESTORING HUMAN CREATURELINESS IN CHRIST

In his essay "'Where Christ Is': Christology and Ethics," John Webster proclaims that "the reality that we have been transferred into the kingdom of God's beloved Son ([Col] 1.13)" is Christ's "decision about what creatures are, and the execution of that decision in time."[23] Webster here emphasizes that humans are *creatures*. The result of redemption needs to be viewed through the lens of creatureliness: we are "summoned to redeemed and perfected creatureliness."[24] Where others speak of deification, Webster trains attention upon the perfecting of our creatureliness. The more we are in Christ, the more we will be creatures, since our fundamental problem—the core of all sin—is our rejection of our status as God's *creatures*.

To hammer home this emphasis on our status as creatures, Webster employs Paul's Letter to the Colossians. On the one hand, as Webster recognizes, nothing could be more christologically focused than Colossians. Paul mentions "Christ" four times in the first four verses. Paul proclaims God's Son (Christ) to be "the image of the invisible God" and to be the one "in whom all things were created" and in whom "all things hold together" (1:15–17). Moving from creation to redemption, Paul praises Christ as "the head of the body, the church," and "preeminent" in everything, including resurrection (1:16). The divine-human status of Christ is strongly affirmed in Paul's summary of Christ's redemptive mission: "For in him all the fulness of God was pleased to dwell, and through him to reconcile to himself all things, whether on earth or in heaven, making peace by the blood of his cross" (1:19–20). The overall message of the letter is well summed up by Colossian 3:11's insistence that among believers, "Christ is all, and in all."[25]

On the other hand, this christological focus does not compete with a strong valuation of creation. Christ holds together all of creation, since all things were created not only "for him" but also "through him" (Col 1:16). The description of Christ as "the image of the invisible God" hearkens back to Genesis 1:26, where God says, "Let us make man in our image, after our likeness." Although in Christ "all the fulness of God was pleased to dwell" (Col 1:19; cf. 2:9), he is human as we are. He is on the side of the Creator, but he is also a creature. In him we receive a "new nature, which is being renewed in knowledge after the image of its creator" (3:10). In all these ways, to focus on Christ according to Colossians is also to focus on creation and creatureliness.

In setting forth what he gains by invoking Jesus Christ according to Colossians 1:17, Webster speaks of the source and goal of "creaturely reality," "creaturely existence," and "creaturely action."[26] In Christ, no "created dominion" can imagine itself to be anything other than "created" and thus utterly governed and nonautonomous.[27] Furthermore, "in and as" Christ, God has radically changed the "condition of creatures."[28] By falling into sin, creatures became less than creaturely (and thus became "lost"); now, in God's inaugurated kingdom, God remakes "creaturely relation to God" and *establishes* creatures."[29] To be a creature is to be in relation to God, and for creatures to rise up against this ontological reality is for creatures to attempt, morally speaking, to overthrow their nature by rejecting the relationality that constitutes creaturehood. Although creatures cannot in fact get rid of their ontological relation to the Creator, rebellious creatures have deeply wounded who they are as creatures and have thereby enslaved themselves to lesser things.

In the work of "God's charity to lost creatures," then, a key task is reestablishing human creatureliness.[30] This is done, as Colossians says, by God delivering "us from the dominion of darkness" through Christ's cross, so that we no longer are in slavery to lesser things but once again are able to acknowledge the sovereignty of our Creator in "the kingdom of his beloved Son" (1:13). In this kingdom, we rediscover ourselves as the creatures that we are: as Webster puts it, "Christ's rule is intelligible and renders intelligible that over which he rules."[31] Webster describes what happens when God draws us into his kingdom: we regain the activities of true human creatureliness, as perfected by Christ himself. In Colossians 3, Paul urges members of the kingdom of God to reorient their desires: "Set your minds on things that are above, not on things that are on earth.... Put to death therefore what is earthly in you: immorality, impurity, passion, evil desire, and covetousness" (3:2, 5). This reorientation is a renewal of creatureliness, freeing us from actions and desires that distort the end or goal of the human creature.[32]

Webster derives from Colossians "a metaphysics of morals — an account of moral natures, a moral ontology."[33] As Webster makes clear, the key aspect here is that the ontology of creatureliness, rooted as it is in relation to God, drives the moral character of creaturely action, which must express and foster relation to God. This relation has a mode proper to each kind of creature, since creatures are not pure relationality but instead have natures. Act follows being; the being or nature that humans possess grounds a particular mode of action to attain the end of human nature. Here we see Webster moving from Colossians' christological doctrine of creation to a scholastic manner of expressing the entailments of this doctrine. In his words, "To act well is to act in accordance with my nature and so to move towards perfection, that is, the entire realization of my nature."[34] To do this is to act in accordance with one's nature as created in, through, and for Christ. The "realization" of one's nature, therefore, involves acting "in fellowship with God," which means within "the eschatological reality of life with God in the new creation."[35] The Holy Spirit transforms our nature by grace, enabling us to perform actions for which our original nature (both as created and as fallen) lacked the capacity. But such action of the Spirit-filled believer in Christ can only be understood, Webster reiterates, by attending to the human nature created by Christ: thus "the antithesis between moral ontology and moral history is specious."[36]

Webster emphasizes that Christ the Redeemer "*constitutes* creaturely reality" *as Creator*, and Christ the Redeemer also reconstitutes "creaturely reality" by turning it toward the Creator and thus restoring the creature to what a creature should be.[37] A redeemed creature becomes what a creature should be precisely in union with Christ:

therefore, we must "pursue his [Christ's] reality and our end in him," since as man he is the true creature.[38] Webster's greatest concern consists in showing that all things fall under the "dominion" or "kingdom" (Col 1:13) of Christ, Creator and Redeemer. I agree with him that outside the inaugurated kingdom of Christ (just as outside Christ as Creator), no creature can be a creature in the full and proper sense willed by God.[39]

Webster warns, too, that we must not "neglect the proper finality of created reality, and so fall into intemperance, crazy attachments which inhibit moral growth towards Christ in whom all things have their end."[40] The key problem with "intemperance" is that it turns created things into ends in themselves, rather than recognizing that creatures are only truly creatures when oriented toward Christ (toward God). For Webster, then, we can only be creatures rightly when we accept that we must be "where Christ is, seated at the right hand of God" (Col 3:1). It is "where Christ is" that creaturely reality shines forth as it should be. Believers must recognize themselves already to be "where Christ is," since there we find the redeemed creatureliness that Webster calls our "own most proper reality: proper first to Christ," and proper to us through "Christ's self-communicative goodness."[41] By recognizing that in fact our "life is hid with Christ in God" (3:3), we come to enjoy true creatureliness, since to be a creature properly (rather than rebelliously) is to be ordered toward God. We encounter here, as Webster says, both "an unsettling of our [fallen] desire to possess ourselves and also a restoration of creaturely nature and vocation."[42] The truth of "creaturely nature" is God oriented, in an integral bodily and spiritual way; and this is why not only bodily temperance is needed but also spiritual temperance, by which we embrace our ordering toward God rather than desiring to be God for ourselves.[43]

In his "The Dignity of Creatures," Webster likewise insists upon the "anthropologically fundamental" status of "creatureliness," by which he means three things: "absolute contingency of origin," "specificity of nature," and destiny "to be the children of God through Jesus Christ (Eph. 1.5)."[44] To be a human "creature" is to be created from nothing with a Godward orientation both by nature and by the grace of adoptive sonship. Webster notes that in the fifteenth century,

Giovanni Pico della Mirandola radically reconceived humans as created without any limits or bounds of divine law other than those humans ordain for themselves.[45] By contrast, Webster holds that "creaturely being is and is available to be known and lived out only within the grace of God's relation to us."[46]

Describing this relation, Webster begins with creation (creation in grace). Human creaturely dignity is rooted in "absolute dependence" upon God, who has given the creature "a given nature" whose powers are ordered to "a specific destiny or end."[47] It follows that sin strikes against true creatureliness rather than being evidence of the exuberance of creaturely freedom. Creaturely self-realization must fit with the givenness of creaturely ontology, and this givenness (or giftedness) involves relation to the Creator and indeed a God-given orientation to fellowship with the Creator. No creaturely dignity can stand "apart from the creator's moving presence."[48] Webster observes that "creaturely dignity is an ontological and moral relation to God."[49] To distort human creatureliness by excluding God from the picture involves human creatures in the indignity of pride. Webster insightfully terms this situation "creatures' trespass upon their own dignity," since the rejection of God is the rejection of the true dignity of creatureliness.[50]

Webster grants that we cannot "abolish" our "creaturely dignity" in the sense that we simply "cannot not be a creature made and called by God's love."[51] But as he observes, sin produces objective alienation from God and subjective misery due to "the futile attempt to have life on conditions other than those established by the creator's love."[52] He explores the ways that we can degrade and abase ourselves, and notably he describes them as involving "carnality and self-responsibility" (rather than accepting God's responsibility for our being).[53] These are helpful terms for describing bodily and spiritual intemperance, by which, as he says, "creatures threaten to become at their own hands what they are not."[54]

Webster eloquently fills out the relationship between creaturely ontology and creaturely perfection. He states that "creaturely dignity is necessarily a task, for it is not simply an inner quality of creatures but a nature which brings with it a commission: the 'metaphysical' is also the 'orientational.'"[55] Indeed, the forgiveness of sins restores relational creaturehood: reconciliation reorients us to the Godward orientation that is the heart of creatureliness. This perfecting reestablishes not only our fellowship with God but also our fellowship with each other. The Holy Spirit "generates, sustains and purifies" this "eschatological fellowship" in Christ (namely, the Church), which is in the truest sense "creaturely."[56] Webster emphasizes that the Church as we know it is not the goal, since it "awaits the consummation" of God's kingdom.[57] Even so, our ecclesial life places us at the service not only of our fellow Christians but also of the whole of humanity, when by setting our "minds on things that are above" (Col 3:2) we bear real witness to the graced perfection of creatureliness — the relational sharing in the Trinitarian communion — that is (despite what may sometimes seem to be the case in this world) the supreme dignity of humans both now and forever.[58]

Aquinas on Humble Creaturehood

Webster's theology of creatureliness emphasizes that sin denies the relational order in which humans actually exist. Bodily intemperance does this by undermining the ordering of human beings to others (and to the family of God), whereas pride, as a form of spiritual intemperance, does this by rebelling against our ordering to God and instead trying to be our own God as autonomous beings. The two are intimately connected, since spiritual rebellion against relation with God (a rebellion moved by our vehement spiritual desires) leads to bodily rebellion against God's order (a rebellion moved by our vehement bodily desires). In order to escape the brokenness to which this rebellion binds us, we need to regain our true creatureliness.

The way to do this is to recover humility through the eschatological outpouring of the Spirit of Christ.[59] Thomas Aquinas builds his theology of humility upon the authoritative testimony of biblical texts, supported by Augustine, Origen, and Gregory the Great.[60] He begins with the example of Mary. In a passage cited by Aquinas, Mary proclaims humbly, "My soul magnifies the Lord, and my spirit rejoices in God my Savior, for he has regarded the low estate of his handmaiden" (Lk 1:46–48).⁶¹ In his *Commentary on Luke*, Origen interprets the key word in Luke 1:48 as "humility" (rather than "low estate"). As Aquinas notes, Origen connects Mary's humility with Christ's statement in Matthew 11:29, "I am gentle and lowly [humble] in heart."⁶²

Other biblical texts cited by Aquinas to support his discussion of humility include Genesis 18:27, "Behold, I [Abraham] have taken upon myself to speak to the Lord, I who am but dust and ashes"; Isaiah 40:17, "All the nations are as nothing before him [God], they are accounted by him as less than nothing and emptiness"; Psalm 131:1, "O Lord, my heart is not lifted up, my eyes are not raised too high"; 1 Corinthians 12:31, "But earnestly desire the higher gifts";⁶³ Philippians 2:3, "Do nothing from selfishness or conceit, but in humility count others better than yourselves"; 1 Corinthians 2:12, "Now we have received not the spirit of the world, but the Spirit which is from God, that we might understand the gifts bestowed on us by God"; 1 Peter 3:3–4, "Let not yours be the outward adorning with braiding of hair, decoration of gold, and wearing of robes, but let it be the hidden person of the heart with the imperishable jewel of a gentle and quiet spirit;"⁶⁴ Luke 12:11, "For every one who exalts himself will be humbled, and he who humbles himself will be exalted"; Colossians 3:14, "And above all these put on love, which binds everything together in perfect harmony"; Luke 18:13–14, "But the tax collector, standing far off, would not even lift up his eyes to heaven, but beat his breast, saying, 'God, be merciful to me a sinner!' I [Jesus] tell you, this man went down to his house justified rather than the other; for every one who exalts himself will be humbled, but he who humbles himself will be exalted"; James 4:6 (quoting Prov 3:34), "God opposes the proud, but gives grace to the humble";⁶⁵ Matthew 6:19–20, "Do not lay up for yourselves treasures on earth, where moth and rust consume and where thieves break in and steal, but lay up for yourselves treasures in heaven"; and Matthew 5:4, "Blessed are those who mourn, for they shall be comforted."⁶⁶

This is quite an extraordinary chain of biblical texts, and offers an instructive biblical theology of humility, drawn from both Testaments and including many of the most definitive and illuminating scriptural passages on the topic. Aquinas follows these biblical texts in their depiction of humble creaturehood. He argues that biblical humility does not require Christians to fail to desire good for themselves, as though humility meant seeking nothing exalted. Instead, the virtuous purpose of humility is "to temper and restrain the mind, lest it tend to high things immoderately."[67] Aquinas's account of humility has in view the biblical depiction of the fall, as I will discuss in more detail below. Fallen humans want to "be like God" (Gen 3:5), and so fallen humans "count equality with God a thing to be grasped" (Phil 2:6). Humility is necessary, then, because God made humans with a certain greatness, as creatures made "in his own image" (Gen 1:27). God created us to "have dominion" (1:28) over the earth, exercising a royal and priestly vocation. The true greatness of our creaturehood, however, is destroyed when in pride we seek to displace or deny God as though we were not creatures at all. Humility moderates our desire for greatness in a manner that enables us to behave as true creatures. As Garrigou-Lagrange states (indebted to Aquinas), "The proper act of humility consists in bowing toward the earth, called *humus* in Latin.... Its proper act consists in abasing oneself before God and before what is of God in every creature."[68]

Aquinas emphasizes that humility pertains to "the subjection of man to God," a subjection that is requisite for the inaugurated kingdom of God.[69] Normally we think of subjection as diminishing the one who is subjected, but since God is love and is the ontologically transcendent giver of all gifts, subjection to God means the flourishing of the human creature, called to image (but not displace) God's royal rule. In humility, the human creature knows "his disproportion to that which surpasses his capacity."[70] The humble person therefore does not try to grasp or claim what is disproportionate to human nature. Instead, the humble person seeks ever greater intimacy with God while recognizing that only God can give this gift. Aquinas states that "it is contrary to humility to aim at greater things through confiding in one's own powers: but to aim at greater things through confidence in God's help, is not contrary to humility; especially since the more one subjects oneself to God, the more is one exalted in God's sight."[71] For the humble person, it is evident that because humans are creatures, "whatever pertains to man's welfare and perfection is God's."⁷² Humility enables us to praise the Giver, an action that perfects us.

Can a humble person lay claim to the eschatological outpouring of the Spirit without boasting? The example of Paul shows that we can and should proclaim and praise the Spirit's gifts to us. Aquinas cites two Pauline texts that pertain to the eschatological forgiveness of sins and outpouring of the Spirit.⁷³ The first is 1 Corinthians 2:12, where Paul rejoices that he and his fellow believers have received "the Spirit which is from God, that we might understand the gifts bestowed on us by God." The second is Ephesians 3:5, where Paul is proclaiming the good news that Christ has come to "reconcile us ... to God in one body through the cross" (Eph 2:16)—a reconciliation that "was not made known to the sons of men in other generations as it has now been revealed to his holy apostles and prophets by the Spirit" (Eph 3:5). In both instances, Paul rejoices in God's gifts without falling into pride.

In this discussion, Aquinas questions whether we must think that other people are better than ourselves, as seems to be required by Philippians 2:3: "In humility count others better than yourselves." Aquinas argues that the humble person must do so, but in a precise way: namely, with respect to the gifts and talents that other people have from God and we ourselves do not yet possess.⁷⁴ In this way, every humble person must recognize the superiority of other persons, since all that a person "has of himself as coming from himself, is inferior to what every other man has from God in the order of nature and that of grace."⁷⁵ As for the gifts and talents that the humble person possesses, since these too come from God, the humble person should not hesitate to recognize and praise God for them, thus avoiding a false humility or an overly low self-esteem (rooted in failure to acknowledge God's good gifts). As Sebastian Carlson comments, "Humility does not demand that one believe his own gifts are less than another's, far less that one consider himself the least perfect creature that ever left God's hands."⁷⁶

Aquinas argues that the "moderation of spirit" that is humility is not the greatest of Christian virtues, despite what might at first glance seem to be the case.⁷⁷ It is not greater than love, which is "above" the other virtues and which "binds everything together in perfect harmony" (Col 3:14; cf. 1 Cor 13:13). Nor does humility stand above faith and hope, whose formal object is God himself. As the moderation of the desire for excellence, humility is also not a "cardinal" virtue.[78] Having made these clarifications, Aquinas shows that the greatness of humility is that it "makes a man a good subject to ordinance of all kinds and in all matters."[79] In other words, the humble person is a "good subject" in God's inaugurated kingdom. As Craig Boyd comments, "Humility involves 'receptivity.'"[80] The proud person rebels against God's law, but the humble person accepts God's law in all its manifestations. The humble person therefore is able to reign in God's inaugurated kingdom, being "subject to God."[81] Aquinas points out that our ordering to God is a rational ordering, and so the virtues that pertain to the intellect, as well as the virtue of justice, are in a certain sense prior to humility — which could not function without them. Yet as Aquinas notes, "Sin is pardoned through humility."[82] The outpouring of the Spirit and the forgiveness of sins take effect in the humble person, whereas the proud person obstructs the efficacy of God's forgiveness. Thus, in this regard humility stands at the source of our being made just (see Luke 18:14).

Aquinas makes clear that although fallen humans can and do acquire virtues using the resources of human nature, we depend for the full Christian life upon even the moral virtues being "infused by God," which happens through the Spirit, who is poured out at Pentecost.[83] We need the eschatological forgiveness of sins and outpouring of the Spirit. As *Gaudium et Spes* says, "Through the Spirit who is the 'guarantee of our inheritance' (Eph 1, 14), the whole person is renewed within."[84] In this healing and elevation of the human person, the Spirit first removes the obstacle of pride. Aquinas observes that here "humility holds the first place, inasmuch as it expels pride . . . and makes man submissive and ever open to receive the influx of Divine grace," just as James 4:6 suggests.[85] So long as we keep in view that faith is the foundation of all the virtues as the first and decisive "step towards God," therefore, we can rightly hold humility to be "the foundation of the spiritual edifice."[86] Indeed, in treating Matthew 11:29 in his *Commentary on the Gospel of Matthew*, Aquinas affirms that "the whole

New Law consists in two things: in meekness and humility," because "humility makes a man capable of being filled with God."[87] In his discussion of humility in the *Summa*'s treatise on temperance, similarly, Aquinas agrees with Gregory the Great that in Matthew 11:29 "the lesson proposed to us in the mystery of our redemption is the humility of God."[88]

Aquinas appreciates that humility "despises earthly things" and thus despises "earthly uplifting."[89] This has importance both for his understanding of virtuous creaturehood and for his understanding of the inaugurated kingdom of God. Virtuous creaturehood humbly seeks exaltation to a deeper relationship with the humble triune God. True humility therefore does not mean a lack of desire for good things, since the humble person wants everlasting union with God in the community of the blessed, which is a great thing indeed. As befits proper self-love, the humble person will also want good things in this world.[90] But what true humility lacks is the driving desire for worldly exaltation. Aquinas quotes Matthew 4:5 and 6:19–20 to underscore that Jesus' kingdom does not involve worldly exaltation, but rather involves earthly mourning and the willingness to give away one's earthly possessions. To belong to Jesus' kingdom, we have to want what he offers, such as forgiveness of sins and communion with God. Such goods greatly impact human life on earth, but they are not earthly goods that directly meet our bodily needs, and they do not foster earthly ambition. *Gaudium et Spes* comments that "the Spirit gives the freedom to deny self-love and to direct all earthly resources towards human life, stretching out towards the future when humanity itself will become an offering acceptable to God."[91]

Aquinas says of the humble person: "To him that despises earthly things, heavenly things are promised."[92] Truly to despise earthly things, one must be humble—because persons who despise earthly things will usually themselves be esteemed less. Those who are most honored and privileged in this life tend to have sought and obtained abundant earthly things. But the paradox of true creaturehood and the kingdom of God is that humility leads to the only true and enduring exaltation of the creature: eternal life as God's adopted children in Christ and his Spirit. Humility, therefore, does not mean lack of ambition, but rather it means a moderated ambition for our true end. If we are proud, we will in spiritual matters follow the path of assertive grasping that often produces success in worldly endeavors but that cannot attain to the God on whose free gifts we utterly depend.[93] Aquinas concludes that "humility is . . . a disposition to man's untrammeled access to spiritual and divine goods," because humility "especially removes the obstacle to man's spiritual welfare consisting in man's aiming at heavenly and spiritual things, in which he is hindered by striving to become great in earthly things."[94]

Before leaving the topic of humility, Aquinas reflects upon the twelve steps or degrees of humility famously traced by Benedict in his monastic rule.[95] These steps include practices of humility such as keeping one's eyes on the ground, speaking softly and with few words, acknowledging oneself to be unprofitable and sinful, displaying patience and obedience vis-à-vis one's religious superior, not focusing on the fulfillment of one's own desires, and fearing and obeying God. Aquinas also mentions Anselm's seven degrees of humility,[96] which include acknowledging one's contemptibleness and patiently bearing being treated with contempt—neither of which a proud person can do.[97] Aquinas suggests that these practices of humility are what fallen humans often need to undertake in order to allow the virtues that the Spirit infuses within us to take full root.[98] We must "[restrain] the outward man" by admitting our contemptibleness, which is a truthful admission even for a virtuous person by comparison with the greatness of God or even by comparison with the perfection that a Christian is called to possess.[99] These practices aid humility in restraining our spiritual "impetuosity" and our temptation to "aim inordinately at [our] own excellence."[100] Humility has at its root interior fear of God,[101] and so the outward signs or practices of humility are not infallible or in all cases necessary. Aquinas defends the value of these practices insofar as they both support and manifest interior humility.[102]

Aquinas points out that while the humble person may recognize his or her own strengths and praise God for them, the humble person will also recognize his or her contemptible "hidden faults."[103] Similarly, he observes that "without falsehood one may avow and believe oneself in all ways unprofitable and useless in respect of one's own capability, so as to refer all one's sufficiency to God," given that every good thing comes from God (see 2 Cor 3:5).[104] The humble person, too, will not be humble only before a respectful person but will also be humble before a disrespectful or hurtful person. A humble person will not fear "external abasement" before others, just as Christ endured the "supreme self-humiliation" of the cross.[105] In his *Commentary on the Gospel of St. Matthew*, Aquinas describes the Holy Spirit as the "Spirit of humility" and concludes that "the more humility a man has, so much the more does he love God, and the more he despises his own excellence, the less he attributes to himself: and so the more charity a man has, the more humility he has."[106] Aquinas is commenting on Matthew 18:4, where Jesus says, "Whoever humbles himself like this child, he is the greatest in the kingdom of heaven."

Many modern philosophers take a dim view of humility, and even Christians sometimes tacitly share this suspicion. The theologian Joseph McInerney observes in this regard, "The lowliness and passivity of humility are the antithesis of power for Nietzsche and serve no purpose that Hume can discern to be beneficial to the individual and human society."[107] Friedrich Nietzsche and David Hume worry that humility, as conceived by Christians such as Aquinas, leads to a lack of earthly ambition and achievement. For Nietzsche, our troubling disease is not pride but rather lack of pride: as the theologian Chad Pecknold comments, "It is precisely the *libido dominandi* that Augustine wants us to reject that Nietzsche thinks we should embrace."[108] For most of us, however, as Nietzsche well knew, there is generally not much chance of us doing anything particularly spectacular in a worldly sense.

Contrasting humility and pride, Aquinas makes clear that pride is neither rare nor beneficial. He notes that "humility observes the rule of right reason whereby a man has true self-esteem. Now pride does not observe this rule of right reason, for he esteems himself greater than he is."[109] As a result, the proud person does not "deign to learn anything from man," let alone from God.[110] Proud people delight in their "own excellence" and "disdain the excellence of truth," because truth overshadows and threatens their autonomy.[111] Proud people imagine themselves to possess goods that in fact they do not possess, and they assume that whatever goods they possess derive from themselves rather than from God or neighbor. The proud person easily "despises others and wishes to be singularly conspicuous."[112]

To put it simply, the proud person lives in an illusory dream of autonomy and understands himself or herself as a fundamentally nonrelational creature. Such self-understanding, while absurd, is all too common. Our gifts come from outside us; we are mere mortals who live only briefly on this earth (see Gen 3:19; Ps 103:14–16).[113] Yet the dream of autonomy—of boasting "of one's goods as though one had them of oneself, or of one's own merits"[114]—is a condition that we find deeply inscribed within ourselves. The reason is that, as Aquinas says, "the root of pride is found to consist in man not being, in some way, subject to God and His rule."[115] The desire not to be subject to anyone, and certainly not to God, is so deeply inscribed within fallen humans that some persons even become absurdly "proud of their humility."[116] When we distort our creaturehood by living as though we had no relation to God, we live irrationally and reverse the true order of reality, with the result that "any kind of sin is naturally liable to arise from pride."[117]

Aquinas on Adam and Eve's Spiritual Intemperance

We need a realistic understanding of our wounded creaturehood, whose fruits are manifested in all the greed, war, corruption, lust, and abuse that characterize this world. To understand the depths of pride's grasp upon us, we should consider the sin of the first humans, who prior to the fall possessed relational creaturehood rooted in true "reverence . . . toward God."[118] Aquinas's treatment of the intemperate pride of original sin exhibits his deep agreement with Webster on what it means to be a creature and on the integration of creation and redemption in the humble Christ. The whole of salvation history, from Adam to the new Adam, finds itself inscribed within Aquinas's theology of humility, a virtue whose ultimate purpose, as Reinhard Feldmeier says, is "not self-denial but self-realization as a life together with God and with the neighbor."[119]

Aquinas begins his discussion of Adam's sin with Romans 5:19: "For as by one man's disobedience many were made sinners, so by one man's obedience many will be made righteous."[120] In an objection, he cites this verse to propose—against his own opinion—that disobedience, not pride, was the first sin. To Romans 5:19, he adds Luke 4:3, Matthew 4:3, Genesis 3:5, and 1 Timothy 2:14 to paint a portrait of Adam rebelling against creaturely limits not through pride but rather through disobedience, gluttony, inappropriate desire for knowledge, and lack of belief in God's goodness.[121] Certainly, the rebellious Adam is a creature who in every way distrusts and dislikes the relational provision made by God. He is a creature who, in sinning, fails to manifest what "creature" means: he takes God as his competitor or rival rather than the gracious ground and goal of his creaturely flourishing.

In reply to the view that pride was not the first sin, Aquinas argues that the root of Adam's skewed creaturehood is in fact pride, with its spiritual intemperance. He states in this regard that "man's first sin consisted in his coveting some spiritual good above his measure."[122] Whereas God is without measure, the creature is measured by God; and this is precisely what Adam rebelled against, since Adam "coveted inordinately . . . his own excellence," by which he (and Eve) sought unmeasured divine status; they would be "like God, knowing good and evil" (Gen 3:5).[123] Adam (and Eve) thereby rebelled against creatureliness, since they freely disobeyed God's good law for human flourishing.

By contrast, Christ the new Adam shows true spiritual temperance—true relational creaturehood—when Satan tempts him to act beyond the creaturely measure: "If you are the Son of God, command these stones to become loaves of bread" (Mt 4:3).[124] Christ responds as Adam and Eve should have done by pointing to the divine measure, to which Christ commits himself in his humanity: "Man shall not live by bread alone, but by every word that proceeds from the mouth of God" (Mt 4:4, quoting Deut 8:3). Given the christological unity of creation and redemption, Adam (and Eve)'s downfall was not their desire for deification. The New Testament makes clear that God created humankind for deification, and Aquinas states that prior to sin

Adam "would not have coveted it [the spiritual good of deification] inordinately, by desiring it according to his measure as established by the Divine rule."[125] Rather, the downfall of Adam (and Eve) was spiritual intemperance in pursuit of deification: "Man's first sin consisted in his coveting some spiritual good above his measure," instead of accepting his divinely given measure.[126]

Aquinas clarifies that the spiritual good that Adam (and Eve) sought in breaking God's commandment was not actual identity or equality with God. He assumes that the first humans were intelligent enough to know that they could not obtain "absolute equality" with God.[127] As creatures made "in the image of God" (Gen 1:27), the first humans could rightly have sought a greater "participation in the Divine likeness," through knowledge and love.[128] Instead, they sought to be autonomous, to give themselves their own law of human flourishing, independent from the order of relational creaturehood in which God rules over creatures. Aquinas compares their sin to God's lamentation over the king of Tyre in Ezekiel 28, where God warns the king of Tyre that mortal calamities will come upon him because his "heart is proud," and he has said, "I am a god," and because he considers himself "as wise as a god" (Ezek 28:2, 6). God compares the fate of the king of Tyre to the expulsion of Adam (and Eve) from Eden. Originally, says God to the king, "you were the signet of perfection, full of wisdom and perfect in beauty. You were in Eden, the garden of God," but as a result of pride "you corrupted your wisdom for the sake of your splendor" (Ezek 28:12–13, 17).[129] In Aquinas's view, like the king of Tyre who claimed divine authority, Adam (joined by Eve) sought that "by his own natural power he might decide what was good, and what was evil for him to do."[130]

Aquinas sums up the problem: like Satan, Adam (joined by Eve) "wished to rely on himself in contempt of the order of the Divine rule."[131] This "order of the Divine rule" is the wise plan of the true King, who knows what will fulfill his royal images. Because God is infinitely good, God's wise order is good for us, and rebelling against it alienates us from the source of our being. The foolishness of human pride consists in the desire to flourish autonomously, in a mode that no longer accepts our creaturely measure.

When Aquinas discusses the sin of Adam—Adam and Eve's rebellion against relational creaturehood—he identifies its punishment as death (see Rom 5:12; 6:23).[132] But Aquinas knows that human bodies, due to their material composition, naturally are subject to disease and death.[133] Humans are, by nature, mortal creatures. Moreover, if death is the punishment of sin, the punishment seems to be poorly distributed: some people die as infants, whereas others live many years. What can be meant, then, by holding that death is a punishment for Adam and Eve's sin?

Prior to their sin, Aquinas suggests, God sustained Adam and Eve's bodies in right order, in accord with the goodness of their souls. In rebelling against the relationality of their creaturely being, they did not succeed in casting off relational creaturehood, but they did manage to reject the relationship with God that originally sustained them in a bodily life free from bodily decay. Thus, their sin led in due time to their deaths, just as the forgiveness of sins in Christ will in due time lead to the (eternal) life of those who are united by faith and love to his saving cross and resurrection.

There was another consequence of Adam and Eve's sin, and this consequence shows the connection between spiritual intemperance and bodily intemperance. Aquinas explains that "inasmuch as through sin man's mind withdrew from subjection to God, the result was that neither were his lower powers wholly subject to his reason, whence there followed so great a rebellion of the carnal appetite against the reason."[134] Paul speaks of this consequence of the fall in terms of the rebellious "flesh" (Rom 8), so that fallen humans now live according to what is lower in us (the "flesh") rather than according to our reason as governed by the Holy Spirit. When we deny our relational creaturehood, the irrationality of this denial leads to our being governed by our passions, since our reason (having in pride embraced irrationality) no longer can govern. The rejection of relational creaturehood, then, leads to reason obeying the strong movements of fallen bodily desires. To live in this way is to let "sin reign in [our] mortal bodies, to make [us] obey their passions" (Rom 6:12).[135]

Aquinas also addresses the other punishments of Adam and Eve's sin, including expulsion from Eden, the difficulty of tilling the earth, pain in childbirth, subjection, and shame. Once we no longer reflect God's wise order because of our rebellion, our disordered relational creaturehood results in problems for all our relationships, not least in "family life," as well as in the shame that we feel due to lust.[136] Aquinas deems that the mutual shame that immediately follows upon Adam and Eve's rebellion—"the eyes of both were opened, and they knew that they were naked" (Gen 3:7)—indicates the first stirring of lustful thoughts, aimed at use of the other person rather than love.[137] When we try to live autonomously, apart from God, we enslave ourselves to "the unhappiness of this life," because we cannot be happy outside of the union with God for which we were made.[138]

When God curses the serpent by stating, "Upon your belly you shall go" (Gen 3:14), Aquinas sees an implied reference to connection between pride and carnal lust, symbolized by the belly.[139] Indeed, in recognizing the extent of our fallenness, we discover that pride and lust mingle in us to such a degree that what we require is the eschatological forgiveness of sins, the outpouring of the Spirit, and the infusion of a deep humility.

I have argued in this chapter that the eschatological forgiveness of sins and outpouring of the Spirit makes Christ's people humble. We Christians must "do nothing from selfishness or conceit, but in humility count others better than [ourselves]" (Phil 2:3). As John Webster points out, "creaturely need and creaturely dignity are not in conflict; indeed, they are inseparable, for need is simply the creature's reference back to God's original bestowal of life, and reference forward to the end to which creatures have been ordained."[140] Our relational creaturehood is utterly dependent and needy, and when we forget this or deny it, we fall into the pride that afflicted the first humans, who "coveted God's likeness inordinately" by seeking to take upon themselves God's role as lawgiver.[141] Webster observes that "the basis of human dignity in the creator's beneficence has to be brought to the fore."[142]

With regard to our awareness of our true dignity, John Tarasievitch takes a dim view. In his *Humility in the Light of St. Thomas*, published in 1935, he states, "Men of our modern times have lost almost every taste for things of a higher order. Only the senses and sensible pleasures are highly appreciated and valued by them."[143] In his study, Tarasievitch focuses upon unfolding the truth of Aquinas's claim that humility is "the foundation of the spiritual edifice."[144] This "spiritual edifice" is the inaugurated kingdom of God, marked by the eschatological forgiveness of sins and the outpouring of the Spirit. We need God to transfer "us to the kingdom of his beloved Son, in whom we have redemption, the forgiveness of sins" (Col 1:13–14). This can only happen when we "embrace the practice of humility" and freely "bow before the higher order of things."[145]

The patristics scholar Warren Smith rightly observes that the kingdom of God, while not yet consummated, is already "a present reality," present here and now "when the children of God become the body of Christ animated by his Spirit to perform works of love in the world."[146] In this inaugurated kingdom of Christ, we experience a "love born out of a sense of profound gratitude and dependence."[147] Healed of pride by the Holy Spirit and given the virtue of humility, we can manifest true relational creaturehood. Christ teaches that "whoever humbles himself will be exalted" (Mt 23:12). Through the forgiveness of sins and the outpouring of the Spirit, it is the humble who are the new Adam's bride, holy Church. Let us join them.

CHAPTER SEVEN

Studiousness

In *Being and Time*, Martin Heidegger addresses the topic of "curiosity."[1] He warns against a curiosity that is focused on "outward appearance" and "is not concerned with comprehending and knowingly being in the truth, but with possibilities of abandoning itself to the world" in the insatiable restlessness of "continual novelty and changing encounters."[2] According to Heidegger, the curious person never mentally dwells anywhere for long and knows things only to be able to include them among the things he or she has known. The curious person avoids any kind of rootedness, and the curious person tragically distracts himself or herself from the "being-in-the-world" that he or she is.[3]

Heidegger clearly does not approve of such curiosity, but he does not describe it as a sin. By contrast, the theologian Ernstpeter Maurer remarks that "human wisdom is deeply involved in the divine struggle with human presumption."[4] He focuses upon the limits of our rational powers, limits that fallen humans wish to disregard. In his view, it is our fallen struggle against the limits of reason that redemption overcomes. Of its own powers, human desire to know cannot in fact attain to "the ultimate foundation of knowledge," since human reason has its excellence in a creaturely way, "within the context of creation and in strict relation to divine wisdom."[5] Maurer concludes in this regard, "There is no chance for self-recognition until persons recognize themselves in their origin, which is God. The false assumption that reason is the supreme authority can be shattered only by the encounter with divine reality."[6] Thus Paul rejoices that the Spirit enables us to share in "the mind of Christ" (1 Cor 2:16) so that we are "transformed by the renewal of [our] mind" (Rom 12:2).[7]

Given the importance of such transformation of the mind, Aquinas considers the virtue of studiousness to be of central importance for life in Christ.[8] In its fallenness, the human desire to know is not neutral but requires divine forgiveness and correction, so that we will be able to desire knowledge as we should. Although they lacked the doctrine of original sin, the Greco-Roman philosophers who first set forth the virtue of studiousness and its opposed vice *curiositas* were well aware that our desire to know needs to be moderated and reformed.[9] In criticizing curiositas, of course, they were not criticizing what the philosopher Todd Kashdan defines as "an orientation toward investigating specific objects, events, and problems to understand them better and be challenged by them."[10] Rather, the Greco-Roman philosophers who formulated the vice of curiositas knew that our "orientation toward investigating"—our desire to know—can be focused rightly, in which case it is the virtue of studiousness, or wrongly, in which case it is the vice of curiositas. As Thomas Kennedy remarks, curiositas "both distracts us from proper attention to that to which we ought to be attending and disposes us to attend *in the wrong sort of way* whenever we do turn to that to which we ought to be attending," namely by using "the goods of the world not to turn out from the self to others, but to turn back in upon oneself."[11]

According to Kennedy, "Curiosity is religiously vicious because it inhibits us from attending appropriately to God's creation and to God's ongoing activity in the world."[12] It follows that the renewal of our minds described by Paul belongs to the healing of God's people through the eschatological forgiveness of sins and outpouring of the Spirit. To make present in our lives the reconciliation that Jesus has accomplished for us, the Holy Spirit acts through the work of "conversion and sanctification, of which the conflict between studiousness and curiosity forms part."[13] John Webster emphasizes that "curiosity" marks our *fallen* desire to know, which entails idolatry and vanity. He contends, "The enactment of our intellectual nature is a function of desire; but in our fallen condition desire can be disordered, and studiousness distorted into its deviant form, curiosity.... What makes curiosity vicious is not the intellectual activity of coming-to-know but the corrupt desire which commands the activity."[14]

As Webster makes clear, the virtue of studiousness in believers is a "fruit of the Holy Spirit's work of regeneration and sanctification," and it brings about "within the realm of created intellect an unexpected, indeed astounding, reality, 'the new nature which is being renewed in knowledge' (Col. 3.10)."[15] Scripturally, Webster additionally draws upon Psalm 119, Titus 2:11–12, 1 Corinthians 2:2, 2 Corinthians 5:17, and Ephesians 4:17–24. In his discussion of the vice of curiosity, Webster quotes Augustine and Bernard of Clairvaux extensively, and he quotes Aquinas seven times, more than any source besides Scripture. The only contemporary work that Webster cites is the theologian Paul Griffiths's *Intellectual Appetite*, whose Augustinian analysis fills out Webster's contention that curiosity "is preoccupied with satisfying the appetite for new objects to be consumed or hoarded."[16]

This final chapter charts roughly the same path as does Webster, though in more detail. First, I sketch some biblical background to the virtue of studiousness, with the goal of showing that the eschatological forgiveness of sins and the outpouring of the Spirit make possible a renewed knowing on the part of the people of God, a knowing that is constituted primarily by knowledge of God and therefore the ability to relate all that one knows to its creative source. Second, to further illumine the central significance of studiousness for the Christian moral life, I survey the central arguments of Griffiths's *Intellectual Appetite*. Griffiths's perspective is informed not only by Christian sources—above all Augustine—but also by contemporary works such as the cultural historian Barbara Benedict's *Curiosity*, which praises curiosity "as ontological transgression, the violation of role, of species, of a public self; it is an invitation to elude identity" and an "ambition to go beyond."[17] Here we can see how apt is Christopher Blum's remark that the "restraint" provided by the virtue of studiousness "is not one that keeps us from climbing to the heights . . . but that keeps us from doing so precipitously."[18]

Third and lastly, I examine Aquinas's theology of studiousness and of curiositas as its opposed vice, with attention to his biblical references. I suggest that Aquinas's approach to the virtue of studiousness unites attention to the scripturally attested work of the eschatological Spirit with the insights of the Augustinian tradition into the place of studiousness in the Christian moral life.[19] Through the forgiveness of sins and the outpouring of the Spirit, studious participants in the inaugurated kingdom share in the building up of what the theologian Matthew Lamb calls the "cathedral of the mind and heart, far more enduring than those of stone, wherein dwells an attentive reverence for the goodness and holiness of genuine knowing and loving. In such a cathedral of the mind and heart every discovery of truth is ultimately a gift, a finite, created participation in the embracing Mystery of Father, Son, and Holy Spirit."[20]

Biblical Background

Scripture emphasizes that we cannot know God in any exhaustive way. God is infinitely beyond us, though he encounters us and teaches us about himself through the created order and through divine revelation.[21] The psalmist says of God's own knowledge, "Such knowledge is too wonderful for me; it is high, I cannot attain it" (Ps 139:6). Refusing to attempt to measure God's knowledge, the psalmist remarks, "How precious to me are thy thoughts, O God! How vast is the sum of them! If I would count them, they are more than the sand" (vv. 17–18). Job makes a similar point: "Will any teach God knowledge, seeing that he judges those that are on high?" (Job 21:22). Job says of human knowledge's natural limits, "Where shall wisdom be found? And where is the place of understanding? Man does not know the way to it, and it is not found in the land of the living" (28:12–13). This can sound despairing, and in Job's mouth it may well be. But it can also sound realistic, as opposed to proud efforts to know more than is possible for us.

Similarly, in the context of criticizing the foolishness of idol worship, God warns Israel through the prophet Isaiah, "To whom will you liken me and make me equal, and compare me, that we may be alike? ... I am God, and there is no other; I am God, and there is none like me" (46:5, 9). Later in the book of Isaiah, God instructs his people not to imagine that they know his will for them, as though his mercy were merely a creaturely mercy. God tells his people, "For my thoughts are not your thoughts, neither are your ways my ways, says the Lord. For as the heavens are higher than the earth, so are my ways higher than your ways and my thoughts higher than your thoughts" (55:8–9).[22]

Yet Scripture also urges that we strive to learn about God and the world. Wisdom of Solomon, for instance, expresses admiration for humans who "investigate the world" (Wis 13:9) and seek to know the elements (fire, air, water) and "the circle of the stars" (13:2), but it bemoans the fact that these humans—the pagan philosophers—failed to rise to a proper knowledge of God. According to Wisdom of Solomon, God gave humans the ability to know that "from the greatness and beauty of created things comes a corresponding perception of their Creator" (Wis 13:5; cf. Rom 1).[23] But what happened instead, as Wisdom of Solomon says, is that humans used their skills in woodcutting and in fashioning gold and silver to make gods for themselves and to pray to them. Wisdom of Solomon adds that one result of this misuse of intelligence was immoral behavior: "Afterward it was not enough for them to err about the knowledge of God, but they live in great strife due to ignorance, and they call such great evils peace" (Wis 14:22). Among the sins that in Wisdom of Solomon's view typify fallen humans are child sacrifice, murder, adultery, theft, lying, ingratitude, "pollution of souls, sex perversion, disorder in marriage, ... and debauchery" (14:26).

Similarly, in Proverbs, we find a lengthy plea to use our intelligence to find out truth about God and reality, rather than wasting our intelligence through ignorance, evildoing, and debauchery. The author of Proverbs urges his children not to "enter the path of the wicked," which "is like deep darkness," since "they do not know over what they stumble" (4:14, 19). Instead, says Proverbs, we must come to be as much like God as we can be through wisdom. Famously, Proverbs 8 contains a paean to (personified) wisdom. Personified Wisdom states that "the Lord created me at the beginning of his work," and personified Wisdom urges: "Hear instruction and be wise, and do not neglect it" (8:22, 33). Proverbs recognizes that wisdom about God and human life is difficult to acquire, and that many people fail to seek it, despite its importance.[24]

The Psalms extol studying the Torah, much as the devout scribe Ezra "set his heart to study the law of the Lord" (Ezra 7:10). In Psalm 119 we read, "Oh, how I love thy law! It is my meditation all the day," and "I have sought thy precepts. . . . I will meditate on thy statutes" (vv. 45, 48, 97). God will instruct, lead, and teach those who are humble, according to Psalm 25. In the words of Psalm 19, "The heavens are telling the glory of God; and the firmament proclaims his handiwork. Day to day pours forth speech, and night to night declares knowledge" (vv. 1–2). The same God whom we learn about by studying the world is the God whose "law . . . is perfect" (19:7).[25] By contrast, "The fool says in his heart, 'There is no God'" (53:1).

Wisdom of Solomon bemoans the fact that bad use of intelligence results in despair about the enduring meaning of life, and the fruits of this despair are pleasure seeking and violence. According to Wisdom of Solomon, those who are fools have "reasoned unsoundly, saying to themselves, 'Short and sorrowful is our life, and there is no remedy when a man comes to his end. . . . Because we were born by mere chance, and hereafter we shall be as though we had never been'" (2:1–2). A better use of intelligence could have spared them this hopeless conclusion. In the book of Isaiah, God complains sadly, "My people go into exile for [lack] of knowledge," because "they do not regard the deeds of the Lord, or see the work of his hands" (Is 5:12–13). Rather than employing their minds to know and obey God's works and his law, the disobedient Israelites instead focus on building bigger homes, drinking alcohol, playing music, and making ornaments and clothing for their bodily adornment.

In the book of Jeremiah, the knowledge of God is connected with the eschatological forgiveness of sins and the outpouring of the Spirit. In Jeremiah 31, God promises, "I will forgive their iniquity, and I will remember their sin no more" (v. 34). This promise of forgiveness is paired with a promise of new knowledge: "No longer shall each man teach his neighbor and each his brother, saying, 'Know the Lord,' for they shall all know me, from the least of them to the greatest" (v. 34). Similarly, in the book of Isaiah, the eschatological "day" of the Lord will bring about the forgiveness of sins and will remove ignorance of God. Isaiah prophesies that God "will destroy on this mountain [Zion] the covering that is cast over all peoples, the veil that is spread over all nations" (Is 25:7). This "veil" is their ignorance of the true God. At the same time, God will "wipe away tears from all faces, and the reproach of his people he will take away from all the earth" (25:8)—signaling the forgiveness of sins and the restoration of Israel. Hosea 6:3 urges, "Let us press on to know the Lord."[26]

The eschatological forgiveness of sins and outpouring of the Spirit provide a powerful stimulus for learning about God, who is known in "the church of the living God, the pillar and bulwark of the truth" (1 Tim 3:15),[27] and who is known through the scripture that "is inspired by God and profitable for teaching, for reproof, for correction, and for training in righteousness" (2 Tim 3:16). In addition, the enlightenment brought by the forgiveness of sins and the outpouring of the Spirit should strengthen our learning about the created order, a learning that is necessary for rightly understanding scripture and for perceiving God in his works. In *De doctrina christiana*, Augustine recommends that those who wish to gain a better knowledge of scripture should study plants and animals, mathematics, history, philosophy, rhetoric, and many other arts, even while keeping in mind that at the center of all learning always remains "know[ing] the love of Christ which surpasses knowledge" (Eph 3:19).[28] It is a matter of God's grace rightly ordering our desire for knowledge and thereby of our knowing the right things in the right way.

PAUL GRIFFITHS ON STUDIOUSNESS AND CURIOSITY

Is it really possible to know things wrongly, due to a problem with our desire to know? No doubt "much study is a weariness of the flesh" (Eccles 12:12), but other than such weariness, it hardly seems that studying can be bad. Contemporary scholars may admit that in the end all knowledge "is vanity" (12:8), but they are generally loath to say that our desire to know can itself be disordered. By contrast, as Paul Griffiths comments, "It was a commonplace for all Latin-using Christian intellectuals from Tertullian at the end of the second century through at least to Bossuet in the seventeenth to say that *curiositas* is a vice, and that it needs to be distinguished from virtuous forms of the desire to know, which, beginning in the third century, began to be called *studiositas*."[29] Today, by contrast, the term "curiosity" functions as a term of praise, since we conceive of curiosity as encouraging the positive dynamisms of intellectual questing, creativity, and discovery. In the eighteenth century, David Hume's influential *A Treatise of Human Nature* praises "curiosity" as simply an open-minded desire to know the truth. Thus "curiosity" today names a virtue, and "studiousness"—when indicating a lack of well-rounded sociability—can even name a vice.

Inquiring into the origins of the Christian view of studiousness, Griffiths points first to 1 Corinthians 3, Colossians 2, and Proverbs 9. Most significantly, he identifies an exegetical tradition that built up around 1 John 2:16, which distinguishes "the lust of the flesh" from "the lust of the eyes." As he explains, "If the eyes can lust, desire inappropriately to see, then surely they can also seek vision (knowledge) chastely and rightly."[30] He adds that the Christian concern about desiring knowledge in a wrong way comes also from Greco-Roman philosophers. For Seneca and Apuleius, for example, *curiositas* is (in Griffiths's words) "a crass, vulgar, and dangerous appetite for knowledge no one should want."[31]

Griffiths probes Augustine's distinction in *De Trinitate* 10.1.3 between the studious soul, which loves that which it knows and therefore desires to know it more, and the curious soul, which loves the unknown and therefore seeks to make it known. On this basis, Griffiths offers a definition of the vice of *curiositas*: "Curiosity is . . . *appetite for the ownership of new knowledge*."[32] Curiositas seeks to grasp completely rather than to know more fully, and so curiositas reflects pride and power, rather than love and wonder.[33] Under the sway of curiositas, knowledge becomes a commodified and claimed object rather than being a deeper understanding of a beloved entity, in which understanding all people share by right. Griffiths remarks that "the studious do not seek to sequester, own, possess, or dominate what they hope to know; they want, instead, to participate lovingly in it, to respond to it knowingly as a gift rather than as a potential possession."[34] The curious treat reality as though it were there to be seized and dominated, while the studious treat reality as though it were a divine gift with its own integrity and inexhaustibility. Griffiths comments, "The curious inhabit a world of objects, which can be sequestered and possessed; the studious inhabit a world of gifts, given things, which can be known by participation, but which, because of their very natures cannot be possessed."[35]

Whether we are Christians or not, we inevitably hold that some human appetites should be encouraged and others discouraged. As a Christian, Griffiths affirms that humans possess a shared "human nature" that is teleologically "ordered to a certain end or goal," so that appetites that hinder the attainment of this goal should be discouraged or reformed.[36] In his view, "appetite is rooted in wonder and has intimacy with some creature or ensemble of creatures as its end."[37] He argues that our nature is made for praising the gifting God, since we are "creatures who are *imagines dei*, especially intimate participants in divine gift."[38] On this view, the appetite or desire for knowledge properly seeks "the participatory conformity of the knower to the known" through accurate judgments about what is known.[39] In no case, Griffiths emphasizes, should what is known be possessed or owned as an objectified entity. He contrasts studious, participatory knowledge with "mathesis," the quest (rooted in *curiositas*) for exhaustive knowledge based on following the right method, a quest devoid of wonder and surprise and aimed at isolation of the object studied, with the goal of eventually "knowing everything that's to be known and knowing it perfectly, without blemish or error."[40]

This understanding of knowledge as meant to be given away and as meant to participate intimately in the reality known leads Griffiths to a theology of scripture and the liturgy. Scripture cannot merely be a bounded (or owned) set of words but must instead be "a set of meanings, or verbal actions," which arises from and is attested to by liturgical proclamation and *confessio*.[41] When understood rightly, scripture is inseparable from the ways in which its words are "given away," as in the liturgy; Griffiths calls the result "Scripture-liturgy or liturgy-scripture."[42] He notes that the first giver of these words is God, and then humans, too, give these words, both as authors and editors, and as preachers to the whole world. Studious Christians study and love the words that God has given in order to participate more deeply in God through Christ and his Spirit and to give back the triune God's words in liturgical praise and proclamation, a proclamation that in turn gives these words to the whole world. To have the virtue of studiousness is to be committed to "grateful receipt" and "stewardly use," participatory intimacy and wonder rather than ownership and exhaustive conceptual mastery of the gifts by which God reveals himself and his love.[43]

Griffiths approves of Augustine's distinction between wisdom and "spectacle," the latter of which lacks the being that it pretends to possess (and thus cannot nourish wise participation in what is real) but succeeds in attracting the curious.[44] I note that the novelist Mario Vargas Llosa has described contemporary Western civilization as a "civilization of the spectacle," namely, "a world in which pride of place, in terms of a scale of values, is given to entertainment, and where having a good time, escaping boredom, is the universal passion"—with the result that the culture becomes banal and frivolous, boring rather than attuned to what is truly real and valuable.[45] How is it that a person can avoid becoming absorbed by mere spectacles? Griffiths proposes two principles: the degree to which sensible things are fallen indicates the extent to which knowledge of them will not satisfy us (since they will not have the "iconicity" and the reality that they should have); and the degree to which sensible things participate in God indicates how much our desire to know will be satisfied by knowing them.[46] If we are truly studious, we will strive to know sensible creatures that participate in a maximal way, according to their kind, in God. Such creatures are icons of the divine beauty to which they give finite expression.[47] When we know them properly, we always at the same time move beyond them to their inexhaustible source, rather than having our minds trapped idolatrously by finite things. Since the greatest sensible thing to know is Christ's humanity, it follows for Griffiths that "all other iconic arrays must be such because of the relation they bear to that one," and "some are exceedingly intimate with it," above all Mary and the Eucharist.[48]

Does this account provide any room for knowing nonsacred things? For Griffiths, nothing is *purely* secular, if by that is meant autonomous, independent of the gifting God and not iconically representative of his infinite wisdom, goodness, and beauty. But Griffiths urges that we should seek to know the "works made by human hands whose beauty gives them a high degree of participation in God, but which have nothing explicitly to do with the events in which God's presence is at a high degree of intensity."[49] Such works include those of the builder, the artist, the gardener, the cook, and so forth. Furthermore, he proposes that each human face is or should be an icon of Christ's face. Turning from human realities to the things of the natural world (the earth's ecosystem and the cosmos), he describes the natural world as damaged by the fall but nonetheless as constituting a vast set of "iconic arrays," less valuable than human realities but certainly worthy of our study.[50] The scope of studious knowing, therefore, is as broad as creation, though it always attends to the ways in which particular creatures are specially related to God (or hypostatically united to God, in the case of Christ's humanity).

By contrast, mere "spectacles" reflect the fallen aspect of ourselves and of the created order. Such spectacles conceal the divine Giver and seek to lock us into an exclusive and exhaustive relationship with sensible things, which are thereby deeply misused. If we assume ourselves to have mastered a sensible thing, we not only do not see it in its true reality (as distinct from our image of it), but also we become bored with it and seek something new. We certainly do not attain the intimacy with it that is the characteristic mark of studious knowing. We fall short of the true intellectual life, which in fact must be "a matter of constant wonder and constant stammering before the openness of what we study to the God who made it."[51]

Griffiths emphasizes that in knowing sensible and changing things, we must allow ourselves to be led upward to unchanging things. Otherwise, we will find ourselves moving from one changing thing to another, in a quest for novelty, or, more precisely, for things that are partly new and that can be therefore newly known. In such a case, the process of seeking knowledge has replaced desire for knowledge itself, since knowledge, once attained, immediately ceases to be novel. As Griffiths points out, the tendency of our minds to require ever new novelties manifests itself in numerous industries today. Since curiosity for new things cannot satisfy the mind, curiosity can only be "a self-replicating desire that cannot be satisfied and that must lead to an agonizing restlessness."[52]

By contrast, studiousness leads to God, who, unlike changing things, can inexhaustibly satisfy the mind via stable participatory intimacy. Studious persons will certainly seek to know and thus to be intimate with changing things, but only from within the recognition that such things participate in God and cannot be mastered or owned except by God.[53] Griffiths underscores that this God-centered way of knowing sensible things accords with that of our participation in the liturgy, which shapes the habit of studiousness. In the liturgy, our knowing of sensible things forms our participation in the changeless (but not static) relational love of the triune God. In this framework of participatory intimacy, studious Christians come to know both God and creatures more deeply, and in this sense come to know previously unknown things, though the goal of the studious knower is deeper intimacy rather than novelty.

For Griffiths, the fundamental way in which we learn studiousness is through the liturgy, where human words are given back in praise to the God who is the Giver of all that is. The key to moving from curiosity to studiousness consists in turning away from the proud desire to own our insights, to master and have dominion over them. The conversion to studiousness requires letting go of knowledge-as-exhaustive-mastery. Griffiths's emphasis on participation, wonder, and gift appreciates that each creature "has the value it has, and the possibilities of intimacy with humans proper to it, only because its face is a particular icon of God's presence."[54] This emphasis is grounded in the revelation of the Giver in Christ, and in the liturgical wonder, praise, and participatory intimacy with the triune God that Christ makes possible by forgiving sins and converting us. Through his Spirit, Christ not only unites us to the forgiveness that he has won on the cross but also reorders our knowing so that we truly know God. As

Jeremiah 31:34 says, "They shall all know me [God], from the least of them to the greatest."

We thereby obtain a renewed intellectual appetite, geared to liturgical praise. Discussing divine revelation, the philosopher Jean-Luc Marion comments that we regain the ability to know that "man, myself, my neighbor, cannot be known in the manner of an object, of an ideal or of an idol, but that he is received, definitively unknowable, as a gift of the God who remains forever unknowable."[55] Our redeemed intellectual desire enables us to see reality as it truly is, as Trinitarian gifting and Trinitarian gift. Quoting Alexander Schmemann, Norman Wirzba remarks along these lines: "True knowledge of the world is apprehension of it as the delectable expression of God's self-giving. The point is not simply to see that everything has its cause in God, 'but also that everything in the world and the world itself is a gift of God's love, a revelation by God of his very self, summoning us in everything to know God, through everything to be in communion with him, to possess everything as life in him.'"[56]

Thomas Aquinas on *Studiositas* and *Curiositas*

Let me now connect these views with Aquinas's succinct reading of the virtue of *studiositas* and its opposed vice *curiositas*. According to Aquinas, *studiositas* is a potential part of temperance because of its moderating of the desire to know. His main point is that the virtue of studiousness moderates the natural human desire to know by ensuring that the mind applies itself to the right things in the right way.

In his first article on studiousness, Aquinas cites four biblical texts: Romans 13:14, "put on the Lord Jesus Christ, and make no provision for the flesh, to gratify its desires"; Jeremiah 6:13, "For from the least to the greatest of them, every one is greedy for unjust gain [Vulgate: every one studies greediness]"; Proverbs 27:11, "Be wise [Vulgate: Study wisdom], my son, and make my heart glad"; and Matthew 6:21, "For where your treasure is, there will your heart be also."[57] Reflection on these texts can help us to appreciate more deeply Aquinas's theology of studiousness.[58]

In the Old Testament, Jeremiah 6:13 bears witness to our condition of sinfulness, including (in its Vulgate version) sinful intellectual appetite. It points forward to Jeremiah 31's prophecy of the new covenant, the eschatological forgiveness of sins, and the renewal of the people's minds to know God. Proverbs 27:11 urges us to seek wisdom as the path of avoiding sin, and therefore also (given our fallen condition) signals the need for the outpouring of the Spirit so that we will turn from sin and obtain wisdom.

The two New Testament texts, in turn, bear witness to the inaugurated kingdom. In the Sermon on the Mount, Jesus, who is "king of the Jews" (Mt 2:2), offers commandments for God's eschatological people to whom he has been "preaching the gospel of the kingdom" (4:23). Crucial to these commandments is the fact that our appetite (including our intellectual appetite, our desire to know) must be focused on the things of God. As Jesus puts it in the passage quoted by Aquinas, "Where your treasure is, there will your heart be also" (6:21). If our desire is not focused on "treasures in heaven" (6:20), then we are still in our sins, still living according to the flesh and not yet studious. Romans 13 urges believers to "wake from sleep" (Rom 13:11) and prepare for the coming of Christ to consummate the kingdom. Our focus must not be "the flesh" but rather must be "the Lord Jesus Christ" (13:14). For both of these New Testament texts, the key point is that God's eschatological people must focus primarily on the things of God.

This focus on divine realities is made possible by the outpouring of the Spirit, since without the Spirit, fallen humans will inevitably live according to the flesh. As Paul says earlier in Romans, "The law of the Spirit of life in Christ Jesus has set me free from the law of sin and death" (8:2). In Christ, Paul tells us, God "condemned sin in the flesh, in order that the just requirement of the law might be fulfilled in us, who walk not according to the flesh but according to the Spirit" (8:3–4).[59]

Aquinas observes that "covetousness craves the acquisition of gain."[60] By contrast, the Christian mind must be focused on God in Christ. Even though the Christian can and should be "skilled in earthly things,"[61] such skills should not deprive the Christian mind of its primary focus. Aquinas remarks that "man has special affection for those things which foster the flesh."[62] Studiousness thus requires a conversion of the mind away from the fallen tendency to focus solely on the "things that foster [our] flesh."

Studiousness involves the mind applying itself to seek to know. Recognizing the problem of laziness, Aquinas points out that "as regards knowledge, man has contrary inclinations. For on the part of the soul, he is inclined to desire knowledge of things; . . . whereas on the part of his bodily nature, man is inclined to avoid the trouble of seeking knowledge."[63] Study tires us quickly, and it hardly seems to amount to much practical benefit. One aspect of the virtue of studiousness, then, is that it inspires us to seek knowledge with more urgency and constancy. Aquinas makes clear, however, that the purpose of the virtue of studiousness is not to produce scholars; rather, studiousness primarily addresses the problem of seeking knowledge "immoderately" by seeking the wrong knowledge in the wrong way.[64]

It might seem that since God knows everything and God created us in his image, we should desire to know without limit. Although Aquinas disagrees with this view, as scriptural evidence in favor of it he quotes Sirach 1:1, "All wisdom comes from the Lord," and Wisdom 7:17, "For it is he [God] who gave me unerring knowledge of what exists, to know the structure of the world and the activity of the elements."[65] He grants that knowledge of earthly things (what today is called "science") is not bad or prohibited, since it is God who makes such knowledge possible for us. Likewise, he affirms that since "all wisdom comes from the Lord," the possession of wisdom per se cannot be sinful. In support of the view that God's images should seek to know without limit, he calls to mind 1 Samuel 2:3, "the Lord is a God of knowledge," and Hebrews 4:13, "before him [God] no creature is hidden, but all are open and laid bare to the eyes of him."[66] In these ways, he presents a strong case for the view that desiring to know without limit is not sinful.

Against this view, however, it is already noteworthy that 1 Samuel 2:3 and Hebrews 4:13 appear in passages of divine judgment. 1 Samuel 2:3 belongs to Hannah's song of praise after she has born her child Samuel. Hannah's song functions to communicate the divine judgment against the priestly house of Eli and against all who are proud and depend upon human resources rather than upon God. The full verse, from which Aquinas takes a segment, reads: "Talk no more so very proudly, let not arrogance come from your mouth; for the Lord is a God of knowledge, and by him actions are weighed." Similarly, Hebrews 4:13 follows upon an admonition to recognize that God is judge and that, if we wish to enter into the perfect Sabbath, we must not sin: "Let us therefore strive to enter that rest, that no one fall by the same sort of disobedience" (Heb 4:11). Thus, 1 Samuel 2:3 and Hebrews 4:13 do more than confirm the goodness of our desire to know; they warn against arrogance and disobedience. In a similar way, Sirach 1:1 should be read in light of the broader passage's point that "to fear the Lord is the beginning of wisdom" (Sir 1:13). When we seek to know in a virtuous manner, we fear and obey God, and we accept our finite limits in knowing. Here Thomas Pfau's critique of the "transformation of knowledge from an interpretive and morally responsible hermeneutic into an open-ended quest for (ostensibly value-neutral) information" comes to mind, given that the latter view of knowing is intrinsically unlimited.[67]

In answering whether it is possible for us to sin in desiring and seeking knowledge, Aquinas cites four further biblical texts that provide the foundation of his account of how we can sin in the pursuit of knowledge: 1 Corinthians 8:1; Jeremiah 9:5; Sirach 3:22, 26; and Colossians 2:8. The first verse, 1 Corinthians 8:1, helps Aquinas to distinguish between vices that pertain to the use of knowledge and the particular vice (curiositas) that is opposed to studiousness. Curiositas is specifically a vice found in "the desire and study in the pursuit of the knowledge of truth."[68] In 1 Corinthians 8:1–3, Paul warns the Corinthians that the inaugurated kingdom is built on how much we love, not on how much we know, since none of us knows much in comparison with God's knowledge. Paul states, "'Knowledge' puffs up, but love builds up. If any one imagines that he knows something, he does not yet know as he ought to know. But if one loves God, one is known by him" (1 Cor 8:1–3). Citing 1 Corinthians 8:1, Aquinas observes that knowledge can puff us up in our own estimation when we do not refer all that we know to God, who cannot be captured by our knowing and who is the source both of our knowing and of all that we know. Thus, when we study to take pride in our knowledge—so that we are ultimately interested only in ourselves rather than in truth about reality[69]—we have become puffed up and have traded studiousness for curiosity.

Similarly, when we hope to "learn something in order to sin," we have also fallen into curiosity.[70] Aquinas applies a warning from Jeremiah to our curious minds: "They have taught their tongue to speak lies" (9:5). This verse from Jeremiah belongs to God's explanation of the exile of his people, which only Christ's eschatological forgiveness of sins and outpouring of the Spirit overcomes.[71] When we desire to know in order to act against God, we have forgotten that the goal of knowledge is deeper participation in God. Aquinas quotes Augustine's observation that curious people who know a vast amount about earthly realities but do not know or seek God, who is the source of these realities, are absurd. They imagine that they know far more than they do, and their knowledge has failed to apprehend the most important thing about what they do know, namely that earthly realities are created.[72]

Natural scientists, historians, economists, and so forth do not need to become theologians. They do need, however, to understand their topics with some reference to God, because otherwise they cannot properly understand their topics.[73] As the philosopher Gregory Reichberg observes, for Aquinas "the assiduous study of creatures is a praiseworthy pursuit,"[74] but since it is the study of *created* things, we must refer in some way to the Creator in order to understand the truth of such things. This point applies most clearly in the human sciences (such as history), since human action involves a personal relation to God. The point also applies to the natural sciences, because the things studied by the natural sciences are apprehended as self-created only through a grave distortion of what they actually are—and of our purposes in studying them.[75] If we deliberately cut off God from any area of our desire to know things, then we have separated ourselves from the purpose of knowing, which (implicitly at least) is to know God and so to attain true happiness.[76] I note that the eschatological community is marked by constant reference to God. In Isaiah's prophecy of the new creation, God foretells that "he who blesses himself in the land shall bless himself by the God of truth" (Is 65:16).[77]

Aquinas observes that it is characteristic of curiositas to focus on sense knowledge. He cites 1 John 2:16, "the lust of eyes," which he (like Augustine and Griffiths) links with the vice of curiosity and which 1 John 2:16 pairs with two other vices focused on sensible things, namely "the lust of the flesh" and "the pride of life."[78] The study of sensible things can be directed to sustaining and improving one's bodily life or to "intellective knowledge, whether speculative or practical."[79] In neither of these ways is the desire to know sensible things sinful. It becomes sinful only when the desire to know sensible things distracts us from more important and useful reflection or when it directs our minds toward "something harmful."[80] The point is that desiring to know sensible things is commendable in itself, but when such a desire is disordered, the vice of curiosity takes over.

Although curiosity focuses our minds on sensible things, Aquinas is certainly not saying that the vice of curiosity can *only* arise with regard to the knowledge of sensible things. With respect to curiosity, Aquinas explains that "there may be sin in the knowledge of certain truths, in so far as the desire of such knowledge is not directed in due manner to the knowledge of the sovereign truth," namely God.[81] One can seek to know God in a way that is not duly ordered to God, for example if one seeks to know God out of pride. Aquinas recognizes that philosophers can make wicked use of the knowledge of God that they seek and obtain. Thus, curiosity is not limited to the study of sensible things, but rather curiosity arises wherever the quest for knowledge involves a disordered self-reference rather than a proper God-reference.

Since curiosity always involves a disordered self-reference, however, curiosity always directs our desire to know away from God and toward earthly things. As Aquinas and Griffiths emphasize, those who seek to know in a spirit of curiosity will generally be focused on using such knowledge for sin or for bodily profit, leaving God out of the picture. For this reason, the connection between curiosity and the "lust of the eyes" described in 1 John 2:16 is appropriate. Curiosity generally "is about pleasures arising from the knowledge acquired through all the senses."[82] The curious person refers his or her knowledge to the self and to the self's pleasures.[83] When this is done, true knowledge is gravely impeded. Paul concludes aptly, "Claiming to be wise, they became fools" (Rom 1:22).

※ ※ ※

Although the fall has not left us bereft of the power to reason, nonetheless, as Reinhard Hütter says, "reasoning can be profoundly misdirected while the intellect's epistemic capacity per se remains unaffected."[84] Paul is all too correct when he recognizes that "'knowledge' puffs up" (1 Cor 8:1). Analysis of the virtue of studiousness and the vice of curiosity explains how this can be so. In Christ's inaugurated kingdom, the Spirit heals our desire to know and enables us to seek knowledge of things while referring them properly to God. Hütter comments that fallen human nature needs the will's "renewal or healing through grace," so as to restore "reasoning's directedness" and to escape "the incurvature of human existence under the condition of sin."[85] Through the forgiveness of sins and outpouring of the Spirit, the studious person comes to desire knowledge not for mastery and domination, but for intimate and liturgical sharing in God and his gifts.

The main task of the virtue of studiousness is to ensure that we desire to know things with reference to God. Norman Wirzba warns that when reference to God is lacking, we will inevitably conceive of "the creatures and gifts of this world as uninteresting and uncherished things, as objects of no special significance or worth."[86] Wirzba contends that "people would gradually learn to forget about God entirely if they could be trained to think that the world is a collection of random facts rather than the site of God's creation, and that every created thing is only an object and not also an expression of God's sustaining Word."[87] When we seek to know things without acknowledging their reference to God, this results in a severe distortion of what things actually are. We destroy, as Griffiths puts it, the "iconicity" of things.

Whereas Griffiths relatively rarely cites scripture, Aquinas returns us to Jeremiah 6 (God's condemnation of Israel and announcement of the impending exile), Jeremiah 9 (the distortion of knowledge by lies), Wisdom 7 and Sirach 1 (God as the source of all wisdom), Matthew 6 (Christ's Sermon on the Mount), Romans 13 (the attitude of the believer awaiting Christ's return and the final consummation), 1 Corinthians 8 (the distortedness of knowledge without love of God), Colossians 2 (the futility of human tradition without Christ), and Hebrews 4 (God's knowledge of all things as judge). This scriptural context reminds us that recovering the iconicity of all things—rather than treating them with respect to isolation and mastery—requires the Spirit's outpouring and the eschatological forgiveness of sins so that we can desire knowledge rightly. Aquinas anchors the virtue of studiousness in the drama of the inaugurated kingdom.

Paul cautions, "If any one imagines that he knows something, he does not yet know as he ought to know. But if one loves God, one is known by him" (1 Cor 8:2–3). Real reference to God deprives our knowledge of its absurd claim to sufficiency and mastery. It is necessary to ground our knowledge in divine praise, as when the psalmist proclaims, "Great are the works of the Lord, studied by all who have pleasure in them" (Ps 111:2). When love orders our desire for knowledge rightly—when the forgiveness of sins and the outpouring of the Spirit shape our knowing—we "abound more and more, with knowledge and all discernment, so that [we] may approve what is excellent, and may be pure and blameless for the day of Christ" (Phil 1:9–10).

Conclusion

Catholic moral theology is rooted in the realities of God the Father's sending of Christ and his Spirit, on the one hand, and the created, renewed, restored, and forgiven people of God on the other. The virtues associated with Christian temperance help to reveal what human nature should be. When we live in this way, we follow the divinely given path of true human flourishing, the path that leads to everlasting beatitude as members of the body of Christ. In concluding this book, therefore, let me reflect once more upon the divinely given path set forth in the Sermon on the Mount.

Discussing the Sermon on the Mount, Servais Pinckaers remarks that "the beatitudes gather together the ancient promises regarding the Promised Land and point them to the Kingdom of heaven."[1] The Sermon's beatitudes reveal that believers are on the way, in a new and definitive exodus, to the consummated "Kingdom of heaven, where all the divine promises will be fulfilled."[2] On this basis, Pinckaers states that Jesus' moral teachings have "all the force of a legislative text determining the life and actions of a people and powerful enough to form a new society, a Kingdom which shall be the special province of the Wisdom and Providence of God."[3]

In our contemporary culture, however, people often fear that an authoritative "legislative text" will restrict and hamper human flourishing and could even place God's mercy out of reach for sinners. Even professed Christians today sometimes seek to ignore or weaken the authoritative teaching of scripture as mediated by the Church over the centuries; we are urged, explicitly or implicitly, to separate ourselves from scripture's outdated moral rules. In fact, as the present book has sought to show, Jesus' moral teachings in the Sermon, and indeed the whole of the scriptural teaching on temperance, constitute a crucial part of his mercy for sinners. He not only dies for our sins as a work of pure mercy but also by his teachings mercifully shows us how to be configured to the image of his self-surrendering love. In this way, his Sermon signals the inauguration of the new creation that is the kingdom of God.

Importantly, this kingdom is a liturgical one, rooted in sacramental sharing in Jesus' Pasch through his Spirit.[4] Participating in the liturgy of the Eucharist, offering our embodied spiritual sacrifices to God in and through Christ and the Spirit, we believers live in the world as royal priests. David Fagerberg observes, "Our entire daily life, excepting nothing, can become a spiritual sacrifice acceptable to God through the supreme and eternal priest, Jesus Christ, who vivifies his mystical members' lives in his Spirit."[5] Fagerberg adds that it is "by operating the leverage of the cross" that "we consecrate the entire world (*consecratio mundi*), and all our daily actions, to God."[6] The moral theologian Livio Melina echoes this insight: "The new sacrifice of Christians, their spiritual cult, is the *caritas* that comes from the sacrifice of Christ with whom we communicate in the Eucharist. . . . If the new center of ethics is given in the Eucharist, that means that life becomes liturgy through mutual love in the community of the body of Christ."[7]

The Sermon on the Mount expresses the ethics of this eucharistic kingdom of self-sacrificial love. As we would expect, therefore, the Sermon proclaims what Fagerberg calls "mundane liturgical theology." In the Sermon, we find the central parts of temperance. Thus, the Sermon warns against anger: "Every one who is angry with his brother shall be liable to judgment" (Mt 5:22). The Sermon warns against lust: "Every one who looks at a woman lustfully has already committed adultery with her in his heart" (5:28). The Sermon commands meekness: "Blessed are the meek, for they shall inherit the earth" (5:5). The Sermon requires fasting: "When you fast, anoint your head and wash your face, that your fasting may not be seen by men but by your Father who is in secret" (6:16). Emphasizing trust in God's provision, the Sermon corrects gluttony: "Is not life more than food . . . ?" (6:25).

The Sermon commends humility: "Why do you see the speck that is in your brother's eye, but do not notice the log that is in your own eye?" (7:3). The Sermon shows that our desire to know, like all our desires, must be ordered to God: "Seek first his kingdom and his righteousness, and all these things shall be yours as well" (6:33).[8]

In a manner that is highly pertinent to the purposes of the present book, N. T. Wright sums up the central meaning of the Sermon's words: "God's future is arriving in the present, in the person and work of Jesus, and you can practice, right now, the habits of life which will find their goal in that coming future."[9] The virtues that Jesus commands to us in the Sermon on the Mount are, as Wright says, "the signs of life, the language of life, the life of new creation, the life of new covenant, the life which Jesus came to bring."[10] Jesus' gift of "the life of new creation" means that Jesus loves us by enabling us, through his Spirit, to live temperately, avoiding insatiable desire for food and drink, sexual lust, enraged anger, self-absorbed pride, and the illusion that we can possess the masterful knowledge of things that only God can possess.

Because the inauguration of the kingdom fulfills rather than negates created human nature, Aquinas draws upon the best teachings of Plato, Aristotle, Cicero, and Seneca about human nature and about the moral virtues of prudence, justice, courage, and temperance (including the various "parts" of temperance). In the Sermon, however, Christ reveals to us not only the depth of the need for fallen nature's healing but also our supernatural end, the consummated kingdom, which is infinitely above the capacities of human nature.[11] Life in Christ therefore requires infused moral virtues, including infused temperance, which the Holy Spirit bestows upon God's people along with faith, hope, and charity. Aquinas explains that the "infused moral virtues, whereby men behave well in respect of their being 'fellow-citizens with the saints, and of the household of God' (Eph 2:19), differ from the acquired virtues, whereby man behaves well in respect of human affairs."[12] Specifically with regard to temperance, Aquinas states, "Both acquired and infused temperance moderate desires for pleasures of touch, but for different reasons . . . wherefore their respective acts are not identical."[13] As the Sermon makes clear, God's wise order for the flourishing of human nature requires that we avoid the vice of lust, but because we are citizens of the inaugurated kingdom it is the *infused* virtue of temperance that enables our chastity to manifest the reality that we are "a new creation" (Gal 6:16) insofar as we "walk by the Spirit" (5:25).

Dare We Trust the Sermon on the Mount?

All this sounds good, but does it really work? After all, even if the Sermon on the Mount proclaims an eschatological ethics of temperance, and even if the Sermon "contains within itself the potential to create, direct, and transform history,"[14] believers obviously remain very weak and imperfect. Stanley Hauerwas notes that "we have been called into a community unimaginable if Christ has not been raised from the dead," but he adds that this cannot be a reason for boasting, since we are still weak.[15] The inauguration of the kingdom of God reveals to us "the light of the world" (Mt 5:14), which, in Christ, we are called to embody. But in order to be this "light," we must hear and obey Christ's words about the moral life, and this means often going against the grain of our fallen desires. To do this, we must obey the instruction of Cardinal Jorge Bergoglio (Pope Francis) to "put ourselves in the presence of the Lord who beholds and loves us."[16] This includes confessing our failings to Jesus and receiving, through his inexhaustible mercy, a new foundation in his kingdom of mercy.

As the Wesleyan theologian Bernie Van De Walle comments, however, in this fallen world we remain all too "prone to excuse our own shortcomings, to vindicate our personal faults."[17] Augustine puts this point with characteristic sharpness, with respect to the "fevers of [our] soul," including lust.[18] He states that when we are ill from such fevers, God "hates" what we have made ourselves to be, and God wants to make us the true images of God that we "are not yet."[19] We need to allow ourselves to be changed by Christ the healer, but—as Augustine says—"how irksome food is to sick people when they are beginning to recover!"[20]

The fact is that most Christians, including me, are still recovering from the lingering consequences of original sin and from acquired vices against temperance. Aquinas explains why this is still the case, notwithstanding the transformative power of the Holy Spirit. He notes that "sometimes the habits of moral virtue experience difficulty in their works, by reason of certain contrary dispositions remaining from previous acts."[21] Infused moral virtue does not obliterate the "contrary dispositions" that we have acquired. Indeed, even persons whom the Church acknowledges to be saints may seem to lack certain virtuous habits "in so far as they experience difficulty in the acts of those virtues."[22]

In such persons, the infused virtuous habits are present. Otherwise such saintly Christians could not truly "love one another" with the consistency that Paul envisions when he commands us to "love one another; for he who loves his neighbor has fulfilled the law" (Rom 13:8).[23] But the point is that when we possess infused moral virtues (such as infused temperance), we may possess them in a manner that is weak or faltering because of the dispositions that belong to our fallen "old self" (6:6). The moral theologian Michael Sherwin remarks that in such a situation, "although the disposition to sin is no longer the principle from which we act, it still can impede our ability to act from our new principle of action, which is infused temperance."[24] Sherwin adds that due to the lingering effects of acquired vices and to the ongoing presence of the *fomes* or "tinder of sin" caused by original sin and inflamed by one's own sins, a believer may find "himself in the unique position of having virtues that he does not psychologically feel like he has."[25] This is one reason why Augustine urges his *Christian* congregation to strive even now to "*become new people*" and truly to "be Christians," in an ongoing transformation that is only possible "because Christ has made himself into a broad road and highway which leads us straight home."[26]

THE ESCHATOLOGICAL HIGHWAY OF CHRISTIAN TEMPERANCE

The present book has sought to map an important portion of this "broad road and highway." In the integral parts of temperance, shame and *honestas*, we found a sign of the eschatological renewal of the temple: the fear of defilement and the interior beauty of the believer, whose body is the "temple of the Holy Spirit" (1 Cor 6:19). In the subjective parts of temperance, abstinence and chastity (along with fasting, sobriety, and virginity), we found a sign of the eschatological restoration of God's people: the reasonable ordering of eating, drinking, and sexuality toward self-giving care for others, in the context of family and communal life. In the potential parts of temperance, including clemency, meekness, humility, and studiousness, we found a sign of the eschatological forgiveness of sins and the outpouring of the Spirit, who makes it possible for us to overcome the guilt and destruction wrought by irrational anger, pride, and self-centered *curiositas*.

By interpreting the parts of temperance in light of the inaugurated eschatological kingdom, I have augmented what Aquinas himself explicitly says. I hope that this heuristic device has shed light upon the motivating factors behind Aquinas's appreciation for temperance's role in Christian life.[27] Indeed, when we seek to apprehend Christian ethics without attending to the eschatological renewal of the temple, restoration of God's people, and forgiveness of sins and outpouring of the Spirit, we have not grasped what is entailed in a biblically grounded moral theology such as Aquinas's.[28] Pinckaers rightly emphasizes that for Aquinas, Christian obedience to divinely revealed law relies upon the eschatological grace of the Holy Spirit that comes to us, as Aquinas says, "through God's Son made man, whose humanity grace filled first, and thence flowed forth to us [see John 1:14–17]."[29]

The theologian W. H. Kane observes that "the great heart of nature is full to overflowing always, like a dripping elm tree, with love and praise to God for His goodness."[30] Human nature displays the divine artistry. God has made rational animals fit for interpersonal communion. The desires that foster our self-preservation pertain not only to bodily sustenance but to the broader realm of meals, marriage, and family that make life so meaningful. Christ's inauguration of the kingdom affects the virtue of temperance in various ways, including by healing and elevating our appetites so that they can serve our goal of attaining true communion with God and neighbor, by giving place for fasting and virginity in the context of the virtues of abstinence and chastity, by providing a graced exemplar of meekness and humility, and by transforming our desire to master the created order into a studious wonder in response to the divine gifting.

Yet, Kane remarks somberly, "Whence then is the warfare, the ruin and ugliness of the cities of men? . . . In man we find the miseries of a narrow, egotistic heart, a fickle will, an unbalanced, violent, capricious character. The miseries of his pride and greed make man vile and contemptible."[31] In our fallen state, not only humanity in general but we ourselves stand accused, and rightly accused. How greatly we need, both as individuals and as God's people, the merciful grace and light of the inaugurated kingdom of Christ and his Spirit. How deeply we hunger, in our fallen condition, for "genuine and deep communion, what we might also call an intimate taste for life."[32]

Fortunately, as Rabbi Jonathan Sacks observes, "Love distinguishes between the person and the deed. An act may be evil, but since the person is free, he or she is not inseparably joined to that evil. . . . Wrongs can be rectified, and harm healed."[33] By God's grace, we can be forgiven, and we can be changed. Proclaiming "the message of reconciliation" (2 Cor 5:19), Kane rejoices that even now "the Holy Spirit waters and tends humble souls in the garden of God."[34]

Therefore, when we are afflicted by lack of temperance, oppressed by interior impurity, vehement desires, bursts of anger that exceed the bounds of reason, absurd pride, and desire to use knowledge to master and control the things of God, let us "draw near to the throne of grace, that we may receive mercy and find grace to help in time of need" (Heb 4:16). Let us beg urgently for God's gracious help in Christ and his Spirit. Imploring God for the renewal and strengthening of the infused virtue of temperance, let us "rely not on ourselves but on God who raises the dead; he delivered us from so deadly a peril, and he will deliver us" (2 Cor 1:9–10). "Then all the assembly shouted loudly and blessed God, who saves those who hope in him" (Dan 13:60).

NOTES

Introduction

1. See Philip G. Ziegler, *The Apocalyptic Turn and the Future of Christian Theology* (Grand Rapids, MI: Baker Academic, 2018); Joshua B. Davis and Douglas Harink, eds., *Apocalyptic and the Future of Theology: With and Beyond J. Louis Martyn* (Eugene, OR: Wipf and Stock, 2012). Against the false antitheses that plague "apocalyptic theology," see N. T. Wright, "Apocalyptic and the Sudden Fulfillment of Divine Promise," in *Paul and the Apocalyptic Imagination*, ed. Ben C. Blackwell, John K. Goodrich, and Jason Maston (Minneapolis: Fortress, 2016), 111–34; R. David Nelson, "Creation and the Problem of Evil after the Apocalyptic Turn," in *Evil and the Doctrine of Creation*, ed. David Luy, Matthew Levering, and George Kalantzis (Bellingham, WA: Lexham, forthcoming).

2. Bernard Häring, *Free and Faithful in Christ: Moral Theology for Clergy and Laity*, vol. 1, *General Moral Theology* (New York: Crossroad, 1978), 19.

3. Pope Francis, *Amoris Laetitia*, Vatican translation (Frederick, MD: The Word Among Us Press, 2016), §314.

4. Ibid., §320. For discussion of divine mercy in light of Pope Francis's homily of March 3, 2016, in which he emphasizes the need to recognize ourselves as sinners as a condition for receiving mercy, see Reinhard Hütter, "Human Sexuality in a Fallen World: An Economy of Mercy and Grace," *Nova et Vetera* 15 (2017): 447.

5. For the danger of an overrealized eschatology, see the cautionary notes sounded by Paula Fredriksen in her review of *Paul and the Faithfulness of God*, by N. T. Wright, *Catholic Biblical Quarterly* 77 (2015): 388. Regarding the goal of the Christian life, Robert Barron points out that "the Catholic Church's job is to call people to sanctity and to equip them for

living saintly lives. Its mission is not to produce nice people, or people with hearts of gold or people with good intentions; its mission is to produce saints, people of heroic virtue" (Barron, *Vibrant Paradoxes: The Both/And of Catholicism* [Skokie, IL: Word on Fire Catholic Ministries, 2016], 6). He compares the Church's teachings on just war with the Church's teachings on sexual matters, observing that in both cases polling data show that the majority of Catholics reject the Church's teachings. In both cases, people (and nations) often fall short of the moral law. He argues, however, that "to dial down the demands because they are hard and most people have a hard time realizing them is to compromise the very meaning and purpose of the Church" (ibid., 7). He adds that the difficulty, for fallen humans, of living up to the moral law—even with the aid of the grace of the Holy Spirit—is recognized by the Church's penitential practice (the sacrament of reconciliation). As he says, "The Church also mediates the infinite mercy of God to those who fail to live up to that ideal (which means practically everyone). This is why its forgiveness is so generous and so absolute" (ibid.). It turns out, too, that to live in accord with the Church's moral law is to live in the way that makes us most fully human, so that we discover that what at first seems an ideal—and what often remains difficult to follow, given our fallen condition—is in fact what makes us "real," what makes us able to live in a fully human way in our families and communities. See also Barron's critique of proportionalist ethics in his *The Priority of Christ: Toward a Postliberal Catholicism* (Grand Rapids, MI: Brazos, 2007), 264–73.

6. All quotations from the Bible are from the Revised Standard Version (RSV) Catholic Edition (San Francisco: Ignatius Press, n.d.).

7. Aquinas is clear that "at all times there have been some persons belonging to the New Testament" through "implicit faith," which in the case of Gentiles can arise simply "through believing in divine providence" (*ST* I-II, q. 106, a. 3, ad 2; *ST* II-II, q. 2, a. 7, ad 3, trans. Fathers of the English Dominican Province [Westminster, MD: Christian Classics, 1981]; all English quotations of *ST* are taken from this translation) and which the Mosaic law stimulated in the Jewish people. For my position on these matters, see my "Aquinas and Supersessionism One More Time: A Response to Matthew A. Tapie's *Aquinas on Israel and the Church*," *Pro Ecclesia* 25 (2016): 395–412. Note that Jewish scholars generally recognize that to fulfill God's commandments we need God's grace: see for example Jon D. Levenson, *The Love of God: Divine Gift, Human Gratitude, and Mutual Faithfulness in Judaism* (Princeton: Princeton University Press, 2016), 158; David Novak, "Response to Matthew Levering's 'Christians and Natural Law,'" in Anver M. Emon, Matthew Levering, and David Novak, *Natural Law: A Jewish, Christian, and Islamic Trialogue* (Oxford: Oxford Univer-

sity Press, 2014), 138. For a Jewish perspective that is optimistic about fallen human capabilities to overcome sin, see Solomon Schimmel, *The Seven Deadly Sins: Jewish, Christian, and Classical Reflections on Human Psychology* (Oxford: Oxford University Press, 1997), 20. For the variety of Second Temple Jewish understandings of grace or divine gift, see John M. G. Barclay, *Paul and the Gift* (Grand Rapids, MI: Eerdmans, 2015), 189–328.

8. James D. G. Dunn, *Jesus Remembered*, vol. 1 of *Christianity in the Making* (Grand Rapids, MI: Eerdmans, 2003), 890.

9. Richard B. Hays, *The Moral Vision of the New Testament: Community, Cross, New Creation; A Contemporary Introduction to New Testament Ethics* (New York: HarperCollins, 1996), 27. Since injustice and death still characterize the world, the inaugurated kingdom is obviously not yet the consummated kingdom. Earlier, Hays notes that for Paul, "the church community is a sneak preview of God's ultimate redemption of the world. This is a grandiose-sounding claim, but its potential triumphalism is tempered by the other side of Paul's eschatological dialectic, the 'not yet'" (ibid., 24). Scot McKnight similarly observes that it is a mistake to "think church and following Jesus are disconnected" ("The New Perspective and the Christian Life: The Ecclesial Life," in *The Apostle Paul and the Christian Life: Ethical and Missional Implications of the New Perspective*, ed. Scot McKnight and Joseph B. Modica [Grand Rapids, MI: Baker Academic, 2016], 128). Indeed, McKnight contends that precisely because Paul knew "that Jesus was Messiah and Lord," the "*church* was Paul's obsession.... The mission of the apostle Paul is to form fellowships in separate cities that embody a new sociopolitical and economic and spiritual order" (ibid., 142–43, 145). See also the section on Pauline "ethics, eschatology and theology" in Richard A. Burridge, *Imitating Jesus: An Inclusive Approach to New Testament Ethics* (Grand Rapids, MI: Eerdmans, 2007), 98–107. After assessing a wide range of views in Pauline studies and examining Paul's letters, Burridge concludes this section: "Because we live in the eschatological tension 'between the times,' ethics is all the more necessary as we work out the consequences of being 'in Christ' and sharing in the Christian community.... Jesus' ethics were primarily concerned with a response to his preaching of the coming of the kingdom into our present now, undertaken within the context of a community of disciples. Paul is often contrasted with Jesus, and seen as responsible for a shift from 'the kingdom of God' to the 'King,' to the person of Christ, and thus the founder of a new religious movement. In fact, this is an unfair distinction since, for Paul, the supreme act of God's sovereignty (i.e., the 'kingdom') is what he has done in Christ: this is how he has brought the whole story of Israel to a climax in Jesus of Nazareth" (ibid., 106–7).

10. For brief background see Philippe Delhaye, *The Christian Conscience*, trans. Charles Underhill Quinn (New York: Desclée, 1968). Delhaye identifies seven "moral systems" developed in the post-Tridentine period: "absolute tutiorism, mitigated tutiorism, probabiliorism, equiprobabilism, probabilism, compensationism, laxism" (ibid., 21).

11. Charles J. Chaput, "The Splendor of Truth in 2017," *First Things*, no. 276 (October 2017): 23. In this essay, Archbishop Chaput defends the teachings of Pope John Paul II's encyclical *Veritatis Splendor*.

12. For a defense of casuistry, see Brian Besong, "Reappraising the Manual Tradition," *American Catholic Philosophical Quarterly* 89 (2015): 557-84. While I think that his critique of Pinckaers is too broad, I agree that casuistry is needed in moral reflection.

13. Stanley Hauerwas, "Why 'The Way the Words Run' Matters: Reflections on Becoming a 'Major Biblical Scholar,'" in *The Word Leaps the Gap: Essays on Scripture and Theology in Honor of Richard B. Hays*, ed. J. Ross Wagner, C. Kavin Rowe, and A. Katherine Grieb (Grand Rapids, MI: Eerdmans, 2008), 3.

14. Thomas Aquinas, *ST* II-II, q. 141, a. 2. Thus temperance has to do with the concupiscible appetite, whereas fortitude has to do with the irascible appetite, since fortitude enables a person "to endure or withstand those things on account of which he forsakes the good of reason" (ibid.).

15. See Andrew Pinsent, *Prudence, Justice, Courage, and Temperance: The Cardinal Virtues* (London: Catholic Truth Society, 2017), 58. He notes, "Those who dissent from this new world order are often ridiculed and may even be criminalised. Pride in sexual immorality cannot, however, wholly disguise some of its dreary and pain-filled consequences. Some of the more obvious examples include promiscuity, marital betrayal and breakdown, the corruption of the young, cynicism, the spread of debilitating diseases, and dealing with unwanted consequences of immorality through contraception, abortion and abortifacients" (ibid.).

16. In his *Hope and Christian Ethics* (Cambridge: Cambridge University Press, 2017), David Elliot comments, "The rise of virtue ethics in the past decades has led to many treatments of the cardinal and theological virtues. Justice, prudence, courage, charity, and the rest have inspired a great many books, articles, dissertations, and conferences. But one ship has not been lifted by this rising tide: the theological virtue of hope" (1). He could have added another such "ship," the Christian virtue of temperance.

17. R. R. Reno, "Redemption and Ethics," in *The Oxford Handbook of Theological Ethics*, ed. Gilbert Meilaender and William Werpehowski (Oxford: Oxford University Press, 2005), 27.

18. Pope Francis, *Evangelii Gaudium*, Vatican translation (Boston: Pauline Books & Media, 2013), §169. Pope Francis is here describing the attitude that evangelizers must take. I am not suggesting that Pope Francis has adequately handled the problems that have arisen from entrenched intemperance (and open rejection of the virtue of temperance) within the Church.

19. David Fagerberg, *On Liturgical Asceticism* (Washington, DC: Catholic University of America Press, 2013), 76. Robert Miner, indebted to Servais Pinckaers, points out that

> sensitive love and pleasure function as images of their spiritual originals. Without the experience of *delectatio*, it would be difficult to have any grasp of what Aquinas means by *gaudium* and *fruitio*, associated with the last end.... The passions constitute a first image of a beatitude that transcends the passions. This does not, however, imply that the passions are solely a means to happiness, conceived as an end existing separately from the means. At the very least, the passions are partly constitutive of the happiness available in this life.... Conceived as a person's total perfection, happiness cannot be limited to the actualization of a part. It must include the whole of her basic powers and appetites. (Miner, *Thomas Aquinas on the Passions* [Cambridge: Cambridge University Press, 2009], 295–96)

He adds that "Aquinas explicitly rejects the view that in perfect happiness [everlasting beatitude] the passions are left behind. On the contrary, because pleasure follows upon the intellect's *operatio*, the passions belong to perfect happiness 'consequently'" (ibid., 297–98). As Miner says, "The design of the 1a2ae is meant to provide a knowledge of the passions that promotes the ascent toward beatitude" (ibid., 299; cf. 94).

20. Fagerberg, *On Liturgical Asceticism*, 77, 91.

21. Pope Francis, *Evangelii Gaudium*, §168.

22. For the history and influence of the temperance movement in America, Great Britain, and Ireland, see chapter 5 of Christopher C. H. Cook, *Alcohol, Addiction and Christian Ethics* (Cambridge: Cambridge University Press, 2006).

23. Chaput, "Splendor of Truth in 2017," 23.

24. Ibid. Note that Chaput is here describing a viewpoint with which he disagrees.

25. In his *A Small Treatise on the Great Virtues: The Uses of Philosophy in Everyday Life*, trans. Catherine Temerson (New York: Metropolitan Books, 2001), 40, André Comte-Sponville defines temperance as

"prudence applied to pleasure, the point being to enjoy as much as possible as well as is possible, by intensifying sensation or our consciousness of it and not by multiplying the objects of pleasure ad infinitum." This Epicurean definition of temperance, however, focuses it entirely on the self and misses the crucial connection of temperance to our relationships with God and neighbor. Comte-Sponville's reflections on love later in his book are much more promising, since he validates selflessness, but in the end he diminishes charity, describing it merely as "the joyful acceptance of the other, of any other, as he is or whatever he may be" (ibid., 285). These diminishments, it seems to me, follow from Comte-Sponville's professed atheism (see 287). He concludes his book, a best seller in France, with the seemingly paradoxical — but actually nonsensical — claim that "love commits us to morality and frees us from it. Morality commits us to love, even in its absence, and must yield before it" (ibid., 290).

26. Timothy G. Gombis, "Participation in the New-Creation People of God in Christ by the Spirit," in McKnight and Modica, *Apostle Paul and the Christian Life*, 124. He adds that believers' "lives together as a community should resemble the self-giving life trajectory of Jesus ([Phil] 2:5–11). As they pursue the cultivation of community habits that embody this reality, it is God himself, dwelling among them by the Spirit of Jesus, who empowers them in this endeavor. The Christian life as the participation (along with others in Christ) in God and thus enjoyment of divine empowerment ought to relieve Protestant concerns about potential anthropological optimism" (ibid.).

27. Hans Urs von Balthasar, *The Moment of Christian Witness*, trans. Richard Beckley (San Francisco: Ignatius Press, 1994), 53, 55. As von Balthasar points out, if the Church's ethics were "a form of adaptation or concession permitted for the benefit of sinners," the Church would

> lose its credibility as something established by Christ, the only-begotten Son, who has communicated God to us. The classical myth for this form of interpretation is Dostoyevsky's Grand Inquisitor, who seeks to make the current form of the Church plausible to the imprisoned Christ as a necessary and, therefore, philanthropic falsification of Christ's true intentions. The institution, which is to say the hierarchy, here relieves the great mass of the people in the Church of their responsibility; they cannot bear such responsibility, the myth continues, because the inner logic of the Lord's demands can be lived only by the chosen few and essentially exceeds the abilities of the mass.... In this way everyone is satisfied: the clergy enjoys the spiritual posi-

tion of power conferred on it and the laity enjoys the resulting exoneration and, in anticipation, the fruits of the spiritual "life-insurance" for heaven which has been accorded to it. By means of this terrible and rightly immortal satire on the "concessionary form" of the Church, Ivan Karamazov seeks to prove two things: how humanly attractive in its logic such a human form of religion can be, and at the same time what a mockery it makes of everything that is Christian. (*The Glory of the Lord: A Theological Aesthetics*, vol. 1, *Seeing the Form*, trans. Erasmo Leiva-Merikakis [San Francisco: Ignatius Press, 1982], 569–70)

28. Rudi te Velde, "How Charity Teaches Us to Be Prudent and Just: Thomas Aquinas on Charity as Source of Moral Virtues," *The Virtuous Life: Thomas Aquinas on the Theological Nature of Moral Virtues*, ed. Harm Goris and Henk Schoot (Leuven: Peeters, 2017), 131. Te Velde explains further that "the moral virtues under command of charity are *infused* virtues, not *acquired* by human acts. 'Infused' means caused by God who through his grace works in us; however, they are infused together with or through the theological virtues which are infused principally. . . . But this does not justify a quietist conclusion as if the human subject remains merely passive and lets God do the work" (ibid., 137).

29. Patricia Lamoureux and Paul J. Wadell, *The Christian Moral Life: Faithful Discipleship for a Global Society* (Maryknoll, NY: Orbis, 2010), 50.

30. Reno, "Redemption and Ethics," 31. At the same time, as Reno recognizes, the demands of the Christian moral life go beyond that of healed human nature, because human nature in Christ has been elevated and transformed by the Holy Spirit so as to manifest the life of the inaugurated kingdom. The dynamisms of graced human nature are misunderstood by Josef Fuchs, S.J., when he writes (misinterpreting the import of Vatican II's pastoral constitution *Gaudium et Spes*):

> If the vocation of Christ had given rise to a moral doctrine that imposed on man in the world of men a behavior different from an (authentic) *humanitas*, Christianity would have become a sect and the Church a ghetto. . . . However, this is not to say that those called in Christ do not nourish their authentically human morality from motives born out of the newness of a transformed heart or from the revelation of a living faith. Nor are the grace of the Christian heart and the content of the Word of God prevented from having their own special insight into genuinely human forms of behavior. (*Personal Responsibility and Christian Morality*, trans. William Cleves et al. [Washington, DC: Georgetown University Press, 1983], 37)

31. *ST* II-II, q. 141, a. 3 and a. 4, ad 1. Romanus Cessario, O.P., comments that "the concupiscible appetites include three pairs of *passiones animae*, namely, the emotions of love and hatred, desire and aversion, pleasure and sadness. . . . As elementary human capacities, the emotions of the concupiscible appetites principally secure goods indispensable for human flourishing" (*The Virtues, or The Examined Life* [London: Continuum, 2002], 177). He adds that

> in order for appetite to operate properly in the human person, there must exist the potential for conformity between the human person and the good that satisfies his or her yearning. In the example of thirsting, for instance, saltwater never satisfies the human appetite for liquid intake. In human conduct, ends are said to draw. By definition, then, the objects of human appetite exercise a specific kind of causal influence on the human person. If the object embodies some good that, when embraced in reasonable measure, perfects human nature, then the drawing attraction of such a good serves to promote the overall well-being of the human person. . . . When, however, the sense appetites settle on objects the embrace of which causes harm to the person, then no virtuous measure can be determined for any inclination toward such objects. (ibid., 179)

For emphasis that temperance is grounded not simply in the concupiscible passions but also "in the *obiecta passionum*," see Miner, *Thomas Aquinas on the Passions*, 292. Miner also provides a helpful discussion of the distinction between the sense (or sensitive) appetite and the rational appetite, as well as the nature and relationship of the "passions" and the distinction between irascible and concupiscible: see ibid., 21–25, 29–87. See also Mark Jordan, "Aquinas's Construction of a Moral Account of the Passions," *Freiburger Zeitschrift für Philosophie und Theologie* 33 (1986): 71–97, as well as the succinct presentation of temperance in Thomas Petri, O.P., *Aquinas and the Theology of the Body: The Thomistic Foundations of John Paul II's Anthropology* (Washington, DC: Catholic University of America Press, 2016), 255–60. Miner's book draws significantly upon Santiago M. Ramírez, O.P., *De passionibus animae in I-II Summae Theologiae divi Thomae exposition (qq. xxii–xlviii)* (Madrid: Instituto de Filosofía Luis Vives, 1973).

32. John Rziha, *The Christian Moral Life: Directions for the Journey to Happiness* (Notre Dame, IN: University of Notre Dame Press, 2017), 259.

33. *ST* II-II, q. 143, a. 1. Karol Wojtyła raises the concern that if temperance is understood as "moderation," this may not be suitable for the

fullness of the virtue of chastity. His concern is, in part, how to distinguish chastity from continence. More specifically, he urges that rather than looking "for the essence of chastity in moderation," the task of showing "the real value and significance of chastity in human life" requires emphasizing "much more forcefully the kinship between chastity and love" (Karol Wojtyła, *Love and Responsibility*, trans. H. T. Willetts [New York: Farrar, Straus and Giroux, 1981], 169). Indeed, he argues that "*Chastity can only be thought of in association with the virtue of love*. Its function is to free love from the utilitarian attitude," that is to say, from "emotional egoism" and "sensual egoism" (ibid., 169–70). He states, "To be chaste means to have a 'transparent' attitude to a person of the other sex—*chastity means just that—the interior 'transparency'* without which love is not itself, for it cannot be itself until the desire to 'enjoy' is subordinated to a readiness to show loving kindness in every situation" (ibid., 170). While insisting upon the importance of the "values of the 'body' and of sex," he adds that "the virtue of chastity is underdeveloped in anyone who is slow to affirm the value of the person and allows the values of sex to reign supreme: these, once they take possession of the will, distort one's whole attitude to a person of the other sex. The essence of chastity consists in quickness to affirm the value of the person in every situation, and in raising to the personal level all reactions to the value of 'the body and sex'" (ibid., 170–71). But this conclusion returns him, in a much more positive way, to the basic understanding of temperance as moderating the concupiscible passions: "For by 'moderating' the feelings and actions connected with the sexual values we serve the values of the person and of love" (ibid., 171). The key is that chastity frees our sexual desire "from that tendency to use a person which is objectively incompatible with 'loving kindness'" (ibid.). As Aquinas makes clear, ungoverned or self-seeking sexual desire is unreasonable—because it does not conduce to our flourishing as individuals, families, and communities—and therefore it cannot and does not accord with charity.

34. *ST* II-II, q. 143, a. 1.
35. Cessario, *Virtues*, 115.
36. Ibid.
37. See R. E. Houser, introduction to *The Cardinal Virtues: Aquinas, Albert, and Philip the Chancellor*, trans. and ed. R. E. Houser (Toronto: Pontifical Institute of Mediaeval Studies, 2004), 79. Houser notes that Aristotle limited temperance to the "virtues connected with the sense of touch" (ibid., 80), which of course play a major (but not exclusive) role in Aquinas's understanding of temperance. For the view that Aquinas's ethics really is not "Aristotelian" at all—a view to which Houser would not subscribe—see Eleonore Stump, "The Non-Aristotelian Character of

Aquinas's Ethics: Aquinas on the Passions," in *Faith, Rationality, and the Passions*, ed. Sarah Coakley (Oxford: Blackwell, 2012), 91–106; Andrew Pinsent, *The Second-Person Perspective in Aquinas's Ethics: Virtues and Gifts* (New York: Routledge, 2012); and Pinsent, "Who's Afraid of the Infused Virtues? Dispositional Infusion, Human and Divine," in Goris and Schoot, *Virtuous Life*, 73–95. Pinsent argues that Aquinas's ethics must not "be interpreted in broadly Aristotelian terms," due not only to the many changes that Aquinas makes to Aristotle's ethics but also to the fact that "the non-Aristotelian virtues and gifts of his [Aquinas's] account can be interpreted as removing a person's spiritual autism, enabling a second-person relationship with God that is different in kind, not merely in degree, from what Aristotle considers to be possible" (*Second-Person Perspective in Aquinas's Ethics*, xii). Pinsent concludes that "Aquinas's virtue ethics is radically non-Aristotelian" (ibid., 104), a claim that I find to be an unhelpful exaggeration, rooted in part in turning the distinction between nature and person into an opposition (see ibid.). Certainly, Aquinas's moral theology differs from Aristotle's ethics in numerous crucial ways (and so Pinsent's insights into the "second-person perspective" are helpful), but Aquinas's moral theology also draws so much upon Aristotle that to describe it as "radically non-Aristotelian" is not adequate to Aristotle's influence. Although I disagree with Stump's suggestion that Aquinas dismisses Aristotelian (acquired) moral virtues, I agree with her that "the virtues around which his ethics is based are the virtues infused by God" and that for Aquinas "the gifts of the Holy Spirit have the effect of anchoring the infused theological [and moral] virtues more deeply in a person's psyche and enabling them to have their desired effect there" (Stump, "Non-Aristotelian Character of Aquinas's Ethics," 96). For a broader perspective on Aquinas's theological use of Aristotle, see the essays in Gilles Emery, O.P., and Matthew Levering, eds., *Aristotle in Aquinas's Theology* (Oxford: Oxford University Press, 2015). See also the balanced perspective of John F. Wippel, "Platonism and Aristotelianism in Aquinas," in *Metaphysical Themes in Thomas Aquinas II* (Washington, DC: Catholic University of America Press, 2007), 272–89.

38. For an example of contemporary "kingdom ethics" — lacking, however, Aquinas's concentrated study of created human nature — see David B. Gushee and Glen H. Stassen, *Kingdom Ethics: Following Jesus in Contemporary Context*, 2nd ed. (Grand Rapids, MI: Eerdmans, 2016). Gushee and Stassen rightly make the Sermon on the Mount the center of their ethics, although I do not share all their interpretations of the Sermon or all the elements that they believe a "kingdom ethics" should include. For a perspective that resonates with my own, see Michael Allen, *Grounded in*

Heaven: Recentering Christian Hope and Life on God (Grand Rapids, MI: Eerdmans, 2018).

39. See for example N. T. Wright, *Paul and the Faithfulness of God* (Minneapolis: Fortress, 2013), 814. In *The New Testament and the People of God* (Minneapolis: Fortress, 1992), 299, Wright puts it this way: "The fundamental Jewish hope was for the liberation from oppression, for the restoration of the Land, and for the proper rebuilding of the Temple." Liberation from oppression is connected with the forgiveness of sins, because YHWH had abandoned the people to foreign rule (so that the "exile" continued) due to their sins. While I value Wright's emphasis on these aspects of the anticipated (and inaugurated) kingdom, I recognize the concerns of biblical scholars, a number of whom would agree with Douglas A. Campbell that even if there is much to praise in Wright's approach to Paul (for example), there are also "basic problems of method and exegesis with Wright's manner of reading Paul's texts, while his engagements with other scholarly interlocutors frequently lapse into mere polemic" (Douglas A. Campbell, "Panoramic Lutheranism and Apocalyptic Ambivalence: An Appreciative Critique of N. T. Wright's *Paul and the Faithfulness of God*," *Scottish Journal of Theology* 69 [2016]: 455).

40. Why align the eschatological renewal of the temple especially with shame and *honestas*? Could not the renewal of the temple also apply to humility? I grant that it could and does. Likewise, although I link the eschatological forgiveness of sins to meekness, humility, and studiousness, the forgiveness of sins could also apply to abstinence. When in chapter 7 I connect the eschatological forgiveness of sins and outpouring of the Spirit with the virtue of studiousness, I argue that the knowledge of God especially pertains to the outpouring of the Spirit, without which the people cannot intimately know God. The link is not arbitrary; yet, at the same time, the knowledge of God also characterizes the eschatologically restored people and renewed temple. Thus, although I have reasons for making the correlations that I do, all the dimensions of the kingdom can be applied to all parts of temperance. The correlations that I make are intended to be heuristically helpful but are not intended to be exclusive.

41. Lamoureux and Wadell, *The Christian Moral Life*, 132.

42. As Lamoureux and Wadell say, "For human beings true honor comes not from wealth, celebrity, fame, or power but from goodness and virtue" (ibid.).

43. Mary M. Keys, *Aquinas, Aristotle, and the Promise of the Common Good* (Cambridge: Cambridge University Press, 2006), 24. See also the fourth chapter (on Aquinas) of my *The Indissolubility of Marriage: Amoris Laetitia in Context* (San Francisco: Ignatius Press, 2019). For a succinct

presentation of the authority of Scripture for Catholic theology, see Guy Mansini, O.S.B., *Fundamental Theology* (Washington, DC: Catholic University of America Press, 2018), 2–3. Robert C. Roberts comments that for Aristotle, "The point of temperance is that these pleasant bodily activities [eating, drinking, sexual activity] should be engaged in rationally, according to the 'rule' (thinking, *logos*) of a wise person. . . . Or more precisely, the *desires and pleasures* associated with the activities should be shaped and governed by wise *logos*" ("Temperance," in *Virtues and Their Vices*, ed. Kevin Timpe and Craig A. Boyd [Oxford: Oxford University Press, 2014], 97). Roberts explains further that for Aristotle, "temperance is a rational state of (disposition for) appetite for food, drink, and sex. It is a dispositional desire or caring for these things that is 'right' for the individual, both as a human being and as the particular human being that she or he is, in her or his circumstances. This particular state of appetite is right because it fits properly with the other aspects of a good life on which the appetites for food, drink, and sex touch: with health, justice to his family and neighbors, with his material means, and with his work and other obligations" (ibid., 98–99).

44. Interestingly, the Hebrew word *yada*, meaning "to know," can also be translated "to embrace": see Robert Alter, *The Five Books of Moses* (New York: Norton, 2004), 29 (footnote on Gen 4:1).

45. Reinhard Hütter, "The Christian Life," in *The Oxford Handbook of Systematic Theology*, ed. John Webster, Kathryn Tanner, and Iain Torrance (Oxford: Oxford University Press, 2007), 297.

46. Lamoureux and Wadell, *Christian Moral Life*, 130. They go on to say,

> Sexual relationships that are guided by the virtue of temperance will be characterized by fidelity and commitment, while intemperate sexual relationships are commonly characterized by selfishness, hedonism, promiscuity, and betrayal. . . . Or think of a person who can never control her anger even if the anger is justified. A lack of temperance in regard to anger can make her malicious and hateful, at which point her anger becomes toxic not only for the person to whom it is directed, but also for herself. Alcohol can bring out the worst in us, leaving us saying and doing things that can be tremendously harmful to others. (ibid., 130–31)

More broadly, Lamoureux and Wadell state that

> what God wills always is a way of living and acting that establishes a person in the stable pursuit of the truly good that is the reign of

God. . . . Living amid the tension of the in-between times when God's reign is here, but not yet, requires an ability to discern what is like and what is contrary to God's presence. The glory of God is present in the world, but so is human sinfulness. . . . We cannot make the journey from sin to life apart from Christ not only because Christ alone can deliver us from sin, but also because our true self is found not in the illusory autonomy of sin, but in faithful discipleship with Christ. To be a Christian is to answer the gospel's call to repentance and conversion; indeed, the Christian life *is* a life of ongoing and forever incomplete repentance and conversion. But we can pursue such a life only as disciples to Christ, as men and women whose lives together are marked by continual openness, deepening surrender, and resilient commitment to Jesus, his proclamation, and his mission. (ibid., 67, 73, 77)

47. Jonathan T. Pennington, *The Sermon on the Mount and Human Flourishing: A Theological Commentary* (Grand Rapids, MI: Baker Academic, 2017), 63; see also Grant Macaskill, *Revealed Wisdom and Inaugurated Eschatology in Ancient Judaism and Early Christianity* (Leiden: Brill, 2007). Pennington frequently cites Macaskill. See also Wayne A. Meeks, *The Origins of Christian Morality: The First Two Centuries* (New Haven: Yale University Press, 1993), 212: "The Christians' lists of virtues and vices were not much different from those common in popular morality. . . . Their leaders borrowed from the topics of philosophical and rhetorical moralizing, though sometimes they twisted them in peculiar ways or set them into unusual contexts." For the view that early Christian and Greco-Roman (specifically, Stoic) moral traditions are related in certain ways but nonetheless are fundamentally incommensurable, see C. Kavin Rowe, *One True Life: The Stoics and Early Christians as Rival Traditions* (New Haven: Yale University Press, 2016). Rowe is concerned that the reality of radical Christian distinctiveness not be forgotten. I share his concern (against classically liberal views of Christianity) even if I think that Pennington and Macaskill are right that in the wisdom context, Christian insistence that Christ has inaugurated the kingdom of God can and does take advantage of truths set forth in pagan virtue ethics. In response to David Garland's critique of eudaemonist ethics (centered in happiness and human flourishing), Pennington rightly warns against "an unnecessary and unhelpful dichotomy" and argues that

> there is a thoroughly Isaianic kingdom-restoring eschatological backdrop to the Beatitudes (indeed, all of Matthew), but this in no way undercuts the vision of human flourishing that the Beatitudes speak to. One is not forced to choose between these or to put asunder what

Second Temple Judaism has joined together.... The point is that the best readings of the Beatitudes will combine and keep in balance the reality of two streams of tradition that are feeding into the encyclopedic background to Jesus's macarisms—the wisdom tradition (Jewish and Greco-Roman) and the Second Temple apocalyptic emphasis on the eschatological reversal of fortunes. (*Sermon on the Mount and Human Flourishing*, 63, 66)

See also the Thomistic analysis of William C. Mattison III, *The Sermon on the Mount and Moral Theology: A Virtue Perspective* (Cambridge: Cambridge University Press, 2017), as well as the New Testament scholar Frank Matera's *The Sermon on the Mount* (Collegeville, MN: Liturgical Press, 2013). As Mattison says, "Matthew did not read Aristotle, but it is extraordinary how closely the text of the Sermon matches up with the conceptual resources of virtue ethics" (*Sermon on the Mount and Moral Theology*, 1). Mattison argues both that "the Sermon on the Mount is fruitfully read with the questions and concerns of virtue ethics in mind" and that "the Sermon on the Mount specifies and illuminates a virtue-centered approach to morality" (ibid., 2).

48. Pennington, *Sermon on the Mount and Human Flourishing*, 63.

49. Ibid., 66.

50. *ST* II-II, q. 29, a. 2, ad 3. Here Aquinas cites Wisdom 14:22: "It was not enough for them to err about the knowledge of God, but they live in great strife due to ignorance, and they call such great evils peace."

51. Bernard McGinn, *Thomas Aquinas's* Summa theologiae: *A Biography* (Princeton: Princeton University Press, 2014), 102. McGinn adds that Aquinas's "treatment here is so detailed that all but the most devoted Thomists may be excused from reading the 916 articles that constitute the *Secunda Secundae*" (ibid.). I hope to show that theologians should certainly read the articles that constitute the treatise on temperance.

52. Mattison, *Sermon on the Mount and Moral Theology*, 15. Mattison refreshingly concludes that "the ultimate end of this project [i.e., his book], as of all things, is the joyous and communal contemplation of God that constitutes eternal happiness" (ibid.).

53. For Aquinas on continence, modesty in outward movements (such as games and laughter), and modesty in dress, see *ST* II-II, qq. 155–56, 168–69. For overviews of the virtue of temperance that locate temperance within Aquinas's broader understanding of the virtues, see Josef Pieper, *The Four Cardinal Virtues*, trans. Daniel F. Coogan et al. (Notre Dame, IN: University of Notre Dame Press, 1966), and Leo J. Elders, S.V.D., "St. Thomas Aquinas's Treatise on Temperance and Aristotle," *Nova et Vetera* 16 (2018):

465–87. See also Reinhard Hütter, "The Virtue of Chastity and the Scourge of Pornography: A Twofold Crisis Considered in Light of Thomas Aquinas's Moral Theology," *Thomist* 77 (2013): 1–39.

54. In his *Spiritual Theology* (London: Bloomsbury, 2017), Jordan Aumann, O.P., comments: "Natural or acquired temperance is regulated simply by the light of natural reason, and therefore contains or restricts the functions of the pleasure emotions within rational or purely human limits; supernatural or infused temperance extends much further because it adds to simple reason the light of faith, which imposes superior and more delicate demands" (297).

55. Frederick Christian Bauerschmidt, *Thomas Aquinas: Faith, Reason, and Following Christ* (Oxford: Oxford University Press, 2013), 262.

56. For Aquinas's reflections on "You shall not commit adultery" and "You shall not covet your neighbor's wife" (Exod 20:14, 17), see *ST* II-II, q. 170, a. 1 (including the sed contra). For discussion of these two commandments in relation to temperance, see Rziha, *Christian Moral Life*, 266–67, 275–76.

57. Describing Karl Barth's view of the "eschatological orientation of the Christian life," John Webster remarks that Christ's outpouring of the Spirit frees the Christian "to be a rebel against the lordless powers which oppress humanity and rob humanity of its dignity and freedom" (*Barth's Ethics of Reconciliation* [Cambridge: Cambridge University Press, 1995], 201, 203). Yet infused moral virtues do not remove weaknesses associated with prior vices (or with hormonal effects) that reflect our inheritance of a fallen human nature. As an example, consider what Cynthia Long Westfall reports about the vice of irrational anger with respect to the distinction between men and women: "A Harvard study has shown that nearly 10 percent of American men have intermittent explosive disorder (IED): 'If the Harvard researchers are correct, almost 1 in 10 adult men routinely display wildly disproportionate aggression, and are so angry that they're likely to damage property, or threaten or injure others. (The researchers estimate that only half as many women suffer from IED.)' While some may argue that this is a recent phenomenon due to cultural developments that discriminate against men, similar patterns of behavior may be detected in other cultures and other time periods. Men murder more and commit more crimes and acts of violence than women" (*Paul and Gender: Reclaiming the Apostle's Vision for Men and Women in Christ* [Grand Rapids, MI: Baker Academic, 2016], 187). Westfall connects this point with Paul's critique of irrational anger in Ephesians 4:31, which she suggests is linked with Paul's instructions to husbands in Ephesians 5:28–29. Overcoming one's own ongoing fallen tendencies (behavioral and/or hormonal) is, for everyone, a necessary part of living the virtues associated with Christian temperance.

58. See Harm Goris, "Acquired and Infused Moral Virtues in Wounded Nature," in Goris and Schoot, *Virtuous Life*, 21–46, especially 40–41; Michael S. Sherwin, O.P., "Infused Virtue and the Effects of Acquired Vice: A Test Case for the Thomistic Theory of Infused Cardinal Virtues," *Thomist* 73 (2009): 29–52. For a critique of Sherwin's approach to this problem, see Nicholas Austin, S.J., *Aquinas on Virtue: A Causal Reading* (Washington, DC: Georgetown University Press, 2017), 192–94. According to Austin, "Since facility involving promptness, ease, and joy is the sign of virtue, the lack of such facility in the new convert is not a sign that infused moral virtue lacks such facility. Rather, it is a sign that she does not possess infused virtue in its complete form.... In the case of Matt Talbot [Sherwin's example], it is more plausible to say not that he possesses infused temperance yet still experiences the inclination to sin but rather that he possesses continence or self-control" (ibid., 194). Austin recognizes that Aquinas understands that "infused moral virtue does not confer facility in the same way as acquired virtue" and that "it can be difficult and painful to exercise infused moral virtue" (ibid., 192). But Austin does not accept Aquinas's explanation for this, which Austin summarizes as follows: "Habituated facility arises from preceding habit or custom; it is characteristic of acquired moral virtue. Agonistic facility belongs to infused moral virtue from its generation; it arises from a strong attachment to virtue's object. For Aquinas the latter kind of facility is compatible with difficulty in acting virtuously due to the hangover from a previous life of sin" (ibid., 193). Austin argues that facility that is not easy or joyful is not facility. But in my view, Aquinas's position is correct. The emphasis should be placed on the "strong attachment to virtue's object" that is a sign of the Spirit's transformative presence.

59. See *ST* II-II, q. 2, a. 7, obj. 1 and ad 1.

60. For discussion of how this works in practice, see Craig Steven Titus, "Moral Development and Connecting the Virtues: Aquinas, Porter, and the Flawed Saint," in *Ressourcement Thomism: Sacred Doctrine, The Sacraments, and the Moral Life; Essays in Honor of Romanus Cessario, O.P.*, ed. Reinhard Hütter and Matthew Levering (Washington, DC: Catholic University of America, 2010), 330–52. Titus is responding to Jean Porter's "Virtue and Sin: The Connection of the Virtues and the Case of the Flawed Saint," *Journal of Religion* 75 (1995): 521–39.

61. Webster, *Barth's Ethics of Reconciliation*, 196. In describing this "Christological-eschatological frame," Webster (like Karl Barth) has in view the final consummation of the kingdom, and Webster wishes to emphasize that human action does not mediate or bring about this final consummation (a point with which Aquinas would agree). Webster and Barth

rightly emphasize God's priority, as does Aquinas—although Aquinas argues for a participation in or cooperation with the action of Christ and his Spirit, whereas Webster and Barth prefer "to think of a set of analogical relations between the action of God and human acts" (ibid., 211). I agree with Livio Melina—though I would accentuate the importance of created (fallen) human nature—that "Christian moral action" can be rightly seen as a Spirit-enabled *"participation in the virtues of Christ* by means of the grace of our ecclesial incorporation into him" (*Sharing in Christ's Virtues: For a Renewal of Moral Theology in Light of "Veritatis Splendor,"* trans. William May [Washington, DC: Catholic University of America Press, 2001], 6). For Barth, moral truth cannot be found outside of Christ, whereas for Aquinas the created order, even in its fallen condition, contains moral truth (though never outside the creative Son, and never outside the actual supernatural order). Webster states, "Barth believes that good human action is generated, shaped, and judged by 'that which is,' and that 'that which is' is a Christological, not a pre-Christological, category" (*Barth's Ethics of Reconciliation*, 214; cf. 220–23 on ethical foundationalism). For a similar viewpoint, see Stanley Hauerwas's "On Keeping Theological Ethics Theological," in *Against the Nations: War and Survival in a Liberal Society* (Notre Dame, IN: University of Notre Dame Press, 1992), 23–50. In later work, Webster's position arguably moves closer to Aquinas on these points. See also Janet Soskice, "The God of Creative Address: Creation, Christology and Ethics," in *The Image of God in an Image Driven Age: Explorations in Theological Anthropology*, ed. Beth Felker Jones and Jeffrey W. Barbeau (Downers Grove, IL: IVP Academic, 2016), 189–201.

62. David W. Fagerberg, *Consecrating the World: On Mundane Liturgical Theology* (Kettering, OH: Angelico Press, 2016), 36.

63. N. T. Wright, *After You Believe: Why Christian Character Matters* (New York: HarperCollins, 2010), 240. Mistakenly in my view, Wright criticizes the "cardinal virtues expounded by Aristotle and others" as "designed to produce . . . grand isolated heroes, leading a nation in politics and war" (ibid., 217–18). But Wright otherwise summarizes his point in a manner with which Aquinas would fully agree: "Precisely because the Christian virtues look upward to the God who made the whole world, and made all people in his image, and outward to that world and all people within it, they cannot be the private preserve of an enclosed community. It isn't a matter of turning our back on the great traditions of virtue developed by pagan and non-Christian philosophers down the centuries. It should be a matter of demonstrating that what they were striving for is fully comprehended within, but also transcended by, this new vision of virtue, which is the vision of Jesus Christ himself" (ibid., 218).

64. Ibid., 241. I note that this overlap is found explicitly in Scripture itself; the four cardinal virtues receive praise in Wisdom of Solomon 8:7: "If any one loves righteousness, her [wisdom's] labors are virtues; for she teaches self-control [temperance] and prudence, justice and courage; nothing in life is more profitable for men than these." Although Wright, as an Anglican, does not consider Wisdom of Solomon to be part of Scripture, it belongs to the Catholic canon.

65. Wright, *After You Believe*, 241. This approach has been challenged (with Aquinas rather than Wright in view) by John M. G. Barclay. He argues that although some Pauline texts "suggest that Paul's soteriology has some connection to categories of 'creation,'" nonetheless even in the interpretation of those texts,

> much . . . has to be supplied *to Paul* from (Aristotle-inspired) speculation about the original human state of "integrity." Paul himself appeals very little to the category of nature (or to "the image of God" in humanity), and where he does (e.g., in 1 Cor 11), he seems to use it to legitimate gender hierarchies that are in-built into ancient (including Aristotelian) versions of "nature" but are clearly cultural constructs and deeply unhelpful today. More to the point, Paul's theology revolves around the great, stark *antitheses* between human sin and divine grace, between flesh and Spirit, between "the present evil age" and "the new creation" (Gal 1:4; 6:15). Paul seems to know only two kinds of human, the fallen human and the saved, not a third, pre-fall human whose rationality and morality is still partly intact in the midst of sin. Paul's theology of inversion and contradiction, of the God who "raises the dead and calls into being the things that do not exist" (Rom 4:17), of the structuring symbols of Cross (death) and resurrection (*newness of life*), is not easily squeezed into a Thomist mold, or if so squeezed, it would be in danger of losing its creative, radical edge. ("A Thomist Reading of Paul? Response and Reflections," *Nova et Vetera* 17 [2019]: 239)

I note, however, that this assumes that Aquinas's moral vision lacks the Pauline "creative, radical edge." This assumption fails to understand how Aquinas conceives Christian morality as shaped by the Holy Spirit all the way down (as seen in the infused theological and infused moral virtues, the seven gifts of the Holy Spirit, the charisms, and so on) and informed by a profound awareness of human sinfulness. Created human nature plays a significant role for Aquinas, and it does so for Paul as well, since created human nature appears not merely in prefall humans but precisely in *fallen* human beings who possess *human* capacities, emotions, and dynamisms, as Paul recognizes. Put another way, in order to retain the antitheses between sin and grace and between the present world and the new creation, it is not necessary to rid theological anthropology (or Paul) of the basic affirmations that flow from the doctrine of creation. Nor does every aspect of Aristotle's view of human nature need to be taken on board in order to appreciate (Aristotelian) virtues and vices. Barclay is influenced by the "apocalyptic" reading of Paul advanced by Ernst Käsemann and J. Louis Martyn, and the weakness of this school of thought consists in an unnecessarily thoroughgoing opposition between creation and new creation. For further discussion (though without reference to Barclay), see my "Sin and Grace in the Church according to Paul and Aquinas," in *Aquinas the Biblical Theologian*, ed. Michael Dauphinais, Scott W. Hahn, and Roger W. Nutt (Steubenville, OH: Emmaus Academic, forthcoming).

66. On this point see for example Ralph McInerny, *The Question of Christian Ethics* (Washington, DC: Catholic University of America Press, 1993); McInerny, *Ethica Thomistica: The Moral Philosophy of Thomas Aquinas*, rev. ed. (Washington, DC: Catholic University of America Press, 1997); Steven A. Long, *The Teleological Grammar of the Moral Act* (Naples, FL: Sapientia Press, 2007); Long, "Creation *ad imaginem Dei*: The Obediential Potency of the Human Person to Grace and Glory," *Nova et Vetera* 14 (2016): 1175–92; Stephen L. Brock, *Action and Conduct: Thomas Aquinas and the Theory of Action* (Edinburgh: T&T Clark, 1998); Alasdair MacIntyre, *Dependent Rational Animals: Why Human Beings Need the Virtues* (Chicago: Open Court, 1999). With a focus on Aristotle rather than Aquinas, see also Talbot Brewer's *The Retrieval of Ethics* (Oxford: Oxford University Press, 2009)—indebted to MacIntyre's work.

67. For an extensive treatment of Aquinas's sources (including his pagan sources), see Houser, introduction to *Cardinal Virtues*, 1–82. Houser comments,

> The theory of four cardinal virtues was a medieval Christian doctrine. Its origins go back to Socrates, to be sure, and Plato was the first thinker to set out an explicit theory about the four virtues of prudence, courage, temperance, and justice. But the phrase 'cardinal virtues' seems to have been invented by Ambrose, Christian Bishop of Milan. Born of anguish and hope, it was first pronounced in the funeral oration he delivered over the body of his brother Satyrus. The Fathers of the Christian Church were able to baptize the Platonic virtues, but a rigorous and thorough doctrine of the cardinal virtues had to wait almost a millennium, for the founding of universities and the teaching of their Masters. . . . Philip, Albert, and Thomas consciously built on

the work of three groups of thinkers: pagan philosophers (*philosophi*), Christian Fathers (*sancti*), and other school-masters (*magistri*). (ibid., 6–7)

For further background, see Rachana Kamtekar's "Ancient Virtue Ethics: An Overview with an Emphasis on Practical Wisdom," in *The Cambridge Companion to Virtue Ethics*, ed. Daniel C. Russell (Cambridge: Cambridge University Press, 2013), 29–48; Jean Porter, "Virtue Ethics in the Medieval Period," in Russell, *Cambridge Companion to Virtue Ethics*, 72–74.

68. Plato, *Republic*, trans. Paul Shorey, in *The Collected Dialogues of Plato*, ed. Edith Hamilton and Huntington Cairns (Princeton: Princeton University Press, 1961), 586a–b, p. 813.

69. Ibid., 586e, p. 814. See Daniel C. Russell, *Plato on Pleasure and the Good Life* (Oxford: Oxford University Press, 2005). Russell treats the following dialogues: the *Euthydemus, Gorgias, Phaedo, Republic, Philebus, Laws, Timaeus*, and *Protagoras*. He argues that Plato offers "a plausible and compelling account of pleasure and the good life" (ibid., 1). Russell differentiates between pleasures that are emotions and pleasures that are sensations, but of course (as he recognizes) the two are often related. Importantly, Russell notes that Plato's view of pleasure in relation to rationality (and virtue) requires "the view that our affective nature is sufficiently subtle to grasp and adopt the direction that our rational nature gives it," but Plato is inconsistent in this regard: sometimes Plato suggests that our affective nature can do this, but at other times Plato suggests that "our affective nature lacks such subtlety and thus will conform to reason only by being restrained and curbed, but not transformed" (ibid., 12–13). In this regard, Russell considers Aristotle to have made an advance. Russell directs attention to Nancy Sherman, *Making a Necessity of Virtue: Aristotle and Kant on Virtue* (Cambridge: Cambridge University Press, 1997), 83–93. Russell rightly opposes George Rudebusch's view that Plato offers a fundamentally hedonist account of pleasure: see Rudebusch, *Socrates, Pleasure, and Value* (Oxford: Oxford University Press, 1999). See also Gerd Van Riel, *Pleasure and the Good Life: Plato, Aristotle, and the Neoplatonists* (Leiden: Brill, 2000); John M. Rist, *Real Ethics: Reconsidering the Foundations of Morality* (Cambridge: Cambridge University Press, 2002).

70. Plato, *Republic* 589b, p. 817.

71. Ibid., 591c, p. 819; 389e, p. 634.

72. See ibid., 430e, p. 672; 442a–d, pp. 684–85. For further discussion, striving to read Plato outside any lens influenced by Christian Platonism, see Julia Annas, "Plato's Ethics," in *The Oxford Handbook of Plato*, ed. Gail Fine (Oxford: Oxford University Press, 2008), 267–85; Annas, *Pla-*

tonic Ethics, Old and New (Ithaca, NY: Cornell University Press, 1999). The constant connection in Plato between political and personal virtue is highlighted with respect to temperance by Robert J. O'Connell, S.J., *Plato on the Human Paradox* (New York: Fordham University Press, 1997), 148–49. See also Houser's excellent summary in his introduction to *Cardinal Virtues*, 9–13. Houser comments,

> The three classes found in a city lead to understanding the three corresponding parts of the soul: reason (*logistikon*), emotion (*thumos*), and desire (*epithumia*), whose virtues are respectively wisdom, courage, and temperance. Wisdom is found wherever reason knows and chooses the good; courage is found wherever the emotions overcome obstacles to the good; and temperance is found wherever desire for pleasure is so controlled as to lead to the good rather than away from it. Each of these virtues is broadly conceived, since it functions in each and every good act of that part of the soul. Justice, however, is in a way ontologically homeless, for it is a harmony produced when each of the three parts functions well. (ibid., 10–11)

73. Aristotle, *Nicomachean Ethics*, trans. H. Rackham (Cambridge, MA: Harvard University Press, 1934), 7.2.6, p. 381. On continence, incontinence, and temperance according to Aristotle, see Sarah Broadie, *Ethics with Aristotle* (New York: Oxford University Press, 1991), 266–312. On pleasure, see Broadie, *Ethics with Aristotle*, 313–65; Amélie O. Rorty, "*Akrasia* and Pleasure: *Nicomachean Ethics* Book 7," in *Essays on Aristotle's Ethics*, ed. Amélie Oksenberg Rorty (Berkeley: University of California Press, 1980), 267–84; Rorty, "The Place of Pleasure in Aristotle's Ethics," *Mind* 83 (1974): 481–97; Julia Annas, "Aristotle on Pleasure and Goodness," in Rorty, *Essays on Aristotle's Ethics*, 285–99. See also Gerd Van Riel, "Does a Perfect Activity Necessarily Yield Pleasure? An Evaluation of the Relation between Pleasure and Activity in Aristotle, *Nicomachean Ethics* VII and X," *International Journal of Philosophical Studies* 7 (1999): 211–24; Van Riel, *Pleasure and the Good Life*.

74. Aristotle, *Nicomachean Ethics* 3.10.1, pp. 173–75.

75. Ibid., 3.10.11 and 3.11.3, p. 179; 3.12.9, p. 187. For contemporary philosophical discussions of Aristotle's ethics (which in my view often tend to be less insightful than medieval discussions of Aristotle, but which remain helpful nonetheless), see also Christopher Shields, *Aristotle* (London: Routledge, 2007), 323–29; Richard Kraut, *Aristotle on the Human Good* (Princeton: Princeton University Press, 1989), 332–45.

76. Roberts, "Temperance," 94. Aquinas follows Aristotle in this view, whereas Bonaventure (among others) follows Plato's position.

Roberts defines Aristotelian temperance as "the appetite for food, drink, or sexual activity insofar as a right thinking concern about the important things of human life on which such appetites and pleasures touch has properly adjusted, qualified, moderated, attuned, softened, firmed up, or steadied them" (ibid., 93). For Bonaventure's understanding of the moral virtues in relation to faith, see Kent Emery, "Reading the World Rightly and Squarely: Bonaventure's Doctrine of the Cardinal Virtues," *Traditio* 39 (1983): 183–218.

77. Cicero, *On Duties*, trans. Walter Miller (Cambridge, MA: Harvard University Press, 1913), 1.4, p. 15. Jean Porter notes that Cicero's "eclectic theory of virtue included both Stoic and Aristotelian elements (the latter mediated predominantly through the Peripatetics), and he played a key role in mediating both approaches to later Christian reflection" ("Virtue Ethics in the Medieval Period," 74). For a summary of Cicero's virtue theory in his *De inventione* and his *De finibus*, see Houser, introduction to *Cardinal Virtues*, 21–30.

78. Cicero, *On Duties* 1.4, pp. 15–17.

79. Ibid., 1.5, p. 17.

80. Ibid., 1.5–6, p. 17.

81. Ibid., 1.23, p. 81.

82. Ibid., 1.30, p. 107.

83. Ibid., p. 109. In his own work *De officiis*, Ambrose transmits the text of Cicero's *De officiis* with a relatively slight (but in certain ways significant) Christian rewriting. I have chosen not to summarize Ambrose here, because it seems to me that his central points are found in Cicero, although Ambrose cites instructive biblical passages. For Ambrose, as for Cicero, "verecundia" is the virtue of reserve, although Ambrose also connects it with modesty. For discussion, see Jean-Paul Bernard, *Les parties integrales de la temperance selon saint Thomas* (Lévis, Quebec: Le Quotidien, 1958), 31–32. I should note that Aquinas draws his account of "shame" (verecundia) from Aristotle and Cicero, whose thought he adapts under the influence of Ambrose, Albert the Great, and others. For Cicero, "shame" is a reserve that we adopt in order to ensure that we do not cause offense to others. Cicero rarely discusses "shame"—by contrast to his many references to "honestas"—and he presents it as a kind of virtue attached to temperance as a potential part. Aristotle describes "shame" as a passion. For discussion see Bernard, *Les parties integrales de la temperance selon saint Thomas*, 29–39.

84. Hans Urs von Balthasar, *Love Alone Is Credible*, trans. D. C. Schindler (San Francisco: Ignatius Press, 2004), 132. Von Balthasar goes on to reject, in light of the irruption of cruciform (and radically theocentric)

love, both "the ancient harmony between the cosmic and the supra-cosmic" and any "new cosmic harmony" (ibid., 134). I think that Aquinas shows that there can be a "harmony," but not if harmony means a simple continuity on the same level. The cross changes everything and bestows supernatural communion, and yet human nature's flourishing is fulfilled, not ruptured or displaced, by the grace of the Holy Spirit.

85. *ST* I, q. 1, a. 8, ad 2.

86. See David Decosimo, *Ethics as a Work of Charity: Thomas Aquinas and Pagan Virtue* (Stanford, CA: Stanford University Press, 2014), 259. As Decosimo points out, "Thomas distinguishes where Augustine seems not to, proceeding as though Augustine had been dividing infused from acquired, perfect from imperfect all along, as if Augustine had never proclaimed the falsity of pagan virtue, only the absolute supremacy of infused (I.II 63.2; 65.2)" (ibid., 262). Decosimo warns against denying or downplaying "the vital difference between the vicious and relatively virtuous pagan, the unjust and imperfectly just—distinctions essential to loving the neighbor and seeking the common good" (ibid., 263). Yet Decosimo makes clear that "Thomas's insistence on the utter incapacity of pagan virtue for salvation clarifies that his welcome has nothing to do with any sort of Pelagianism," and he adds that "Thomas counts infused virtues primary; they alone are perfect and true *simpliciter*, the prime analogue in relation to which acquired virtues are *secundum quid*" (ibid., 264). Decosimo would agree, of course, with the point made by Nicholas Lombardo, O.P., that since Aquinas's treatise on temperance presumes the sanctifying grace of the Holy Spirit, the treatise would be misunderstood if interpreted as simply a reprising of pagan virtue, not least because it generally has infused moral virtues in view and because it adds new virtues such as fasting, virginity, and humility (see Lombardo, *The Logic of Desire: Aquinas on Emotion* [Washington, DC: Catholic University of America Press, 2011], 189). For concern that Decosimo concedes too much to pagan virtue, see Thomas M. Osborne Jr., "What Is at Stake in the Question of Whether Someone Can Possess the Natural Moral Virtues without Charity?," in Goris and Schoot, *Virtuous Life*, 128–29.

87. Albert Plé, O.P., *Chastity and the Affective Life*, trans. Marie-Claude Thompson (New York: Herder and Herder, 1966), 125. Along similar lines, see Servais Pinckaers, O.P., "Reappropriating Aquinas's Account of the Passions," trans. Craig Steven Titus, in *The Pinckaers Reader: Renewing Thomistic Moral Theology*, ed. John Berkman and Craig Steven Titus (Washington, DC: Catholic University of America Press, 2005), 273–87; Pinckaers, *Passions and Virtue*, trans. Benedict M. Guevin, O.S.B. (Washington, DC: Catholic University of America Press, 2015);

Marie-Dominique Chenu, O.P., "Les passions vertueuses: L'anthropologie de saint Thomas," *Revue philosophique de Louvain* 72 (1974): 11–18; Cornelius Williams, O.P., "The Hedonism of Aquinas," *Thomist* 38 (1974): 257–90.

88. Diana Fritz Cates offers a nice summary of Aquinas's understanding of the passion of anger:

> Thomas holds that anger is an embodied movement of the irascible part of the sense appetite whose nature can be specified with reference to its causes, objects, and effects. The causes of anger are an unmerited slight to one's excellence, a self-loving desire to be justly regarded for one's excellence, a sorrow over the injury inflicted on that excellence, a denouncing of the injury, and a hope of avenging it by causing its perpetrator pain. The objects of anger are the perpetrator of the slight regarded under the aspect of evil, and vengeance toward him regarded under the aspect of good. Anger seeks vengeance as a means to the reestablishment of right relationship. Finally, the effects of anger are a powerful bodily commotion and a pleasure that attends the righting of a wrong. ("Thomas Aquinas and Audre Lorde on Anger," in *Aquinas and Empowerment: Classical Ethics for Ordinary Lives*, ed. G. Simon Harak, S.J. [Washington, DC: Georgetown University Press, 1996], 63)

89. Plé, *Chastity and the Affective Life*, 126.

90. Pinsent, *Prudence, Justice, Courage, and Temperance*, 61.

91. See the insightful summary by G. Simon Harak, S.J., of what he calls Aquinas's "moral project":

> Thomas surely considers physical movement as part of his description of what it means to be a human being. But what is most characteristic of humans is movement in accord with their rational *appetitus*.... The lifelong moral project of a human being would thus be to complete and fulfill the integration of the self, so that the whole self becomes fully rational. I hesitate as I write these words, because of our modern sense of the word "rational." We have images from Descartes of the intellect or our "thinking part" warring against the passions. But the fact that Thomas says that all dimensions of the human being are ordered toward rationality forbids us from using the model of "the intellect against the lower passions." Perhaps it will help to recall what *Thomas* means by "rational." It means seeing and being drawn by the Supreme Good. In fact, if we recall how Thomas began his discussion of God (with the inadequacy of intellect), we can see that the primary way of being drawn to God in the first place is *not* by what we would call

exclusively "the intellect," or "thinking." It is the dynamic of *wanting*, of desiring, which is most properly and best drawn to God.... We can summarize Thomas' understanding of the moral project a different way. As a sensate being, we are, like the animals, drawn to particular goods, perceptible to our senses. As rational beings, we are drawn to the Supreme Good, whose loveliness attracts us. As integrated beings, we must see each particular good in light of the Supreme Good, and enjoy the Supreme Good in every particular good. Thomas sees this project not just as personally integrative, but also as interactive. All others are good (in that they exist) and all good is attractive to us. We must order all those others such that they are aligned with the vision of God's goodness. (*Virtuous Passions: The Formation of Christian Character* [Mahwah, NJ: Paulist Press, 1993], 66–68)

See also Diana Fritz Cates, *Aquinas on the Emotions: A Religious-Ethical Inquiry* (Washington, DC: Georgetown University Press, 2009), 185–86.

92. See David Bentley Hart, *The Experience of God: Being, Consciousness, Bliss* (New Haven: Yale University Press, 2013), 152–237, 295–300; Edward Feser, *Aquinas: A Beginner's Guide* (Oxford: Oneworld, 2009); James D. Madden, *Mind, Matter, and Nature: A Thomistic Proposal for the Philosophy of Mind* (Washington, DC: Catholic University of America Press, 2013). See also Robert P. George and Patrick Lee, *Body-Self Dualism in Contemporary Ethics and Politics* (Cambridge: Cambridge University Press, 2009).

93. Réginald Garrigou-Lagrange, O.P., *The Three Ages of the Interior Life*, vol. 1, trans. M. Timothea Doyle, O.P. (St. Louis: B. Herder, 1947), 35.

94. For awareness of this need for mercy and of its mediation in the Church of Christ through the sacraments, see Maria C. Morrow, *Sin in the Sixties: Catholics and Confession, 1955–1975* (Washington, DC: Catholic University of America Press, 2016). Morrow argues that the period of 1966–1975 produced "a much reduced penitential sensibility" among Catholics in America, and she points out that this situation calls today for a renewal of Catholics' penitential sensibility (ibid., 244). Häring's chapter on the "fundamental option" makes clear why the sacrament of reconciliation fell into disuse: see Häring, *Free and Faithful in Christ*, 1:211–16.

CHAPTER ONE. Aquinas and the Ethics of the Inaugurated Kingdom

1. Herbert McCabe, O.P., *The Good Life: Ethics and the Pursuit of Happiness*, ed. Brian Davies, O.P. (London: Continuum, 2005).

2. Rebecca Konyndyk DeYoung, Colleen McCluskey, and Christina Van Dyke, *Aquinas's Ethics: Metaphysical Foundations, Moral Theory, and Theological Context* (Notre Dame, IN: University of Notre Dame Press, 2009), 187. I agree with Oliver O'Donovan that "the essential note of an evangelical ethics will be missing if the freedom of the Gospel is not understood as *life in the Spirit*. Failure on this point must mean the failure of Theological Ethics as a whole" (*Ethics as Theology*, vol. 2, *Finding and Seeking* [Grand Rapids, MI: Eerdmans, 2014], 2, emphasis added). O'Donovan appreciatively cites Johannes Fischer's *Leben aus dem Geist* (Zurich: Theologischer Verlag Zürich, 1994).

3. Diana Fritz Cates, "The Virtue of Temperance (IIa IIae, qq. 141–170)," in *The Ethics of Aquinas*, ed. Stephen J. Pope (Washington, DC: Georgetown University Press, 2002), 334.

4. Ibid.

5. Ibid. See also Laurent Sentis, "La lumière dont nous faisons usage: La règle de la raison et la loi divine selon Thomas d'Aquin," *Revue des sciences philosophiques et théologiques* 79 (1995): 49–69.

6. Serge-Thomas Bonino, O.P., "Les beatitudes au coeur de la théologie de saint Thomas d'Aquinas," *Nova et Vetera* 89 (2014): 429. See also William C. Mattison III, "Beatitude and the Beatitudes in the *Summa Theologiae* of St. Thomas Aquinas," *Josephinum Journal of Theology* 17 (2010): 233–49; Olivier Bonnewijn, *La beatitude et les beatitudes: Une approche thomiste de l'éthique* (Rome: Pontificio Istituto Giovanni Paolo II, 2001). For further background, see Michael Dauphinais, "Gregory of Nyssa and Augustine on the Beatitudes," *Nova et Vetera* 1 (2003): 141–63; William C. Mattison III, "The Beatitudes and Moral Theology: A Virtue Ethics Approach," *Nova et Vetera* 11 (2013): 819–48.

7. Rowan Williams, *Being Disciples: Essentials of Christian Life* (Grand Rapids, MI: Eerdmans, 2016), 15.

8. Regarding the relatively widespread contemporary rejection of the concept of "human nature," Joseph Ratzinger notes that in contemporary culture, it is assumed that "everyone is free to give to his personal *libido* the content considered suitable for himself" (Ratzinger with Vittorio Messori, *The Ratzinger Report: An Exclusive Interview on the State of the Church*, trans. Salvator Attanasio and Graham Harrison [San Francisco: Ignatius Press, 1985], 85). Ratzinger remarks that at the root of this situation is a rejection of "human nature" as such, namely, the requirements for human flourishing that human nature inscribes. See also Pope Benedict XVI, *Deus Caritas Est*, Vatican translation (Boston: Pauline Books & Media, 2006), §11. Without the application to sexual ethics, John Milbank and Adrian Pabst likewise insist that "goodness is *given* in nature and not

something we contrive with difficulty from time to time" (*The Politics of Virtue: Post-Liberalism and the Human Future* [Lanham, MD: Rowman & Littlefield, 2016], 5). Milbank and Pabst argue that "while, for liberalism, avoiding pain and maximising pleasure are seen as the best way of liberating the individual, in reality liberal utilitarianism hands over life to the forces of the state and the market, treating it as a commodity that can be traded or dispensed with without regard to its intrinsic worth" (ibid., 275). In addition, see Joseph W. Koterski, S.J., "The Concept of Nature: Philosophical Reflections in the Service of Theology," in *Theology Needs Philosophy: Acting against Reason Is Contrary to the Nature of God*, ed. Matthew L. Lamb (Washington, DC: Catholic University of America Press, 2016), 54–73.

9. On the kingdom and the Church, see Avery Dulles, S.J., "The Church and the Kingdom: A Study of Their Relationship in Scripture, Tradition, and Evangelization," *Letter & Spirit* 3 (2007): 23–38. In accord with the Second Vatican Council and with chapter 5 of the Congregation of the Doctrine of the Faith's *Dominus Iesus*, Vatican trans. (Boston: Pauline Books & Media, 2000), Dulles holds that since the kingdom is the perfected body of Christ, "the Church ... cannot be detached from the kingdom, but is ordered to it as the 'sign and instrument' in which the kingdom is mysteriously present" ("Church and the Kingdom," 36). I note that insofar as the Church is even now the body of Christ, the Church is the inaugurated kingdom—which means not that the Church is coterminous with the kingdom but that "the kingdom is mysteriously present" in the Church due to Christ's salvific work and his outpouring of the Spirit, by which we have been made "children of God, and if children, then heirs, heirs of God and fellow heirs with Christ, provided we suffer with him in order that we may also be glorified with him" (Rom 8:16–17). On the Spirit and the Church, see Yves Congar, O.P., *I Believe in the Holy Spirit*, trans. David Smith (New York: Crossroad, 1997), book 2, pp. 5–64; Anscar Vonier, O.S.B., *The Spirit and the Bride* (London: Burns, Oates, and Washbourne, 1935). Jean-Pierre Torrell, O.P., comments that for Aquinas, the "Christian is first and foremost a member of the ecclesial Body" (Torrell, *Spiritual Master*, vol. 2 of *Saint Thomas Aquinas* [Washington, DC: Catholic University of America Press, 2003], 376).

10. See *ST* I-II, q. 106, a. 4. For discussion—clearly warning against certain postconciliar developments—see Henri de Lubac, S.J., *La postérité spirituelle de Joachim de Flore*, vol. 1, *De Joachim à Schelling* (Paris: Éditions Lethielleux, 1979). See also Ernst Benz, "Joachim-Studien III: Thomas von Aquin und Joachim de Fiore. Die katholische Antwort auf die spiritualistische Kirchen- und Geschichtsauffassung," *Zeitschrift für Kirchengeschichte* 53 (1934): 52–116.

11. In response to Wright's work, see for example Burridge, *Imitating Jesus*, 42–43, 49–50; Dunn, *Jesus Remembered*; Craig A. Evans, "Jesus and the Continuing Exile," in *Jesus and the Restoration of Israel: A Critical Assessment of N. T. Wright's "Jesus and the Victory of God,"* ed. Carey C. Newman (Downers Grove, IL: InterVarsity Press, 1999), 77–100; Luke Timothy Johnson, "A Historiographical Response to Wright's Jesus," in Newman, *Jesus and the Restoration of Israel*, 210–12; Steven M. Bryan, *Jesus and Israel's Traditions of Judgment and Restoration* (Cambridge: Cambridge University Press, 2002); Brant Pitre, *Jesus, the Tribulation, and the End of Exile: Restoration Eschatology and the Origin of the Atonement* (Grand Rapids, MI: Baker Academic, 2005); Matthew J. Thomas, *Paul's "Works of the Law" in the Perspective of Second Century Reception* (Tübingen: Mohr Siebeck, 2018). Although he thinks that Wright exaggerates in certain important ways, Dunn observes that "there was a widespread belief [Dunn footnotes a large range of biblical and extra-biblical Second-Temple texts] that after a period of dispersion among the nations, the outcasts/scattered of Israel would be gathered again and brought back to the promised land, the unity of the twelve tribes reestablished, and the relation of Israel as God's people, and Yahweh as Israel's God, restored" (Dunn, *Jesus Remembered*, 393). Dunn provides a list of fourteen "clearly attested and most relevant motifs which suggest the sort of expectations that were cherished and may have been evoked by Jesus' kingdom talk among Jews living in the land of Israel in the first century CE," including the motif of the end of exile (ibid.).

12. Stanley Hauerwas, "Habit Matters: The Bodily Character of the Virtues," in *Approaching the End: Eschatological Reflections on Church, Politics, and Life* (Grand Rapids, MI: Eerdmans, 2013), 172. Miguel A. De La Torre comments from the perspective of liberation theology, "If conversion is understood as a rupture with and a turning away from sin (sin caused by individual actions *and* sin caused by social institutions), then salvation can occur only through the raising of consciousness to a level that can recognize the personal and communal sins preventing the start of a new life in Jesus" (De La Torre, *Doing Christian Ethics from the Margins* [Maryknoll, NY: Orbis, 2004], 42). De La Torre does not treat the virtues associated with temperance, in part because he fears that "concentrating solely on personal morality or virtues without engaging the actual structures responsible for producing injustices will only lead to discouraging results. A change of heart of individuals usually is insufficient to produce a more just social order. The social structures themselves require transformation and conversion" (ibid., 44). In this regard see the helpful defense of virtue ethics offered by Hauerwas, "Virtue in Public," in *Christian Existence*

Today: Essays on Church, World, and Living In Between (Grand Rapids, MI: Baker, 1988), 191–97, as well as Luke Timothy Johnson's argument that liberation theology tends to oversimplify our problem (which in fact is a "disease of the human heart") and turns salvation into a matter of getting "human social reform" right rather than a matter that only God can accomplish (*The Living Gospel* [London: Continuum, 2004], 193–94). With political (liberation) theology in view, Ratzinger remarks that an "'eschatological' attitude" is what "allows us to be healthy," since earthly life and merely human agency cannot give us what we need and demand (Ratzinger, *Values in a Time of Upheaval*, trans. Brian McNeil [San Francisco: Ignatius Press, 2006], 71).

13. Wright, *Paul and the Faithfulness of God*, 814. James W. Thompson praises Wright's central approach: "I am in basic agreement that Paul, a very Jewish thinker, has reconfigured basic Jewish beliefs around the Messiah. To start from Israel's narrative and the place of the Messianic people within that story is an appropriate way to begin a theology of Paul" (review of N. T. Wright, *Paul and the Faithfulness of God*, *Restoration Quarterly* 56 [2014]: 247). Like others noted above, however, Thompson adds some cautionary notes: "I am convinced, with Professor Wright, that Paul envisioned the communities that he founded as the people of God returned from exile as described in Deut 30–31, the recipients of the good news announced in Deutero-Isaiah, the people on whom the Spirit had been poured, as anticipated in Ezekiel, the people of the Messiah who live out Israel's destiny. I am not always convinced that this narrative accounts for Paul's theological reflection as comprehensively as Professor Wright maintains" (ibid.).

14. Wright, *Paul and the Faithfulness of God*, 814.

15. Ibid.

16. Ibid.

17. Ibid., 833.

18. Ibid., 1013. See also Burridge, *Imitating Jesus*, 107–110. Burridge argues persuasively against Richard Hays's argument that "love" is too vague and broad to be made a pillar of contemporary retrieval of Paul's ethics. Burridge draws upon a variety of sources, including Victor P. Furnish, *The Love Command in the New Testament* (Nashville: Abingdon, 1972); Raymond F. Collins, *Christian Morality: Biblical Foundations* (Notre Dame, IN: University of Notre Dame Press, 1986), especially 137–48; Wolfgang Schrage, *The Ethics of the New Testament*, trans. David E. Green (Philadelphia: Fortress, 1988), 211–17; Douglas A. Campbell, *The Quest for Paul's Gospel: A Suggested Strategy* (London: T&T Clark, 2005), 117.

19. Wright, *Paul and the Faithfulness of God*, 1019, 1021. See also Brant Pitre, *Jesus and the Last Supper* (Grand Rapids, MI: Eerdmans, 2015).

20. Wright, *Paul and the Faithfulness of God*, 1037. Note that for Paul, according to Wright,

> Torah, as now redefined around Messiah and spirit, retains its community-shaping and community-defining function. This then produces new paradoxes: neither circumcision nor uncircumcision matters, since what matters is "keeping God's commandments" [1 Cor 7:19]! But, with this new-covenant redefinition, we find the characteristically Pauline rejection of any attempt to go on defining the covenant community by "works of Torah" in the earlier sense. . . . Once again, there are two reasons. First, if Torah-works such as circumcision and food laws defined the new covenant people, that would perpetuate the Jew/Gentile division which has now been overcome in the Messiah and spirit. "The law of commandments and ordinances" functioned like a wall to keep the pagans out, but it is now demolished. Second, even within the apparent safety of an Israel living within the "fence" of Torah, there was no way through to the new covenant

due to the sinfulness of all humanity, including Israel (Wright, *Paul and the Faithfulness of God*, 1036–37).

21. N. T. Wright, *The Day the Revolution Began: Reconsidering the Meaning of Jesus's Crucifixion* (New York: HarperCollins, 2016), 76.

22. Ibid.

23. Ibid., 385. For a fuller exposition of these themes, see Wright, *After You Believe*, chapters 6 and 7. In *After You Believe*, Wright likewise describes "the new way of being human—not only some new and previously unheard-of virtues, but a new definition of virtue itself, a whole new way of humanity" (ibid., 218). Wright's fellow Anglican, the late moral theologian Daniel A. Westberg, criticizes *After You Believe* for "a certain vagueness and lack of precision" and for setting "aside the framework of the classical moral virtues," which Christians "share in common with other people" (*Renewing Moral Theology: Christian Ethics as Action, Character and Grace* [Downers Grove, IL: IVP Academic, 2015], 148). I partly agree with this critique—especially insofar as it magnifies the importance of philosophical anthropology and human nature—but I nonetheless find Wright's book to be quite helpful. See also, for work that prepares for and finds a place in *After You Believe*, Wright's "Faith, Virtue, Justification, and the Journey to Freedom," in Wagner, Rowe, and Grieb, *Word Leaps the Gap*, 472–97. Westberg worries about the neglect of the cardinal virtues in Anglican moral theology: see *Renewing Moral Theology*, 198–99.

24. Wright, *Day the Revolution Began*, 395.

25. See Gary Wilson, *Your Brain on Porn: Internet Pornography and the Emerging Science of Addiction* (Margate, Kent: Commonwealth Publishing, 2014); Matt Fradd, *The Porn Myth: Exposing the Reality behind the Fantasy of Pornography* (San Francisco: Ignatius Press, 2017), 194–95. See also the critique of pornography offered by Fabrice Hadjadj, "Ce que la pornographie nous cache," *Nova et Vetera* [Swiss edition] 92 (2017): 219–30. Hadjadj concludes that "pornography is the exaltation of techno-economic mastery, because the body is absent, and sex is deprived of its most proper powers, and the flesh is overwhelmed on a screen" (ibid., 230). Unless otherwise noted, all translations of non-English texts in quotations are my own.

26. Wright, *Day the Revolution Began*, 398. Wright notes that "Jesus himself was quite clear, following in the prophetic tradition: the human heart is deceitful, and out of it come all kinds of things that defile people, that is, make them unable to function as genuine human beings, as the royal priesthood they were called to be. . . . The victory won through suffering on the cross is implemented, here as elsewhere, through the suffering of Jesus' followers, most of whom will continue to be troubled from time to time by temptation in relation to money and sex and many other things besides" (ibid.). Regarding self-control, Romano Guardini makes the helpful point that "everyone who knows the tendency of human nature toward self-indulgence also knows how necessary it is to impose upon ourselves voluntary exercises in self-control" (*Learning the Virtues That Lead You to God* [Manchester, NH: Sophia Institute Press, 1998], 89). As Guardini points out, too, "The motive for true asceticism does not lie in . . . a struggle to overcome the urges, but in the necessity of bringing them into proper order" (ibid., 88).

27. Wright, *Day the Revolution Began*, 398. See also Wright's insightful remark in *After You Believe*, in his chapter "Virtue in Action: The Royal Priesthood": "The life of worship, then, is itself a corporate form of virtue. It expresses and in turn reinforces the faith, hope, and love which are themselves the key Christian virtues. From this activity there flow all kinds of other things in terms of Christian life and witness. But worship is central, basic, and in the best sense habit-forming" (*After You Believe*, 225).

28. Second Vatican Council, *Dei Verbum*, §24, in *The Conciliar and Post Conciliar Documents*, ed. Austin Flannery, O.P., rev. ed., vol. 1 of *Vatican Council II* (Northport, NY: Costello, 1996), 763–64.

29. Second Vatican Council, *Optatam Totius*, §16, in Flannery, *Conciliar and Post Conciliar Documents*, 719.

30. Ibid., 720.

31. See my "Supplementing Pinckaers: The Old Testament in Aquinas's Ethics," in *Reading Sacred Scripture with Thomas Aquinas: Hermeneutical Tools, Theological Questions and New Perspectives*, ed. Piotr Roszak and Jörgen Vijgen (Turnhout: Brepols, 2015), 349–73. My engagement with Pinckaers in this section is drawn from this article.

32. Torrell, *Spiritual Master*, 378. See also my *Paul in the* Summa Theologiae (Washington, DC: Catholic University of America Press, 2014).

33. Servais Pinckaers, *The Sources of Christian Ethics*, trans. Mary Thomas Noble, O.P. (Washington, DC: Catholic University of America Press, 1995), xviii. See also Servais Pinckaers, O.P., "Scripture and the Renewal of Moral Theology," trans. Mary Thomas Noble, in *Pinckaers Reader*, 46–63, as well as Craig Steven Titus, "Servais Pinckaers and the Renewal of Catholic Moral Theology," *Journal of Moral Theology* 1 (2012): 43–68. See also William C. Spohn's comment,

> In the pre–Vatican II Catholicism in which I was raised, the person of Jesus played an important role in devotional life while being largely ignored in Catholic moral theology. . . . Moral theology bracketed specifically Christian religious experience; that was relegated to "ascetical" and "mystical" theology. Natural law looked to the "proper end of man" and derived objective moral principles to guide the journey toward human fulfillment. The closest ally of moral theology was not the New Testament but the intricate system of obligations and regulations calibrated in canon law. Catholic moralists showed great skill in resolving the conflicting obligations that created "cases of conscience." (*Go and Do Likewise: Jesus and Ethics* [New York: Continuum, 2007], 185)

With respect to temperance, see for example Joseph Fuchs, S.J., *De castitate et ordine sexuali: Conspectus praelectionum theologiae moralis ad usum auditorium*, 2nd ed. (Rome: Editrice Università Gregoriana, 1960); B. H. Merkelbach, O.P., *Quaestiones de castitate et luxuria quas in utilitatem cleri*, 6th ed. (Paris: Casterman, 1936); P. Chrétien, *De castitate: Tractatus ad usum confessariorum quem in seminario metensi proponebat* (Metz, France: Le Lorrain, 1938). Note that during this period, there were also manuals on the ascetic and spiritual life.

34. Pinckaers, *Sources of Christian Ethics*, 114.

35. Ibid., 116.

36. Ibid., 117.

37. Phenomenologically, Karol Wojtyła connects humility and chastity in an evocative manner that is worth noting here: "The human body

must be 'humble' in the face of the greatness represented by the person: for in the person resides the true and definitive greatness of man. Furthermore, the human body must 'humble itself' in face of the magnitude represented by love—and here 'humble itself' means subordinate itself. Chastity is conducive to this. . . . 'The body' must also show humility in face of human happiness. How often does it insinuate that it alone possesses the key to the secret of happiness. 'Happiness,' if this were so, would have to be identified with mere enjoyment, with the sum of the pleasures which the 'body and sex' can bring to the relationship between man and woman. But this superficial view of happiness for one thing obscures the truth that man and woman can and must seek their temporal, earthly happiness in a lasting union which has an interpersonal character, since it is based in each of them on unreserved affirmation of the value of the person. Still more certainly does the 'body'—if it is not 'humble,' not subordinate to the full truth about the happiness of man—obscure the vision of the ultimate happiness: the happiness of the human person in union with a personal God. This is the sense in which we should understand Christ's words in the Sermon on the Mount: 'Blessed are the pure in heart, for they shall see God'" (Wojtyła, *Love and Responsibility*, trans. H. T. Willetts [New York: Farrar, Straus and Giroux, 1981], 172–73).

38. Pinckaers, *Sources of Christian Ethics*, 138.

39. For the scope of Aquinas's indebtedness to Augustine, see Leo J. Elders, S.V.D., "Les citations de saint Augustin dans la *Somme Théologique* de saint Thomas d'Aquin," *Doctor Communis* 40 (1987): 115–67; Georg von Hertling, "Augustinuszitate bei Thomas von Aquin," in *Sitzungsberichte der Bayerischen Akademie der Wissenschaften* (Munich: Verlag der Bayerischen Akademie der Wissenschaften, 1914), 535–602; and the essays in Michael Dauphinais, Barry David, and Matthew Levering, eds., *Aquinas the Augustinian* (Washington, DC: Catholic University of America Press, 2007).

40. Pinckaers, *Sources of Christian Ethics*, 150. See also Giuseppe Abbà, *Felicità, vita buona e virtù: Saggio di filosofia morale* (Rome: LAS, 1989). Note that for Pinckaers, prayer (both private and communal/liturgical)—which can seem "useless" to a world focused on productivity—is at the center of Christian life, and thus Christian ethics cannot be separated from a contemplative spirit. See Pinckaers, *Passions and Virtue*, 135. For Aquinas's spirituality and theology of prayer, see also Paul Murray, O.P., *Aquinas at Prayer: The Bible, Mysticism and Poetry* (London: Bloomsbury, 2013); Murray, *Praying with Confidence: Aquinas on the Lord's Prayer* (London: Continuum, 2010).

41. See *ST* I-II, q. 68, a. 4; II-II, q. 141, a. 1, ad 3. In both places he cites Psalm 119:120, "My flesh trembles for fear of thee, and I am afraid of thy judgments."

42. *ST* I-II, q. 68, a. 4, ad 4.

43. *ST* I-II, q. 68, a. 5.

44. Pinckaers, *Sources of Christian Ethics*, 162.

45. See also Servais Pinckaers, O.P., *The Spirituality of Martyrdom . . . to the Limits of Love*, trans. Patrick M. Clark and Annie Hounsokou (Washington, DC: Catholic University of America Press, 2016).

46. Pennington, *Sermon on the Mount and Human Flourishing*, 289. Much like Pinckaers (though in a Protestant context focused on the problem of merit), Pennington adds that

> the history of the church manifests a loss of this eudaimonistic understanding of the nature of the faith and its ethics. The loss of focus on human flourishing—indeed, the latent *fear* of speaking this way that plagues many faithful Christians, including many within the assorted Reformed, Lutheran, and evangelical traditions—often comes from a rightful and biblical desire to highlight a "God-centeredness" that keeps God and his creatures in a proper relationship of hierarchy and in proper focus; too much talk of the importance of humanity sounds to many like a slippery slope to the loss of the Bible's focus first on God. I think this fear of theological human flourishing is also motivated by an awareness that Jesus calls his followers to self-sacrifice (Mark 8:34–35; Luke 9:23–24), to cross carrying (Matt. 10:38; Luke 14:27), to considering others as more important than themselves (Phil. 2:3–8). However, as I have argued above, this cannot be construed as a flat-footed denial of one's own reward, recompense, satisfaction, or ultimate flourishing. Indeed, every time Jesus calls people to sacrifice it is based on promises of future reward and recompense, even as we saw in the Sermon (e.g., 6:1–21). (ibid., 291–92)

See also, for works allied with Pennington's perspective, Ellen Charry, *God and the Art of Happiness* (Grand Rapids, MI: Eerdmans, 2010); Brent Strawn, ed., *The Bible and the Pursuit of Happiness: What the Old and New Testaments Teach Us about the Good Life* (Oxford: Oxford University Press, 2012). Pennington appreciatively discusses Pinckaers's work in *Sermon on the Mount and Human Flourishing*, 61–62, and he recognizes that N. T. Wright's *After You Believe* "provides a creative and robust biblical argument for an eschatological, virtue-ethics understanding" (*Sermon on the Mount and Human Flourishing*, 290n2).

47. Pennington, *Sermon on the Mount and Human Flourishing*, 289.

48. On the infused moral virtues in relation to the acquired moral virtues, see Diana Fritz Cates, *Choosing to Feel: Virtue, Friendship, and Compassion for Friends* (Notre Dame, IN: University of Notre Dame Press, 1997), 38–45. In Cates's view, the infused moral virtues displace the acquired moral virtues within the unified action of a charitable person. For recent scholarship about the relationship of the infused and acquired moral virtues, see Angela McKay Knobel, "Can Aquinas's Infused and Acquired Virtues Coexist in the Christian Life?," *Studies in Christian Ethics* 23 (2010): 381–96; Knobel, "Relating Aquinas's Infused and Acquired Virtues: Some Problematic Texts for a Common Interpretation," *Nova et Vetera* 9 (2011): 411–31; William C. Mattison III, "Can Christians Possess the Acquired Moral Virtues?," *Thomist* 72 (2011): 558–85. Knobel suggests that "Aquinas's silence about the relationship between the infused and acquired virtues" means that accounts of their relationship must arise from sources other than his texts ("Relating Aquinas's Infused and Acquired Virtues," 431). For Knobel and Mattison, Christians in a state of grace actively possess only the infused moral virtues. By contrast, Réginald Garrigou-Lagrange, O.P., states with regard to the virtue of chastity, "Infused chastity, received at baptism, causes the light of grace to descend into the sensible part of the soul; it makes use of acquired chastity somewhat as the intellect makes use of the imagination. They are exercised together; acquired chastity is thus at the service of infused chastity" (*Three Ages of the Interior Life*, 2:133–34). Cajetan Chereso, O.P., adds a further helpful consideration: "When St. Thomas takes great care in delineating the nature of an acquired moral virtue [as often in his treatise on temperance], his intent is theological. One cannot, after all, understand the infused moral virtues, since they are essentially supernatural, except by analogy with the acquired or natural moral virtues. Since grace supposes nature, the natural moral virtue gives some explanation of the nature of the corresponding infused virtue, providing that the essential diversity of the latter be noted, namely, that its consonance and proportion depend upon a supernatural end conceived by reason illumined by Faith" (*The Virtue of Honor and Beauty according to St. Thomas Aquinas: An Analysis of Moral Beauty* [River Forest, IL: Aquinas Library, 1960], xv–xvi). Michael S. Sherwin, O.P., argues that in cases where the person lacks a particular acquired moral virtue, it is the infused virtue that enables the person to acquire the particular virtue, so that "we become well ordered to our temporal community by first becoming citizens of heaven in the gift of grace" ("Infused Virtue and the Effects of Acquired Vice," 51; cf. his view that "the (elicited) acts of the

acquired moral virtues are commanded by the infused moral virtues," and "for many adult converts, the infused moral virtues are what make developing the acquired virtues possible at all" [ibid., 50–51]). See also, in Goris and Schoot, *Virtuous Life*, the contrasting views of (on the one side) Knobel, "A Confusing Comparison: Interpreting *De Virtutibus in Communi* a. 10 ad 4," 97–115, and Mattison, "Infused Virtues in the Scriptures: Infused Prudence in *Matthew* 6, 19–34," 281–300, and (on the other side, but in certain important respects differing from each other) David Decosimo, "More to Love: Ends, Ordering, and the Compatibility of Acquired and Infused Virtues," 47–72, and Osborne, "What Is at Stake in the Question," 117–30. For a creative attempt to resolve the problem by appeal to the Salamancan school of Thomism, see Austin, *Aquinas on Virtue*, 202–5. His proposal is that "a moral virtue's specifying target is somewhat indeterminate and capable of being filled out either naturally or supernaturally. A moral virtue is related to a natural or supernatural end neither intrinsically and directly (as for the traditional Thomist position) nor extrinsically (as for the Scotists) but only 'as a condition'" (ibid., 205). Notwithstanding their disagreements, the above scholars agree in contesting the view of "medieval thinkers such as Duns Scotus and his followers" who "did not see the need nor the biblical support for asserting the existence of infused cardinal virtues" (Michael S. Sherwin, O.P., *On Love and Virtue: Theological Essays* [Steubenville, OH: Emmaus Academic, 2018], 163).

49. Yves Congar, O.P., "The Holy Spirit in the Thomistic Theology of Moral Action," trans. Susan Mader Brown and Joseph G. Mueller, S.J., in Congar, *Spirit of God: Short Writings on the Holy Spirit*, ed. Mark E. Ginter, Susan Mader Brown, and Joseph G. Mueller, S.J. (Washington, DC: Catholic University of America Press, 2017), 150. Congar goes on to point out that Aquinas, in laboring to connect each theological and cardinal virtue with a specific gift and beatitude, "seems to have had trouble attributing a gift and a beatitude" to temperance, finally settling upon "fear and either the 'beati pauperes [blessed are the poor]' or the 'qui esurient et sitiunt iustitiam [those who hunger and thirst for justice]'" (ibid., 152). He directs attention to S. Lyonnet, S.J., "Liberté chrétienne et loi de l'Esprit selon s. Paul," *Christus* 4 (1954): 6–27, as well as to his own "Variations sur le thème 'Loi-Grâce,'" *Revue Thomiste* 71 (1971): 429–38. Congar emphasizes that Aquinas "sees all that is external rule, and even the letter of Scripture (1a2ae q. 106, a. 2), as wholly subsumed by grace, wholly referred to the relationship between faith and love, wholly measured by love" ("Holy Spirit in the Thomistic Theology of Moral Action," 155). This is so, but here we need to be careful to insist also upon the givens of human nature and the goodness of divine law.

50. As Sherwin has observed, "Pinckaers repeatedly affirmed the importance of the infused cardinal virtues for the moral life. For Pinckaers, what is at stake in this doctrine is the difference that grace makes in the life of virtue. Grace transforms the source and character of moral excellence" ("Infused Virtue and the Effects of Acquired Vice," 29).

51. Porter, "Virtue Ethics in the Medieval Period," 85. For a critique of Aquinas's "idea that the virtues arrive all at once in the soul by infusion," see Austin, *Aquinas on Virtue*, 196. He notes that

> Cajetan thinks that someone persisting in mortal sin after baptism could well have received faith and hope but still lacks charity: the mortally sinful acts of the convert prevent the generation of charity in the soul by infusion. Whatever we make of the plausibility of this case, it nevertheless provides Cajetan the occasion for making a valuable distinction between the *infusion* of the virtues, which in the strict and formal sense is an activity of God, and their *reception*, which is something that may happen in the soul as a consequence of God's action but only on condition that the person is appropriately disposed. Cajetan therefore restates the simultaneity thesis this way: the habits of theological virtues are infused at the same time "*on the part of the one infusing and by the rationale of infusion*, although the opposite may happen *from the disposition of the one receiving*" (emphasis added). In other words, infusion *as infusion* of all the virtues happens simultaneously since God does not hold back on His gifts; yet one or other of the virtues may fail to be generated or increased because of a person's lack of openness to this infusion. (ibid.)

I think Aquinas would have accepted Cajetan's proposal.

52. *ST* I-II, q. 68, a. 7, ad 1.

53. See also Yves Congar, O.P., "Réflexion et propos sur l'originalité d'une ethique chrétienne," *Studia Moralia* 15 (1977): 40: "It is a *theonomy* of the living God, a *Christonomy*, which cannot be a legalism. A purely *moral* ethics is replaced by a *theological* and *spiritual* ethics, that is, dependent upon the gift of the Spirit." Daniel Westberg nicely sums up the approach of Pinckaers as being "centered on recapturing the 'realist' moral theology of Aquinas, locating it within sacred doctrine as a whole, stressing the virtues and the role of the Spirit in the Christian moral life. Human action and natural law certainly are part of this description, but put in a theological context of the human being as the image of God. This way of reading Aquinas preserves the necessary elements of moral reasoning and gives them the proper theological and spiritual context" (*Renewing Moral*

Theology, 24). Westberg identifies the "necessary elements of moral reasoning" as including "a renewed biblical basis," "a sound moral psychology," "the proper place for law in ethics," and "spirituality" (ibid., 25–26)—and to this list should be added an adequate anthropology. Westberg directs attention to Fergus Kerr, O.P., "Doctrine of God and Theological Ethics according to Thomas Aquinas," in *The Doctrine of God and Theological Ethics*, ed. Alan Torrance and Michael Banner (London: T&T Clark, 2006), 71–84. See also Melina, *Sharing in Christ's Virtues*, as well as (on Christ and *sacra doctrina*) Gilles Mongeau, S.J., *Embracing Wisdom: The Summa theologiae as Spiritual Pedagogy* (Toronto: Pontifical Institute of Mediaeval Studies, 2015).

54. Pope John Paul II, *Fides et Ratio*, §68. For work along these lines, see McInerny, *Question of Christian Ethics*. See also the essays in Tobias Hoffmann, Jörn Müllet, and Matthias Perkams, eds., *Aquinas and the "Nicomachean Ethics"* (Cambridge: Cambridge University Press, 2013), as well as the essays in John P. O'Callaghan and Thomas S. Hibbs, eds., *Recovering Nature: Essays in Natural Philosophy, Ethics, and Metaphysics in Honor of Ralph McInerny* (Notre Dame, IN: University of Notre Dame Press, 1999).

55. See Patrick M. Clark, *Perfection in Death: The Christological Dimension of Courage in Aquinas* (Washington, DC: Catholic University of America Press, 2015). Clark investigates the virtue of courage via extensive consideration not only of Aquinas and Christian doctrine but also of the figures of Achilles and Socrates in light of Aristotle's account of courage.

56. Highlighting the impact of Christ's resurrection, Sarah Bachelard observes that "some of our deepest moral questions concern the treatment of those human beings whom the modern moral philosopher renders marginal to the moral community" (such as the unborn, the dying, and the mentally disabled), but "merely repeating a formula expressing sincere conviction *about* the sanctity of all human life will not 'effect' the conversion that is needed to keep such people morally among us" (*Resurrection and Moral Imagination* [Burlington, VT: Ashgate, 2014], 182). Instead what is needed is the "revelatory power" of "resurrection ethics," which "calls for the involvement of the whole person who is in the process of undergoing transformation" (ibid., 182–83). Oddly, however, Bachelard contrasts "resurrection ethics" with Christian ethical teaching about marriage as between a man and a woman. She thereby neglects aspects of (in her words) "what is deepest in the human condition" (ibid., 183). Her definition of what "resurrection ethics" means needs to be integrated more profoundly both with divine revelation (including Scripture) and with reflection upon created human nature: "Practising ethics from resurrection

means touching and deepening moral imagination, our active sense of how life is transformed by not having to be afraid, and not having to be 'over against' anything in order to be" (ibid.). Certainly, she is right that "those seeking to be good by comparison with those who are bad *cannot* love their neighbours as themselves," insofar as comparison breeds self-righteousness (ibid., 188), but this simple point is in itself a moral evaluation (of some persons in comparison with others), thereby showing that moral evaluation in itself is necessary and that "genuine neighbour love" (ibid., 189) requires more biblical, theological, and philosophical specification than she provides. For a more adequate formulation of "resurrection ethics," even if in my view overly wedded to a critique of both "law" and philosophical ethics (but rightly emphasizing that our identity is God's gift and that we must not fear vulnerability and failure as though God were not the victor over sin and death), see Rowan Williams, "Resurrection and Peace: More on New Testament Ethics," in *On Christian Theology* (Oxford: Blackwell, 2000), 265–75. See also the criticism by Brian V. Johnstone, C.S.s.R., of Pinckaers's *Sources of Christian Ethics* for failing to make the resurrection of Jesus central to the moral life: Johnstone, "Transformation Ethics," in *The Resurrection: An Interdisciplinary Symposium on the Resurrection of Jesus*, ed. Stephen T. Davis, Daniel Kendall, S.J., and Gerald O'Collins, S.J. (Oxford: Oxford University Press, 1997), 341. In my view, Pinckaers's understanding of Christian ethics is suffused by his understanding of the inauguration of the kingdom and the outpouring the Spirit brought about by Jesus' cross, resurrection, and ascension, and therefore radiates with a resurrection-guided understanding of human freedom and destiny (beatitude). Mistakenly in my view, Johnstone also criticizes Oliver O'Donovan's *Resurrection and Moral Order: An Outline for Evangelical Ethics* (Grand Rapids, MI: Eerdmans, 1986), for failing to enable "resurrection belief" to "shape or illumine the form of the moral life" ("Transformation Ethics," 343). Johnstone's position is that "love for the risen Jesus generates responsibility, and this becomes absolute commitment to others, the victims and potential victims whom one encounters in the world.... Responsibility to this real person [the risen Jesus] founds our responsibility to all other persons, who are meant to share his destiny" (ibid., 346–47). I contend that the perspective shaped by the inaugurated kingdom allows for a deeper engagement with creation and grace, one that includes the responsibility generated by love for the risen Jesus. Indeed, Johnstone moves in this direction when he advocates "an ethic of virtue, but virtue transformed in the light of the resurrection" (ibid., 350).

57. For the Catholic Church's teachings on sexuality as "prophetic" in the sense of upholding crucial Christian values but feasible only for an

elite—"a vocation offered only to some and perhaps similar in this respect to the teaching of Jesus on permanent celibacy"—see John Mahoney, *The Making of Moral Theology: A Study of the Roman Catholic Tradition* (Oxford: Oxford University Press, 1987), 284–86.

58. Roberts, "Temperance," 99. It might still seem that "temperance" does not have anything to do with such a kingdom, because temperance often now stands for a negative moralism or rigorism, whereas God's covenantal people (according to Jonathan Sacks) "are commanded to serve God in joy out of the abundance of good things, not through self-denial" (Jonathan Sacks, *To Heal a Fractured World: The Ethics of Responsibility* [New York: Schocken Books, 2005], 35). Temperance, however, is not about self-denial per se but rather is about human flourishing in families and communities, and indeed as the eschatological family of God that Jesus has inaugurated. See also Rebecca Konyndyk DeYoung, *Glittering Vices: A New Look at the Seven Deadly Sins and Their Remedies* (Grand Rapids, MI: Brazos Press, 2009), 170: "Our sexual desires and pleasures should be integrated into our personal and social and spiritual lives such that they serve to enhance our full humanness and the possibility of loving each other. Our control over them helps them serve us; our indulgence of them makes them our masters, even as they leave us empty."

59. See Aquinas, *ST* II-II, q. 156, a. 2. Aquinas notes that "incontinence," when it has to do with food, drink, or sex, "is a sin for two reasons: first, because the incontinent man goes astray from that which is in accord with reason; secondly, because he plunges into shameful pleasures" (ibid.).

60. See Aquinas, *ST* II-II, q. 156, a. 3.

61. David A. deSilva, *Honor, Patronage, Kinship and Purity: Unlocking New Testament Culture* (Downers Grove, IL: InterVarsity Press, 2000), 92.

62. Barclay, *Paul and the Gift*, 518. Barclay adds that for Paul, "God's grace does not exclude, deny, or displace believing agents; they are not reduced to passivity or pure receptivity. Rather, it generates and grounds an active, willed conformity to the Christ-life, in which believers become, like Christ, truly human, as obedient agents" (ibid., 519).

63. Pope Francis, *Amoris Laetitia*, §234. On the nature of accompaniment that is truly "sympathetic," see John S. Grabowski's discussion of "an authentic gradualism" in *Sex and Virtue: An Introduction to Sexual Ethics* (Washington, DC: Catholic University of America Press, 2003), 162–63. Grabowski notes,

> In his Apostolic Exhortation *Familiaris consortio* Pope John Paul II makes a distinction between what he calls "the law of gradualness" and

"the gradualness of the law." The "law of gradualness" refers to the fact that conversion is an ongoing process in the life of a Christian.... The idea behind the "gradualness of the law" is rather different. In this view, there are "different degrees or forms of precept in God's law for different individuals and situations." Hence if particular groups find some moral norm too burdensome, it ought to be changed or at least accommodated to them in some fashion. (ibid., 162, citing *Familiaris Consortio*, apostolic exhortation, November 22, 1981, §34, available at the Vatican website, http://w2.vatican.va/content/vatican/en.html)

Grabowski rightly points out that

> it is negative norms that exclude certain behaviors that provide a foundation for subsequent growth in moral freedom. To undermine these first principles of moral growth is to significantly damage the possibility of the development of virtue that capacitates one for the beatitude of union with God. Followers of Jesus need to continually be challenged to the full measure of excellence and flourishing, even if they fall short of it. The answer to this aspect of the human condition is not to attempt to change norms that flow from the biblical witness and the Church's tradition, but to recall the constant mercy of God that precedes and undergirds the whole of the Christian moral life. (*Sex and Virtue*, 163)

Grabowski is responding to such works as Margaret Farley, R.S.M., "An Ethic for Same-Sex Relations," in *A Challenge to Love: Gay and Lesbian Catholics in the Church*, ed. Robert Nugent (New York: Crossroad, 1983), 93–106. Earlier in his analysis of moral growth (an analysis drawn from Pinckaers's *Sources of Christian Ethics*, 359–71), Grabowski explains that "moral norms such as those prohibiting extramarital or anti-procreative forms of sexual activity can lay a foundation for a person's growth in freedom. But this only occurs through the interiorization of these norms and the moral goods that they serve to protect through repeated moral choices and the interior work of the Holy Spirit" (*Sex and Virtue*, 161). Against the modern tendency toward an individualistic ethics, see Sacks, *To Heal a Fractured World*; Milbank and Pabst, *Politics of Virtue*.

64. Pope Francis, *Amoris Laetitia*, §234.

65. Pope Francis, *Evangelii Gaudium*, §170. In *Amoris Laetitia*, Pope Francis takes up the question of the canonical status vis-à-vis the Eucharist of those who have been divorced and remarried in civil law without an ecclesiastical annulment of their first marriage. He argues, "When a responsible and tactful person, who does not presume to put his or her

desires ahead of the common good of the Church, meets with a pastor capable of acknowledging the seriousness of the matter before him, there can be no risk that a specific discernment may lead people to think that the Church maintains a double standard" (*Amoris Laetitia*, §300). Although Pope Francis is here referring to a "double standard" on the part of priest-counselors allowing exceptions for those whom they favor, I note that the Church cannot adopt a "double standard" about whether a valid sacramental marriage is dissoluble. Here the magisterium of the Church, guided by the Holy Spirit, has been consistent over twenty centuries in its interpretation of Christ's words about the indissolubility of marriage—words that were offensive and surprising to his disciples, who replied, "If such is the case of a man with his wife, it is not expedient to marry" (Mt 19:10). Pope Francis has repeatedly underscored that he does not intend to weaken or undermine the Church's teaching on the indissolubility of sacramental marriage, which is the standard by which pastoral strategies must be judged. See also the analysis offered by Paul Josef Cardinal Cordes, "'Without Rupture or Discontinuity,'" in *Eleven Cardinals Speak on Marriage and the Family: Essays from a Pastoral Viewpoint*, trans. Michael J. Miller et al., ed. Winfried Aymans (San Francisco: Ignatius Press, 2015), 17–38, as well as Stephan Kampowski's "A Promise to Keep: Which Bond, Whose Fidelity?," *Nova et Vetera* 13 (2015): 489–514. See also the essays in Margaret Harper McCarthy, ed., *Torn Asunder: Children, the Myth of the Good Divorce, and the Recovery of Origins* (Grand Rapids, MI: Eerdmans, 2017). For the timely point that both the Council of Trent and magisterial teaching since Trent have taught definitively "that the bond of a Christian marriage is indissoluble" and "that this is a truth of divine revelation," so that "the doctrine of absolute indissolubility cannot not be true" (unless one holds that the Catholic Church has no power to interpret Scripture authoritatively, which is the contrary of what the Church has always understood to be the case, and which would de facto invalidate all Church teaching as an authoritative guide to the meaning of divine revelation), see E. Christian Brugger, *The Indissolubility of Marriage and the Council of Trent* (Washington, DC: Catholic University of America Press, 2017), 146–47.

66. Andy Johnson, *Holiness and the Missio Dei* (Eugene, OR: Cascade, 2016), 191.

67. Aristotle, *Politics*, trans. Benjamin Jowett (New York: Random House, 1943), 1.2.1253a1, p. 54. David Hume would agree that many of temperance's associated virtues are social virtues: "Meekness, beneficence, charity, generosity, clemency, moderation, equity bear the greatest figure among the moral qualities, and are commonly denominated the *social* virtues, to mark their tendency to the good of society" (Hume, *A Treatise of*

Human Nature, ed. Ernest C. Mossner [London: Penguin, 1969], 629). Against the view that the ethics of happiness is self-centered or self-serving, Daniel Russell points out that "we can easily recognize that people usually live happy lives in taking the good of others as an end of their own. Such ends are ones that happy people usually choose to love in their lives: helping the poor or the homeless can be such an end, but more commonly people take devotion to a partner as an end, or raising their children" (Daniel C. Russell, "Virtue Ethics, Happiness, and the Good Life," in Russell, *Cambridge Companion to Virtue Ethics*, 22). He devotes extensive attention to showing that "if one's final end is eudaimonia, then doing well by others is much more than something he just *might* do; it is something he would *have* to do.... A crucial part of our humanity is our sociality" (ibid., 24). Russell also emphasizes the importance of living rationally: "Whatever human happiness is ... it must be the happiness of a creature whose characteristic mode of life is to live by directing itself through practical reasoning" (ibid., 13; cf. 17).

68. Sacks, *To Heal a Fractured World*, 243.

69. Stanley Hauerwas, *A Community of Character: Toward a Constructive Christian Social Ethic* (Notre Dame, IN: University of Notre Dame Press, 1981), 5.

70. Ibid. In light of the contemporary ideal of "the autonomous, self-sufficient, free person," Hauerwas adds, "In our society the family has been rendered problematic by the attempt to create the limited state in the name of the freedom of the individual. The social roles of the family have been sacrificed in the interest of creating an individualistic economic and political order. This kind of society did not seem directly inimical to the interest of the family, since the individual could decide to start a family if he or she so desired. The crucial point, however, is that the political units were assumed to be, not the state and the family, but the state and the individual.... The family in our society thus appears morally irrational. It is simply part of the necessities of our life that the free person should learn to outgrow. For to be part of a family is to accept a limit that I have not chosen" (ibid., 170–71). He extends these points to the Church. See also Hauerwas's *Character and the Christian Life: A Study in Theological Ethics* (Notre Dame, IN: University of Notre Dame Press, 1994), originally published by Trinity University Press in 1975.

71. *ST* I-II, q. 110, a. 3; I-II, q. 112, a. 1, ad 2.

72. *ST* I, q. 43, a. 3. Kenneth M. Loyer summarizes Aquinas's understanding of the eschatological outpouring of the Holy Spirit: "For Aquinas, the same Spirit who proceeds eternally as the bond of love between the Father and the Son is sent, in temporal mission, to inhabit the hearts of the

faithful in the gift of sanctifying grace, to make them like God by grace, and to draw them into the life and love of God" (*God's Love through the Spirit: The Holy Spirit in Thomas Aquinas and John Wesley* [Washington, DC: Catholic University of America Press, 2014], 157). See also my *Engaging the Doctrine of the Holy Spirit: Love and Gift in the Trinity and the Church* (Grand Rapids, MI: Baker Academic, 2016), as well as Christopher J. H. Wright, *Cultivating the Fruit of the Spirit: Growing in Christlikeness* (Downers Grove, IL: IVP Academic, 2017).

73. Gilles Emery, O.P., "The Holy Spirit in Aquinas's Commentary on Romans," in *Reading Romans with St. Thomas Aquinas*, ed. Matthew Levering and Michael Dauphinais (Washington, DC: Catholic University of America Press, 2012), 127. For a demonstration of the same point, see Emery, "Holy Spirit," in *The Cambridge Companion to the "Summa Theologiae,"* ed. Philip McCosker and Denys Turner (Cambridge: Cambridge University of America Press, 2016), 129–41. See also the argument of Jean-Marc Laporte, S.J., that "the Spirit, and God as beginning and end, play a key role in the structuring of the *Summa*. But so does Christ. His role is pervasive" (Christ in Aquinas's *Summa theologiae*: Peripheral or Pervasive?," *Thomist* 67 [2003]: 248). And see the conclusions of Dominic Legge, O.P., *The Trinitarian Christology of St Thomas Aquinas* (Oxford: Oxford University Press, 2017), 238–40. For Emery's broader approach, see his collection of essays *Présence de Dieu et union à Dieu* (Paris: Parole et Silence, 2017).

74. Marie-Dominique Chenu, O.P., *Aquinas and His Role in Theology*, trans. Paul Philibert, O.P. (Collegeville, MN: Liturgical Press, 2002), 107. Chenu emphasizes that the notion that the sense appetites can become virtuous is not a given in Christian theology: "In contrast to Bonaventure (and to many others after him down to our days), Thomas Aquinas held that the virtues of temperance and fortitude (as they are technically named) are seated not in the will but in the emotive powers of the sensitive appetites" (ibid., 108).

75. Edgardo A. Colón-Emeric, *Wesley, Aquinas, and Christian Perfection: An Ecumenical Dialogue* (Waco, TX: Baylor University Press, 2009), 93. See also Daria Spezzano's chapter "The Grace of the Holy Spirit," in *The Glory of God's Grace: Deification according to St. Thomas Aquinas* (Ave Maria, FL: Sapientia Press, 2015), 105–51, as well as Bernhard Blankenhorn's chapter "Grace in Thomas," in *The Mystery of Union with God: Dionysian Mysticism in Albert the Great and Thomas Aquinas* (Washington, DC: Catholic University of America Press, 2015), 249–95. For the implications of Aquinas's doctrine of the gifts of the Holy Spirit, see Steven A. Long, "The Gifts of the Holy Spirit and Their Indispensability for

the Christian Moral Life: Grace as *Motus*," *Nova et Vetera* 11 (2013): 357–73; M. J. Nicholas, "Les dons du Saint-Esprit," *Revue Thomiste* 92 (1992): 141–53. For the view that "the operative effects of the gifts supplement the imperfect possession of the virtues by the subject," see John M. Meinert, *The Love of God Poured Out: Grace and the Gifts of the Holy Spirit in St. Thomas Aquinas* (Steubenville, OH: Emmaus Academic, 2018), 269. Jennifer Herdt notes correctly that for Aquinas, "charity does not take away the specific character of the other virtues but allows an act of virtue to serve its own proximate end while also being directed to the ultimate end" (*Putting on Virtue: The Legacy of the Splendid Vices* [Chicago: University of Chicago Press, 2012], 85).

76. *ST* I-II, q. 112, a. 1, ad 2. Here and elsewhere, I have changed "Holy Ghost" to "Holy Spirit." See also Reginald M. Lynch, O.P., *The Cleansing of the Heart: The Sacraments as Instrumental Causes in the Thomistic Tradition* (Washington, DC: Catholic University of America Press, 2017). Lynch observes that "theological discussion of the sacraments in the mid- to late twentieth century has been centered on liturgical praxis or experience within the context of the Church, rather than on the nature of instrumental causality," but in fact "our attempts to understand the sacramental reality of grace at work in the Church must necessarily raise the question of the way in which the sacraments have this effect" (ibid., 65).

77. Thomas Aquinas, *Commentary on the Gospel of St. Matthew*, trans. Paul M. Kimball (n.p.: Dolorosa Press, 2012), 292 (commenting on Mt 6:33).

78. Frederick Christian Bauerschmidt, "Doctrine: Knowing and Doing," in *The Morally Divided Body: Ethical Disagreement and the Disunity of the Church*, ed. Michael Root and James J. Buckley (Eugene, OR: Cascade, 2012), 40–41.

79. Schimmel, *Seven Deadly Sins*, 9.

80. The virtues associated with temperance can appear to be focused solely on the individual. Indeed, as Jean Porter comments, "Both fortitude and temperance are primarily ordered towards maintaining the individual's equilibrium between passions and reasoned judgments about the overall good, and in that sense they both have the good of the individual as their primary focus" ("Virtue Ethics in the Medieval Period," 85). As Porter and Aquinas know, however, the "good of the individual" is not the good of the individual *in isolation*. Temperance, while perfective of the individual, has large social implications. Thus, the passion of shame keeps us attuned to how our actions affect the needs of families and communities; the virtue of abstinence (the opposite of gluttony) enables us to eat and drink with awareness that others in our families and communities need to be able to

eat and drink too; the virtue of chastity recalls us to the truth that our sexual actions bear profoundly upon others, especially children, who need to be raised by their parents; the virtues of clemency and meekness help us keep our anger from overflowing in explosive ways that destroy families and communities; the virtue of humility properly relates us to others, so that we appreciate the great good that we find in others and we do not overestimate our own talents in ways that deeply damage our ability to interact with and work with others; and the virtue of studiousness ensures that we seek knowledge in order to share it joyfully with others rather than for self-aggrandizement, mastery, and control.

81. Aquinas, *Commentary on the Gospel of St. Matthew*, 292, 403 (commenting on Mt 6:33 and 11:11).

82. Ibid., 88 (commenting on Mt 3:2); *ST* III, q. 69, a. 5. For discussion see Richard Cross, "Thomas Aquinas," in *The Spiritual Senses: Perceiving God in Western Christianity*, ed. Paul L. Gavrilyuk and Sarah Coakley (Cambridge: Cambridge University Press, 2012), 181.

83. Jean Porter, "Right Reason and the Love of God: The Parameters of Aquinas' Moral Theology," in *The Theology of Thomas Aquinas*, ed. Rik Van Nieuwenhove and Joseph Wawrykow (Notre Dame, IN: University of Notre Dame Press, 2005), 170.

84. Fradd, *Porn Myth*, 23. Gary Wilson notes that people are vulnerable to pornography not least because it "can be a form of self-medication for boredom, frustration, stress or loneliness," but he shows that it actually causes a deeper boredom, frustration, and loneliness (*Your Brain on Porn*, 113). As he points out, what we need is real human connection. See also Everett Fritz, *Freedom: Battle Strategies for Conquering Temptation* (San Francisco: Ignatius Press, 2015).

85. Wright, *After You Believe*, 242. Wright's full sentence is more pointed and indicates that he may not have yet read or assimilated the work of Pinckaers: "I hope that among the effects of this book will be that I have alerted virtue theoreticians to the wealth and depth of material in the New Testament, which they have normally ignored by going straight for the major subsequent exponents, such as Aristotle and Aquinas" (ibid.). See also Daniel Harrington, S.J., and James Keenan, S.J., *Jesus and Virtue Ethics: Building Bridges between New Testament Studies and Moral Theology* (Lanham, MD: Rowman & Littlefield, 2002), although I think that this book, while rightly attentive to the inaugurated kingdom, does not rise to the level of Aquinas's understanding of biblical ethics and virtue (or, concomitantly, of the order of creation and human nature), as can be seen not least when particular moral issues are discussed. Keenan holds that the kingdom of God "is not something to be removed from history" but, as

revealed, "emerges through history," but I note that this claim mistakenly grounds revelation in the historical experience of the economically poor over the centuries, rather than in Jesus' words and deeds in the presence of his disciples (ibid., 108). In his *A History of Catholic Moral Theology in the Twentieth Century: From Confessing Sins to Liberating Consciences* (New York: Continuum, 2010), Keenan barely mentions Pinckaers and strangely deems Pope John Paul II's 1993 encyclical *Veritatis Splendor* an exemplar of "neo-manualism" (128). For the problematic views critiqued by *Veritatis Splendor* and held by Keenan and many others, see William E. May, "Theologians and Theologies in the Encyclical," *Anthropotes* 10 (1994): 39–59. Livio Melina comments that in fact it is those criticized by *Veritatis Splendor* who are the inheritors of the problems (but not the strengths) associated with manualist moral theology: see Melina, *Sharing in Christ's Virtues*, 4–5; see also the insights of William F. Murphy Jr., "Revisiting the Biblical Renewal of Moral Theology in Light of *Veritatis Splendor*," *Nova et Vetera* 2 (2004): 420–29, and my "Pinckaers and Häring on Conscience," *Journal of Moral Theology* 8: Special Issue 2 (2019): 134–65.

86. Second Vatican Council, *Optatam Totius*, §16, in Flannery, *Conciliar and Post Conciliar Documents*, 719–20.

87. Second Vatican Council, *Lumen Gentium*, §3 and §5, in *Trent to Vatican II*, vol. 2 of *Decrees of the Ecumenical Councils*, ed. Norman P. Tanner, S.J. (Washington, DC: Georgetown University Press, 1990), 850–51. For Aquinas on the kingdom of God, see for example his *Commentary on the Sentences of Peter Lombard*, book 4, dist. 49, q. 1, a. 2, in Aquinas, *Opera Omnia* (Paris, 1874), vol. 11, p. 470.

88. Joseph Ratzinger, "The Church's Teaching Authority—Faith—Morals," in *Principles of Christian Morality*, ed. Heinz Schürmann, Joseph Ratzinger, and Hans Urs von Balthasar, trans. Graham Harrison (San Francisco: Ignatius Press, 1986), 65.

CHAPTER TWO. Shame and *Honestas*

1. Michael J. Gorman, *Apostle of the Crucified Lord: A Theological Introduction to Paul and His Letters*, 2nd ed. (Grand Rapids, MI: Eerdmans, 2017), 13. See also David A. deSilva, *Honor, Patronage, Kinship and Purity: Unlocking New Testament Culture* (Downers Grove, IL: InterVarsity Press, 2000), chapters 1 and 2; deSilva, *Despising Shame: Honor Discourse and Community Maintenance in the Epistle to the Hebrews* (Atlanta: Scholars Press, 1995). In support of his contention that "the culture of the first-century world was built on the foundational social values of

honor and dishonor," deSilva cites a number of Greco-Roman philosophers, including Isocrates, Aristotle, Seneca, and Quintilian (*Honor, Patronage, Kinship and Purity*, 23). In the same vein, deSilva also cites Proverbs and Sirach. DeSilva directs attention also to John H. Elliott, "Disgraced yet Graced: The Gospel according to 1 Peter in the Key of Honor and Shame," *Biblical Theology Bulletin* 24 (1994): 166–78; Bruce J. Malina and Jerome H. Neyrey, "Honor and Shame in Luke-Acts: Pivotal Values of the Mediterranean World," in *The Social World of Luke-Acts: Models for Interpretation*, ed. Jerome H. Neyrey (Peabody, MA: Hendrickson, 1991), 25–66; Jerome H. Neyrey, *Honor and Shame in the Gospel of Matthew* (Louisville: Westminster John Knox, 1998).

2. Gorman, *Apostle of the Crucified Lord*, 216.

3. Ibid., 222.

4. DeSilva states in sociological terms, "If honor signifies respect for being the kind of person and doing the kinds of things the group values, shame signifies, in the first instance, being seen as less than valuable because one has behaved in ways that run contrary to the values of the group.... In a second sense, however, shame can signify a positive character trait, namely a sensitivity to the opinion of the group such that one avoids those actions that bring disgrace. Out of shame of this kind, a woman refuses an adulterous invitation" (deSilva, *Honor, Patronage, Kinship and Purity*, 25).

5. See ibid., 44–45, 51–84.

6. See ibid., 67.

7. Chereso, *Virtue of Honor and Beauty according to St. Thomas Aquinas*, 73. Chereso adds a further clarification, indebted to Cardinal Cajetan:

> It seems that flight from disgrace, and love of spiritual beauty are not more attributable to temperance than to the other moral virtues. It is certain that *verecundia* and *honestas* are common to all the moral virtues; for, in every matter of moral virtue, it is always dishonorable to recede from reason, and honorable to be conformed with it. Therefore, *verecundia* and *honestas* are not the names of integral parts of temperance only. It can be conceded that shamefacedness and *honestas* are general conditions which are necessary for the perfection of any moral virtue. Nevertheless, *honestas*—with shamefacedness—is especially appropriated as an integral part of temperance for the same reason that the general name of 'temperance' or 'moderation' is appropriated to the special, cardinal virtue of temperance: the matters of temperance and intemperance present a special need and difficulty with regards to moderation and proportioning, and are apt to exhibit the greatest kind

of ugliness or beauty. Hence, while the disgrace which temperance flees, and the beauty which it loves are confined to its own particular matters, that disgrace and that beauty share more in the 'generic' notions of beauty and disgrace and are therefore more conspicuous than the peculiar disgrace or beauty of any other of the moral vices or virtues. (ibid., 73–74)

8. See ibid., 64–65, 81.
9. N. T. Wright, *Jesus and the Victory of God* (Minneapolis: Fortress, 1996), 204–5.
10. Ibid., 205. See also Jon D. Levenson's Jewish biblical theology, *Sinai and Zion: An Entry into the Jewish Bible* (San Francisco: Harper & Row, 1985), for its discussion of the theology of the temple.
11. For succinct historical-critical background to the text of Ezekiel 8–11, see Joseph Blenkinsopp, *Ezekiel* (Louisville: Westminster John Knox, 2012), 52–64. In the temple precincts, too, there are "women weeping for Tammuz," and—worst of all—men turning their backs upon the sacred altar of God in order to worship the sun (Ezek 8:14, 16). Blenkinsopp offers a helpful explanation of Tammuz:

> The cult of this god, identical with the Sumerian Dumuzi known from the third millennium B.C., may have been introduced into the country by the Assyrians. As with his counterpart Baal-hadad among the Canaanites (cf. Zech. 12:11) and Adonis among the Greeks, the life cycle of Tammuz corresponded to the unchanging round of the agrarian calendar in the Middle East. With the onset of the dry season he disappeared into the underworld, was sought for and lamented by his lover and consort Ishtar (Inanna, Anath, Aphrodite), and in the course of time rose from the realm of the dead to new life with the rebirth of the vegetation. (ibid., 55).

12. For discussion of Ezekiel's portrait of the eschatological temple, see also G. K. Beale, *The Temple and the Church's Mission: A Biblical Theology of the Dwelling Place of God* (Downers Grove, IL: InterVarsity Press, 2004), 110–12, 335–64.
13. Blenkinsopp, *Ezekiel*, 196.
14. For discussion, see Mark A. Throntveit, *Ezra-Nehemiah* (Louisville: Westminster John Knox, 1992), 124–26.
15. Wright, *Jesus and the Victory of God*, 205. For a defense of Wright's view on the return from exile, see Craig A. Evans, "Jesus and the Continuing Exile of Israel."
16. Wright, *Jesus and the Victory of God*, 434.

17. Ibid., 437. See also Nicholas Perrin, *Jesus the Temple* (Grand Rapids, MI: Baker Academic, 2010).

18. Wright, *Paul and the Faithfulness of God*, book 2, p. 711.

19. Ibid., 712–13. As Wright notes, believers' status as the temple of God relates to the fact that God's Spirit is dwelling with them, with the result that they are journeying on the new exodus inaugurated by Christ's Passover and thereby are sharing in Christ's tribulation, strengthened by his Spirit. See ibid., 714, 717–27. As Wright says, "Paul clearly saw the events concerning Jesus as constituting the new Exodus and hence saw the life of the church, indwelt and led by the spirit, as constituting the new version of the time of wilderness wandering" (ibid., 727).

20. In the chapter "Virtue in Action: The Royal Priesthood," in *After You Believe*, Wright points out that "the 'royal' vocation of Jesus's followers must give rise to the hard-won virtues of seeking, generating, and sustaining justice and beauty in a world where both have been at a discount for too long. . . . The line that runs forward from Aristotle's insistence on 'the beautiful and the just' at the start of his *Nicomachean Ethics* is one which Christians should celebrate and advance" (231).

21. Ibid., 232.

22. Perrin, *Jesus the Temple*, ix.

23. Ibid., 10.

24. Ibid. Perrin adds, "This eschatological temple was nothing less than the heavenly temple, the basis for Moses' instructions (Exod. 25.40), come down to earth" (ibid., 11).

25. Ibid., 12, 14.

26. Ibid., 47.

27. Ibid., 55. See also Paul M. Hoskins, *Jesus as the Fulfillment of the Temple in the Gospel of John* (Milton Keynes: Paternoster, 2006); Mary L. Coloe, *God Dwells with Us: Temple Symbolism in the Fourth Gospel* (Collegeville, MN: Liturgical Press, 2001).

28. Perrin, *Jesus the Temple*, 70. Perrin argues that "for Paul the redemptive-historical shift has occurred in Christ and as a result those who are of Christ and filled with the Holy Spirit corporately make up the new locus of God's presence. As members of the eschatological temple, these believers are also ordained to priestly suffering, thereby partaking in the messianic sufferings, for the furtherance of the gospel mission" (ibid.).

29. See ibid., 71–75. See also Gary A. Anderson, *Charity: The Place of the Poor in the Biblical Tradition* (New Haven: Yale University Press, 2013). Timothy J. M. Ling points to "a religious social practice of radical discipleship: the surrender of property, sharing a common purse, and giving alms" (*The Judaean Poor and the Fourth Gospel* [Cambridge: Cam-

bridge University Press, 2006], 145). According to Perrin, Jesus' cleansing of the temple had to do mainly "with the economic injustices of the temple" (Perrin, *Jesus the Temple*, 95; cf. 97, 114–48). Perrin explains these injustices: "By being in a position to leverage usurious, high-risk loans, the temple financiers were then able to foreclose quickly and efficiently on landholders struggling to eke out an existence. Increased temple landholdings eventually meant more wealth for the priestly elite, more wealth meant even more high-interest loans, more high-interest loans meant more foreclosures on the land" (ibid., 97). For further discussion of almsgiving's place in the gospels, see Nathan Eubank, *Wages of Cross-Bearing and Debt of Sin: The Economy of Heaven in Matthew's Gospel* (Berlin: Walter de Gruyter, 2013); Anthony Giambrone, O.P., *Sacramental Charity, Creditor Christology, and the Economy of Salvation in Luke's Gospel* (Tübingen: Mohr Siebeck, 2017).

30. Perrin, *Jesus the Temple*, 179.

31. Building upon the biblical link between cultic purity and sexual purity, Aquinas argues that "purity belongs properly to chastity" (*ST* II-II, q. 151, a. 4, sed contra).

32. Wright, *After You Believe*, 234, 251–52. Before turning to his account of the fundamental Christian moral virtues, including chastity or self-control (temperance), Wright notes that "we should expect that God's glory will be reflected out into the world when Jesus's followers learn the habits of mind, heart, and life that imitate the generous love of Jesus and thus bring new order, beauty, and freedom to the world. It is hugely important that we see these habits precisely as *virtues*, not simply as 'principles' to be 'applied' or 'values' to be 'embraced'" (ibid., 234). Spelling this out further, Wright asks and answers an important question: "Is there a complete disjunction between the *theory* of virtue, as (for instance) in Aristotle or Seneca, and the theory we have seen developing in the proclamation of Jesus and the teaching of Paul? No. . . . For Aristotle, we become virtuous by doing virtuous deeds: 'second nature' develops, and we grow into the full attainment of that which, glimpsing the 'goal' of complete human flourishing, we have begun to practice. So for Paul, taking 1 Corinthians 13 as the obvious example: here is the goal, the state of being *teleios*, complete; here are the qualities of character which contribute to it; here are the steps you must take to practice that quality of character. . . . What Paul is arguing for is a Christian form of the ancient pagan theory of virtue. But it has indeed been thoroughly Christianized" (ibid., 239–40). Wright identifies the new Christian virtue of humility as evidence of this Christianizing.

33. *ST* II-II, q. 143, a. 1.

34. Ibid.

35. *ST* II-II, q. 141, a. 2, ad 3.

36. Wright, *After You Believe*, 242.

37. Chereso's whole passage is worth quoting: "The integral parts of the virtue of temperance may be derived by considering the requirements for its perfect operation. Since temperance must expel that which is most disgraceful and ugly for man, it is necessary that he have a fear of—even a revulsion for—the most disgraceful of vices. He must have this fear and revulsion to the extent that he will flee instinctively every occasion of contracting the disgrace and ugliness of intemperance. This fear of, and flight from anything even merely suggestive of the disgrace of intemperance is an integral part which St. Thomas calls 'shamefacedness'—*verecundia*.... But a man will fear and flee the shameful vice of intemperance only when he has a love—an instinctive appreciation and aptitude—for the opposite good, for love is the principle or root of all the movements of the soul. Therefore, since the opposite of the disgracefulness of intemperance is the *honestas* or spiritual beauty of temperance, man will fear and fly from the ugliness of intemperance in the proportion that he loves the beauty of temperance. And inasmuch as an act is specified by its object, the very act of loving the *honestas* of temperance is also called *honestas*" (*Virtue of Honor and Beauty according to St. Thomas Aquinas*, 72–73).

38. *ST* II-II, q. 144, a. 1, citing John of Damascus, *On the Orthodox Faith*, 2.15. Somewhat differently, the modern English text of Damascene's work here reads "a fear due to the perpetration of a shameful act": see John of Damascus, "An Exact Exposition of the Orthodox Faith," in John of Damascus, *Writings*, trans. Frederic H. Chase Jr. (Washington, DC: Catholic University of America Press, 1958), 240–41. See also Albert Plé, O.P., *Chastity and the Affective Life*, trans. Marie-Claude Thompson (New York: Herder and Herder, 1966), 131–34. Plé emphasizes that the "two passions, *verecundia* and *honestas*, must not be confused with the virtue of temperance: they prepare it and dispose to it" (ibid., 134). He notes that even honestas is only "a favorable passional disposition to virtue; it changes into virtue in proportion as the superior powers of the rational order exert their action" (ibid.).

39. *ST* II-II, q. 144, a. 1.

40. *ST* II-II, q. 144, a. 1; Chereso, *Virtue of Honor and Beauty according to St. Thomas Aquinas*, 73. See also the helpful discussion of shame and honestas in Paul J. Wadell, *The Primacy of Love: An Introduction to the Ethics of Thomas Aquinas* (Mahwah, NJ: Paulist Press, 1992), 133–36. Wadell rightly recognizes that "Aquinas saw no division between the moral

and the spiritual life. For him they were one, and to attempt to separate them was to forget that the overall purpose of the moral life was to make us the kind of people whose lives are songs of praise to a God whose love is unending. Thomas knew that the moral life is the Christian life, that to grow in goodness is to be transfigured in holiness, and that charity is no idle love, but is the virtue that makes our whole life an offering to God" (ibid., 1). He opposes the view that Aquinas's moral theology is "overly rationalistic, excessively formal, and too scholastic to be of use to us today" (ibid.). Perhaps because of the time in which he was writing—the early 1990s—he does not recognize how unified Aquinas's understanding of natural law is with his understanding of the virtues. Wadell somewhat undervalues the importance of reason, by negatively contrasting "acts of reason" with "strategies of love whereby those devoted to God are transformed in God's goodness" (ibid.).

41. *ST* II-II, q. 144, a. 2, obj. 1.

42. Ibid., obj. 3.

43. Ibid., obj. 4. Aquinas accepts that shame can also be present in people who possess virtue imperfectly, and who therefore become ashamed (despite themselves) when their virtuous actions incur public reproach (see ibid., ad 1). It is easy to say, "Fear not the reproach of men, and be not dismayed at their revilings" (Is 51:7), but when people are enduring such revilings, they may feel shame despite themselves. People may also feel ashamed about their virtuous deeds because the community no longer perceives these deeds as virtuous (though in fact they are).

44. *ST* II-II, q. 144, a. 2, sed contra. See Chereso, *Virtue of Honor and Beauty according to St. Thomas Aquinas*, xvii–xviii.

45. See also Jonathan Sacks, *Essays on Ethics: A Weekly Reading of the Jewish Bible* (New Milford, CT: Maggid Books, 2016), 147.

46. *ST* II-II, q. 144, a. 2.

47. *ST* II-II, q. 144, a. 4.

48. *ST* II-II, q. 144, a. 4, obj. 1.

49. *ST* II-II, q. 144, a. 4.

50. Gabriele Taylor, *Pride, Shame, and Guilt: Emotions of Self-Assessment* (Oxford: Oxford University Press, 1985), 80. Thus, I see a positive place for shame among those who have sinned, even though shame is praiseworthy especially when it helps to restrain sin. More critically with respect to shame, Thomas J. Bushlack states: "For more advanced practitioners of Christian mindfulness awareness of one's sinfulness and of the ongoing struggle with vices then becomes a call to return to quiet contemplation. Personal struggles with disordered passions foster mindfulness of

one's total dependency upon God in each moment, rather than encouraging moments of recoiling from God in shame" ("Mindfulness and the Discernment of Passions: Insights from Thomas Aquinas," *Spiritus: A Journal of Christian Spirituality* 14 [2014]: 157). Shame before God has both negative and positive aspects, as Bushlack would likely agree.

51. *ST* II-II, q. 144, a. 3.
52. See *ST* II-II, q. 144, a. 3, ad 2.
53. *ST* II-II, q. 144, a. 3 and ad 1.
54. See *ST* II-II, q. 144, a. 4, ad 4.
55. *ST* II-II, q. 144, a. 4.
56. Aquinas remarks, for example, that "the sin of gluttony is diminished . . . both on account of the necessity of taking food, and on account of the difficulty of proper discretion and moderation in such matters" (*ST* II-II, q. 148, a. 3).
57. *ST* II-II, q. 144, a. 4, obj. 1.
58. *ST* II-II, q. 144, a. 4, ad 1.
59. *ST* II-II, q. 144, a. 4, ad 4.
60. *ST* II-II, q. 144, a. 4.
61. Taylor, *Pride, Shame, and Guilt*, 81. Taylor admits that the person "may or may not be right in his view of what needs protecting, he may be muddled and misguided in this matter, and so concentrate his energies on protecting a part of himself that is not worth protecting" (ibid.).
62. See *ST* II-II, q. 145, a. 4. For discussion, see Bernard, *Les parties integrales de la temperance selon saint Thomas*, 47–52, 57–58. Bernard also explores the influence of Albert the Great.
63. *ST* II-II, q. 145, a. 1.
64. For discussion, see Chereso, *Virtue of Honor and Beauty according to St. Thomas Aquinas*, 38–42. He points out that "the essential interiority of virtue, and the exteriority implied by *honestum* are reconcilable. As Aristotle teaches, virtue is principally an interior choice. But this interior election of virtue cannot be known—and honored—by other men unless it be externalized in virtuous activity. And yet, exterior conduct has the nature of *honestum* only insofar as it echoes interior rectitude. Radically, therefore, *honestas* consists in internal choice. Exterior activity is merely its expression or manifestation" (ibid., 42).
65. *ST* II-II, q. 145, a. 1, ad 1.
66. As Chereso notes, "It has been generally observed that the Angelic Doctor has not written an *ex professo* work on the nature of the beautiful. The few, broad esthetic principles that he does enunciate are scattered throughout his works, and, at that, are usually occasioned by his preoccupation with other notions which must be distinguished from that of beauty.

And yet, St. Thomas Aquinas has focused his attention on a particular phase of beauty: moral or spiritual beauty. The treatise that he has left on spiritual beauty might easily go unnoticed because it is not found in a separate work and under a special title, but rather makes its appearance in the *Secunda Secundae* of his *Summa Theologiae*—in the *De Honestate* question in the tract on temperance" (*Virtue of Honor and Beauty according to St. Thomas Aquinas*, xi). Chereso treats Aquinas on beauty, arguing that it is a transcendental, in chapter 1 of his study (see also 78–80), and he notes that beauty involves "integrity or perfection, due proportion or consonance, and clarity" (ibid., 15; cf. 80–82). For contemporary discussion of Aquinas on beauty (and for the view that beauty is not a transcendental for Aquinas), see Jan A. Aertsen, *Medieval Philosophy and the Transcendentals: The Case of Thomas Aquinas* (Leiden: Brill, 1996). See also Michael Waddell, "Integrating Beauty: Reflections on the Psychology, Ontology and Etiology of Thomas Aquinas's *Summa Theologiae* 1.5.4," *Saint Anselm Journal* 8 (2012): 1–18.

67. *ST* II-II, q. 145, a. 2, obj. 2.

68. Chereso points out that the Vulgate version of 1 Corinthians 12:12–26 provides Aquinas with "a parallel drawn between *inhonesta* and *turpia* on the one hand, and between *honesta* and *pulchra* on the other. *Inhonesta* translates the Greek, aschèmona, which means, literally, those things which are lacking in form; *honesta* translates the Greek, euschèmona, and this refers to things which are well formed" (*Virtue of Honor and Beauty according to St. Thomas Aquinas*, xvii).

69. *ST* II-II, q. 145, a. 2.

70. Ibid.

71. For an extended discussion of this point, see Chereso, *Virtue of Honor and Beauty according to St. Thomas Aquinas*, 42–51. He notes that "virtue is that by which man's whole life is proportioned according to the spiritual clarity of reason. Virtue, therefore, is the same as spiritual beauty. And inasmuch as *honestum* is the same as virtue, it is also the same as the spiritually beautiful" (ibid., 47).

72. *ST* II-II, q. 145, a. 2, citing Augustine's *Eighty-Three Different Questions*, q. 30. See Chereso, *The Virtue of Honor and Beauty according to St. Thomas Aquinas*, 47.

73. Aquinas adds that when we perceive something to be beautiful, we take it to be good and therefore "an object of desire" (*ST* II-II, q. 145, a. 2, ad 1). Similarly, whatever we recognize to be honorable and praiseworthy, we take to have "clarity" (ibid., ad 2). Thus reasonable self-control in our appetites for food, drink, and sex does not mean a repressed and unattractive puritanical bent, but rather reflects honor, desirability, and beauty.

Such persons, as beautiful temples of God, can fulfill natural appetites in a manner that gives glory to God and that truly cares for neighbor.

74. See *ST* II-II, q. 145, a. 3 (including the sed contra and ad 1). Chereso comments that "neither *honestas*, nor beauty can be formally identified with utility and delight. When the Angelic Doctor divides the transcendentally good into *honestum*, the useful, and the delightful, he warns that the division is not one of opposed entities, but of opposed formalities.... While *honestas*, utility, and delight are materially the same and formally distinct, . . . *honestas* and spiritual beauty are one and the same formality" (*Virtue of Honor and Beauty according to St. Thomas Aquinas*, 50). Chereso adds that virtue "always contains three distinct formalities: *honestas* because of the beauty it has from reason's order and clarity; delight because the appetite rests in the possession of virtue as in the possession of a natural and fitting good; and utility because it leads to final happiness" (ibid., 51).

75. *ST* II-II, q. 145, a. 3.

76. Ibid.

77. *ST* II-II, q. 145, a. 4, obj. 3. For discussion of this problem, see Chereso, *Virtue of Honor and Beauty according to St. Thomas Aquinas*, chapter 3. Chereso remarks that given Aquinas's "singling out of the general condition of moderation or proportion as significant for beauty," it follows that "if there is one of the four cardinal virtues which is especially noted for its work of moderation or consonance, then that virtue will exhibit spiritual beauty in a more noticeable way" (ibid., 53).

78. See *ST* II-II, q. 145, a. 4, obj. 3.

79. *ST* II-II, q. 145, a. 4. Chereso states that "the particular excellence and honorableness of temperance is due to its work of placing a check and measure on man's vehement propensity to renounce and desert reason in favor of those pleasures which enslave him to the order of brute nature" (*Virtue of Honor and Beauty according to St. Thomas Aquinas*, 59–60). Note that the comparison with animals here indicates not a degradation of animals, but what happens when a rational animal tries to act like an irrational animal. Romano Guardini remarks, with some exaggeration but still along insightful lines: "No animal follows the drive toward food as much as a man who makes the pleasure its own end and thereby harms himself. In no animal does the sexual urge reach the boundless extent which it has in a man who permits it to destroy his honor and his life. No animal has the urge to kill that man has. His wars have no real counterpart in the animal kingdom. All that we can call an urge operates differently in a man than in an animal. The spirit gives a unique freedom to the life-impulses; they become stronger and deeper, with far greater possibilities of demand

and response. But at the same time, they lose the protection of the organic order which binds and secures them in the animal" (Guardini, *Learning the Virtues That Lead You to God* [Manchester, NH: Sophia Institute Press, 1998], 86–87). In accord with Aquinas's perspective, Guardini finds that "by the spirit, man acquires the possibility of ordering and forming the urge, and so leading it to greater heights, to its own perfection, even as an urge" (ibid., 87)—though I would add that after the fall, this will generally require not simply the human spirit but the action of the Holy Spirit.

80. The citation of Paul here is my own, not Aquinas's.

81. Thomas Aquinas, *Commentary on the Letter of Saint Paul to the Romans*, trans. F. R. Larcher, O.P., ed. J. Mortensen and E. Alarcón (Lander, WY: Aquinas Institute for the Study of Sacred Doctrine, 2012), §617, p. 208.

82. Chereso, *Virtue of Honor and Beauty according to St. Thomas Aquinas*, 63. Of course, Chereso recognizes that "because of the substantial union between the rational and animal in man, man retains his physical integrity even when he is intemperate. Nevertheless, intemperance destroys that integrity virtually, or effectively speaking, that is, inasmuch as an intemperate man fails to act like a man" (ibid., 64). He concludes, "Since, therefore, the greatest degree of ugliness is found in beastly voluptuousness—the condition of the concupiscible appetite which has declared its independence from reason's ordering light—the good of reason which integrates and moderates the desires for voluptuous pleasures shines forth most manifestly in the virtue of temperance" (ibid., 66). See also Aquinas's comments on Romans 13:12: "Here the works of sin are called works of darkness: first, because in themselves they lack the light of reason with which man's works should be illumined: *the wise man has eyes in his head, but the fool walks in darkness* (Eccl 2:14). . . . They [the virtues] are called the armor of light, because they are decorated and perfected by the light of reason; hence it says in Proverbs: *The path of the just is like the light of dawn* (Prov 4:18); and because they are tested by light: *he who does what is true comes to the light* (John 3:2)" (Aquinas, *Letter of Saint Paul to the Romans*, §§1071–72, p. 364).

83. Bernard, *Les parties integrales de la temperance selon saint Thomas*, 59.

84. Pieper, *Four Cardinal Virtues*, 152.

85. Wright, *After You Believe*, 253. Pieper comments similarly with respect to temperance: "For man there are two modes of this turning toward the self: a selfless and a selfish one. Only the former makes for self-preservation; the latter is destructive. In modern psychology we find this thought: genuine self-preservation is the turning of man toward himself, with the essential stipulation, however, that in this movement he does

not become fixed upon himself. ('Whoever fixes his eyes upon himself gives no light.') Temperance is selfless self-preservation. Intemperance is self-destruction through the selfish degradation of the powers which aim at self-preservation" (*Four Cardinal Virtues*, 148; cf. 204–5 on temperance as "liberating").

86. *Sacrosanctum Concilium* §10, in Tanner, *Trent to Vatican II*, 823.

87. Beale, *Temple and the Church's Mission*, 391–92. Beale observes that "the redemptive-historical development may be explained as proceeding from God's unique presence in the structural temple in the Old Testament to the God-man, Christ, the true temple. As a result of Christ's resurrection, the Spirit continued building the end-time temple, the building materials of which are God's people, thus extending the temple into the new creation in the new age. This building process will culminate in the eternal new heavens and earth as a paradisal city-temple. Or, more briefly, the temple of God has been transformed into God, his people and the rest of the new creation as the temple" (ibid., 392–93).

88. DeSilva, *Honor, Patronage, Kinship and Purity*, 78–79. Drawing upon the psychologist Robert Karen, deSilva offers a helpful clarification regarding healthy and unhealthy kinds of shame: "The first [kind of shame] is the 'feeling' or 'experience' of shame (the warmth under the skin and extreme self-consciousness that overtakes an individual when he or she has done something that provokes public disapproval or ridicule); the second is a 'sense' of shame, the 'healthy attitudes that define a wholesome character,' the predilection for avoiding certain behaviors that bring shame.... The third kind of shame, however, is what Karen describes as 'repressed but hounding shame, something activated to the level of gnawing self-doubt, occasionally reaching the intensity of fully inflamed self-hatred,' a kind of shame about who we are that 'drives people toward perfectionism, withdrawal, diffidence, combativeness,' 'a festering negative self-portrait against which one is repeatedly trying to defend'" (ibid., 89). Aquinas, of course, has the second kind of shame in view. DeSilva cites Robert Karen, "Shame," *Atlantic Monthly*, February 1992, 42, 58.

89. Bernard, *Les parties integrales de la temperance selon saint Thomas*, 60.

90. See Pieper, *Four Cardinal Virtues*, 150.

CHAPTER THREE. ABSTINENCE AND SOBRIETY

1. Robert B. Kruschwitz, "Gluttony and Abstinence," in Timpe and Boyd, *Virtues and Their Vices*, 147. For application of this point to the

Eucharist, see Eugene LaVerdiere, S.S.S., *Dining in the Kingdom of God: The Origins of Eucharist in the Gospel of Luke* (Chicago: Liturgy Training Publications, 1994). See also Wendell Berry, "The Pleasures of Eating," in *What Are People For? Essays* (New York: North Point Press, 1990), 145–52, cited in Kruschwitz, "Gluttony and Abstinence," 147. Admittedly, although I wish to minimize human-caused animal misery and to reduce chemical usage, I worry that if animals, vegetables, and fruits had to be raised or cultivated in the specific ways that Berry describes, there would not be enough food, and certainly not enough affordable food, to provide healthy diets at reasonable cost to the people currently living on this planet, with the result being the starvation of the poor. On inevitable conflicts between human needs and those of other species, see Martha C. Nussbaum's observations in her *Frontiers of Justice: Disability, Nationality, Species Membership* (Cambridge, MA: Harvard University Press, 2006), 402.

2. See also Norman Wirzba, *Food and Faith: A Theology of Eating* (Cambridge: Cambridge University Press, 2011), 25; Fred Bahnson, *Soil and Sacrament: A Spiritual Memoir of Food and Faith* (New York: Simon & Schuster, 2013), 9. Aquinas would have agreed with Wirzba that we need to ask such questions as whether "the eating we enjoy deprive[s] others of the ability to eat well" (*Food and Faith*, 201). For Christian vegetarianism, see Stephen H. Webb, *Good Eating* (Grand Rapids, MI: Brazos Press, 2001); David Grumett and Rachel Muers, *Theology on the Menu: Asceticism, Meat and Christian Diet* (London: Routledge, 2010); and many of the essays in David Grumett and Rachel Muers, eds., *Eating and Believing: Interdisciplinary Perspectives on Vegetarianism and Theology* (London: T&T Clark, 2008). For Wirzba's persuasive biblical defense of eating animals, see Wirzba, *Food and Faith*, 132–37. For a fitting emphasis on thanksgiving, see ibid., 179–210. But I am hesitant to join in Wirzba's sharp criticisms of "our desire for 'cheap food'" (ibid., 177) and of the range of methods by which cheap food is made possible, since I fear jeopardizing the lives of countless economically impoverished people alive today. For a Catholic ecological perspective, see Jeanne Heffernan Schindler's "Catholic Social Thought and Environmental Ethics in a Global Context," in *Gathered for the Journey: Moral Theology in Catholic Perspective*, ed. David Matzko McCarthy and M. Therese Lysaught (Grand Rapids, MI: Eerdmans, 2007), 329–48.

3. Dennis Okholm, *Dangerous Passions, Deadly Sins: Learning from the Psychology of the Ancient Monks* (Grand Rapids, MI: Brazos Press, 2014), 12, notes that the topic of gluttony "has been virtually neglected by modern theologians." Similarly, David Grumett and Rachel Muers criticize

"modern theologians and Christian ethicists" for "their failure to take proper account of the theological importance of everyday eating" (Grumett and Muers, *Theology on the Menu*, vii). Although Okholm, Grumett, and Muers are generally correct in this assessment, it is also the case, as the previous endnote shows, that a number of books on virtuous Christian eating have appeared recently, inspired by the ecological movement and by vegetarian perspectives. Norman Wirzba treats gluttony in his *Food and Faith*, 139–40. Okholm notes that the topic of eating has great importance for Christians not least because "eating is not only an absolute necessity for us, it is also centrally important in our lives. Given USDA statistics, between ages twenty and fifty the average person spends about 28,000 hours eating—over 1160 days. Our daily schedules are often planned around mealtimes" (*Dangerous Passions, Deadly Sins*, 12). Okholm recognizes that "eating is crucial in biblical narratives as well. Our first parents plunged the human race into sin by violating a prohibition against eating. The Hebrews were given a sense of identity in a meal that signifies the defining moment in their history—the Passover. The second Adam was victorious over a temptation involving the production and consumption of bread. Christians celebrate their life together in Christ around a family meal initiated by Jesus—one which anticipates the eschatological banquet that will mark the consummation of salvation history" (ibid., 13). On gluttony, Okholm cites Mary Louise Bringle, *The God of Thinness: Gluttony and Other Weighty Matters* (Nashville: Abingdon, 1992).

4. Wirzba, *Food and Faith*, 139. See also the remark of Angel F. Méndez-Montoya, *Theology of Food: Eating and the Eucharist* (Oxford: Wiley-Blackwell, 2009), 112: "If God is superabundant sharing, then theologians must look at how—or not—this divine sharing is repeated in the world's daily exchanges of food."

5. Robert J. Karris, O.F.M., *Eating Your Way through Luke's Gospel* (Collegeville, MN: Liturgical Press, 2006), 97.

6. Pope Benedict XVI, *Deus Caritas Est*, Vatican translation (Boston: Pauline Books & Media, 2006), §32.

7. For background, see John M. Wilkins and Shaun Hill, *Food in the Ancient World* (Oxford: Blackwell, 2006).

8. Okholm, *Dangerous Passions, Deadly Sins*, 20. See also Adalbert de Vogüé, O.S.B., *To Love Fasting: The Monastic Experience* (Petersham, MA: St. Bede's Publications, 1989). In a passage quoted in Scot McKnight's *Fasting: Fasting as Body Talk in the Christian Tradition* (Nashville: Thomas Nelson, 2009), 62, de Vogüé states: "I think the cause [of my joy] is that a certain mastery of the primordial appetite, eating, permits a greater mastery of the other manifestations of the libido and aggressiveness. It is as if the

man who fasts were more himself, in possession of his true identity, and less dependent on exterior objects and the impulses they arouse in him" (*To Love Fasting*, 10). McKnight cautions that "the disciplinary fasting he [de Vogüé] advocates cannot be found explicitly in the pages of the Bible" (*Fasting*, 63). It seems to me, however, that it is present in a sufficiently clear way, as for example in Paul's statement "I pommel my body and subdue it, lest after preaching to others I myself should be disqualified" (1 Cor 9:27). Disagreeing somewhat with Dallas Willard (though largely agreeing with him in the end), McKnight argues: "In spite of Willard's enthusiasm for the disciplines as the embodied training ground for growth in spirituality, one must observe that Paul does not explicitly connect his statement about beating the body to fasting. In the book of Acts, it is said that Paul fasted at his conversion (9:9) and that he participated in group fasting to gain guidance from God (13:2–3; 14:23). But only twice did Paul himself address anything that can be understood today as disciplinary fasting [2 Corinthians 6:4–5 and 11:27].... Is someone else depriving Paul of food and water, or is this Paul's own discipline? The evidence, in my judgment, is not clear. But in light of Paul's comparison of ongoing moral development to athletic discipline, it is quite likely that Paul was an early proponent of fasting as body discipline" (McKnight, *Fasting*, 69–70). I agree with this conclusion.

9. Wright, *New Testament and the People of God*, 234.

10. See also, with regard to the Torah's dietary laws, David Kraemer, *Jewish Eating and Identity through the Ages* (New York: Routledge, 2007).

11. For theological discussion of the manna—and the Eucharist as the new manna—see Méndez-Montoya, *Theology of Food*, 123–42.

12. Among the Torah's instances of fasting, McKnight includes the Day of Atonement as described in Leviticus 23. He identifies three elements to the fasting on the Day of Atonement: "First, this is a grievous sacred moment of confessing sin and finding atonement and forgiveness. Second, Israel's response to the sacredness of this moment is to deny itself of food as well as physical comfort and pleasure. Third, the whole person engages in the act of repentance—not just the heart or the soul or the mind or the spirit" (McKnight, *Fasting*, 27).

13. See Wright, *New Testament and the People of God*, 234–35. For aspects of the Gospels' understanding of the restoration of Israel (and background in biblical and Second Temple sources), see also such studies as Rodrigo J. Morales, *The Spirit and the Restoration of Israel* (Tübingen: Mohr Siebeck, 2010); Michael E. Fuller, *The Restoration of Israel* (Berlin: Walter de Gruyter, 2006); Young S. Chae, *Jesus as the Eschatological Davidic Shepherd* (Tübingen: Mohr Siebeck, 2006); Max Turner, *Power from*

on High: The Spirit in Israel's Restoration and Witness in Luke-Acts (Sheffield: Sheffield Academic, 2000). Regarding the theme of the eschatological restoration of Israel in Galatians, Morales points out that "Paul develops this theme with regard to the daily life of the community. The life that the Spirit gives is not some abstract principle; rather, it is the empowerment the Galatians need to order their lives properly" (*Spirit and the Restoration of Israel*, 163).

14. See Brant Pitre, *Jesus the Bridegroom: The Greatest Love Story Ever Told* (New York: Random House, 2014).

15. For discussion see Arthur Just, *The Ongoing Feast: Table Fellowship and Eschatology at Emmaus* (Collegeville, MN: Liturgical Press, 1993); Brendan Byrne, S.J., *The Hospitality of God: A Reading of Luke's Gospel* (Collegeville, MN: Liturgical Press, 2000); Willi Braun, *Feasting and Social Rhetoric in Luke 14* (Cambridge: Cambridge University Press, 1995); John Koenig, *New Testament Hospitality: Partnership with Strangers as Promise and Mission* (Philadelphia: Fortress, 1985).

16. Pitre, *Jesus and the Last Supper*, 477, 511. See also Pitre's comment, citing 2 Chronicles 30:1–26, that "the idea that Jesus sought to restore the twelve tribes of Israel by celebrating the Passover with representatives of the Twelve tribes is also plausible within a first-century context, since in the Old Testament, it is the Passover feast that King Hezekiah uses as the mechanism in his attempt to restore the twelve tribes of Israel and the unity of the Davidic kingdom" (ibid., 500). For further discussion, see Brant Pitre, "Jesus, the Messianic Wedding Banquet, and the Restoration of Israel," *Letter & Spirit* 8 (2013): 35–54; Scott W. Hahn, *The Kingdom of God as Liturgical Empire: A Theological Commentary on 1–2 Chronicles* (Grand Rapids, MI: Baker Academic, 2012).

17. Pitre, *Jesus and the Last Supper*, 511.

18. Ibid., 512. Pitre adds, "As his teaching regarding the banquet with the patriarchs and his vow at the Last Supper show, for Jesus, as in Second Temple Jewish apocalyptic literature, the kingdom of God was not only an eschatological reality to be tasted at the 'end of the world,' but a heavenly reality that already existed in the invisible transcendent realm. Far too many studies of Jesus and Jewish apocalyptic have placed all of the emphasis on the eschatological and failed to take into account apocalyptic literature's concomitant (and sometimes greater) emphasis on heavenly realities. In this way, the Last Supper itself, as well as the remembrance of it to be celebrated by the disciples after his death, becomes the mechanism of the eschatological restoration of Israel. As the prophetic sign performed by Jesus with the Twelve disciples makes abundantly clear, it is not a geographical restoration Jesus envisaged (any more than it was a biological re-

unification of the twelve tribes), but a cultic restoration—we might even call it a 'eucharistic' restoration—in which the scattered descendants of Israel and the nations spoken of by Isaiah are already beginning to be gathered into the banquet of the heavenly and eschatological kingdom by eating and drinking alongside the patriarchs and the Son of Man himself in the covenant meal instituted by Jesus" (ibid., 516).

19. Ibid., 517. See also Brant Pitre, *Jesus and the Jewish Roots of the Eucharist: Unlocking the Secrets of the Last Supper* (New York: Doubleday, 2011), 177: "Like the Jews at the time of the Temple, Christians are pilgrims journeying toward Jerusalem. However, in the case of the new Passover, the destination is no longer the earthly city of the earthly land, but the new Jerusalem of the heavenly city of God."

20. See also LaVerdiere, *Dining in the Kingdom of God*, 194–99.

21. For discussion, see Wirzba, *Food and Faith*, 150–53. Wirzba argues, "Paul is making the point that life at its best is a Christ-inspired membership of self-offering. Though people may exist as individuals, they do not become fully alive until they are intimately joined to others and committed to their well-being" (ibid., 152). Extending this point by reference to the Orthodox theologian Alexander Schmemann, Wirzba adds that we should "see Eucharistic eating as manifesting God's heavenly kingdom because it *participates* in what it manifests. By eating at the Lord's Table, people are given here and now a glimpse of heaven as the sort of life God desires for the whole creation. . . . [Jesus Christ] instituted a new way of eating in which followers are invited to give their lives to each other" (ibid., 153, referring to Schmemann, *The Eucharist: Sacrament of the Kingdom* [Crestwood, NY: St. Vladimir's Seminary Press, 2003], 200–201).

22. Wirzba, *Food and Faith*, 154. See also the similar perspective of Méndez-Montoya, *Theology of Food*. Wirzba emphasizes the relation of the human eater to what is eaten, whereas my focus is on the relation of the (virtuous or unvirtuous) eater to other people and to God. The two emphases need not be at odds, of course, and Wirzba shows the interrelationship of the two. Though I differ from Wirzba in that I do not prioritize certain modes of cultivation and distribution of food in the way that he does, I am still sympathetic with his point that "if the scope of God's reconciling work extends to the whole creation, then it becomes evident that eating, understood as our most intimate joining with the bodies of creation, must be a primary site and means through which this reconciliation becomes visible. In our eating we are not simply to be reconciled to fellow human eaters. We must also be reconciled to what we eat. How we prepare to eat, as well as the character of the eating itself, demonstrates whether or not we appreciate the wide scope of God's reconciling ways with the

world" (*Food and Faith*, 175). I hold that how we prepare to eat and how we eat are important, but I do not share all the prudential judgments that Wirzba brings to the topic, and in my view other areas of contemporary moral life are more important—though without denying the importance of virtuous eating.

23. Karl Olav Sandnes, *Belly and Body in the Pauline Epistles* (Cambridge: Cambridge University Press, 2002), 92–93.

24. See ibid., 97.

25. Ibid., 105.

26. Ibid., 111.

27. See ibid., 117–20. For background, emphasizing the connections with Stoic philosophy, see Carlos Lévy, "Philo's Ethics," trans. Ada Bronowski, in *The Cambridge Companion to Philo*, ed. Adam Kamesar (Cambridge: Cambridge University Press, 2009), 146–71.

28. Sandnes, *Belly and Body in the Pauline Epistles*, 140; cf. 143. Regarding the identity of those whom Paul criticizes in Philippians 3:19, Gordon D. Fee observes: "Who these people are can only be speculated. Some things remind us of the 'dogs' with which the section began; but their (apparently) libertine ways clearly do not. Most likely Paul is here picking up on the major concerns of his personal narrative in 3:4–14, by reminding the Philippians again of some about whom he has often told them in the past, who have left the way of the cross and are pursuing present, earthly concerns. He is probably describing some itinerants whose view of the faith allows them a great deal of undisciplined self-indulgence. In any case, they have not appeared heretofore in the letter and do not appear again" (*Philippians* [Downers Grove, IL: InterVarsity Press, 1999], 163–64). It would be an unwarranted stretch, in my view, to suppose that in Philippians 3:19 Paul has in view Jewish Christians who continue to practice circumcision and the food laws of Israel.

29. Sandnes, *Belly and Body in the Pauline Epistles*, 151.

30. Ibid., 153; cf. 178. As Sandnes goes on to say, for Paul, "the body is either an instrument for glorifying Christ or a means of worshipping oneself" (ibid., 164; cf. 180).

31. Ibid., 177, 198. Sandnes remarks in his book's conclusion, "Being crucified and raised with Christ must be worked out in a commitment to a new way of life; i.e. enslavement to sin, body and desires belonged to the past. Devoting oneself again to the power of the belly was thus tantamount to nullifying Christ's crucifixion" (ibid., 268).

32. Ibid., 198.

33. Ibid., 199.

34. Ibid., 271.

35. Ibid., 205. Commenting on 1 Corinthians 10, Sandnes states that "the desire of some of the Corinthians to join the tables in the temples is a passion for forbidden food, just as the Jews were longing for meat, not finding God's providence sufficient. . . . The whole tenor of Paul's text evokes the cries for the flesh-pots of Egypt, so widely attested in the Exodus traditions" (ibid., 204–5). Note too that "Philo views the Golden Calf episode as a story about what might happen when the stomach and sexual organs are in control" (ibid., 207). Philo, of course, is here building not only upon the exodus narrative but also upon the Greco-Roman philosophical emphasis on the value of mastery of the bodily passions. As Sandnes observes,

> Plato's anthropology was the basis for the thinking of most moral philosophers. Reason and mind represented a divine element or kinship in human beings, while desires were located in the stomach and the organs below it, i.e. the genitals. These parts of the human body were marks of an earthly identity. The desires of the unruly belly had therefore to be mastered. Mastery of desires became a philosophical commonplace in antiquity, designed to keep the desires of the belly, such as eating, drinking and copulating, under control. All these passions would keep on demanding, take hold of a person and rule him. . . . Persons living like this become selfish and egoistic, their main concern becomes to satisfy their own belly. (ibid., 265–66)

Sandnes adds that Paul, while informed by Greco-Roman philosophical culture, has the exodus narrative centrally in view: "The model which he [Paul] brings out explicitly, in order to explain what belly-worship is all about, is the desert-generation. On a continuous basis they demanded food, and longed for the flesh-pots of Egypt. Finally, they devoted themselves to idolatry, in whose wake followed eating, drinking and copulation. The major contrast figure was . . . Christ" (ibid., 267).

36. Ibid., 213. See at this juncture Sandnes's insightful critique of Dale B. Martin's *The Corinthian Body* (New Haven: Yale University Press, 1995).

37. Hays, *Moral Vision of the New Testament*, 125. Hays here has politics in view, and he is specifically discussing the perspective of Luke-Acts. His position anticipates the insightful perspective of C. Kavin Rowe, *World Upside Down: Reading Acts in the Graeco-Roman Age* (Oxford: Oxford University Press, 2009).

38. For a broader treatment of Christian hospitality, see Christine Pohl, *Making Room: Recovering Hospitality as a Christian Tradition* (Grand Rapids, MI: Eerdmans, 1999). See also John Navone, S.J., "Divine and Human Hospitality," *New Blackfriars* 85 (2004): 329–40.

39. A recent exception is William C. Mattison III's *Introducing Moral Theology: True Happiness and the Virtues* (Grand Rapids, MI: Baker Academic, 2008), which discusses fasting on pages 325–29. Mattison observes that for the believer, "The natural end of eating is not taken away; rather, it is fulfilled and transcended in the broader context of one's supernatural destiny" (ibid., 329). By contrast, unless I have missed it, Hays's *Moral Vision of the New Testament* does not mention fasting. Allen Verhey's textbook on New Testament ethics mentions fasting, but does so somewhat dismissively and without paying it much attention: "The ethic of Jesus is an ethic of response to the coming act of God and its present impact in Jesus himself. The response can be summarized—and was summarized by Mark (1:15) and Matthew (4:17)—as 'repentance.' Repentance is not merely an uneasy conscience prompted by introspection or meditation on the law. It is surely not merely the external gestures of sackcloth and ashes (Mt. 11:21 and par.) or the pious rituals of fasting (Mt. 6:16–18; Mk. 2:18–22 par.)" (Verhey, *The Great Reversal: Ethics and the New Testament* [Grand Rapids, MI: Eerdmans, 1984], 16). Verhey emphasizes that "the great reversal of the coming kingdom does not make its power felt in a rigorous asceticism" (ibid., 19), and he adds that Jesus' followers are "free to live beyond scrupulous observance of fasts and Sabbaths" (ibid., 52). Frank J. Matera's *New Testament Ethics* (Louisville: Westminster John Knox, 1996) recognizes that in the Sermon on the Mount "Jesus explains how disciples are to practice the righteous deeds of almsgiving, prayer, and fasting" (47), but so far as I can tell, Matera does not mention fasting elsewhere in his book.

40. Mary Healy, *The Gospel of Mark* (Grand Rapids, MI: Baker Academic, 2008), 62.

41. Matta El-Maskeen [Matthew the Poor], *The Communion of Love* (Crestwood, NY: St. Vladimir's Seminary Press, 1984), 122. Fr. Matta El-Maskeen, a hermit and later a monk of the Monastery of St. Macarius in the desert of Scetis (Wadi El-Natroon), was born in 1919 and died in 2006.

42. See Curtis Mitch and Edward Sri, *The Gospel of Matthew* (Grand Rapids, MI: Baker Academic, 2010), 102.

43. Healy, *Gospel of Mark*, 63.

44. Wirzba, *Food and Faith*, 137. See also Méndez-Montoya, *Theology of Food*, 154.

45. Wirzba, *Food and Faith*, 137. Wirzba discusses biblical fasting, as well as the witness of the Fathers to fasting, on p. 141. He draws attention to Kent D. Berghuis, *Christian Fasting: A Theological Approach* (Richardson, TX: Biblical Studies Press, 2007), with its translation of Basil the Great's sermon on fasting. As Wirzba says, "When we fast, we learn that

in many of our actions we presume that the world's gifts exist for our own exclusive enjoyment (hence the need to tame the greed and develop the restraint that are at the basis of all just relationships). Fasting, in other words, leads us to a realization about the responsibilities of life together. When we refrain from eating, we not only demonstrate solidarity with those who do not have food to eat but we also demonstrate that food is the precious gift of a self-giving God. It is a gift not to be taken for granted or to be presumed upon. We need to refrain from eating from time to time so that we can more fully appreciate food as a gracious gift, and then also practice the self-offering that will enable others to eat when they don't have enough" (*Food and Faith*, 142).

46. *ST* II-II, q. 143, a. 1.

47. *ST* II-II, q. 141, aa. 2 and 4.

48. *ST* II-II, q. 141, a. 4.

49. *ST* II-II, q. 141, a. 8, obj. 2. Cajetan Chereso, O.P., remarks in this regard, "Experience proves . . . that it is easier to observe justice in external relations with other men than to restrain movements of lust in oneself. For while man has 'despotical' or absolute dominion over his exterior members, he has only 'political' or persuasive dominion over his passions. Then, too, while fear of death might be stronger than lust, the former is of rare occurrence, while the latter arises more frequently, and lies lurking in the makeup of man during his whole life time" (Chereso, *Virtue of Honor and Beauty according to St. Thomas Aquinas*, 61).

50. DeYoung, *Glittering Vices*, 147. Aquinas puts the point technically: "Something can be natural to man in two ways: in one way inasmuch as he is an animal, and in this way it is natural to him that generally speaking the concupiscible power is moved to what is enjoyable according to the senses; in the other way inasmuch as he is a man, i.e., a rational animal, and in this way it is natural to him that the concupiscible power be moved to what is sensually enjoyable according to the order of reason" (Aquinas, *De Malo*, q. 4, a. 2, ad 1; for the English translation see *On Evil*, trans. John A. Oesterle and Jean T. Oesterle [Notre Dame, IN: University of Notre Dame Press, 1995]).

51. See *ST* I-II, q. 33, a. 4. For discussion of the Aristotelian and Augustinian elements of Aquinas's account here, see Kevin White, "Pleasure, a Supervenient End," in *Aquinas and the Nicomachean Ethics*, ed. Tobias Hoffmann, Jörn Müllet, and Matthias Perkams (Cambridge: Cambridge University Press, 2013), 220–38. White explains that for Aquinas "pleasure perfects action in the manner of an *end*, in the secondary sense of *that* term, the sense in which every good that supervenes by way of completion can be called an end. It supervenes on an action as a further good, the good of repose of appetite" (ibid., 237).

52. Aquinas warns that in our fallen state, we are inclined to pursue physical pleasures rather than spiritual pleasures, and to pursue physical pleasures in a wrong way. He observes, "The reason why more [people] seek bodily pleasures is because sensible goods are known better and more generally: and, again, because men need pleasures as remedies for many kinds of sorrow and sadness: and since the majority cannot attain spiritual pleasures, which are proper to the virtuous, hence it is that they turn aside to seek those of the body" (*ST* I-II, q. 31, a. 5, ad 1).

53. Spiritual pleasure or enjoyment of God as the ultimate end "may be said to be the greatest among human goods" (*ST* I-II, q. 34, a. 3). Regarding taking pleasure in things that we should not take pleasure in, Aquinas explains briefly that it can happen that "something which is not natural to man, either in regard to reason, or in regard to the preservation of the body, becomes connatural to this individual man, on account of there being some corruption of nature in him. And this corruption may be either on the part of the body,—from some ailment; thus to a man suffering from fever, sweet things seem bitter, and vice versa,—or from an evil temperament; thus some take pleasure in eating earth and coals and the like; or on the part of the soul; thus from custom some take pleasure in cannibalism or in the unnatural intercourse of man and beast, or other such like things, which are not in accord with human nature" (*ST* I-II, q. 31, a. 7). For discussion of Aquinas's criticism of insensibility to pleasure, see DeYoung, *Glittering Vices*, 148–49.

54. Quoted in *ST* II-II, q. 146, a. 1, obj. 1.

55. *ST* II-II, q. 146, a. 1, ad 1.

56. See Wirzba, *Food and Faith*, 140. See also Okholm, *Dangerous Passions, Deadly Sins*, 15; Daniel A. Westberg, *Renewing Moral Theology: Christian Ethics as Action, Character and Grace* (Downers Grove, IL: IVP Academic, 2015), 213.

57. See DeYoung, *Glittering Vices*, 150–51.

58. Ibid., 151.

59. *ST* II-II, q. 146, a. 1, ad 4. DeYoung summarizes, "Greater discipline about food may help us focus on spiritual goods in a way that discipleship requires. Our eating should not be ruled by our desire for pleasure; instead, it should be regulated by what befits this higher goal and our flourishing as spiritual beings" (*Glittering Vices*, 151–52).

60. *ST* II-II, q. 146, a. 2, obj. 3.

61. *ST* II-II, q. 146, a. 2 and ad 2.

62. McKnight, *Fasting*, 150. From a similar Evangelical perspective, see John Piper, *A Hunger for God: Desiring God through Fasting and Prayer* (Wheaton, IL: Crossway, 1997), 14: "Half of Christian fasting is that our

physical appetite is lost because our homesickness for God is so intense. The other half is that our homesickness for God is threatened because our physical appetites are so intense." Piper's book begins, "Beware of books on fasting.... The discipline of self-denial is fraught with dangers—perhaps only surpassed by the dangers of indulgence" (ibid., 9). But Piper is aware that "the weakness of our hunger for God is not because he is unsavory, but because we keep ourselves stuffed with 'other things.' Perhaps, then, the denial of our stomach's appetite for food might express, or even increase, our soul's appetite for God.... What we hunger for most, we worship" (ibid., 10). Like McKnight, Piper seeks to chart a course "between the dangers of self-denial and self-indulgence" (ibid.). He calls for fasting to remind ourselves that we do not live by bread alone, fasting with a radical God-orientation, fasting to remind us of our hunger for Christ's coming in glory, fasting in times of discernment so as to hear God's will, fasting for the sake of feeding and serving the poor and overcoming our own consumerist self-indulgence, and fasting in mourning and protest over injustice toward the poor.

63. See *ST* II-II, q. 146, a. 1, obj. 4.

64. Sandnes, *Belly and Body in the Pauline Epistles*, 274.

65. *ST* II-II, q. 147, a. 1, obj. 2. For discussion of Aquinas's theology of fasting, see Stephen J. Loughlin, "Thomas Aquinas and the Importance of Fasting to the Christian Life," *Pro Ecclesia* 17 (2008): 343–61; see also Loughlin, *Aquinas' Summa Theologiae* (London: T&T Clark International, 2010), 249–73.

66. For the connection of gluttony and lust, see Okholm, *Dangerous Passions, Deadly Sins*, 16–17, 37–39. See also the reflections on the connection between eating and *eros* found in Isabel Allende, *Aphrodite: A Memoir of the Senses* (London: Flamingo, 1998). McKnight warns, "Some see the body as a *monster of desires* that needs to be tamed by imposing spirit over the body to conquer these unwanted desires. These folks are *ascetics*. For those who have a body-as-monster body image, fasting attempts to control the desires of the body. Some with this view become radical ascetics intent on keeping desires suppressed. People with this body image are often dedicated to purity or holiness or service, and they focus their spirituality on the kingdom to come, on heaven. Some with this view of the body have become saints; some starved themselves to death" (McKnight, *Fasting*, 7). I agree with McKnight that some "radical ascetics" have gone overboard in their bodily mortifications, including excessive fasting; he names in this regard St. Francis and St. Catherine of Siena (ibid., 76). They fasted excessively (as Catherine herself recognized too late, leading her to beg her correspondents not to follow her example of excessive fasting in her youth

that irreversibly compromised her digestive system), although their spirituality and understanding of the body were not what McKnight seems to suggest. For McKnight, radical asceticism emerges when Christians fail to integrate body and soul, and thereby see their body as a "monster." But as McKnight recognizes, we can have an integrated understanding of body and soul and can recognize the body as good, while still valuing the "negative" reasons for fasting. McKnight approves of fasting as a valuable (and biblical) part of expressing mourning and repentance, on the grounds that "at the very core of fasting is empathy with the divine or participation in God's perception of a sacred moment" (ibid., 20). Recognizing that fasting as body discipline was present in the Jewish world and (after Jesus' death and resurrection) among Jesus' disciples, McKnight sums up his position: "I believe body discipline is a legitimate development of biblical and early Christian practice and belief. But I believe there is potential here for body discipline to become a dangerous exaggeration. It all has to do with body image: as long as the person is seen holistically—body and soul—and as long as fasting is a response to a grievous sacred moment, Christian developments of fasting will be healthy. Yet the minute the body becomes the temporary location of evil desire, fasting can easily become unhealthy" (ibid., 74). McKnight's concern may be simply a matter of words (i.e., a concern that positive words about body discipline will lead to an overreaction and to the deadly fruit of anorexia), since while he rejects thinking of the body as "the temporary location of evil desire," he grants the presence of disordered desires in fallen humans: "The healthy side of the early Christian development was the moderate disciplinary fast designed to keep the coals of desire—mostly sexual, but also gluttonous—from falling out and setting the entire Christian on fire" (ibid., 75; cf. 79). Yet he insists that "the Bible shows almost no interest in fasting as a means to conquer the monster—that is, as a means for the spirit to overcome the passions" (ibid., 77). Without considering the body a "monster" or thinking in terms of the domination (rather than healing) of the passions, I think that McKnight, seeking to highlight "the goodness of our sexuality and dining" (ibid., 80), underestimates the presence (often, admittedly, implicit) of body discipline in Paul's letters.

    67. Richard Foster, *Celebration of Discipline: The Path to Spiritual Growth*, rev. ed. (San Francisco: Harper & Row, 1988), 55. See also Lynne M. Baab, *Fasting: Spiritual Freedom beyond Our Appetites* (Downers Grove, IL: InterVarsity Press, 2006); Dallas Willard, *The Spirit of the Disciplines: Understanding How God Changes Lives* (San Francisco: HarperSanFrancisco, 1991). Lest fasting be seen as something valued most by Catholics or Orthodox (note that the authors listed in this footnote are all

Protestants), McKnight helpfully points out how central fasting was for John Wesley: see McKnight, *Fasting*, 81–82, quoting John Wesley, *Works of John Wesley* (Grand Rapids, MI: Zondervan, 1958), 4:94. McKnight has high praise for the traditional place of fasting in the Church's liturgical calendar (as found in the Anglican Book of Common Prayer and in Catholic and Orthodox communions), which mirrors in certain valuable ways the liturgical calendar of Israel. As McKnight concludes, speaking to Protestant readers, "Should not many of us reconsider the body calendar of the Bible and the church?" (ibid., 98). He directs attention to Archimandrite Akakios's *Fasting in the Orthodox Church: Its Theological, Pastoral, and Social Implications* (Etna, CA: Center for Traditionalist Orthodox Studies, 1996).

68. Healy, *Gospel of Mark*, 62.

69. *ST* II-II, q. 147, a. 1.

70. Margaret R. Miles, *Fullness of Life: Historical Foundations for a New Asceticism* (Philadelphia: Westminster, 1981), 147, 149. Miles notes that "the body as foil" was "unacceptable to Augustine as a rationale for asceticism," since people rightly love and care for their bodies (ibid., 147; cf. her account of Augustine's anthropology in 62–78). As she observes,

> Augustine was *interested* in the human body. He saw that Christian authors had not integrated their view of the body with their affirmation of the fully human incarnation of the Word and their insistence on resurrection of the body, and he set out to remedy this. Without glossing over the problems of human embodiment, he attempted to describe the body's participation in the suffering, beauty, and pathos of this life, and its ultimate participation in the resurrection. Like all of us, Augustine was partially thwarted by his personal predilections and cultural assumptions, but this should not obscure the immensity of the task he set for himself, the skill and commitment with which he worked on it, or the value of his achievement—the description of the integrity and continuity of embodied experience. (ibid., 78)

Regarding Aquinas, to whose anthropology she devotes fifteen pages, she remarks that "he advocates neither harsh asceticism nor bodily neglect" (ibid., 133). For reflections on early Christian asceticism, with particular interest in the practice of fasting (often in relation to sex), see Veronika Grimm, *From Feasting to Fasting, the Evolution of a Sin: Attitudes to Food in Late Antiquity* (London: Routledge, 1996); Teresa Shaw, *The Burden of the Flesh: Fasting and Sexuality in Early Christianity* (Minneapolis: Fortress, 1998). See also Peter Brown, *The Body and Society: Men, Women, and Sexual Renunciation in Early Christianity* (New York: Columbia

University Press, 1988). Comparing Acts 2:42, 46 with a letter of St. Jerome, Grimm suggests that the worldviews expressed are completely opposed to each other: "Hospitality, loving kindness, and cheerful conviviality on the one hand and on the other contempt for the world, mortification of the flesh, weeping and groaning are held up by the authors of these passages as ideal patterns of Christian behaviour. Approximately three hundred years passed between the writing of these Christian texts and a veritable abyss seems to separate the attitudes expressed in them" (*From Feasting to Fasting*, 1). Grimm devotes lengthy discussions to Jewish fasting (which was prompted by desire for atonement or by mourning over national disasters); Greco-Roman medical advice (with its critique of gluttony and extravagance with food); the positions of Greco-Roman philosophers (especially regarding ascesis with respect to food, and thus also the practice of vegetarianism); and fasting and eating according to Paul and Acts, Clement of Alexandria, Tertullian, Origen, Eusebius, Ambrose, Jerome, and Augustine. Her survey indicates more unity than she implies at the outset, although obviously some Christian writers take an extreme and unfortunate stance (for example, Jerome). She notes, "To be fair, Augustine was more charitable than many of the famous athletes of asceticism, and did caution his monks against a too severe mortification of their bodies by extreme fasting. Rather, he suggested, the body, as a slave, should be restrained but its legitimate needs should be attended to, within limits.... Fasting does *not* mean giving up food, but only food that one likes" (ibid., 189). Augustine approved eating meat and drinking wine, but he warned against the tendency of pleasurable food and drink to become an idol. Teresa Shaw cites unfortunate examples, encouraged by some fathers of the Church, of "the ravaging of female features through asceticism" so as to become essentially androgynous as, for some fathers, the first Edenic human was — or at least so as to become fully separated from the constraining sexual and childbearing norms for women (*Burden of the Flesh*, 243; cf. 247). Shaw's lack of sympathy for the authors, texts, and practices she describes results in exaggerations on her part — for example her suggestion that behind male Christian piety was fear of women's power: "The male delineation of the contours of female piety seems driven by *fear* of the power and sexual danger ascribed to the female body and to female 'nature'" (ibid., 252). But there is no doubt that she has identified some baneful passages and practices.

71. *ST* II-II, q. 147, a. 1, ad 2.
72. Ibid.
73. See *ST* II-II, q. 147, aa. 6–7.

74. *ST* II-II, q. 147, a. 8. Daniel A. Westberg provides helpful context: "People who pursue the avenue of personal development/destruction involving immoderate sensual pleasure often experience unhappiness and irritation that they then mask or deal with by further temporary pleasures, a pattern often leading to addiction and loss of freedom. The Thomistic approach sees in this the fact that the selfish form of self-love and the pursuit of pleasure is something fundamentally unnatural, in the sense that our human nature, including of course our bodies, was created to function when ordered toward its proper end: in right relation to self, to other people and to God. 'Selfless self-love' seeks a proper measure of life's pleasures in right relationship to true reality and requires the insight, wisdom and the Holy Spirit for the fullest and most accurate understanding of the reality of our physical, psychological and spiritual world" (*Renewing Moral Theology*, 210).

75. See *ST* II-II, q. 147, a. 3. For discussion, see Bridget Ann Henisch, *Fast and Feast: Food in Medieval Society* (University Park: Pennsylvania State University Press, 1976). See also David Grumett and Rachel Muers, *Theology on the Menu*, 22–27. Henisch reports that, not surprisingly, many people hated the rigors of the Lenten fast, not least because the fast forbade not only meat but also dairy products and eggs (which strikes me as overly rigorous). Grumett and Muers comment that "dried cod, known as 'stockfish,' was the best option available to most people. This fish was preserved by drying and beating with hammers for at least an hour, and rehydrated for a minimum of two hours. It was finally boiled and eaten with butter or mustard. Such fare, it can easily be imagined, did little to satisfy appetites, and was a source of continual resentment during what were, at the best of times, naturally bleak months" (*Theology on the Menu*, 26–27). Notably, in 1538, after the English Reformation, Henry VIII "repealed the Lenten ban on the consumption of dairy products, including milk, butter, eggs and cheese, in order to relieve pressure on fish stocks during the season and probably also to appease the populace by making the fast a little easier" (ibid., 28).

76. *ST* II-II, q. 147, a. 3, ad 3.

77. Ibid.

78. See Miles, *Fullness of Life*; Sarah Coakley, *The New Asceticism: Sexuality, Gender and the Quest for God* (London: Bloomsbury, 2015). Coakley's book, with which I differ on certain important points, has wide ecclesiastical and theological goals, set within the context of Anglican debates over same-sex "marriage." Her overarching point, which makes sense to me, is that "the task for the Anglican communion today is, at its deepest

level, theological and spiritual: not merely to reconsider its subtle and distinctive heritage regarding scripture, tradition and 'reason,' but to reenliven its demanding vision of the 'devout life'" (Coakley, *New Asceticism*, 143).

79. Miles grants that "asceticism was, in some notorious instances, shamefully misused, but this does not license us to caricature it as against life or masochistic. If we take seriously the admonition that changes in the habits and condition of the body open the soul to greater insight, we understand the need for a new asceticism. We too find ourselves cluttered with habits and addictions that deaden our sense of lifelulness" (Miles, *Fullness of Life*, 163).

80. See *ST* II-II, q. 147, a. 2. Miles makes the general observation—applicable here—that "typically, Christian authors insist that what is good for the soul *is* good for the body, so that, far from implying a pejorative view of the body, its 'best interests' are served in practices that enhance the soul's energy" (Miles, *Fullness of Life*, 13). While rejecting a simple repetition of the "old asceticism," she strongly affirms that "there are forms of bodily discipline that are clearly beneficial and energy-producing for both body and soul" (ibid., 15–16).

81. See *ST* II-II, q. 147, a. 4, sed contra.

82. Ibid.

83. *ST* II-II, q. 147, a. 4.

84. Ibid., ad 3.

85. Ibid., ad 4.

86. Ibid., ad 5.

87. Ibid.

88. Wirzba, *Food and Faith*, 142. In her *Gluttony* (Oxford: Oxford University Press, 2003), Francine Prose directs our attention, for a positive appraisal of gluttony, to M. F. K. Fisher's *The Art of Eating* (New York: Vintage, 1976). Prose quotes Fisher:

> As often as possible, when a really beautiful bottle is before me, I drink all I can of it, even when I know I have had more than I want physically. That is gluttonous. But I think to myself, when again will I have this taste upon my tongue. Where else in the world is there just such wine as this, with just this bouquet, at just this heat, in just this crystal cup. And when again will I be alive to it as I am this very minute, sitting here on a green hillside above the sea, or here in this dim, murmuring, richly odorous restaurant." This always subversive and fresh writer alters our view of this deadly sin as a fast ticket to ill health or hell, and obliges us to acknowledge it as an affirmation of pleasure and of passion. (Prose, *Gluttony*, 85, citing Fisher, *Art of Eating*, 615)

Here I should underscore that Aquinas's viewpoint is not opposed to the pleasure of eating, or to passion. Reasonable eating and drinking should have pleasure and passion. The line is crossed when we become self-seeking in our pleasure and do not care for others (or, properly, for ourselves). Prose argues that "there's something about the serious glutton (or in any case, *some* serious gluttons) that inspires a certain respect for the life force—the appetite—asserting itself in all that prodigious feasting. It's not unlike our secret feelings about various Don Juans and Casanovas; even as we understand the compulsive quality of their behavior and destructive effects it has on their hapless lovers, we can't help feeling a grudging regard for so much sheer sexual energy" (*Gluttony*, 85–86). From the perspective of Aquinas, we can admire the ontological goodness of their power of appetite and the goods toward which their appetite is directed, without admiring the ordering of their appetites, an ordering that is in fact destructive to their neighbor and to themselves. If we find ourselves obsessed with thinking about prodigious feasts, then we ourselves have become disordered; but this does not mean that we have to pretend that we do not gladly anticipate a good meal or a true feast.

89. *ST* II-II, q. 142, a. 1.

90. In the Vulgate version of Daniel (based on the Septuagint), we read, "In those days I, Daniel, was mourning for three weeks. I ate no delicacies, no meat or wine entered my mouth, nor did I anoint myself at all, for the full three weeks" (Dan 10:2–3). Cited by Aquinas in *ST* II-II, q. 142, a. 1, obj. 1.

91. *ST* II-II, q. 142, a. 1, ad 1.

92. See for example Thomas Merton, *New Seeds of Contemplation* (Boston: Shambhala, 2003); Donald Haggerty, *The Contemplative Hunger* (San Francisco: Ignatius Press, 2016).

93. *ST* II-II, q. 180, a. 7.

94. See *ST* II-II, q. 180, a. 3, obj. 4 and ad 4.

95. *ST* II-II, q. 142, a. 1, ad 2.

96. As McKnight notes, this includes appreciating the relationship of the various "kingdom practices," including fasting's relationship to almsgiving and to the pursuit of justice for the poor (or "solidarity"): "When a group protests by fasting, they both negate one relationship—with the haves—and they affirm another relationship—with the have-nots. And since the structures of power always have sufficient food, fasting is not only refusing relationship, but it is also protesting the power structures that exist" (*Fasting*, 106). With regard to the inaugurated kingdom, McKnight adds that "fasting is to union with God what a marriage ring is to a loving couple. As the ring is not what prompts their union, so also the fasting is

not what prompts union with God. . . . A more complete view of fasting suggests that it is the combination of our yearning to know God and our present state of not knowing God intimately enough that prompts the person to fast with the hope of encountering God" (ibid., 113–14).

97. *ST* II-II, q. 142, a. 2. For Aquinas on gluttony, see Tiziana Suarez-Nani, "Du goût et de la gourmandise selon Thomas d'Aquin," *Micrologus* 10 (2002): 313–34; M. V. Dougherty, "Moral Luck and the Capital Vices in *De malo*: Gluttony and Lust," in *Aquinas's Disputed Questions on Evil: A Critical Guide*, ed. M. V. Dougherty (Cambridge: Cambridge University Press, 2016), 222–34.

98. *ST* II-II, q. 142, a. 2. Note that Aquinas never envisions concupiscence in terms of the soul over against the body, as though the solution is to control or dominate (rather than virtuously orient) bodily desire. On this point, see G. J. McAleer, "The Politics of the Flesh: Rahner and Aquinas on *Concupiscentia*," *Modern Theology* 15 (1999): 355–65. McAleer argues that

> [Karl] Rahner explains concupiscence quite literally as a metaphysical problem inherent to human nature as a material composite, whilst Thomas regards the phenomenon strictly in terms of the soul as a political community. . . . Rahner's development of flesh in terms of the dualism between nature and person will relocate the event of concupiscence away from the soul and the political analysis of the community of its parts. Instead, concupiscence comes to be described as an antagonism of parts so foreign to one another that only a coercive authority can stabilize desire, albeit temporarily. . . . For Thomas [Aquinas], concupiscence or flesh describes a frontier within human nature that is simultaneously soul and body, matter and form, or, in Rahner's terminology, person and nature. Where Rahner identifies a division and opposition, Aquinas articulates a gradation within human nature that partakes of both constituent principles. For this reason, Thomas explains the relationship between reason and flesh in terms of a political community. Reason, he says, rules the flesh by a political or royal rule as when a governor rules over free men. Which is to say, rational appetite as the superior has the role of commanding the lower sensitive appetite but also the responsibility to ensure that the sensitive appetite is able to satisfy its legitimate wants. The model of a political community is designed to alert the reader that the human is a composite of needs which must be brought into a well-ordered community of mutual satisfaction. (ibid., 356–57)

McAleer is critiquing Rahner's "The Theological Concept of Concupiscentia," in Rahner, *Theological Investigations*, vol. 1, *God, Christ, Mary and Grace*, trans. Cornelius Ernst, O.P. (Baltimore: Helicon, 1961), 347–82.

99. Kruschwitz, "Gluttony and Abstinence," 137.
100. Cited in *ST* II-II, q. 148, a. 1, obj. 1.
101. *ST* II-II, q. 148, a. 1.
102. *ST* II-II, q. 148, a. 2.
103. See C. S. Lewis, *The Screwtape Letters* (New York: HarperCollins, 2000), 87–88; DeYoung, *Glittering Vices*, 142–43. DeYoung shows that the "Christian dieting" advice of Gwen Shamblin, founder of the Weigh Down Workshop, in fact combines "dainty" and "sumptuous" eating and thus is a form of gluttony.
104. DeYoung, *Glittering Vices*, 145.
105. *ST* II-II, q. 148, a. 5, obj. 3.
106. *ST* II-II, q. 148, a. 3.
107. Ibid. Francine Prose caricatures the Christian view of gluttony when she implies that Christian theologians held simply that "eating too much or enjoying one's food is a crime against God, a profound moral failure for which we will be promptly dispatched to hell" (Prose, *Gluttony*, 4). More positively, she adds that for the patristic and medieval theologians

> the specter of gluttony was never meant to prevent the faithful from eating. Although the pious were duly warned against the insidious ways in which concupiscence and pleasure could masquerade as necessity, the early Christian theologians had a surprising and comparatively ... tolerant attitude toward the occasional overindulgence. The sin of gluttony *was* one of degree, but the degree that appeared to matter most was not so much excessive consumption as excessive appetite, desire, and attention: the fixation on food, the pleasure derived from taste; the self-inflicted pain of starvation; and, especially, the ways in which all these related fixations turned one's attention away from the more important and urgent needs of the soul and the spirit. (ibid., 38–41)

Oddly, Prose suggests that the struggle to maintain a certain weight is an example of the virtue of abstinence and of "the daunting challenge of overcoming the fierce temptations of gluttony" (ibid., 2). She thereby misunderstands what the virtue of abstinence is, although she correctly recognizes that "from the early Middle Ages until the early Renaissance, centuries during which mass consciousness was formed and dominated by the tenets of Christianity, the principal danger of gluttony was thought to reside in its nature as a form of idolatry, the most literal sort of navel gazing, of worshiping the belly as a God" (ibid., 3; cf. 13–14, as well as her at times sarcastic treatment of patristic and monastic viewpoints on 26–30, 33–37). Suggesting that Aquinas's theology was affected by the fact that he himself was overweight, Prose finds in Aquinas a "notably soft line on gluttony" (ibid., 38).

108. Kruschwitz, "Gluttony and Abstinence," 152.

109. DeYoung, *Glittering Vices*, 146.

110. *ST* II-II, q. 148, a. 6. I should draw attention to the valuable friendly correction offered here by Robert Kruschwitz. Kruschwitz notes that according to Aquinas, a "capital vice," such as gluttony, is supposed to lead to other vices by "*formal* causation," through proposing a false happiness toward which the subordinate vices aim. The subordinate vices named by Aquinas in the case of gluttony, however, simply result from gluttony. Kruschwitz offers a helpful suggestion: "We can do better in applying the official doctrine [namely, "*formal* causation"] to the case of gluttony. Our earlier discussion suggests there will be offspring vices of the sort the theory predicts—including inhospitality, mistaken social policy priorities, false entitlements, and damaging social constructions of desire—that beset the glutton whose thinking is disoriented by the pleasures and ready availability of the preferred foods and drinks" (Kruschwitz, "Gluttony and Abstinence," 151). I agree with Kruschwitz here, while still finding Aquinas's list of subordinate vices that result from gluttony to be apropos.

111. *ST* II-II, q. 148, a. 6.

112. DeYoung, *Glittering Vices*, 146.

113. Catherine of Siena, *The Dialogue*, trans. Suzanne Noffke, O.P. (Mahwah, NJ: Paulist Press, 1980), 89.

114. See *ST* II-II, q. 149, a. 2, obj. 2 and ad 2.

115. For analysis, see the MA thesis of L. William Uhl, "The Virtue of Sobriety in Aquinas' *Summa Theologiae*," Washington, DC, School of Philosophy of the Catholic University of America, 1994. For a study that accords with Aquinas's views, Uhl cites John C. Ford, S.J., *Man Takes a Drink: Facts and Principles about Alcohol* (New York: P. J. Kennedy and Sons, 1955). The recreational use of mind-altering drugs might also be considered here, but such drug use does not properly belong to temperance because there is no amount of consumption that is good. For discussion of recreational (illicit) drug use, see the *Catechism of the Catholic Church*, 2nd ed. (Vatican City: Libreria Editrice Vaticana, 1997), which treats such drug use under the fifth commandment ("Thou shalt not kill"): "The *use of drugs* inflicts very grave damage on human health and life. Their use, except on strictly therapeutic grounds, is a grave offense" (§2291).

116. *ST* II-II, q. 149, a. 1, sed contra.
117. Cited in *ST* II-II, q. 149, a. 1.
118. *ST* II-II, q. 149, a. 1.
119. In the RSV, this verse reads quite differently: "I searched my mind how to cheer my body with wine—my mind still guiding me with wisdom."
120. *ST* II-II, q. 149, a. 3, sed contra.
121. *ST* II-II, q. 149, a. 3.
122. Cook, *Alcohol, Addiction and Christian Ethics*, 51.
123. See *ST* II-II, q. 149, a. 3, ad 1 and ad 3.
124. *ST* II-II, q. 149, a. 3, ad 3. Cook surveys a book from the nineteenth-century Catholic temperance movement, Thomas Edward Bridgett's *The Discipline of Drink: An Historical Enquiry into the Principles and Practice of the Catholic Church regarding the Use, Abuse, and Disuse of Alcoholic Liquors, Especially in England, Ireland, and Scotland, from the 6th to the 16th Century* (London, 1876). Cook points out, "Bridgett emphasised that total abstinence had never been imposed upon the clergy by the Church, although drunkenness was forbidden. The option of total abstinence was open to them, however, and Bridgett argued (on the basis of scant evidence) that this option was taken up by some from the earliest times.... Bridgett recognised that some ascetics, through individual choice, pursued total abstinence, but was unaware of any monastic rule that ever imposed this.... For the laity also, Bridgett was clear, the Church had never imposed total abstinence" (*Alcohol, Addiction and Christian Ethics*, 109). Anselm of Canterbury imposed canonical discipline against priests going to drinking parties.
125. See *ST* II-II, q. 149, a. 4, sed contra.
126. *ST* II-II, q. 149, a. 4.
127. Ibid.
128. Ibid.
129. *ST* II-II, q. 150, a. 1, sed contra. For drunkenness arising from ignorance or weakness, see also *ST* I-II, q. 88, a. 5.
130. *ST* II-II, q. 150, a. 1.
131. *ST* II-II, q. 150, a. 2, sed contra.
132. *ST* II-II, q. 150, a. 2.
133. *ST* II-II, q. 150, a. 3, sed contra.
134. *ST* II-II, q. 150, a. 3, ad 1.
135. *ST* II-II, q. 150, a. 4. Aquinas cites the discussion of Lot in book 22 of Augustine's *Contra Faustum*. See Augustine, *Answer to Faustus, a Manichean*, trans. Roland Teske, S.J. (Hyde Park, NY: New City Press, 2007). Christopher Cook sums up his survey of Aquinas on drunkenness:

"Aquinas quoted scripture and the Church Fathers in support of his arguments, but he relied principally upon philosophical argument and natural law as the basis for his conclusions. Human beings are created for the ultimate end of the *ratio boni*, and drunkenness, by impairing reason, acts contrary to this good" (*Alcohol, Addiction and Christian Ethics*, 65–66). Although Cook's study is generally quite helpful, he falls into an unnecessary opposition here, one that he repeats on 73. In fact, Aquinas's condemnation of drunkenness flows from Scripture as much as from natural law, and indeed he does not conceive of "natural law" as though it were somehow cut off from the scriptural testimony to the Creator God of Israel or from Christ, who fulfills the law and reveals our call to deification. Having introduced this opposition, Cook mistakenly contrasts Aquinas with Martin Luther, who, as Cook says, "saw drunkenness as sinful on the basis that it is expressly forbidden in scripture" (ibid., 69). Aquinas agrees with this point, and he also sees natural law as rooted in Scripture, even if not therefore accessible only by means of Scripture (since natural law is knowable by human reason, given the kind of creatures that we are). Similarly, Cook makes an unnecessary opposition when he writes: "For Augustine, it [drunkenness] represented a failure to strive to please God alone. For Aquinas, it was understood as impairment of the ability of human beings to fulfil the rational function for which they were created" (ibid., 73; cf. 184–86). This "rational function" for which God created humankind is, Aquinas holds, to know and love God above all else both now and forever (which requires, in our fallen state, Christ's eschatological work), and so the opposition between Augustine and Aquinas here is fundamentally mistaken.

136. In contemporary American culture, one of three adults is addicted to nicotine and one of eight adults is addicted to alcohol or illegal drugs. See Kent Dunnington, *Addiction and Virtue: Beyond the Models of Disease and Choice* (Downers Grove, IL: IVP Academic, 2011), 100.

137. Cook helpfully remarks that "Aquinas' concept of the mean of virtues offers a potentially broad base for understanding the ethics of drinking. Such a concept has the potential to relate 'normal' drinking ethically to drunkenness and to other alcohol-related problems. Given that scientists now consider that alcohol use and misuse are closely related at the population level, this would appear to offer a closer correspondence between epidemiology, social psychology and ethics than would an ethical framework which treats drunkenness as a completely separate issue" (*Alcohol, Addiction and Christian Ethics*, 75–76). For Cook, however, Aquinas made a mistake in supposing that drunkenness "either is present or is not present," and Aquinas should also have given more attention to the norms present

in the cultural context (ibid., 76). I think that Aquinas is right that the key to the presence of drunkenness is the loss of the ability to direct one's rational powers, but certainly there can be other negative forms of alcohol dependency.

138. Dunnington, *Addiction and Virtue*, 91. See also Cook's discussion of addiction as an instance of divided will in *Alcohol, Addiction and Christian Ethics*, 156–63.

139. Dunnington, *Addiction and Virtue*, 94.

140. Cook, *Alcohol, Addiction and Christian Ethics*, 162. On the insufficiency of shame, see Dunnington, *Addiction and Virtue*, 106. Both Dunnington and Cook make clear that the category of sin is not rightly cut off from the category of addiction. In a passage reflective of much of Cook's approach, Dunnington states: "There is room within the doctrine of sin to recognize, as Augustine does, the bondage of the human will in the face of temptation. . . . Persons with addictions claim that their addictive behavior is admittedly destructive yet, in some very real sense, beyond the immediate control of their willpower. Similarly the doctrine of sin teaches that human beings act in ways that are destructive of right relationship with God yet those actions often flow out of habits and fundamental orientations that are not amenable to reform through immediate exertion of will" (ibid., 132). Though addiction can therefore be a sinful habit, nonetheless conflating "addiction" and "sin" (so that all sin is simply addiction) would be a mistake, as Dunnington recognizes. For a book that exemplifies this mistaken approach, see Patrick McCormick, C.M., *Sin as Addiction* (New York: Paulist Press, 1989). Dunnington rightly notes that "many instances of addiction are not appropriately labeled as sin," for example when a person has mental illness or when a person's addiction has arisen out of "experiences of trauma or victimization," although in this latter case there remains a possibility for the behaviors that flow from the addiction to be rightly labeled "sin" (*Addiction and Virtue*, 136). Cook draws especially upon H. G. Frankfurt, "Freedom of the Will and the Concept of a Person," *Journal of Philosophy* 68 (1971): 5–20; Alistair McFadyen, *Bound to Sin: Abuse, Holocaust, and the Christian Doctrine of Sin* (Cambridge: Cambridge University Press, 2000); and Eleonore Stump, "Augustine on Free Will," in *The Cambridge Companion to Augustine*, ed. Eleonore Stump and Norman Kretzmann (Cambridge: Cambridge University Press, 2002), 124–47.

141. Dunnington argues that "the lure of addiction increases to the extent that we lack other intelligible means of ordering our lives" (*Addiction and Virtue*, 105; cf. 152). As an example, he points to the fact that "addiction is disproportionately prevalent on Native American reservations

where few of the traditional modes of understanding and ordering the moral life remain and the possibilities that are on offer are in total discontinuity from these traditional ways" (*Addiction and Virtue*, 105). He directs attention to such works as James Nelson, *Thirst: God and the Alcoholic Experience* (Louisville: Westminster John Knox, 2004), and Bruce Wilshire, *Wild Hunger: The Primal Roots of Modern Addiction* (Lanham, MD: Rowman & Littlefield, 1998).

142. See Cook, *Alcohol, Addiction and Christian Ethics*, 169–70, 183, 187; Bill Wilson, *Alcoholics Anonymous: The Story of How Many Thousands of Men and Women Have Recovered from Alcoholism*, 3rd ed. (New York: Alcoholics Anonymous Press, 1976). Cook notes that "addiction is concerned with the way in which relationships are disordered by making a particular substance or behaviour an object of desire for its own sake. Similarly, the Twelve Steps of Alcoholics Anonymous, which have been one of the prime sources of inspiration for the literature on addiction and spirituality, focus on the importance of making amends in relationships that have been damaged by addiction to alcohol, and on the need to reorientate life around a Higher Power, or God" (*Alcohol, Addiction and Christian Ethics*, 183). These points make crystal clear that, as he later adds, addiction to alcohol is "set in the context of further-reaching goals and desires than simply those concerned with drug use. Abstinence from alcohol is unlikely to be a satisfactory treatment goal when more profound and widely-reaching issues are not addressed" (ibid., 189). This is Dunnington's central point as well. For Cook and Dunnington, as for Aquinas's eschatological ethics, "Christ alone providences that grace which is able to set people free from the broader experience of captivity that the divided self represents. It is therefore no surprise to find that there are many accounts in the literature of spiritual and religious experience associated with recovery from addiction" (*Alcohol, Addiction and Christian Ethics*, 198).

143. Ellen F. Davis, *Scripture, Culture, and Agriculture: An Agrarian Reading of the Bible* (Cambridge: Cambridge University Press, 2009), 70. The story of the manna suggests, for Davis, that God intends for Israel to understand the land and food production in terms of divine generosity and presence. Davis's concern is to criticize agribusiness and large-scale agricultural exports, which in my view may well be necessary for raising and distributing affordable food for a world population of 7.5 billion or more. I am profoundly grateful that many people are alive today on our planet who in earlier centuries would have died young of now-curable (or preventable) diseases—as in my own case—or else would have starved to death.

144. *ST* II-II, q. 141, a. 7, ad 2 and ad 3.

145. Prose, *Gluttony*, 41. In the "Foreword to the Paperback Edition" of his *The Hungry Soul: Eating and the Perfecting of Our Nature* (Chicago: University of Chicago Press, 1999), xi–xvii, Leon R. Kass grants that contemporary cultural interest in good food may involve "affluent people . . . engaged, quite literally, in conspicuous consumption, seeking to sample the strange, to buy the best, to be first among their friends to try this or that" (xiii). But he adds, "More optimistically, the new preoccupations with finer eating may represent, at least for some, a genuine delight in taste and refinement, a cultivation of the aesthetic dimension of life to which (as I argue) eating provides a regular opening" (ibid.). I agree with Kass that good eating and good feasting are an important and morally laudable part of life. See Wirzba, *Food and Faith*, 138: "When people feast together they gratefully acknowledge their place in the memberships of creation and the generosity of the Creator." Wirzba adds the point that eating enables us to appreciate what God's creation offers to the hungry person: "Eating, like sexual life, is among the most intimate ways we know for relating to others. Here we have the chance to approach and savor another, taking in its full flavor and life" (ibid., 156). Wirzba advocates "Eucharistic eating," through which we learn how "to respect and respond to what is other than me" (ibid., 158). See also Méndez-Montoya, *Theology of Food*, 149–50, 154.

146. Ben Witherington III, *Making a Meal of It: Rethinking the Theology of the Lord's Supper* (Waco, TX: Baylor University Press, 2007), 142. For the way in which all meals belong, in Christ, to our priestly offering of creation to God, see Robert Farrar Capon, *The Supper of the Lamb: A Culinary Reflection* (New York: Modern Library, 2002).

147. Kass, *Hungry Soul*, 229. In Kass's view, "We face serious dangers from our increasingly utilitarian, functional, or 'economic' attitudes toward food. True, fast food, TV dinners, and eating on the run save time, meet our need for 'fuel,' and provide close to instant gratification. But for these very reasons, they diminish opportunities for conversation, communion, and aesthetic discernment; they thus shortchange the other hungers of the soul. . . . Meals eaten before the television turn eating into feeding. Wolfing down food dishonors both the human effort to prepare it and the lives of those plants and animals sacrificed on our behalf. Not surprisingly, incivility, insensitivity, and ingratitude learned at the family table can infect all other aspects of one's life. Conversely, good habits and thoughtful attitudes regarding food and eating will have far-reaching benefits. Self-restraint and self-command, consideration for others, politeness, fairness, generosity, tact, discernment, good taste, and the art of friendly conversation—all learnable and practiced at the table—enrich and ennoble all of human life" (ibid., 229–30).

CHAPTER FOUR. Chastity

1. Wright, *Paul and the Faithfulness of God*, 1509. See also John H. Walton, *The Lost World of Genesis One: Ancient Cosmology and the Origins Debate* (Downers Grove, IL: IVP Academic, 2009).

2. Wright, *Paul and the Faithfulness of God*, 1509.

3. See Grabowski, *Sex and Virtue*, 96–103; Francis Martin, "Male and Female He Created Them: A Summary of the Teaching of Genesis Chapter One," *Communio* 20 (1993): 240–65. By contrast, the biblical scholar Calum Carmichael argues that Jesus' reference to Genesis 1:27 and 2:24 in Matthew 19:5 — from which Jesus draws the conclusion that "they [the husband and wife] are no longer two but one" — is in fact evidence of Jesus' view that "marriage is a return to the original androgynous state that God created at the beginning of time" (*Sex and Religion in the Bible* [New Haven: Yale University Press, 2010], 9). Carmichael argues that for Jesus and Paul, "The pre-sexual, first being that possesses the image of God is of a higher order than the males and the females who come after Eve issues from Adam's body. The eventual, end-time reversal of the separate conditions of maleness and femaleness represents the return to the ideal of a sexually free state, the attainment of an original, undifferentiated gender ready for incorporation into God. This is why, according to Jesus, after the Resurrection the institution of marriage will not exist (Mark 12:25)" (ibid.). I note, however, that Jesus does not say in Mark 12 that there will be no more male and female. Jesus says only that marriage, the context for sexual intercourse and procreation, will no longer exist, which makes sense if one supposes that in the final consummation no further procreation will be needed, since God's creation will be complete and soul-body intimacy with God and neighbor will be all in all. Carmichael later argues,

> As a state in which a man cleaves to his wife (touching rib cages, so to speak) and becomes one flesh with her, an androgynous idea underlies the description of marriage in Genesis 2:23, 24. The married couple is male and female in one, a notion that links marriage to the original creation of man. A major implication is that any interference with this union constitutes an offense against the created order. It therefore follows, as the rabbis long ago saw (*b. San.* 58a), that a rule prohibiting adultery is implicit in Genesis 2:23, 24: adultery breaks the bond of the united male and female that God originally intended at creation. It is this rich background that accounts for the appearance of the prohibition of adultery in the Decalogue. (ibid., 102)

But why suppose that the prohibition of adultery derives from the presence in the original "created order" of an androgynous human, rather than rooting the prohibition in the husband-wife relationship? For further eccentric views, see David Wheeler-Reed, *Regulating Sex in the Roman Empire: Ideology, the Bible, and the Early Christians* (New Haven: Yale University Press, 2017). Wheeler-Reed exaggerates the degree to which Paul (or Jesus) was "antifamily" (ibid., xix), arguing that "the oldest Christian view of marriage maintains that sex is a prophylactic against *porneia* and has nothing to do with procreation" (ibid., 121).

4. Wright, *After You Believe*, 228. On the formation and meaning of God's family in the Torah, see Olivier Bonnewijn, *La famille dans la Bible: Quand Abraham, Joseph et Moïse éclairent nos propres histoires* (Paris: Mame, 2014).

5. Okholm, *Dangerous Passions, Deadly Sins*, 51. See also Milbank and Pabst, *Politics of Virtue*, 270–71: "The ever-increasing separation of sex from procreation (such that the palliative and accurate sense that one's natural sexual drive is the drive of nature to sustain itself scarcely comes any longer to male consciousness) is regarded naively if we do not realise that this is what the state covertly wants—such being the central theme of Aldous Huxley's *Brave New World*. In terms of partially deliberate but mainly objective intentional drift, it desires a 'Malthusian' control over reproduction that is more easily attained through self-release and permission than through self-discipline. This allows the state to deal with the individual directly, rather than through the mediation of couples and families, which are too much like micro-states within states."

6. See Edward Feser, "In Defense of the Perverted Faculty Argument," in his *Neo-Scholastic Essays* (South Bend, IN: St. Augustine's Press, 2015), 378–415. As Feser says, Aquinas "presupposes an *essentialism* according to which natural substances possess essences that are objectively real (rather than inventions of the human mind or mere artifacts of language) and immanent to things themselves (rather than existing in a Platonic third realm); and a *teleologism* according to which the activities and processes characteristic of a natural substance are 'directed toward' certain ends or outcomes, and *inherently* so, by virtue of the nature of the thing itself (rather than having a 'directedness' that is purely extrinsic or entirely imposed from outside, the way artifacts do)" (ibid., 379–80). Aquinas does not have a mechanistic view of nature (including human nature); created things have a proper form and a goal or purpose. See also Feser's *Scholastic Metaphysics: A Contemporary Introduction* (Heusenstamm: Editiones Scholasticae, 2014), 211–41, as well as Gerard M. Verschuuren, *Aquinas and Modern Science: A New Synthesis of Faith and Reason* (Kettering, OH:

Angelico Press, 2016), 127–42, and Marie-Dominique Chenu's observation that for Aquinas "each substance realizes its true end according to its own nature within the general goal-orientation of the universe" (*Aquinas and His Role in Theology*, 96). For further discussion see Alexander Pruss, "Christian Sexual Ethics and Teleological Organicity," *Thomist* 64 (2000): 71–100; Petri, *Aquinas and the Theology of the Body*, 219–26; Nicholas J. Healy Jr., "Christian Personalism and the Debate over the End of Marriage," *Communio* 39 (2012): 186–200. For the opposite perspective, see the chapter "Caresses" in Paul J. Griffiths, *Christian Flesh* (Stanford: Stanford University Press, 2018). Proceeding philosophically and theologically without engagement with biblical texts—though with reference to Mary's flesh and to Jesus' flesh and caresses—Griffiths argues against the view that human sexual acts are only rightly ordered within the marital bond with its inseparable procreative and unitive ends. In his view, sexual pleasures such as "masturbation, fellatio, sodomy, cunnilingus, and much more" (ibid., 141) need to be reclaimed by Christians as often good when done for personal pleasure or as part of loving caresses toward another person (whether same sex or opposite sex), without there being any procreative and unitive teleological bodily order. Regarding "the extent to which sodomitic caresses contribute to a mutually supportive intertwined life of a kind intimate with Jesus's love for the Church," Griffiths concludes that "often they do and often they don't, just as is the case with the copulative [male-female] caress" (ibid., 144). For Griffiths human bodies have no teleology regarding sexuality other than to be a locus of pleasurable and/or "mutually supportive" intimate caress. The result is a reductive viewpoint in which the human spirit engages human flesh without attending to any bodily ordering deeper than flesh's ability to give and enjoy pleasurable caresses. By emphasizing the injustices that take place among male-female married couples, Griffiths also suggests that the injustices caused by rejecting male-female bodily teleology are no more significant than are injustices within relationships approved by the Church, but this is mistaken. I make this case in detail—with regard to social justice—in my forthcoming *Engaging the Doctrine of Marriage* (Eugene, OR: Cascade).

7. John Grabowski notes that Aquinas "successfully integrates an account of human nature and its inclinations into a larger framework of virtue. Chastity enables the person's sexual powers to be exercised intelligently and freely in accord with the goods of human nature—particularly the inclination to procreate, educate, and care for offspring" (Grabowski, *Sex and Virtue*, 82). He adds, "Chastity, as presented by St. Thomas, is the virtue that enables human beings to use their sexual powers wisely and well. In so doing they contribute not only to their own flourishing, but to a

well-ordered society that reflects God's plan for human sexuality" (ibid., 84). He cites Patrick Riley, *Civilising Sex: On Chastity and the Common Good* (Edinburgh: T&T Clark, 2000). Jean Porter praises Aquinas's broader discussion of chastity but finds his "analysis of the sins of lust (*Summa theologiae* II-II 154)" to be "perhaps the least attractive aspect of his moral theology" ("Chastity as a Virtue," *Scottish Journal of Theology* 58 [2005]: 285). Porter is put off by Aquinas's ranking of the sexual sins (though she fails to mention that he would rank them quite differently if he were ranking them with regard to the order of justice and the order of charity), but more importantly she disagrees with his list of sins, including his view that homosexual acts are sinful. In a better approach, she thinks,

> the ideal of chastity would play somewhat the same role in our lives as does the ideal of moderation with respect to food and drink; that is to say, it would combine broad, socially mediated standards for appropriateness with considerable flexibility at the level of individual appropriation. It would acknowledge the appropriateness and necessity of substantive ideals of chaste behaviour, including (for example) the foregoing of casual sex and faithfulness to one's partner, while still allowing for considerable room for adaptation to one's individual circumstances and dispositions. Thus, it would be flexible enough to allow for differences in sexual orientation, as well as for more diffuse factors such as one's natural level of sexual desire, the practical possibilities of forming a long-term partnership, and the like. (ibid., 289)

See the rejoinder offered by Kevin L. Flannery, S.J., "Marriage, Thomas Aquinas, and Jean Porter," *Journal of Catholic Social Thought* 8 (2011): 277–89.

8. Attempting to describe this fullness of meaning, Hans Urs von Balthasar describes the "incomprehensible wonder that fills them [the man and woman] with unexpected delight" in encountering the "independent spirit-person" who comes forth from them and reveals the deepest intrinsic meaning of the sexual act. See Hans Urs von Balthasar, *Theo-Logic: Theological Logical Theory*, vol. 2, *Truth of God*, trans. Adrian J. Walker (San Francisco: Ignatius Press, 2004), 61. See also Marie LeBlanc, O.S.B., "Amour et procréation dans la théologie de saint Thomas," *Revue Thomiste* 92 (1992): 433–59.

9. See Mark Regnerus, *Cheap Sex: The Transformation of Men, Marriage, and Monogamy* (Oxford: Oxford University Press, 2017). At the root of this development, Regnerus argues, is "artificial hormonal contraception. It was a quiet but monumental grand bargain that has resulted in some unintended fallout in the domain of marriage and relationship

formation and continuity" (ibid., 173). In his conclusion, Regnerus predicts that "the share of Americans who will marry will continue to slide," despite the fact that "marriage remains powerfully associated [statistically] with all manner of optimal outcomes in American life—among children, adolescents, and adults" (ibid., 205). He argues that "we will find that as marriage retreats so will enduring love, giving way to the dominance of confluent love. And with it will recede less expensive forms of stable social order" (ibid., 206; on "confluent love" and its impact on adults and children, see 194–96). At the same time, he thinks, Christian communities can no longer be counted upon to uphold the morality of the New Testament: sociologically speaking, at least, "the new American Christian cosmology privileges individual rights and the pursuit of happiness—wherever it may lead—over notions of solidarity and the common good" (ibid., 211). In Regnerus's view, because sex is a motivator for many men, the easy availability of sex (and thus the lack of motivation to work hard as part of attracting a sexual partner) is one factor, though not the only one, behind the demonstrable fact that "more and more men are considered less and less marriageable" (ibid., 152). From a different perspective, but aware of the lack of marriageable men, Kathryn Edin and Maria Kefalas remark, "No modern marriage can, or even should, survive the ravages of domestic abuse, chronic infidelity, alcoholism or drug addiction, repeated incarceration, or a living made from crime. Given the prevalence of these problems in the low-income population, promoting marriage will do more harm than good unless policymakers figure out a way to make low-skilled men safer prospects for long-term relationships with women and children" (Edin and Kefalas, *Promises I Can Keep: Why Poor Women Put Motherhood before Marriage*, 2nd ed. [Berkeley: University of California Press, 2011], 217). Before policy makers can make much headway, however, I think that the virtue of chastity (among other virtues) will have an important part to play.

10. For exegetical discussion of 1 Corinthians 7:1–9, see Hays, *Moral Vision of the New Testament*, 47–52. For Augustine's and Aquinas's interpretations of 1 Corinthians 7:1–9, and for the development of the Catholic Church's teaching on the *remedium concupiscentiae* (emphasizing that marriage does not represent an outlet for lust, which must rather be healed by chastity in marriage), see Cormac Burke, *The Theology of Marriage: Personalism, Doctrine, and Canon Law* (Washington, DC: Catholic University of America Press, 2015), chapter 8, although I think that Burke's view of the *remedium concupiscentiae* is too negative. For clarification see Jörgen Vijgen, "The Intelligibility of Aquinas' Account of Marriage as *Remedium Concupiscentiae* in His Commentary on 1 Corinthians 7, 1–9," in *Towards a Biblical Thomism: Thomas Aquinas and the Renewal of Biblical*

Theology, ed. Piotr Roszak and Jörgen Vijgen (Pamplona: EUNSA, 2018), 219–41. See also DeYoung, *Glittering Vices*, 162–63.

11. As the evangelical moral theologian Dennis P. Hollinger states,

> God's design is that humans enter the world through the most intimate, loving relationship on earth—the one-flesh covenant relationship of marriage. We know historically, and increasingly in today's world, that large numbers of children are born outside of such a union. But God's intention from creation is that children be born out of a sexual union that is covenantal, permanent, loving, enjoyable, and responsible. We know well, though some deny it or shut their eyes to it, that many problems in society emerge because procreation becomes dislodged from the commitments and stability of marriage. Not only is it God's intention that children are born through the sexual intimacy of a covenant relationship, but that sex itself always remains an inherently procreative act. Until modern times, the link between sex and procreation was virtually unchallenged. Of course there was much sex outside of marriage, but humans knew by nature that this was a procreative act.... As we examine God's designs, however, we see that sex is inherently procreative. We cannot develop the Christian meaning of sex by setting aside this dimension. Children are the fruit of sexual love. Though couples engaging in sex need not intend to have children through a given act, they must always be open to that possibility, for sex is by nature procreative. It is part of its essential meaning. (*The Meaning of Sex: Christian Ethics and the Moral Life* [Grand Rapids, MI: Baker Academic, 2009], 102)

Hollinger, however, allows for the goodness of masturbation and contraception in the context of marriage, on the grounds that so long as the context of marriage is in place, then sexual acts will have a procreative context that provides sufficient unity between the procreative and unitive dimensions. Here more attention is needed to the specificity and ends of individual acts.

12. Thomas Gilby, O.P., "Appendix 3: Natural and Unnatural in Morals (2a2ae. 154, 11)," in St. Thomas Aquinas, *Summa theologiae*, vol. 43, *Temperance* (2a2ae. 141–54), trans. Thomas Gilby, O.P. (London: Eyre & Spottiswoode, 1968), 254. Oliver O'Donovan notes that this "right" is one of "the inherent goods of creaturely existence" (O'Donovan, *Church in Crisis: The Gay Controversy and the Anglican Communion* [Eugene, OR: Cascade Books, 2008], 98). See also in this regard William B. May's *Getting the Marriage Conversation Right: A Guide for Effective Dialogue* (Steubenville, OH: Emmaus Road Publishing, 2012), 5–7; Douglas Farrow,

Nation of Bastards: Essays on the End of Marriage (Toronto: BPS Books, 2007), 13. See also critical rejoinders to Sherif Girgis, Ryan T. Anderson, and Robert P. George's *What Is Marriage? Man and Woman; A Defense* (New York: Encounter Books, 2012), as found in Andrew Forsyth, "Defining Marriage," *Soundings: An Interdisciplinary Journal* 97 (2014): 297–322; Rebekah Johnston, "Marriage and the Metaphysics of Bodily Union: Framing the Same-Sex Marriage Debate," *Social Theory and Practice* 39 (2013): 288–312. Joshua Madden rightly points out that "Johnston's argument derives its principles from a nominalism that sweeps away any intelligibility intrinsic to human action and sexuality. . . . Claiming that the sexual act . . . is ordered toward procreation is not to instrumentalize human sexuality in any way but to claim for it what is naturally its own" (Madden, "Marriage, 'Bodily Union,' and Natural Teleology: A Response to Rebekah Johnston and the New Natural Law Theorists," *National Catholic Bioethics Quarterly* 16 [2016]: 93).

13. Janet E. Smith, "The Universality of Natural Law and the Irreducibility of Personalism," *Nova et Vetera* 11 (2013): 1143. Regarding pleasure, Aquinas observes that "in the moral order, there is a good pleasure, whereby the higher or lower appetite rests in that which is in accord with reason; and an evil pleasure, whereby the appetite rests in that which is discordant from reason and the law of God" (*ST* I-II, q. 34, a. 1). He adds that in sexual intercourse the pleasure can certainly be "in accord with reason" (ibid., ad 1), and indeed he considers that "an operation cannot be perfectly good, unless there be also pleasure in good" (*ST* I-II, q. 34, a. 4, ad 3). See also Pope John Paul II [Karol Wojtyła], *Love and Responsibility*, as well as Adrian J. Reimers, *Truth about the Good: Moral Norms in the Thought of John Paul II* (Ave Maria, FL: Sapientia Press, 2011), and Melina, *Sharing in Christ's Virtues*, 59–91. The value of Janet Smith's work is on full display in her *Self-Gift: Essays on* Humanae Vitae *and the Thought of John Paul II* (Steubenville, OH: Emmaus Academic, 2018).

14. Adrian Thatcher, *Theology and Families* (Oxford: Blackwell, 2007), 45. However, Thatcher argues in favor of "extending the rite and the right of marriage to couples of the same sex" (ibid., 137). It seems to me that Thatcher does not think through a number of matters in this regard, including the fact that homosexual sexual acts cannot procreate children, and therefore children raised by same-sex couples (many of whom will inevitably desire to have children) will have been willfully deprived of either their biological father or their biological mother—an injustice that I note more than once in this chapter. In the end, Thatcher's case rests upon a fundamentally Cartesian account of "marital values" (ibid.).

15. Grabowski comments, "Much of the postconciliar discussion [of the need to renew moral theology through attention to Scripture] has been sidetracked by debates over whether Scripture poses any concrete norms that could not be known by the natural light of human reason (i.e., the natural law). The reduction of morality to law presupposed by these disagreements reveals the enduring influence of a morality of obligation. Further problems arise from the growing specialization found within the discrete areas of biblical studies that threaten to make it inaccessible to both theologians and laypersons" (Grabowski, *Sex and Virtue*, 25). As an example of the main problem, Grabowski points to the essays in *The Distinctiveness of Christian Ethics*, ed. Charles Curran and Richard McCormick, S.J. (New York: Paulist Press, 1980); and he also cites John R. Donahue, S.J., "The Challenge of Biblical Renewal to Moral Theology," in *Riding Time Like a River: The Catholic Moral Tradition since Vatican II*, ed. William J. O'Brien (Washington, DC: Georgetown University Press, 1993), 59–80. For helpful guidelines to employing scripture within moral theology, see Grabowski, *Sex and Virtue*, 26–28.

16. Grabowski, *Sex and Virtue*, 63. Grabowski adds, "Life in the Spirit is enfleshed in the body and indeed in sexuality" (ibid., 64).

17. Beth Felker Jones, *Faithful: A Theology of Sex* (Grand Rapids, MI: Zondervan, 2015), 41–42. As she adds, "Good, married sex isn't just about the self. It's *for* others: for the spouse, for the world, and for God.... God provides us with manifold goods—including fidelity and fruitfulness and grace [Augustine's three "goods" of marriage]—that order our sexuality away from idols, that turn our sexuality from ingrown selfishness to kingdom work, and that train us to point our whole lives—body and soul, sex included—toward the only One who can truly satisfy the animals that we are, the God we have met in Jesus Christ" (ibid., 42–43). See also Jonathan Grant, *Divine Sex: A Compelling Vision for Christian Relationships in a Hypersexualized Age* (Grand Rapids, MI: Brazos Press, 2015).

18. *ST* I-II, q. 106, a. 4, ad 4.

19. Joseph C. Atkinson, *Biblical and Theological Foundations of the Family: The Domestic Church* (Washington, DC: Catholic University of America Press, 2014), 71–72.

20. Wright, *Paul and the Faithfulness of God*, 1508. Richard Hays states similarly, "Many of his [Paul's] standards for sexual morality... are carried forward directly from Jewish tradition" (*Moral Vision of the New Testament*, 41). For further background, see Markus Bockmuehl, "The Noachide Commandments and the New Testament," in *Jewish Law in Gentile Churches: Halakhah and the Beginning of Christian Public Ethics*

(Grand Rapids, MI: Baker Academic, 2000), 145–73; Richard B. Hays, "The Conversion of the Imagination: Scripture and Eschatology in 1 Corinthians," in *Torah Ethics and Early Christian Identity*, ed. Susan J. Wendel and David M. Miller (Grand Rapids, MI: Eerdmans, 2016), 151–73; S. A. Cummins, "Torah, Jesus, and the Kingdom of God in the Gospel of Mark," in Wendel and Miller, *Torah Ethics and Early Christian Identity*, 59–74; Brian S. Rosner, *Paul, Scripture and Ethics: A Study of 1 Corinthians 5–7* (Leiden: Brill, 1994). See also Chaim Rapoport, *Judaism and Homosexuality: An Authentic Orthodox View*, with a foreword by Jonathan Sacks (London: Valentine Mitchell, 2004); David Novak, "Jewish Marriage: Nature, Covenant, and Contract," in *Jewish Justice: The Contested Limits of Nature, Law, and Covenant* (Waco, TX: Baylor University Press, 2017), 101–23.

21. Aquinas quotes Galatians 5:19 in *ST* II-II, q. 154, a. 1, obj. 6.
22. Wright, *Paul and the Faithfulness of God*, 1112.
23. Wright, *New Testament and the People of God*, 448. Wright adds, "If one belonged to it, one did not belong any more, certainly not in the same way, to one's previous unit, whether familial or racial" (ibid.); but Wright here is not denying the importance of families (in the standard sense).
24. Joseph H. Hellerman, *When the Church Was a Family: Recapturing Jesus' Vision for Authentic Christian Community* (Nashville: B&H Academic, 2009), 142. See also Ephesians 3:14–19, directing our minds Godward: "For this reason I bow my knees before the Father, from whom every family in heaven and on earth is named, that according to the riches of his glory he may grant you to be strengthened with might through his Spirit in the inner man, and that Christ may dwell in your hearts through faith; that you, being rooted and grounded in love, may have power to comprehend with all the saints what is the breadth and length and height and depth, and to know the love of Christ which surpasses knowledge, that you may be filled with all the fulness of God."
25. Wright, *Paul and the Faithfulness of God*, 1113. Wright comments further that "Paul is thinking of the formation of a genuine humanity who will reflect the divine image into the world; and the things which mar this image are to be left behind in dying with the Messiah in baptism, in the sanctifying presence of the spirit" (ibid.).
26. On Colossians 3:5, see N. T. Wright, *The Epistles of Paul to the Colossians and to Philemon: An Introduction and Commentary* (Grand Rapids, MI: Eerdmans, 1986), 134: "The word here translated *sexual immorality* refers to any intercourse outside marriage: in the ancient world, as in the modern, intercourse with a prostitute would be a specific, and in

pagan culture a frequent, instance of this. *Impurity* highlights the contamination of character effected by immoral behaviour. The word rendered *lust* could refer to any overmastering passion, but regularly, as here, indicates uncontrolled sexual urges."

27. I recognize that this passage is missing from the earliest manuscripts, but no doubt the Holy Spirit had good reason for its inclusion in the canonical gospel.

28. See for example N. T. Wright, "The Letter to the Romans," in *The New Interpreter's Bible* (Nashville: Abingdon, 2002), 10:435.

29. Ibid., 436; cf. 769.

30. N. T. Wright, *The Last Word: Beyond the Bible Wars to a New Understanding of the Authority of Scripture* (New York: HarperCollins, 2005), 43.

31. In a Barthian vein, Christopher R. J. Holmes—whose more recent work has taken an instructive Thomistic turn—argues that "concreteness in ethics is achieved by Christ's ongoing activity as living minister" and that scripture "is the chief form of his ministering presence" (*Ethics in the Presence of Christ* [London: T&T Clark International, 2012], 149). I agree, though I would add (as I believe Holmes would agree) that scripture is written and mediated by God's people and that those in search of concrete Christian ethics are called to hear scripture in the Spirit-guided Church, whose head is the living Christ. In hearing God's word in the Church, which is governed by the incarnate Word, one also becomes attuned to the way in which Scripture's moral claims draw upon and require (without being reducible to) philosophical claims rooted in the created order, as befits the creative Word Jesus Christ.

32. Wright, *Last Word*, 51.

33. Ibid., 54.

34. Ibid., 61. Wright critiques later allegorical exegesis and the four "senses" of Scripture, but in my view, he exaggerates the problems with these approaches and does not appreciate the biblical grounds for why ecclesial tradition (under the guidance of the Spirit) was and is held in such esteem by Catholics. On this point, see the introduction to my *Was the Reformation a Mistake? Why Catholic Doctrine Is Not Unbiblical*, with a response by Kevin J. Vanhoozer (Grand Rapids, MI: Zondervan, 2017), where I describe the biblically warranted modes for determining what is biblical doctrine (perhaps misled by the book's subtitle, Vanhoozer misunderstands me to be proposing that certain Catholic doctrines are merely "not unbiblical" rather than "biblical"). Wright's basic account of scripture's function, nonetheless, accords with the patristic and medieval understanding of scripture's function.

35. Wright, *Last Word*, 103. This of course is the crucial issue. For further reflection, see my *Engaging the Doctrine of Revelation: The Mediation of the Gospel through Church and Scripture* (Grand Rapids, MI: Baker Academic, 2014).

36. Wright, *Last Word*, 114.

37. Ibid., 116.

38. Ibid., 125. From a different angle, but with the same recognition that the authority of scripture and God's history with his covenantal people are inseparable, see Joseph Ratzinger / Pope Benedict XVI's observation in his foreword to the first volume of his *Jesus of Nazareth*:

> The Scripture emerged from within the heart of a living subject—the pilgrim People of God—and lives within this same subject. One could say that the books of Scripture involve three interacting subjects. First of all, there is the individual author or group of authors to whom we owe a particular scriptural text. But these authors are not autonomous writers in the modern sense; they form part of a collective subject, the "People of God," from within whose heart and to whom they speak. Hence, this subject is actually the deeper "author" of the Scriptures. And yet likewise, this people does not exist alone; rather, it knows that it is led, and spoken to, by God himself, who—through men and their humanity—is at the deepest level the one speaking. The connection with the subject we call "People of God" is vital for Scripture. On one hand, this book—Scripture—is the measure that comes from God, the power directing the people. On the other hand, though, Scripture lives precisely within this people, even as this people transcends itself in Scripture. Through their self-transcendence (a fruit, at the deepest level, of the incarnate Word) they become the people of *God*. The People of God—the Church—is the living subject of Scripture; it is in the Church that the words of the Bible are always in the present. This also means, of course, that the People has to receive its very self from God, ultimately from the incarnate Christ; it has to let itself be ordered, guided, and led by him. (Joseph Ratzinger [Pope Benedict XVI], *Jesus of Nazareth: From the Baptism in the Jordan to the Transfiguration*, trans. Adrian J. Walker [New York: Doubleday, 2007], xx–xxi)

See also Pope Benedict XVI, *Verbum Domini*, Vatican trans. (Boston: Pauline Books & Media, 2010), as well as the arguments of my *Participatory Biblical Exegesis: A Theology of Biblical Interpretation* (Notre Dame, IN: University of Notre Dame Press, 2008). More recently see the valuable contributions of Joseph K. Gordon, *Divine Scripture in Human Under-*

standing: A Systematic Theology of the Christian Bible (Notre Dame, IN: University of Notre Dame Press, 2019).

39. Margaret A. Farley, R.S.M., *Just Love: A Framework for Christian Sexual Ethics* (New York: Continuum, 2006), 183. Another Catholic moral theologian, Christine E. Gudorf, makes the same point: "Internal contradiction, beginning with the New Testament itself, forces us to set aside large parts of the Christian tradition.... Again and again in scripture, and in subsequent theological tradition, texts conflict, and we must choose that which accords better with the overall message of the gospel as that gospel is experienced in our individual lives and in communities" (Gudorf, *Body, Sex, and Pleasure: Reconstructing Christian Sexual Ethics* [Cleveland, OH: Pilgrim Press, 1994], 13). Gudorf emphasizes, therefore, that the fact that "all scripture and theology" are "historically conditioned" is not the reason why she advocates "jettison[ing] large parts of the Christian sexual tradition" (ibid., 12).

40. Farley, *Just Love*, 195.

41. Ibid., 194. Arguing that "large parts of the Christian sexual tradition are incompatible with the God we experience and worship," Gudorf states that "experience is, and always has been, the most reliable source for discerning God's will. Today it is experience of sexuality within the contemporary church which has led many to question or reject those aspects of the Christian tradition which present sexuality as morally dangerous or sinful, devoid of the capacity to reveal God" (Gudorf, *Body, Sex, and Pleasure*, 12). See also the conclusion of Andrew Fiala: "Jesus does seem to advocate a certain sort of tolerance even though he maintains a fairly stringent and traditional idea of sex and gender. This contradiction is not easily resolved within the Christian framework. To resolve it properly, we need a fuller defense of individual liberty, a more comprehensive account of sexuality, and a less patriarchal view of women. In other words, we need to go beyond the Bible and develop a more comprehensive and rational theory of sexual ethics" (*What Would Jesus Really Do? The Power and Limits of Jesus' Moral Teachings* [Lanham, MD: Rowman & Littlefield, 2007], 112).

42. Farley, *Just Love*, 195. From a different perspective, drawing upon the work of Stephen Fowl, David Matzko McCarthy argues, "Insofar as we learn the virtues and practices of Christian community, we are learning how to approach Scripture well. An incarnational approach to the function of Scripture and the significance of Jesus for today will invite us into practices of steadfast love, the confession of our sins, forgiveness, reconciliation, and a discernment of the Spirit in our lives" ("Jesus Christ, Scripture, and Ethics," in *Gathered for the Journey: Moral Theology in Catholic*

Perspective, ed. David Matzko McCarthy and M. Therese Lysaught [Grand Rapids, MI: Eerdmans, 2007], 64). McCarthy urges that we do not "have to get the theory right or have expert knowledge before we put our understanding into practice (i.e., that we must know precisely what a biblical text means before we can put it into practice)" (ibid., 65). While I agree with McCarthy that living a Christian life helps us to understand what scripture teaches about the moral life to which followers of Christ are called, I think that McCarthy's essay neglects the way in which scripture contains concrete moral teachings whose basic meaning can be understood by believers and nonbelievers alike (for example, the commandment not to commit adultery). We should not suppose that scripture's ethical teachings can only be cognitively apprehended by those who are living as Christians. See also Stephen Fowl, *Engaging Scripture: A Model of Theological Interpretation* (Oxford: Blackwell, 1998). McCarthy also directs attention to Spohn, *Go and Do Likewise*. According to McCarthy, "Spohn proposes that a primary function of Scripture in the moral life is to allow us to begin to see the world from God's point of view (however challenging that might be) and to experience our lives in light of this vision of the world. We are called not only to experience the call of God in Scripture, but also to become experienced listeners and readers of Scripture. We become experienced not merely by opening a book, but through prayer, common worship (especially the celebration of the Eucharist), and following Jesus' way of love" ("Jesus Christ, Scripture, and Ethics," 65).

43. Todd A. Salzman and Michael G. Lawler accept that "Christians automatically appeal to their sacred scripture, believed to be *Dei verbum*, the very word of God, to substantiate their theological claims, including their moral theological claims" (Salzman and Lawler, *The Sexual Person: Toward a Renewed Catholic Anthropology* [Washington, DC: Georgetown University Press, 2008], 12). But they point out that scripture developed within history and its moral teachings are historically conditioned, as are the moral teachings of the Church through the centuries. They suggest that a "historical-critical hermeneutic" (ibid., 13) shows that particular acts consistently condemned in the New Testament and throughout the course of the Church's history may in fact be licit. As Salzman and Lawler say,

> Because the scriptural rule of faith and the theological writings selectively derived from it are historically and culturally conditioned, they will require translation, interpretation, and inculturation to truly disclose God in every different historical and cultural situation. Because the translators, interpreters, and inculturators may stand in different sociohistorical contexts, their interpretations of the classic tradition

> will almost certainly be pluriform, which will lead to dialectic. That dialectic will be resolved only by intellectually, morally, religiously, and psychically converted theologians in respectful dialogue. Discovering what scripture says about sexual morality, therefore, is never as straightforward as simply reading the text. . . . It is never enough simply to read the text to find out what it says about sexual morality. Its original sociohistorical context must first be clarified and then the text can be translated, interpreted, and inculturated in a contemporary context. (ibid., 14)

Salzman and Lawler then point out that the entirety of scripture and almost all (or all) of the centuries of the Church's interpretation of scripture are marked by patriarchy, although there are also liberative elements in scripture and tradition. Given the distortion that patriarchy causes, "if we accept the Bible as a source for moral judgments about sexual morality, the Catholic tradition requires that we first examine the sociocultural assumptions that underpin what is said about sexual morality" (ibid., 15). On this basis, Salzman and Lawler rule out any "unidirectional instruction from the Bible and Christian tradition to human sexual experience," and they require that "contemporary human experience and understanding of sexuality and sexual activity are equal partners in the moral dialogue" (ibid., 16). They conclude that Farley is right in affirming the moral goodness of homosexual intercourse that "is mutually freely chosen, just, and loving" (ibid., 234). Similarly, they support the licitness, where loving couples are involved, of "the occasional use of artificial means to bring about conception without a sexual act, or to avoid conception with a sexual act" (ibid., 249). They support embryo adoption to "provide, for lesbian couples, an opportunity to participate in both the gestational and nurturing dimensions of parenthood" and observe that "there is no credible social scientific evidence to support the claim that homosexual parenting has a negative impact on children" (ibid., 253)—despite the radical injustice done to the child who is thereby deprived of his or her father. We are here very far from the biblical text, whose actual teachings about sexual ethics are on this view not intended to be normative for followers of Jesus, or at least should not be received today as normative. Salzman and Lawler have historicized the teaching of scripture and the Church in a manner that evacuates that teaching of any normative value, and they have also made "nature" into a purely "socially constructed category" (ibid., 259). As a result, they greatly undervalue God's effective communication of true teachings about sexual ethics in scripture and tradition. For a cognate position, see Lisa Sowle Cahill, "Same-Sex Marriage and Catholicism: Dialogue, Learning, and

Change," in *Inquiry, Thought, and Expression*, ed. J. Patrick Hornbeck II and Michael A. Norko, vol. 2 of *More than a Monologue: Sexual Diversity and the Catholic Church* (New York: Fordham University Press, 2014), 141–55. Cahill argues, "For Aquinas, moral values and norms are not known deductively but practically—by the practical reason engaged with the world and human relationships, discerning what does and does not lead to human fulfillment and to the enjoyment of the goods 'natural' to humans" (ibid., 144). Missing here, however, is the relation of prudence and synderesis, and also the instruction given to fallen practical reason by divine revelation in scripture and tradition. Citing Salzman and Lawler, Cahill argues that Christians should conclude that "both heterosexual and homosexual acts and relationships are moral if they exhibit holistic complementarity, equality, freedom, mutuality, and commitment" (ibid., 147). The significance of actual male and female bodiliness—and thus ultimately of father and mother—ends up with no real place, in part because sexual acts are denuded of their teleological bodily grounding, and in part because sexual relationships are presented simply in terms of consenting individuals (rather than in light of children). Cahill strenuously attempts to avoid the latter problem, as when (in an earlier book) she observes with concern that "a new generation of sexual attitudes and practices in liberal democratic societies presents mutual consent as practically the sole behavior-guiding norm, and hardly encourages ongoing responsibility either for one's sexual partner, or for the procreative potentials of sex" (*Sex, Gender, and Christian Ethics* [Cambridge: Cambridge University Press, 1996], 10; cf. 206). Indeed, she recognizes that women primarily "seek . . . a mutually responsible and intimate human relationship in sex, including an experience of maternity that flows from and represents such reciprocity," but she balances this insight with the concern that "for women, marriage and family are dangerous, at least as traditionally practiced" (due to patriarchy), and she warns that attending to male-female bodily teleology in sexual acts leads to an unrealistic and burdensome (especially upon women) requirement that sexual acts must *achieve* procreation and embody *perfect* self-gift (ibid., 198–205). In *Sex, Gender, and Christian Ethics*, Cahill is willing to grant that "the Christian family may be seen as a biologically-based sphere of affections" and that "incorporating homosexual people in the Christian community does not necessarily denigrate the ideals of virginity (introduced by Christians) or faithful, mutual, heterosexual marriage (transformatively appropriated by Christians from cultural trends)," while indicating support for homosexual sexual acts within appropriate relationships (ibid., 158–59, 210). In "Same-Sex Marriage and Catholicism," however, she abandons the biological dimension of marriage and family while arguing that same-sex marriage can in fact be equally "procreative- and family-focused" in its understanding of marriage (155)—which means that the absence from the outset of father (or mother) is not an injustice to the child (a claim that, were it true, would explode any "procreative- and family-focused" understanding of sexual intercourse, marital or otherwise). See also the reflections on historical consciousness and rejection of absolute norms in moral matters in Charles E. Curran, *The Development of Moral Theology: Five Strands* (Washington, DC: Georgetown University Press, 2013). For better practical and philosophical foundations for reflecting on these issues, see Helen M. Alvaré, *Putting Children's Interests First in US Family Law and Policy: With Power Comes Responsibility* (Cambridge: Cambridge University Press, 2018); Ryan J. Brady, *Conforming to Right Reason: On the Ends of the Moral Virtues and the Roles of Prudence and Synderesis* (Steubenville, OH: Emmaus Academic Press, forthcoming).

44. Farley, *Just Love*, 33.
45. Ibid., 34, 36.
46. Ibid., 38.
47. She states, "The Christian Testament, like the Hebrew Bible, is also not a very helpful source if our question has to do with moral prohibitions or permissions regarding same-sex relationships" (ibid., 274).
48. Ibid. She gives particular attention to John Boswell, *Christianity, Social Tolerance, and Homosexuality: Gay People in Western Europe from the Beginning of the Christian Era to the Fourteenth Century* (Chicago: University of Chicago Press, 1980); Hays, *Moral Vision of the New Testament*, chapter 16; Hays, "Relations Natural and Unnatural: A Response to John Boswell's Exegesis of Romans 1," *Journal of Religious Ethics* 14 (1986): 184–215; and Dale B. Martin, "Heterosexism and the Interpretation of Romans 1:18–31," *Biblical Interpretation* 3 (1995): 332–55. In her view, Martin and Boswell have the best of the argument, against Hays's view that Romans 1:26–27 rules out homosexual activity for Christians today. In favor of her perspective, she could also have cited the Catholic theologian Daniel A. Helminiak's influential best seller *What the Bible Really Says about Homosexuality*, rev. ed. (Tajique, NM: Alamo Square Press, 2000), though Helminiak argues that homosexual "sex with youth in the ancient world was generally not child abuse as we understand it today" (130) and suggests that David was the homosexual lover of both Saul and Jonathan. Farley also argues that

> the story of Sodom and Gomorrah (Gen. 19:1–29), today popularly thought to present a threatened crime of homosexual rape at the heart of the sins of the cities (Gen. 1–11), has no such meaning when looked

at more carefully. In its earliest interpretations—that is, in other Hebrew Bible and apocryphal texts—the extreme moral depravity of the citizens of Sodom and other cities of the plain was identified not with homosexuality but with violations of moral requirements of hospitality, as well as with injustice, arrogance, and hatred of foreigners (Ezek. 16:49; Sirach 16:8; Wisd. Of Sol. 10:6–8; 19:13–15). In the Christian Testament, where Sodom is referenced, again there is no mention of homosexuality (Luke 10:12; Matt. 10:15). What influenced later Christians to introduce an identification of homosexual sins as central to this story was probably the interpretation of first century C.E. Jewish writers, in particular the historian Josephus and the Hellenistic philosopher Philo. (Farley, *Just Love*, 274)

Farley grants that homosexual acts (at least, in her view, between men) are condemned as sinful by the Hebrew Bible. Farley's discussion of Romans 1:26–27 and of the biblical teaching on homosexual acts is very brief and relies upon her preference for interpretations that go against the grain of the plain sense of the biblical texts and upon her dismissal of the Church's consistent interpretation of these texts. For a thorough study of the moral status of homosexual actions according to Scripture, which takes its bearings from Genesis 1–2 and thus locates the key texts within a full scriptural framework, see Robert A. J. Gagnon, *The Bible and Homosexual Practice: Texts and Hermeneutics* (Nashville: Abingdon, 2002). Gagnon painstakingly demonstrates that biblically speaking, homosexual acts are immoral.

49. Farley, *Just Love*, 41. For a thorough exposition and defense of Augustine's views (in their historical context, and in light of their reception over the centuries), see Anthony Dupont, Wim François, Paul van Geest, and Mathijs Lamberigts, "Sex," in *The Oxford Guide to the Historical Reception of Augustine*, vol. 3, ed. Karla Pollmann (Oxford: Oxford University Press, 2013), 1726–35.

50. Farley, *Just Love*, 231. Farley dismisses the contributions of Aquinas: "Thomas Aquinas wrote in the thirteenth century when rigorism regarding sex already prevailed in Christian teaching and church discipline. His remarkable synthesis of Christian theology did not offer much that was innovative in the area of sexual ethics" (ibid., 43–44).

51. For a valuable response to Farley's *Just Love* (and to Todd Salzman and Michael Lawler's *Sexual Person*), see John S. Grabowski, *Transformed in Christ: Essays on the Renewal of Moral Theology* (Ave Maria, FL: Sapientia Press, 2017), 233–50. Grabowski points out,

> A concept of justice invoked as a source for the moral evaluation of human sexual activity must be able to account for the basic equality of

dignity and rights of all persons grounded by a shared human nature *and* the irreducible differences between men and women as persons, which are the basis of marriage itself both naturally and sacramentally.... The concept of justice invoked by Farley, and by Salzman and Lawler who rely on her, presupposes a view of persons as autonomous and largely self-creating subjects who must be treated as basically interchangeable. Justice understood as mere fairness must abstract itself from the contingencies of difference and the body and view all individuals, relationships, and sexual activity on equal and interchangeable terms. Conversely, the concept of justice defended by the Church is specified by reference to the body, by sexual difference and its life-giving potential, even while defending the dignity and rights of persons grounded in a shared human nature. But more than this it is specified by the demands of justice toward the Creator, who made male and female in his own image and endowed them with the capacity to become cocreators with him in the generation of new human life. (ibid., 248; see also Pope John Paul II [Wojtyła], *Love and Responsibility*, 211–61)

The only significant discussions of scriptural texts that Farley provides in her book, so far as I can tell, have to do with homosexual actions (ibid., 273–76); with the ambiguities and tensions in the New Testament's teachings on marriage and family (ibid., 255–57); and with the differentiation between male and female found in Genesis 1:27 and called into question by Galatians 3:28 (ibid., 140–44). See also the Congregation for the Doctrine of the Faith's 2012 "Notification on the Book *Just Love: A Framework for Christian Sexual Ethics*, by Sr. Margaret A. Farley, R.S.M.," available via the Vatican website, http://www.vatican.va/roman_curia/congregations/cfaith/documents/rc_con_cfaith_doc_20120330_nota-farley_en.html. The CDF points out that Farley, by presenting her claims as though there were no authoritative magisterial interpretations of the scriptural teaching about sexual ethics and the indissolubility of marriage (and thereby de facto assuming that the Church cannot definitively guide the faithful on these matters), "does not present a correct understanding of the role of the Church's Magisterium as the teaching authority of the Bishops united with the Successor of Peter, which guides the Church's ever deeper understanding of the Word of God as found in Holy Scripture and handed on faithfully in the Church's living tradition." The CDF concludes that Farley's book is not "a valid expression of Catholic teaching."

52. Second Vatican Council, *Dei Verbum*, §§6–7, in Flannery, *Conciliar and Post Conciliar Documents*, 752–53.

53. Second Vatican Council, *Optatam Totius*, §16, in Flannery, *Conciliar and Post Conciliar Documents*, 720.

54. Marie-Dominique Chenu, O.P., *Toward Understanding Saint Thomas*, trans. A.-M. Landry, O.P., and D. Hughes, O.P. (Chicago: Henry Regnery, 1964), 68. Philosophical reflection on human nature pertains to this goal of understanding God's Word more deeply.

55. Wright, *Paul and the Faithfulness of God*, 1113.

56. *ST* I, q. 93, a. 4. See also David Braine, *The Human Person: Animal and Spirit* (Notre Dame, IN: University of Notre Dame Press, 1992). I discuss humans as the image of God in my *Jewish-Christian Dialogue and the Life of Wisdom: Engagements with the Theology of David Novak* (London: Continuum, 2010), chapter 3, and my *Engaging the Doctrine of Creation: Cosmos, Creatures, and the Wise and Good Creator* (Grand Rapids, MI: Baker Academic, 2017), chapter 4.

57. See *ST* I-II, q. 90, a. 2. Mary M. Keys notes that "Aquinas's connection of moral rectitude, or goodness of will, with the common good is not primarily a matter of negatives, of *not desiring* particular goods, but rather desiring especially the highest or intrinsically most common" (*Aquinas, Aristotle, and the Promise of the Common Good*, 123). She explains that for Aquinas, "the cultivation of the ethical virtues should not be done solely with a view to benefit the individual, but should also extend to serve the family, the civic community, and the community of the universe, all under God and ultimately for the sake of God" (ibid., 131; cf. François Daguet, O.P., *Du politique chez Thomas d'Aquin* [Paris: J. Vrin, 2015], 60–65). See also Michael Waldstein, "Children as the Common Good of Marriage," *Nova et Vetera* 7 (2009): 697–709. Waldstein notes that in much discussion of marriage, "attention is focused on the individual person, on his or her dignity, on the mutual love between two unique persons, yet in such a way that the importance of the common good, its importance *precisely as the good of the person*, tends to fade from view" (ibid., 697). In addition to its citations from Clement of Alexandria, John Chrysostom, Thomas Aquinas, Matthias Scheeben, and Karol Wojtyła/John Paul II on the common good, Waldstein's essay retrieves the important book of Charles De Koninck, published in English translation as "On the Primacy of the Common Good: Against the Personalists," trans. Sean Collins, *Aquinas Review* 4 (1997): 1–71. For expansion upon De Koninck's argument, connecting it with natural law, see Stephen L. Brock, "The Primacy of the Common Good and the Foundations of Natural Law in St. Thomas," in Hütter and Levering, *Ressourcement Thomism*, 234–55.

58. *ST* II-II, q. 151, a. 1. As Daniel A. Westberg says, "Even while we want to affirm the inherent goodness of sexual desire and activity, when in

accordance with God's will, we need to be aware of the strength and potential for corruption of sexual desire when it is misplaced, disordered, excessive, and not directed by prudence" (*Renewing Moral Theology*, 218). To understand Aquinas's viewpoint here it is important to avoid "the conflation of 'subjection' (the condition of politic rule [reason's political rule of the passions]) with 'domination' or 'control'" (Miner, *Thomas Aquinas on the Passions*, 108). Furthermore, for Aquinas "concupiscence" is a passion (rather than a mere sinful tendency), even though the human passion of concupiscence is affected by human fallenness, and so when Aquinas speaks of concupiscence, he often has lust in view. For discussion see Miner, *Thomas Aquinas on the Passions*, 150–59. Miner remarks,

> As an appetite for sensible good, concupiscence might be regarded as simply a bodily thing, bearing no relation to the spirit. Against this view, Aquinas reminds us that what desires is not the body, but the whole person. . . . As part of our nature, *concupiscentia*, desire for things pleasing to the senses, is in itself good. It goes wrong only when it refuses to be subordinated to the rational appetite for the immaterial good. But even here, blame lies less in the passion itself and more in the will's decision to choose the lower good as if it were the higher good. (ibid., 151–52, 159)

Note that Miner is willing to use the term "control," properly understood, as are most commentators. See Giuseppe Butera, "On Reason's Control of the Passions in Aquinas's Theory of Temperance," *Mediaeval Studies* 68 (2006): 133–60.

59. See Grabowski, *Sex and Virtue*, 77: "According to the Bishop of Hippo [Augustine], *concupiscentia* is the result of original sin and disorders all human desires—the more intense the desire, the greater the disorder. Because of its intensity, sexual desire is profoundly affected by concupiscence." In his *Making of Moral Theology*, 45, John Mahoney, S.J., blames Augustine for introducing a "sombre pessimism" that is "dogmatic and devastating" into Catholic moral theology. Allowing for the corrections to Augustine that Aquinas and others introduce, it needs to be said that Mahoney's view of Augustine is a serious exaggeration. The "sombre pessimism" is already present in scripture itself, and the reason it is there has to do not with a Manichaean spirit, but with the fact that human sexuality is fallen. Mahoney opposes "the theory of moral absolutes as it has derived from Aquinas," especially moral absolutes regarding human sexual acts (ibid., 313; cf. 317–19).

60. Westberg, *Renewing Moral Theology*, 215.

61. *ST* II-II, q. 151, a. 1, ad 1.

62. Plé, *Chastity and the Affective Life*, 141; cf. 146–48.

63. For discussion see Petri, *Aquinas and the Theology of the Body*, 275–308; Feser, "In Defense of the Perverted Faculty Argument," 388–92. Aquinas observes that there is properly "the greatest friendship between husband and wife, for they are united not only in the act of fleshly union, which produces a certain gentle association even among beasts, but also in the partnership of the whole range of domestic activity" (*Summa contra gentiles* III, q. 123; in Aquinas, *Summa contra gentiles*, book 3, "Providence," part 2, trans. Vernon J. Bourke [Notre Dame, IN: University of Notre Dame Press, 1975], 148). See also the superb discussion of marital friendship (according to Aquinas) in Gondreau, "'Inseparable Connection,'" 754–58. For a view that relativizes the procreative end, see Lisa Fullam, "Toward a Virtue Ethics of Marriage: Augustine and Aquinas on Friendship in Marriage," *Theological Studies* 73 (2012): 663–92; see the response to Fullam in Ron Haflidson, "Outward, Inward, Upward: Why Three Goods of Marriage for Augustine?," *Studies in Christian Ethics* 29 (2016): 51–68.

64. *ST* I, q. 91, a. 3. For discussion see Jan Aertsen, *Nature and Creature: Thomas Aquinas's Way of Thought* (Leiden: Brill, 1988), 162–65, 335; Norbert Luyten, "The Significance of the Body in a Thomistic Anthropology," *Philosophy Today* 7 (1963): 175–93; Paul Gondreau, "The 'Inseparable Connection' between Procreation and Unitive Love (*Humanae Vitae*, §12) and Thomistic Hylemorphic Anthropology," *Nova et Vetera* 6 (2008): 736–38, 751–53. Gondreau observes that for Aquinas "the body is the necessary condition for the existence of the soul, even while the soul, for whose sake the body exists, is necessary for the realization of the body" (737). I note that the evolutionary development of human bodies, under the guidance of divine providence, does not mean that we can no longer intelligibly speak of "human nature." On this point see the succinct remarks of Alasdair MacIntyre in the preface to his *After Virtue*, 3rd ed. (Notre Dame, IN: University of Notre Dame Press, 2007), as well as Michele M. Schumacher, "The Nature of Nature in Feminism, Old and New: From Dualism to Complementary Unity," in *Women in Christ: Toward a New Feminism*, ed. Michele M. Schumacher (Grand Rapids, MI: Eerdmans, 2004), 17–51, and John Finnis, "The Natural Law, Objective Morality, and Vatican II," in *Principles of Catholic Moral Life*, ed. William E. May (Chicago: Franciscan Herald, 1980), 141–42. Although he does not agree with many of the Catholic Church's teachings on sexual ethics, Stephen J. Pope rightly recognizes that "human nature is . . . teleological in that it is naturally oriented both to specific goods and, more importantly, to the good as

such" ("Reason and Natural Law," in Meilaender and Werpehowski, *Oxford Handbook of Theological Ethics*, 161). From a proportionalist perspective, however, Pope argues that we should focus our attention on the "concrete goods and evils at stake in particular situations" (ibid., 163). This opens the door for acts such as adultery to be judged morally good in particular situations, given sufficient concrete goods in relation to the concrete evils. A deeper understanding of the ordering of body-soul human nature would help Pope to see that the morality of human actions is not as situation-dependent as he implies, even though the moral evaluation of human actions always includes the circumstances. Jesus and the apostle Paul rightly condemn a variety of kinds of actions as simply incompatible with the kingdom of God.

65. Gondreau, "The 'Inseparable Connection' between Procreation and Unitive Love (*Humanae Vitae*, §12) and Thomistic Hylemorphic Anthropology," 749. Gondreau's paragraph is worth quoting in full:

> In the sexual sphere, the Cartesian view has certainly played a significant role in the post-modern tendency to consider the body a pure instrument without value in and of itself. Not infrequently, the body today is treated as a kind of morally neutral playground, as a kind of Never-Never Land, where, like Peter Pan, we prefer perpetually to play without a proper grown-up sense of moral responsibility. The body's sole aim, at least sexually speaking, is utilitarian, namely, to provide pleasure or enjoyment for the "self" (the soul). "Consent," provided by the "self" (the soul), is the only essential ingredient to morally acceptable sexual activity. (ibid.)

Obviously Gondreau strongly disagrees with this contemporary perspective. As Gondreau says, "To speak of the procreative process as if it were a mere machine is deeply revealing of a disdain for the organic beauty of the human body and of a supposition that the procreative dimension is purely accidental to our sexuality" (ibid., 753). Karol Wojtyła, in an article originally published in Italian in 1978 while he was still a cardinal, remarks similarly (with an emphasis on the personal dimension of human natural teleology) that "there seems to weigh on the modern mentality the division of a Cartesian type that opposes in man his understanding, his consciousness, and his body," and he notes that Pope Paul VI's encyclical *Humanae Vitae* "considers the body not as an autonomous being, with its own structure and dynamic, but as a component of the whole man in his personal constitution.... The respect due to the body, particularly in its procreative functions—functions rooted in the whole specific somatic quality of sex—

is respect for the human being, that is, for the dignity of the man and the woman" ("The Anthropological Vision of *Humanae Vitae*," trans. William E. May, *Nova et Vetera* 7 [2009]: 746). See also Steven A. Long, "Natural Law, the Moral Object, and *Humanae Vitae*," in *Ressourcement Thomism*, 285–311.

66. On "eternal law," see especially *ST* I-II, q. 93, aa. 1–6. See also John Rziha, *Perfecting Human Actions: St. Thomas Aquinas on Human Participation in Eternal Law* (Washington, DC: Catholic University of America Press, 2009). For Aquinas, as J. Budziszewski points out, "Eternal law is the foundation and origin of all law, its *sine qua non*. . . . If eternal law does not exist, then neither does natural law. In fact, properly speaking, we have no nature at all" (*Commentary on Thomas Aquinas's "Treatise on Law"* [Cambridge: Cambridge University Press, 2014], 159).

67. For further discussion see Rziha, *Christian Moral Life*, 267–69. Rziha remarks with regard to natural family planning (periodic abstinence, in accord with the woman's fertility cycle, due to a reasonable need to avoid having another child),

> (1) If a couple believes that the proper end of the sexual act is procreation and unity and they want to avoid pregnancy, then they will abstain. The act of abstaining emphasizes that the proper ends of the sexual act are procreation and unity; (2) If a couple does *not* believe that sex is ordered to procreation and unity, then they will use contraception in order to avoid pregnancy. . . . Does having sex when they [the couple] believe they are infertile violate the higher end of procreation? It does not. The sexual act is still open to procreation, since it is something *outside* of the sexual act [namely, the woman's infertility] that impedes procreation. (ibid., 272)

68. Odozor, *Morality Truly Christian, Truly African*, 267.

69. As Edward Feser observes, "We are talking about *nature's* ends here, not ours" (Feser, "In Defense of the Perverted Faculty Argument," 389; see 391 for a fuller explanation). See also the observation of Perry J. Cahall, *The Mystery of Marriage: A Theology of the Body and the Sacrament* (Chicago: Hillenbrand Books, 2016), 29: "While animal sexual union serves to reproduce a species, human sexual union is an encounter of persons that serves not only to create with God (procreate) another unrepeatable human person, but also to express the self-donation of personal love." Cahall is indebted especially to Pope John Paul II, *Man and Woman He Created Them: A Theology of the Body*, trans. Michael Waldstein (Boston: Pauline Books & Media, 2006), as well as to the personalist shift (though not a shift rejecting the procreative end) initiated in 1929 by Dietrich von

Hildebrand's *Marriage: The Mystery of Faithful Love* (Manchester, NH: Sophia Institute Press, 1991). For discussion of John Paul II's thought in relation to Aquinas's, see Petri, *Aquinas and the Theology of the Body*. See also the analysis of Mary Shivanandan, *Crossing the Threshold of Love: A New Vision of Marriage in the Light of John Paul II's Anthropology* (Washington, DC: Catholic University of America Press, 1999).

70. J. Budziszewski, *On the Meaning of Sex* (Wilmington, DE: ISI Books, 2012), 24. He adds that

> apart from the link between sexual powers and new life, any explanation of why we have sexual powers at all would be woefully incomplete. I think even the most ardent Darwinist would concede this point. . . . If the procreative meaning of sex is granted, the unitive meaning follows. We aren't designed like guppies, who cooperate only for a moment. For us, procreation requires an enduring partnership between two beings, the man and the woman, who are different, but in ways that enable them to complete and balance each other. Union, then, characterizes the distinctly human mode of procreation. A parent of each sex is necessary to make the child, to raise the child, and to teach the child. Both are needed to make them, because the female provides the egg, the male fertilizes it, and the female incubates the resulting zygote. Both are needed to raise him, because the male is better suited to protection, the female to nurture. Both are needed to teach him, because he needs a model of his own sex, a model of the other, and a model of the relationship between them. Mom and dad are jointly irreplaceable. Their partnership in procreation continues even after the kids are grown, because the kids need the help and counsel of their parents to establish their own new families. (ibid., 25–26)

Among many sociological studies he could cite as further evidence for his point, Budziszewski refers to Sara McLanahan and Gary Sandefur, *Growing Up with a Single Parent: What Hurts, What Helps* (Cambridge, MA: Harvard University Press, 1994). Budziszewski's point is particularly helpful given the fact that, as David Matzko McCarthy observes, most contemporary "theological accounts of marriage have . . . been shaped by efforts to deny, on the one hand, that procreation is a necessary end of marriage and, on the other hand, that homosexual acts can be justified. The dismissal of procreation as necessary to sex is usually taken as common sense and receives little argument. With procreation unnecessary, virtually all the weight of marriage is carried by the communion of husband and wife" (McCarthy, *Sex and Love in the Home: A Theology of the Household*, 2nd ed. [London: SCM Press, 2004], 217). As McCarthy recognizes, the view that "procreation is a necessary end of marriage" means that sexual intercourse must be open to procreation (and the raising of children) and intrinsically ordered to it, not that sexual intercourse on the part of an infertile husband and wife is illicit. McCarthy summarizes the Catholic position and suggests that there might be a way of making a "concession" or "exception" to allow for homosexual unions (a "concession" that depends on a presumption of the general impossibility of expecting celibacy from persons with homosexual inclinations, which in my view is neither correct nor a basis for such an exception), but McCarthy leaves his own position unclear.

71. See G. J. McAleer, *Ecstatic Morality and Sexual Politics: A Catholic and Antitotalitarian Theory of the Body* (New York: Fordham University Press, 2005).

72. Adoption of children is a noble action, insofar as it generously provides children who would otherwise lack parents with a mother and a father. For discussion of the practice of adopting children, see Russell Moore, *Adopted for Life: The Priority of Adoption for Christian Families and Churches*, 2nd ed. (Wheaton, IL: Crossway, 2015). More broadly, the *Catechism of the Catholic Church* observes,

> A child is not something *owed* to one, but is a *gift*. The "supreme gift of marriage" is a human person. A child may not be considered a piece of property, an idea to which an alleged "right to a child" would lead. In this area, only the child possesses genuine rights: the right "to be the fruit of the specific act of the conjugal love of his parents," and "the right to be respected as a person from the moment of his conception." The gospel shows that physical sterility is not an absolute evil. Spouses who still suffer from infertility after exhausting legitimate medical procedures should unite themselves with the Lord's Cross, the source of all spiritual fecundity. They can give expression to their generosity by adopting abandoned children or performing demanding services for others. (*Catechism of the Catholic Church*, §§2378–79, citing the Congregation of the Doctrine of the Faith's *Donum Vitae* [available at www.vatican.va])

See also Tony Merida and Rick Morton, *Orphanology: Awakening to Gospel-Centered Adoption and Orphan Care* (Birmingham, AL: New Hope Publishers, 2011); Kelley Nikondeha, *Adopted: The Sacrament of Belonging in a Fractured World* (Grand Rapids, MI: Eerdmans, 2017).

73. See Gondreau, "'Inseparable Connection,'" 762. Gondreau emphasizes "how misleading it is to stick pejorative labels like 'physicalist' or 'biological' onto those moral (natural law) accounts of human sexu-

ality which place such heavy emphasis upon the procreative dimension. Not only is the procreative for the sake of (or even internal to) the unitive love between spouses, but procreation itself signifies something much broader than a mere 'biological' or 'physicalist' act. . . . Human biology does not function as a kind of free-floating mechanism in isolation from a social unit" (ibid., 761–62). Feser demonstrates that emphasis on the mutual self-donation of the spouses or on the language of the body still relies, for its argumentative force, upon implicitly or explicitly affirming the Aristotelian-Thomistic view of "the natural ends of our faculties" ("In Defense of the Perverted Faculty Argument," 413)—without denying that charity governs the Christian use of our sexual faculties. See also the salutary personalist arguments of Eduardo J. Echeverria, *"In the Beginning . . .": A Theology of the Body* [Eugene, OR: Pickwick, 2011], 259); Nigel Zimmermann, *Facing the Other: John Paul II, Levinas, and the Body* (Eugene, OR: Cascade, 2015); Kevin Schemenauer, *Conjugal Love and Procreation: Dietrich von Hildebrand's Superabundant Integration* (Lanham, MD: Lexington Books, 2011); and Angel Perez-Lopez, *Procreation and the Spousal Meaning of the Body: A Thomistic Argument Grounded in Vatican II* (Eugene, OR: Pickwick, 2017).

74. Grabowski, *Transformed in Christ*, 57. In deeming masturbation to be morally wrong because it eschews the proper ordering of sexual activity, the *Catechism of the Catholic Church* similarly remarks that in individual cases, "to form an equitable judgment about the subjects' moral responsibility and to guide pastoral action, one must take into account the affective immaturity, force of acquired habit, conditions of anxiety, or other psychological or social factors that can lessen, if not even reduce to a minimum, moral culpability" (§2352).

75. Indeed, when, in the context of condemning lust, Jesus adds that "if your right hand causes you to sin, cut it off and throw it away" (Mt 5:30), he is most likely referring to masturbation. See W. D. Davies and Dale C. Allison Jr., *A Critical and Exegetical Commentary on the Gospel according to Saint Matthew*, vol. 1, *Introduction and Commentary on Matthew I–VII* (London: T&T Clark International, 2004), 525–26. Davies and Allison's point is that Jesus, in strongly condemning lust in Matthew 5:28, knew of the strong connection between male masturbation (using one's "right hand" [Mt 5:30]) and lust. See also Gushee and Stassen, *Kingdom Ethics*, 261. Gushee and Stassen direct attention here to Davies and Allison's interpretation of Matthew 5:30, but they note, "We are not arguing that self-touching is inherently wrong" (*Kingdom Ethics*, 261). At the same time, however, they observe that a "frequent aspect of the transition from spark of attraction to adultery is masturbation," and they warn against the

fantasizing involved in masturbation (ibid.), which might seem to make masturbation (at least the intentional kind that involves fantasizing) "inherently wrong."

76. *ST* I, q. 98, a. 2, ad 3. In the corpus of this article, Aquinas critiques Gregory of Nyssa's view that there would have been no sexual intercourse in the state of innocence and indeed that human generation would have occurred in some other way. Aquinas states that Gregory holds that "God made man male and female before sin, because He foreknew the mode of generation which would take place after sin, which He foresaw" (*ST* I, q. 98, a. 2). To this view, Aquinas responds: "But this is unreasonable. For what is natural to man was neither acquired nor forfeited by sin. Now it is clear that generation by coition is natural to man by reason of his animal life, which he possessed even before sin . . . , just as it is natural to other perfect animals, as the corporeal members [reproductive organs] make it clear. So we cannot allow that these members [reproductive organs] would not have had a natural use, as other members had, before sin" (ibid.).

77. *ST* I, q. 98, a. 2, ad 3; see also Aquinas's discussion of the nature and function of pleasure in *ST* I-II, qq. 31–34, including his position that all good operations will be pleasurable in some way. For further discussion of Aquinas (and Aristotle) on pleasure, see Miner, *Thomas Aquinas on the Passions*, 160–87; Plé, *Chastity and the Affective Life*, 76–111, emphasizing Aquinas's appreciation for pleasure (in contradistinction to Immanuel Kant and William of Ockham). Plé sums up Aquinas's view of pleasure:

> The moral end of man is thus, all in one: the reality of the honest good, the act which gives it to him, and the pleasure which accompanies this act. It can thus be concluded that the virtuous man's pleasure is included in the last end which he gives to himself. It is included in it, but it is not its only component, not even its main component. . . . Pleasure is felt in all its truth and fruitfulness to the extent that it is caught up in a movement and in a dynamism which end in and are regulated by Good loved for itself. (ibid., 88)

See also the insights into Greek philosophical views of pleasure contained in Van Riel, *Pleasure and the Good Life*.

78. Plé, *Chastity and the Affective Life*, 124. Miner gives the example of how we take pleasure in the use of food: "No matter how pleasing the sensation of tasting chocolate pie, a temperate person is repulsed by the idea of eating the whole pie at a single sitting. She would not will such a thing; such a volition would bring her no pleasure. The self-indulgent man, by contrast, takes pleasure in doing such things. It is not that he enjoys the

taste of the pie more than the temperate person does" (Miner, *Thomas Aquinas on the Passions*, 186).

79. Plé, *Chastity and the Affective Life*, 125.

80. See especially Alexander Pruss, *One Body: An Essay in Christian Sexual Ethics* (Notre Dame, IN: University of Notre Dame Press, 2013). For a constructive Thomistic theology of marriage, see Paul Gondreau, "The Redemption and Divinization of Human Sexuality through the Sacrament of Marriage: A Thomistic Approach," *Nova et Vetera* 10 (2012): 383–413. See also Petri, *Aquinas and the Theology of the Body*, chapter 8; Angela McKay [Knobel], "Aquinas on the End of Marriage," in *Human Fertility: Where Faith and Science Meet*, ed. Richard J. Fehring and Theresa Notare (Milwaukee: Marquette University Press, 2008), 53–70; Mary Catherine Sommers, "Marriage Vows and 'Taking Up a New State,'" *Nova et Vetera* 7 (2009): 679–95; Peter Kwasniewski, "St. Thomas on the Grandeur and Limitations of Marriage," *Nova et Vetera* 10 (2012): 415–36; Guy de Broglie, S.J., "La conception thomiste des deux finalités du marriage," *Doctor Communis* 30 (1974): 3–41; Joseph W. Koterski, S.J., "Aquinas on the Sacrament of Marriage," in *Rediscovering Aquinas and the Sacraments: Studies in Sacramental Theology*, ed. Matthew Levering and Michael Dauphinais (Chicago: Hillenbrand Books, 2009), 102–13. Much more critically, focusing on power relationships, see Colleen McCluskey, "An Unequal Relationship of Equals: Thomas Aquinas on Marriage," *History of Philosophy Quarterly* 24 (2007): 1–18. For contemporary developments with regard to Ephesians 5, see John S. Grabowski, "Mutual Submission and Trinitarian Self-Giving," *Angelicum* 84 (1997): 489–512.

81. Hütter, "Virtue of Chastity and the Scourge of Pornography," 35. Hütter specifies that "in the extant providential order, due to the wounds of original sin, chastity is restored, preserved, and perfected from above, that is, by way of healing and sanctifying grace" (ibid.). He adds, "The restoration and protection of chastity, however, call especially for *communal* intercessory prayers. For such communal practices of prayer acknowledge explicitly the fact that the restoration and protection of chastity depend on the providence and grace of God" (ibid., 36). As an exemplary mode of such communal practices, he gives the example of the Angelic Warfare Confraternity promoted by the Dominican Order. He directs attention here to Brian T. Mullady, O.P., *The Angelic Warfare Confraternity*, 4th ed. (New Hope, KY: St. Martin de Porres Lay Dominicans, 2006). Such practices are necessary in any culture, but particularly in ours, given that "our modern popular entertainment culture and media . . . surround us at every turn and threaten to engulf us in body and soul with blatant incitements to

lust. They have become so highly sexualized for profit that our consciences may become numb" (Kevin Vost, *The Seven Deadly Sins: A Thomistic Guide to Vanquishing Vice and Sin* [Manchester, NH: Sophia Institute Press, 2015], 162). See also the important work of William C. Struthers, *Wired for Intimacy: How Pornography Hijacks the Male Brain* (Downers Grove, IL: InterVarsity Press, 2009).

82. See *ST* II-II, q. 151, a. 4, where Aquinas comments that "purity regards venereal matters properly, and especially the signs thereof, such as impure looks, kisses, and touches. And since the latter are more wont to be observed, purity regards rather these external signs, while chastity regards rather sexual union. Therefore purity is directed to chastity, not as a virtue distinct therefrom, but as expressing a circumstance of chastity." For further discussion see Mattison, *Sermon on the Mount and Moral Theology*, 106–7. See also Mattison's "Movements of Love: A Thomistic Perspective on *Eros* and *Agape*," *Journal of Moral Theology* 1 (2012): 31–60.

83. For a contemporary appreciation of consecrated virginity, see Raniero Cantalamessa, O.F.M. Cap., *Virginity: A Positive Approach to Celibacy for the Sake of the Kingdom of Heaven*, trans. Charles Serignat (New York: Alba House, 1995). Cantalamessa notes with regard to virginity (either prior to marriage or permanent) that contemporary

> secular culture casts suspicion and even ridicule on this traditional value which nature itself defends by surrounding it with the delicate yet sturdy safeguard of modesty. Young men and women are pressured by their surroundings—often even by the school environment which ought to help them mature—to be ashamed of their chastity.... Celibacy and virginity, it is sometimes said, prevent healthy, complete personal development. They keep a man from being fully a man, and a woman from being fully a woman.... The fact is that virginity for the Kingdom is a splendid value which changing times and fashions cannot alter. (ibid., x–xi)

For a critique of the Catholic Church's theology of virginity, see Mark D. Jordan, *The Ethics of Sex* (Oxford: Blackwell, 2002), chapter 3. For extensive patristic background to the theology of virginity, as well as for the full text of Pope Pius XII's encyclical *Sacra Virginitas* (1954), see Joseph-Marie Perrin, O.P., *La virginité chrétienne* (Paris: Desclée de Brouwer, 1955). See also the erudite study of John Bugge, *Virginitas: An Essay in the History of a Medieval Ideal* (The Hague: Martinus Nijhoff, 1975), which suggests—mistakenly in my view—that Christians' valuation of virginity came about because sex was thought to be a product of the fall and thereby sinful. Edward Schillebeeckx, O.P., argues against "the *abolition* of celibacy for priests" but, perhaps, in favor of admitting "married persons not only to the diaconate . . . but also to the priesthood": see his *Celibacy*, trans. C. A. L. Jarrott (New York: Sheed and Ward, 1968), 132, 141. See more recently the valuable theological study by Gary Selin, *Priestly Celibacy: Theological Foundations* (Washington, DC: Catholic University of America Press, 2016).

84. For discussion see Cantalamessa, *Virginity*, 3–8. Jordan argues against the traditional interpretation of this verse: "Jesus' saying is indeed obscure. As some contemporary readers have noted, it is introduced here by a discussion of divorce, and so it may refer to conduct within marriage. To live in a marriage according to the severe standard announced by Jesus is to make oneself a eunuch for the sake of the Kingdom. But many older Christian traditions did not read the saying as an illustration of the rigors of marriage. They read it as an invitation to renounce marriage for the sake of the kingdom. To these readers the passage seemed a counsel of virginity or celibacy" (Jordan, *Ethics of Sex*, 48). See, however, the discussion of this verse in W. D. Davies and Dale C. Allison Jr., *A Critical and Exegetical Commentary on the Gospel according to Saint Matthew*, vol. 3, *Commentary on Matthew XIX–XXVIII* (London: T&T Clark International, 2004), 22–27. See also Grabowski, *Sex and Virtue*, 52–53:

> The radical nature of Jesus' summons is made even more clear in the call given to some to renounce sex and marriage altogether in order to follow him more closely. Diverse New Testament traditions make it clear that this practice, modeled on the witness of John the Baptist and Jesus himself, was highly regarded in early Christian communities (cf. Mt 19:12; 1 Cor 7:7–9, 32–35). In a world dominated by concern to reproduce offspring for one's city or nation, the practice of sexual renunciation was itself a dramatic proclamation of the gospel message. To deliberately step outside the seemingly endless cycle of reproduction, birth, growth, sickness, decay, and death was an announcement writ in bodies and behavior that in Jesus, time as it had been previously known had come to an end and a new era of immortality had broken into human existence.

85. Fagerberg, *On Liturgical Asceticism*, 81. Fagerberg draws here upon a variety of sources, including Karl Rahner, S.J., "Reflections on the Theology of Renunciation," in *Theological Investigations*, vol. 3, *The Theology of the Spiritual Life*, trans. Karl-H. Kruger and Boniface Kruger (Baltimore: Helicon, 1967), 47–57.

86. See *ST* I, q. 12.

87. *ST* II-II, q. 152, a. 2, ad 1. Cajetan Chereso, O.P., discusses the "beauty" of virginity in his *Virtue of Honor and Beauty according to St. Thomas Aquinas*, 69–71.

88. Cantalamessa notes that consecrated virginity

> is a prophetic existence. There has been much discussion in the past about whether virginity is a more prefect state than marriage, and if so in what sense. I believe that it is not *ontologically* (that is, in itself) *a more perfect* state, but it is an *eschatologically more advanced* state, in the sense that it is more like the definitive state towards which we are all journeying. . . . For married people, virginity is a reminder of the primacy of the spirit and of God. It reminds them that God has made us for Himself and that therefore our hearts will always be "unsatisfied," until they rest in Him. It is a reminder, too, that marriage and the family cannot be turned into an idol to which everything and everyone is sacrificed, a kind of absolute in life. Everyone knows how easy it is to hide behind one's family duties ("I have a wife and children") in order to avoid the radical demands of the Gospel, and how easy it is to make a good marriage the supreme ideal and purpose in life, even using its success to measure the success of one's own life. And since the first casualty of such undue absolutization is marriage itself, which is crushed by these disproportionate expectations which it will never be able to satisfy, this is why I say that virginity comes to the aid of married people themselves. (*Virginity*, 7–8; cf. 19–37)

Cantalamessa recognizes that Christian marriage is a sign of the eschatological union of Christ and his Church, and so he does not deny that all Christian life (not only virginity) is eschatological in character. As Paul says about the married and the unmarried, "each has his own special gift from God, one of one kind and one of another" (1 Cor 7:7). By emphasizing that consecrated virginity has to do with "the primacy of the spirit and of God," as Aquinas also does in his own way, Cantalamessa offers a helpful interpretation of Paul's conclusion that "he who marries his betrothed does well; and he who refrains from marriage will do better" (1 Cor 7:38). See also the point made by Sara Butler, M.S.B.T., commenting upon the reception of Vatican II's *Perfectae Caritatis*, that consecrated virginity "has always been considered to have an 'objective superiority' (or 'excellence') as 'a way of showing forth the Church's holiness' because those who embrace it reproduce—as nearly as possible and from a desire to be completely conformed to him—the poverty, chastity, and obedience of Jesus" ("*Perfectae Caritatis*," in *The Reception of Vatican II*, ed. Matthew L. Lamb and Matthew Levering [Oxford: Oxford University Press, 2017], 221).

89. *ST* II-II, q. 152, a. 5, ad 3. See Cantalamessa, *Virginity*, 13.

90. *ST* II-II, q. 153, a. 4, ad 3. See also Hütter, "Virtue of Chastity and the Scourge of Pornography," 34–35. Hütter directs attention here to Craig Steven Titus, *Resilience and the Virtue of Fortitude: Aquinas in Dialogue with the Psychosocial Sciences* (Washington, DC: Catholic University of America Press, 2006), 146.

91. Note that Aquinas ranks the gravity of sexual sins in accord with the ways in which they are "against nature," but I do not discuss these degrees of gravity here because, although they rightly insist upon an "order of nature," they cause unnecessary (and often profound) misunderstanding. For helpful discussions of this topic, see Michael Nolan, "Aquinas and the Act of Love," *New Blackfriars* 92 (March 1996): 115–30; Grabowski, *Sex and Virtue*, 81; Ronald Lawler, O.F.M. Cap., Joseph Boyle, and William E. May, *Catholic Sexual Ethics: A Summary Explanation and Defense*, 2nd ed. (Huntingdon, IN: Our Sunday Visitor, 1998), 58. See also Gilby, "Natural and Unnatural in Morals," although Gilby mistakenly suggests that sexual acts that are not "biographically evaluated" are thereby necessarily evaluated in an impersonal manner.

92. Along similar lines, Cantalamessa—commenting on Galatians 5:24, "those who belong to Christ Jesus have crucified the flesh with its passions and desires"—observes, "It is no joke to crucify one's flesh with its passions and desires, especially sexual desire, which is among the most imperious of all. The desires of the flesh—self-indulgence—are always in opposition to the Spirit (cf. Gal 5:17)" (*Virginity*, 40). Galatians 5:16–17 has to do with self-indulgence, and the import of these verses needs to be taken seriously today: "But I say, walk by the Spirit, and do not gratify the desires of the flesh. For the desires of the flesh are against the Spirit, and the desires of the Spirit are against the flesh."

93. Colleen McCluskey argues that Aquinas's account of virtuous sexual activity "is too narrow insofar as he sees every case of sex not for the sake of reproduction, even within marriage, as objectification" (McCluskey, "Lust and Chastity," in Timpe and Boyd, *Virtues and Their Vices*, 133). I note that Aquinas considers that sex is intrinsically ordered to procreation (or reproduction), but he certainly does *not* hold either that sex must be solely for the sake of reproduction or that a married couple that is infertile (whether because of the woman's monthly cycle, a physical defect, or menopause) cannot licitly have sex. With regard to whether it is licit for a married person to have sex with his or her spouse *solely* for the sake of pleasure, rather than also for interpersonal communion (and thus openness

to the new life that can come from sexual intercourse), McCluskey affirms that "Aquinas is correct in holding that pursuing sexual activity for the sake of pleasure can be problematic ... because it can involve objectification" (ibid., 129), and she agrees with Aquinas that "love of friendship" (i.e., charity) "rules out the pursuit of pleasure solely for its own sake.... If pleasure becomes the primary object, LOF [love of friendship] is destroyed" and objectification results (ibid., 133). McCluskey's point about the danger of "the pursuit of pleasure solely for its own sake" is what is missing in Corey L. Barnes's misleading assertion, "Aquinas restricted the rational end of sex to reproduction. This restriction denigrates the natural good of sexual pleasure by reducing it to an irrational and accompanying good" ("Thomas Aquinas on the Body and Bodily Passions," in *The Embrace of Eros: Bodies, Desires, and Sexuality in Christianity*, ed. Margaret D. Kamitsuka [Minneapolis: Fortress, 2010], 96–97). Going further, Christine Gudorf warns strongly against "procreationism," which "is the assumption that sex is naturally oriented toward creation of human life" (*Body, Sex, and Pleasure*, 29). She objects to this assumption because, among other things, "it denigrates sexual relationships in which coitus is not possible. From a procreationist perspective, lesbians do not have real or legitimate sex, but 'only' foreplay, because real/legitimate sex requires an impregnating penis" (ibid., 30). Gudorf observes that "if sex is to be mutually pleasurable, then as a society we need to address the fears that stalk contemporary sexual activity. Fear of pregnancy is an old fear which still haunts sex, especially among the young. A variety of effective contraceptives need to be made available to all men and women, along with counseling as to the most appropriate form in particular circumstances" (ibid., 151). This advice, which is so commonplace today, supposes that the fears associated with sexual intercourse—with its deep interpersonal vulnerability—can be substantially resolved by more effective technologies and better use of them.

94. *ST* II-II, q. 153, a. 3, obj. 2 and ad 2.

95. *ST* II-II, q. 153, a. 3, ad 2.

96. Michael Waldstein points out, "The most insidious and destructive error about the common good is to conceive it as an alien good, as the good of the community as opposed to the person" ("Children as the Common Good of Marriage," 699). Pierpaolo Donati remarks in a similar vein, "The dignity of the human person, if considered as a common good, shows us that such a quality is not an individual one, but it is connected and inherent to the relations of the person with the whole creation, with God and with other human persons" ("The Common Good as a Relational Good," *Nova et Vetera* 7 [2009]: 611).

97. *ST* II-II, q. 153, a. 3.

98. *ST* II-II, q. 153, a. 5.

99. Plé, *Chastity and the Affective Life*, 135. Plé adds, "It thus behooves the virtue of chastity, in order to accomplish its object, to moderate, to 'temper' the passions, and even, when they are too vehement and rebellious, to have recourse to force in order to master them. It is necessary to 'correct' them as one corrects a child. But the correction, in this case, too, if it has to use force, must be educative. The struggle against the passions should have no other aim than to favor the awakening of these passions to their participation in the reasonable order" (ibid., 136; cf. 161). Plé goes on to describe the relationship of chastity to the other virtues, including the other virtues of temperance. Like Karol Wojtyła/Pope John Paul II, Plé affirms that "the sexual act is a language of the body" (ibid., 166). This is the problem with masturbation (which Plé ascribes normally to incontinence rather than intemperance): "He who masturbates is a man who speaks to himself. In doing so, he hurts himself; for he stops in himself the felicitous evolution of the affectivity of the child towards the oblativity of the adult" (ibid.), as can be seen in our pornography-saturated culture, in which a number of divorces arise from use of pornography. On the impact of pornography upon our relationship with our spouse (or "romantic partner"), see Nathaniel M. Lambert et al., "A Love That Doesn't Last: Pornography Consumption and Weakened Commitment to One's Romantic Partner," *Journal of Social and Clinical Psychology* 31 (2012): 410–38.

100. Cited by Aquinas in *ST* II-II, q. 153, a. 5.

101. *ST* II-II, q. 153, a. 5.

102. See Janet E. Smith and Paul Check, eds., *Living the Truth in Love: Pastoral Approaches to Same-Sex Attraction* (San Francisco: Ignatius Press, 2015).

103. Aquinas distinguishes fornication—which involves people who are not virgins—from seduction, "which denotes the unlawful violation of a virgin" (*ST* II-II, q. 154, a. 6). I can see the point of this distinction, since seduction certainly adds something to the sin of fornication on the part of the seducer, but for my purposes here the distinction is not particularly important. Aquinas also treats the way in which kissing and sexual touching prepare persons for fornication and are therefore, when undertaken with a spirit desirous of or open to fornication, sinful in themselves: see *ST* II-II, q. 154, a. 4. The key element, however, is fornication itself as "contrary to the good of the human race, in so far as it is prejudicial to the individual begetting of the one man that may be born" (*ST* II-II, q. 154, a. 3, ad 3).

104. *ST* II-II, q. 154, a. 2, sed contra.

105. For the instance of Judah, see *ST* II-II, q. 154, a. 2, obj. 3. Aquinas does not here quote Mt 15:19.

106. These two verses of 1 Corinthians are cited by Aquinas in *ST* II-II, q. 154, a. 3, obj. 2 and 3.

107. For discussion of the harm that lust causes, see DeYoung, *Glittering Vices*, 170–72.

108. David Hume, operating from a quite different understanding of virtue, applies this same argument but applies it only to women; he holds that men generally do not need this virtue. He states, "Whoever considers the length and feebleness of human infancy, with the concern which both sexes naturally have for their offspring, will easily perceive, that there must be an union of male and female for the education of the young, and that this union must be of considerable duration. But in order to induce the men to impose on themselves this restraint, and undergo chearfully all the fatigues and expences, to which it subjects them, they must believe, that the children are their own" (Hume, *A Treatise of Human Nature*, ed. Ernest C. Mossner [London: Penguin Books, 1969], 621). Hume argues that to meet this need, the force of social custom imposes strict rules of chastity and reputation upon women that do not strictly apply to men. In this regard, he comments that it is "contrary to the interest of civil society, that men shou'd have an *entire* liberty of indulging their appetites in venereal enjoyment: But as this interest is weaker than in the case of the female sex, the moral obligation, arising from it, must be proportionably weaker. And to prove this we need only appeal to the practice and sentiments of all nations and ages" (ibid., 622).

109. See the similar conclusion of Gushee and Stassen, *Kingdom Ethics*, 257. Note that although fornication often includes the use of contraceptives, the procreative end is not repressible in human sexuality, and so a culture with high rates of fornication will have high rates of out-of-wedlock births, as ours does (even despite massive use of contraceptives and relatively frequent recourse to abortion). Criticizing Pope Paul VI's encyclical *Humanae Vitae*, which confirms the Catholic Church's condemnation of contraceptive modes that separate acts of sexual intercourse from their intrinsic ordering to the end of procreation, Tatha Wiley argues: "The church presents moral and immoral sex as if its generative purpose were self-evident. Its argument 'sees' the function of complementary heterosexual genitals and 'knows' from the biology that the moral purpose of sex is procreative" ("*Humanae vitae*, Sexual Ethics, and the Roman Catholic Church," in Kamitsuka, *Embrace of Eros*, 105). I do not think that it is "the biology" that primarily drives the Church's conclusion—though bodies (which Wiley dismisses as mere "biological structures" [ibid., 107]) are certainly important for moral reasoning—but rather the Church's conclusion arises from rational attention, supported by Genesis 1:23–24, Ephe-

sians 5:31–32, and other biblical texts (as shown in Pope John Paul II's *Man and Woman He Created Them: A Theology of the Body*), to the real connection between the love expressed in the activity of sexual intercourse (with its soul-body teleology) and the begetting and raising of children by their father and mother in a stable and intimate union of love. Separating the unitive dimension of sexual intercourse from the procreative ordering of sexual intercourse changes the embodied meaning of the act and undermines the complete (even if imperfect) body-soul self-giving of the partners that the act should express.

110. *ST* II-II, q. 154, a. 8. Sirach 22:22–23 reads, "So it is with a woman who leaves her husband and provides an heir by a stranger. For first of all, she has disobeyed the law of the Most High; second, she has committed an offense against her husband; and third, she has committed adultery through harlotry and brought forth children by another man." See also Sirach 22:18–21: "A man who breaks his marriage vows says to himself, 'Who sees me? Darkness surrounds me, and the walls hide me, and no one sees me. Why should I fear? The Most High will not take notice of my sins.' His fear is confined to the eyes of men, and he does not realize that the eyes of the Lord are ten thousand times brighter than the sun; they look upon all the ways of men, and perceive even the hidden places. Before the universe was created, it was known to him; so it was also after it was finished. This man will be punished in the streets of the city, and where he least suspects it, he will be seized."

111. For reflection on the contemporary cultural situation in which less than a third of children born in the United States today will reach age eighteen living with both their biological parents, see for example the work of the Yale medical doctor and child-development scholar Kyle D. Pruett, *Fatherneed: Why Father Care Is as Essential as Mother Care for Your Child* (New York: Free Press, 2000). Pruett states, "If co-parenting is indeed the dominant expectation during this era when nuclear families are becoming so uncommon, then we have an urgent need to understand how kids and their dads and moms are going to stay connected to each other during the time when it matters most to the healthy development of our country's children" (ibid., 2). Christine Gudorf offers an opposite perspective: "No one marital or family pattern is normative, and all others defective in some way. Families do not need to include children. Families need not include blood kin. Families need not be based on marriage. Families can be collections of persons who are committed to the physical, moral, spiritual, social, and intellectual development of other members of the collective unit in an ongoing way" (Gudorf, *Body, Sex, and Pleasure*, 79). Gudorf adds, "Marriage can take many shapes and forms. Institutions such as churches and

states should allow various forms of marriage, and should be open to any marital roles/patterns which are non-abusive, just, and socially responsible" (ibid.). I evaluate and respond to this kind of viewpoint in my *Engaging the Doctrine of Marriage*.

112. Pope Francis, *Amoris Laetitia*, §172, p. 130, quoting the Australian Bishops' Conference, *Don't Mess with Marriage*, pastoral letter (November 24, 2015), 13, available at the website of the Catholic Church in Australia, https://www.catholic.org.au/marriage/don-t-mess-with-marriage. This is the central point of the Jewish philosopher Shimon Cowen's intervention in the Australian debate over same-sex marriage, *Homosexuality, Marriage and Society* (Brisbane: Connor Court Publishing, 2016).

113. *ST* II-II, q. 154, a. 2.

114. Ibid. For further discussion see Waldstein, "Children as the Common Good of Marriage." Colleen McCluskey argues that Aquinas's position here is that "women are not capable by themselves to care for offspring that should result from sexual union," because "women lack sufficient rationality to provide educational and moral guidance to their children and depend upon the father to provide these resources" ("Lust and Chastity," 119). I think that Aquinas's essential point holds, when separated from his faulty understanding of women; and I also think that Aquinas's view of women (given that he thinks that the greatest human friendship is between husband and wife) is hardly as negative as McCluskey suggests. McCluskey grants that "raising children is arduous. Even if women are able to (and in fact do) raise children successfully on their own, it is undeniable that on the whole, children benefit from the engagement of both their parents" (ibid., 131). At the same time, McCluskey argues that marriage itself is often deeply problematic—a point with which I agree, though it is almost always far less problematic than the alternatives, and not problematic in all the ways that McCluskey has in view. In this regard she directs attention to Claudia Card's *The Atrocity Paradigm: A Theory of Evil* (Oxford: Oxford University Press, 2002). See the important historical and constructive work of Prudence Allen, R.S.M., *The Concept of Woman*, vol. 1, *The Aristotelian Revolution (750 B.C.–A.D. 1250)*; vol. 2, *The Early Humanist Reformation, 1250–1500*; vol. 3, *The Search for Communion of Persons, 1500–2015* (Grand Rapids, MI: Eerdmans, 1997–2016). Allen criticizes Platonic, Cartesian, and postmodern models as "philosophers' dreams rather than living realities" (*Concept of Woman*, 3:490), and she sets forth insightful "fundamental principles of integral gender complementarity" (ibid.). See also *Not Just Good, but Beautiful: The Complementary Relationship between Man and Woman*, ed. Helen Alvaré and Steven Lopes (Walden, NY: Plough, 2015).

115. Rziha, *Christian Moral Life*, 267. Rziha adds that "the best way for humans to develop so that they can perform their proper actions is for them to be born into a stable environment where they can observe and receive the unconditional and permanent love of their mother and their father.... Although some animals are naturally inclined to have sex outside of monogamous relationships, humans are naturally inclined to have sex only within a monogamous relationship that is built upon lifelong love between the spouses" (ibid.).

116. *ST* II-II, q. 154, a. 2. He observes that in this regard, adultery is even worse than fornication, since by having sexual intercourse with someone who is not one's spouse, one destabilizes both one's own marriage (thus harming one's own children or potential children) and the marriage of one's partner in adultery (thus harming the children or potential children of one's partner). See *ST* II-II, q. 154, a. 8. On "human nature" and the "natures" of things as understood by Aquinas, in light of contemporary considerations, see Kenneth L. Schmitz, *Person and Psyche* (Arlington, VA: Institute for the Psychological Sciences Press, 2009), 17–32.

117. *ST* II-II, q. 154, a. 2, ad 1.

118. Ibid.

119. *ST* II-II, q. 154, a. 2, ad 2.

120. *ST* II-II, q. 154, a. 3, ad 1. I note that in book 6 of his *Laws*, Plato deems the sexual appetite to be "our ... most imperious need and fiercest passion," which "fires men to all manner of frenzies" with its "blaze of wanton appetite" (*Laws* 783a, in Plato, *Laws*, trans. A. E. Taylor, in *The Collected Dialogues of Plato*, 1358). Plato argues that the solution consists in making "the procreation of children follow on our regulations of marriages, and on their procreation, their nurture, and education" (ibid. [783b]).

121. See *ST* II-II, q. 154, a. 7.

122. On this ugly subject, see for example a recent article by Vanessa Brown in the lurid British tabloid *The Sun*, June 11, 2016, "Breaking Taboos: Incest Pornography Is Becoming More Popular and Game of Thrones Could Be to Blame," https://www.thesun.co.uk/living/1268468/incest-pornography-is-becoming-more-popular-and-game-of-thrones-could-be-to-blame/. See also Catherine Itzin, "Incest, Paedophilia, Pornography and Prostitution: Making Familial Males More Visible as the Abusers," *Child Abuse Review* 10 (2001): 35–48.

123. *ST* II-II, q. 154, a. 9, ad 3.

124. *ST* II-II, q. 154, a. 10.

125. For works arguing in favor of the moral goodness of homosexual acts from a Christian perspective, see for example Jordan, *Ethics of Sex*;

Mark D. Jordan, *The Invention of Sodomy in Christian Theology* (Chicago: University of Chicago Press, 1997); Jordan, *The Silence of Sodom: Homosexuality in Modern Catholicism* (Chicago: University of Chicago Press, 2002); Jordan, "'Baptizing' Queer Characters," in Kamitsuka, *Embrace of Eros*, 151–63; Eugene F. Rogers Jr., *Sexuality and the Christian Body: Their Way into the Triune God* (Oxford: Blackwell, 1999); L. William Countryman and M. R. Ritley, *Gifted by Otherness: Gay and Lesbian Christians in the Church* (Harrisburg, PA: Morehouse Publishing, 2001). Jean Porter argues that "marriage" should include unions between partners of the same sex in her "The Natural Law and Innovative Forms of Marriage: A Reconsideration," *Journal of the Society of Christian Ethics* 30 (2010): 79–97. Along similar lines, though even less sympathetic to Aquinas's perspective, see Stephen J. Pope, "The Magisterium's Arguments against 'Same-Sex Marriage': An Ethical Analysis and Critique," *Theological Studies* 65 (2004): 530–65. In *Ethics of Sex*, Jordan notes,

> We cannot talk about "Christian" ideals of celibacy, chastity, or virginity without admitting that the most significant alternatives to these have been excluded from the churches as anti-Christian, that is, as heretical. Beginning with the Corinthian 'libertines' of Paul's first letter, many individuals and groups have been ruled out of communion or church membership for advocating different ideals of Christian sexual behavior. Many of these "heretics" typically considered themselves to be faithful followers of Jesus. They didn't see contradictions between their views about sex and their faith in the Lord. The judgment that their views are un- or anti-Christian is the judgment of the orthodox, that is, of the victors in the doctrinal struggles. (71)

Jordan here has in view "heretics" of centuries long past, but he is obviously speaking about the present as well, and he goes on to critique the "rule of procreation" (ibid., 116). In his "'Baptizing' Queer Characters," Jordan warns against the position of those who approve the licitness of homosexual acts but do so only when those acts are subsumed "under the general rules for heterosexuals [e.g., monogamy]. This assimilation reduces significant differences between same-sex and other-sex relations—or among types of same-sex relations" (162). For Rogers's spirited but in my view mistaken defense of the adoption of children by gay and lesbian Christians—arguing that this serves as a sign of Christians' primary covenantal, graced, christological, and eschatological identity—see *Sexuality and the Christian Body*, 260–65. In a tone of respect, Rogers critiques Aquinas's treatment of homosexual acts; see *Sexuality and the Christian Body*, 91–139. Whereas Jordan points out that homosexual acts take up little space in the *Summa*, Rogers challenges the understanding of "nature" with which Aquinas is working. Gudorf finds that "homosexual couples, both gay and lesbian, are generally agreed to have been more successful than heterosexual couples in constructing egalitarian couples, as well as egalitarian groups and subcultures" (*Body, Sex, and Pleasure*, 148). For the point that research shows that "two women are significantly more apt to break up than other pair combinations" and that "we should expect non-monogamy to characterize a significant share of gay men's unions," see Regnerus, *Cheap Sex*, 157, 206–7. My view is that Aquinas's understanding of the created and graced ordering of human sexuality to the fostering of families in which children are raised by their mother and father is the truth of the matter, in accord with what Richard B. Hays calls "the New Testament's diagnosis of homosexual activity as a sign of human alienation from God's design" (Hays, *Moral Vision of the New Testament*, 397).

126. Wesley Hill, *Spiritual Friendship: Finding Love in the Church as a Celibate Gay Christian* (Grand Rapids, MI: Brazos Press, 2015), 78. Hill would agree—as would I—with the point made by M. R. Ritley that we need to have "a kind of compassion and tenderness not only for the wounds that gay men and lesbians carry, but also for the people whose blindness and fear are so monstrous that they are led to demonize" gay men and lesbians (Countryman and Ritley, *Gifted by Otherness*, 16). Such demonization is indeed monstrous and anti-Christian. In the view of Countryman and Ritley, however, it is necessary to affirm that desire for same-sex sexual acts is a gift from God. I think that desire to engage in same-sex sexual acts is in fact a manifestation of human fallenness, but persons who experience such desires are most certainly gifts from God. Ritley states, "Despite their corporate acts of injustice, oppression, and hatred, I am forced to take the gospel seriously and admit that heterosexuals are as apt to show saintliness as gay men and women. They do not need my permission to be baptized, communicated, blessed, or ordained" (ibid., 25). I certainly agree with Ritley that neither persons with heterosexual desires nor persons with homosexual desires should be excluded from the sacraments. Yet persons who act upon these desires in (heterosexual or homosexual) ways that do not accord with God's wisdom for human flourishing or with the eschatological restoration of God's family can and should be asked to repent of such actions and to avoid such actions in the future, as requisite for approaching the sacraments in charity. For Ritley, the fact that "there is not a single named gay man or lesbian person in the Scriptures" constitutes "a genuine act of psychic genocide" (ibid., 28), but in my view Scripture is right to make clear that same-sex acts are not in accord with human flourishing while at the same time refusing to identify *persons* by means of their

orientation toward particular sexual acts. Ritley holds that if homosexual actions are not affirmed as morally good, this is tantamount to a rejection of the full presence of persons with homosexual orientations in the Christian community. Thus she states, "We have paid our pledges, taught in Sunday schools, laid down our lives in defense of others, fed the hungry, and—yes, in the midst of it—made love to those of our own genders and built caring communities" (ibid., 28). See also along these lines Carter Heyward, *Touching Our Strength: The Erotic as Power and the Love of God* (San Francisco: Harper & Row, 1989); Charles Hefling, ed., *Ourselves, Our Souls and Bodies: Sexuality and the Household of God* (Cambridge, MA: Cowley, 1996); Richard Cleaver, *Know My Name: A Gay Liberation Theology* (Louisville: Westminster John Knox, 1995). For a better way forward, calling upon Christians to recognize (with repentance) that people with homosexual inclinations have unjustly "suffered intense and even violent rejection" (150) but also affirming "fidelity to Church teaching on chastity" (154), see Eve Tushnet, *Gay and Catholic: Accepting My Sexuality, Finding My Community, Living My Faith* (Notre Dame, IN: Ave Maria Press, 2014). Tushnet argues, "To call homosexuality 'objectively disordered,' always directed toward and fulfilled in sexual acts, is to reduce the tangle of emotional experiences we've decided to call 'homosexuality' to only those expressions that are forbidden by the *Catechism* and ignore all the expressions that aren't" (ibid., 181). I grant that what "homosexuality" means experientially goes well beyond same-sex sexual acts. In this chapter on chastity, my purpose is not to condemn or demean that range of experience, but I think that desire to engage in same-sex sexual acts is a desire that is not ordered to the fullness of human individual and familial flourishing.

127. Second Vatican Council, *Gaudium et Spes*, §48, in Tanner, *Trent to Vatican II*, 1100. The same paragraph of *Gaudium et Spes* adds:

> The institution of marriage and married love are, of their nature, directed to the begetting and upbringing of children and they find their culmination in this. Thus it is that a man and a woman, who "are no longer two but one flesh" (Mt 19, 6) in their marital covenant, help and serve each other in their intimate union of persons and activities, and from day to day experience and increase their sense of oneness. Such intimacy, as a mutual giving of two persons, as well as the good of their children requires complete faithfulness between the partners, and call for their union being indissoluble.

As Paulinus I. Odozor notes, therefore, any Catholic discussion of same-sex marriage must account for "the question of the moral significance of sexual difference, the idea that man and woman both lack the perfections and capabilities of the opposite sex," and "the issue of marriage as intrinsically connected to reproduction and rearing of children" ("The Same Sex Marriage Debate: Matters Arising," in *Families*, ed. Susan A. Ross, Lisa Cahill, Erik Borgman, and Sarojini Nadar [London: SCM Press, 2016], 128). See the similar point, with regard to the multifaceted and lengthy work of raising children, in Rziha, *Christian Moral Life*, 267. To hold that mother and father are complementary and that both are needed for the raising of children is not the same as holding to rigid gender roles. In his "The Church of the Future: Pressing Moral Issues from *Ecclesia in Africa*," Emmanuel Katongole bemoans the fact that work on "'the most pressing moral issues' often ends up obscuring the reality of the church in its theological, historical, and social context," and "in relation to sexuality, the pressing moral question easily gets reduced to whether one is for or against gay rights" ("The Church of the Future: Pressing Moral Issues from *Ecclesia in Africa*," in *The Church We Want: African Catholics Look to Vatican III*, ed. Agbonkhianmeghe E. Orobator [Maryknoll, NY: Orbis, 2016], 161, 164). Katongole critiques the Bultmannian hermeneutics of Elias Bongmba as articulated in Bongmba, "Hermeneutics and the Debate on Homosexuality in Africa," *Religion and Theology* 22 (2015): 69–99. See also Julie Hanlon Rubio, *A Christian Theology of Marriage and Family* (Mahwah, NJ: Paulist Press, 2003), written before the debate about same-sex marriage took off in Catholic circles, and thus able to focus on other issues.

128. In their *Public Faith in Action: How to Think Carefully, Engage Wisely, and Vote with Integrity* (Grand Rapids, MI: Brazos Press, 2016), Miroslav Volf and Ryan McAnnally-Linz emphasize the importance of families: "Other than strong families, there is no viable way that we know of to provide for the rearing of every child in society. Families, then, are necessary for flourishing" (87). But they also hold that "Christians should support providing the same set of legal protections and provisions to same-sex as to other-sex unions" (ibid., 88), by which they mean supporting the view that same-sex unions are "marriage." They argue that "both of the reasons for the importance of marriage—founding stable families for the rearing of children and forming deep covenantal commitments—are applicable to same-sex unions" (ibid., 89). I think that this is not the case, because family life—rooted in the importance of being raised by one's mother and father—is undermined by same-sex unions, even if one were to suppose that homosexual acts in themselves conduce to human flourishing, which I do not suppose. I affirm that the care that two people of the same

sex give to each other is a genuine good, but I do not think that homosexual acts are a genuine good, even if (like all sinful acts) they are certainly not without some good.

129. *ST* II-II, q. 154, a. 12, ad 4. See Rziha, *Christian Moral Life*, 270: "Homosexual actions ... violate both the procreative and unitive ends of sex. The procreative end is violated because these actions cannot result in the procreation of life. The unitive end is violated because these actions cannot take place within a divinely established marriage, since God only unites men and women within marriage." Lest this seem to cut at the core of the dignity of persons with homosexual orientation, Oliver O'Donovan makes a crucial point: "Homosexuality is not the determining factor in any human being's existence; therefore it cannot be the determining factor in the way we treat a human being, and should not be the determining factor in the way a human being treats him- or herself" (O'Donovan, *Church in Crisis*, 105). Gushee and Stassen, in the second edition of their *Kingdom Ethics* (by contrast with the first edition, a contrast that is sharpened by the fact that Stassen died before work on the second edition could begin, though Gushee says that Stassen's views were evolving alongside his own), note with approval the view of many people that homosexual inclinations are generally so deep-seated that persons with these inclinations cannot truly be loved by those who reject the goodness of acting upon homosexual inclinations: "They ['LGBT Christians'] do not find in anything less than full acceptance any kind of transforming initiative that can bring wholeness and life. . . . They find it implausible that the Jesus they love, and that they encounter in Scripture and in personal relationship, would give them anything less than a full embrace" (*Kingdom Ethics*, 267, in view of the issue of "church recognition of the same kinds of covenanted sexual-romantic relationships that 'straight' Christians seek" [ibid.]). In my experience, many persons with homosexual inclinations recognize that they are lovable—and that I love them—without requiring acceptance of the moral goodness of acting upon these inclinations. I think that Jesus certainly gives persons with homosexual inclinations "a full embrace." But we must say more than do Gushee and Stassen when they conclude simply that "human beings require stable, rightly ordered sexual relationships in order to flourish" (ibid., 269).

130. Rziha, *Christian Moral Life*, 270.

131. See Paulinus Ikechukwu Odozor, *Morality Truly Christian, Truly African: Foundational, Methodological, and Theological Considerations* (Notre Dame, IN: University of Notre Dame Press, 2014), 264. Odozor describes his encounter with an Igbo elder: "When asked what he thought about the debate on same-sex marriage, the old man simply said to me that

growing up in this part of the world he had never doubted that his mother was not his father or that there is a difference biologically, anatomically, and sexually between him and his wife. He said he did not think that these facts were morally insignificant" (ibid.). As Odozor goes on to say, the ground for according "the status of marriage to the relationship between persons of the same sex" has its roots in

> the so-called sexual revolution, which has characterized Western society for a while now. The idea of free love, which Vatican II spoke of (*Gaudium et Spes* 52–54), and the contraceptive mentality that has characterized the West since then are very much part of the issue. What these two trends did was to sunder the unitive from the procreative aspects of human sexuality. With sex losing its connection to procreation, the way was opened not only to massive pornography but to all other relationships in which people believed one should "just do it," as the Nike ad puts it, with whomever one feels like. It was therefore a very logical step to the day when, in President Barack Obama's words, "people should feel free to marry whomever they are in love with." The point here is that the current same-sex debate is indicative of the various traditions of moral discourse in contemporary society. (ibid., 265)

132. Janet E. Smith, *Humanae Vitae: A Generation Later* (Washington, DC: Catholic University of America Press, 1991), 80. See also Mansini and Welch, "Revelation, Natural Law, and Homosexual Unions," 343–44:

> There is one thing in the argument of *Humanae Vitae*, as well as in the argument against same-sex unions, that really should be taken as obvious, and that is the procreative finality of sexual acts. If this is obvious, *and* if we see the rightness of never impeding this finality because of the dignity and fundamentality of the good it is ordered to, *and* if we take the world as created, then the moral obligations themselves become "obvious" as a matter of "natural law." . . . The heterosexual and procreative meaning of sexual acts is nonetheless something that one can ignore. One turns away from such givens as the desire to penetrate, and the capacity of semen, and changes the subject.

Although this point is missed by Stephen Pope (and Charles Curran), Aquinas is well aware that "human reason does not exist in itself, abstractly, and it does not operate unconditioned by history, culture, sin, grace" (ibid., 347). See *ST* I-II, q. 94, a. 6; I-II, q. 99, a. 2, ad 2. See also Hittinger, *First Grace*, chapters 1 and 2.

133. Ellen F. Davis, *Preaching the Luminous Word: Biblical Sermons and Homiletical Essays* (Grand Rapids, MI: Eerdmans, 2016), 112.

134. William M. Shea, "An Agenda for Evangelicals and Catholics," *Pro Ecclesia* 26 (2017): 12. Shea argues that "'the Catholic problem' is its own hierarchical/sacerdotal structure that to me seemed under the last two popes to be choking the Church to death. The Church cannot go on living with this notion of divinely underwritten structure, but would the church be Catholic without it? To me this question of the 'divinity' of the hierarchical structure is not only not 'definitively closed,' as Joseph Ratzinger would have it, but wide open" (ibid., 20). I am struck by the notion that the pontificates of John Paul II and Benedict XVI were responsible for "choking the Church to death," by which I presume is meant leading the members of the Church away from true faith and true moral life (since that would cause the "death" of the Church). For further reflections on postconciliar Catholicism, see my *An Introduction to Vatican II as an Ongoing Theological Event* (Washington, DC: Catholic University of America Press, 2017).

135. Grabowski, *Sex and Virtue*, 52, 61.

136. McCluskey, "Lust and Chastity," 115. She gives the example of Simon Blackburn's *Lust* (Oxford: Oxford University Press, 2004). See also Randall G. Colton, "Two Rival Versions of Sexual Virtue: Simon Blackburn and John Paul II on Lust and Chastity," *Thomist* 70 (2006): 71–101. Colton criticizes Blackburn's "reduction of sexual activity to pleasure" (ibid., 100). Colton explains that for Blackburn "pleasure does not merely accompany or complete sexual activity but defines it. The couple engaged in it is engaged in the activity of *producing sexual pleasure*. If pleasures are defined by the kind of activity they accompany, then the kind of pleasure the couple experiences is the pleasure of producing pleasure. This circularity—sexual pleasure accompanies an activity whose point is to produce sexual pleasure—undermines the significance of sexual unity, since it blocks any attempt to articulate the point of the pleasure in terms of an intrinsically worthwhile activity. Typically, pleasures that seem separated from otherwise meaningful activity in this way appear trivial. Think, for example, of the pleasure of scratching an itch" (ibid., 99). Colton and McCluskey both point out that Blackburn and Aquinas, in speaking of "lust," define very differently what they mean by the term. See also the excellent discussion of pleasure in Pruss, *One Body*.

137. Joseph A. Selling, *Reframing Catholic Theological Ethics* (Oxford: Oxford University Press, 2016), 19. See also the criticisms of Pope John Paul II's encyclical *Veritatis Splendor* in the essays in Joseph Selling

and Jan Jans, eds., *The Splendor of Accuracy: An Examination of the Assertions Made by* Veritatis Splendor (Grand Rapids, MI: Eerdmans, 1994). In response, see William E. May's "*The Splendor of Accuracy*: How Accurate?," *Thomist* 59 (1995): 465–84. See also the essays in J. A. DiNoia, O.P., and Romanus Cessario, O.P., eds., *Veritatis Splendor and the Renewal of Moral Theology* (Chicago: Midwest Theological Forum, 1999).

138. For this position, see also Curran's *Development of Moral Theology*. For insight into *Humanae Vitae* from perspectives concordant with my own, see Janet E. Smith, "Conscious Parenthood," *Nova et Vetera* 6 (2008): 927–50; Smith, *Humanae Vitae*; Hans Urs von Balthasar, "Ephesians 5:21–33 and 'Humanae Vitae': A Meditation," in *Christian Married Love*, ed. Raymond Dennehy (San Francisco: Ignatius Press, 1981), 55–73; and the essays collected in Janet E. Smith, ed., *Why* Humanae Vitae *Was Right: A Reader* (San Francisco: Ignatius Press, 1993), and Janet E. Smith, ed., *Why* Humanae Vitae *Is Still Right* (San Francisco: Ignatius Press, 2018).

139. Selling, *Reframing Catholic Theological Ethics*, 45. For background to Selling's approach, see the ethical theory articulated in Häring, *Free and Faithful in Christ*, vol. 1, *General Moral Theology*, as well as Fuchs, *Personal Responsibility and Christian Morality*, 36 and elsewhere. For a cogent critique of this ethical theory, which focuses on a person's "fundamental option," see John Paul II, *Veritatis Splendor*, encyclical, August 6, 1993, §§65–68, available via the Vatican website, http://w2.vatican.va/content/vatican/en.html).

140. Selling, *Reframing Catholic Theological Ethics*, 39.

141. Ibid.

142. Selling argues that Aquinas agrees with Selling's perspective:

> If I had to single out one thing that characterizes Thomas's uniqueness in our Western, ethical tradition, it would have to be his insistence that the moral evaluation of human activity begins with the integrity of moral intention, which is subsequently followed by a consideration of behavioural options. Who one is, the moral character that the acting person exhibits, is by far more important than the sometimes clumsy, uninformed, or simply mistaken behavioural choices that we make. As a corollary to this, we should be able to appreciate why Thomas never refers to something that would be akin to the notion of an act, a behaviour, that is "intrinsically evil." In his approach, behaviour is always secondary to one's intentional commitment. Things that we might "never" consider doing under "normal circumstances," we might willingly perform when the need is great enough. (ibid., 82–83)

Tatha Wiley echoes this reading of Aquinas in her *"Humanae vitae, Sexual Ethics, and the Roman Catholic Church,"* 112–13, with a focus on happiness as "authenticity," which is "realized when judgments of value are the product of responsible choices and actions" arising from "the couple's own complex discernment of authentic value." For accounts of Aquinas's moral theory that correct this limited (and fundamentally Kantian) reading of Aquinas, see Kevin Flannery, S.J., *Acts amid Precepts: The Aristotelian Logical Structure of Thomas Aquinas's Moral Theory* (Washington, DC: Catholic University of America Press, 2001); David S. Oderberg, *Moral Theory: A Non-Consequentialist Approach* (Oxford: Blackwell, 2000); Christopher Kaczor, *Proportionalism and the Natural Law Tradition* (Washington, DC: Catholic University of America Press, 2002).

143. Samuel Johnson, *Selected Essays*, ed. David Womersley (London: Penguin, 2003), 41.

144. Wendell Berry, *Sex, Economy, Freedom and Community: Eight Essays* (New York: Pantheon Books, 1993), 125. Berry has in view the atomization of households and communities caused, he argues, by "the exceedingly profitable [to companies] 'sexual revolution'" (ibid., 124). Berry argues further,

> The sexuality of community life, whatever its inevitable vagaries, is centered on marriage, which joins two living souls as closely as, in this world, they can be joined. This joining of two who know, love, and trust one another brings them in the same breath into the freedom of sexual consent and into the fullest earthly realization of the image of God. From their joining, other living souls come into being, and with them great responsibilities that are unending, fearful, and joyful. The marriage of two lovers joins them to one another, to forebears, to descendants, to the community, to Heaven and earth. (ibid., 138–39)

See also Gregory Wolfe's observation (in commenting on Berry's work), "What have we lost in abstracting marriage from family, community, and history? Throughout much of Western history, marriage was considered not only a private reality but a *public* one as well—part of the larger web of obligations that hold a community together, a hard-won victory over the temptations of the restless human heart" (Wolfe, *Beauty Will Save the World: Recovering the Human in an Ideological Age* [Wilmington, DE: ISI Books, 2011], 161). I disagree, therefore, with Traci C. West's understanding of a "feminist/womanist liberative ethics" (West, *Disruptive Christian Ethics: When Racism and Women's Lives Matter* [Louisville: Westminster John Knox, 2006], xii), because I do not think that her views are liberative.

See also Wendell Berry, "Feminism, the Body, and the Machine," in *What Are People For?*, 178–96.

145. Fabrice Hadjadj, *Qu'est-ce qu'une famille?* (Paris: Salvator, 2014), 37. See also Hadjadj's reflections on marriage in his *La profondeur des sexes: Pour une mystique de la chair* (Paris: Éditions du Seuil, 2008).

CHAPTER FIVE.   Clemency and Meekness

1. Pope Francis, *Lumen Fidei*, Vatican translation (San Francisco: Ignatius Press, 2013), §26, p. 47.

2. John Barton, *Ethics in Ancient Israel* (Oxford: Oxford University Press, 2014), 253. Barton goes on to say, "Do Old Testament writers not *themselves* show an ability to distinguish between what 'we' but also they find attractive and unattractive aspects of the divine character? A fair answer would seem to me to be that sometimes they do, as in Job, and sometimes they do not, as in Joshua" (ibid., 271). Barton recognizes that "there was a sense among some ancient Israelites that *God and humans shared certain moral perceptions*, and that God was accordingly not wholly inscrutable in his judgements of human action, nor in his own doings as they affected the human race. Despite the 'dark side' of God, which undoubtedly exists in the Old Testament, on the whole the literature we have tries to show that God is just according to standards human beings also recognize—despite the consequent risk of therefore blaming human agents whenever anything goes wrong" (ibid.; see also for the same point Barton's remarks on 260).

3. Ibid., 249, drawing upon Andrew Davies, *Double Standards in Isaiah: Re-evaluating Prophetic Ethics and Divine Justice* (London: T&T Clark, 2000). Barton comments, "Even if we grant that there is something wrong with the women of Isaiah 3:16–4:1, who take such pleasure in their jewellery and cosmetics, it is impossible to find any human moral principle that would justify the cruel and degrading punishment with which the prophet threatens them: this is not so much an eye for an eye as an eye for an eyelash. The whole thing is grossly disproportionate" (Barton, *Ethics in Ancient Israel*, 249). In his survey of the literature, Barton directs particular attention to Fredrik Lindström's *God and the Origin of Evil: Contextual Analysis of Alleged Monistic Evidence in the Old Testament* (Lund: CWK Gleerup, 1983).

4. Augustine, *On Christian Doctrine*, trans. D. W. Robertson Jr. (New York: Macmillan, 1958), 3.12.18, p. 90. See also Mark Sheridan,

O.S.B., *Language for God in Patristic Tradition: Wrestling with Biblical Anthropomorphism* (Downers Grove, IL: IVP Academic, 2015); Michael Graves, *The Inspiration and Interpretation of Scripture: What the Early Church Can Teach Us* (Grand Rapids, MI: Eerdmans, 2014).

5. As Jon C. Laansma points out in a chapter titled "The Meek King and God's Promise of Rest," "The theme of Christ's lowliness is pervasive in Matthew's Gospel" (Laansma, *'I Will Give You Rest': The Rest Motif in the New Testament with Special Reference to Mt 11 and Heb 3–4* [Tübingen: Mohr Siebeck, 1997], 223). According to Laansma, "It is his [Jesus'] on-going presence *as the humble king* which mediates rest" (ibid., 238). Jesus is the "gentle king, in whose work . . . the long awaited kingdom of God is present" (ibid., 248). Laansma notes that "here, a 'high' Christology is strongly implied when Jesus not only claims to bring to fulfilment the Sabbath rest and God's promise of rest, but takes to himself the authority hitherto reserved for YHWH, his Father" (ibid., 249).

6. Bernard of Clairvaux, *On the Song of Songs II*, trans. Kilian Walsh, O.C.S.O. (Kalamazoo, MI: Cistercian Publications, 1983), sermon 38 ("Ignorance of God Leads to Despair; The Beauty of the Bride"), p. 187.

7. Okholm, *Dangerous Passions, Deadly Sins*, 94. He cites Gregory the Great, *Morals on the Book of Job*, 3 vols., trans. J. Bliss (Oxford: John Henry Parker, 1850), vol. 3, commentary on Job 39:25.

8. For Aquinas on the passion of anger, see *ST* I-II, qq. 46–48, as well as the valuable discussion in Miner, *Thomas Aquinas on the Passions*, 268–86.

9. William C. Mattison III, "Jesus' Prohibition of Anger (Mt 5:22): The Person/Sin Distinction from Augustine to Aquinas," *Theological Studies* 68 (2007): 858. See also Mattison, "Virtuous Anger? From Questions of *Vindicatio* to the Habituation of Emotion," *Journal of the Society of Christian Ethics* 24 (2004): 159–79; Michael Rota, "The Moral Status of Anger: Thomas Aquinas and John Cassian," *American Catholic Philosophical Quarterly* 81 (2007): 395–418. Rota, like Mattison, defends Aquinas's view that anger, as a passion, is a positive good, although it becomes sinful if not directed by reason. As Miner notes, Aquinas is well aware that "bodily *perturbatio* and the consequent impairment of reason are typical effects of anger in the fallen nature," though the passion of anger in itself does not necessitate these effects (*Thomas Aquinas on the Passions*, 285; cf. 274 on immoderate anger). Okholm notes that Aquinas's position that virtuous anger is possible differs from the position of ascetics such as John Cassian and Evagrius Ponticus but concurs with the position of Gregory the Great. See Okholm, *Dangerous Passions, Deadly Sins*, 102. See also the helpful discussion of Cassian, Evagrius, Gregory, and Aquinas in DeYoung,

Glittering Vices, 117–21. For extended engagement with Evagrius's perspective, see Gabriel Bunge, O.S.B., *Dragon's Wine and Angel's Bread: The Teaching of Evagrius Ponticus on Anger and Meekness*, trans. Anthony P. Gythiel (Crestwood, NY: St. Vladimir's Seminary Press, 2009).

10. Although Nicholas Wolterstorff has proposed that Jesus Christ explicitly rules out retributive punishment—see Wolterstorff, *Justice in Love* (Grand Rapids, MI: Eerdmans, 2011)—I argue against this view on exegetical and theological grounds in my *Engaging the Doctrine of Creation*, chapter 7.

11. Okholm, *Dangerous Passions, Deadly Sins*, 94. Somewhat similarly, but from a different (broadly Buddhist) perspective, Robert A. F. Thurman distinguishes between hate-filled anger, which "is never useful, never justifiable, always harmful to self as well as others," and the "raw, neutral energy of anger" that can function as a "fire . . . to destroy the suffering of other beings" (*Anger* [Oxford: Oxford University Press, 2005], 8). For Thurman, however, the "raw, neutral energy of anger" is in fact not anger at all, but a "fierce energy" of the enlightened mind, a "liberating, transcendent wisdom" (ibid., 9). For Aquinas, as Robert Miner says, "considered 'in themselves' (*secundum se*), purely as acts in common with other animals, the passions are morally neutral," but insofar as in human beings the passions are "placed under the command of reason and will," they "cannot be morally neutral" (*Thomas Aquinas on the Passions*, 89). Indeed, for Aquinas, "if an act done out of rational judgment is accompanied by a passion that obeys reason, the presence of that passion will increase the moral goodness of that act" (ibid., 91). For Aquinas's critique of the Stoic view that passions are evil, see *ST* I-II, q. 24, aa. 2–3.

12. See Gary Chapman, *Anger: Taming a Powerful Emotion* (Chicago: Moody Publishers, 2015), 9, 19. See also Chapman's chapter "When Anger Can Do Good," in ibid., 25–32. As Chapman says, "Anger can be a powerful and positive motivator, useful to move us toward loving action to right wrongs and correct injustice—but it also can become a raging, uncontrolled force" (ibid., 32; cf. 39). A good number of Chapman's Christian approaches to healing destructive anger find a parallel in the mindfulness, compassionate listening, and loving speech described in Buddhist author Thich Nhat Hanh's *Anger: Wisdom for Cooling the Flames* (New York: Riverhead Books, 2001), although Hanh adds the recommendation to "let go of the illusion called self" (124).

13. Chapman, *Anger*, 58, 83. Chapman observes, "Explosive, angry behavior is never constructive. It not only hurts the person at whom it is directed, it destroys the self-esteem of the person who is out of control. . . . In the heat of such angry explosions, people say and do things they later

regret. Undisciplined anger that expresses itself in verbal and physical explosions will ultimately destroy relationships" (ibid., 85). Chapman does not recommend suppressing one's anger; instead he explores ways of releasing one's anger appropriately, either by confronting the person with the cause of one's anger or by giving over one's anger to God, knowing that God mercifully loves all of us sinners and will ensure that justice is done. Rebecca Konyndyk DeYoung concludes, "In a world full of injustice, it is hard to imagine a right response [to injustice] that doesn't include anger. At the same time, given how much of our anger is selfish, rather than just, practicing the regular purgation of anger would likely be a worthwhile discipline for us" (*Glittering Vices*, 119). She adds that "anger must be directed at the sin to be put right, not at the sinner," and that "the fittingness of anger's expression is measured by whether it effectively furthers the goal of justice" (ibid., 119, 121).

14. Tobias Hägerland, *Jesus and the Forgiveness of Sins: An Aspect of His Prophetic Mission* (Cambridge: Cambridge University Press, 2012), 253.

15. Wright, *New Testament and the People of God*, 301.

16. Dunn, *Jesus Remembered*, 788.

17. Note that forgiveness is linked with repentance. Gary Chapman sums up, "God's forgiveness toward us serves as a model of how we are to forgive others. The Scriptures say that we are to forgive each other, 'just as God through Christ has forgiven you' (Ephesians 4:32). In this divine model, there are two essential elements—confession and repentance on the part of the sinner and forgiveness on the part of the one sinned against. In the Scriptures, these two are never separated.... Never does God agree to reconcile while Israel continues in sin. There can be no reconciliation without repentance" (*Anger*, 115; cf. 119, citing Mt 18:15–17). Regarding those who have wronged us and remain unrepentant (he gives the example of a husband who has committed adultery), Chapman states, "We pray for them; we seek to be kind to them, but we do not treat them as though they were innocent, for they are not. Remember, all sin brings separation. The separation is not removed by our choosing to overlook the sin. Sin always creates barriers in human relationships, and the barriers only come down when there is genuine repentance and genuine forgiveness" (ibid., 120). The same view is argued persuasively by Wolterstorff, *Justice in Love*, 172–75. Wolterstorff emphasizes that we must always be willing and eager to forgive (and thus cannot be bitter or hate filled in any way), but full forgiveness requires the perpetrator acknowledging the wrongness of the action by an act of repentance. For the opposite position, see Miroslav Volf, *Free of Charge: Giving and Forgiving in a Culture Stripped of Grace* (Grand

Rapids, MI: Zondervan, 2005), 208: "Even when offenders are unrepentant, we can and should forgive." See also Daniel Philpott, *Just and Unjust Peace: An Ethic of Political Reconciliation* (Oxford: Oxford University Press, 2012), 260–76. Philpott argues that "unilateral forgiveness [in which the perpetrator of the injustice does not repent] . . . is justifiable though not required" (ibid., 272). Margaret Urban Walker argues that we need not suppose that there is "a single correct idea of forgiveness," since "forgiveness is a variable human process and a practice with culturally distinctive versions" (*Moral Repair: Reconstructing Moral Relations after Wrongdoing* [Cambridge: Cambridge University Press, 2006], 152). For the intrinsic connection between reconciliation and repentance (or "lament"), see Emmanuel Katongole and Chris Rice, *Reconciling All Things: A Christian Vision for Justice, Peace and Healing* (Downers Grove, IL: InterVarsity Press, 2008), 87–90.

18. Walter Brueggemann comments, "All inclination to resist, refuse, or disobey will have evaporated, because the members of the new community of covenant are transformed people who have rightly inclined hearts. There will be easy and ready community between God and reconstituted Israel. . . . All the newness is possible *because* Yahweh has forgiven. . . . Jewish faith is deeply rooted in forgiveness" (*A Commentary on Jeremiah: Exile and Homecoming* [Grand Rapids, MI: Eerdmans, 1998], 293–94).

19. For discussion, see the essays in Bernd Janowski and Peter Stuhlmacher, eds., *The Suffering Servant: Isaiah 53 in Jewish and Christian Sources*, trans. Daniel P. Bailey (Grand Rapids, MI: Eerdmans, 2004).

20. Davies and Allison, *Gospel according to Saint Matthew*, vol. 1, *Matthew I–VII*, 210.

21. W. D. Davies and Dale C. Allison, Jr., *A Critical and Exegetical Commentary on the Gospel according to Saint Matthew*, vol. 2, *Commentary on Matthew VIII–XVIII* (London: T&T Clark International, 2004), 290.

22. Michael J. Gorman, *Cruciformity: Paul's Narrative Spirituality of the Cross* (Grand Rapids, MI: Eerdmans, 2001), 5.

23. Ibid., 236, 252.

24. Ibid., 262.

25. See ibid., 281. For discussion see Timothy B. Savage, *Power through Weakness: Paul's Understanding of the Christian Ministry in 2 Corinthians* (Cambridge: Cambridge University Press, 1996); Hans Urs von Balthasar, *Paul Struggles with His Congregation: The Pastoral Message of the Letters to the Corinthians*, trans. Brigitte L. Bojarska (San Francisco: Ignatius Press, 1992). For the view that Paul was power hungry and domineering, see Elizabeth Castelli, *Imitating Paul: A Discourse of Power*

(Louisville: Westminster John Knox, 1991). Gorman responds to Castelli by arguing that although "Paul is consciously willing to exercise power," Paul rejects "arrogant, human power that boasts in particular and irrelevant human accomplishments and status indicators rather than in the cross of Christ" (*Cruciformity*, 294–95).

26. Gorman, *Cruciformity*, 292–93. See also von Balthasar's *Love Alone Is Credible*. In his *Inhabiting the Cruciform God*, Gorman develops this thesis into a critique of all "sacred violence," all violence that in virtue of an "(allegedly) good end is believed to have divine approval" (*Inhabiting the Cruciform God: Kenosis, Justification, and Theosis in Paul's Narrative Soteriology* [Grand Rapids, MI: Eerdmans, 2009], 160). Richard B. Hays argues that "Christendom's long-held and clearly formulated just war tradition is finally incompatible with the New Testament vision of the church as a people called to take up the cross and follow Jesus" (*Moral Vision of the New Testament*, 297). For a biblical response to the argument that the New Testament mandates pacifism, see Allen Verhey, "Neither Devils nor Angels: Peace, Justice, and Defending the Innocent; A Response to Richard Hays," in Wagner, Rowe, and Grieb, *Word Leaps the Gap*, 599–625. I argue in favor of Verhey's position, in light of Aquinas's account of just war, in chapter 7 of my *The Betrayal of Charity: The Sins That Sabotage Divine Love* (Waco, TX: Baylor University Press, 2011).

27. Walter Brueggemann holds that according to the Old Testament, "YHWH is a jealous God who is capable of irrational destructiveness," but Brueggemann nonetheless shows God's clemency and mercy, which he describes as God's "soft underside to which appeal can be made" and as God's "readiness to be engaged with and exposed for the sake of the partner [Israel, the human person, the nations, creation]" (Brueggemann, *The Unsettling God: The Heart of the Hebrew Bible* [Minneapolis: Fortress, 2009], 168). Brueggemann's *The Unsettling God* reprises material (in a revised form) from part 3 of his *Theology of the Old Testament: Testimony, Dispute, Advocacy* (Minneapolis: Fortress, 1997).

28. With Exodus 32:9–14 explicitly in view, Jon D. Levenson puts the divine clemency in covenantal terms, grounding it in the gift of covenantal election: "There is something about biblical covenant that locks in the dispositions characteristic of the idyllic situation and makes them normative for both parties. That is why, to the surprise of some, the horrors that follow never cancel the pertinence of God's initial love, and though the covenant repeatedly seems on the verge of dissolution, it is never, in fact, ended but always renewed" (Levenson, *Love of God*, 58).

29. See Martin Hengel, *Saint Peter: The Underestimated Apostle*, trans. Thomas H. Trapp (Grand Rapids, MI: Eerdmans, 2010), 44.

30. Wright, *New Testament and the People of God*, 301.
31. See *ST* II-II, q. 157, a. 1, sed contra; Aquinas cites Seneca's *De clementia* 2.3. John Calvin wrote his first academic work on Seneca's *De clementia*, which further indicates the importance of this treatise for Christian moral reflection. See Seneca, *De clementia*, in Seneca, *Moral Essays*, vol. 1, trans. John W. Basore (Cambridge, MA: Harvard University Press, 1928), 435: clemency "means restraining the mind [Clementia est temperantia animi] from vengeance when it has the power to take it, or the leniency of a superior towards an inferior in fixing punishment"; clemency is "the inclination of the mind towards leniency in exacting punishment." Basore translates "clementia" as "mercy," which is misleading.
32. *ST* II-II, q. 157, a. 1.
33. Here Aquinas is indebted to Aristotle's *Nicomachean Ethics*. In his "A Study of Virtuous and Vicious Anger," in Timpe and Boyd, *Virtues and Their Vices*, 207, Zac Cogly points out that "Aristotle is more comfortable with the idea that revenge can be justified than most contemporary philosophers; he holds that sometimes the angry desire for revenge is the right desire to have because it virtuously motivates vengeful actions. Aquinas follows Aristotle in agreeing that anger involves a desire to punish in the service of revenge and that such retribution can be just if properly motivated and proportionate to the offense."
34. For an extended discussion of this point, in response to Nicholas Wolterstorff, see chapter 7 of my *Engaging the Doctrine of Creation*.
35. *ST* II-II, q. 157, a. 1, ad 3.
36. Cited in *ST* II-II, q. 157, a. 4, obj. 2. The RSV reads "his throne is upheld by righteousness" (Prov 20:28).
37. *ST* II-II, q. 157, a. 4, ad 2.
38. *ST* II-II, q. 157, a. 4, obj. 2.
39. Aquinas cites this verse in *ST* II-II, q. 157, a. 2, obj. 3.
40. *ST* II-II, q. 157, a. 4.
41. Cited in *ST* II-II, q. 157, a. 4, obj. 2.
42. *ST* II-II, q. 157, a. 4, ad 3.
43. See *ST* I-II, q. 106, a. 1, ad 3; I-II, q. 106, a. 3, ad 2. Aquinas also recognizes with regard to the Church's manifestation of holiness (or general lack thereof) that "the state of the New Law is subject to change with regard to various places, times, and persons, according as the grace of the Holy Spirit dwells in man more or less perfectly" (*ST* I-II, q. 106, a. 4).
44. *ST* II-II, q. 157, a. 4.
45. The quotation of Seneca comes from *ST* II-II, q. 157, a. 2, sed contra, and Aquinas attributes this quotation to Seneca's *De clementia* 2.5. Aquinas mentions Aristotle's praise of meekness in *ST* II-II, q. 157, a. 1,

obj. 1, and II-II, q. 157, a. 2 and ad 2. For discussion of Seneca on anger—focusing on his *De ira*, which is among the treatises included in Seneca's *Moral Essays*—see Nancy Sherman, "Virtue and a Warrior's Anger," in *Working Virtue: Virtue Ethics and Contemporary Moral Problems*, ed. Rebecca L. Walker and Philip J. Ivanhoe (Oxford: Oxford University Press, 2007), 260–66. Sherman also appreciatively treats Aristotle's account of anger in his *Rhetoric* and *Nicomachean Ethics*. Sherman concludes,

> Seneca argues persuasively that unrestrained anger, whether of rage, bitterness, revenge, or indignation, is more often than not inappropriate. But Seneca insists that the way to guard against these excesses is to ostracize *all* anger from our lives. And we are to achieve that end through a robust use of defensive techniques that we today know as disassociation and splitting. On Seneca's version of splitting, competing desires don't mingle or mix, modify or moderate each other. There is no Aristotelian notion of unwelcome emotions becoming tamed by more congenial ones, or excesses in each direction finding more moderate forms by mutual adjustments. Instead, there is only containment. (ibid., 273)

46. See *ST* II-II, q. 157, a. 4, obj. 3; Aquinas cites Augustine, *De sermone Domini in monte* 1.2.

47. *ST* II-II, q. 157, a. 3, ad 3.

48. *ST* II-II, q. 157, a. 3, ad 1.

49. *ST* II-II, q. 157, a. 1, ad 2.

50. Cited by Aquinas in *ST* I, q. 21, a. 4, obj. 1.

51. *ST* I, q. 21, a. 4, ad 1.

52. *ST* II-II, q. 157, a. 2, ad 2. For discussion see Adrian J. Reimers, *Hell and the Mercy of God* (Washington, DC: Catholic University of America Press, 2017).

53. Cited by Aquinas in *ST* II-II, q. 158, a. 2, sed contra.

54. See *ST* II-II, q. 158, a. 2, obj. 3 and obj. 4.

55. *ST* II-II, q. 158, a. 2.

56. Ibid. DeYoung observes, "Aquinas says that anger is an ally of justice and courage, but only if it *follows* a reasonable judgment about what is right. This is a major caveat. Too often, we begin with anger and make our best judgments its puppet" (*Glittering Vices*, 123).

57. See *ST* II-II, q. 158, a. 2, ad 3.

58. See *ST* II-II, q. 158, a. 3, obj. 1 and obj. 2.

59. *ST* II-II, q. 158, a. 1, ad 3. On Christ's reasonable anger, see *ST* III, q. 15, a. 9. Aquinas cites John 2:17, which belongs to the Gospel of John's account of Jesus' cleansing of the temple (John 2:14–17).

60. *ST* II-II, q. 158, a. 1, ad 3.
61. Cited by Aquinas in *ST* II-II, q. 158, a. 3, sed contra.
62. *ST* II-II, q. 158, a. 3.
63. Ibid.
64. *ST* II-II, q. 158, a. 5, ad 3.
65. *ST* II-II, q. 158, a. 4, obj. 1 and 2.
66. *ST* II-II, q. 158, a. 4, sed contra; citing Augustine's *Letter 211*.
67. See *ST* II-II, q. 158, a. 5, sed contra.
68. *ST* II-II, q. 158, a. 5.
69. *ST* II-II, q. 158, a. 7.
70. *ST* II-II, q. 159, a. 1, ad 2.
71. Ibid.; see also ad 3.
72. *ST* II-II, q. 159, a. 1.
73. Von Balthasar, *Paul Struggles with His Congregation*, 85.
74. *ST* II-II, q. 159, a. 2.
75. For discussion, see DeYoung, *Glittering Vices*, 128–30. DeYoung points out, "Anger, when it is a *holy* emotion, has *justice* as its object and *love* as its root. Both love and justice are focused on the good of others. Justice concerns giving to another what that other is due. Good anger is expressed in passionate efforts to make sure others get the respect they deserve, to bring about the end of oppression and tyranny, to give due punishment to those who cause injury and damage, to honor covenants and promises, to give equal treatment to the marginalized, and to uphold the law. Motivated by good anger, we hunger and thirst for righteousness, an appetite that depends on justice for its object, but on love for its right expression. Anger in these cases adds energy and passion to the execution of justice. The love that underlies it, however, keeps it in check, for love does not seek to destroy the other, but to set things right. In this way, our anger can imitate God's in its object" (ibid., 130).
76. Davies and Allison, *Gospel according to Saint Matthew*, vol. 1, *Matthew I–VII*, 449.
77. Ibid.
78. DeYoung therefore argues that the virtue of "meekness" or gentleness "is probably better described as 'self-possession.' People with this virtue keep anger as a finely tuned instrument of their will and do not let it master them" (*Glittering Vices*, 131). In my view, the explicit connection with biblical "meekness" should be retained.
79. For the "connection between pride and anger," see Gabriele Taylor, *Deadly Vices* (Oxford: Oxford University Press, 2006), 82–91.
80. DeYoung, *Glittering Vices*, 130. DeYoung notes that for Aquinas, anger's "job is to aid the will in executing justice," but anger must "proceed

with its eyes open, rather than blindly lashing out" (ibid., 134–35). She adds, "Because wrath is so often rooted in unholy expectations—both of what we are due and what others are due—dealing with this vice requires setting realistic expectations and realizing that the claims we make on the world may be overinflated by our fragile or arrogant egos" (ibid., 136).

81. Niccolò Machiavelli, *The Discourses*, trans. Christian E. Detmold, 2.28, in *The Prince and The Discourses* (New York: Random House, 1950), 379.

82. DeYoung, *Glittering Vices*, 133. For the same example, see Cogly, "Study of Virtuous and Vicious Anger," 210–16.

83. DeYoung, *Glittering Vices*, 133.

84. Catherine of Siena, *Dialogue*, 75.

85. See ibid., 39. Here Catherine alludes to the counsel of St. Paul that I partly quote in this paragraph: "Repay no one evil for evil, but take thought for what is noble in the sight of all. If possible, so far as it depends upon you, live peaceably with all.... Do not be overcome by evil, but overcome evil with good" (Rom 12:17–18, 21).

86. DeYoung, *Glittering Vices*, 137. DeYoung observes, "Those with the virtue of gentleness [meekness] have mastered their anger, rather than being mastered by it. When they act with anger, they channel its power rather than being swept away by it. But gentleness as a character trait—a deeply embedded virtue—depends on much more than just the power of self-restraint. Gentleness depends closely on humility in that it does not put what is due oneself at the center of attention. It does not have to hold the reins of the universe. It responds instead from a heart that acknowledges and trusts the mysterious combination of justice and mercy that is God's way of setting things right.... In wrath, we ultimately want our own way. In gentle self-mastery, we pray, 'Thy will be done'" (ibid., 137–38).

87. Michel de Montaigne, "Of Anger," in *The Complete Works: Essays, Travel Journal, Letters*, trans. Donald M. Frame (New York: Knopf, 2003), 655. For Montaigne, "anger is always an imperfection" (ibid., 659). Describing cruelty, Montaigne bemoans the fact that some people in his own day "sharpen their wits to invent unaccustomed torments and new forms of death, without enmity, without profit, and for the sole purpose of enjoying the pleasing spectacle of the pitiful gestures and movements, the lamentable groans and cries, of a man dying in anguish" (Montaigne, "Of Cruelty," in *Complete Works*, 372–86, at 383).

88. As Luke Timothy Johnson cogently remarks, "Sin is not a matter of the spirit being polluted by the body, nor is it a matter of people being enslaved by an unjust social order. It is a disease of freedom itself that is so profound, so complex, so entrenched, so *enslaved*, that only God—who

has created us as free creatures—has power enough of knowledge and love to redirect that freedom rightly" (*Living Gospel*, 195). I note that Johnson's book also includes a challenge to the Church to ask whether "homosexuality and holiness of life" are "compatible," and to ask "whether the Church can recognize the possibility of homosexual committed and covenantal love, in the way that it recognizes such sexual/personal love in the sacrament of marriage" (ibid., 64–65). Certainly homosexual inclinations (as distinct from same-sex sexual acts) are compatible with holiness of life, and certainly the friendships between persons with homosexual inclinations are often deeply rich in various ways. For the reasons given in chapter 4, however, I think that same-sex sexual acts have a negative relationship to holiness. Lest it seem as though I am singling out persons with homosexual inclinations, however, I note that the full scope of chastity includes the rejection of many actions toward which heterosexuals, as fallen humans, are inclined. In this regard, Johnson refers to "the heterosexual '*Playboy/Cosmo* lifestyle'" (ibid., 64), and he could also have mentioned pornography (which of course also afflicts persons with homosexual inclinations). It is also worth pointing out that there are likely to be cases of invincible ignorance, where the persons involved in the actions have been taught by society that the actions are right and just, even though the actions are not so. Christians, therefore, will judge the state of no one's soul, though Christians can and should assess the moral status of actions in light of revelation and reason and should make clear that some actions separate a person from the body of Christ. Johnson grants that "the Church, cannot, should not, define itself in response to political pressure or popularity polls" (ibid., 65). See also my "Knowing What Is 'Natural': Thomas Aquinas and Luke Timothy Johnson on Romans 1–2," *Logos* 12 (2009): 117–42.

CHAPTER SIX. Humility

1. Wright, *Paul and the Faithfulness of God*, 1068.
2. Johnson, *Living Gospel*, 112.
3. Wright, *Paul and the Faithfulness of God*, 1072; cf. 770.
4. Ibid., 1072, 770.
5. Jonathan Sacks similarly observes that in the Torah "there is a connection between idolatry and sexual lawlessness": see Sacks, *Essays on Ethics*, xxvii. For Sacks, Judaism and Christianity must insist upon "the fundamental importance of sexual ethics ... and of the sanctity of marriage and the family as the matrix of society and the place where children are inducted into the moral life" (ibid., xxviii).

6. Cantalamessa, *Virginity*, 57. Cantalamessa adds, "Lust is carnal pride and pride is spiritual lust" (ibid.).

7. See Sebastian Carlson, O.P., *The Virtue of Humility* (Dubuque, IA: Wm. C. Brown Co., 1952), 11: "The matter of humility is the appetition of personal excellence." In chapter 7 of his book, Carlson compares humility with magnanimity. He notes that magnanimity "and humility seem to approach and blend together, like shadows. They are in the same part of the soul, the irascible appetite. They have the same material object: remotely, every excellence; proximately, the appetite for arduous good. They possess the same formal object, the rationalizing of [the passion of] hope" (ibid., 64; cf. 3–7). But "humility is concerned with every good *conceived of* as an excellence, magnanimity only with things objectively great" (ibid., 65). For discussions and critiques of Aristotle's account of magnanimity, see MacIntyre, *Dependent Rational Animals*, 127; Craig A. Boyd, "Pride and Humility: Tempering the Desire for Excellence," in Timpe and Boyd, *Virtues and Their Vices*, 247–51. For Aquinas on Aristotelian magnanimity, see especially Marc D. Guerra, "Moderating the Magnanimous Man: Aquinas on Greatness of Soul," in *Theology Needs Philosophy: Acting Against Reason Is Contrary to the Nature of God*, ed. Matthew L. Lamb (Washington, DC: Catholic University of America Press, 2016), 253–66, as well as Keys, *Aquinas, Aristotle, and the Promise of the Common Good*, 143–72; Rebecca Konyndyk DeYoung, "Aquinas's Virtues of Acknowledged Dependence: A New Measure of Greatness," *Faith and Philosophy* 21 (2006): 214–27.

8. Taylor, *Pride, Shame, and Guilt*, 51.

9. Alasdair MacIntyre, *Whose Justice? Which Rationality?* (Notre Dame, IN: University of Notre Dame Press, 1988), 163.

10. Ibid. It is the fruitfulness of this biblical understanding, alive even in our culture today, that refutes Edith Wyschogrod's charge that MacIntyre's project is a mere nostalgia, what she describes as "impossible dreams such as Alasdair MacIntyre's hope for the restoration of a monastic ethic or a return to an Aristotelian version of the good life as one governed by the classical virtues" (Wyschogrod, *Saints and Postmodernism: Revisioning Moral Philosophy* [Chicago: University of Chicago Press, 1990], 257). Wyschogrod's own constructive proposal strikes me as a truly impossible dream, in that she does not seem to account sufficiently for either the depths of sin or the greatness of our need for divine grace. She sketches her vision as follows: "Borrowing the compassionate strands of the world's religious traditions, the absurdist gestures of recent modernist art and literature, and modern technologies, saints try to fashion lives of compassion and generosity. They may remain uncanonized, for postmodernism does

not encourage institutional canonization, but this does not mean that they need to go unrecognized or unappreciated. The names of saints, revealed under the 'rotten sun' (Bataille) of postmodern existence, are written *sous rature*, under erasure (Derrida), and show as faint traces of alterity (Levinas) beneath the catena of altruistic actions that constitute postmodern hagiography" (ibid.).

11. Anthony Bash notes, "Both the Hebrew Scriptures and the Christian Scriptures presuppose that repentance is the starting point for forgiveness" (*Forgiveness: A Theology* [Eugene, OR: Cascade, 2015], 42). Full reconciliation requires not only divine (and human) forgiveness but also repentance on the part of the wrongdoer so that the wrongdoer can receive the forgiveness and be truly changed by it. If the wrongdoer acknowledges no need for forgiveness, the wrongdoer can be offered forgiveness but is unable to receive it.

12. Reinhard Feldmeier, *Power, Service, Humility: A New Testament Ethic*, trans. Brian McNeil (Waco, TX: Baylor University Press, 2014), 61. Feldmeier notes that by contrast to Greco-Roman literature, "a somewhat narrower Old Testament tradition and a broader early Jewish tradition, in addition to some logia of Jesus, attest a high religious appreciation of lowliness, which Paul takes up" (ibid., 62). His Old Testament examples of praise of humility include Psalm 149:4; Sirach 10:14–15; Proverbs 11:2; 15:33; 18:12; 22:4; 29:23. He adds, "There is only one formulation in the Gospel tradition in which Jesus calls himself *tapeinos tê[i] kardia[i]*, which we can translate as 'humble' (Matt 11:29). It was Paul who employed the noun *tapeinophrosunê* as a concept that expressed the positive appreciation of the attitude that refrains from self-exaltation. It is first in the sphere of influence of the Pauline theology that humility is given a home. After the Letters to the Colossians and the Ephesians, the First Letter of Peter represents the next important stage on the path taken by the ideal of humility" (ibid., 63). Feldmeier grants that there was *some* positive background in Greco-Roman literature:

> "Humility" was an inflammatory term already in classical antiquity, a culture that was oriented to the ideal of the free man and of his honor. For example, the Stoic philosopher Epictetus criticizes it as an undignified self-abasement. It is indeed true that the word group *tapeinos ktl.* can sometimes also denote something positive in classical literature, in that the human being in question is not behaving presumptuously. This means that A. Dihle's verdict that the idea of humility is foreign "to the whole of ancient ethics" is perhaps somewhat too apodictic; and we may add, with H. Wojtkowiak, that even the pagan

"ethos [offers] a point of contact for the demand for an attitude of lowliness, that is to say, the good of the community." In general, however, it remains true that nothing outside the Jewish-Christian sphere corresponds to the ideal formulated by Paul, that one should regard the other in humility as higher than one's own self (Phil 2:3). (ibid., 65–66)

He refers to Albrecht Dihle, "Demut," *Reallexikon für Antike und Christentum* 3 (1957): 735–78; Heiko Wojtkowiak, *Christologie und Ethik im Philipperbrief: Studien zur Handlungsorientierung einer frühchristlichen Gemeinde in paganer Umwelt* (Göttingen: Vandenhoeck & Ruprecht, 2012), 155; Wolfgang Schrage, *Ethik des Neuen Testaments*, 5th ed. (Göttingen: Vandenhoeck & Ruprecht, 1989); Gudrun Guttenberger Ortwein, *Status und Statusverzicht im Neuen Testament und seiner Umwelt* (Freiburg, Switzerland: Universitätsverlag, 1999); Stefan Rehrl, *Das Problem der Demut in der profangriechischen Literatur im Vergleich zu Septuaginta und Neuem Testament* (Münster: Aschendorff, 1961). For Augustine's critique of Stoicism as fostering pride, see Christopher Brooke, *Philosophic Pride: Stoicism and Political Thought from Lipsius to Rousseau* (Princeton: Princeton University Press, 2012), 1–11.

13. Porter, "Virtue Ethics in the Medieval Period," 70–71. For the concern that Aquinas underestimates humility in his *Summa theologiae*—due to his reliance upon Cicero's pagan philosophical way of organizing virtues (Cicero places humility under modesty)—see especially Sheryl Overmyer, "Exalting the Meek Virtue of Humility in Aquinas," *Heythrop Journal* 56 (2015): 650–62.

14. Servais Pinckaers, O.P., "The Sources of the Ethics of St. Thomas Aquinas," trans. Mary Thomas Noble, O.P., with Michael Sherwin, O.P., in *Pinckaers Reader*, 14.

15. *ST* II-II, q. 162, a. 5. See also, for the way that pride (as understood by Aquinas) can cause us to reject any form of political rule over ourselves, Paul J. Weithman's "Thomistic Pride and Liberal Vice," *Thomist* 60 (1996): 241–74. Weithman is responding to the fact that pride "is a vice that many philosophers now consider unworthy of attention," often because they desire to "sever the connection between religion on the one hand and moral and political philosophy on the other" (ibid., 242–43). Arguing that Aquinas's account of pride remains of value even for nontheists, Weithman has in view especially the work of Thomas Nagel, Martha Nussbaum, and Judith Shklar. According to Weithman, "Shklar neglects pride expressly because she rejects the moral agenda that Augustine and others thought biblical religion set for political theory" (ibid., 245). See Shklar, *Ordinary Vices* (Cambridge, MA: Harvard University Press, 1984).

16. *ST* II-II, q. 162, a. 4, ad 1. By contrast, building upon his theory that "moral distinctions depend entirely on certain peculiar sentiments of pain and pleasure, and that whatever mental quality in ourselves or others gives us a satisfaction . . . is of course virtuous" (Hume, *A Treatise of Human Nature*, ed. Ernest C. Mossner [London: Penguin Books, 1969], 625), David Hume argues for the virtuousness of pride (and the viciousness of humility). On this view, pride arises simply from qualities in ourselves that cause pleasure, since "moral good and evil are . . . distinguish'd by our *sentiments*, not by *reason*" (ibid., 640): "The merit of pride or self-esteem is deriv'd from two circumstances, *viz.* its utility and its agreeableness to ourselves; by which it capacitates us for business, and, at the same time, gives us an immediate satisfaction" (ibid., 650). For Hume, humility is simply a "disagreeable passion" (ibid., 651). For a valuable response to Hume, see Gabrielle Taylor, *Pride, Shame, and Guilt*, chapter 2.

17. *ST* II-II, q. 162, a. 5; *ST* II-II, q. 162, a. 7, ad 2.

18. John Webster, *Holiness* (Grand Rapids, MI: Eerdmans, 2003), 23.

19. Ibid., 25.

20. Julia Annas, *Intelligent Virtue* (Oxford: Oxford University Press, 2011), 161.

21. Garrigou-Lagrange, *Three Ages of the Interior Life*, 1:387.

22. Carlson notes that for some (though not for most) classical Thomist commentators, humility should be divided into three virtues: "an acquired humility of the sense appetite"; a "second acquired humility, subjected in the will, [that] has as its object submission to every created superior"; and "the third and noblest humility, likewise inhering in the will, . . . not acquired by man's efforts but infused by God, and motivated by reverence for the designs of His Providence" (*Virtue of Humility*, 69). As Carlson explains, commentators who take this position are influenced to do so "(a) by the needlessness of any virtue in the will assisting it to attain its own good; (b) by the apparent impossibility of the appetition of excellence by the lower irascible; (c) by the fact that humility seems to be just as much concerned with external human relations (the object of justice) as it is with the passion and affection of hope; and (d) by the identity of its formal motive and that of religion" (ibid., 70). Carlson shows in detail that humility is in fact one virtue, properly described by Aquinas. See also Stephan Ernst, "Die bescheidene Rolle der Demut. Christliche und philosophische Grundhaltungen in der speziellen Tugendlehre," in *Thomas von Aquin: Die Summa theologiae: Werkinterpretationen*, ed. Andreas Speer (Berlin: Walter de Gruyter, 2005), 343–76.

23. John Webster, "'Where Christ Is': Christology and Ethics," in *God without Measure: Working Papers in Christian Theology*, vol. 2, *Virtue and Intellect* (London: Bloomsbury, 2016), 5–27, at 14.

24. Ibid. Marie-Dominique Chenu, O.P., describes Aquinas's doctrine of relational creaturehood: "When creation came about, at the heart of the being that it receives from God is placed an ontological link—a pure relation where the poverty of the created one is expressed—and the creature is thus bound to God even as it is set forth in existence. To be created is first of all to *be*: the being is of one who is dependent, always linked to its source of being, but whose dependence only has significance because it is something that *is*" (*Aquinas and His Role in Theology*, 87). This latter point, Chenu argues, means that creatures have an integrity or "autonomy," pre-eminently realized in human intelligence and freedom but always rooted in "radical dependency" on God (ibid.). Chenu couches this point within a polemical, and in my view exaggerated, contrast between Augustine and Aquinas. Rightly, however, Chenu suggests that it is a fully God-centered perspective that allows for the integrity of relational creaturehood: "In the world's destiny, God's role is not that of the helper of human beings within a shared partnership in which God would provide power and courage along with some assurance of eternal happiness. God controls history, precisely because events *are totally human* within this creative providence. The very transcendence of God is the reason for the real efficacy of nature, of causes, and of events—the 'the will of God, if we understand that it is beyond the order of things, is the cause penetrating the depths of being in its totality, all distinctions included'" (ibid., 89; the internal quotation is from Aquinas's *Commentary on the Peri Hermeneias of Aristotle*, book 1, lect. 14, no. 197 [Turin: Marietti, 1955]).

25. For discussion of Colossians, see Wright, *Epistles of Paul to the Colossians and to Philemon*.

26. Webster "'Where Christ Is,'" 7.

27. Ibid.

28. Ibid., 8.

29. Ibid.

30. Ibid.

31. Ibid.

32. Here the work of Eugen Drewermann deserves mention, especially his three-volume analysis of Genesis 2–11, *Strukturen des Bösen: Sonderausgabe; Die jahwistische Urgeschichte in exegetischer/ psychoanalytischer/ philosophischer Sicht* (Paderborn: Schöningh, 1985–86), which I encountered in Sandra M. Schneiders's *Jesus Risen in Our Midst: Essays on the Resurrection of Jesus in the Fourth Gospel* (Collegeville, MN: Liturgical Press, 2013), chapter 6. Schneiders nicely sums up the thesis of this massive work: "Drewermann calls up the 'usual suspects' for the motivation of our first parents' sin—greed, lust, pride, disobedience—and finds all these hy-

potheses incoherent. He proposes that the fundamental motive for the originating sin was fear—existential fear of annihilation born of the ontological 'wound' of creaturehood. What humanity rejects, Drewermann says, is contingency, the fact that we are not God. Our existential terror stems from our realization that—even though made in God's image and likeness—we, unlike God, are not the source of our own existence" (*Jesus Risen in Our Midst*, 155). Precisely what Drewermann describes, however, is what Aquinas and Webster understand to be the sin of pride. For an influential psychoanalytic approach to death and dying that follows a path somewhat similar to that of Drewermann, but without belief in God, see Ernest Becker, *The Denial of Death* (New York: Free Press, 1997). See also Matthias Beier, *A Violent God-Image: An Introduction to the Work of Eugen Drewermann* (New York: Continuum, 2004). Schneiders describes the christological solution: "Jesus is God's incarnate overture to alienated humans grasping for divinity as the only security against the contingency of creaturehood. In Jesus, God demonstrates that divinity—equality with God—is not something to be coveted, because divinity is not something God exploits at our expense. In Jesus, God takes on the very form that humanity, instructed by the tempter, regards as slavery, namely, creaturehood, to demonstrate that creaturehood is not a condition of existential peril rooted in ontological deficiency" (*Jesus Risen in Our Midst*, 157).

33. Webster, "'Where Christ Is,'" 11.

34. Ibid., 12.

35. Ibid., 12–13.

36. Ibid., 13. Webster here is responding to the early Barth, to Bonhoeffer, and to Hans Ulrich. See Karl Barth, *Ethics* (Edinburgh: T&T Clark, 1981); Dietrich Bonhoeffer, *Ethics* (Minneapolis: Fortress, 1996); Hans Ulrich, *Wie Geschöpfe leben: Konturen evangelischer Ethik* (Münster: LIT, 2005). As Webster goes on to say, "Moral ontology concerns the creature's appointment to be a certain kind of being, the creature's being moved in order to engage in a certain movement. Yet that moral *movement* is imperfectly undertaken without apprehension of moral *nature*, without intelligence of who and where we are, and of by whom we are met" (Webster, "'Where Christ Is,'" 14).

37. Webster, "'Where Christ Is,'" 22.

38. Ibid., 23.

39. See also Second Vatican Council, *Gaudium et Spes*, §22, in Tanner, *Trent to Vatican II*, 1081: "It is Christ, the last Adam, who fully discloses humankind to itself and unfolds its noble calling."

40. Webster, "'Where Christ Is,'" 24.

41. Ibid.

42. Ibid.

43. Webster rightly warns against "an over-realized eschatology," as though "moral time" were over and we were fully the creatures we are called to be, in the consummated "kingdom of his beloved Son" (Col 1:13). See ibid., 24. Webster does not explicitly discuss moral failure on the part of Christians. Instead he notes that the "new nature" that we have "put on" (Col 3:10) is still "hidden," so that when we talk about this "new nature," non-Christians may not know what we are talking about, and we may experience "ignominy" due to "the occlusion of life in Christ" and "the world's negation of its true basis and direction" (ibid., 25).

44. Webster, "The Dignity of Creatures," in *God without Measure*, 30.

45. See Giovanni Pico della Mirandola, "Oration on the Dignity of Man," in *The Renaissance Philosophy of Man*, ed. E. Cassirer and P. Kristeller (Chicago: University of Chicago Press, 1949), 223–54. For a more positive assessment of Pico on human nature, see M. V. Dougherty, "Three Precursors to Pico della Mirandola's Roman Disputation and the Question of Human Nature," in *Pico della Mirandola: New Essays*, ed. M. V. Dougherty (Cambridge: Cambridge University Press, 2007), 114–51.

46. Webster, "Dignity of Creatures," 33.

47. Ibid., 34.

48. Ibid., 36.

49. Ibid., 44.

50. Ibid., 38.

51. Ibid., 40. Webster refers to sin as "creatures' deadly trespass upon their own dignity" (ibid.). Aquinas argues that "by sinning man departs from the order of reason, and consequently falls away from the dignity of his manhood, in so far as he is naturally free, and exists for himself, and he falls into the slavish state of the beasts [by enslaving himself irrationally to sin]" (*ST* II-II, q. 64, a. 2, ad 3). Aquinas makes clear that the (minimal) dignity of possessing the image of God cannot be effaced, since even the human being in a state of sin "possesses a natural aptitude for understanding and loving God," an aptitude that "consists in the very nature of the mind" (*ST* I, q. 93, a. 4).

52. Webster, "Dignity of Creatures," 39.

53. Ibid., 40.

54. Ibid. Webster adds that "creaturely dignity is not protected by the promulgation of a moral ideal (law), but by a divine mission of reconciliation (gospel)" (ibid.). Although of course we receive forgiveness of sins through the gospel, I think that a more positive account of law would be helpful here.

55. Ibid., 45.

56. Ibid., 44–45.

57. Ibid., 45.

58. See Leonard J. DeLorenzo, *Work of Love: A Theological Reconstruction of the Communion of Saints* (Notre Dame, IN: University of Notre Dame Press, 2017), especially chapter 6. DeLorenzo writes movingly in his acknowledgments, "Who I am, what I believe, how I think, and why I 'do' theology are all tied up in my relationships with those who love me, inspire me, teach me, and hold me accountable to the gifts I have received. Truly, I am not myself by myself. Any good that I may have achieved in this work redounds to those who have shared and who continue to share their goodness with me. The greatest good I have received is the gift of faith, without which I would be incapable of doing theology at all" (ibid., xi).

59. The inclusion of humility within "temperance" may be initially surprising. Recall that for Aquinas, humility is among the "potential parts" of temperance. Strictly speaking, temperance moderates our desire for the pleasures of food, drink, and sex. But Aquinas argues that "any virtue that is effective of moderation in some matter or other, and restrains the appetite in its impulse towards something, may be reckoned a part of temperance, as a virtue annexed thereto" (*ST* II-II, q. 143, a. 1). See my introduction to this book for further discussion.

60. For a constructive theology of humility that builds upon Aquinas and numerous other saints, see Father Canice, O.F.M. Cap., *Humility: The Foundation of the Spiritual Life* (Westminster, MD: Newman Press, 1951).

61. For the patristic and medieval background to Aquinas's theology of humility, see Carlson, *Virtue of Humility*, 95–102. Aquinas cites Luke 1:48 in *ST* II-II, q. 161, a. 1, sed contra. He discusses Luke 1:48 in conjunction with Origen's commentary on the passage. For an English edition of the text Aquinas cites, see Origen, *Homilies on Luke*, trans. Joseph T. Lienhard, S.J. (Washington, DC: Catholic University of America Press, 1996), homily 8, pp. 33–36. Origen comments,

> Someone might object and say, "I understand how God could look upon his handmaid's justice and wisdom. But it is not quite clear how he could look upon her humility." The one who asks such questions should consider that, in the Scriptures, humility is declared to be one of the virtues. For the Savior says, "Learn from me, for I am gentle and humble in heart, and you will find rest for your souls." If you wish to hear the name of this virtue, how even the philosophers designate it, listen: the humility that God looks upon is the same virtue that they call ἀτυφία ("modesty") or μετριότης ("moderation"). (*Homilies on Luke*, 35)

In a footnote, the translator (Lienhard) remarks, "The Greeks never considered humility to be a virtue, and the word used for it at Lk 1.48 always had, in secular Greek, a negative connotation. Morally, it meant 'baseness' or 'vileness,' socially, 'lowness of position.' In this paragraph, Origen struggles to present humility as a virtue to an audience of catechumens who are not used to thinking of it as such" (ibid., 35n15).

62. See *ST* II-II, q. 161, a. 1, sed contra. Aquinas also quotes Matthew 11:29 in *ST* II-II, q. 161, a. 5, obj. 4. For a discussion of Mary's humility, see Canice, *Humility*, 88–90; John Tarasievitch, "Humility in the Light of St. Thomas" (STD diss., University of Fribourg, 1935), 186–96.

63. Recall that humility has to do with proper desire for spiritual gifts and proper estimation of the ways in which God has gifted us.

64. The broader context of 1 Peter 3 is noteworthy here, since 1 Peter 3:8 urges all Christians to have "a humble mind." In addition, 1 Peter 5:5–6 commands, "Clothe yourselves, all of you, with humility toward one another, for 'God opposes the proud, but gives grace to the humble.' Humble yourselves therefore under the mighty hand of God, that in due time he may exalt you." For discussion see Feldmeier, *Power, Service, Humility*, 83–88.

65. For discussion of James 4, see Feldmeier, *Power, Service, Humility*, 88–92. Feldmeier concludes his discussion of James with the suggestion that hierarchical structures are opposed to humility, a position that I argue against in my *Christ and the Catholic Priesthood: Ecclesial Hierarchy and the Pattern of the Trinity* (Chicago: Hillenbrand Books, 2010).

66. See *ST* II-II, q. 161, a. 1, ad 1 and ad 4; q. 161, a. 2, obj. 1 and obj. 2; q. 161, a. 3, sed contra; q. 161, a. 3; q. 161, a. 4; q. 161, a. 5, obj. 3; q. 161, a. 5, sed contra; q. 161, a. 5, ad 1–3.

67. *ST* II-II, q. 161, a. 1.

68. Garrigou-Lagrange, *Three Ages of the Interior Life*, 144. After quoting this passage, Carlson helpfully inquires: "If the essential act of humility is the moderate quest of excellence, how can its 'principal' act be the subjection of the heart to God? The two seem to move in different directions. In reality, however, they are *specifically the same act*. The former is the motion of the appetite toward the object of humility, the latter is its motion toward the formal motive of the virtue" (*Virtue of Humility*, 31).

69. *ST* II-II, q. 161, a. 1, ad 5.

70. *ST* II-II, q. 161, a. 2. See Canice's observation: "When a mortal is confronted by the Lord or when he kneels before the tabernacle and dwells prayerfully on the divine perfections, the holiness, the power, the immensity of God, he sees the overwhelming contrast between God and himself. He recognizes his absolute inferiority before these infinite attri-

butes. He adores; and in this act of supreme worship the enormous antithesis is apparent to him: his own lowliness and nothingness is contrasted with the immeasurable greatness and immense majesty of the Lord" (Canice, *Humility*, 14). Or as Garrigou-Lagrange puts it, "The more this distance appears to us in a living and concrete manner, the more humble we are. However lofty the creature may be, this abyss is always infinite; and the higher we ascend, the more evident does this infinite abyss become for us. In this sense, the highest soul is the most humble, because the most enlightened" (*Three Ages of the Interior Life*, 2:145).

71. *ST* II-II, q. 161, a. 2, ad 2.

72. *ST* II-II, q. 161, a. 3. Garrigou-Lagrange points out, "If all that comes from God were taken away from even our best free acts, strictly speaking nothing would remain, for in such an act one part does not come from us and the other from God. The act is entirely from God as from its first cause, and it is entirely from us as from its second cause.... We should recognize practically that without God, the Creator and Preserver of all things, we are nothing" (*Three Ages of the Interior Life*, 2:146). He adds that in Christ "we cannot take the slightest step forward, or perform the least salutary and meritorious act without the help of an actual grace. We need this grace particularly to persevere to the end and should, consequently, humbly ask for it. Even if we had a high degree of sanctifying grace and charity, ten talents for example, we should still need an actual grace for the least salutary act. And especially for a happy death we need the great gift of final perseverance" (ibid., 147). The Christian life involves recognizing our radical dependence upon the gifts of God, and thus the Christian life must be one of humility.

73. *ST* II-II, q. 161, a. 3.

74. See Boyd, "Pride and Humility," 264–65. Canice comments that "it is unquestionable that all men are not equal in merit, that one is better than another and that one person is superior to his fellows. Humility never departs from the truth. It acts by making each of us consider what he has *of himself*, his nothingness and his sins, and it makes us consider in our neighbor what he has *from God*, his virtues, his gifts of nature and of grace. At the contrast, we should acknowledge our inferiority and humble ourselves" (*Humility*, 23). At the same time, Canice admits that "few there are, however, who get as far as this in the virtue. Their self-knowledge does not go deep enough. It is a grace not given to all" (ibid., 24). In this discussion, Canice draws upon Columba Marmion, O.S.B., *Christ, the Ideal of the Monk* (New Pekin, IN: Refuge of Sinners Publications, 1926). See also Dennis Okholm, *Dangerous Passions, Deadly Sins*, 176–78.

75. Garrigou-Lagrange, *Three Ages of the Interior Life*, 2:150.

76. Carlson, *Virtue of Humility*, 39. Following Aquinas, Carlson emphasizes that it is not "a sin against lowliness of heart to feel that one is not the greatest sinner in the world," although one must recognize the gifts of God in others and be aware in oneself of resistance to God's gifts (ibid.; cf. 40–43).

77. *ST* II-II, q. 161, a. 4.

78. For humility's relationship to the other virtues, see Carlson, *Virtue of Humility*, 44–61. Carlson suggests that Christianity gives humility such a high standing because of humility's "uniquely wide participation in the good of reason, the fact that, subjecting the entire appetite out of reverence for God, it renders it docile to the voice of reason" (ibid., 61). Carlson is relying in significant part on Cardinal Cajetan's commentary on the *Summa theologiae*. Obviously, as Carlson says, "there are various viewpoints from which the perfection of the virtues can be regarded, and . . . their rank will vary with each consideration" (ibid., 53).

79. *ST* II-II, q. 161, a. 5.

80. Boyd, "Pride and Humility," 259.

81. *ST* II-II, q. 161, a. 4, obj. 1.

82. *ST* II-II, q. 161, a. 5, ad 1.

83. *ST* II-II, q. 161, a. 5, ad 2. See my *Engaging the Doctrine of the Holy Spirit*, especially chapter 5. See also Emery, "Holy Spirit in Aquinas's Commentary on Romans."

84. Second Vatican Council, *Gaudium et Spes*, §22, in Tanner, *Trent to Vatican II*, 1082.

85. *ST* II-II, q. 161, a. 5, ad 2.

86. Ibid. For discussion see Canice, *Humility*, 35–36.

87. Aquinas, *Commentary on the Gospel of St. Matthew*, 419. In Matthew 11:29, Jesus says, "Take my yoke upon you, and learn from me; for I am gentle [meek] and lowly in heart [humble], and you will find rest for your souls."

88. *ST* II-II, q. 161, a. 5, obj. 4, quoting Gregory the Great, *The Book of Pastoral Rule*, 3.1.

89. *ST* II-II, q. 161, a. 5, ad 3.

90. See *ST* II-II, q. 26, aa. 4–5. See also Canice, *Humility*, 15, for the affirmation that "a man must esteem himself if he desires to live properly."

91. Second Vatican Council, *Gaudium et Spes*, §38, in Tanner, *Trent to Vatican II*, 1092. *Gaudium et Spes* here has Romans 15:16 in view.

92. *ST* II-II, q. 161, a. 5, ad 3.

93. Canice observes that "in the world of the supernatural, ours is an innate and absolute helplessness without God. . . . When we realize our incompetence we see immediately that self-depreciation is the logical and

correct course of action, and that self-exaltation or self-glorification is wild and most absurd" (Canice, *Humility*, 52–53).

94. *ST* II-II, q. 161, a. 5, ad 4.

95. For discussion see especially Carlson, *Virtue of Humility*, 74–82. Carlson notes, "Thomas evidently did not have the *Rule* itself to refer to, for he gives them in inverse order. His first degree, 'Always to display humility in heart and body,' is Benedict's twelfth. Yet, he certainly wished to follow the original order and thought he was doing so" (ibid., 74). Carlson directs attention to Cyrille Lambot, O.S.B., "L'ordre et le text des degrés d'humilité dans s. Thomas," *Revue Bénédictine* 39 (1927): 129–35. Lambot shows that Aquinas solely possessed the *capitula*, posthumously prefaced to Bernard's treatise *De humilitate et superbia* with the purpose of summarizing the chapter on humility found in Benedict's rule. Carlson points out, however, that Aquinas "begins his commentary on it [the *capitula*] from the twelfth degree of his own text (Benedict's first), thus employing it in its original order" (*Virtue of Humility*, 75–76).

96. Carlson observes that Aquinas finds Anselm's seven degrees to be "reducible to two of the twelve given by Benedict" (ibid., 74). See also Garrigou-Lagrange's appreciation of Anselm's seven degrees: *Three Ages of the Interior Life*, 2:153.

97. See Bernard of Clairvaux, *On the Song of Songs II*, trans. Kilian Walsh, O.C.S.O. (Kalamazoo, MI: Cistercian Publications, 1983), sermon 34 ("True Humility"), pp. 161–63. Bernard states, "There are some who meet humiliation with rancor, some with patience, some again with cheerfulness. The first kind are culpable, the second are innocent, the last just" (ibid., 162).

98. See Canice, *Humility*, 80–81. Canice remarks, "We have it on the authority of St. Bernard that we cannot be humble unless we are humbled, and that humiliation is the way to humility just as study leads to knowledge" (ibid., 90).

99. *ST* II-II, q. 161, a. 6, ad 2. Canice notes, "We have reason to be humble when we think of our sins. Though not the primary reason for the virtue, they afford the greatest ground for it" (*Humility*, 56). He adds, "The Church, in one of the collects [Second Sunday of Lent], makes us admit that we are destitute of every virtue, and yet we esteem ourselves so excessively that we are troubled if others do not esteem us also. This is due to a failure in remembering our sins, and a resultant lack of proper self-knowledge" (ibid., 57).

100. *ST* II-II, q. 161, a. 6.

101. In *ST* II-II, q. 19, a. 9, ad 4, Aquinas roots humility in the Holy Spirit's gift of filial fear: "Fear cuts off the source of pride, for which reason

it is bestowed as a remedy against pride. Yet it does not follow that it is the same as the virtue of humility, but that it is its origin. For the gifts of the Holy Spirit are the origin of the intellectual and moral virtues . . . while the theological virtues are the origin of the gifts." Aquinas adds in *ST* II-II, q. 19, a. 12, that "it belongs to filial fear to show reverence and submission to God. . . . Now from the very fact that a man submits to God, it follows that he ceases to seek greatness either in himself or in another but seeks it only in God." For discussion, see Carlson, *Virtue of Humility*, 80–92. As Carlson says, "Humility increases as filial fear of God increases, for . . . it depends on that fear for its very being. But filial fear grows only as charity does" (ibid., 80; cf. 90).

102. Note that in certain respects, Aquinas is correcting the monastic tradition even while he agrees with it. John Tarasievitch notes that the monastic and ascetical tradition overly associates humility with "belittlement" and "depreciation" ("Humility in the Light of St. Thomas," 45). Regarding the positive end of humility (namely, exaltation to divine intimacy), Tarasievitch observes, "God is the end of every virtue. Therefore St. Bernard should have specified this, while defining humility. Of course he knew very well that he practiced it solely to please God; hence even humiliations and abasements brought him nearer to God; were animated by him with the spirit of moral perfection; were instituted by him as a special domain wherein lowliness and abjection would be suddenly and mysteriously transformed into an effective and glorious power of leading his soul closer to his Heavenly Father. He [Bernard] took for granted that everyone would see humility in this light, and consequently, love it ardently and practice it assiduously. St. Thomas, indeed, saw it in this light; therefore commentated on it; incorporated St. Bernard's teachings on the degrees of humility in the body of his own teachings; and followed his example in loving and practicing it. . . . The fact, however, remains that for common mortals, humility as defined by the mellifluous doctor [Bernard] is not by any means a lovable virtue but a repellent habit. That is why the Angelic Doctor defined it quite otherwise" (ibid., 48). See also Carlson, *Virtue of Humility*, 36.

103. *ST* II-II, q. 161, a. 6, ad 1. As Carlson points out, in fact, "It is the knowledge of God, of His power and mercy, that keeps humility from collapsing in despair under the weight of human nothingness and sin" (*Virtue of Humility*, 24). He quotes Louis-Marie Grignon de Montfort's observation: "We are naturally prouder than peacocks, more grovelling on the earth than toads, more vile than unclean animals, more envious than serpents, more gluttonous than hogs, more furious than tigers, lazier than tortoises, weaker than reeds, and more capricious than weathercocks" (de Montfort, *True Devotion to the Blessed Virgin*, trans. F. W. Faber [New

York: 1909], 55; quoted in *Virtue of Humility*, 26). See also Bernard of Clairvaux, *On the Song of Songs II*, sermon 37 ("Knowledge and Ignorance of God and of Self"), p. 181: "No one is saved without self-knowledge, since it is the source of that humility on which salvation depends, and of the fear of the Lord that is as much the beginning of salvation as of wisdom."

104. *ST* II-II, q. 161, a. 6, ad 1.

105. *ST* II-II, q. 161, a. 6, ad 3; Canice, *Humility*, 66. On Christ's humility, see Garrigou-Lagrange, *Three Ages of the Interior Life*, vol. 2, chapter 13. Canice offers helpful examples of external abasement:

> Someone in authority will admonish; he will overlook us in giving offices or in bestowing attention and sympathy. Colleagues will treat us awkwardly; they will contradict or pass disparaging remarks about our work; they will show a lack of due regard; they will ask another for his opinion, as if ours were of little use; they will show anger at an inoffensive word. All these slights and many more may originate from inadvertence or from frailty or (very rarely) from malice. But it should not matter. Those who humble us do us a genuine service. . . . Our acceptance of these involuntary humiliations is a sign of true and sincere humility. (*Humility*, 92–93)

106. Aquinas, *Commentary on the Gospel of St. Matthew*, 605–6. Carlson comments, "Charity is opposed to pride as directly as love of God is opposed to love of self; and humility is as intimate with charity as subjection to God is with love of Him" (*Virtue of Humility*, 79).

107. McInerney, *Greatness of Humility*, 187. See David Hume, *An Enquiry concerning the Principles of Morals*, ed. J. B. Schneewind (Indianapolis: Hackett, 1983), §9—Conclusion, pp. 73–74:

> Celibacy, fasting, penance, mortification, self-denial, humility, silence, solitude, and the whole train of monkish virtues; for what reason are they everywhere rejected by men of sense, but because they serve to no manner of purpose; neither to advance a man's fortune in the world, nor render him a more valuable member of society; neither qualify him for the entertainment of company, nor increase his power of self-enjoyment? We observe, on the contrary, that they cross all those desirable ends; stupify the understanding and harden the heart, obscure the fancy and sour the temper. We justly, therefore, transfer them to the opposite column, and place them in the catalogue of vices; nor has any superstition force sufficient among men of the world, to pervert entirely these natural sentiments."

108. C. C. Pecknold, foreword to McInerney, *Greatness of Humility*, ix. For a defense of Nietzsche's concerns as grounded in Christian abuses of humility, see Feldmeier, *Power, Service, Humility*, 64. See also Kent Dunnington's argument that "Augustine envisions Christian humility as expressed through submission to God grounded in a disposition of the will to embrace radical dependence and accordingly to guard against the drive to establish an intelligible, secure, and self-sufficient identity" ("Humility: An Augustinian Perspective," *Pro Ecclesia* 25 [2016]: 34). Dunnington affirms, as a matter of faith, that "there is an intelligible, coherent content to the identity of 'Christian'" (ibid., 35), but he downplays and indeed negates this content by arguing that "knowledge of Christian identity is perpetually deferred this side of eternity" (ibid.). Dunnington would have benefited from following more closely Augustine's understanding of the virtues (in addition to humility), and thereby gaining more insight into the content and ontological grounding of what Dunnington insightfully calls "a way of being a self in which relationship, receptivity, and self-donation are constitutive" (ibid., 38). Early in his essay, he provides a striking summary of the misunderstanding of humility prevalent among contemporary secular philosophers:

> Norvin Richards, for example, claims that according to the traditional Christian view, "to be humble is to have a low opinion of oneself" (1988, 253). Daniel Statman claims humility entered Western civilization through the Jewish and Christian religions, both of which took the virtue to consist in "a certain kind of (low) self-assessment" (1992, 432). G. F. Schueler claims the "Christian view of the virtue called 'humility' accepts a 'low-opinion' account" (1997, 470). Stephen Hare says of humility that "the term for many denotes low self-regard" and notes such an understanding of the term is connected to Christian theological assumptions (1996, 235). No account in the secular philosophical literature on humility offers anything other than a "low-estimate" definition of Christian humility. (ibid., 19)

See Daniel Statman, "Modesty, Pride and Realistic Self-Assessment," *Philosophical Quarterly* 42 (1992): 420–38; G. F. Schueler, "Why Modesty Is a Virtue," *Ethics* 107 (1997): 467–85; Stephen Hare, "The Paradox of Moral Humility," *American Philosophical Quarterly* 33 (1996): 235–41; Norvin Richards, "Is Humility a Virtue?," *American Philosophical Quarterly* 25 (1988): 253–59.

109. *ST* II-II, q. 162, a. 3, ad 2. On prudence as "right reason of things to be done" (*ST* I-II, q. 57, a. 4), see Boyd, "Pride and Humility," 261–63.

See also Frank Yartz, "Order and Right Reason in Aquinas's Ethics," *Mediaeval Studies* 37 (1975): 407–18.

110. *ST* II-II, q. 162, a. 3, ad 1.

111. Ibid. For discussion of pride and "vainglory" according to the patristic ascetic tradition, see Okholm, *Dangerous Passions, Deadly Sins*, chapter 8.

112. *ST* II-II, q. 162, a. 4.

113. See *ST* II-II, q. 162, a. 6.

114. *ST* II-II, q. 162, a. 4, ad 1. See Boyd, "Pride and Humility," 256.

115. *ST* II-II, q. 162, a. 5. Okholm observes that "salvation requires what pride cannot allow: an admission by the fallen creature of his non-superior sinful standing before God, of his *need* for grace, and of *faith*, which is absolute trust in God, not in self (see Rom 3:27; 4:2–5; James 4:6)" (*Dangerous Passions, Deadly Sins*, 170).

116. *ST* II-II, q. 162, a. 5, ad 3.

117. *ST* II-II, q. 162, a. 7, ad 1. Carlson points out that humility "is that which removes from the soul the greatest obstacle to the infusion and increase of the virtues: pride. Its worth is the worth of a *removens prohibens*, no more, no less. It is in this sense that humility is the foundation of all the virtues, and that which conserves them in being. . . . The friendship with God which we call charity of its very nature implies humble subjection: it is a friendship of master and servant, of Creator and creature" (*Virtue of Humility*, 81–82).

118. *ST* II-II, q. 161, a. 6.

119. Feldmeier, *Power, Service, Humility*, 96.

120. *ST* II-II, q. 163, a. 1, obj. 1.

121. For Adam's sin as a sin of pride and gluttony, see Alexander Schmemann, *Great Lent: Journey to Pascha*, rev. ed. (Crestwood, NY: St. Vladimir's Seminary Press, 1974), 94–95:

> The unfathomable tragedy of Adam is that he ate for its own sake. More than that, he ate "apart" from God in order to be independent of Him. And if he did it, it is because he believed that food had life in itself and that he, by partaking of that food, could be like God, i.e., have life in himself. To put it very simply: he *believed in food*, whereas the only object of belief, of faith, of dependence is God and God alone. World, food, became his gods, the sources and principles of his life. He became their slave.

See also, for original sin as an act of bad eating, Méndez-Montoya, *Theology of Food*, 79–84. Méndez-Montoya points out that for Schmemann, the eucharistic banquet embodies the reversal of the bad eating of Adam (and Eve): see Méndez-Montoya, *Theology of Food*, 85–89, summarizing Schmemann, *For the Life of the World: Sacraments and Orthodoxy* (Crestwood, NY: St. Vladimir's Seminary Press, 1973).

122. *ST* II-II, q. 163, a. 1.
123. Ibid., ad 1.
124. Cited in *ST* II-II, q. 163, a. 1, obj. 2.
125. *ST* II-II, q. 163, a. 1. See Daniel A. Keating, *Deification and Grace* (Ave Maria, FL: Sapientia Press, 2007); Keating, "Justification, Sanctification and Divinization in Thomas Aquinas," in *Aquinas on Doctrine: Critical Essays*, ed. Thomas G. Weinandy, O.F.M. Cap., Daniel A. Keating, and John P. Yocum (New York: T&T Clark, 2004), 139–58.
126. *ST* II-II, q. 163, a. 1.
127. *ST* II-II, q. 163, a. 2.
128. Ibid.
129. Aquinas quotes Ezekiel 28:12 in ibid.
130. *ST* II-II, q. 163, a. 2.
131. Ibid.
132. Aquinas quotes Romans 5:12 in *ST* II-II, q. 164, a. 1, sed contra. For a defense of the reality of original sin and its punishment (death), see chapter 6 of my *Engaging the Doctrine of Creation*. For discussion of human dying as we experience it in our fallen condition, see my *Dying and the Virtues* (Grand Rapids, MI: Eerdmans, 2018).
133. For discussion see Randall S. Rosenberg, "Being-Toward-a-Death-Transformed: Aquinas on the Naturalness and Unnaturalness of Human Death," *Angelicum* 83 (2006): 747–66; David Albert Jones, *Approaching the End: A Theological Exploration of Death and Dying* (Oxford: Oxford University Press, 2007), chapter 5: "In One Way Natural, in Another Unnatural: Death in the Thought of Thomas Aquinas."
134. *ST* II-II, q. 164, a. 1.
135. See Lombardo, *Logic of Desire*, chapters 4 and 5. See also Paul Gondreau, "The Passions and the Moral Life: Appreciating the Originality of Aquinas," *Thomist* 71 (2007): 419–50.
136. *ST* II-II, q. 164, a. 2.
137. *ST* II-II, q. 164, a. 2, ad 9.
138. *ST* II-II, q. 164, a. 2, ad 6. There would be no need for the forgiveness of sins if Adam and Eve, and all other humans, could simply have remained in a state of innocence. Is God therefore to blame for our needing the forgiveness of sins, because he failed to protect Adam and Eve from the wiles of Satan? Aquinas notes that as befits the created order, angelic creatures interact with humans, and do so both to help (i.e., the good angels)

and to tempt (i.e., the bad angels). He defends God's permitting the fallen angel to communicate with the first humans. Indebted to Sirach 34, which extols the value of experience (and which in his Latin version specifically pertains to the value of trial or testing), he notes that as temporal creatures, humans learn through experience—including experience with angels— rather than learning everything all at once (see *ST* II-II, q. 165, a. 1, sed contra). God, however, tempts no one. Here Aquinas quotes James 1:13, to which I add verses fourteen and fifteen: "Let no one say when he is tempted, 'I am tempted by God'; for God cannot be tempted with evil and he himself tempts no one; but each person is tempted by his own desire. Then desire when it has conceived gives birth to sin; and sin when it is full-grown brings forth death" (*ST* II-II, q. 165, a. 1, ad 1). Our relational creaturehood makes it suitable that Eden contained the diverse kinds of creatures, even fallen ones, with whom we interact. Aquinas adds with respect to Adam that "no creature outside himself could harm him against his own will" (*ST* II-II, q. 165, a. 1). Since Adam (and Eve) could freely resist demonic temptation and did not have to give in to it, God did not need to prevent the bad and good angels from interacting with the first humans. Remarking that God "knew that man was able, by his free will, to resist the tempter" and to do so "without any difficulty," Aquinas holds that human nature itself required that God not force human freedom (*ST* II-II, q. 165, a. 1, ad 2 and ad 3). He quotes Sirach 15:14: "It was he [God] who created man in the beginning, and he left him in the power of his own inclination" (*ST* II-II, q. 165, a. 2). See also the concerns raised for later Thomism by David Bentley Hart, "Impassibility as Transcendence: On the Infinite Innocence of God," in *Divine Impassibility and the Mystery of Human Suffering*, ed. James F. Keating and Thomas Joseph White, O.P. (Grand Rapids, MI: Eerdmans, 2009), 299–323, as well as my *Predestination: Biblical and Theological Paths* (Oxford: Oxford University Press, 2011).

139. See *ST* II-II, q. 165, a. 2, ad 4.
140. Webster, "Dignity of Creatures," 35.
141. *ST* II-II, q. 163, a. 2.
142. Webster, "Dignity of Creatures," 37. J. Warren Smith cautions that we Christians, in our zeal for Christ, can fall into an "intemperate boldness" that must be healed by admitting that when we face trials we all too easily abandon Christ: see Smith, *The Lord's Prayer: Confessing the New Covenant* (Eugene, OR: Cascade, 2015), 117.
143. Tarasievitch, "Humility in the Light of St. Thomas," 306.
144. *ST* II-II, q. 161, a. 5, ad 2, cited in Tarasievitch, "Humility in the Light of St. Thomas," 307. Tarasievitch understands the Catholic Church to be "the Divine Kingdom on earth" (ibid., 309), and thus not yet fully the consummated kingdom (the Church triumphant).

145. Tarasievitch, "Humility in the Light of St. Thomas," 119, 310.
146. Smith, *Lord's Prayer*, 60, 63.
147. Ibid., 62.

CHAPTER SEVEN. Studiousness

1. Martin Heidegger, *Being and Time*, trans. Joan Stambaugh with revisions by Dennis J. Schmidt (Albany: State University of New York Press, 2010), 165.
2. Ibid., 166.
3. Ibid. Josef Pieper similarly describes the plight of the person who "refuses assent to reality as a whole" and "refuses to approve the fact of his own existence": "He is driven out of his own house—into the hurly-burly of work-and-nothing-else, into the fine-spun exhausting game of sophistical phrase-mongering, into incessant 'entertainment' by empty stimulants—in short, into a no man's land which may be quite comfortably furnished, but which has no place for the serenity of intrinsically meaningful activity, for contemplation, and certainly not for festivity" (*In Tune with the World: A Theory of Festivity*, trans. Richard and Clara Winston [South Bend, IN: St. Augustine's Press, 1999], 27–28).
4. Ernstpeter Maurer, "The Perplexity and Complexity of Sinful and Redeemed Reason," in *Reason and the Reasons of Faith*, ed. Paul J. Griffiths and Reinhard Hütter (New York: T&T Clark International, 2005), 196.
5. Ibid., 196, 220. For implications for the modern (Catholic) university, see Christopher O. Blum, "A Fruitful Restraint: The Perennial Relevance of the Virtue of Studiousness," *Nova et Vetera* 11 (2013): 953–68; Thomas S. Hibbs, "The Research University in Crisis (Again): MacIntyre's *God, Philosophy, Universities*," *Nova et Vetera* 9 (2011): 947–66; Reinhard Hütter, "God, the University, and the Missing Link—Wisdom: Reflections on Two Untimely Books," *Thomist* 73 (2009): 241–77. See also the important insights of my late mentor Matthew L. Lamb, "The Millennial Challenges Facing Catholic Intellectual Life," *Nova et Vetera* 11 (2013): 969–91; Alasdair MacIntyre, *God, Philosophy, Universities: A Selective History of the Catholic Philosophical Tradition* (Lanham, MD: Rowman & Littlefield, 2009). Whereas MacIntyre focuses on undergraduate study, Lamb pays attention to the importance of graduate study. Lamb offers the following defense of the ongoing project of the Catholic university:

> A long procession of saints, scholars, scientists, and artists in the last two centuries of the second millennium sought to defend the dignity of human life and to overcome the fragmentation of an instrumentalist

degradation of human reason. . . . Whenever Catholics feel lost in a maze of modernity or post-modernity and are tempted to break off participation in the procession, to withdraw into a total rejection of contemporary science, scholarship, and art, we need to recall, with Flannery O'Connor, that a procession is not a march or regimented parade. These latter she saw as Pelagian efforts to march mechanically with a false conviction that human progress has replaced Divine Providence: ever forwards, never backwards or sideways. In comparison with such marches, processions tend to meander, depending upon countless interactions of the participants, each moving in answer to a Divine Call of the Teacher, being fascinated by this or that object or person. ("Millennial Challenges Facing Catholic Intellectual Life," 990)

6. Maurer, "Perplexity and Complexity of Sinful and Redeemed Reason," 210. See also Lamb's observation that "the importance of holiness and the theological virtues cannot be overestimated for participation in this Catholic intellectual procession as the Church makes her way at the beginning of her third millennium" (Lamb, "Millennial Challenges Facing Catholic Intellectual Life," 991).

7. See Maurer, "Perplexity and Complexity of Sinful and Redeemed Reason," 210.

8. See Christian Trottmann, "Studiositas et superstitio dans la Somme de Théologie de Thomas d'Aquin, enjeux de la défiance à l'égard des 'sciences curieuses,'" in *Ratio et superstitio: Essays in Honor of Graziella Federici-Vescovini*, ed. G. Marchetti, O. Rignani, and V. Sorge (Louvain-la-Neuve: Fidem, 2003), 137–54; Serge-Thomas Bonino, O.P., "Du bon usage de l'étude: Réflexions autour de la vertu de studiosité selon saint Thomas d'Aquin," in *L'amour du Christ nous presse: Mélanges offerts à Mgr Pierre Debergé*, ed. M.-T. Urvoy and L.-T. Somme (Versailles: Éditions du Paris, 2013), 375–90 ; Pierre Blanchard, "Studiosité et curiosité: Le vrai savoir d'après saint Thomas d'Aquin," *Revue Thomiste* 53 (1953): 551–62.

9. For Plato on "the virtues of philosophic character," namely "intellectual moderation" and "intellectual spiritedness," see Gregory M. Reichberg, "*Studiositas*, the Virtue of Attention," in *The Common Things: Essays on Thomism and Education*, ed. Daniel McInerny (Mishawaka, IN: American Maritain Association, 1999), 144–46. Reichberg emphasizes Plato's "focus on the appetitive side of truth-seeking" (ibid., 146). On Aristotle's presentation of the pleasure of study in his *Nicomachean Ethics*, see James V. Schall, *The Life of the Mind: On the Joys and Travails of Thinking* (Wilmington, DE: ISI Books, 2006), 82.

10. Todd B. Kashdan, "Curiosity," in *Character Strengths and Virtues: A Handbook and Classification*, ed. Christopher Peterson and Martin E. P.

Seligman (Oxford: Oxford University Press, 2004), 129. The distinction between "novelty seeking (diversive curiosity)" and "specific curiosity," a distinction that Kashdan finds very helpful, emerges from theories that build upon and go beyond the "cognitive process theory" (ibid., 128).

11. Thomas D. Kennedy, "Curiosity and the Integrated Self: A Postmodern Vice," *Logos* 4 (2001): 46–47. Kennedy suggests that curiosity is a particularly dangerous vice in the culture of postmodernity, and he notes that the modern university has been organized in ways that foster the vice of curiosity.

12. Ibid., 48.

13. John Webster, "Curiosity," in *The Domain of the Word: Scripture and Theological Reason* (London: T&T Clark International, 2012), 193.

14. Ibid., 195.

15. Ibid., 200. Without specific reference to the virtue of studiousness (since he has in view the relationship of the intellectual and moral virtues, arguing that the former cannot be expected to sustain the latter), the need for the eschatological outpouring of the Holy Spirit to transform our intellectual desire is expressed by John Henry Newman: "Quarry the granite rock with razors, or moor the vessel with a thread of silk; then you may hope with such keen and delicate instruments as human knowledge and human reason to contend against those giants, the passion and the pride of man" (*The Idea of a University*, ed. Martin J. Svaglic [Notre Dame, IN: University of Notre Dame Press, 1982], 91). Christopher Blum cites this text in his "Fruitful Restraint," 956.

16. Webster, "Curiosity," 202.

17. Barbara M. Benedict, *Curiosity: A Cultural History of Early Modern Inquiry* (Chicago: University of Chicago Press, 2001), 254. The key questions are what the curious person is going beyond and where the curious person seeks to go. Phrases such as "to elude identity" and "ontological transgression" often have little real signification, but they can also entail an attempt to reject our relational creaturehood, as discussed in the previous chapter. Without an adequate account of human nature and human happiness, reflection on curiosity rapidly descends into boilerplate, as in the following sociological assessment by Todd Kashdan: "Curiosity, novelty-seeking, and openness to experience are all associated with desirable psychosocial outcomes. This includes general positive affect, willingness to challenge stereotypes, creativity, preference for challenge in work and play, perceived control, and negative relationships with perceived stress and boredom" (Kashdan, "Curiosity," 134). By contrast, for a focus on patristic authors (Tertullian, Augustine, Gregory the Great) and medieval authors (Peter Damien, Peter Abelard, Bernard of Clairvaux, Albert

the Great, Aquinas) with attention to their roots in ancient Roman philosophy, see Gunther Bös, *Curiositas: Die Rezeption eines antiken Begriffes durch christliche Autoren bis Thomas von Aquin* (Paderborn: Ferdinand Schöningh, 1995). Bös displays Aquinas's synthesis of a lengthy tradition. See also Neil Kenny, *Curiosity in Early Modern Europe Word Histories* (Wiesbaden: Harrassowitz Verlag, 1998); André Labhardt, "Curiositas: Notes sur l'histoire d'un mot et d'une notion," *Museum Helveticum* 17 (1960): 206–24; Richard Newhauser, "Towards a History of Human Curiosity: A Prolegomenon to Its Medieval Phase," *Deutsche Vierteljahrsschrift für Literaturwissenschaft und Geistesgeschichte* 56 (1982): 559–75, responding to the treatment of curiosity in Hans Blumenberg, *The Legitimacy of the Modern Age*, trans. R. M. Wallace (Cambridge, MA: Harvard University Press, 1983).

18. Blum, "Fruitful Restraint," 959. Blum draws attention to *ST* II-II, q. 53, a. 3, where Aquinas treats the vice of precipitousness. Blum includes "Fruitful Restraint" in his valuable collection of essays, *Rejoicing in the Truth: Wisdom and the Educator's Craft* (Front Royal, VA: Christendom Press, 2015).

19. Reichberg describes the Augustinian character of Aquinas's reflections on *studiositas* and *curiositas*: "Fundamental, in my estimation, is his [Aquinas's] emphasis on the moral or ethical dimensions of knowing. In this respect, St. Thomas is very much the disciple of St. Augustine, whose *Confessions*, in particular, are replete with comments about the intentions which ought (and ought not) to guide the student in his or her pursuit of knowledge. Augustine faults himself, for instance, for having sought intellectual cultivation, not for the sake of insight about himself and God, but rather in order to impress his classmates and professors" (Reichberg, "*Studiositas*, the Virtue of Attention," 151). Reichberg also fittingly directs attention to Simone Weil's "Reflections on the Right Use of School Studies with a View to the Love of God," in Weil, *Waiting for God*, trans. Emma Craufurd (New York: G. P. Putnam's Sons, 1951), 104–16.

20. Lamb, "Millennial Challenges Facing Catholic Intellectual Life," 991.

21. For discussion, see Serge-Thomas Bonino, O.P., "The Incomprehensible Wisdom of God in the *Expositio super Iob*," in *Reading Job with St. Thomas Aquinas*, ed. Matthew Levering, Piotr Roszak, and Jörgen Vijgen (Washington, DC: Catholic University of America Press, forthcoming).

22. Brevard Childs comments, "By God's thoughts are intended his plans and purpose, which differ in kind from those of human beings as greatly as that distance dividing heaven and earth" (*Isaiah: A Commentary* [Louisville: Westminster John Knox, 2001], 437).

23. For discussion of Wisdom 13 and Romans 1, see my *Engaging the Doctrine of Revelation*, chapter 8, as well as the background presented in my *Proofs of God: Classical Arguments from Tertullian to Barth* (Grand Rapids, MI: Baker Academic, 2016), 12–20. For debate over whether Paul agrees with Wisdom of Solomon (I think he does), see Douglas A. Campbell, *The Deliverance of God: An Apocalyptic Rereading of Justification in Paul* (Grand Rapids, MI: Eerdmans, 2009), 360–62, 542; Wright, *Paul and the Faithfulness of God*, 766–67.

24. For background see Tremper Longman III, *Proverbs* (Grand Rapids, MI: Baker Academic, 2006).

25. Ellen T. Charry comments, "Psalm 19 hopes to attract us to the glory of God in stages. Beginning with the Creator . . . the psalmist lures us to consider the wisdom of God the legislator as he carries us into deeper water" (Charry, *Psalms 1–50: Sighs and Songs of Israel* [Grand Rapids, MI: Brazos Press, 2015], 97).

26. Richard Alan Fuhr Jr. and Gary E. Yates comment on Hosea 6:1–3, "If Israel were to pursue the knowledge of God (6:3a), returning to the Lord (6:1a), she could expect that God would be faithful to respond" (*The Message of the Twelve: Hearing the Voice of the Minor Prophets* [Nashville: B&H Academic, 2016], 76).

27. For discussion see George T. Montague, S.M., *First and Second Timothy, Titus* (Grand Rapids, MI: Baker Academic, 2008), 86–87.

28. See Augustine, *On Christian Doctrine*, trans. D. W. Robertson Jr. (New York: Macmillan, 1958), book 2.

29. Paul J. Griffiths, *Intellectual Appetite: A Theological Grammar* (Washington, DC: Catholic University of America Press, 2009), 9. See also Christopher O. Blum, "The Studiousness of Jacques-Bénigne Bossuet," *Nova et Vetera* 8 (2010): 17–32. Blum provides helpful background to the demise of the virtue of studiousness in the seventeenth century:

> Two texts from the late Renaissance are particularly helpful for laying bare the inordinate desire for knowledge that characterized the new learning: Gabriel Naudé's *Advis pour dresser une Bibliothèque* (1627) and Pierre Gassendi's *Viri illustris Nicolai Claudii Fabricii de Peiresc, senatoris Aquisextiensis, vita* (1641). . . . In these two treatises can be seen three common characteristics of the new learning: first, that the word curiosity had become the name of a positive character trait and even of an ideal; second, that the ideal consisted in the lack of restraint in the pursuit of knowledge; third, that new institutions were emerging to support and instantiate the new ideal. (ibid., 19)

30. Griffiths, *Intellectual Appetite*, 11.

31. Ibid., 13.
32. Ibid., 20.
33. See also Anthony T. Flood, "What We Can Learn from the Medieval Rejection of Curiosity," *Northern Plains Ethics Journal* 1 (2013): 47–54. Flood draws attention to Aquinas's account of wonder (*admiratio*) in *ST* I-II, q. 3, a. 8, and I-II, q. 32, a. 8. He comments that for Aquinas, "the full experience of wonder has at least four essential parts: desire for knowledge, awareness of our own ignorance, hope of obtaining the truth, and a fear of error" ("What We Can Learn from the Medieval Rejection of Curiosity," 48).
34. Griffiths, *Intellectual Appetite*, 21. Griffiths emphasizes that studious persons do not approach intellectual work with the desire of accumulating intellectual property or owning ideas. As Wendell Berry puts it, in writing a book "I am being paid only for my work in arranging the words; my property is that arrangement. The thoughts in this book, on the contrary, are not mine. They came freely to me, and I give them freely away. I have no 'intellectual property,' and I think that all claimants to such property are thieves" (*Sex, Economy, Freedom and Community*, xviii).
35. Griffiths, *Intellectual Appetite*, 22. Griffiths holds that for a human person to exist is "to participate in God, as is true of all creatures" (ibid., 79)—though Griffiths denies that one can truly describe ontologically (in terms of causality and substantiality) what such participation involves. He uses "the category of 'participation'" as "a figure," not "as a category in an ontological system.... The importance of the figure is that it maintains the possibility of the created order disclosing its creator while at the same time banning circumscription of God by the categories of an ontological system" (ibid., 86–87). As fallen and damaged creatures, we "participate in God less fully" than God created us to do, and so the entire cosmos groans for redemption (ibid., 91; see Rom 8).
36. Ibid., 112. This contrasts with Griffiths's more recent *Christian Flesh*, which as a whole diverges sharply from his 2009 work with regard to its perspective toward the Catholic tradition.
37. Griffiths, *Intellectual Appetite*, 125.
38. Ibid., 116.
39. Ibid., 125, 129, 135.
40. Ibid., 153. See also Philip E. Dow, *Virtuous Minds: Intellectual Character Development* (Downers Grove, IL: IVP Academic, 2013), 74–75: "The academic world is particularly plagued by the poison of intellectual pride. For instance, when a lab produces a major breakthrough in the fight against some disease, the reaction of the competing labs is usually not joy that this breakthrough will save thousands of lives but jealousy that the

breakthrough was not theirs.... Those who treat truth as a commodity to be bought and sold are unlikely to simply give it away without getting something in return. Like Gollum's self-destructive obsession with the ring in Tolkien's novels, when we see knowledge as something to possess, not only do we miss out on the fulfillment of seeing that knowledge positively influence the lives of those around us, but we miss out on the rich personal growth that results from participation in a free give and take of truth."

41. Griffiths, *Intellectual Appetite*, 178.
42. Ibid., 181.
43. Ibid., 156.
44. See ibid., 188. For Augustine's understanding of the "spectacle," primarily referencing gladiatorial exhibitions and pagan shows in honor of gods and goddesses, see Joseph Torchia, O.P., *Restless Mind: Curiositas and the Scope of Inquiry in St. Augustine's Psychology* (Milwaukee: Marquette University Press, 2013), 200, 224. Augustine contrasts wisdom (*sapientia*), which is knowledge of eternal realities, with "*scientia*, the knowledge derived from the experience of mutable temporal realities" (ibid., 188). In Augustine's view, we can easily become absorbed by interest in temporal realities or images, and such absorption is curiositas. Along somewhat related lines, though without Augustine's guiding concern that we will become absorbed by interest in this-worldly realities (rather than attending to God and understanding temporal things in light of God), Norman Wirzba argues that

> modern cultures tend to reduce the world to a spectacle.... Because so few people have direct and regular involvement with the sources of their livelihood, it is inevitable that the world will be experienced in superficial and ephemeral ways. In the age of the spectacle, things are lifted out of their ecological and cultural contexts so they can be re-presented in fairly stylized ways.... Because images are the products of (mostly) unknown corporate interests—how many people really know where food products come from or how they are processed?—both things and the people who purchase them are increasingly alienated from the life-contexts that make them possible. Rather than identifying with the animal or field, one identifies with a brand. In the separation of consumption from production and the erosion of an individual's creative participation in the means of life, people invariably become passive and bored. (*Food and Faith: A Theology of Eating* [Cambridge: Cambridge University Press, 2011], 182)

I do not think that the movement away from agrarian life necessarily causes an increase in fallen human desire for "spectacle" rather than for wisdom, since this fallen desire, it seems to me, no doubt finds ways to thrive in agrarian communities. Nonetheless, I think that much of what Wirzba is reacting against is indeed rooted in the fallen human desire for "spectacle." Wirzba directs attention to Guy Debord, *The Society of the Spectacle* (New York: Zone Books, 1994), originally published in French in 1967. See also Jean-Luc Marion's reflections on "spectacle" in his *The Crossing of the Visible*, trans. James K. A. Smith (Stanford, CA: Stanford University Press, 2004), chapters 3–4. Without rejecting prudent forms of industrial and digital work, I can agree with Wirzba that "in a world of simulacra, creatures and things lose their depth. Reality is depleted by industrial processing, digital manipulation, the proliferation of images and fantasies, and the endless variations on style" (*Food and Faith*, 190). For background to Wirzba's agrarianism (which I appreciate but do not share), see the texts included in *The Essential Agrarian Reader: The Future of Culture, Community, and the Land*, ed. Norman Wirzba (Lexington: University Press of Kentucky, 2003).

45. Mario Vargas Llosa, *Notes on the Death of Culture: Essays on Spectacle and Society*, ed. and trans. John King (New York: Farrar, Straus and Giroux, 2015), 23–24. In its original Spanish edition, Vargas Llosa's book is titled *Civilización del espectáculo*. Vargas Llosa offers examples of what concerns him:

> Fashionable bands and singers attract huge crowds to their concerts, which, like the Dionysian pagan festivals that celebrated irrationality in ancient Greece, are collective ceremonies of excess and catharsis, worshipping instinct, passion and unreason. The same can be said, of course, of the packed electronic music parties, raves, where people dance in the darkness, listen to trance-inducing music and get high on ecstasy. It is not too far-fetched to compare these celebrations to the great religious popular festivals of old. For we find, in secular form, a religious spirit that, in keeping with the spirit of the age, has replaced the liturgy and catechisms of traditional religions with these displays of musical mysticism where, to the rhythm of raw voices and instruments, both amplified to an inaudible level, individuals are no longer individuals; they become a mass, and unwittingly return to the primitive times of magic and the tribe. This is the modern and, of course, much more amusing way of achieving the ecstasy that St Teresa or St John of the Cross found through asceticism, prayer and faith. In these crowded parties and concerts young people today commune, confess, achieve redemption and find fulfilment through this intense, elemental experience of becoming lost to themselves. (ibid., 29)

He also gives the example of soccer games played in huge stadiums, which, "like the Roman circuses, function mainly as a pretext for irrationality, the regression of individuals to the tribe, to being part of a collective, where, in the anonymous warmth of the stands, spectators can give free rein to their aggressive instincts, to the symbolic (and at times real) conquest and annihilation of the opposition" (ibid., 30). To this he adds an insightful comment on drug use, again with the "civilization of the spectacle" in view:

> Today, the mass consumption of marijuana, cocaine, ecstasy, crack, heroin, etc., is a response to a social environment that pushes men and women towards quick and easy pleasure, that immunizes them against worries and responsibility, allowing them to turn their backs on any self-knowledge that might be gained through thought and introspection, two eminently intellectual activities that are now considered tedious in our fickle, ludic culture.... For millions of people drugs now have the role, previously played by religions and high culture, of assuaging doubts and questions about the human condition, life, death, the beyond, the sense or senselessness of existence. (ibid., 31–32)

46. Note that Augustine does not reject learning about temporal things: on the contrary, he himself devotes a great deal of labor to acquiring such learning, and recommends such learning in his *On Christian Doctrine* (among other writings). As Torchia says, Augustine is concerned to show that reason must not "rest content with the appearances of things alone, no matter how pleasing or alluring they are to the senses. Ultimately, it [reason] seeks unchanging principles without which things could not be designated as 'good' or 'beautiful' at all" (Torchia, *Restless Mind*, 249).

47. See also Jean-Luc Marion, *In Excess: Studies of Saturated Phenomena*, trans. Robyn Horner and Vincent Berraud (New York: Fordham University Press, 2002), especially chapter 5: "The Icon or the Endless Hermeneutic." Indebted to Emmanuel Levinas, Marion reflects particularly upon the human face.

48. Griffiths, *Intellectual Appetite*, 195.

49. Ibid., 196.

50. Ibid., 198. On this damage, see Paul J. Griffiths, *Decreation: The Last Things of All Creatures* (Waco, TX: Baylor University Press, 2014), 4 and elsewhere.

51. Griffiths, *Intellectual Appetite*, 202.

52. Ibid., 211.

53. As C. S. Lewis remarks in *The Screwtape Letters*, 114, "The word 'Mine' in its fully possessive sense cannot be uttered by a human being about anything."

54. Griffiths, *Intellectual Appetite*, 120.

55. Jean-Luc Marion, *Believing in Order to See: On the Rationality of Revelation and the Irrationality of Some Believers*, trans. Christina M. Gschwandtner (New York: Fordham University Press, 2017), 82.

56. Wirzba, *Food and Faith*, 199, quoting Schmemann, *Eucharist*, 177. Wirzba goes on to say, "When people forget God, memory, vision, and desire turn away from the gift of creation and turn inward. Rather than perceiving and engaging each other as gifts of God, others are reduced to means or possessions that serve a narrow, self-preoccupied end" (*Food and Faith*, 200). Wirzba also appreciatively notes Martin Heidegger's "account of thinking as thanking and thanking as thinking" (ibid., 198): see Heidegger, *What Is Called Thinking* (New York: Harper & Row, 1968). For further critique of what Wirzba calls "a flat and boring world in which things have significance primarily in terms of their ability to satisfy an ego's desires"—a world in which things are "idols" rather than "icons" (*Food and Faith*, 31)—see Rowan Williams, *Dostoevsky: Language, Faith, and Fiction* (Waco, TX: Baylor University Press, 2008); Philip Sherrard, *The Rape of Man and Nature: An Inquiry into the Origins and Consequences of Modern Science* (Ipswich: Golgonooza Press, 1987). See also Sergei Bulgakov, *Philosophy of Economy: The World as a Household*, trans. Catherine Evtuhov (New Haven: Yale University Press, 2000), whose main arguments are set forth in Méndez-Montoya, *Theology of Food*, 89–96.

57. *ST* II-II, q. 166, a. 1 (see specifically obj. 2 and 3; sed contra; ad 2).

58. When Aquinas places four biblical texts in the first article of a question, one has to pay attention—and in this case we see the call to God's eschatological people to live as people whose sins have been forgiven and whose minds have been renewed by the wisdom of Christ. Aquinas often sets forth the biblical background for a topic by scattering the key biblical texts in the objections, sed contra, and answers to the objections. The small function of a particular biblical text (for example in an objection) does not indicate Aquinas's valuation of its importance in shaping his view of the topic at hand. For further discussion, see my *Paul in the Summa Theologiae*.

59. On the fulfillment of the law by love—in accord with Romans 13:8, 10: "He who loves his neighbor has fulfilled the law. . . . Love does no wrong to a neighbor; therefore love is the fulfilling of the law"—see Burridge, *Imitating Jesus*, 110–12. See also Michael B. Thompson, *Clothed with Christ: The Example and Teaching of Jesus in Romans 12.1–15.13* (Sheffield: Sheffield Academic Press, 1991), 126; Matera, *New Testament Ethics*, 201.

60. *ST* II-II, q. 166, a. 1, ad 3.

61. Ibid.

62. *ST* II-II, q. 166, a. 1, ad 2.

63. *ST* II-II, q. 166, a. 2, ad 3. See Reichberg, "*Studiositas*, the Virtue of Attention," 150: "In its secondary role, *studiositas* reinforces intellectual desire.... The essential problem is to overcome the body's resistance to the effort involved in the acquisition of knowledge."

64. *ST* II-II, q. 166, a. 2, ad 3. See Alice Ramos, "Studiositas and Curiositas," *Educational Horizons* 83 (2005): 272–81.

65. Cited in *ST* II-II, q. 167, a. 1, obj. 2.

66. Cited in ibid.

67. Thomas Pfau, *Minding the Modern: Human Agency, Intellectual Traditions, and Responsible Knowledge* (Notre Dame, IN: University of Notre Dame Press, 2013), 586. Pfau is here appreciatively appropriating Samuel Taylor Coleridge's critique of modernity.

68. *ST* II-II, q. 167, a. 1.

69. This problem is the subject of Harry G. Frankfurt's *On Bullshit* (Princeton: Princeton University Press, 2005). Flood provides a helpful summary of Frankfurt's book: "Bullshit is not lying; to lie involves saying something that you believe to be false. The bull-shitter does not think what she says is false, but she lacks any substantive reason for thinking it is true. One of the consequences for a culture of bull-shitters is the prevailing belief that we are all experts about everything, which really amounts to the belief that there are no experts. Frankfurt argues that this development should be of a grave concern as it undermines the role truth should play in rational discourse" (Flood, "What We Can Learn from the Medieval Rejection of Curiosity," 53–54).

70. *ST* II-II, q. 167, a. 1.

71. For discussion see R. E. Clements, *Jeremiah* (Atlanta: John Knox Press, 1988), 61.

72. See *ST* II-II, q. 167, a. 1.

73. *ST* II-II, q. 167, a. 1. Ralph McInerny observes that "a deliberate and a priori restriction of intellectual interest to the finite, to the neutral, existentially speaking, is regarded as a vice by Aquinas. Such a judgment involves an attitude toward the whole context of man's pursuit of knowledge. Why is man a knower? Why has he been given this capacity? What is the ultimate import of his natural desire to know?" (*Thomism in an Age of Renewal* [Garden City, NY: Doubleday, 1966], 127). More pointedly, and quite accurately, Christopher Blum has commented that this third way "came to typify the new learning of the Renaissance.... It would be hard to imagine a more perfect embodiment of the vice [of *curiositas*] than the new learning of the seventeenth century. Consider, for instance, Descartes's

prohibition of the search for final causes, or, more provocatively, the name Bacon gave to his imaginary academy, the College of the Six Days Works, a name suggesting that productive work and not contemplation was man's highest good" (Blum, "Studiousness of Jacques-Bénigne Bossuet," 19).

74. Reichberg, "*Studiositas*, the Virtue of Attention," 149. Hence the impossible desire of the "intemperate inquirer" who "seeks full intellectual satisfaction in dwelling upon the inexhaustible variety of natural phenomena" without reference to God (ibid., 150).

75. On this point see especially Michael Hanby, *No God, No Science: Theology, Cosmology, Biology* (Oxford: Wiley-Blackwell, 2013). Other ways in which our desire to know can fall into curiositas include the desire to devote our mind to something less important than what our particular job or vocation requires or to seek to learn things from the dark arts (see Col 2:8). Our desire to know can also be inordinate when despite the evident limitations of our cognitive capacity, we insist upon trying to know things that are beyond our cognitive limits. The result of such perseverance will not be the reward of understanding, but rather will be some kind of error rooted in lack of understanding (see Sirach 3:21, cited in *ST* II-II, q. 167, a. 1, ad 3).

76. See *ST* II-II, q. 167, a. 1, ad 1. Michael S. Sherwin, O.P., rightly distinguishes happiness from "pleasure" or "a pleasantly satisfied state of well-feeling," which was John Locke's view of the meaning of "happiness." See Sherwin, "Happiness and Its Discontents," *Logos* 13 (2010): 36. Locke urged that in this life, we should seek happiness (as he understood it). By contrast, Sherwin asks, "Is the world a happy place and does God wish us to enjoy contented prosperity in this life? Is this God's primary concern for us?" (ibid., 42). As Sherwin points out, "Sooner or later the sensitive person discovers that none of the goods of this life, not even the life of the mind or the good activity of virtue so vaunted by the classical tradition, constitutes our proper and perfect happiness. None of these goods constitute the essence of our happiness because none of them is permanent. We desire perfect and lasting happiness, a happiness that fulfills all our desires and cannot be lost, and we discover that no created thing or activity proper to this life can grant it to us" (ibid., 45). He goes on to say,

> Although the pagans could discover that happiness consists in union with God, it is only in the light of Christian revelation that we discover Christ as the way to this union. From the Christian perspective, the inevitable experience of sickness, suffering, and death points not only to the fact that perfect happiness belongs only to heaven, it also points

to our need for salvation. Death alone will not bring happiness. We must be freed from sin and pass from death to life—to a new life in the Trinity that includes a resurrected and glorified body. Thus, salvation and redemption in Christ are what make eternal happiness possible. Indeed, Christ's salvific love even enables us to enjoy an inchoate participation of eternal happiness in this life. (ibid., 46)

In this light, Sherwin explains why eternal contemplation of God in love, experiencing with grateful joy the full self-revelation of the triune God, is true happiness. Sherwin also explains why the way of the cross—the way of true charity—is the way to this happiness.

77. See *ST* II-II, q. 167, a. 1, ad 3.
78. See *ST* II-II, q. 167, a. 2, sed contra.
79. *ST* II-II, q. 167, a. 2.
80. Ibid.
81. *ST* II-II, q. 167, a. 1, ad 1.
82. Ibid.
83. *ST* II-II, q. 167, a. 1, obj. 1.
84. Reinhard Hütter, *Dust Bound for Heaven: Explorations in the Theology of Thomas Aquinas* (Grand Rapids, MI: Eerdmans, 2012), 57.
85. Ibid., 61, 63–64.
86. Wirzba, *Food and Faith*, 182.
87. Ibid. Wirzba draws this point from Capon, *Supper of the Lamb*, 111. Wirzba comments further, "Living creatures as well as nonliving things can cease to be expressions of God's love and instead become commodified bits that serve a narrow, perhaps exclusively utilitarian meaning. People can become exiles in the world in which they live when fellow creatures cease to evoke in them the marvel and delight that marks God's own Sabbath encounter with the world" (*Food and Faith*, 183). He rightly highlights the role of charity in overcoming this distortion: "In loving what one sees, or, more precisely, by letting love be the form through which perception happens, the grace of the world begins to appear. Things cease to be merely what we take them or want them to be. They begin to stand in the light of God as the graced and gifted beings that they are. As Josef Pieper puts it, contemplation is the highest form of human happiness because it affords 'a direct perception of the presence of God' as 'the acting basis of everything that exists'" (ibid., 185, citing Pieper, *Happiness and Contemplation*, trans. Richard and Clara Winston [South Bend, IN: St. Augustine's Press, 1998], 78–80). See also Elizabeth Theokritoff, *Living in God's Creation: Orthodox Perspectives on Ecology* (Crestwood, NY: St. Vladimir's Seminary Press, 2009), 186, cited in Wirzba, *Food and Faith*, 187n21.

Conclusion

1. Servais Pinckaers, O.P., *The Pursuit of Happiness—God's Way: Living the Beatitudes*, trans. Mary Thomas Noble, O.P. (New York: Alba House, 1998),10.
2. Ibid.
3. Ibid.
4. See Hahn, *Kingdom of God as Liturgical Empire*. See also Melina, *Sharing in Christ's Virtues*, 150: "The moment in which the bond between the ecclesial sense and morality is established and documented with the maximum theological conciseness is in the sacrament of the Eucharist. This is the place from which the Church springs and, at the same time, the place in which we are given the new commandment of Christian morality. The Eucharist is the true 'dwelling' of the new man from which derives all his ethics." Melina here draws upon Carlo Caffarra, *Living in Christ: Fundamental Principles of Catholic Moral Teaching*, trans. Christopher Ruff (San Francisco: Ignatius Press, 1987). Melina goes on to commend "a eucharistic morality" (*Sharing in Christ's Virtues*, 152), with reference to Matthias Joseph Scheeben, *The Mysteries of Christianity*, trans. Cyril Vollert, S.J. (St. Louis: Herder, 1946), 558–66.
5. Fagerberg, *Consecrating the World*, 96.
6. Ibid.
7. Melina, *Sharing in Christ's Virtues*, 154.
8. See Mattison, *Sermon on the Mount and Moral Theology*, 163, 183–84, 196–97.
9. Wright, *After You Believe*, 103 (italics removed). Wright adds a contrast with Aristotle that, while correct about the fulfillment of Israel's hopes, is also a bit unnecessary (since of course Aristotelian "happiness" could not know of God's work of new creation): "Here is the goal, the *telos*: not 'happiness' in the sense of Aristotle's *eudaimonia*, but 'blessedness' in the Hebrew sense of *ashre* or *baruch* (Greek *makarios*). That, by the way, is why translations of the Beatitudes (the familiar series of Sermon sayings announcing blessings) which say 'happy' instead of 'blessed' are precisely missing the point. And the key point about 'bless,' 'blessing,' and 'blessed'—one of the things that marks Jesus out over against Aristotle in terms of the source and driving energy of the 'virtues'—is that this *includes* 'happiness,' but it includes it *as the result of something else*—namely, the loving action of the creator God" (ibid., 103–4). This is why Aquinas underscores that for the believer, the theological and moral virtues are infused, even if moral virtues can be acquired.
10. Ibid., 106.

11. Jennifer A. Herdt points out that late medieval theologians, emphasizing God's freedom and ours, expressed concerns about Aquinas's perspective on infused virtue. She states, "While Aquinas understood divine and human agency in noncompetitive terms, nominalist thinkers, intending to preserve freedom, tended to think disjunctively of divine gift and human responsive action. Within this context, Aquinas's recognition of infused moral virtues seemed problematic, for these seemed to infringe on the space within which human persons were responsible for themselves and their own action. Even the notion of infused virtues as such, at once both divine gift and intrinsic disposition of the human agent, might seem to muddy the waters. It might seem more natural to affirm that God's agency within human persons displaces human agency, that what God gives is not an intrinsic modification of human character but God's own self, uncreated rather than created grace" (*Putting on Virtue*, 93). She draws attention specifically to John Duns Scotus, *Ordinatio* III, distinction 36, in *Duns Scotus on the Will and Morality*, ed. Allan Wolter, O.F.M. (Washington, DC: Catholic University of America Press, 1986), 414–16.

12. *ST* I-II, q. 63, a. 4.

13. *ST* I-II, q. 63, a. 4, ad 2.

14. Fagerberg, *Consecrating the World*, 12.

15. Hauerwas, "Bearing Reality," in *Approaching the End*, 156–57. Hauerwas quips, "If ever there was a language that seems to be on a holiday, 'to see history doxologically' seems a ready candidate" (ibid., 156). As a Christian pacifist, Hauerwas has in view the costs of following a nonviolent Lord rather than trying to control or master history through violence. Although I accept just war doctrine and the prudential use of violence in the defense of the weak and vulnerable, I agree with Hauerwas's insistent repudiation of the tendency of the Church in each country to side with its military, which almost inevitably becomes an idol of "security," blinding Christians to the horrific realities of war for combatants and noncombatants alike. Hauerwas directs attention to John Howard Yoder, "To Serve Our God and to Rule the World," in *The Royal Priesthood: Essays Ecclesiological and Ecumenical*, ed. Michael Cartwright (Grand Rapids, MI: Eerdmans, 1994), 128–40; Yoder, *The Politics of Jesus: Vicit Agnus Noster*, 2nd ed. (Grand Rapids, MI: Eerdmans, 1995); J. Alexander Sider, *To See History Doxologically: History and Holiness in John Howard Yoder's Ecclesiology* (Grand Rapids, MI: Eerdmans, 2011).

16. Jorge Mario Bergoglio [Pope Francis], *Open Mind, Faithful Heart: Reflections on Following Jesus*, trans. Joseph V. Owens, S.J. (New York: Crossroad, 2013), 169.

17. Bernie A. Van De Walle, *Rethinking Holiness: A Theological Introduction* (Grand Rapids, MI: Baker Academic, 2017), 65.

18. Augustine, *Sermons*, vol. 1, *Sermons 1–19*, trans. Edmund Hill, O.P., ed. John E. Rotelle, O.S.A. (Brooklyn, NY: New City Press, 1990), sermon 9.10, p. 268.

19. Ibid., sermon 9.9, p. 267.

20. Ibid., sermon 9.10, p. 268.

21. *ST* I-II, q. 65, a. 3, ad 2. See Sherwin, "Infused Virtue and the Effects of Acquired Vice." Discussing the experience of Matthew Talbot, an alcoholic who experienced a profound conversion to Christ, Sherwin notes that even after his conversion, "The thought of getting drunk and of all the practices integral to the life of a drunkard (the illusory camaraderie, the bravado, etc.) still brought him great pleasure. Such a life still felt connatural to him. His whole character was inclined to it" (ibid., 43). Sherwin points out that Aquinas "refuses . . . to portray these lingering dispositions themselves as vices because they are no longer the principles of our action. . . . What remains is not the '*habitus intemperantiae*' properly so called, but a certain disposition on the way to corruption" (ibid., 44).

22. *ST* I-II, q. 65, a. 3, ad 2.

23. Cited by Aquinas in *ST* I-II, q. 65, a. 3, sed contra. For example, if we have love but lack chastity, we could not act consistently in a loving way toward our neighbors and ourselves. In such a condition, we could not fulfill the law of Christ.

24. Sherwin, "Infused Virtue and the Effects of Acquired Vice," 44. Sherwin adds the important point, "Even though some Christians in the state of grace fail to perform acts of moral virtue with ease and pleasure, this does not imply that therefore infused moral virtues do not exist. It means only that the ease, promptness, and joy proper to infused moral virtue can be impeded by the lingering dispositions caused by our previous sinful actions" (ibid., 44–45).

25. Sherwin, "Infused Virtue and the Effects of Acquired Vice," 46. See also Harm Goris's helpful explanation:

> Habitual grace does not totally remove these effects of original sin and of personal sins. It does take away the stain of guilt (*macula culpae*) and the liability for punishment (*reatus poenae*), but it does not completely heal the wounds of human nature. Through habitual grace, original sin disappears *reatu* but remains *actu*. Our will may be ordered and elevated to God as our supernatural goal through habitual grace, but our mind and our senses remain infected and corrupted. At

the same time, the tinder for sin is "diminished" (*minuitur*) by grace so that it, including the acquired personal sinful vices, no longer dominates or functions as an active principle for our behaviour. But the tinder or infection and the "contrary dispositions" still linger on. Therefore, the healing activity of God's *auxilium gratiae*, which had already begun before receiving habitual grace, must continue in the person who has grace and it will only come to an end in the state of glory when our nature will be totally cured. . . . During our lifetime, the ordering to the supernatural end remains fragile and delicate. ("Acquired and Infused Moral Virtues in Wounded Nature," 40–41, 43)

Equally cogently, Goris adds that acquired virtues, in those who do not possess habitual grace, are "the result of God's gracious help and healing in preparing humans for receiving grace as a habitual gift" (ibid., 45).

26. Augustine, *Sermons*, vol. 1, sermon 9.16, p. 273; sermon 9.21, p. 277; sermon 9.21, p. 278 (emphasis added).

27. A full accounting of the virtue of temperance, of course, would need a detailed discussion of many philosophical topics that I have been unable to discuss at length in this book.

28. For Aquinas's ethics, the dictum of David W. Fagerberg holds true: "Theology does not begin in the card catalogue, it begins in fasting, and the end of theology is not becoming a professor, it is becoming a saint" (Fagerberg, *On Liturgical Asceticism*, 168). Or as Andrew Prevot puts it, "A theology that does not find its motivations and greatest significance in spirituality—that is, in a life formed through the dramatic inter-*action* of divine and creaturely freedoms—is a dead theology complicit in the 'death of God,' the 'death of man,' and innumerable other deaths in the modern age. It is a 'theology' in name only. Christ did not leave the world with only the distant memory of his incarnate glory and word, which might be endlessly theorized, but rather offered us his Spirit as a lasting source of vitality, holiness, and liberative action in every age" (*Thinking Prayer* [Notre Dame, IN: University of Notre Dame Press, 2015], 332–33). It should go without saying that these excellent points should not lead to positing a necessary opposition between the life of the professor and the life of the saint, or to depreciating the value of dogmatic truth and *theoria*.

29. *ST* I-II, q. 108, a. 1. See also John A. Cuddeback, "Law, Pinckaers, and the Definition of Christian Ethics," *Nova et Vetera* 7 (2009): 301–25. Cuddeback rightly urges that law should receive more positive attention from Pinckaers. On obedience according to Aquinas, see Hugues Bohineust, O.S.B., *Obéissance du Christ, obeisance du Chrétien: Christologie et morale chez saint Thomas d'Aquin* (Paris: Parole et Silence, 2017).

Bohineust comments, "Before being a virtue, obedience is a gift, and, before being a law, it is a grace.... To live in a spirit of obedience is to be more and more docile to the promptings of the Holy Spirit" (ibid., 728–29).

30. W. H. Kane, O.P., preface to Carlson, *Virtue of Humility*, vii.

31. Ibid.

32. Wirzba, *Food and Faith*, 181. See also Gaetano Mary da Bergamo, O.F.M. Cap., *Humility of Heart*, trans. Herbert Cardinal Vaughan (Westminster, MD: Newman Bookshop, 1944), 27.

33. Jonathan Sacks, *The Dignity of Difference: How to Avoid the Clash of Civilizations*, rev. ed. (London: Bloomsbury, 2003), 180.

34. Kane, preface, vii.

BIBLIOGRAPHY

Abbà, Giuseppe. *Felicità, vita buona e virtù: Saggio di filosofia morale.* Rome: LAS, 1989.
Aertsen, Jan A. *Medieval Philosophy and the Transcendentals: The Case of Thomas Aquinas.* Leiden: Brill, 1996.
———. *Nature and Creature: Thomas Aquinas's Way of Thought.* Leiden: Brill, 1988.
Akakios, Archimandrite. *Fasting in the Orthodox Church: Its Theological, Pastoral, and Social Implications.* Etna, CA: Center for Traditionalist Orthodox Studies, 1996.
Allen, Michael. *Grounded in Heaven: Recentering Christian Hope and Life on God.* Grand Rapids, MI: Eerdmans, 2018.
Allen, Prudence, R.S.M. *The Concept of Woman.* Vol. 1, *The Aristotelian Revolution (750 B.C.–A.D. 1250)*; Vol. 2, *The Early Humanist Reformation, 1250–1500*; Vol. 3, *The Search for Communion of Persons, 1500–2015.* Grand Rapids, MI: Eerdmans, 1997–2016.
Allende, Isabel. *Aphrodite: A Memoir of the Senses.* London: Flamingo, 1998.
Alter, Robert. *The Five Books of Moses.* New York: Norton, 2004.
Alvaré, Helen M. *Putting Children's Interests First in US Family Law and Policy: With Power Comes Responsibility.* Cambridge: Cambridge University Press, 2018.
Alvaré, Helen, and Steven Lopes, eds. *Not Just Good, but Beautiful: The Complementary Relationship between Man and Woman.* Walden, NY: Plough, 2015.
Anderson, Gary A. *Charity: The Place of the Poor in the Biblical Tradition.* New Haven: Yale University Press, 2013.
Annas, Julia. "Aristotle on Pleasure and Goodness." In *Essays on Aristotle's Ethics*, edited by Amélie Oksenberg Rorty, 285–99. Berkeley: University of California Press, 1980.

———. *Intelligent Virtue.* Oxford: Oxford University Press, 2011.
———. *Platonic Ethics, Old and New.* Ithaca, NY: Cornell University Press, 1999.
———. "Plato's Ethics." In *The Oxford Handbook of Plato,* edited by Gail Fine, 267–85. Oxford: Oxford University Press, 2008.
Aquinas, Thomas. *Commentary on the Gospel of St. Matthew.* Translated by Paul M. Kimball. n.p.: Dolorosa Press, 2012.
———. *Commentary on the Letter of Saint Paul to the Romans.* Translated by F. R. Larcher, O.P. Edited by J. Mortensen and E. Alarcón. Lander, WY: Aquinas Institute for the Study of Sacred Doctrine, 2012.
———. *Commentary on the Sentences of Peter Lombard.* In Thomas Aquinas, *Opera Omnia,* vol. 11. Paris, 1874.
———. *On Evil.* Translated by John A. Oesterle and Jean T. Oesterle. Notre Dame, IN: University of Notre Dame Press, 1995.
———. *Summa contra gentiles.* Book 3, "Providence," part 2. Translated by Vernon J. Bourke. Notre Dame, IN: University of Notre Dame Press, 1975.
———. *Summa theologiae.* Translated by the Fathers of the English Dominican Province. Westminster, MD: Christian Classics, 1981.
———. *Summa theologiae.* Vol. 43, *Temperance (2a2ae. 141–54).* Translated by Thomas Gilby, O.P. London: Eyre & Spottiswoode, 1968.
Aristotle. *Nicomachean Ethics.* Translated by H. Rackham. Cambridge, MA: Harvard University Press, 1934.
———. *Politics.* Translated by Benjamin Jowett. New York: Random House, 1943.
Arkes, Hadley. *Constitutional Illusions and Anchoring Truths: The Touchstone of the Natural Law.* Cambridge: Cambridge University Press, 2010.
Atkinson, Joseph C. *Biblical and Theological Foundations of the Family: The Domestic Church.* Washington, DC: Catholic University of America Press, 2014.
Augustine. *Answer to Faustus, a Manichean.* Translated by Roland Teske, S.J. Hyde Park, NY: New City Press, 2007.
———. *On Christian Doctrine.* Translated by D. W. Robertson Jr. New York: Macmillan, 1958.
———. *Sermons.* Vol. 1, *Sermons 1–19.* Translated by Edmund Hill, O.P. Edited by John E. Rotelle, O.S.A. Brooklyn, NY: New City Press, 1990.
Aumann, Jordan, O.P. *Spiritual Theology.* London: Bloomsbury, 2017.
Austin, Nicholas, S.J. *Aquinas on Virtue: A Causal Reading.* Washington, DC: Georgetown University Press, 2017.

Australian Bishops' Conference. *Don't Mess with Marriage*. Pastoral letter, November 24, 2015. Available at the website of the Catholic Church in Australia, https://www.catholic.org.au/marriage/don-t-mess-with-marriage.
Baab, Lynne M. *Fasting: Spiritual Freedom beyond Our Appetites*. Downers Grove, IL: InterVarsity Press, 2006.
Bachelard, Sarah. *Resurrection and Moral Imagination*. Burlington, VT: Ashgate, 2014.
Bahnson, Fred. *Soil and Sacrament: A Spiritual Memoir of Food and Faith*. New York: Simon & Schuster, 2013.
Barclay, John M. G. *Paul and the Gift*. Grand Rapids, MI: Eerdmans, 2015.
———. "A Thomist Reading of Paul? Response and Reflections." *Nova et Vetera* 17 (2019): 235–44.
Barnes, Corey L. "Thomas Aquinas on the Body and Bodily Passions." In Kamitsuka, *Embrace of Eros*, 83–97.
Barron, Robert. *The Priority of Christ: Toward a Postliberal Catholicism*. Grand Rapids, MI: Brazos, 2007.
———. *Vibrant Paradoxes: The Both/And of Catholicism*. Skokie, IL: Word on Fire Catholic Ministries, 2016.
Barth, Karl. *Ethics*. Edinburgh: T&T Clark, 1981.
Barton, John. *Ethics in Ancient Israel*. Oxford: Oxford University Press, 2014.
Bash, Anthony. *Forgiveness: A Theology*. Eugene, OR: Cascade, 2015.
Bauerschmidt, Frederick Christian. "Doctrine: Knowing and Doing." In *The Morally Divided Body: Ethical Disagreement and the Disunity of the Church*, edited by Michael Root and James J. Buckley, 25–42. Eugene, OR: Cascade, 2012.
———. *Thomas Aquinas: Faith, Reason, and Following Christ*. Oxford: Oxford University Press, 2013.
Beale, G. K. *The Temple and the Church's Mission: A Biblical Theology of the Dwelling Place of God*. Downers Grove, IL: InterVarsity Press, 2004.
Becker, Ernest. *The Denial of Death*. New York: Free Press, 1997.
Beier, Matthias. *A Violent God-Image: An Introduction to the Work of Eugen Drewermann*. New York: Continuum, 2004.
Benedict, Barbara M. *Curiosity: A Cultural History of Early Modern Inquiry*. Chicago: University of Chicago Press, 2001.
Benedict XVI, Pope. *Deus Caritas Est*. Vatican translation. Boston: Pauline Books & Media, 2006.
———. *Verbum Domini*. Vatican translation. Boston: Pauline Books & Media, 2010.

Benz, Ernst. "Joachim-Studien III: Thomas von Aquin und Joachim de Fiore; Die katholische Antwort auf die spiritualistische Kirchen- und Geschichtsauffassung." *Zeitschrift für Kirchengeschichte* 53 (1934): 52–116.

Bergamo, Gaetano Mary da, O.F.M. Cap. *Humility of Heart*. Translated by Herbert Cardinal Vaughan. Westminster, MD: Newman Bookshop, 1944.

Berghuis, Kent D. *Christian Fasting: A Theological Approach*. Richardson, TX: Biblical Studies Press, 2007.

Bernard, Jean-Paul. *Les parties integrales de la temperance selon saint Thomas*. Lévis, Quebec: Le Quotidien, 1958.

Bernard of Clairvaux. *On the Song of Songs II*. Translated by Kilian Walsh, O.C.S.O. Kalamazoo, MI: Cistercian Publications, 1983.

Berry, Wendell. "Feminism, the Body, and the Machine." In *What Are People For?*, 178–96.

———. "The Pleasures of Eating." In *What Are People For?*, 145–52.

———. *Sex, Economy, Freedom and Community: Eight Essays*. New York: Pantheon Books, 1993.

———. *What Are People For? Essays*. New York: North Point Press, 1990.

Besong, Brian. "Reappraising the Manual Tradition." *American Catholic Philosophical Quarterly* 89 (2015): 557–84.

Blackburn, Simon. *Lust*. Oxford: Oxford University Press, 2004.

Blanchard, Pierre. "Studiosité et curiosité: Le vrai savoir d'après saint Thomas d'Aquin." *Revue Thomiste* 53 (1953): 551–62.

Blankenhorn, Bernhard, O.P. "Aquinas as Interpreter of Augustinian Illumination in Light of Albertus Magnus." *Nova et Vetera* 10 (2012): 689–713.

———. *The Mystery of Union with God: Dionysian Mysticism in Albert the Great and Thomas Aquinas*. Washington, DC: Catholic University of America Press, 2015.

Blenkinsopp, Joseph. *Ezekiel*. Louisville: Westminster John Knox, 2012.

Blum, Christopher O. "A Fruitful Restraint: The Perennial Relevance of the Virtue of Studiousness." *Nova et Vetera* 11 (2013): 953–68.

———. *Rejoicing in the Truth: Wisdom and the Educator's Craft*. Front Royal, VA: Christendom Press, 2015.

———. "The Studiousness of Jacques-Bénigne Bossuet." *Nova et Vetera* 8 (2010): 17–32.

Blumenberg, Hans. *The Legitimacy of the Modern Age*. Translated by R. M. Wallace. Cambridge, MA: Harvard University Press, 1983.

Bockmuehl, Markus. *Jewish Law in Gentile Churches: Halakhah and the Beginning of Christian Public Ethics.* Grand Rapids, MI: Baker Academic, 2000.

———. "The Noachide Commandments and the New Testament." In *Jewish Law in Gentile Churches,* 145–73.

Bohineust, Hugues, O.S.B. *Obéissance du Christ, obeisance du Chrétien: Christologie et morale chez saint Thomas d'Aquin.* Paris: Parole et Silence, 2017.

Bongmba, Elias. "Hermeneutics and the Debate on Homosexuality in Africa." *Religion and Theology* 22 (2015): 69–99.

Bonhoeffer, Dietrich. *Ethics.* Minneapolis: Fortress, 1996.

Bonino, Serge-Thomas, O.P. "Les beatitudes au coeur de la théologie de saint Thomas d'Aquinas." *Nova et Vetera* 89 (2014): 429–44.

———. "Du bon usage de l'étude: Réflexions autour de la vertu de studiosité selon saint Thomas d'Aquin." In *L'amour du Christ nous presse: Mélanges offerts à Mgr Pierre Debergé,* edited by M.-T. Urvoy and L.-T. Somme, 375–90. Versailles: Éditions du Paris, 2013.

———. "The Incomprehensible Wisdom of God in the *Expositio super Iob.*" In *Reading Job with St. Thomas Aquinas,* edited by Matthew Levering, Piotr Roszak, and Jörgen Vijgen. Washington, DC: Catholic University of America Press, forthcoming.

Bonnewijn, Olivier. *La beatitude et les beatitudes: Une approche thomiste de l'éthique.* Rome: Pontificio Istituto Giovanni Paolo II, 2001.

———. *La famille dans la Bible: Quand Abraham, Joseph et Moïse éclairent nos propres histoires.* Paris: Mame, 2014.

Bös, Gunther. *Curiositas: Die Rezeption eines antiken Begriffes durch christliche Autoren bis Thomas von Aquin.* Paderborn: Ferdinand Schöningh, 1995.

Boswell, John. *Christianity, Social Tolerance, and Homosexuality: Gay People in Western Europe from the Beginning of the Christian Era to the Fourteenth Century.* Chicago: University of Chicago Press, 1980.

Boyd, Craig A. "Pride and Humility: Tempering the Desire for Excellence." In Timpe and Boyd, *Virtues and Their Vices,* 245–66.

Braine, David. *The Human Person: Animal and Spirit.* Notre Dame, IN: University of Notre Dame Press, 1992.

Braun, Willi. *Feasting and Social Rhetoric in Luke 14.* Cambridge: Cambridge University Press, 1995.

Brewer, Talbot. *The Retrieval of Ethics.* Oxford: Oxford University Press, 2009.

Bridgett, Thomas Edward. *The Discipline of Drink: An Historical Enquiry into the Principles and Practice of the Catholic Church regarding the*

Use, Abuse, and Disuse of Alcoholic Liquors, Especially in England, Ireland, and Scotland, from the 6th to the 16th Century. London, 1876.
Bringle, Mary Louise. *The God of Thinness: Gluttony and Other Weighty Matters.* Nashville: Abingdon, 1992.
Broadie, Sarah. *Ethics with Aristotle.* New York: Oxford University Press, 1991.
Brock, Stephen L. *Action and Conduct: Thomas Aquinas and the Theory of Action.* Edinburgh: T&T Clark, 1998.
———. "Natural Inclination and the Intelligibility of the Good in Thomistic Natural Law." *Vera Lex* 6 (2005): 57–78.
———. "Natural Law, the Understanding of Principles, and Universal Good." *Nova et Vetera* 9 (2011): 671–706.
———. "The Primacy of the Common Good and the Foundations of Natural Law in St. Thomas." In Hütter and Levering, *Ressourcement Thomism*, 234–55.
Broglie, Guy de, S.J. "La conception thomiste des deux finalités du mariage." *Doctor Communis* 30 (1974): 3–41.
Brooke, Christopher. *Philosophic Pride: Stoicism and Political Thought from Lipsius to Rousseau.* Princeton: Princeton University Press, 2012.
Brown, Peter. *The Body and Society: Men, Women, and Sexual Renunciation in Early Christianity.* New York: Columbia University Press, 1988.
Brown, Vanessa. "Breaking Taboos: Incest Pornography Is Becoming More Popular and Game of Thrones Could Be to Blame." *Sun* [UK], June 11, 2016. https://www.thesun.co.uk/living/1268468/incest-pornography-is-becoming-more-popular-and-game-of-thrones-could-be-to-blame/.
Brueggemann, Walter. *A Commentary on Jeremiah: Exile and Homecoming.* Grand Rapids, MI: Eerdmans, 1998.
———. *Theology of the Old Testament: Testimony, Dispute, Advocacy.* Minneapolis: Fortress, 1997.
———. *The Unsettling God: The Heart of the Hebrew Bible.* Minneapolis: Fortress, 2009.
Brugger, E. Christian. *The Indissolubility of Marriage and the Council of Trent.* Washington, DC: Catholic University of America Press, 2017.
Bryan, Steven M. *Jesus and Israel's Traditions of Judgment and Restoration.* Cambridge: Cambridge University Press, 2002.
Budziszewski, J. *Commentary on Thomas Aquinas's "Treatise on Law."* Cambridge: Cambridge University Press, 2014.
———. *On the Meaning of Sex.* Wilmington, DE: ISI Books, 2012.

Bugge, John. *Virginitas: An Essay in the History of a Medieval Ideal*. The Hague: Martinus Nijhoff, 1975.
Bulgakov, Sergei. *Philosophy of Economy: The World as a Household*. Translated by Catherine Evtuhov. New Haven: Yale University Press, 2000.
Bunge, Gabriel, O.S.B. *Dragon's Wine and Angel's Bread: The Teaching of Evagrius Ponticus on Anger and Meekness*. Translated by Anthony P. Gythiel. Crestwood, NY: St. Vladimir's Seminary Press, 2009.
Burke, Cormac. *The Theology of Marriage: Personalism, Doctrine, and Canon Law*. Washington, DC: Catholic University of America Press, 2015.
Burridge, Richard A. *Imitating Jesus: An Inclusive Approach to New Testament Ethics*. Grand Rapids, MI: Eerdmans, 2007.
Bushlack, Thomas J. "Mindfulness and the Discernment of Passions: Insights from Thomas Aquinas." *Spiritus: A Journal of Christian Spirituality* 14 (2014): 141–65.
Butera, Giuseppe. "On Reason's Control of the Passions in Aquinas's Theory of Temperance." *Mediaeval Studies* 68 (2006): 133–60.
Butler, Sara, M.S.B.T. "*Perfectae Caritatis*." In *The Reception of Vatican II*, edited by Matthew L. Lamb and Matthew Levering, 208–33. Oxford: Oxford University Press, 2017.
Byrne, Brendan, S.J. *The Hospitality of God: A Reading of Luke's Gospel*. Collegeville, MN: Liturgical Press, 2000.
Cahall, Perry J. *The Mystery of Marriage: A Theology of the Body and the Sacrament*. Chicago: Hillenbrand Books, 2016.
Cahill, Lisa Sowle. "Same-Sex Marriage and Catholicism: Dialogue, Learning, and Change." In *Inquiry, Thought, and Expression*, edited by J. Patrick Hornbeck II and Michael A. Norko, 141–55. Vol. 2 of *More than a Monologue: Sexual Diversity and the Catholic Church*. New York: Fordham University Press, 2014.
———. *Sex, Gender, and Christian Ethics*. Cambridge: Cambridge University Press, 1996.
Campbell, Douglas A. *The Deliverance of God: An Apocalyptic Rereading of Justification in Paul*. Grand Rapids, MI: Eerdmans, 2009.
———. "Panoramic Lutheranism and Apocalyptic Ambivalence: An Appreciative Critique of N. T. Wright's *Paul and the Faithfulness of God*." *Scottish Journal of Theology* 69 (2016): 453–73.
———. *The Quest for Paul's Gospel: A Suggested Strategy*. London: T&T Clark, 2005.
Canice, Father, O.F.M. Cap. *Humility: The Foundation of the Spiritual Life*. Westminster, MD: Newman Press, 1951.

Cantalamessa, Raniero, O.F.M. Cap. *Virginity: A Positive Approach to Celibacy for the Sake of the Kingdom of Heaven*. Translated by Charles Serignat. New York: Alba House, 1995.

Capon, Robert Farrar. *The Supper of the Lamb: A Culinary Reflection*. New York: Modern Library, 2002.

Card, Claudia. *The Atrocity Paradigm*. Oxford: Oxford University Press, 2002.

Carlson, Sebastian, O.P. *The Virtue of Humility*. Dubuque, IA: Wm. C. Brown Co., 1952.

Carmichael, Calum. *Sex and Religion in the Bible*. New Haven: Yale University Press, 2010.

Castelli, Elizabeth. *Imitating Paul: A Discourse of Power*. Louisville: Westminster John Knox, 1991.

Catechism of the Catholic Church. 2nd ed. Vatican City: Libreria Editrice Vaticana, 1997.

Cates, Diana Fritz. *Aquinas on the Emotions: A Religious-Ethical Inquiry*. Washington, DC: Georgetown University Press, 2009.

———. *Choosing to Feel: Virtue, Friendship, and Compassion for Friends*. Notre Dame, IN: University of Notre Dame Press, 1997.

———. "Thomas Aquinas and Audre Lorde on Anger." In Harak, *Aquinas and Empowerment*, 47–88.

———. "The Virtue of Temperance (IIa IIae, qq. 141–170)." In *The Ethics of Aquinas*, edited by Stephen J. Pope, 321–39. Washington, DC: Georgetown University Press, 2002.

Catherine of Siena. *The Dialogue*. Translated by Suzanne Noffke, O.P. Mahwah, NJ: Paulist Press, 1980.

Cessario, Romanus, O.P. *The Virtues, or The Examined Life*. London: Continuum, 2002.

Chae, Young S. *Jesus as the Eschatological Davidic Shepherd*. Tübingen: Mohr Siebeck, 2006.

Chapman, Gary. *Anger: Taming a Powerful Emotion*. Chicago: Moody Publishers, 2015.

Chappell, Timothy. "Virtue Ethics in the Twentieth Century." In Russell, *Cambridge Companion to Virtue Ethics*, 149–71.

Chaput, Charles J. "The Splendor of Truth in 2017." *First Things*, no. 276 (October 2017): 21–26.

Charry, Ellen. *God and the Art of Happiness*. Grand Rapids, MI: Eerdmans, 2010.

———. *Psalms 1–50: Sighs and Songs of Israel*. Grand Rapids, MI: Brazos, 2015.

Chenu, Marie-Dominique, O.P. *Aquinas and His Role in Theology.* Translated by Paul Philibert, O.P. Collegeville, MN: Liturgical Press, 2002.
———. "Les passions vertueuses: L'anthropologie de saint Thomas." *Revue philosophique de Louvain* 72 (1974): 11–18.
———. *Toward Understanding Saint Thomas.* Translated by A.-M. Landry, O.P., and D. Hughes, O.P. Chicago: Henry Regnery, 1964.
Chereso, Cajetan, O.P. *The Virtue of Honor and Beauty according to St. Thomas Aquinas: An Analysis of Moral Beauty.* River Forest, IL: Aquinas Library, 1960.
Childs, Brevard. *Isaiah: A Commentary.* Louisville: Westminster John Knox, 2001.
Chrétien, P. *De castitate: Tractatus ad usum confessariorum quem in seminario metensi proponebat.* Metz, France: Le Lorrain, 1938.
Cicero. *On Duties.* Translated by Walter Miller. Cambridge, MA: Harvard University Press, 1913.
Clark, Patrick M. *Perfection in Death: The Christological Dimension of Courage in Aquinas.* Washington, DC: Catholic University of America Press, 2015.
Cleaver, Richard. *Know My Name: A Gay Liberation Theology.* Louisville: Westminster John Knox, 1995.
Clements, R. E. *Jeremiah.* Atlanta: John Knox Press, 1988.
Coakley, Sarah. *The New Asceticism: Sexuality, Gender and the Quest for God.* London: Bloomsbury, 2015.
Cogly, Zac. "A Study of Virtuous and Vicious Anger." In Timpe and Boyd, *Virtues and Their Vices,* 199–224.
Collins, Raymond F. *Christian Morality: Biblical Foundations.* Notre Dame, IN: University of Notre Dame Press, 1986.
Coloe, Mary L. *God Dwells with Us: Temple Symbolism in the Fourth Gospel.* Collegeville, MN: Liturgical Press, 2001.
Colón-Emeric, Edgardo A. *Wesley, Aquinas, and Christian Perfection: An Ecumenical Dialogue.* Waco, TX: Baylor University Press, 2009.
Colton, Randall G. "Two Rival Versions of Sexual Virtue: Simon Blackburn and John Paul II on Lust and Chastity." *Thomist* 70 (2006): 71–101.
Comte-Sponville, André. *A Small Treatise on the Great Virtues: The Uses of Philosophy in Everyday Life.* Translated by Catherine Temerson. New York: Metropolitan Books, 2001.
Congar, Yves, O.P. "The Holy Spirit in the Thomistic Theology of Moral Action." Translated by Susan Mader Brown and Joseph G. Mueller, S.J. In *Spirit of God,* 145–61.

---. *I Believe in the Holy Spirit*. Translated by David Smith. New York: Crossroad, 1997.

---. "Réflexion et propos sur l'originalité d'une ethique chrétienne." *Studia Moralia* 15 (1977): 31–40.

---. *Spirit of God: Short Writings on the Holy Spirit*. Edited by Mark E. Ginter, Susan Mader Brown, and Joseph G. Mueller, S.J. Washington, DC: Catholic University of America Press, 2017.

---. "Variations sur le thème 'Loi-Grâce.'" *Revue Thomiste* 71 (1971): 429–38.

Congregation for the Doctrine of the Faith. *Dominus Iesus*. Vatican translation. Boston: Pauline Books & Media, 2000.

---. "Notification on the Book *Just Love: A Framework for Christian Sexual Ethics*, by Sr. Margaret A. Farley, R.S.M." Available via the Vatican website, http://www.vatican.va/roman_curia/congregations/cfaith/documents/rc_con_cfaith_doc_20120330_nota-farley_en.html.

Cook, Christopher C. H. *Alcohol, Addiction and Christian Ethics*. Cambridge: Cambridge University Press, 2006.

Cordes, Paul Josef Cardinal. "'Without Rupture or Discontinuity.'" In *Eleven Cardinals Speak on Marriage and the Family: Essays from a Pastoral Viewpoint*, translated by Michael J. Miller et al., edited by Winfried Aymans, 17–38. San Francisco: Ignatius Press, 2015.

Countryman, L. William, and M. R. Ritley. *Gifted by Otherness: Gay and Lesbian Christians in the Church*. Harrisburg, PA: Morehouse Publishing, 2001.

Cowen, Shimon. *Homosexuality, Marriage and Society*. Brisbane: Connor Court Publishing, 2016.

Cross, Richard. "Thomas Aquinas." In *The Spiritual Senses: Perceiving God in Western Christianity*, edited by Paul L. Gavrilyuk and Sarah Coakley, 174–89. Cambridge: Cambridge University Press, 2012.

Cuddeback, John A. "Law, Pinckaers, and the Definition of Christian Ethics." *Nova et Vetera* 7 (2009): 301–26.

Cuddeback, Matthew. "Thomas Aquinas on Divine Illumination and the Authority of the First Truth." *Nova et Vetera* 7 (2009): 579–602.

Cummins, S. A. "Torah, Jesus, and the Kingdom of God in the Gospel of Mark." In Wendel and Miller, *Torah Ethics and Early Christian Identity*, 59–74.

Curran, Charles E. *The Development of Moral Theology: Five Strands*. Washington, DC: Georgetown University Press, 2013.

Curran, Charles E., and Richard McCormick, S.J., eds. *The Distinctiveness of Christian Ethics*. New York: Paulist Press, 1980.

Daguet, François, O.P. *Du politique chez Thomas d'Aquin*. Paris: J. Vrin, 2015.
Dauphinais, Michael. "Gregory of Nyssa and Augustine on the Beatitudes." *Nova et Vetera* 1 (2003): 141–63.
Dauphinais, Michael, Barry David, and Matthew Levering, eds. *Aquinas the Augustinian*. Washington, DC: Catholic University of America Press, 2007.
Davies, Andrew. *Double Standards in Isaiah: Re-evaluating Prophetic Ethics and Divine Justice*. London: T&T Clark, 2000.
Davies, W. D., and Dale C. Allison Jr. *A Critical and Exegetical Commentary on the Gospel according to Saint Matthew*. Vol. 1, *Introduction and Commentary on Matthew I–VII*. London: T&T Clark International, 2004.
——— . *A Critical and Exegetical Commentary on the Gospel according to Saint Matthew*. Vol. 2, *Commentary on Matthew VIII–XVIII*. London: T&T Clark International, 2004.
——— . *A Critical and Exegetical Commentary on the Gospel according to Saint Matthew*. Vol. 3, *Commentary on Matthew XIX–XXVIII*. London T&T Clark International, 2004.
Davis, Ellen F. *Preaching the Luminous Word: Biblical Sermons and Homiletical Essays*. Grand Rapids, MI: Eerdmans, 2016.
——— . *Scripture, Culture, and Agriculture: An Agrarian Reading of the Bible*. Cambridge: Cambridge University Press, 2009.
Davis, Joshua B., and Douglas Harink, eds. *Apocalyptic and the Future of Theology: With and Beyond J. Louis Martyn*. Eugene, OR: Wipf and Stock, 2012.
Debord, Guy. *The Society of the Spectacle*. Translated by Donald Nicholson-Smith. New York: Zone Books, 1994.
Decosimo, David. *Ethics as a Work of Charity: Thomas Aquinas and Pagan Virtue*. Stanford, CA: Stanford University Press, 2014.
——— . "More to Love: Ends, Ordering, and the Compatibility of Acquired and Infused Virtues." In Goris and Schoot, *Virtuous Life*, 47–72.
De Koninck, Charles. "On the Primacy of the Common Good: Against the Personalists." Translated by Sean Collins. *Aquinas Review* 4 (1997): 1–71.
De La Torre, Miguel A. *Doing Christian Ethics from the Margins*. Maryknoll, NY: Orbis, 2004.
Delhaye, Philippe. *The Christian Conscience*. Translated by Charles Underhill Quinn. New York: Desclée, 1968.

DeLorenzo, Leonard J. *Work of Love: A Theological Reconstruction of the Communion of Saints*. Notre Dame, IN: University of Notre Dame Press, 2017.
de Lubac, Henri, S.J. *La postérité spirituelle de Joachim de Flore*. Vol. 1, *De Joachim à Schelling*. Paris: Éditions Lethielleux, 1979.
DeSilva, David A. *Despising Shame: Honor Discourse and Community Maintenance in the Epistle to the Hebrews*. Atlanta: Scholars Press, 1995.
———. *Honor, Patronage, Kinship and Purity: Unlocking New Testament Culture*. Downers Grove, IL: InterVarsity Press, 2000.
de Vogüé, Adalbert. *To Love Fasting: The Monastic Experience*. Petersham, MA: St. Bede's Publications, 1989.
DeYoung, Rebecca Konyndyk. "Aquinas's Virtues of Acknowledged Dependence: A New Measure of Greatness." *Faith and Philosophy* 21 (2006): 214–27.
———. *Glittering Vices: A New Look at the Seven Deadly Sins and Their Remedies*. Grand Rapids, MI: Brazos, 2009.
DeYoung, Rebecca Konyndyk, Colleen McCluskey, and Christina Van Dyke. *Aquinas's Ethics: Metaphysical Foundations, Moral Theory, and Theological Context*. Notre Dame, IN: University of Notre Dame Press, 2009.
Di Blasi, Fulvio. "Practical Syllogism, *Proairesis*, and the Virtues: Toward a Reconciliation of Virtue Ethics and Natural Law Ethics." *Nova et Vetera* 2 (2004): 21–42.
DiNoia, J. A., O.P., and Romanus Cessario, O.P. *Veritatis Splendor and the Renewal of Moral Theology*. Chicago: Midwest Theological Forum, 1999.
Donahue, John R., S.J. "The Challenge of Biblical Renewal to Moral Theology." In *Riding Time Like a River: The Catholic Moral Tradition since Vatican II*, edited by William J. O'Brien, 59–80. Washington, DC: Georgetown University Press, 1993.
Donati, Pierpaolo. "The Common Good as a Relational Good." *Nova et Vetera* 7 (2009): 603–24.
Dougherty, M. V. "Moral Luck and the Capital Vices in *De malo*: Gluttony and Lust." In *Aquinas's "Disputed Questions on Evil": A Critical Guide*, edited by M. V. Dougherty, 222–34. Cambridge: Cambridge University Press, 2016.
———. "Three Precursors to Pico della Mirandola's Roman Disputation and the Question of Human Nature." In *Pico della Mirandola: New Essays*, edited by M. V. Dougherty, 114–51. Cambridge: Cambridge University Press, 2007.

Dow, Philip E. *Virtuous Minds: Intellectual Character Development*. Downers Grove, IL: IVP Academic, 2013.
Drewermann, Eugen. *Strukturen des Bösen: Sonderausgabe; Die jahwistische Urgeschichte in exegetischer/psychoanalytischer/philosophischer Sicht*. Paderborn: Schöningh, 1985–86.
Dulles, Avery, S.J. "The Church and the Kingdom: A Study of Their Relationship in Scripture, Tradition, and Evangelization." *Letter & Spirit* 3 (2007): 23–38.
Dunn, James D. G. *Jesus Remembered*. Vol. 1 of *Christianity in the Making*. Grand Rapids, MI: Eerdmans, 2003.
Dunnington, Kent. *Addiction and Virtue: Beyond the Models of Disease and Choice*. Downers Grove, IL: IVP Academic, 2011.
———. "Humility: An Augustinian Perspective." *Pro Ecclesia* 25 (2016): 18–43.
Dupont, Anthony, Wim François, Paul van Geest, and Mathijs Lamberigts. "Sex." In *The Oxford Guide to the Historical Reception of Augustine*, vol. 3, edited by Karla Pollmann, 1726–35. Oxford: Oxford University Press, 2013.
Echeverria, Eduardo J. *"In the Beginning...": A Theology of the Body*. Eugene, OR: Pickwick, 2011.
Edin, Kathryn, and Maria Kefalas. *Promises I Can Keep: Why Poor Women Put Motherhood before Marriage*. 2nd ed. Berkeley: University of California Press, 2011.
Elders, Leo J., S.V.D. "Les citations de saint Augustin dans la *Somme Théologique* de saint Thomas d'Aquin." *Doctor Communis* 40 (1987): 115–67.
———. "St. Thomas Aquinas's Treatise on Temperance and Aristotle." *Nova et Vetera* 16 (2018): 465–87.
Elliot, David. *Hope and Christian Ethics*. Cambridge: Cambridge University Press, 2017.
Elliott, John H. "Disgraced Yet Graced: The Gospel according to 1 Peter in the Key of Honor and Shame." *Biblical Theology Bulletin* 24 (1994): 166–78.
Emery, Gilles, O.P. "Holy Spirit." In *The Cambridge Companion to the "Summa Theologiae,"* edited by Philip McCosker and Denys Turner, 129–41. Cambridge: Cambridge University of America Press, 2016.
———. "The Holy Spirit in Aquinas's Commentary on Romans." In *Reading Romans with St. Thomas Aquinas*, edited by Matthew Levering and Michael Dauphinais, 127–62. Washington, DC: Catholic University of America Press, 2012.

———. *Présence de Dieu et union à Dieu*. Paris: Parole et Silence, 2017.
Emery, Gilles, O.P., and Matthew Levering, eds. *Aristotle in Aquinas's Theology*. Oxford: Oxford University Press, 2015.
Emery, Kent. "Reading the World Rightly and Squarely: Bonaventure's Doctrine of the Cardinal Virtues." *Traditio* 39 (1983): 183–218.
Emon, Anver M., Matthew Levering, and David Novak. *Natural Law: A Jewish, Christian, and Islamic Trialogue*. Oxford: Oxford University Press, 2014.
Ernst, Stephan. "Die bescheidene Rolle der Demut: Christliche und philosophische Grundhaltungen in der speziellen Tugendlehre." In *Thomas von Aquin: Die "Summa theologiae": Werkinterpretationen*, edited by Andreas Speer, 343–76. Berlin: Walter de Gruyter, 2005.
Evans, Craig A. "Jesus and the Continuing Exile." In Newman, *Jesus and the Restoration of Israel*, 77–100.
Fagerberg, David W. *Consecrating the World: On Mundane Liturgical Theology*. Kettering, OH: Angelico Press, 2016.
———. *On Liturgical Asceticism*. Washington, DC: Catholic University of America Press, 2013.
Farley, Margaret, R.S.M. "An Ethic for Same-Sex Relations." In *A Challenge to Love: Gay and Lesbian Catholics in the Church*, edited by Robert Nugent, 93–106. New York: Crossroad, 1983.
———. *Just Love: A Framework for Christian Sexual Ethics*. New York: Continuum, 2006.
Farrow, Douglas. *Nation of Bastards: Essays on the End of Marriage*. Toronto: BPS Books, 2007.
Fee, Gordon D. *Philippians*. Downers Grove, IL: InterVarsity Press, 1999.
Feldmeier, Reinhard. *Power, Service, Humility: A New Testament Ethic*. Translated by Brian McNeil. Waco, TX: Baylor University Press, 2014.
Feser, Edward. *Aquinas: A Beginner's Guide*. Oxford: Oneworld, 2009.
———. "In Defense of the Perverted Faculty Argument." In *Neo-Scholastic Essays*, 378–415.
———. *Neo-Scholastic Essays*. South Bend, IN: St. Augustine's Press, 2015.
———. *Scholastic Metaphysics: A Contemporary Introduction*. Heusenstamm: Editiones Scholasticae, 2014.
Fiala, Andrew. *What Would Jesus Really Do? The Power and Limits of Jesus' Moral Teachings*. Lanham, MD: Rowman & Littlefield, 2007.
Finnis, John. "The Natural Law, Objective Morality, and Vatican II." In *Principles of Catholic Moral Life*, edited by William E. May, 113–49. Chicago: Franciscan Herald, 1980.
Fischer, Johannes. *Leben aus dem Geist*. Zurich: Theologischer Verlag Zürich, 1994.

Fisher, M. F. K. *The Art of Eating.* New York: Vintage, 1976.
Flannery, Austin, O.P., ed. *Vatican Council II.* Vol. 1, *The Conciliar and Post Conciliar Documents*, rev. ed. Northport, NY: Costello Publishing Company, 1996.
Flannery, Kevin L., S.J. *Acts amid Precepts: The Aristotelian Logical Structure of Thomas Aquinas's Moral Theory.* Washington, DC: Catholic University of America Press, 2001.
———. "Marriage, Thomas Aquinas, and Jean Porter." *Journal of Catholic Social Thought* 8 (2011): 277–89.
Flood, Anthony T. "What We Can Learn from the Medieval Rejection of Curiosity." *Northern Plains Ethics Journal* 1 (2013): 47–54.
Ford, John C., S.J. *Man Takes a Drink: Facts and Principles about Alcohol.* New York: P. J. Kennedy and Sons, 1955.
Forsyth, Andrew. "Defining Marriage." *Soundings: An Interdisciplinary Journal* 97 (2014): 297–322.
Foster, Richard. *Celebration of Discipline: The Path to Spiritual Growth.* Rev. ed. San Francisco: Harper & Row, 1988.
Fowl, Stephen. *Engaging Scripture: A Model of Theological Interpretation.* Oxford: Blackwell, 1998.
Fradd, Matt. *The Porn Myth: Exposing the Reality behind the Fantasy of Pornography.* San Francisco: Ignatius Press, 2017.
Francis, Pope. *Amoris Laetitia.* Apostolic exhortation. Vatican translation. Frederick, MD: The Word Among Us Press, 2016.
———. *Evangelii Gaudium.* Apostolic exhortation. Vatican translation. Boston: Pauline Books & Media, 2013.
———. *Lumen Fidei.* Encyclical. Vatican translation. San Francisco: Ignatius Press, 2013.
Francis, Pope [Jorge Mario Bergoglio]. *Open Mind, Faithful Heart: Reflections on Following Jesus.* Translated by Joseph V. Owens, S.J. New York: Crossroad, 2013.
Frankfurt, Harry G. "Freedom of the Will and the Concept of a Person." *Journal of Philosophy* 68 (1971): 5–20.
———. *On Bullshit.* Princeton: Princeton University Press, 2005.
Fredriksen, Paula. Review of *Paul and the Faithfulness of God*, by N. T. Wright. *Catholic Biblical Quarterly* 77 (2015): 387–91.
Fritz, Everett. *Freedom: Battle Strategies for Conquering Temptation.* San Francisco: Ignatius Press, 2015.
Fuchs, Joseph, S.J. *De castitate et ordine sexuali: Conspectus praelectionum theologiae moralis ad usum auditorium.* 2nd ed. Rome: Editrice Università Gregoriana, 1960.

———. *Personal Responsibility and Christian Morality*. Translated by William Cleves et al. Washington, DC: Georgetown University Press, 1983.

Fuhr, Richard Alan, Jr., and Gary E. Yates. *The Message of the Twelve: Hearing the Voice of the Minor Prophets*. Nashville: B&H Academic, 2016.

Fullam, Lisa. "Toward a Virtue Ethics of Marriage: Augustine and Aquinas on Friendship in Marriage." *Theological Studies* 73 (2012): 663–92.

Fuller, Michael E. *The Restoration of Israel*. Berlin: Walter de Gruyter, 2006.

Furnish, Victor P. *The Love Command in the New Testament*. Nashville: Abingdon, 1972.

Gagnon, Robert A. J. *The Bible and Homosexual Practice: Texts and Hermeneutics*. Nashville: Abingdon, 2002.

Garrigou-Lagrange, Réginald, O.P. *The Three Ages of the Interior Life*. Vol. 1. Translated by M. Timothea Doyle, O.P. St. Louis: B. Herder, 1947.

———. *The Three Ages of the Interior Life*. Vol. 2, *Prelude of Eternal Life*. Translated by M. Timothea Doyle, O.P. St. Louis: B. Herder, 1954.

George, Robert P., and Patrick Lee. *Body-Self Dualism in Contemporary Ethics and Politics*. Cambridge: Cambridge University Press, 2009.

Gilby, Thomas, O.P. "Appendix 3: Natural and Unnatural in Morals (2a2ae. 154, 11)." In Aquinas, *Summa theologiae*, vol. 43, *Temperance (2a2ae. 141–54)*, 254–55.

Girgis, Sherif, Ryan T. Anderson, and Robert P. George. *What Is Marriage? Man and Woman; A Defense*. New York: Encounter Books, 2012.

Gombis, Timothy G. "Participation in the New-Creation People of God in Christ by the Spirit." In McKnight and Modica, *Apostle Paul and the Christian Life*, 103–24.

Gondreau, Paul. "The 'Inseparable Connection' between Procreation and Unitive Love (*Humanae Vitae*, §12) and Thomistic Hylemorphic Anthropology." *Nova et Vetera* 6 (2008): 731–64.

———. "The Natural Law Ordering of Human Sexuality to (Heterosexual) Marriage: Towards a Thomistic Philosophy of the Body." *Nova et Vetera* 8 (2010): 553–92.

———. "The Passions and the Moral Life: Appreciating the Originality of Aquinas." *Thomist* 71 (2007): 419–50.

———. "The Redemption and Divinization of Human Sexuality through the Sacrament of Marriage: A Thomistic Approach." *Nova et Vetera* 10 (2012): 383–413.

Gordon, Joseph K. *Divine Scripture in Human Understanding: A Systematic Theology of the Christian Bible.* Notre Dame, IN: University of Notre Dame Press, 2019.
Gordon, Richard A. *Eating Disorders: Analysis of a Social Epidemic.* Oxford: Blackwell, 2000.
Goris, Harm. "Acquired and Infused Moral Virtues in Wounded Nature." In Goris and Schoot, *Virtuous Life*, 21–46.
Goris, Harm, and Henk Schoot, eds. *The Virtuous Life: Thomas Aquinas on the Theological Nature of the Moral Virtues.* Leuven: Peeters, 2017.
Gorman, Michael J. *Apostle of the Crucified Lord: A Theological Introduction to Paul and His Letters.* 2nd ed. Grand Rapids, MI: Eerdmans, 2017.
———. *Cruciformity: Paul's Narrative Spirituality of the Cross.* Grand Rapids, MI: Eerdmans, 2001.
———. *Inhabiting the Cruciform God: Kenosis, Justification, and Theosis in Paul's Narrative Soteriology.* Grand Rapids, MI: Eerdmans, 2009.
Grabowski, John S. "Mutual Submission and Trinitarian Self-Giving." *Angelicum* 84 (1997): 489–512.
———. *Sex and Virtue: An Introduction to Sexual Ethics.* Washington, DC: Catholic University of America Press, 2003.
———. *Transformed in Christ: Essays on the Renewal of Moral Theology.* Ave Maria, FL: Sapientia Press, 2017.
Grant, Jonathan. *Divine Sex: A Compelling Vision for Christian Relationships in a Hypersexualized Age.* Grand Rapids, MI: Brazos, 2015.
Graves, Michael. *The Inspiration and Interpretation of Scripture: What the Early Church Can Teach Us.* Grand Rapids, MI: Eerdmans, 2014.
Gregory the Great. *Morals on the Book of Job.* 3 vols. Translated by J. Bliss. Oxford: John Henry Parker, 1850.
Griffiths, Paul J. *Christian Flesh.* Stanford, CA: Stanford University Press, 2018.
———. *Decreation: The Last Things of All Creatures.* Waco, TX: Baylor University Press, 2014.
———. *Intellectual Appetite: A Theological Grammar.* Washington, DC: Catholic University of America Press, 2009.
Grimm, Veronika. *From Feasting to Fasting, the Evolution of a Sin: Attitudes to Food in Late Antiquity.* London: Routledge, 1996.
Grumett, David, and Rachel Muers. *Theology on the Menu: Asceticism, Meat and Christian Diet.* London: Routledge, 2010.
———, eds. *Eating and Believing: Interdisciplinary Perspectives on Vegetarianism and Theology.* London: T&T Clark, 2008.

Guardini, Romano. *Learning the Virtues That Lead You to God.* Manchester, NH: Sophia Institute Press, 1998.
Gudorf, Christine E. *Body, Sex, and Pleasure: Reconstructing Christian Sexual Ethics.* Cleveland, OH: Pilgrim Press, 1994.
Guerra, Marc D. "Moderating the Magnanimous Man: Aquinas on Greatness of Soul." In *Theology Needs Philosophy: Acting against Reason Is Contrary to the Nature of God,* edited by Matthew L. Lamb, 253–66. Washington, DC: Catholic University of America Press, 2016.
Gushee, David B., and Glen H. Stassen. *Kingdom Ethics: Following Jesus in Contemporary Context.* 2nd ed. Grand Rapids, MI: Eerdmans, 2016.
Hadjadj, Fabrice. "Ce que la pornographie nous cache." *Nova et Vetera* 92 (2017): 219–30.
———. *La profondeur des sexes: Pour une mystique de la chair.* Paris: Éditions du Seuil, 2008.
———. *Qu'est-ce qu'une famille?* Paris: Salvator, 2014.
Haflidson, Ron. "Outward, Inward, Upward: Why Three Goods of Marriage for Augustine?" *Studies in Christian Ethics* 29 (2016): 51–68.
Hägerland, Tobias. *Jesus and the Forgiveness of Sins: An Aspect of His Prophetic Mission.* Cambridge: Cambridge University Press, 2012.
Haggerty, Donald. *The Contemplative Hunger.* San Francisco: Ignatius Press, 2016.
Hahn, Scott W. *The Kingdom of God as Liturgical Empire: A Theological Commentary on 1–2 Chronicles.* Grand Rapids, MI: Baker Academic, 2012.
Hanby, Michael. *No God, No Science: Theology, Cosmology, Biology.* Oxford: Wiley-Blackwell, 2013.
Harak, G. Simon, S.J., ed. *Aquinas and Empowerment: Classical Ethics for Ordinary Lives.* Washington, DC: Georgetown University Press, 1996.
———. *Virtuous Passions: The Formation of Christian Character.* Mahwah, NJ: Paulist Press, 1993.
Hare, Stephen. "The Paradox of Moral Humility." *American Philosophical Quarterly* 33 (1996): 235–41.
Häring, Bernard. *Free and Faithful in Christ: Moral Theology for Clergy and Laity.* Vol. 1, *General Moral Theology.* New York: Crossroad, 1978.
Harrington, Daniel, S.J., and James Keenan, S.J., eds. *Jesus and Virtue Ethics: Building Bridges between New Testament Studies and Moral Theology.* Lanham, MD: Rowman & Littlefield, 2002.
Hart, David Bentley. *The Experience of God: Being, Consciousness, Bliss.* New Haven: Yale University Press, 2013.

———. "Impassibility as Transcendence: On the Infinite Innocence of God." In *Divine Impassibility and the Mystery of Human Suffering*, edited by James F. Keating and Thomas Joseph White, O.P., 299–323. Grand Rapids, MI: Eerdmans, 2009.

Hauerwas, Stanley. *Against the Nations: War and Survival in a Liberal Society*. Notre Dame, IN: University of Notre Dame Press, 1992.

———. *Approaching the End: Eschatological Reflections on Church, Politics, and Life*. Grand Rapids, MI: Eerdmans, 2013.

———. "Bearing Reality." In *Approaching the End*, 139–57.

———. *Character and the Christian Life: A Study in Theological Ethics*. Notre Dame, IN: University of Notre Dame Press, 1994.

———. *Christian Existence Today: Essays on Church, World, and Living In Between*. Grand Rapids, MI: Baker, 1988.

———. *A Community of Character: Toward a Constructive Christian Social Ethic*. Notre Dame, IN: University of Notre Dame Press, 1981.

———. "Habit Matters: The Bodily Character of the Virtues." In *Approaching the End*, 158–75.

———. "On Keeping Theological Ethics Theological." In *Against the Nations*, 23–50.

———. "Virtue in Public." In *Christian Existence Today*, 191–97.

———. "Why 'The Way the Words Run' Matters: Reflections on Becoming a 'Major Biblical Scholar.'" In Wagner, Rowe, and Grieb, *Word Leaps the Gap*, 1–19.

Hays, Richard B. "The Conversion of the Imagination: Scripture and Eschatology in 1 Corinthians." In Wendel and Miller, *Torah Ethics and Early Christian Identity*, 151–73.

———. *The Moral Vision of the New Testament: Community, Cross, New Creation; A Contemporary Introduction to New Testament Ethics*. New York: HarperCollins, 1996.

———. "Relations Natural and Unnatural: A Response to John Boswell's Exegesis of Romans 1." *Journal of Religious Ethics* 14 (1986): 184–215.

Healy, Mary. *The Gospel of Mark*. Grand Rapids, MI: Baker Academic, 2008.

Healy, Nicholas J., Jr. "Christian Personalism and the Debate over the End of Marriage." *Communio* 39 (2012): 186–200.

Hefling, Charles, ed. *Ourselves, Our Souls and Bodies: Sexuality and the Household of God*. Cambridge, MA: Cowley, 1996.

Heidegger, Martin. *Being and Time*. Translated by Joan Stambaugh with revisions by Dennis J. Schmidt. Albany: State University of New York Press, 2010.

———. *What Is Called Thinking*. New York: Harper & Row, 1968.
Hellerman, Joseph H. *When the Church Was a Family: Recapturing Jesus' Vision for Authentic Christian Community*. Nashville: B&H Academic, 2009.
Helminiak, Daniel A. *What the Bible Really Says about Homosexuality*. Rev. ed. Tajique, NM: Alamo Square Press, 2000.
Hengel, Martin. *Saint Peter: The Underestimated Apostle*. Translated by Thomas H. Trapp. Grand Rapids, MI: Eerdmans, 2010.
Henisch, Bridget Ann. *Fast and Feast: Food in Medieval Society*. University Park: Pennsylvania State University Press, 1976.
Herdt, Jennifer. *Putting on Virtue: The Legacy of the Splendid Vices*. Chicago: University of Chicago Press, 2012.
Hertling, Georg von. "Augustinuszitate bei Thomas von Aquin." In *Sitzungsberichte der Bayerischen Akademie der Wissenschaften*, 535–602. Munich: Verlag der Bayerischen Akademie der Wissenschaften, 1914.
Heyward, Carter. *Touching Our Strength: The Erotic as Power and the Love of God*. San Francisco: Harper & Row, 1989.
Hibbs, Thomas S. "The Research University in Crisis (Again): MacIntyre's *God, Philosophy, Universities*." *Nova et Vetera* 9 (2011): 947–66.
Hildebrand, Dietrich von. *Marriage: The Mystery of Faithful Love*. Manchester, NH: Sophia Institute Press, 1991.
Hill, Wesley. *Spiritual Friendship: Finding Love in the Church as a Celibate Gay Christian*. Grand Rapids, MI: Brazos, 2015.
Hittinger, Russell. *The First Grace: Rediscovering the Natural Law in a Post-Christian World*. Wilmington, DE: ISI Books, 2003.
———. "Human Nature and States of Nature in John Paul II's Theological Anthropology." In *Human Nature in Its Wholeness: A Roman Catholic Perspective*, edited by Daniel N. Robinson, Gladys M. Sweeney, and Richard Gill, L.C., 9–33. Washington, DC: Catholic University of America Press, 2006.
Hoffmann, Tobias, Jörn Müllet, and Matthias Perkams, eds. *Aquinas and the "Nicomachean Ethics."* Cambridge: Cambridge University Press, 2013.
Hollinger, Dennis P. *The Meaning of Sex: Christian Ethics and the Moral Life*. Grand Rapids, MI: Baker Academic, 2009.
Holmes, Christopher R. J. *Ethics in the Presence of Christ*. London: T&T Clark International, 2012.
Hoskins, Paul M. *Jesus as the Fulfillment of the Temple in the Gospel of John*. Milton Keynes: Paternoster, 2006.
Houser, R. E. Introduction to *The Cardinal Virtues: Aquinas, Albert, and Philip the Chancellor*, translated and edited by R. E. Houser, 1–82. Toronto: Pontifical Institute of Mediaeval Studies, 2004.

Hume, David. *An Enquiry concerning the Principles of Morals*. Edited by J. B. Schneewind. Indianapolis: Hackett, 1983.
———. *A Treatise of Human Nature*. Edited by Ernest C. Mossner. London: Penguin, 1969.
Hütter, Reinhard. "The Christian Life." In *The Oxford Handbook of Systematic Theology*, edited by John Webster, Kathryn Tanner, and Iain Torrance, 285–305. Oxford: Oxford University Press, 2007.
———. *Dust Bound for Heaven: Explorations in the Theology of Thomas Aquinas*. Grand Rapids, MI: Eerdmans, 2012.
———. "God, the University, and the Missing Link—Wisdom: Reflections on Two Untimely Books." *Thomist* 73 (2009): 241–77.
———. "Human Sexuality in a Fallen World: An Economy of Mercy and Grace." *Nova et Vetera* 15 (2017): 433–64.
———. "The Virtue of Chastity and the Scourge of Pornography: A Twofold Crisis Considered in Light of Thomas Aquinas's Moral Theology." *Thomist* 77 (2013): 1–39.
Hütter, Reinhard, and Matthew Levering, eds. *Ressourcement Thomism: Sacred Doctrine, The Sacraments, and the Moral Life; Essays in Honor of Romanus Cessario, O.P.* Washington, DC: Catholic University of America Press, 2010.
Itzin, Catherine. "Incest, Paedophilia, Pornography and Prostitution: Making Familial Males More Visible as the Abusers." *Child Abuse Review* 10 (2001): 35–48.
Janowski, Bernd, and Peter Stuhlmacher, eds. *The Suffering Servant: Isaiah 53 in Jewish and Christian Sources*. Translated by Daniel P. Bailey. Grand Rapids, MI: Eerdmans, 2004.
Jensen, Steven J. *Knowing the Natural Law: From Precepts and Inclinations to Deriving Oughts*. Washington, DC: Catholic University of America Press, 2015.
John of Damascus. "An Exact Exposition of the Orthodox Faith." In *Writings*, by John of Damascus, translated by Frederic H. Chase Jr., 165–406. Washington, DC: Catholic University of America Press, 1958.
John Paul II, Pope. *Familiaris Consortio*. Apostolic exhortation, November 22, 1981. Available via the Vatican website, http://w2.vatican.va/content/vatican/en.html.
———. *Fides et Ratio*. Encyclical, September 14, 1998. Available via the Vatican website, http://w2.vatican.va/content/vatican/en.html.
———. *Man and Woman He Created Them: A Theology of the Body*. Translated by Michael Waldstein. Boston: Pauline Books & Media, 2006.
———. *Veritatis Splendor*. Encyclical, August 6, 1993. Available via the Vatican website, http://w2.vatican.va/content/vatican/en.html.

Johnson, Andy. *Holiness and the* Missio Dei. Eugene, OR: Cascade, 2016.
Johnson, Luke Timothy. "A Historiographical Response to Wright's Jesus." In Newman, *Jesus and the Restoration of Israel*, 206–24.
———. *The Living Gospel*. London: Continuum, 2004.
Johnson, Samuel. *Selected Essays*. Edited by David Womersley. London: Penguin, 2003.
Johnston, Rebekah. "Marriage and the Metaphysics of Bodily Union: Framing the Same-Sex Marriage Debate." *Social Theory and Practice* 39 (2013): 288–312.
Johnstone, Brian V., C.S.s.R. "Transformation Ethics." In *The Resurrection: An Interdisciplinary Symposium on the Resurrection of Jesus*, edited by Stephen T. Davis, Daniel Kendall, S.J., and Gerald O'Collins, S.J., 339–60. Oxford: Oxford University Press, 1997.
Jones, Beth Felker. *Faithful: A Theology of Sex*. Grand Rapids, MI: Zondervan, 2015.
Jones, David Albert. *Approaching the End: A Theological Exploration of Death and Dying*. Oxford: Oxford University Press, 2007.
Jordan, Mark D. "Aquinas's Construction of a Moral Account of the Passions." *Freiburger Zeitschrift für Philosophie und Theologie* 33 (1986): 71–97.
———. "'Baptizing' Queer Characters." In Kamitsuka, *Embrace of Eros*, 151–63.
———. *The Ethics of Sex*. Oxford: Blackwell, 2002.
———. *The Invention of Sodomy in Christian Theology*. Chicago: University of Chicago Press, 1997.
———. *The Silence of Sodom: Homosexuality in Modern Catholicism*. Chicago: University of Chicago Press, 2002.
Just, Arthur. *The Ongoing Feast: Table Fellowship and Eschatology at Emmaus*. Collegeville, MN: Liturgical Press, 1993.
Kaczor, Christopher. *Proportionalism and the Natural Law Tradition*. Washington, DC: Catholic University of America Press, 2002.
Kamitsuka, Margaret E., ed. *The Embrace of Eros: Bodies, Desires, and Sexuality in Christianity*. Minneapolis: Fortress, 2010.
Kampowski, Stephan. "A Promise to Keep: Which Bond, Whose Fidelity?" *Nova et Vetera* 13 (2015): 489–514.
Kamtekar, Rachana. "Ancient Virtue Ethics: An Overview with an Emphasis on Practical Wisdom." In Russell, *Cambridge Companion to Virtue Ethics*, 29–48.
Kane, W. H., O.P. Preface to Carlson, *Virtue of Humility*, vii–viii.
Karen, Robert. "Shame." *Atlantic Monthly*, February 1992, 40–70.

Karris, Robert J., O.F.M. *Eating Your Way through Luke's Gospel.* Collegeville, MN: Liturgical Press, 2006.
Kashdan, Todd B. "Curiosity." In *Character Strengths and Virtues: A Handbook and Classification,* edited by Christopher Peterson and Martin E. P. Seligman, 125–41. Oxford: Oxford University Press, 2004.
Kass, Leon R. *The Hungry Soul: Eating and the Perfecting of Our Nature.* Chicago: University of Chicago Press, 1999.
Katongole, Emmanuel. "The Church of the Future: Pressing Moral Issues from *Ecclesia in Africa.*" In *The Church We Want: African Catholics Look to Vatican III,* edited by Agbonkhianmeghe E. Orobator, 161–73. Maryknoll, NY: Orbis, 2016.
Katongole, Emmanuel, and Chris Rice. *Reconciling All Things: A Christian Vision for Justice, Peace and Healing.* Downers Grove, IL: InterVarsity Press, 2008.
Keating, Daniel A. *Deification and Grace.* Ave Maria, FL: Sapientia Press, 2007.
———. "Justification, Sanctification and Divinization in Thomas Aquinas." In *Aquinas on Doctrine: Critical Essays,* edited by Thomas G. Weinandy, O.F.M. Cap., Daniel A. Keating, and John P. Yocum, 139–58. New York: T&T Clark, 2004.
Keenan, James, S.J. *A History of Catholic Moral Theology in the Twentieth Century: From Confessing Sins to Liberating Consciences.* New York: Continuum, 2010.
Kennedy, Thomas D. "Curiosity and the Integrated Self: A Postmodern Vice." *Logos* 4 (2001): 33–54.
Kenny, Neil. *Curiosity in Early Modern Europe Word Histories.* Wiesbaden: Harrassowitz Verlag, 1998.
Kerr, Fergus, O.P. "Doctrine of God and Theological Ethics according to Thomas Aquinas." In *The Doctrine of God and Theological Ethics,* edited by Alan Torrance and Michael Banner, 71–84. London: T&T Clark, 2006.
Keys, Mary M. *Aquinas, Aristotle, and the Promise of the Common Good.* Cambridge: Cambridge University Press, 2006.
Klein, Jacob. "Stoic Eudaimonism and the Natural Law Tradition." In *Reason, Religion, and Natural Law: From Plato to Spinoza,* edited by Jonathan A. Jacobs, 57–80. Oxford: Oxford University Press, 2012.
Knobel, Angela McKay. "Can Aquinas's Infused and Acquired Virtues Coexist in the Christian Life?" *Studies in Christian Ethics* 23 (2010): 381–96.

———. "A Confusing Comparison: Interpreting *De Virtutibus in Communi* a. 10 ad 4." In Goris and Schoot, *Virtuous Life*, 97–115.

———. "Relating Aquinas's Infused and Acquired Virtues: Some Problematic Texts for a Common Interpretation." *Nova et Vetera* 9 (2011): 411–31.

Koenig, John. *New Testament Hospitality: Partnership with Strangers as Promise and Mission*. Philadelphia: Fortress, 1985.

Koterski, Joseph W., S.J. "Aquinas on the Sacrament of Marriage." In *Rediscovering Aquinas and the Sacraments: Studies in Sacramental Theology*, edited by Matthew Levering and Michael Dauphinais, 102–13. Chicago: Hillenbrand Books, 2009.

———. "The Concept of Nature: Philosophical Reflections in the Service of Theology." In *Theology Needs Philosophy: Acting against Reason Is Contrary to the Nature of God*, edited by Matthew L. Lamb, 54–73. Washington, DC: Catholic University of America Press, 2016.

Kraemer, David. *Jewish Eating and Identity through the Ages*. New York: Routledge, 2007.

Kraut, Richard. *Aristotle on the Human Good*. Princeton: Princeton University Press, 1989.

Kruschwitz, Robert B. "Gluttony and Abstinence." In Timpe and Boyd, *Virtues and Their Vices*, 137–55.

Kwasniewski, Peter. "St. Thomas on the Grandeur and Limitations of Marriage." *Nova et Vetera* 10 (2012): 415–36.

Laansma, Jon C. *"I Will Give You Rest": The Rest Motif in the New Testament with Special Reference to Mt 11 and Heb 3–4*. Tübingen: Mohr Siebeck, 1997.

Labhardt, André. "Curiositas: Notes sur l'histoire d'un mot et d'une notion." *Museum Helveticum* 17 (1960): 206–24.

Lamb, Matthew L. "The Millennial Challenges Facing Catholic Intellectual Life." *Nova et Vetera* 11 (2013): 969–91.

Lambert, Nathaniel M., et al. "A Love That Doesn't Last: Pornography Consumption and Weakened Commitment to One's Romantic Partner." *Journal of Social and Clinical Psychology* 31 (2012): 410–38.

Lambot, Cyrille, O.S.B. "L'ordre et le text des degrés d'humilité dans s. Thomas." *Revue Bénédictine* 39 (1927): 129–35.

Lamoureux, Patricia, and Paul J. Wadell. *The Christian Moral Life: Faithful Discipleship for a Global Society*. Maryknoll, NY: Orbis, 2010.

Laporte, Jean-Marc, S.J. "Christ in Aquinas's *Summa theologiae*: Peripheral or Pervasive?" *Thomist* 67 (2003): 221–48.

LaVerdiere, Eugene, S.S.S. *Dining in the Kingdom of God: The Origins of Eucharist in the Gospel of Luke*. Chicago: Liturgy Training Publications, 1994.

Lawler, Ronald, O.F.M. Cap., Joseph Boyle, and William E. May. *Catholic Sexual Ethics: A Summary Explanation and Defense*. 2nd ed. Huntingdon, IN: Our Sunday Visitor, 1998.

LeBlanc, Marie, O.S.B. "Amour et procréation dans la théologie de saint Thomas." *Revue Thomiste* 92 (1992): 433–59.

Legge, Dominic, O.P. *The Trinitarian Christology of St Thomas Aquinas*. Oxford: Oxford University Press, 2017.

Leo XIII, Pope. *Providentissimus Deus*. Encyclical, November 18, 1893. Available via the Vatican website, http://w2.vatican.va/content/vatican/en.html.

Levenson, Jon D. *The Love of God: Divine Gift, Human Gratitude, and Mutual Faithfulness in Judaism*. Princeton: Princeton University Press, 2016.

———. *Sinai and Zion: An Entry into the Jewish Bible*. San Francisco: Harper & Row, 1985.

Levering, Matthew. "Aquinas and Supersessionism One More Time: A Response to Matthew A. Tapie's *Aquinas on Israel and the Church*." *Pro Ecclesia* 25 (2016): 395–412.

———. *The Betrayal of Charity: The Sins That Sabotage Divine Love*. Waco, TX: Baylor University Press, 2011.

———. *Biblical Natural Law: A Theocentric and Teleological Approach*. Oxford: Oxford University Press, 2008.

———. *Christ and the Catholic Priesthood: Ecclesial Hierarchy and the Pattern of the Trinity*. Chicago: Hillenbrand Books, 2010.

———. "Christians and Natural Law." In Emon, Levering, and Novak, *Natural Law*, 66–110.

———. *Dying and the Virtues*. Grand Rapids, MI: Eerdmans, 2018.

———. *Engaging the Doctrine of Creation: Cosmos, Creatures, and the Wise and Good Creator*. Grand Rapids, MI: Baker Academic, 2017.

———. *Engaging the Doctrine of Revelation: The Mediation of the Gospel through Church and Scripture*. Grand Rapids, MI: Baker Academic, 2014.

———. *Engaging the Doctrine of the Holy Spirit: Love and Gift in the Trinity and the Church*. Grand Rapids, MI: Baker Academic, 2016.

———. *The Indissolubility of Marriage: Amoris Laetitia in Context*. San Francisco: Ignatius Press, 2019.

———. *An Introduction to Vatican II as an Ongoing Theological Event*. Washington, DC: Catholic University of America Press, 2017.

———. *Jesus and the Demise of Death: Resurrection, Afterlife, and the Fate of the Christian*. Waco, TX: Baylor University Press, 2012.

———. *Jewish-Christian Dialogue and the Life of Wisdom: Engagements with the Theology of David Novak.* London: Continuum, 2010.

———. "Knowing What Is 'Natural': Thomas Aquinas and Luke Timothy Johnson on Romans 1–2." *Logos* 12 (2009): 117–42.

———. *Participatory Biblical Exegesis: A Theology of Biblical Interpretation.* Notre Dame, IN: University of Notre Dame Press, 2008.

———. *Paul in the* Summa Theologiae. Washington, DC: Catholic University of America Press, 2014.

———. "Pinckaers and Häring on Conscience." *Journal of Moral Theology* 8: Special Issue 2 (2019): 134–65.

———. *Predestination: Biblical and Theological Paths.* Oxford: Oxford University Press, 2011.

———. *Proofs of God: Classical Arguments from Tertullian to Barth.* Grand Rapids, MI: Baker Academic, 2016.

———. "Sin and Grace in the Church according to Paul and Aquinas." In *Aquinas the Biblical Theologian*, edited by Michael Dauphinais, Scott W. Hahn, and Roger W. Nutt. Steubenville, OH: Emmaus Academic, forthcoming.

———. "Supplementing Pinckaers: The Old Testament in Aquinas's Ethics." In *Reading Sacred Scripture with Thomas Aquinas: Hermeneutical Tools, Theological Questions and New Perspectives*, edited by Piotr Roszak and Jörgen Vijgen, 349–73. Turnhout: Brepols, 2015.

———. *Was the Reformation a Mistake? Why Catholic Doctrine Is Not Unbiblical.* With a response by Kevin J. Vanhoozer. Grand Rapids, MI: Zondervan, 2017.

Lévy, Carlos. "Philo's Ethics." Translated by Ada Bronowski. In *The Cambridge Companion to Philo*, edited by Adam Kamesar, 146–71. Cambridge: Cambridge University Press, 2009.

Lewis, C. S. *The Screwtape Letters.* New York: HarperCollins, 2000.

Lindström, Fredrik. *God and the Origin of Evil: Contextual Analysis of Alleged Monistic Evidence in the Old Testament.* Lund: Gleerup, 1983.

Ling, Timothy J. M. *The Judaean Poor and the Fourth Gospel.* Cambridge: Cambridge University Press, 2006.

Lombardo, Nicholas, O.P. *The Logic of Desire: Aquinas on Emotion.* Washington, DC: Catholic University of America Press, 2011.

Long, Steven A. "Creation *ad imaginem Dei*: The Obediential Potency of the Human Person to Grace and Glory." *Nova et Vetera* 14 (2016): 1175–92.

———. "The Gifts of the Holy Spirit and Their Indispensability for the Christian Moral Life: Grace as *Motus.*" *Nova et Vetera* 11 (2013): 357–73.

———. "Natural Law, the Moral Object, and *Humanae Vitae*." In Hütter and Levering, *Ressourcement Thomism*, 285–311.
———. *The Teleological Grammar of the Moral Act*. Naples, FL: Sapientia Press, 2007.
Longman, Tremper, III. *Proverbs*. Grand Rapids, MI: Baker Academic, 2006.
Loughlin, Stephen J. *Aquinas' Summa Theologiae*. London: T&T Clark International, 2010.
———. "Thomas Aquinas and the Importance of Fasting to the Christian Life." *Pro Ecclesia* 17 (2008): 343–361.
Loyer, Kenneth M. *God's Love through the Spirit: The Holy Spirit in Thomas Aquinas and John Wesley*. Washington, DC: Catholic University of America Press, 2014.
Luyten, Norbert. "The Significance of the Body in a Thomistic Anthropology." *Philosophy Today* 7 (1963): 175–93.
Lynch, Reginald M., O.P. *The Cleansing of the Heart: The Sacraments as Instrumental Causes in the Thomistic Tradition*. Washington, DC: Catholic University of America Press, 2017.
Lyonnet, S., S.J. "Liberté chrétienne et loi de l'Esprit selon s. Paul." *Christus* 4 (1954): 6–27.
Macaskill, Grant. *Revealed Wisdom and Inaugurated Eschatology in Ancient Judaism and Early Christianity*. Leiden: Brill, 2007.
Machiavelli, Niccolò. *The Discourses*. Translated by Christian E. Detmold. In *The Prince and The Discourses*, 101–540.
———. *The Prince and The Discourses*. New York: Random House, 1950.
MacIntyre, Alasdair. *After Virtue*. 3rd ed. Notre Dame, IN: University of Notre Dame Press, 2007.
———. *Dependent Rational Animals: Why Human Beings Need the Virtues*. Chicago: Open Court, 1999.
———. *God, Philosophy, Universities: A Selective History of the Catholic Philosophical Tradition*. Lanham, MD: Rowman & Littlefield, 2009.
———. *Whose Justice? Which Rationality?* Notre Dame, IN: University of Notre Dame Press, 1988.
Madden, James D. *Mind, Matter, and Nature: A Thomistic Proposal for the Philosophy of Mind*. Washington, DC: Catholic University of America Press, 2013.
Madden, Joshua. "Marriage, 'Bodily Union,' and Natural Teleology: A Response to Rebekah Johnston and the New Natural Law Theorists." *National Catholic Bioethics Quarterly* 16 (2016): 83–98.
Mahoney, John, S.J. *The Making of Moral Theology: A Study of the Roman Catholic Tradition*. Oxford: Oxford University Press, 1987.

Malina, Bruce J., and Jerome H. Neyrey. "Honor and Shame in Luke-Acts: Pivotal Values of the Mediterranean World." In *The Social World of Luke-Acts: Models for Interpretation*, edited by Jerome H. Neyrey, 25–66. Peabody, MA: Hendrickson, 1991.

Mansini, Guy, O.S.B. *Fundamental Theology*. Washington, DC: Catholic University of America Press, 2018.

Mansini, Guy, O.S.B., and Lawrence J. Welch. "Revelation, Natural Law, and Homosexual Unions." *Nova et Vetera* 2 (2004): 337–66.

Marion, Jean-Luc. *Believing in Order to See: On the Rationality of Revelation and the Irrationality of Some Believers*. Translated by Christina M. Gschwandtner. New York: Fordham University Press, 2017.

———. *The Crossing of the Visible*. Translated by James K. A. Smith. Stanford, CA: Stanford University Press, 2004.

———. *In Excess: Studies of Saturated Phenomena*. Translated by Robyn Horner and Vincent Berraud. New York: Fordham University Press, 2002.

Marmion, Columba, O.S.B. *Christ, the Ideal of the Monk*. New Pekin, IN: Refuge of Sinners Publications, 1926.

Martin, Dale B. *The Corinthian Body*. New Haven: Yale University Press, 1995.

———. "Heterosexism and the Interpretation of Romans 1:18–31." *Biblical Interpretation* 3 (1995): 332–55.

Martin, Francis. "Male and Female He Created Them: A Summary of the Teaching of Genesis Chapter One." *Communio* 20 (1993): 240–65.

Matera, Frank J. *New Testament Ethics: The Legacies of Jesus and Paul*. Louisville: Westminster John Knox, 1996.

———. *The Sermon on the Mount*. Collegeville, MN: Liturgical Press, 2013.

Matta El-Maskeen [Matthew the Poor]. *The Communion of Love*. Crestwood, NY: St. Vladimir's Seminary Press, 1984.

Mattison, William C., III. "Beatitude and the Beatitudes in the *Summa Theologiae* of St. Thomas Aquinas." *Josephinum Journal of Theology* 17 (2010): 233–49.

———. "The Beatitudes and Moral Theology: A Virtue Ethics Approach." *Nova et Vetera* 11 (2013): 819–48.

———. "Can Christians Possess the Acquired Moral Virtues?" *Thomist* 72 (2011): 558–85.

———. "Infused Virtues in the Scriptures: Infused Prudence in *Matthew* 6, 19–34." In Goris and Schoot, *Virtuous Life*, 281–300.

———. *Introducing Moral Theology: True Happiness and the Virtues*. Grand Rapids, MI: Baker Academic, 2008.

---. "Jesus' Prohibition of Anger (Mt 5:22): The Person/Sin Distinction from Augustine to Aquinas." *Theological Studies* 68 (2007): 839–64.
---. "Movements of Love: A Thomistic Perspective on *Eros* and *Agape*." *Journal of Moral Theology* 1 (2012): 31–60.
---. *The Sermon on the Mount and Moral Theology: A Virtue Perspective*. Cambridge: Cambridge University Press, 2017.
---. "Virtuous Anger? From Questions of *Vindicatio* to the Habituation of Emotion." *Journal of the Society of Christian Ethics* 24 (2004): 159–79.
Maurer, Ernstpeter. "The Perplexity and Complexity of Sinful and Redeemed Reason." In *Reason and the Reasons of Faith*, edited by Paul J. Griffiths and Reinhard Hütter, 194–220. New York: T&T Clark International, 2005.
May, William B. *Getting the Marriage Conversation Right: A Guide for Effective Dialogue*. Steubenville, OH: Emmaus Road Publishing, 2012.
May, William E. "*The Splendor of Accuracy*: How Accurate?" *Thomist* 59 (1995): 465–84.
---. "Theologians and Theologies in the Encyclical." *Anthropotes* 10 (1994): 39–59.
McAleer, G. J. *Ecstatic Morality and Sexual Politics: A Catholic and Antitotalitarian Theory of the Body*. New York: Fordham University Press, 2005.
---. "The Politics of the Flesh: Rahner and Aquinas on *Concupiscentia*." *Modern Theology* 15 (1999): 355–65.
McCabe, Herbert, O.P. *The Good Life: Ethics and the Pursuit of Happiness*. Edited by Brian Davies, O.P. London: Continuum, 2005.
McCarthy, David Matzko. "Jesus Christ, Scripture, and Ethics." In *Gathered for the Journey: Moral Theology in Catholic Perspective*, edited by David Matzko McCarthy and M. Therese Lysaught, 43–67. Grand Rapids, MI: Eerdmans, 2007.
---. *Sex and Love in the Home: A Theology of the Household*. 2nd ed. London: SCM Press, 2004.
McCarthy, Margaret Harper. *Torn Asunder: Children, the Myth of the Good Divorce, and the Recovery of Origins*. Grand Rapids, MI: Eerdmans, 2017.
McCluskey, Colleen. "Lust and Chastity." In Timpe and Boyd, *Virtues and Their Vices*, 115–35.
---. "An Unequal Relationship of Equals: Thomas Aquinas on Marriage." *History of Philosophy Quarterly* 24 (2007): 1–18.

McCormick, Patrick, C.M. *Sin as Addiction*. New York: Paulist Press, 1989.
McFadyen, Alistair. *Bound to Sin: Abuse, Holocaust, and the Christian Doctrine of Sin*. Cambridge: Cambridge University Press, 2000.
McGinn, Bernard. *Thomas Aquinas's* Summa theologiae: *A Biography*. Princeton: Princeton University Press, 2014.
McInerney, Joseph J. *The Greatness of Humility: St. Augustine on Moral Excellence*. Eugene, OR: Pickwick, 2016.
McInerny, Ralph. *Ethica Thomistica: The Moral Philosophy of Thomas Aquinas*. Rev. ed. Washington, DC: Catholic University of America Press, 1997.
———. *The Question of Christian Ethics*. Washington, DC: Catholic University of America Press, 1993.
———. *Thomism in an Age of Renewal*. Garden City, NY: Doubleday, 1966.
McKay [Knobel], Angela. "Aquinas on the End of Marriage." In *Human Fertility: Where Faith and Science Meet*, edited by Richard J. Fehring and Theresa Notare, 53–70. Milwaukee: Marquette University Press, 2008.
McKnight, Scot. *Fasting: Fasting as Body Talk in the Christian Tradition*. Nashville: Thomas Nelson, 2009.
———. "The New Perspective and the Christian Life: The Ecclesial Life." In McKnight and Modica, *Apostle Paul and the Christian Life*, 125–51.
McKnight, Scot, and Joseph B. Modica, eds. *The Apostle Paul and the Christian Life: Ethical and Missional Implications of the New Perspective*. Grand Rapids, MI: Baker Academic, 2016.
McLanahan, Sara, and Gary Sandefur. *Growing Up with a Single Parent: What Hurts, What Helps*. Cambridge, MA: Harvard University Press, 1994.
Meeks, Wayne A. *The Origins of Christian Morality: The First Two Centuries*. New Haven: Yale University Press, 1993.
Meilaender, Gilbert, and William Werpehowski, eds. *The Oxford Handbook of Theological Ethics*. Oxford: Oxford University Press, 2005.
Melina, Livio. *Sharing in Christ's Virtues: For a Renewal of Moral Theology in Light of "Veritatis Splendor."* Translated by William May. Washington, DC: Catholic University of America Press, 2001.
Méndez-Montoya, Angel F. *Theology of Food: Eating and the Eucharist*. Oxford: Wiley-Blackwell, 2009.
Merida, Tony, and Rick Morton. *Orphanology: Awakening to Gospel-Centered Adoption and Orphan Care*. Birmingham, AL: New Hope Publishers, 2011.

Merkelbach, B. H., O.P. *Quaestiones de castitate et luxuria quas in utilitatem cleri*. 6th ed. Paris: Casterman, 1936.
Merton, Thomas. *New Seeds of Contemplation*. Boston: Shambhala, 2003.
Milbank, John, and Adrian Pabst. *The Politics of Virtue: Post-Liberalism and the Human Future*. Lanham, MD: Rowman & Littlefield, 2016.
Miles, Margaret R. *Fullness of Life: Historical Foundations for a New Asceticism*. Philadelphia: Westminster, 1981.
Miller, Fred D., Jr. "The Rule of Reason in Plato's *Laws*." In *Reason, Religion, and Natural Law: From Plato to Spinoza*, edited by Jonathan A. Jacobs, 31–56. Oxford: Oxford University Press, 2012.
Miner, Robert. *Thomas Aquinas on the Passions*. Cambridge: Cambridge University Press, 2009.
Mitch, Curtis, and Edward Sri. *The Gospel of Matthew*. Grand Rapids, MI: Baker Academic, 2010.
Mongeau, Gilles, S.J. *Embracing Wisdom: The "Summa theologiae" as Spiritual Pedagogy*. Toronto: Pontifical Institute of Mediaeval Studies, 2015.
Montague, George T., S.M. *First and Second Timothy, Titus*. Grand Rapids, MI: Baker Academic, 2008.
Montaigne, Michel de. *The Complete Works: Essays, Travel Journal, Letters*. Translated by Donald M. Frame. New York: Knopf, 2003.
———. "Of Anger." in *Complete Works*, 655–61.
Moore, Russell. *Adopted for Life: The Priority of Adoption for Christian Families and Churches*. 2nd ed. Wheaton, IL: Crossway, 2015.
Morales, Rodrigo J. *The Spirit and the Restoration of Israel*. Tübingen: Mohr Siebeck, 2010.
Morrow, Maria C. *Sin in the Sixties: Catholics and Confession, 1955–1975*. Washington, DC: Catholic University of America Press, 2016.
Mühlum, Christoph. *Zum Wohl des Menschen: Glück, Gesetz, Gerechtigkeit und Gnade als Bausteine einer theologischen Ethik bei Thomas von Aquin*. Bonn: Bernstein-Verlag, 2009.
Mullady, Brian T., O.P. *The Angelic Warfare Confraternity*. 4th ed. New Hope, KY: St. Martin de Porres Lay Dominicans, 2006.
Murphy, William F., Jr. "Revisiting the Biblical Renewal of Moral Theology in Light of *Veritatis Splendor*." *Nova et Vetera* 2 (2004): 403–44.
Murray, Paul, O.P. *Aquinas at Prayer: The Bible, Mysticism and Poetry*. London: Bloomsbury, 2013.
———. *Praying with Confidence: Aquinas on the Lord's Prayer*. London: Continuum, 2010.
Navone, John, S.J. "Divine and Human Hospitality." *New Blackfriars* 85 (2004): 329–40.

Nelson, Daniel Mark. *The Priority of Prudence: Virtue and Natural Law in Thomas Aquinas and the Implications for Modern Ethics*. University Park: Pennsylvania State University Press, 1992.

Nelson, James. *Thirst: God and the Alcoholic Experience*. Louisville: Westminster John Knox, 2004.

Nelson, R. David. "Creation and the Problem of Evil after the Apocalyptic Turn." In *Evil and the Doctrine of Creation*, edited by David Luy, Matthew Levering, and George Kalantzis. Bellingham, WA: Lexham, forthcoming.

Newhauser, Richard. "Towards a History of Human Curiosity: A Prolegomenon to Its Medieval Phase." *Deutsche Vierteljahrsschrift für Literaturwissenschaft und Geistesgeschichte* 56 (1982): 559–75.

Newman, Carey C. *Jesus and the Restoration of Israel: A Critical Assessment of N. T. Wright's Jesus and the Victory of God*. Downers Grove, IL: InterVarsity Press, 1999.

Newman, John Henry. *The Idea of a University*. Edited by Martin J. Svaglic. Notre Dame, IN: University of Notre Dame Press, 1982.

Neyrey, Jerome H. *Honor and Shame in the Gospel of Matthew*. Louisville: Westminster John Knox, 1998.

Nhat Hanh, Thich. *Anger: Wisdom for Cooling the Flames*. New York: Riverhead Books, 2001.

Nicholas, M. J. "Les dons du Saint-Esprit." *Revue Thomiste* 92 (1992): 141–53.

Nolan, Michael. "Aquinas and the Act of Love." *New Blackfriars* 92 (March 1996): 115–30.

Novak, David. *Jewish Justice: The Contested Limits of Nature, Law, and Covenant*. Waco, TX: Baylor University Press, 2017.

———. "Response to Matthew Levering's 'Christians and Natural Law.'" In Emon, Levering, and Novak, *Natural Law: A Jewish, Christian, and Islamic Trialogue*, 126–43.

Nussbaum, Martha C. *Frontiers of Justice: Disability, Nationality, Species Membership*. Cambridge, MA: Harvard University Press, 2006.

O'Callaghan, John P., and Thomas S. Hibbs, eds. *Recovering Nature: Essays in Natural Philosophy, Ethics, and Metaphysics in Honor of Ralph McInerny*. Notre Dame, IN: University of Notre Dame Press, 1999.

O'Connell, Robert J., S.J. *Plato on the Human Paradox*. New York: Fordham University Press, 1997.

Oderberg, David S. *Moral Theory: A Non-Consequentialist Approach*. Oxford: Blackwell, 2000.

O'Donovan, Oliver. *Church in Crisis: The Gay Controversy and the Anglican Communion*. Eugene, OR: Cascade, 2008.

———. *Ethics as Theology*. Vol. 2, *Finding and Seeking*. Grand Rapids, MI: Eerdmans, 2014.

———. *Resurrection and Moral Order: An Outline for Evangelical Ethics*. Grand Rapids, MI: Eerdmans, 1986.

Odozor, Paulinus Ikechukwu. *Morality Truly Christian, Truly African: Foundational, Methodological, and Theological Considerations*. Notre Dame, IN: University of Notre Dame Press, 2014.

———. "The Same Sex Marriage Debate: Matters Arising." In *Families*, edited by Susan A. Ross, Lisa Cahill, Erik Borgman, and Sarojini Nadar, 126–33. London: SCM, 2016.

Okholm, Dennis. *Dangerous Passions, Deadly Sins: Learning from the Psychology of the Ancient Monks*. Grand Rapids, MI: Brazos, 2014.

Origen. *Homilies on Luke*. Translated by Joseph T. Lienhard, S.J. Washington, DC: Catholic University of America Press, 1996.

Osborne, Thomas M., Jr. "What Is at Stake in the Question of Whether Someone Can Possess the Natural Moral Virtues without Charity?" In Goris and Schoot, *Virtuous Life*, 117–30.

Ouellet, Mark. *Mystery and Sacrament of Love: A Theology of Marriage and the Family for the New Evangelization*. Translated by Michelle K. Borras and Adrian J. Walker. Grand Rapids, MI: Eerdmans, 2015.

Overmyer, Sheryl. "Exalting the Meek Virtue of Humility in Aquinas." *Heythrop Journal* 56 (2015): 650–62.

Pecknold, C. C. Foreword to McInerney, *Greatness of Humility*, vii–ix.

Pennington, Jonathan T. *The Sermon on the Mount and Human Flourishing: A Theological Commentary*. Grand Rapids, MI: Baker Academic, 2017.

Perez-Lopez, Angel. *Procreation and the Spousal Meaning of the Body: A Thomistic Argument Grounded in Vatican II*. Eugene, OR: Pickwick, 2017.

Perrin, Joseph-Marie, O.P. *La virginité chrétienne*. Paris: Desclée de Brouwer, 1955.

Perrin, Nicholas. *Jesus the Temple*. Grand Rapids, MI: Baker Academic, 2010.

Petri, Thomas, O.P. *Aquinas and the Theology of the Body: The Thomistic Foundations of John Paul II's Anthropology*. Washington, DC: Catholic University of America Press, 2016.

Pfau, Thomas. *Minding the Modern: Human Agency, Intellectual Traditions, and Responsible Knowledge*. Notre Dame, IN: University of Notre Dame Press, 2013.

Philpott, Daniel. *Just and Unjust Peace: An Ethic of Political Reconciliation*. Oxford: Oxford University Press, 2012.

Pico della Mirandola, Giovanni. "Oration on the Dignity of Man." In *The Renaissance Philosophy of Man*, edited by E. Cassirer and P. Kristeller, 223–54. Chicago: University of Chicago Press, 1949.

Pieper, Josef. *The Four Cardinal Virtues*. Translated by Daniel F. Coogan et al. Notre Dame, IN: University of Notre Dame Press, 1966.

———. *In Tune with the World: A Theory of Festivity*. Translated by Richard and Clara Winston. South Bend, IN: St. Augustine's Press, 1999.

Pinckaers, Servais, O.P. *Morality: The Catholic View*. Translated by Michael Sherwin, O.P. South Bend, IN: St. Augustine's Press, 2003.

———. *Passions and Virtue*. Translated by Benedict M. Guevin, O.S.B. Washington, DC: Catholic University of America Press, 2015.

———. *The Pinckaers Reader: Renewing Thomistic Moral Theology*. Edited by John Berkman and Craig Steven Titus. Washington, DC: Catholic University of America Press, 2005.

———. *The Pursuit of Happiness—God's Way: Living the Beatitudes*. Translated by Mary Thomas Noble, O.P. New York: Alba House, 1998.

———. "Reappropriating Aquinas's Account of the Passions." Translated by Craig Steven Titus. In *Pinckaers Reader*, 273–87.

———. "Scripture and the Renewal of Moral Theology." Translated by Mary Thomas Noble, O.P. In *Pinckaers Reader*, 46–63.

———. *The Sources of Christian Ethics*. Translated by Mary Thomas Noble, O.P. Washington, DC: Catholic University of America Press, 1995.

———. "The Sources of the Ethics of St. Thomas Aquinas." Translated by Mary Thomas Noble, O.P., with Michael Sherwin, O.P. In *Pinckaers Reader*, 3–25.

———. *The Spirituality of Martyrdom . . . to the Limits of Love*. Translated by Patrick M. Clark and Annie Hounsokou. Washington, DC: Catholic University of America Press, 2016.

Pinsent, Andrew. *Prudence, Justice, Courage, and Temperance: The Cardinal Virtues*. London: Catholic Truth Society, 2017.

———. *The Second-Person Perspective in Aquinas's Ethics: Virtues and Gifts*. New York: Routledge, 2012.

———. "Who's Afraid of the Infused Virtues? Dispositional Infusion, Human and Divine." In Goris and Schoot, *Virtuous Life*, 73–95.

Piper, John. *A Hunger for God: Desiring God through Fasting and Prayer*. Wheaton, IL: Crossway, 1997.

Pitre, Brant. *Jesus and the Jewish Roots of the Eucharist: Unlocking the Secrets of the Last Supper*. New York: Doubleday, 2011.

———. *Jesus and the Last Supper*. Grand Rapids, MI: Eerdmans, 2015.

———. *Jesus the Bridegroom: The Greatest Love Story Ever Told*. New York: Random House, 2014.

———. "Jesus, the Messianic Wedding Banquet, and the Restoration of Israel." *Letter & Spirit* 8 (2013): 35–54.

———. *Jesus, the Tribulation, and the End of Exile: Restoration Eschatology and the Origin of the Atonement*. Grand Rapids, MI: Baker Academic, 2005.

Plato. *Laws*. Translated by A. E. Taylor. In *The Collected Dialogues of Plato*, edited by Edith Hamilton and Huntington Cairns, 1226–1513. Princeton: Princeton University Press, 1961.

———. *Republic*. Translated by Paul Shorey. In *The Collected Dialogues of Plato*, edited by Edith Hamilton and Huntington Cairns, 576–844. Princeton: Princeton University Press, 1961.

Plé, Albert, O.P. *Chastity and the Affective Life*. Translated by Marie-Claude Thompson. New York: Herder and Herder, 1966.

Pohl, Christine. *Making Room: Recovering Hospitality as a Christian Tradition*. Grand Rapids, MI: Eerdmans, 1999.

Pope, Stephen J. *Human Evolution and Christian Ethics*. Cambridge: Cambridge University Press, 2007.

———. "The Magisterium's Arguments against 'Same-Sex Marriage': An Ethical Analysis and Critique." *Theological Studies* 65 (2004): 530–65.

———. "Reason and Natural Law." In Meilaender and Werpehowski, *Oxford Handbook of Theological Ethics*, 148–67.

———. "Scientific and Natural Law Analyses of Homosexuality." *Journal of Religious Ethics* 29 (2001): 89–126.

Porter, Jean. "Chastity as a Virtue." *Scottish Journal of Theology* 58 (2005): 285–301.

———. "The Natural Law and Innovative Forms of Marriage: A Reconsideration." *Journal of the Society of Christian Ethics* 30 (2010): 79–97.

———. *Nature as Reason: A Thomistic Theory of the Natural Law*. Grand Rapids, MI: Eerdmans, 2005.

———. "Right Reason and the Love of God: The Parameters of Aquinas' Moral Theology." In *The Theology of Thomas Aquinas*, edited by Rik Van Nieuwenhove and Joseph Wawrykow, 167–91. Notre Dame, IN: University of Notre Dame Press, 2005.

———. "Virtue and Sin: The Connection of the Virtues and the Case of the Flawed Saint." *Journal of Religion* 75 (1995): 521–39.

———. "Virtue Ethics in the Medieval Period." In Russell, *Cambridge Companion to Virtue Ethics*, 70–91.

Prevot, Andrew. *Thinking Prayer*. Notre Dame, IN: University of Notre Dame Press, 2015.

Prose, Francine. *Gluttony.* Oxford: Oxford University Press, 2003.
Pruett, Kyle D. *Fatherneed: Why Father Care Is as Essential as Mother Care for Your Child.* New York: Free Press, 2000.
Pruss, Alexander. "Christian Sexual Ethics and Teleological Organicity." *Thomist* 64 (2000): 71–100.
———. *One Body: An Essay in Christian Sexual Ethics.* Notre Dame, IN: University of Notre Dame Press, 2013.
Rahner, Karl, S.J. "Reflections on the Theology of Renunciation." In *Theological Investigations*, vol. 3, *The Theology of the Spiritual Life*, translated by Karl-H. Kruger and Boniface Kruger, 47–57. Baltimore: Helicon, 1967.
———. "The Theological Concept of Concupiscentia." In Karl Rahner, *Theological Investigations*, vol. 1, *God, Christ, Mary and Grace*, translated by Cornelius Ernst, O.P., 347–82. Baltimore: Helicon, 1961.
Ramage, Matthew J. *Dark Passages of the Bible: Engaging Scripture with Benedict XVI and Thomas Aquinas.* Washington, DC: Catholic University of America Press, 2013.
Ramírez, Santiago M., O.P. *De passionibus animae in I-II Summae Theologiae divi Thomae exposition (qq. xxii–xlviii).* Madrid: Instituto de Filosofía Luis Vives, 1973.
Ramos, Alice. "Studiositas and Curiositas." *Educational Horizons* 83 (2005): 272–81.
Rapoport, Chaim. *Judaism and Homosexuality: An Authentic Orthodox View.* With a Foreword by Jonathan Sacks. London: Valentine Mitchell, 2004.
Ratzinger, Joseph. "The Church's Teaching Authority—Faith—Morals." In *Principles of Christian Morality*, edited by Heinz Schürmann, Joseph Ratzinger, and Hans Urs von Balthasar, translated by Graham Harrison, 45–73. San Francisco: Ignatius Press, 1986.
——— [Pope Benedict XVI]. *Jesus of Nazareth: From the Baptism in the Jordan to the Transfiguration.* Translated by Adrian J. Walker. New York: Doubleday, 2007.
———. *Values in a Time of Upheaval.* Translated by Brian McNeil. San Francisco: Ignatius Press, 2006.
Ratzinger, Joseph, with Vittorio Messori. *The Ratzinger Report: An Exclusive Interview on the State of the Church.* Translated by Salvator Attanasio and Graham Harrison. San Francisco: Ignatius Press, 1985.
Regnerus, Mark. *Cheap Sex: The Transformation of Men, Marriage, and Monogamy.* Oxford: Oxford University Press, 2017.
Reichberg, Gregory M. "*Studiositas*, the Virtue of Attention." In *The Common Things: Essays on Thomism and Education*, edited by Daniel

McInerny, 143–52. Mishawaka, IN: American Maritain Association, 1999.
Reimers, Adrian J. *Hell and the Mercy of God*. Washington, DC: Catholic University of America Press, 2017.
———. *Truth about the Good: Moral Norms in the Thought of John Paul II*. Ave Maria, FL: Sapientia Press, 2011.
Reno, R. R. "Redemption and Ethics." In Meilaender and Werpehowski, *Oxford Handbook of Theological Ethics*, 25–40.
Richards, Norvin. "Is Humility a Virtue?" *American Philosophical Quarterly* 25 (1988): 253–59.
Riley, Patrick. *Civilising Sex: On Chastity and the Common Good*. Edinburgh: T&T Clark, 2000.
Rist, John M. *Real Ethics: Reconsidering the Foundations of Morality*. Cambridge: Cambridge University Press, 2002.
Roberts, Robert C. "Temperance." In Timpe and Boyd, *Virtues and Their Vices*, 93–111.
Rogers, Eugene F., Jr. *Sexuality and the Christian Body: Their Way into the Triune God*. Oxford: Blackwell, 1999.
Rorty, Amélie O. "*Akrasia* and Pleasure: *Nicomachean Ethics* Book 7." In *Essays on Aristotle's Ethics*, edited by Amélie Oksenberg Rorty, 267–84. Berkeley: University of California Press, 1980.
———. "The Place of Pleasure in Aristotle's Ethics." *Mind* 83 (1974): 481–97.
Rosenberg, Randall S. "Being-toward-a-Death-Transformed: Aquinas on the Naturalness and Unnaturalness of Human Death." *Angelicum* 83 (2006): 747–66.
Rosner, Brian S. *Paul, Scripture and Ethics: A Study of 1 Corinthians 5–7*. Leiden: Brill, 1994.
Rota, Michael. "The Moral Status of Anger: Thomas Aquinas and John Cassian." *American Catholic Philosophical Quarterly* 81 (2007): 395–418.
Rowe, C. Kavin. *One True Life: The Stoics and Early Christians as Rival Traditions*. New Haven: Yale University Press, 2016.
———. *World Upside Down: Reading Acts in the Graeco-Roman Age*. Oxford: Oxford University Press, 2009.
Rubio, Julie Hanlon. *A Christian Theology of Marriage and Family*. Mahwah, NJ: Paulist Press, 2003.
Rudebusch, George. *Socrates, Pleasure, and Value*. Oxford: Oxford University Press, 1999.
Russell, Daniel C., ed. *The Cambridge Companion to Virtue Ethics*. Cambridge: Cambridge University Press, 2013.

———. *Plato on Pleasure and the Good Life.* Oxford: Oxford University Press, 2005.

———. "Virtue Ethics, Happiness, and the Good Life." In Russell, *Cambridge Companion to Virtue Ethics*, 7–28.

Rziha, John. *The Christian Moral Life: Directions for the Journey to Happiness.* Notre Dame, IN: University of Notre Dame Press, 2017.

———. *Perfecting Human Actions: St. Thomas Aquinas on Human Participation in Eternal Law.* Washington, DC: Catholic University of America Press, 2009.

Sacks, Jonathan. *The Dignity of Difference: How to Avoid the Clash of Civilizations.* Rev. ed. London: Bloomsbury, 2003.

———. *Essays on Ethics: A Weekly Reading of the Jewish Bible.* New Milford, CT: Maggid Books, 2016.

———. *To Heal a Fractured World: The Ethics of Responsibility.* New York: Schocken Books, 2005.

Salzman, Todd A., and Michael G. Lawler. *The Sexual Person: Toward a Renewed Catholic Anthropology.* Washington, DC: Georgetown University Press, 2008.

Sandnes, Karl Olav. *Belly and Body in the Pauline Epistles.* Cambridge: Cambridge University Press, 2002.

Savage, Timothy B. *Power through Weakness: Paul's Understanding of the Christian Ministry in 2 Corinthians.* Cambridge: Cambridge University Press, 1996.

Schall, James V. *The Life of the Mind: On the Joys and Travails of Thinking.* Wilmington, DE: ISI Books, 2006.

Scheeben, Matthias Joseph. *The Mysteries of Christianity.* Translated by Cyril Vollert, S.J. St. Louis: B. Herder, 1946.

Schemenauer, Kevin. *Conjugal Love and Procreation: Dietrich von Hildebrand's Superabundant Integration.* Lanham, MD: Lexington Books, 2011.

Schillebeeckx, Edward, O.P. *Celibacy.* Translated by C. A. L. Jarrott. New York: Sheed and Ward, 1968.

Schimmel, Solomon. *The Seven Deadly Sins: Jewish, Christian, and Classical Reflections on Human Psychology.* Oxford: Oxford University Press, 1997.

Schindler, Jeanne Heffernan. "Catholic Social Thought and Environmental Ethics in a Global Context." In *Gathered for the Journey: Moral Theology in Catholic Perspective*, edited by David Matzko McCarthy and M. Therese Lysaught, 329–48. Grand Rapids, MI: Eerdmans, 2007.

Schmemann, Alexander. *The Eucharist: Sacrament of the Kingdom.* Crestwood, NY: St. Vladimir's Seminary Press, 2003.

———. *Great Lent: Journey to Pascha*. Rev. ed. Crestwood, NY: St. Vladimir's Seminary Press, 1974.
Schmitz, Kenneth L. *Person and Psyche*. Arlington, VA: Institute for the Psychological Sciences Press, 2009.
Schneiders, Sandra M. *Jesus Risen in Our Midst: Essays on the Resurrection of Jesus in the Fourth Gospel*. Collegeville, MN: Liturgical Press, 2013.
Schrage, Wolfgang. *The Ethics of the New Testament*. Translated by David E. Green. Philadelphia: Fortress, 1988.
Schueler, G. F. "Why Modesty Is a Virtue." *Ethics* 107 (1997): 467–85.
Schumacher, Michele M. "The Nature of Nature in Feminism, Old and New: From Dualism to Complementary Unity." In *Women in Christ: Toward a New Feminism*, edited by Michele M. Schumacher, 17–51. Grand Rapids, MI: Eerdmans, 2004.
Second Vatican Council. *Dei Verbum*. In Flannery, *Conciliar and Post Conciliar Documents*, 750–65.
———. *Gaudium et Spes*. In Tanner, *Trent to Vatican II*, 1069–1135.
———. *Lumen Gentium*. In Tanner, *Trent to Vatican II*, 849–900.
———. *Optatam Totius*. In Flannery, *Conciliar and Post Conciliar Documents*, 707–24.
Selin, Gary. *Priestly Celibacy: Theological Foundations*. Washington, DC: Catholic University of America Press, 2016.
Selling, Joseph A. *Reframing Catholic Theological Ethics*. Oxford: Oxford University Press, 2016.
Selling, Joseph A., and Jan Jans, eds. *The Splendor of Accuracy: An Examination of the Assertions Made by* Veritatis Splendor. Grand Rapids, MI: Eerdmans, 1994.
Seneca. *De clementia*. In *Moral Essays*, 1:356–447.
Seneca. *Moral Essays*. Vol. 1. Translated by John W. Basore. Cambridge, MA: Harvard University Press, 1928.
Sentis, Laurent. "La lumière dont nous faisons usage: La règle de la raison et la loi divine selon Thomas d'Aquin." *Revue des sciences philosophiques et théologiques* 79 (1995): 49–69.
Shaw, Teresa. *The Burden of the Flesh: Fasting and Sexuality in Early Christianity*. Minneapolis: Fortress, 1998.
Shea, William M. "An Agenda for Evangelicals and Catholics." *Pro Ecclesia* 26 (2017): 11–24.
Sheridan, Mark, O.S.B. *Language for God in Patristic Tradition: Wrestling with Biblical Anthropomorphism*. Downers Grove, IL: IVP Academic, 2015.
Sherman, Nancy. *Making a Necessity of Virtue: Aristotle and Kant on Virtue*. Cambridge: Cambridge University Press, 1997.

———. "Virtue and a Warrior's Anger." In *Working Virtue: Virtue Ethics and Contemporary Moral Problems*, edited by Rebecca L. Walker and Philip J. Ivanhoe, 251–77. Oxford: Oxford University Press, 2007.

Sherrard, Philip. *The Rape of Man and Nature: An Inquiry into the Origins and Consequences of Modern Science.* Ipswich: Golgonooza Press, 1987.

Sherwin, Michael S., O.P. "Happiness and Its Discontents." *Logos* 13 (2010): 35–59.

———. "Infused Virtue and the Effects of Acquired Vice: A Test Case for the Thomistic Theory of Infused Cardinal Virtues." *Thomist* 73 (2009): 29–52.

———. "St. Thomas and the Common Good: The Theological Perspective; An Invitation to Dialogue." *Angelicum* 70 (1993): 307–28.

Shields, Christopher. *Aristotle*. London: Routledge, 2007.

Shivanandan, Mary. *Crossing the Threshold of Love: A New Vision of Marriage in the Light of John Paul II's Anthropology*. Washington, DC: Catholic University of America Press, 1999.

Shklar, Judith. *Ordinary Vices*. Cambridge, MA: Harvard University Press, 1984.

Sider, J. Alexander. *To See History Doxologically: History and Holiness in John Howard Yoder's Ecclesiology*. Grand Rapids, MI: Eerdmans, 2011.

Smith, Janet E. "Conscious Parenthood." *Nova et Vetera* 6 (2008): 927–50.

———. *Humanae Vitae: A Generation Later*. Washington, DC: Catholic University of America Press, 1991.

———. *Self-Gift: Essays on* Humanae Vitae *and the Thought of John Paul II*. Steubenville, OH: Emmaus Academic, 2018.

———. "The Universality of Natural Law and the Irreducibility of Personalism." *Nova et Vetera* 11 (2013): 1129–47.

———, ed. *Why* Humanae Vitae *Is Still Right*. San Francisco: Ignatius Press, 2018.

———, ed. *Why* Humanae Vitae *Was Right: A Reader*. San Francisco: Ignatius Press, 1993.

Smith, Janet E., and Paul Check, eds. *Living the Truth in Love: Pastoral Approaches to Same-Sex Attraction*. San Francisco: Ignatius Press, 2015.

Smith, J. Warren. *The Lord's Prayer: Confessing the New Covenant*. Eugene, OR: Cascade, 2015.

Sommers, Mary Catherine. "Marriage Vows and 'Taking Up a New State.'" *Nova et Vetera* 7 (2009): 679–95.

Soskice, Janet. "The God of Creative Address: Creation, Christology and Ethics." In *The Image of God in an Image Driven Age: Explorations*

in *Theological Anthropology*, edited by Beth Felker Jones and Jeffrey W. Barbeau, 189–201. Downers Grove, IL: IVP Academic, 2016.
Spezzano, Daria. *The Glory of God's Grace: Deification according to St. Thomas Aquinas.* Ave Maria, FL: Sapientia Press, 2015.
Spohn, William C. *Go and Do Likewise: Jesus and Ethics.* New York: Continuum, 2007.
Statman, Daniel. "Modesty, Pride and Realistic Self-Assessment." *Philosophical Quarterly* 42 (1992): 420–38.
Strawn, Brent, ed. *The Bible and the Pursuit of Happiness: What the Old and New Testaments Teach Us about the Good Life.* Oxford: Oxford University Press, 2012.
Struthers, William C. *Wired for Intimacy: How Pornography Hijacks the Male Brain.* Downers Grove, IL: InterVarsity Press, 2009.
Stump, Eleonore. "Augustine on Free Will." In *The Cambridge Companion to Augustine*, edited by Eleonore Stump and Norman Kretzmann, 124–47. Cambridge: Cambridge University Press, 2002.
———. "The Non-Aristotelian Character of Aquinas's Ethics: Aquinas on the Passions." In *Faith, Rationality, and the Passions*, edited by Sarah Coakley, 91–106. Oxford: Blackwell, 2012.
Suarez-Nani, Tiziana. "Du goût et de la gourmandise selon Thomas d'Aquin." *Micrologus* 10 (2002): 313–34.
Tanner, Kathryn. "Eschatology and Ethics." In Meilaender and Werpehowski, *Oxford Handbook of Theological Ethics*, 41–56.
Tanner, Norman P., ed. *Trent to Vatican II.* Vol. 2 of *Decrees of the Ecumenical Councils.* Washington, DC: Georgetown University Press, 1990.
Tarasievitch, John. "Humility in the Light of St. Thomas." STD diss., University of Fribourg, 1935.
Taylor, Gabriele. *Deadly Vices.* Oxford: Oxford University Press, 2006.
———. *Pride, Shame, and Guilt: Emotions of Self-Assessment.* Oxford: Oxford University Press, 1985.
te Velde, Rudi. "How Charity Teaches Us to Be Prudent and Just: Thomas Aquinas on Charity as Source of Moral Virtues." In Goris and Schoot, *Virtuous Life*, 131–41.
Thatcher, Adrian. *Theology and Families.* Oxford: Blackwell, 2007.
Theokritoff, Elizabeth. *Living in God's Creation: Orthodox Perspectives on Ecology.* Crestwood, NY: St. Vladimir's Seminary Press, 2009.
Thomas, Matthew J. *Paul's "Works of the Law" in the Perspective of Second Century Reception.* Tübingen: Mohr Siebeck, 2018.
Thompson James W. Review of *Paul and the Faithfulness of God*, by N. T. Wright. *Restoration Quarterly* 56 [2014]: 245–51.

Thompson, Michael B. *Clothed with Christ: The Example and Teaching of Jesus in Romans 12.1–15.13*. Sheffield: Sheffield Academic, 1991.
Throntveit, Mark A. *Ezra-Nehemiah*. Louisville: Westminster John Knox, 1992.
Thurman, Robert A. F. *Anger*. Oxford: Oxford University Press, 2005.
Timpe, Kevin, and Craig A. Boyd, eds. *Virtues and Their Vices*. Oxford: Oxford University Press, 2014.
Titus, Craig Steven. "Moral Development and Connecting the Virtues: Aquinas, Porter, and the Flawed Saint." In Hütter and Levering, *Ressourcement Thomism*, 330–52.
———. *Resilience and the Virtue of Fortitude: Aquinas in Dialogue with the Psychosocial Sciences*. Washington, DC: Catholic University of America Press, 2006.
———. "Servais Pinckaers and the Renewal of Catholic Moral Theology." *Journal of Moral Theology* 1 (2012): 43–68.
Torchia, Joseph, O.P. *Restless Mind: Curiositas and the Scope of Inquiry in St. Augustine's Psychology*. Milwaukee: Marquette University Press, 2013.
Torrell, Jean-Pierre. *Spiritual Master*. Vol. 2 of *Saint Thomas Aquinas*. Washington, DC: Catholic University of America Press, 2003.
Trottmann, Christian. "Studiositas et superstitio dans la Somme de Théologie de Thomas d'Aquin, enjeux de la défiance à l'égard des 'sciences curieuses.'" In *Ratio et superstitio: Essays in Honor of Graziella Federici-Vescovini*, edited by G. Marchetti, O. Rignani, and V. Sorge, 137–54. Louvain-la-Neuve: Fidem, 2003.
Turner, Max. *Power from on High: The Spirit in Israel's Restoration and Witness in Luke-Acts*. Sheffield: Sheffield Academic, 2000.
Tushnet, Eve. *Gay and Catholic: Accepting My Sexuality, Finding My Community, Living My Faith*. Notre Dame, IN: Ave Maria Press, 2014.
Uhl, L. William. "The Virtue of Sobriety in Aquinas' *Summa Theologiae*." MA thesis, Washington, DC, School of Philosophy of the Catholic University of America, 1994.
Ulrich, Hans. *Wie Geschöpfe leben: Konturen evangelischer Ethik*. Münster: LIT, 2005.
Van De Walle, Bernie A. *Rethinking Holiness: A Theological Introduction*. Grand Rapids, MI: Baker Academic, 2017.
VanDrunen, David. *Divine Covenants and Moral Order: A Biblical Theology of Natural Law*. Grand Rapids, MI: Eerdmans, 2014.
Van Riel, Gerd. "Does a Perfect Activity Necessarily Yield Pleasure? An Evaluation of the Relation between Pleasure and Activity in Aristotle,

Nicomachean Ethics VII and X." *International Journal of Philosophical Studies* 7 (1999): 211–24.

———. *Pleasure and the Good Life: Plato, Aristotle, and the Neoplatonists.* Leiden: Brill, 2000.

Vargas Llosa, Mario. *Notes on the Death of Culture: Essays on Spectacle and Society.* Edited and translated by John King. New York: Farrar, Straus and Giroux, 2015.

Verhey, Allen. *The Great Reversal: Ethics and the New Testament.* Grand Rapids, MI: Eerdmans, 1984.

———. "Neither Devils nor Angels: Peace, Justice, and Defending the Innocent; A Response to Richard Hays." In Wagner, Rowe, and Grieb, *Word Leaps the Gap*, 599–625.

Verschuuren, Gerard M. *Aquinas and Modern Science: A New Synthesis of Faith and Reason.* Kettering, OH: Angelico Press, 2016.

Vijgen, Jörgen. "The Intelligibility of Aquinas' Account of Marriage as *Remedium Concupiscentiae* in His Commentary on 1 Corinthians 7, 1–9." In *Towards a Biblical Thomism: Thomas Aquinas and the Renewal of Biblical Theology*, edited by Piotr Roszak and Jörgen Vijgen, 219–41. Pamplona: EUNSA, 2018.

Volf, Miroslav. *Free of Charge: Giving and Forgiving in a Culture Stripped of Grace.* Grand Rapids, MI: Zondervan, 2005.

Volf, Miroslav, and Ryan McAnnally-Linz. *Public Faith in Action: How to Think Carefully, Engage Wisely, and Vote with Integrity.* Grand Rapids, MI: Brazos, 2016.

von Balthasar, Hans Urs. "Ephesians 5:21–33 and 'Humanae Vitae': A Meditation." In *Christian Married Love*, edited by Raymond Dennehy, 55–73. San Francisco: Ignatius Press, 1981.

———. *Explorations in Theology.* Vol. 1, *The Word Made Flesh.* Translated by A. V. Littledale with Alexander Dru. San Francisco: Ignatius Press, 1989.

———. *The Glory of the Lord: A Theological Aesthetics.* Vol. 1, *Seeing the Form.* Translated by Erasmo Leiva-Merikakis. San Francisco: Ignatius Press, 1982.

———. *Love Alone Is Credible.* Translated by D. C. Schindler. San Francisco: Ignatius Press, 2004.

———. *The Moment of Christian Witness.* Translated by Richard Beckley. San Francisco: Ignatius Press, 1994.

———. *Paul Struggles with His Congregation: The Pastoral Message of the Letters to the Corinthians.* Translated by Brigitte L. Bojarska. San Francisco: Ignatius Press, 1992.

———. *Theo-Logic: Theological Logical Theory.* Vol. 2, *Truth of God.* Translated by Adrian J. Walker. San Francisco: Ignatius Press, 2004.
Vonier, Anscar, O.S.B. *The Spirit and the Bride.* London: Burns, Oates, and Washbourne, 1935.
Vost, Kevin. *The Seven Deadly Sins: A Thomistic Guide to Vanquishing Vice and Sin.* Manchester, NH: Sophia Institute Press, 2015.
Waddell, Michael. "Integrating Beauty: Reflections on the Psychology, Ontology and Etiology of Thomas Aquinas's *Summa Theologiae* 1.5.4." *Saint Anselm Journal* 8 (2012): 1–18.
Wadell, Paul J. *The Primacy of Love: An Introduction to the Ethics of Thomas Aquinas.* Mahwah, NJ: Paulist Press, 1992.
Wagner, J. Ross, C. Kavin Rowe, and A. Katherine Grieb, eds. *The Word Leaps the Gap: Essays on Scripture and Theology in Honor of Richard B. Hays.* Grand Rapids, MI: Eerdmans, 2008.
Waldstein, Michael. "Children as the Common Good of Marriage." *Nova et Vetera* 7 (2009): 697–709.
Walker, Margaret Urban. *Moral Repair: Reconstructing Moral Relations after Wrongdoing.* Cambridge: Cambridge University Press, 2006.
Walton, John H. *The Lost World of Genesis One: Ancient Cosmology and the Origins Debate.* Downers Grove, IL: IVP Academic, 2009.
Webb, Stephen H. *Good Eating.* Grand Rapids, MI: Brazos, 2001.
Webster, John. *Barth's Ethics of Reconciliation.* Cambridge: Cambridge University Press, 1995.
———. "Curiosity." In *Domain of the Word*, 193–202.
———. "The Dignity of Creatures." In *God without Measure*, 2:29–47.
———. *The Domain of the Word: Scripture and Theological Reason.* London: T&T Clark International, 2012.
———. *God without Measure: Working Papers in Christian Theology.* Vol. 2, *Virtue and Intellect.* London: Bloomsbury, 2016.
———. *Holiness.* Grand Rapids, MI: Eerdmans, 2003.
———. "'Where Christ Is': Christology and Ethics." In *God without Measure*, 2:5–27.
Weil, Simone. *Waiting for God.* Translated by Emma Craufurd. New York: G. P. Putnam's Sons, 1951.
Weithman, Paul J. "Thomistic Pride and Liberal Vice." *Thomist* 60 (1996): 241–74.
Welch, Lawrence J. "Christ, the Moral Law, and the Teaching Authority of the Magisterium." *Irish Theological Quarterly* 64 (1999): 16–28.
———. "Faith and Reason: The Unity of the Moral Law in Christ." *Irish Theological Quarterly* 66 (2001): 249–58.

Wendel, Susan J., and David M. Miller, eds. *Torah Ethics and Early Christian Identity*. Grand Rapids, MI: Eerdmans, 2016.
Wesley, John. *Works of John Wesley*. Grand Rapids, MI: Zondervan, 1958.
West, Traci C. *Disruptive Christian Ethics: When Racism and Women's Lives Matter*. Louisville: Westminster John Knox, 2006.
Westberg, Daniel A. *Renewing Moral Theology: Christian Ethics as Action, Character and Grace*. Downers Grove, IL: IVP Academic, 2015.
Westfall, Cynthia Long. *Paul and Gender: Reclaiming the Apostle's Vision for Men and Women in Christ*. Grand Rapids, MI: Baker Academic, 2016.
Wheeler-Reed, David. *Regulating Sex in the Roman Empire: Ideology, the Bible, and the Early Christians*. New Haven: Yale University Press, 2017.
Whidden, David L. *Christ the Light: The Theology of Light and Illumination in Thomas Aquinas*. Minneapolis: Fortress, 2014.
White, Kevin. "Pleasure, a Supervenient End." In *Aquinas and the "Nicomachean Ethics,"* edited by Tobias Hoffmann, Jörn Müllet, and Matthias Perkams, 220–38. Cambridge: Cambridge University Press, 2013.
Wiley, Tatha. "*Humanae Vitae*, Sexual Ethics, and the Roman Catholic Church." In Kamitsuka, *Embrace of Eros*, 99–114.
Wilkins, John M., and Shaun Hill. *Food in the Ancient World*. Oxford: Blackwell, 2006.
Willard, Dallas. *The Spirit of the Disciplines: Understanding How God Changes Lives*. San Francisco: HarperSanFrancisco, 1991.
Williams, Cornelius, O.P. "The Hedonism of Aquinas." *Thomist* 38 (1974): 257–90.
Williams, Rowan. *Being Disciples: Essentials of Christian Life*. Grand Rapids, MI: Eerdmans, 2016.
———. *Dostoevsky: Language, Faith, and Fiction*. Waco, TX: Baylor University Press, 2008.
———. "Resurrection and Peace: More on New Testament Ethics." In *On Christian Theology*, 265–75. Oxford: Blackwell, 2000.
Wilshire, Bruce. *Wild Hunger: The Primal Roots of Modern Addiction*. Lanham, MD: Rowman & Littlefield, 1998.
Wilson, Bill. *Alcoholics Anonymous: The Story of How Many Thousands of Men and Women Have Recovered from Alcoholism*. 3rd ed. New York: Alcoholics Anonymous Press, 1976.
Wilson, Gary. *Your Brain on Porn: Internet Pornography and the Emerging Science of Addiction*. Margate, Kent: Commonwealth Publishing, 2014.

Wippel, John F. *Metaphysical Themes in Thomas Aquinas II*. Washington, DC: Catholic University of America Press, 2007.

———. "Platonism and Aristotelianism in Aquinas." In *Metaphysical Themes in Thomas Aquinas II*, 272–89.

Wirzba, Norman, ed. *The Essential Agrarian Reader: The Future of Culture, Community, and the Land*. Lexington: University Press of Kentucky, 2003.

———. *Food and Faith: A Theology of Eating*. Cambridge: Cambridge University Press, 2011.

Witherington, Ben, III. *Making a Meal of It: Rethinking the Theology of the Lord's Supper*. Waco, TX: Baylor University Press, 2007.

Wojtyła, Karol. "The Anthropological Vision of *Humanae Vitae*." Translated by William E. May. *Nova et Vetera* 7 (2009): 731–50.

———. *Love and Responsibility*. Translated by H. T. Willetts. New York: Farrar, Straus and Giroux, 1981.

Wolfe, Gregory. *Beauty Will Save the World: Recovering the Human in an Ideological Age*. Wilmington, DE: ISI Books, 2011.

Wolterstorff, Nicholas. *Justice in Love*. Grand Rapids, MI: Eerdmans, 2011.

Wright, Christopher J. H. *Cultivating the Fruit of the Spirit: Growing in Christlikeness*. Downers Grove, IL: IVP Academic, 2017.

Wright, N. T. *After You Believe: Why Christian Character Matters*. New York: HarperCollins, 2010.

———. "Apocalyptic and the Sudden Fulfillment of Divine Promise." In *Paul and the Apocalyptic Imagination*, edited by Ben C. Blackwell, John K. Goodrich, and Jason Maston, 111–34. Minneapolis: Fortress, 2016.

———. *The Day the Revolution Began: Reconsidering the Meaning of Jesus's Crucifixion*. New York: HarperCollins, 2016.

———. *The Epistles of Paul to the Colossians and to Philemon: An Introduction and Commentary*. Grand Rapids, MI: Eerdmans, 1986.

———. "Faith, Virtue, Justification, and the Journey to Freedom." In Wagner, Rowe, and Grieb, *Word Leaps the Gap*, 472–97.

———. *Jesus and the Victory of God*. Minneapolis: Fortress, 1996.

———. *The Last Word: Beyond the Bible Wars to a New Understanding of the Authority of Scripture*. New York: HarperCollins, 2005.

———. "The Letter to the Romans." In *The New Interpreter's Bible*, edited by Leander E. Keck, 10:393–770. Nashville: Abingdon, 2002.

———. *The New Testament and the People of God*. Minneapolis: Fortress, 1992.

———. *Paul and the Faithfulness of God*. Minneapolis: Fortress, 2013.

———. "Virtue in Action: The Royal Priesthood." In *After You Believe*, 219–55.
Wyschogrod, Edith. *Saints and Postmodernism: Revisioning Moral Philosophy*. Chicago: University of Chicago Press, 1990.
Yartz, Frank. "Order and Right Reason in Aquinas's Ethics." *Mediaeval Studies* 37 (1975): 407–18.
Yoder, John Howard. *The Politics of Jesus: Vicit Agnus Noster*. 2nd ed. Grand Rapids, MI: Eerdmans, 1995.
———. *The Royal Priesthood: Essays Ecclesiological and Ecumenical*. Edited by Michael Cartwright. Grand Rapids, MI: Eerdmans, 1994.
Ziegler, Philip G. *The Apocalyptic Turn and the Future of Christian Theology*. Grand Rapids, MI: Baker Academic, 2018.
Zimmermann, Nigel. *Facing the Other: John Paul II, Levinas, and the Body*. Eugene, OR: Cascade, 2015.

INDEX

abstinence, vii, 6, 8, 21, 28, 30, 51–78, 178, 191n40, 225n80, 257n107, 259n124, 262n142, 286n67
Adam, and Eve, 8, 91, 94, 129, 131, 133, 146–51, 239–40n3, 264n3, 327n39, 337n121, 338–39n138
addiction, 18, 61, 67, 75, 76, 253n74, 254n79, 261n138, 261n140–41, 262n142, 267–68n9
adopted children in Christ, 143
adoptive sonship, 136
adultery, 2, 11, 40, 81, 83, 85, 86, 89, 98, 101, 104, 157, 174, 195n55, 264–65n3, 275–76n42, 284–85n64, 289n75, 299n110, 306n116, 314n17
agrarian calendar, 229n11
agrarian life, 346n44
Albert the Great, 7, 202n83, 234n62
alcohol, 4, 18, 72–76, 158, 192n46, 260nn136–37, 262n142, 355n21
    Alcoholics Anonymous, 75, 76, 262
    alcoholism, 61, 75, 267–68n9
Allison, Dale C., Jr., 113, 125, 289n75
almsgiving, 37, 60, 230–31n29, 246n39, 255n96
Ambrose, 43, 199n67, 202n83, 251–52n70

Angelic Warfare Confraternity, 291n81
angels and angelic creatures, 40, 95, 112, 338–39n138
anger, 15, 29, 73, 107, 108–10, 115–22, 124, 127, 174, 175, 178, 179, 192n46, 195n57, 204n88, 225–26n80, 312n9, 313nn11–13, 317n33, 317–18n45, 318n56, 319n75, 319n78, 319n80, 320nn86–87, 335n105
    angry behavior, 313n13
    irrational anger, 107, 109, 119, 120, 124, 126, 127, 178, 195n57
animal flesh, 66
animal products, 66
Annas, Julia, 132
annulment, 221n65
anoint, 55, 59, 174, 255
Anselm of Canterbury, 259n109
Anselm's seven degrees of humility, 144, 333n96
anthropological optimism, 186
anthropology, 217–18n53, 245n35, 251n70
    philosophical, 210n23
    theological, 198–99n65
apocalyptic action, 114
apocalyptic theologians, 1

apostasy, 36
apostles, 141
appetite, 3, 6, 10, 13, 17, 27, 57, 59, 61, 63, 77, 155, 160, 161, 166, 178, 185n19, 188n31, 191–92n43, 201–2n76, 235n73, 236n74, 240n8, 247n51, 248–49n62, 253n75, 254–55n88, 257n107, 270n13, 282–83n58, 298n108, 301n120, 319n75, 322n7, 329n59, 330n68, 332n78
   carnal, 149
   concupiscible, 27, 47, 97, 184n14, 188n31, 237n82
   intellectual, 44, 165, 166
   irascible, 184n14, 322n7
   lower, 47, 270n13
   natural, 235n73
   physical, 248–49n62
   rational appetite (rational *appetitus*), 188n31, 204n91, 256n98, 282–83n58
   sense/sensitive, 120, 188n31, 204n88, 224n74, 256n98, 325n22
Aristotle, 13, 29, 118, 130, 175, 189–90n37, 191–92n43, 193–94n47, 197n63, 198n65, 199n66, 200n69, 201n73, 201nn75–76, 202n83, 218n55, 226n85, 227n1, 230n20, 231n32, 234n64, 290n77, 317n33, 317n45, 322n7, 341n9, 353n9
arrogance, 35, 168, 279–80n48
ascension, 7, 20, 25, 129, 218–19n56
   ascending in glory, 2
asceticism, 4, 65, 67, 77, 108, 211, 212n33, 246n39, 249–50n66, 251–52n70, 254nn79–80, 259n124, 312n9, 334n102, 337n111, 347n45
Assyrians, 54, 229

atheism, 185–86n25
Atkinson, Joseph, 82
Augustine, 18, 23, 45, 64, 65, 66, 68, 89, 108, 119, 122, 130, 131, 138, 145, 155, 159, 160, 162, 169, 170, 176, 177, 203n86, 251–52n70, 259–60n135, 261n140, 271n17, 280n49, 283n59, 323–24n12, 324n15, 326n24, 336n108, 342n17, 343n19, 346n44, 348n46
Aumann, Jordan, O.P., 195n54
Austin, Nicholas, S.J., 196n58, 215–16n48, 217n51
autonomy, 145, 146, 193, 326n24

Babylon/Babylonians, 32, 33, 54, 115
Bachelard, Sarah, 218n56
banquet, 55, 57, 239–40n3, 242–43n18, 337n121
   messianic banquet, 37, 60, 65
   pagan banquets, 57
   wedding banquet, 54
baptism, 22, 87, 102, 215n48, 217n51, 272n25
Barclay, John M. G., 26, 198n65, 220n62
Barnes, Corey L., 296
Barron, Robert, 181n5
Barth, Karl, 195n57, 196n61, 327n36
Barton, John, 107, 108, 311nn2–3
Bash, Anthony, 323n11
Bauerschmidt, Frederick Christian, 11, 28
Beale, G. K., 48, 238n87
Beatitudes, 2, 9, 18, 23, 131, 173, 193n47, 353n9
beauty, 4, 10, 14, 29, 32, 35, 36, 38, 44, 45, 95, 97, 107, 111, 148, 157, 162, 163, 178, 228–29n7, 230n20,

Index   409

231n32, 234–35n66, 235n73,
  236n74, 236n77, 251n70, 285n65,
  294n87
beauty of temperance, 30, 38, 39,
  232n37
external beauty, 14, 36
interior beauty, 14, 35, 36, 37, 38,
  45, 49, 178
physical beauty, 44
spiritual beauty, 7–8, 32, 43, 44, 45,
  46, 47, 48, 228n7, 232n37,
  234–35n66, 235n71, 236n74,
  236n77
Bede, 68
bellies, 8, 13, 35, 37, 48, 56, 57, 58, 64,
  65, 76, 77, 150, 244n31, 245n35,
  257–58n107
Benedict, Barbara, 155
Benedict XVI, Pope, 52, 274n38,
  308n134
  Ratzinger, Joseph, 30, 206n8,
    208–9n12, 274n38, 308n134
Bernard, Jean-Paul, 47, 49
Bernard of Clairvaux (St. Bernard),
  108, 155, 333n98, 334n102,
  342n17
Berry, Wendell, 105, 345
bestiality, 123
biblical scholar(s), 1, 3, 5, 7, 8, 9, 22,
  26, 31, 52, 60, 65, 78, 79, 82, 103,
  107, 110, 113, 114, 129, 131,
  191n39, 264n3
biblical vision, 9
Blackburn, Simon, 308n136
blasphemy, 121, 122
Blenkinsopp, Joseph, 33, 229n11
blessedness, 96, 353n9
body of Christ, 18, 27, 37, 47, 56, 87,
  151, 173, 174, 207n9, 320–21n88
Bohineust, Hugues, O.S.B., 356n29
Bonaventure, 201n76–77, 224n74

Boswell, John, 279n48
Boyd, Craig, 142
bridegroom, 54, 67, 68, 113
Bridgett, Thomas Edward, 259n124
Brueggemann, Walter, 315n18,
  316n27
brutality, 123
Budziszewski, J., 93, 286n66, 287n70
Burridge, Richard A., 183n9, 209n18
Bushlack, Thomas J., 233n50
Butler, Sara, 294n88

Cahall, Perry J., 286n69
Cahill, Lisa Sowle, 276–78n43,
  304–5n127
Cajetan, Cardinal, 228n7, 332n78
Calvin, John, 317n31
Campbell, Douglas A., 191n39
Canice, Father, 331n74, 332n93,
  333n98, 335n105
Cantalamessa, Raniero, 130, 292n83,
  294n88, 295n92, 322n6
capitula, 333n95
Carlson, Sebastian, 141
Carmichael, Calum, 264n3
carnality, 137
Castelli, Elizabeth, 315n25
casuistry, 184n12
Cates, Diana Fritz, 17, 204n88
Catholic Church, 104, 181n5,
  219n57, 221–22n65, 268n10,
  284n64, 292n83, 298n109,
  300n112, 339n144
causality, 225n76, 345n35
cause
  divine cause, 44
  formal causation, 258n110
  primary cause, 10
celibacy, 95, 102, 219n57, 287–88n70,
  292n83, 293n84, 301–2n125,
  335n107

Cessario, Romanus, O.P., 6, 188n31
Chapman, Gary, 313nn12–13, 314n17
Chaput, Charles, Archishop, 3, 4, 184n11, 185n24
charity, 5, 19, 23, 24, 27, 60, 71, 96, 117, 130, 134, 145, 175, 184n16, 185–86n25, 187n28, 203n86, 217n51, 222n67, 224n75, 232–33n40, 266–67n7, 288–89n73, 295–96n93, 303n126, 331n72, 333–34n101, 335n106, 337n117, 351–52n76, 352n87
chastity, 1, 6, 8, 22, 28, 30, 37, 64, 79–106, 130, 176, 178, 188–89n33, 212–13n37, 215n48, 225–26n80, 231nn31–32, 266n7, 267–68n9, 268n10, 292nn82–83, 294n88, 297n99, 298n108, 301–2n125, 303–4n126, 320–21n88, 355n23
  chastity belt, 80
  Christian chastity, 86, 105
  sexual chastity, 8, 65
Chenu, Marie-Dominique, O.P., 90, 224n74, 265–66n6, 326n24
Chereso, Cajetan, O.P., 32, 39, 46, 215n48, 228n7, 232n37, 234n66
children of God, 136, 151, 207n9
Childs, Brevard, 343n22
Christian Fathers, 199n67
Christianity, 4, 37, 187n30, 193n47, 257n107, 321n5, 332n78
Christian life, 8, 11, 16, 23, 26, 142, 178, 181n5, 183n9, 186n26, 192–93n46, 195n57, 211n27, 213n40, 232–33n40, 275–76n42, 294n88, 331n72
Christians, 3, 5, 11, 15, 20, 21, 24, 25, 26, 31, 38, 42, 48, 51, 52, 55, 57, 58, 69, 70, 73, 77, 84, 88, 95, 96, 100, 101, 102, 104, 120, 124, 138, 140, 145, 161, 162, 164, 173, 174, 176, 177, 193n47, 210n23, 214n46, 215n48, 230n20, 239–40n3, 243n19, 244n28, 249–50n66, 265–66n6, 275–76n42, 276–78n43, 279n48, 292n83, 301–2n125, 303–4n126, 305n128, 306n129, 320–21n88, 328n43, 330n64, 339n142, 354n15, 355n24
"Christological-eschatological frame," 12, 196n61
Chrysostom, John, 68, 282n57
Church Fathers, 259–60n135
Cicero, 7, 13, 14, 43, 175, 202n77, 202n83, 324n13
circumcision, 210n20, 244n28
Clark, Patrick, 218n55
clemency, 6, 8, 29, 30, 107, 108, 109–10, 114–17, 118–20, 123, 124, 125–26, 178, 222n67, 225–26n80, 251–52n70, 316n27, 317n31
clergy, 3, 74, 186n27, 259n124
clothing, 64, 158
Coakley, Sarah, 67, 253n78
Cogly, Zac, 317n33
cognitive process theory, 341n10
coition, 290n76
Colton, Randall G., 308n136
commandments, 2, 3, 11, 12, 20, 24, 70, 82, 83, 101, 166, 182n7, 210n20
  Decalogue, 11, 23, 85, 98, 264n3
communal eating, 53
community, 3, 18, 19, 29, 37, 41, 42, 55, 58, 59, 64, 75, 87, 88, 114, 120, 123, 126, 143, 174, 176, 186n26, 197n63, 210n20, 215n48, 218n56, 233n43, 241n13, 256n98, 282n57, 296n96, 310n144, 315n18, 323–24n12

Christian community, 74, 104, 183n9, 275n42, 276–78n43, 303–4n126
Comte-Sponville, André, 185–86n25
concupiscence, 66, 69, 74, 91, 256n98, 257n107, 282–83n58, 283n59
Congar, Yves, O.P., 24, 216n49
Congregation of the Doctrine of the Faith, 207n9, 288n72
conscience, 3, 26, 246n39, 291n81
consumerist images, 3
contemplation, 10, 66, 68, 69, 73, 95, 194n52, 340n3, 350n73, 351–52n76
  contemplative ascent, 66
  contemplatives, 69, 73
  contemplative spirit, 213n40
  eternal contemplation, 351–52n76
continence, 10, 13, 40, 189n32, 194n53, 196n58, 201n73
contraception, 184n15, 267n9, 269n11, 286n67
contraceptives, 295–96n93, 298n109, 306–7n131
conversion, 12, 86, 164, 167, 193, 208n12, 220–21n63, 240–41n8, 355n21
Cook, Christopher, 73, 75, 259–60n135, 261n140, 262n142
Council of Trent, 221–22n65
Countryman, L. William, 303n126
courage, 14, 46, 175, 198n64, 199n67, 200–201n72, 218n55, 318n56, 326n24
covenant, 20, 53, 110, 115, 129, 242–43n18, 269n11, 315n18, 316n28, 319n75
  marital covenant, 304n127
  new covenant, 20, 111, 166, 175, 210n20
Cowen, Shimon, 300n112

creation, 9, 11, 18, 19, 20, 22, 24, 26, 38, 44, 48, 49, 79, 80, 82, 85, 87, 95, 131, 133, 134, 135, 137, 146, 147, 153, 154, 163, 169, 171, 174, 175, 176, 198–99n65, 218–19n56, 226n85, 238n87, 243nn21–22, 263nn145–46, 264n3, 269n11, 295–96n93, 296n96, 316n27, 326n24, 349n56, 353n9
Creator, 20, 48, 88, 96, 134–37, 150, 157, 169, 259–60n135, 263n145, 280–81n51, 331n72, 337n117, 344n25, 345n35, 353n9
creature(s), 18, 46, 48, 91, 131, 133–37, 140, 141, 143, 146–50, 161–64, 167, 169, 171, 214n46, 222–23n67, 259–60n135, 320–21n88, 326n24, 327n36, 328n43, 328n51, 330n70, 337n115, 337n117, 338n138, 345n35, 346–47n44, 352n87
  rational creatures, 46,
  redeemed creature/creatureliness, 135, 136
creaturehood, 134, 138, 140, 143, 146, 147, 326–27n32
  relational creaturehood, 132, 138, 146–51, 326n24, 338–39n138, 342n17
creaturely ontology, 137
cross, 2, 7, 14, 15, 20, 25, 48, 56, 58, 114, 115, 117, 129, 133, 134, 141, 145, 149, 164, 174, 198n65, 202n84, 211n26, 214n46, 218–19n56, 244n28, 288n72, 315n25, 316n26, 335n107, 347n45, 351–52n76
crucifixion, 114, 129, 244n31
cruelty, 29, 107, 109, 123, 125, 325n87
Cuddeback, John A., 356n29
cultic purity, 37, 231n31

curiositas, 154, 156, 160, 161, 165, 168, 170, 178, 343n19, 346n44, 350n73, 351n75
curiosity, 132, 153–55, 159, 160, 164, 169–71, 341n10, 342n11, 342–43n17, 344n29
Curran, Charles, 307n132
customs, 196n58, 248n53, 298n108
  Greco-Roman customs, 4

Davies, W. D., 113, 125, 289n75
Davis, Ellen, 76, 103, 262n143
Day of Atonement, 241n12
death, 16, 19, 20, 46, 55, 60, 83, 85, 114, 124, 130, 131, 135, 149, 166, 183n9, 198n65, 218–19n56, 242n18, 247n49, 249n66, 262n143, 293n84, 308n134, 320n87, 326–27n32, 331n72, 338–39n138, 347–48n45, 351–52n76, 356n28
Decosimo, David, 203n86
defilement, 35, 38, 178
deification, 133, 147, 148, 259–60n135
De La Torre, Miguel A., 208n12
delectatio, 185n19
Delhaye, Philippe, 184n10
de Montfort, Louis-Marie Grignon, 334n103
Descartes, 204n91, 350n73
deSilva, David, 26, 48, 227n1, 228n4, 238n88
desire
  bodily desire(s), 47, 57, 64, 65, 130, 138, 149, 256n98
  intellectual desire, 165, 342n15, 350n63
  rational and sense desires, 15
despair, 22, 97, 158, 334n103

de Vogüé, Adalbert, O.S.B., 240–41n8
devotional life, 212n33
DeYoung, Rebecca Konyndyk, 17, 62, 64, 71, 72, 125, 126, 220n58, 248n59, 257n103, 313–14n13, 318n56, 319n75, 319n78, 319n80, 320n86
dignity, 99, 102, 122, 130, 137, 138, 150, 195n57, 280–81n51, 282n57, 285n65, 296n96, 306n129, 307n132, 328n51, 328n54, 340n5
disciple(s), 1, 2, 27, 34, 54, 55, 59, 60, 68, 113, 117, 125, 183n9, 192–93n46, 221–22n65, 226–27n85, 242n18, 246n39, 249–50n66, 343n19
discipleship, 18, 86, 103, 192–93n46, 230n29, 248n59
disgrace, 13, 32, 38, 39, 40, 42, 48, 228n4, 228–29n7, 232n37
disobedience, 147, 168, 326n32
disposition(s), 43, 47, 144, 177, 191–92n43, 217n51, 232n38, 266–67n7, 316n28, 336n108, 354n11, 355n21, 355nn24–25
divine bridegroom, 54
divine empowerment, 5, 186n26
divine names or attributes, 44
divorce, 21, 79, 84, 89, 221n65, 293n84, 297n99
doctrine, 27, 135, 154, 187n30, 198–99n65, 199n67, 217n50, 217n53, 218n55, 221–22n65, 258n110, 261n140, 273n34, 326n24, 354n15
Donati, Pierpaolo, 296n96
Drewermann, Eugen, 326–27n32
drink(s), 6, 13, 25, 29, 35, 38, 46, 48, 51–52, 54, 55–59, 61, 62, 68, 69, 71, 72–75, 76, 77–78, 96, 109,

Index 413

126, 130, 158, 175, 178,
    191–92n43, 201–2n76, 220n59,
    225–26n80, 235n73, 242–43n18,
    245n35, 251–52n70, 254–55n88,
    258n110, 259n124, 260n137,
    266–67n7, 329n59
drought, 53
drunkard(s), 36, 54, 57, 70, 105,
    355n21
drunkenness, 40, 49, 57, 58, 61, 69,
    72–77, 259n124, 259–60n135,
    260n137
dualism/dualist, 104, 256n98,
    265–66n6
Dulles, Avery, S.J., 207n9
Dunn, James, 110, 208n11
Dunnington, Kent, 75, 261nn140–41,
    262n142, 336n108
Duns Scotus, John, 215–16n48,
    354n11

eating, 13, 25, 46, 48, 51–59, 61–66,
    69, 70–73, 76–78, 96, 130, 178,
    191–92n43, 225n80, 239nn2–3,
    240n8, 242–43n18, 243nn21–22,
    245n35, 246n39, 246n45, 248n53,
    248n59, 249n66, 251–52n70,
    253n75, 254–55n88, 257n103,
    257n107, 263n145, 263n147,
    290n78
ecological movement, 239–40n3
Eden, 148, 149, 338–39n138
    Edenic human, 251–52n70
Edin, Kathryn, 267–68n9
Egypt, 76, 82, 245n35
Eleazar, 46
Elliot, David, 184n16
embryo adoption, 276–77n43
emotion(s), 6, 43, 188n31, 195n54,
    198n65, 200n69, 200–201n72,
    317–18n45, 319n75

end
    end of procreation, 98, 99, 102,
        103, 286n67, 298n109
    procreative end, 80, 92, 93, 94,
        265–66n6, 306n129
    teleological end, 92
    unitive ends, 80, 92, 93, 94,
        265–66n6, 306n129
English Reformation, 253n75
Epictetus, 323n12
eschatology
    eschatological attitude, 208–9n12
    eschatological beings, 5
    eschatological vision, 34, 68
essentialism, 265n6
eternal life, 130, 143, 149
ethics
    Aristotle's ethics, 189–90n37,
        201n75
    biblical ethics, 1, 226n85
    Christian ethics, 3, 14, 16, 22, 23,
        27, 81, 86, 88, 92, 178, 213n40,
        218–19n56, 273n31
    individualistic ethics, 220–21n63
    kingdom ethics, 190n38
    liberative ethics, 310n144
    New Testament ethics, 59, 246n39
    pagan ethics, 1
    proportionalist ethics, 181–82n5
    resurrection ethics, 218n56
    sexual ethics, 8, 81, 82, 84, 85, 86,
        87, 88, 89, 90, 206n8, 275n41,
        276–77n43, 280nn50–51, 284n64,
        321n5
    virtue ethics, 10, 24, 29, 184n15,
        189–90n37, 193–94n47, 208n12,
        214n46
Eucharist, 48, 52, 77, 163, 174,
    221n65, 275–76n42, 353n4
    banquet, 337n121
    body, 56

eating, 243n21, 263n145
Eucharistic table, 56
    kingdom, 174
    liturgy, 20, 48, 174
    meal, 56
    morality, 353n4
    restoration, 55, 242–43n18
eudaimonia, 222–23n67, 353n9
evangelization, 60
evolutionary development, 284n64
exegesis, 191n39, 273n34
exile(s), 33, 34, 54, 59, 110, 131, 158, 169, 171, 191n39, 208n11, 209n13, 229n15, 352n87
    Babylonian exile, 59, 111
exodus, 36, 53, 58, 76, 115, 129, 173, 245n35
    new exodus, 20, 55, 58, 86, 111, 230n19
exorcisms, 37
exterior conduct, 234n64

Fagerberg, David W., 4, 12, 95, 184, 356n28
faith, 4, 9, 12, 19, 20, 22–24, 27, 30, 63, 87, 88, 105, 107, 118, 142, 149, 175, 182n7, 187n30, 195n54, 201–2n76, 211n27, 214n46, 215n48, 216n49, 217n51, 244n28, 272n24, 276n43, 301–2n125, 308n134, 315n18, 329n58, 336n108, 337n115, 337n121, 347n45
fallen condition, 62, 80, 91, 119, 155, 166, 179, 181–82n5, 196–97n61
fallenness, 3, 26, 88, 150, 154, 282–83n58, 303n126
fallen state, 9, 70, 179, 248n52, 259–60n135
family, 2, 20, 27, 29, 52, 61, 64, 71, 75, 77, 78, 80–82, 84, 85, 90, 93, 94, 97, 101, 102, 105, 150, 178, 191–92n43, 223n70, 239–40n3, 263n147, 265n4, 272n24, 276–79n43, 280–81n51, 282n57, 286n67, 294n88, 299n111, 303n126, 305n128, 310n144, 321n5
    covenantal family, 4
    family-centered, 8
    family of God, 4, 8, 52, 67, 76, 80, 84, 85, 90, 102–4, 138, 220n58
Farley, Margaret, R.S.M., 81, 88–90, 104, 276–77n43, 279–80n48, 280nn50–51
fasting, 6, 8, 51–55, 59–61, 65–69, 71, 72, 76, 77, 174, 178, 203n86, 240–41n8, 241n12, 246n39, 246n45, 248–49n62, 249nn65–66, 250–51n67, 251–52n70, 253n75, 254n88, 255n96, 335n107, 356n28
Father, the, 2, 4, 26, 40, 42, 55, 57, 113, 129, 156, 173, 174, 223n72, 272n24, 312n5, 334n102
fear(s), 23, 24, 39, 40, 41, 42, 49, 57, 112, 119, 145, 168, 173, 178, 208n12, 214n41, 214n46, 216n49, 218–19n56, 232nn37–38, 233n43, 239n2, 247n49, 251–52n70, 295–96n93, 299n110, 303n126, 326–27n32, 333n101, 345n33
    fear of God, 35, 144, 333–34n101
    fear of reproach, 40, 41
    fear of the Lord, 23, 24, 49, 334n103
    filial fear, 333–34n101
feast(s), 13, 35, 52–55, 61, 77, 242n16, 254–55n88, 263n145
Fee, Gordon D., 244n28
Feldmeier, Reinhard, 131, 146, 323n12, 330n65

Index 415

Feser, Edward, 265n6, 286n69, 288–89n73
festivals, 53, 347n45
Fiala, Andrew, 275n41
fidelity, 4, 82, 110, 118, 192n46, 271n17, 303–4n126
fighting, 124, 125
first century, 48, 227n1, 242n16
Fisher, M. F. K., 254n88
flesh, 30, 35, 46–48, 60, 66, 67, 73, 74, 79, 82, 86, 91, 94, 102, 104, 149, 159, 160, 165, 166, 167, 170, 198n65, 211n25, 214n41, 245n35, 251–52n70, 256n98, 264n3, 265–66n6, 269n11, 295n92, 304n127
food(s), 3, 6, 13, 18, 25, 28, 29, 35, 38, 51, 52, 53, 55, 56, 57, 61–68, 70–72, 76–77, 109, 174–76, 191–92n43, 201–2n76, 210n20, 220n59, 234n56, 235n73, 236n79, 238–39n1, 239n2, 240n4, 240–41n8, 241n12, 243n22, 244n28, 245n35, 246n45, 248n59, 248–49n62, 251–52n70, 255n96, 257n107, 258n110, 262n143, 263n145, 263n147, 266–67n7, 290n78, 329n59, 337n121, 346n44
forgiveness, 7, 8, 11, 19–21, 29, 109–12, 114, 116, 118–27, 129, 130, 132–33, 137, 141–43, 149, 150–51, 154–56, 158–59, 164, 166, 169, 171–73, 178, 179, 181–82n5, 191nn39–40, 241n12, 275n42, 314n17, 315n18, 323n11, 328n54, 338n138, 349n58
fornication, 85, 86, 98–102, 297n103, 298n109, 301n116
fortitude, 184n14, 224n74, 225n80
Foster, Richard, 65
four "senses" of Scripture, 273n34

Francis, Pope, 4, 26, 99, 107, 176, 181n4, 185n18, 221–22n65
  Bergoglio, Jorge Mario, Cardinal, 4, 26, 99, 107, 176, 181n4, 185n18, 221n65
freedom(s), 5, 26, 36, 67, 89, 137, 143, 195n57, 206n2, 218–19n56, 220–21n63, 223n70, 231n32, 236n79, 253n74, 276–78n43, 310n144, 320–21n88, 326n24, 338–39n138, 354n11, 356n28
  Christian freedom, 67, 109
  spiritual freedom, 66
free love, 188–89n33, 306–7n131
friendship(s), 41, 42, 75, 85, 284n63, 295–96n93, 300n114, 320–21n88, 337n117
fruitio, 185n19
Fuchs, Joseph, S.J., 187n30
funeral oration, 199n67

Gagnon, Robert A.J., 279–80n48
Garland, David, 193n47
Garrigou-Lagrange, Réginald, O.P., 16, 132, 140, 215n48, 330n70, 331n72
Gentiles, 20, 52, 84, 100, 118, 126, 182n7
gift
  gifts of the Holy Spirit, 23, 24, 27, 104, 189–90n37, 198n65, 333–34n101
  spiritual gifts, 330n63
gluttony, 40, 56–58, 61, 64, 65, 69–72, 77, 147, 174, 225n80, 234n56, 239n3, 251–52n70, 257n103, 257–58n107, 258n110
God-centered, 8, 91, 95, 164, 214n46, 326n24
God's family, 2, 52, 82, 303n126
golden calf, 53, 115, 129, 245n35

Gombis, Timothy G., 5, 186n26
Gondreau, Paul, 284n64, 285n65, 288n73
good
　"honest" good, 45
　human goods, 8, 72, 248n53
　"pleasant" good, 45
　"useful" good, 45
　goodness, 4, 31, 38, 65, 82, 85, 95, 136, 147, 149, 156, 163, 168, 178, 191n42, 204–5n91, 206n8, 216n49, 249–50n66, 254–55n88, 269n11, 282nn57–58, 306n129, 329n58
　moral goodness,14, 38, 43, 276–77n43, 301n125, 306n129, 313n11
Gorman, Michael, 31, 114, 315n25, 316n26
Gospel, 4, 23, 25, 37, 52, 54, 60, 82, 90, 94, 112, 113, 142, 145, 166, 192–93n46, 206n2, 230nn28–29, 241n13, 273n27, 275n39, 288n72, 293n84, 294n88, 303n126, 312n5, 318n59, 323n12, 328n54
Grabowski, John S., 93, 103, 220–21n63, 266n7, 271nn15–16, 280n51, 283n59, 293n84
grace
　actual grace, 331n72
　divine grace, 76, 142, 198n65, 322n10
　grace of the Holy Spirit, 10, 11, 20, 26, 30, 48, 81, 93, 100, 105, 178, 181–82n5, 202n84, 203n86, 317n43
　habitual grace, 355–56n25
　sanctifying grace, 11, 27, 94, 203n86, 223n72, 291n81, 331n72
Greece, 89, 347n45
greed, 13, 57, 70, 105, 124, 146, 165, 179, 246n45, 326n32

Gregory of Nyssa, 40, 290n76
Gregory the Great, 70, 71, 75, 108, 120, 122, 138, 143, 312n9, 342n17
Griffiths, Paul J., 265–66n6
Grumett, David, 239–40n3, 253n75
Guardini, Romano, 211n26, 236n79
Gudorf, Christine E., 275n39, 275n41, 295–96n93, 299n11, 301–3n125
guilt, 39, 111, 116, 178, 355n25
Gushee, David B., 190n38, 289n75, 298n109, 306n129

habit(s), 18, 48, 57, 74, 164, 175, 177, 186, 196n58, 211n27, 217n51, 231n32, 254n79, 261n140, 263n147, 289n74, 334n102
habitus intemperantiae, 355n21
Hadjadj, Fabrice, 105, 211n25
Hägerland, Tobias, 110
happiness, 2, 23, 26, 28, 48, 169, 185n19, 193n47, 212–13n37, 222–23n67, 236n74, 258n110, 267–68n9, 309–10n142, 342n17, 351–52n76, 352n87, 353n9
　eternal happiness, 194n52, 326n24, 351–52n76
　perfect happiness, 185n19, 351n76
Harak, G. Simon, S.J., 204n91
Häring, Bernard, 1, 2, 205n94, 309n139
harmony, 13, 14, 32, 139, 142, 200–201n72, 202n84
Hauerwas, Stanley, 3, 26, 27, 176, 223n70, 354n15
Hays, Richard B., 183n9, 303n25, 316n26
healing(s), 6, 12, 16, 25, 26, 37, 88, 94, 116, 124, 142, 154, 171, 175, 178, 249–50n66, 291n81, 313n12, 355–56n25

health insurance, 63
Healy, Mary, 60, 65
heaven(s), 3, 16, 32, 37, 58, 78, 79, 95, 113, 131, 133, 139, 145, 157, 158, 166, 173, 186–87n27, 215n48, 238n87, 243n21, 249n66, 272n24, 310n144, 343n22, 351n76
   citizen of heaven, 58
Hebrew Bible, 89, 279nn47–48
hedonism, 59, 192n46
Heidegger, Martin, 153, 349n56
Hellenistic philosophy, 2, 279–80n48
Hellerman, Joseph, 84
Helminiak, Daniel A., 279n48
Henry VIII, 253n75
Herdt, Jennifer A., 224n75
hermeneutic(s), 168, 276n43, 304–5n127, 348n47
heterosexuals, 301–2n125, 303n126, 320–21n88
hierarchy, 186n27, 214n46
Hill, Wesley, 102, 303n126
holiness, 5, 11, 20, 21, 26, 34, 35, 42, 81, 96, 132, 156, 232–33n40, 249n66, 294n88, 317n43, 320–21n88, 330n70, 341n6, 356n28
Hollinger, Dennis P., 269n11
Holmes, Christopher R. J., 273n31
Holy Spirit, 2, 4, 5–8, 10–12, 18–28, 30, 32, 35, 37–40, 42, 45, 47, 48, 49, 62, 81, 82, 86, 87, 90, 93, 94, 96, 100, 104, 105, 109, 110, 112, 118, 119, 129, 130, 132, 135, 138, 145, 149, 151, 154–56, 175, 177, 178, 179, 181–82n5, 187n30, 189–90n37, 198n65, 202n84, 203n86, 207n9, 216n49, 220–21n63, 221–22n65, 223n72, 224n75, 225n76, 230n28, 236n79, 253n74, 273n27, 317n43, 332n83, 333n101, 342n15, 356n29

homesickness (for God), 248–49n62
homosexual(s), 105, 276–78n43, 303n126, 320–21n88
   couples, 57, 301–3n125
   desires, 102, 303n126
   homosexuality, 89, 279–80n48, 303–4n126, 306n129, 320–21n88
   inclinations, 93, 287–88n70, 303–4n126, 306n129, 320–21n88
   sexual acts, 83, 86, 102, 103, 266–67n7, 270n14, 276–78n43, 279–80n48, 280–81n51, 287n70, 301–3n125, 303–4n126, 305n128, 306n129
   unions, 287–88n70
honesty
   honestas, vii, 7, 8, 29, 30, 31–49, 177, 191n40, 202n83, 228n7, 232nn37–38, 232n40, 234n64, 236n74
   honestum, 14, 234n64, 235n71, 236n74
   honesty, 38, 45
hope(s), 5, 9, 11, 23, 27, 52, 54, 81, 96, 142, 161, 169, 175, 178, 179, 184n16, 191n39, 199n67, 204n88, 211n27, 217n51, 255n96, 322n7, 322n10, 325n22, 342n15, 344n25, 345n33, 353n9
Houser, R. E., 189n37, 199n67, 200–201n72
Humanae Vitae, 104, 285n65, 298n109, 307n132
human flourishing, xi, 9, 24, 80, 90, 91, 92, 100–102, 147, 148, 173, 188n31, 193n47, 206n8, 214n46, 220n58, 231n32, 303n126, 305n128
humanitas, 187n30
humanity, 6, 9, 11, 114, 138, 143, 147, 162, 163, 178, 179, 195n57, 198n65, 210n20, 210n23, 214n46,

humanity (*cont.*)
     222–23n67, 272n25, 274n38, 326–27n32
human will, 10, 261n140
Hume, David, 145, 160, 222n67, 298n108, 325n16
humility, vii, 6, 8, 22, 25, 28, 29, 30, 114, 118, 129–51, 175, 178, 191n40, 203n86, 212–13n37, 225–26n80, 231n32, 320n86, 322n7, 323–24n12, 324n13, 325n16, 325n22, 329nn59–61, 330nn62–65, 330n68, 331n72, 331n74, 332n78, 333n95, 333n98, 333–34n101, 334nn102–3, 335nn105–7, 336n108, 337n117
  false humility, 141
  twelve steps or degrees of humility (St. Benedict), 144
Hütter, Reinhard, 8, 94, 171
Huxley, Aldous, 265n5
hylomorphic, 15
hypocrisy, 45

idolatry, 32, 47, 58, 83, 84, 107, 132, 154, 245n35, 257n107, 321n5
idols, 20, 21, 35, 111, 271n17, 349n56
ignorance, 157, 159, 194n50, 259n129, 312n6, 320–21n88, 334n103, 345n33
image of God, 148, 198n65, 217n53, 264n3, 310n144, 328n51
  divine image, 82, 272n25
  "image-bearers," 79
  imagines dei, 161
immaterial elements, 15
immoral behavior, 157
immorality, 35, 37, 39, 84, 85, 135, 184n15
  sexual immorality, 184n15, 272n26
impatience, 65
impediment, 4

impurity, 47, 84, 85, 130, 135, 272n26
incarnate Word, 115, 273n31, 274n38
incarnation, 251n70, 275n42
incest, 75, 83, 89, 101, 301n122
incontinence, 25, 48, 201n73, 220n59, 297n99
indignation, 108, 115, 122, 317–18n45
indulgence, 56, 211n26, 220n58, 244n28, 248–49n62, 295n92
iniquity, 45, 111, 112, 116, 158
injustice(s), 108, 110, 121, 124, 126, 127, 183n9, 208n12, 230–31n29, 248–49n62, 265–66n6, 270n14, 276–79n43, 279–80n48, 303n126, 313nn12–13, 314–15n17
instinct(s), 14, 29, 347n45
integral parts, 6, 7, 29, 31, 32, 37, 38, 39, 40, 43, 47, 177, 228n7, 232n37
integrity, 7, 47, 161, 198n65, 234–35n66, 237n82, 251n70, 309n142, 326n24
  original human state of "integrity," 198n65
intellect, 6, 27, 142, 155, 171, 185n19, 204n91, 215n48
intellectual pride, 345n40
intellectual property, 345n34
intelligence, 157, 158, 326n24, 327n36
intention(s), 23, 60, 63, 75, 82, 87, 104, 113, 115, 181–82n5, 186n27, 265n5, 269n11, 289n75, 309n142, 343n19
interior rectitude, 234n64
intermittent explosive disorder (IED), 195n57
intrinsically evil, 309n142
Ishtar, 229n11
Isidore, 38, 43
Israel, 10, 11, 19, 32–33, 34, 36, 41, 44, 45, 47, 52–53, 54–55, 57, 59,

60, 64, 76, 77, 82, 83, 84, 86, 87, 97, 110, 111, 112, 115, 116, 129, 131, 156, 159, 171, 183n9, 208n11, 209n13, 210n19, 229n15, 241nn12–13, 242n16, 242n18, 244n28, 250–51n67, 259–60n135, 262n143, 314n17, 315n18, 316n27, 344n26, 353n9
  restoration of Israel, 34, 54, 55, 60, 86, 110, 111, 159, 241n13, 242n18
Israelite(s), 19, 36, 46, 110, 111, 115, 158, 311n2

Jeremiah, 53, 111, 115, 158, 169
Jerusalem, 33, 36, 44, 108, 111, 115, 243n19
  heavenly Jerusalem, 58
  new Jerusalem, 33, 37, 55, 243n19
Jewish people, the, 182n7
John of Damascus (Damascene), 39, 40, 232n38
John Paul II, Pope, 184n11, 220n63, 226–27n85, 282n57, 286n69, 297n99, 298n109, 308n134, 308n137
  Wojtyła, Karol, 188n33, 212n37, 282n57, 285n65, 297n99
Johnson, Luke Timothy, 129, 208–9n12, 320–21n88
Jones, Beth Felker, 82, 271n17
Jordan, Mark D., 293n84, 301–2n125
joy, 23, 25, 33, 44, 48, 60, 62, 65, 72, 79, 91, 95, 130, 196n58, 220n58, 240n8, 345n40, 351–52n76, 355n24
jubilee, 36
Judaism, 89, 113, 321n5
Judea, 54
judgment(s), 15, 56, 59, 67, 86, 91, 111, 113, 118, 119, 120, 121–22, 124, 126, 127, 161, 167, 174, 214n41, 225n80, 240–41n8, 243–44n22, 276–77n43, 289n74, 301–2n125, 309–10n142, 313n11, 318n56, 350n73
justice, 9, 14, 22, 23, 28, 46, 88, 109, 111, 117, 119, 121, 126, 129, 130, 142, 175, 184n16, 191–92n43, 198n64, 199n67, 200–201n72, 216n49, 230n20, 247n49, 255n96, 266–67n7, 280n51, 313–14n13, 318n56, 319n75, 319n80, 320n86, 325n22, 329n61
  social justice, 89, 265–66n6
just war, 181–82n5, 316n26, 354n15

Kane, W. H., 178, 179
Karamazov, Ivan, 186–87n27
Karen, Robert, 238n88
Kashdan, Todd, 154, 342n17
Kass, Leon R., 78
Katongole, Emmanuel, 304–5n127, 314–15n17
Keenan, James, 226n85
Kefalas, Maria, 267–68n9
Kennedy, Thomas, 154
Keys, Mary, 8
King, the, 20, 34, 44, 111, 112, 113, 132, 148, 166, 183n9, 312n5
King David, 83
  Davidic kingdom, 242n16
  Davidic kingship, 34, 54
kingdom
  consummation of the kingdom, 18, 57, 60, 66, 86, 95, 104, 138, 166, 173, 175, 183n9, 196n61, 328n43, 339n144
  heavenly kingdom, 55, 243n21
  inaugurated kingdom, 1, 2, 4, 5, 7, 9, 10, 14, 16, 17–30, 42, 47, 51, 58, 59, 60, 62, 63, 65, 67, 69, 74, 77, 82, 95, 110, 114, 116, 118, 119, 121, 124, 126, 132, 134, 136,

420 Index

kingdom (cont.)
    140, 142, 143, 151, 156, 166,
    168, 171, 172, 176, 179, 183n9,
    187n30, 191n39, 207n9,
    218–19n56, 226n85, 255n96
  kingdom of God, 1–3, 7, 11, 12, 16,
    18, 28–30, 55, 58, 59, 62, 63, 73,
    82, 94, 96, 100, 105, 113, 121,
    132, 133, 135, 140, 143, 151, 174,
    176, 183n9, 193n47, 226n85,
    227n87, 242n18, 284–85n64,
    312n5
  kingdom practices, 37, 60, 67, 77,
    255n96
King Hezekiah, 242n16
King of Tyre, 148
King Solomon, 83, 107
Knobel, Angela McKay, 215n48
knowledge, 9, 10, 22, 29, 40, 53, 90,
    131, 134, 147–48, 153–62,
    164–65, 167–72, 175, 179,
    185n19, 191n40, 194n50,
    225–26n80, 272n24, 275–76n42,
    320–21n88, 331n74, 333nn98–99,
    334n103, 336n108, 342n15,
    343n19, 344n26, 344n29, 345n33,
    345n40, 346n44, 347–48n45,
    350n63, 350n73
Kruschwitz, Robert, 70, 71,
    238–39n1, 258n110

laity, 3, 186–87n27, 259n124
Lamb, Matthew, 156
Lambot, Cyrille, O.S.B., 333n95
Lamoureux, Patricia, 5, 7, 9, 191n42,
    192n46
Laporte, Jean-Marc, S.J., 224n73
Last Supper, 55, 242n18
law
  canon law, 212n33
  divine law, 18, 137, 216n49
  eternal law, 92, 286n66

  food law(s), 57, 64, 70, 210n20,
    244n28
  law of gradualness, 220–21n63
  moral law, 182
  Mosaic law, 84, 182n7
  natural law, 8, 9, 66, 100, 212n33,
    217n53, 232–33n40, 259–60n135,
    271n15, 286n66, 288n73,
    307n132
  New Law, 23, 24, 27, 143, 317n43
Lawler, Michael G., 276n43
leaven, 53
legalism, 3, 4, 217n53
Levenson, Jon D., 182n7, 229n10,
    316n28
liberalism, 206–7n8
liberation, 191n39
  liberation theology, 208–9n12
  sexual "liberation," 48
libido, 145, 206n8, 240n8
Ling, Timothy J. M., 230n29
liturgical cycle, 54, 68
liturgical year, 52
liturgies, 53, 161, 162, 164, 174,
    347n45
Lombardo, Nicholas, O.P., 203n86
Lord, the, 11, 22–24, 32–34, 37, 41,
    44, 46, 49, 53–57, 59, 69, 74, 75,
    77, 78, 85, 95, 96, 104, 105, 111,
    112, 115, 118, 119, 123, 127,
    130, 131, 138, 139, 157, 158,
    159, 165–68, 172, 176, 183n9,
    186–87n27, 243n21, 288n72,
    299n110, 301–2n125, 330n70,
    334n103, 344n26, 354n15
Lot, 75, 82, 259n135
Loyer, Kenneth M., 223n72
lust, 5, 11, 15, 43, 48, 57, 65, 71, 74,
    82, 83, 85, 91, 93, 94, 96, 97, 101,
    103, 104, 130, 146, 150, 160, 170,
    174, 175, 176, 247n49, 249n66,
    266–67n7, 268n10, 272n26,

282–83n58, 289n75, 291n81, 298n107, 308n136, 322n6, 326n32
animal lust(s), 13, 46
sexual lust, 82, 85, 175
Luther, Martin, 259–60n135

Macaskill, Grant, 9, 193n47
Machiavelli, Niccolò, 125
MacIntyre, Alasdair, 130, 322n10, 340n5
Macrobius, 7
"mad-bellies," 13
Madden, Joshua, 269–70n12
magisterium, 222, 280–81n51, 301–2n125
Mahoney, John, S.J., 283n59
manna, 53, 55, 76, 241n11, 262n143
Mansini, Guy, O.S.B., 307n132
manuals, 212n33
Marion, Jean-Luc, 165, 346–47n44, 348n47
marital bond, 265–66n6
marriage, 21, 79, 80, 85, 89, 95, 98, 99, 100, 102, 103, 157, 178, 218n56, 221n65, 253n78, 255n96, 264n3, 265–66n6, 267n9, 268n10, 269nn11–12, 270n14, 271n17, 272n26, 276–79n43, 280–81n51, 282n57, 287n70, 288n72, 291n80, 292n83, 293n84, 294n88, 295n93, 296n96, 299nn110–11, 300n112, 300n114, 301n116, 301n120, 301–2n125, 304n127, 305n128, 306n129, 306n131, 310n144, 311n145, 320–21n88, 321n5
Martin, Dale B., 279n48
Mary, 69, 112, 138, 139, 163, 265–66n6, 330n62
masturbation, 89, 92, 93, 265–66n6, 269n11, 289nn74–75, 297n99
Matera, Frank J., 246n39

material goods, 13
Matta El-Maskeen (Matthew the Poor), 60, 246n41
Mattison, William C., III, 10, 108, 193–94n47, 194n52, 215n48, 246n39, 312n9
Maurer, Ernstpeter, 153
McAleer, G. J., 256n98
McAnnally-Linz, Ryan, 305n128
McCarthy, David Matzko, 275–76n42, 287n70
McCluskey, Colleen, 17, 104, 295–96n93, 300n114, 308n136
McGinn, Bernard, 10, 194n51
McInerney, Joseph, 145
McInerny, Ralph, 199n66, 350n73
McKnight, Scot, 65, 183n9, 240–41n8, 241n12, 248–49n62, 249–50n66, 250–51n67, 255n96
meals, 37, 178, 263nn146–47
medicine, 63
meditation, 14, 158, 246n39
Mediterranean culture, 31
meekness, 6, 8, 16, 25, 28, 29, 30, 107–27, 143, 174, 178, 191n40, 222n67, 225–26n80, 312n5, 317n45, 319n78, 320n86, 332n87
Meeks, Wayne A., 193n47
Melina, Livio, 174, 196–97n61, 226–27n85, 353n4
Méndez-Montoya, Angel F., 240n4, 337n121
mercilessness, 123
mercy, 16, 25, 41, 102, 105, 110, 112–13, 114, 115–16, 119, 123, 127, 157, 173, 174, 176, 179, 181nn4–5, 205n94, 220–21n63, 316n27, 317n31, 320n86, 334n103
Messiah, 20, 38, 76, 183n9, 209n13, 210n20, 272n25
messianic community, 19, 42

Milbank, John, 206n8
Miles, Margaret R., 251n70
mind(s), 14, 43, 46, 56, 63, 66, 70, 73, 74, 77, 86, 87, 88, 108, 111, 115, 118, 119, 122, 125, 132, 135, 138, 140, 149, 154, 156, 158, 159, 162, 164, 165–67, 168, 169, 170, 193–94n47, 231n32, 241n12, 245n35, 259n119, 265n6, 272n24, 313n11, 317n31, 328n51, 330n64, 349n58, 351nn75–76, 355n25
mind-altering drugs, 258n115
Miner, Robert, 185n19, 188n31, 282–83n58, 290n78, 312n9, 313n11
Mirandola, Giovanni Pico della, 137
mission, 55, 60, 87, 116, 133, 181–82n5, 183n9, 192–93n46, 230n28, 328n54
    temporal mission, 223n72
moderation, 6, 14, 15, 59, 71, 72, 107, 109, 116, 125, 141, 142, 188–89n33, 222n67, 228n7, 234n56, 236n77, 266–67n7, 329n59, 329n61, 341n9
modesty, 10, 194n53, 202n83, 292n83, 324n13, 329n61
monastic rule, 144, 259n124
monastic tradition, 131, 334n102
money, 21, 120, 211n26
Montaigne, Michel de, 126, 320n87
morality, 3, 4, 81, 103, 185–86n25, 187n30, 193–94n47, 198n65, 208n12, 267–68n9, 271n15, 271n20, 276–77n43, 284–85n64, 353n4
    Christian morality, 1, 22, 198n65, 353n4
    moralism, 3, 220n58
    moral judgmentalism, 105
    norms, 220–21n63

    ontology, 135, 327n36
    popular morality, 193n47
    project, 204–5n91
    systems, 184n10
    theology, 1, 5, 7, 10, 12, 17, 18, 19, 21–22, 23–24, 25, 27, 29, 59, 90, 173, 178, 189–90n37, 210n23, 212n33, 217n53, 226–27n85, 232–33n40, 266–67n7, 271n15, 283n59
    triumphalism, 16
Morrow, Maria C., 205n94
Moses, 53, 54, 83, 113, 115, 230n24
Mount Sinai, 53, 83
Muers, Rachel, 239n3, 253n75

nations, 11, 34, 76, 112, 139, 159, 181–82n5, 208n11, 242–43n18, 298n108, 316n27
natural family planning, 286n67
nature
    affective nature, 200n69
    creaturely nature, 136
    fallen nature, 12, 119, 175, 312n9
    human nature, 4, 9, 10, 12, 14, 15, 17, 18, 25, 100, 103, 119, 135, 140, 142, 161, 171, 173, 175, 176, 178, 187n30, 188n33, 190n38, 195n57, 196–97n61, 198–99n65, 202n84, 206n8, 210n23, 211n26, 216n49, 218n56, 226n85, 248n53, 253n74, 256n98, 265n6, 266n7, 280–81n51, 282n54, 284n64, 301n116, 328n45, 338–39n138, 342n17, 355n25
neighbors, 2, 46, 47, 48, 51, 52, 55, 56, 58, 63, 64, 65, 70–72, 73, 74–75, 76–77, 84, 93, 105, 108, 117, 121, 122, 126, 146, 159, 165, 177, 178, 186, 191–92n43, 195n56, 203n86, 235n73, 254–55n88, 264n3, 331n74, 349n59, 355n23

Nemesius, 40
neo-manualism, 226–27n85
new exodus, 20, 55, 58, 86, 111, 230n19
Newman, John Henry, 342n15
New Testament, 1, 2, 4, 7, 8, 9, 23, 29, 31, 54, 55, 59, 81, 84, 86, 87, 89, 90, 103, 104, 129, 131, 147, 166, 182n7, 193–94n47, 212n33, 218–19n56, 226n85, 267–68n9, 275n39, 276n43, 280–81n51, 293n84, 301–3n125, 316n26
Nietzsche, Friedrich, 145
nobility, 13
nominalism, 269–70n12
nominalist thinkers, 354n11

obedience, 19, 103, 130, 144, 147, 178, 294n88, 356n29
O'Donovan, Oliver, 206n2, 218–19n56, 269n12, 306n129
Odozor, Paulinus Ikechukwu, 92, 103, 304n127, 306–7n131
Okholm, Dennis, 80, 108, 109, 239n3, 312n9, 313n11, 337n115
Old Testament, 22, 57, 102, 117, 118, 166, 238n87, 242n16, 311n2, 316n27, 323n12
ontological relation, 134
operatio, 185n19
oppression, 59, 109, 114, 191n39, 303n126, 319n75
order
  "inner order," 49
  relational order, 109, 138
organs
  reproductive organs, 92, 93, 290n76
  sexual organs, 80, 92, 96, 97, 102, 103, 245n35
Origen, 138, 139, 251–52n70, 329–30n61

overeating, 71, 72
overindulgence, 257n107

Pabst, Adrian, 206–7n8, 265n5
pacifism, 316n26
pagan culture, 48, 272n26
paganism, 57
parable(s), 37, 113
participatory knowledge, 161
Pasch, 27, 174
passion(s), 4, 5, 6, 11, 13, 14, 15, 25, 35, 38, 39, 40, 45, 46, 47, 58, 80, 84, 96, 97, 109, 115, 116, 117, 120, 121–22, 124, 125, 126, 127, 135, 149, 162, 185n19, 188n31, 188–89n33, 202n83, 203n87, 204n88, 204n91, 225n80, 232n38, 233n50, 245n35, 247n49, 249–50n66, 254n88, 272n26, 282–83n58, 295n92, 297n99, 301n120, 312nn8–9, 313n11, 319n75, 322n7, 325n16, 325n22, 342n15, 347n45
  concupiscible passions, 14, 188n31, 188–89n33
  passiones animae, 188n31
Passover, 34, 53, 55, 230n19, 239–40n3, 242n16, 243n19
  lamb, 55
  meal, 34, 56
patience, 126, 144, 333n97
patriarchy, 276–78n43
Paul, 4, 5, 7, 8, 12, 16, 20, 22, 23, 26, 31, 32, 34, 35, 37, 39, 41, 42, 46, 47, 52, 55, 56, 57, 60, 62, 64, 69, 73, 74, 75, 84, 85, 86, 87, 89, 90, 98, 100, 102, 105, 109, 113, 114, 119, 120, 121, 122, 123, 124, 126, 129, 130, 131, 133, 135, 141, 149, 154, 166, 168, 171, 172, 177, 183n9, 191n39, 195n57, 198n65, 209n13, 209n18, 210n20, 220n62,

Paul (cont.)
   230n19, 230n28, 231n32, 237n80,
   240–41n8, 241n13, 243n21,
   244n28, 244n30, 245n35, 250n77,
   251–52n70, 264n3, 271n20,
   272n25, 284–85n64, 294n88,
   301–2n125, 315n25, 320n85,
   323n12, 344n23
Paul VI, Pope, 104, 285n65,
   298n109
Pecknold, Chad, 145
Pelagianism, 203n86
Pennington, Jonathan T., 9, 10, 23,
   24, 193n47, 214n46
Pentecost, 24, 27, 130, 142
people of God, 7, 20, 33, 52, 55,
   56–57, 58, 59, 61, 63, 66, 67, 76,
   77, 78, 84, 86, 106, 116, 119,
   122, 155, 173, 186n26, 191n39,
   209n13, 272n23, 274n38
   God's people, 8, 20, 29, 48, 52, 53,
      54, 56–57, 58, 59, 65, 80, 86, 98,
      100, 109, 154, 175, 178, 179,
      208n11, 238n87, 273n31
Perfectae Caritatis, 294n88
perfection, 6, 11, 24, 27, 39, 44, 74,
   96, 135, 138, 141, 144, 148,
   185n19, 228n7, 234–35n66,
   236n79, 238n88, 304–5n127,
   330n70, 332n78, 334n102
Perrin, Nicholas, 32, 36, 37, 230n24,
   230nn28–29
Persian king, 44
Pfau, Thomas, 168, 350n67
Pharisees, 3, 45, 113, 124
Philip the Chancellor, 7
Philo, 57, 245n35, 279–80n48
philosophers, 1, 8, 12, 13, 14, 17, 25,
   81, 93, 105, 116, 130, 132, 145,
   154, 160, 165, 169, 170, 197n63,
   227n1, 251–52n70, 279–80n48,
   300n112, 300n114, 317n33,
   323n12, 324n15, 329n61,
   336n108
   moral philosopher(s), 70, 218n56,
      245n35
   pagan philosophers, 9, 12, 23, 157,
      199n67
Philpott, Daniel, 314–15n17
Pieper, Joseph, 48, 237n85, 340n3,
   352n87
Pinckaers, Servais, 19, 22, 23, 131,
   173, 178, 184n12, 185n19,
   212n31, 213n40, 214n46, 217n50,
   217n53, 218–19n56, 226n85,
   356n29
Pinsent, Andrew, 15, 184n15, 189–
   90n37
Piper, John, 248–49n62
Pitre, Brant, 52, 55, 242n16, 242n18,
   243n19
Plato, 13, 175, 199n67, 200n69,
   200–201n72, 201n76, 245n35,
   301n120, 341n9
Plé, Albert, 15, 91, 94, 203n87,
   232n38, 290n77, 297n99
pleasure
   bodily pleasure(s), 6, 38, 47, 61, 62,
      69, 71, 248n52
   "food-pleasures," 51
   lustful pleasures, 96
   physical pleasure(s), 13, 28, 46, 62,
      69, 248n52
   pleasure seeking, 158
   sensual pleasure(s), 14, 74, 253n74
   sexual pleasure(s), 62, 80, 81, 94,
      97, 98, 103, 265–66n6,
      295–96n93, 308n136
   shameful pleasures, 220n59
political community, 256n98
poor, 36, 37, 49, 55, 59, 60, 67, 77,
   109, 125, 131, 216n49,
   222–23n67, 226–27n85,
   238–39n1, 248–49n62, 255n96

Pope, Stephen J., 284–85n64, 307n132
pornography, 21, 81, 93, 101, 211n25, 226n84, 297n99, 306–7n131, 320–21n88
Porter, Jean, 24, 29, 131, 202n77, 225n80, 266–67n7, 301–2n125
postmodernity, 342n11
potential part(s) (of temperance), 6, 7, 8, 109, 130, 165, 178, 202n83, 329n59
prayer(s), 57, 60, 69, 213n40, 246n39, 250–51n67, 275–76n42, 291n81, 347n45
preaching, 2, 166, 183n9, 240–41n8
prejudices, 4, 5
Prevot, Andrew, 356n28
priest(s), 21, 33, 37, 79, 174, 221–22n65, 259n124, 292n83
  royal priesthood, 20, 21, 36, 37, 79, 174, 211n26
procreation, 69, 89, 92, 93, 98, 99, 101, 102, 103, 264–65n3, 265n5, 269nn11–12, 276–78n43, 286n67, 287–88n70, 288–89n73, 295n93, 298n109, 301n120, 301–2n125, 306n129, 306–7n131
  procreative act, 269n11
  procreative end, 91, 92, 93, 94, 96, 102, 284n63, 286n69, 298n109, 306n129
promised land, 55, 173, 208n11
prophetic tradition, 211n26
prophetic visions, 32, 33
prophet(s), 36, 53, 59, 60, 65, 66, 68, 104, 110, 115, 131, 141, 156, 311n3
Prose, Francine, 77, 254–55n88, 257–58n107
prostitute(s), 57, 83, 84, 98, 272n26
Protestant, 186n26, 214n46, 250–51n67

prudence, 14, 175, 184n16, 185–86n25, 198n64, 199n67, 276–78n43, 282–83n58, 336n109
Pruett, Kyle D., 299n111
Pseudo-Dionysius (Dionysius), 44, 45
punishment, 83, 85, 107, 108, 115–21, 123, 125, 126, 131, 149, 299n110, 311n3, 313n10, 317n31, 317n33, 319n75, 338n132, 355n25
purity, 37, 38, 94, 179, 231n31, 249n66, 292n82
  cultic purity, 37, 231n31
  interior purity, 38, 179
  sexual purity, 231n31

radical dependency, 326n24
Rahner, Karl, 256–57n98
rape, 82, 83, 101, 279n48
rationality, 13, 47, 73, 198n65, 200n69, 204n91, 300n114
realism, 100
reality, 4, 8, 9, 19, 27, 34, 60, 93, 97, 101, 102, 107, 133, 134, 135, 136, 146, 151, 154, 155, 157, 161, 162, 163, 165, 169, 176, 186n26, 193–94n47, 206–7n8, 225n76, 242n18, 253n74, 290n77, 304–5n127, 310n144, 338n132, 340n3, 346–47n44
reason
  fallen reason, 9, 15
  human reason, 9, 100, 153, 259–60n135, 271n15, 307n132, 340–41n5, 342n15
  right reason, 8, 44, 64, 91, 94, 98, 100, 101, 145, 336n109
reconciliation, 102, 112, 120, 122, 138, 141, 154, 179, 181–82n5, 205n94, 243n22, 275n42, 314–15n17, 323n11, 328n54

redemption, 11, 16, 36, 54, 129, 131, 133, 135, 136, 143, 146, 147, 151, 153, 165, 183n9, 345n35, 347n45, 351–52n76
Regnerus, Mark, 80, 267–68n9
Reichberg, Gregory, 169, 341n9, 343n19, 350n63
reign of God, 5, 18
relationality, 134, 135, 149
religious movement, 183n9
remarried, 221n65
remedium concupiscentiae, 268n10
renewal, 4, 22, 23, 45, 135, 154, 166, 171, 179, 205n94
Reno, R. R., 4, 6, 187n30
repentance, 6, 16, 19, 25, 40, 41, 48, 53, 66, 86, 98, 102, 105, 111, 119, 130, 192–93n46, 241n12, 246n39, 249–50n66, 303–4n126, 314–15n17, 323n11
restoration
  cultic restoration, 242–43n18
  eschatological restoration, 7-9, 20, 29, 52, 54, 67, 76, 80, 82, 110, 111, 178, 241n13, 242n18, 303n126
  restoration of God's people, 8, 20, 29, 52, 54, 56, 57, 59, 65, 80, 100, 178
  restoration of the Land, 191n39
  restoration of the people of God, 7, 52
resurrection, 7, 15, 20, 25, 55, 84, 95, 129, 133, 149, 198n65, 218n56, 236n87, 249–50n66, 251n70, 264n3
  rising from the dead, 2
retribution, 121, 124, 317n33
revelation, 97, 100, 105, 164, 165, 187n30, 226–27n85, 320–21n88, 351–52n76

divine revelation, 21, 81, 82, 89, 100, 156, 165, 218n56, 221–22n65, 276–78n43
revelatory power, 218n56
revenge, 121, 122, 125, 317n33, 317–18n45
reverence, 23, 146, 156, 325n22, 332n78, 333–34n101
rigorism, 220n58, 280n50
Ritley, M. R., 303–4n126
Roberts, Robert C., 14, 25, 191–92n43, 201–2n76
Rowe, C. Kavin, 193n47, 245n37
Rudebusch, George, 200n69
Russell, Daniel C., 200n69, 222–23n67
Rziha, John, 100, 286n67, 301n115, 306n129

Sabbath, 33, 60, 124, 168, 246n39, 312n5, 352n111
Sacks, Jonathan, Rabbi, 26, 179, 220n58, 321n5
sacrifice, 28, 38, 61, 64, 104, 157, 174, 214n46, 223n70, 263n147, 294n88
sacrilege, 102
saint(s), 16, 63, 175, 177, 181–82n5, 249n66, 272n24, 322–23n10, 340n5, 356n28
Salamancan school of Thomism, 215–16n48
salvation, 16, 21, 27, 76, 90, 112, 127, 203n86, 208–9n12, 334n103, 337n115, 351–52n76
  history, 146, 239–40n3
Salzman, Todd A., 276–78n43, 280–81n51
same-sex
  attractions, 102
  couples, 270n14

Index   427

debate, 306–7n131
marriage, 253n78, 276–79n43, 300n112, 304–5n127, 306n131
relationships, 89, 279n47, 301–2n125
sexual acts, 92, 303–4n126, 320–21n88
sexual partnerships, 102
unions, 305n128, 307n132
sanctity, 108, 181n5, 218n56, 321n5
Sandnes, Karl Olav, 8, 52, 57, 58, 65, 244nn30–31, 245n35
Satan, 116, 147, 148, 338n138
savagery, 123
Schillebeeckx, Edward, O.P., 292n83
Schmemann, Alexander, 165, 243n21, 337n121
Schneiders, Sandra M., 326–27n32
school-masters (*magistri*), 199n67
scientia, 346n44
scribe(s), 3, 45, 46, 158
Scripture, 10, 21, 22, 24, 25, 29, 47, 52, 81, 82, 86, 87, 88, 89, 90, 98, 101, 107, 108, 120, 155, 156, 157, 159, 161, 162, 171, 173, 191–92n43, 198n64, 216n49, 218n56, 221–22n65, 253n78, 259–60n135, 271n15, 273n31, 273n34, 274n38, 275n39, 275–76n42, 276–78n43, 279–80n48, 280–81n51, 283n59, 303n126, 306n129, 314n17, 323n11, 329n61
Second Temple Judaism, 23, 32, 193–94n47
Second Vatican Council (Vatican II), 21, 23, 29, 89, 90, 103, 187n30, 294n88, 306–7n131
pre-Vatican II, 212n33
seduction, 3, 61, 101, 297n103
self-centeredness, 8, 51, 59, 63, 77, 178, 222–23n67
self-consciousness, 238n88
self-control, 5, 21, 37, 63, 196n58, 198n64, 211n26, 231n32, 235n73
self-denial, 146, 220n58, 248–49n62, 335n107
self-destruction, 237n85
self-esteem, 28, 141, 145, 313n13, 325n16
self-indulgence, 56, 211n26, 244n28, 248–49n62, 295n92
selfless service, 31
self-offering, 51, 61, 68, 243n21, 246n45
self-possession, 319n78
self-preservation, 76, 178, 237n85
self-protection, 43
self-respect, 7, 41, 130
self-responsibility, 137
self-restraint, 13, 263n147, 320n86
self-sacrifice, 214n46
self-satisfaction, 51
Selling, Joseph, 104, 309n142
Seneca, 116, 118, 160, 175, 231n32, 317n31, 317–18n45
sensible things, 162, 163, 164, 170
Sermon on the Mount, 2, 10, 18, 23, 24, 54, 112, 117, 124, 131, 166, 171, 173, 174, 175, 176, 190n38, 193–94n47, 212–13n37, 246n39
servant, 34, 47, 112, 113, 126, 337n117
sex, 3, 6, 13, 21, 25, 27, 29, 35, 38, 46, 48, 62, 64, 80, 82, 89, 96, 98, 102–3, 105, 109, 130, 157, 188–89n33, 191–92n43, 211nn25–26, 212–13n37, 220n59, 235n73, 251n70, 264–65n3, 265nn5–6, 266–67n7, 267–68n9, 269n11, 270n14, 271n17, 275n41,

sex (cont.)
    276–78n43, 279n48, 280nn49–50,
    285n65, 286n67, 287n70,
    292nn83–84, 295n93,
    298nn108–9, 301n115,
    301–2n125, 304–5n127, 305n128,
    306n129, 306–7n131,
    329n59
sexual activity, 80, 81, 91, 94,
    191–92n43, 201n76, 220–21n63,
    276–77n43, 280–81n51, 285n65,
    289n74, 295–96n93, 308n136
sexual desire, 4, 79, 85, 91, 94, 96, 97,
    99, 101, 103, 105, 188–89n33,
    220n58, 266–67n7, 282–83n58,
    283n59, 295n92
sexual holiness, 35
sexual intercourse, 84, 94, 95, 98, 99,
    101, 248n53, 264n3, 270n13,
    272n26, 276–79n43, 287–88n70,
    290n76, 295–96n93, 298n109,
    301n116
sexual intimacy, 80, 269n11
sexual morality, 4, 81, 103, 271n20,
    276–77n43
sexual orientation, 266–67n7
sexual partnerships, 80, 102,
    267–68n9, 276–78n43
sexual relationship(s), 101, 104,
    192n46, 276–78n43, 295–96n93,
    306n129
sexual revolution, 306–7n131,
    310n144
sexual unity, 308n136
shame, vii, 7, 9, 29, 31–49, 63, 75, 150,
    177, 191n40, 202n83, 225n80,
    228n4, 232n40, 233n43, 233n50,
    238n88
shamefacedness, 32, 38, 40, 41, 43,
    228n7, 232n37
Shaw, Teresa, 251–52n70

Shea, William M., 103, 308n134
Sherwin, Michael S., O.P., 177,
    196n58, 215n48, 217n50, 351n76,
    355n21, 355n24
sickness, 66, 293n84, 351n76
sin(s), 2, 5, 7, 8, 11–12, 16, 19–21, 26,
    29, 39–42, 49, 63, 65–66, 68,
    70–71, 74–77, 82, 84–86, 90, 96,
    98, 100, 107–16, 118–27, 129–34,
    137–38, 141–43, 146–51, 153–59,
    164, 166, 168–72, 174, 177–78,
    182–83n7, 191nn39–40,
    192–93n46, 196n58, 198n65,
    198–99n65, 208n12, 218–19n56,
    220n59, 233n50, 234n56, 237n82,
    239–40n3, 241n12, 244n31,
    254n88, 257n107, 261n140,
    266–67n7, 275n42, 279n48,
    289n75, 290n76, 297n103,
    299n110, 307n132, 313–14n13,
    314n17, 320n88, 322n10, 326n32,
    328n51, 328n54, 331n74, 332n76,
    333n99, 334n103, 337n121,
    338n138, 349n58, 351–52n76,
    355–56n25
    human sin(s), 108, 198n65
    mortal sin, 71, 121, 122, 217n51
    national sin, 107
    original sin, 11, 133, 146, 154, 176,
        177, 283n59, 291n81, 337n121,
        338n132, 355n25
    personal sin(s), 11, 355n25
    sexual sin(s), 86, 101, 103,
        266–67n7, 295n91
    venial sin, 121
sinner(s), 2, 11, 16, 26, 39–41, 48, 54,
    63, 66, 113, 115, 117–19, 139,
    147, 173, 174, 181n4, 186n27,
    313–14n13, 314n17, 332n76
sixth century BC, 33
Smith, Janet, 81

Index   429

Smith, J. Warren, 151, 339n142
sobriety, vii, 6, 8, 51–78, 178, 238
social order, 208n12, 267–68n9, 320n88
social structures, 208n12
Socrates, 13, 199n67, 218n55
Sodom, 82, 279–80n48
Solomon, 32, 83, 107
  Solomon's Temple, 32, 37
Son, 85, 113, 129, 133, 134, 147, 151, 156, 178, 186n27, 196–97n61, 223n72, 242–43n18
Son of Man, 31, 33, 40, 113, 242–43n18
soul(s), 13, 14, 15, 21, 24, 57, 66, 72, 73, 92, 105, 118, 119, 123, 130, 138, 149, 157, 160, 167, 176, 179, 200n72, 215n48, 217n51, 232n37, 241n12, 248n53, 248–49n62, 249–50n66, 254nn79–80, 256n98, 257n107, 263n147, 264n3, 271n17, 284n64, 285n65, 291n81, 298–99n109, 310n144, 320–21n88, 322n7, 329n61, 330–31n70, 332n87, 334n102, 337n117
sovereignty, 134, 183n9
spirit
  outpouring of the Spirit, 7, 8, 16, 19, 20, 21, 29, 123–27, 130, 133, 138, 141, 142, 150, 151, 154–56, 158, 159, 166, 169, 171, 172, 178, 191n40, 195n57, 207n9
  poor in spirit, 49, 131
spiritual "impetuosity," 144
Spohn, William C., 212n33, 275–76n42
starvation, 71, 238–39n1, 257n107
Stassen, Glen H., 190n38, 289n75, 306n129
state of innocence, 290n76, 338n138

St. Catherine of Siena, 72, 126, 249n66
St. Jerome, 251–52n70
Stoic(s), 7, 120, 193n47, 202n77, 313n11, 323n12
  Roman Stoicism, 88
stomach, 57, 73, 245n35, 248–49n62
studiositas, 160, 165, 343n19, 350n63
studiousness, 6, 8, 25, 28, 30, 153–72, 178, 191n40, 225–26n80, 340n5, 342n15, 344n29, 350–51n73
study, 8, 9, 14, 21, 47, 90, 108, 110, 151, 158, 159, 162, 163, 165, 167, 168–70, 190n38, 195n57, 207n9, 234–35n66, 258n115, 259–60n135, 279–80n48, 292n83, 317n33, 333n98, 340n5, 341n9
Stump, Eleonore, 189n37, 261n140
subjective parts (of temperance), 6, 8, 61, 178
suffering, 19, 37, 58, 211n26, 248n53, 251n70, 313n11, 351n76
  messianic sufferings, 230n28
  priestly suffering, 230n28
Supreme Good, 204n91
Susanna, 97
symbolic actions, 53

Talbot, Matthew, 196n58, 199n66, 355n21
talents, 141, 225–26n80, 331n72
Tammuz, 229n11
Tarasievitch, John, 150, 151, 334n102, 339n144
Taylor, Gabriele, 41, 130, 233n50
teleologism, 265n6
temperance movement, 4
temple(s), 7, 19, 20, 21, 23, 29, 31, 32–40, 42, 44–46, 47, 48–49, 54, 57, 60, 79, 82, 110, 120, 178, 182–83n7, 191nn39–40,

430 Index

temple(s) (*cont.*)
    193–94n47, 208n11, 229nn10–12, 230n19, 230n24, 230nn28–29, 235n73, 238n87, 241n13, 242n18, 243n19, 245n35, 318n59
    cleansing of the temple, 34, 230–31n29, 318n59
    eschatological temple, 36, 37, 38, 42, 229n12, 230n24, 230n28
    Ezekiel's temple, 33
    first temple, 32
    God's temple, 29, 34, 35, 39
    heavenly temple, 230n24
    messianic counter-temple movements, 37
    new temple, 35, 37
    rebuilding of the Temple, 33, 34, 191n39
    renewal of the temple/renewed temple, 7, 19, 20, 29, 31–35, 37–39, 44, 46, 47, 49, 178, 191n40
    Second Temple, 19, 32, 34, 36, 37, 54, 57, 110, 182–83n7, 193–94n47, 208n11, 241n13, 242n18
    sixth-century temple, 33
    temple of the Holy Spirit, 21, 32, 35, 38, 40, 47, 49, 178
temptation(s), 15, 54, 64, 85, 96, 144, 211n26, 239–40n3, 257n107, 261n140, 310n144, 338–39n138
te Velde, Rudi, 187n28
Thatcher, Adrian, 270n14
theologian(s), 1, 3, 4, 5, 6–7, 8, 10, 11, 15, 16, 17, 18, 22, 24, 51, 65, 80, 81, 82, 84, 92, 103, 104, 124, 130, 132, 145, 153, 155, 156, 169, 174, 176, 177, 178, 194n51, 210n23, 239–40n3, 240n4, 243n21, 257n107, 269n11, 271n15, 275n39, 276–77n43, 279n48, 354n11

theology, 1, 2, 4, 10, 12, 16, 17, 21, 23, 29, 39, 51, 53, 61, 66, 82, 86, 87, 90, 138, 146, 156, 161, 165, 174, 181n1, 183n9, 191n43, 198n65, 209n13, 210n23, 212n33, 213n40, 224n74, 226–27n85, 229n10, 249n65, 257–58n107, 275n39, 280n50, 291n80, 292n83, 323n12, 329n58, 329nn60–61, 356n28
    biblical theology, 139, 229n10
    liberation theology, 208–9n12
    liturgical theology, 174
    moral theology, 1, 5, 7, 10, 12, 17, 18, 19, 21–25, 27, 29, 59, 90, 173, 178, 189–90n37, 210n23, 212n33, 217n53, 226–27n85, 232–33n40, 266–67n7, 271n15, 283n59
Thompson, James W., 209n13
Thurman, Robert A. F., 313n11
Torah, 19, 20, 46, 53, 57, 60, 70, 110, 111, 116, 158, 210n20, 241n10, 241n12, 265n4, 321n5
Torchia, Joseph, 348n46
Torrell, Jean-Pierre, O.P., 22, 207n9
transfiguration, 116
transformation, 5, 19, 22, 24, 25, 27, 58, 110, 126, 129, 154, 168, 177, 208n12, 218n56
transcendental, 234–35n66, 236n74
tribulation, 36, 37, 54, 58, 111, 230n19
Trinitarian communion, 138
triumphalism, 16, 183n9
truth(s), 11, 25, 26, 27, 29, 37, 42, 86, 87, 88, 90, 103, 106, 118, 136, 145, 151, 153, 156, 157, 159, 160, 168, 169, 170, 184n11, 184n15, 193n47, 196–97n61, 212n37, 221n65, 225–26n80, 290n77, 302–3n125, 331n74, 341n9, 345n33, 345n40, 350n69, 356n28

Tushnet, Eve, 303–4n126
twelve tribes, 52, 55, 208n11, 242n16, 242–43n18

ugliness, 39, 179, 228–29n7, 232n37, 237n82
unchaste, 104, 105
unhappiness, 123, 150, 253n74
union with God, 46, 47, 143, 150, 220–21n63, 255n96, 351n76
utilitarian, 188–89n33, 206–7n8, 263n147, 285n65, 352n87

vainglory, 337n111
Van De Walle, Bernie, 176
Vargas Llosa, Mario, 162, 347n45
vegetarianism, 239nn2–3, 251–52n70
vengeance and vengefulness, 8, 82, 107, 114, 118, 119, 120, 121, 204n88, 317n31, 317n33
Verhey, Allen, 246n39, 316n26
vice(s), 11, 46, 48, 61, 69, 71, 72, 75, 77, 85, 94, 96, 104, 120, 121, 123, 131, 154, 155, 156, 160, 165, 168, 170, 171, 176, 177, 193n47, 195n57, 198–99n65, 228–29n7, 232n37, 233n50, 248n53, 258n110, 319–20n80, 324n15, 335n107, 342n11, 343n18, 350n73, 355n21, 355–56n25
  capital vice, 258n110
  vicious acts, 40
violence, 83, 101, 114, 158, 195n57, 316n26, 354n15
  sacred violence, 316n26
virgin(s) and virginity, 6, 21, 82, 90, 101, 111, 178, 203n86, 276–78n43, 292n83, 293n84, 294nn87–88, 297n103, 301–2n125
  consecrated virginity/virgin(s), 94, 95, 101, 294n88
  vow of virginity, 101

virtue
  acquired moral virtues, 10, 190, 196n58, 215n48
  cardinal virtue(s), 2, 6, 14, 15, 24, 49, 131, 142, 197n63, 198n64, 199n67, 210n23, 215n48, 216n49, 217n50, 228n7, 236n77
  Christian virtue, 1, 15, 26, 29, 80, 105, 141, 184, 197n63, 211n27, 231n32
  infused moral virtues, 10, 24, 27, 94, 175, 177, 195n57, 196n58, 198n65, 203n86, 215n48, 354n11, 355n24
  infused virtue(s), 16, 24, 93, 176, 179, 187n28, 189–90n37, 196n58, 203n86, 215n48, 354n11
  moral virtue(s), 5, 8, 10, 24, 27, 43, 94, 142, 175, 177, 187n28, 189–90n37, 195n57, 196n58, 198n65, 201–2n76, 203n86, 210n23, 215n48, 228n7, 231n32, 333–34n101, 342n15, 353n9, 354n11, 355n24
  pagan virtue, 24, 193n47, 203n86
  political and personal virtue, 200–201n72
  principal virtue, 7
  social virtues, 26, 222n67
  theological virtue(s), 5, 24, 27, 184n16, 187n28, 217n51, 333–34n101, 341n6
vitality, 15, 356n27
vocation(s), 19, 20, 21, 22, 29, 61, 90, 96, 102, 136, 140, 187n30, 219–20n57, 230n20, 351n75
  rational vocation, 46
Volf, Miroslav, 305n128, 314n17
von Balthasar, Hans Urs, 5, 14, 123, 186n27, 202n84, 267n8
Vulgate, 44, 68, 72, 73, 117, 165, 166, 235n68, 255n90

432   Index

Wadell, Paul J., 232n40
Waldstein, Michael, 282n57, 296n96
Walker, Margaret Urban, 314–15n17
war(s), 83, 124, 125, 146, 181–82n5, 197n63, 236n79, 316n26, 354n15
weakness, 3, 9, 11, 22, 24, 25, 112, 114, 195n57, 198–99n65, 248–49n62, 259n129
Webster, John, 8, 12, 132, 133, 150, 154, 195n57
wedding banquet, 54
Weithman, Paul J., 324n15
Welch, Lawrence J., 307n132
Wesley, John, 250–51n67
Westberg, Daniel A., 91, 210n23, 217–18n53, 253n74, 282n58
Western culture, 51
Westfall, Cynthia Long, 195n57
Wheeler-Reed, David, 264–65n3
White, Kevin, 247n51
wicked, 40, 157, 170
wickedness, 16, 31, 41, 83, 123
Wiley, Tatha, 298n109, 309–10n142
Willard, Dallas, 240–41n8
Wilson, Gary, 226n84
Wirzba, Norman, 51, 56, 61, 68, 165, 171, 239nn2–3, 243nn21–22, 246n45, 263n145, 346–47n44, 349n56, 352n87
Wisdom of God, 5, 344n25

Wisdom of Solomon, 59, 157, 158, 198n64, 344n23
wise *logos*, 191–92n43
Witherington, Ben, III, 78
Wolfe, Gregory, 310n144
wonder, 8, 29, 345n33
Word of God, 22, 23, 90, 119, 187n30, 276n43, 280–81n51
worship, 21, 31, 36, 37, 38, 39, 42, 44–45, 46, 47, 48–49, 53, 58, 59, 63, 64, 65, 70, 76, 79, 101, 115, 129, 156, 211n27, 229n11, 244n30, 245n35, 248–49n62, 257–58n107, 275n41, 275–76n42, 330–31n70, 347n45
"rational worship," 46, 49
"spiritual worship," 38
worshiping, 39, 58, 59, 64, 70, 76, 257–58n107
worshiping God, 39, 64, 70, 76
worship of God, 31, 47, 70, 101
Wright, N. T., 7, 12, 19, 29, 32, 52, 79, 81, 84, 110, 129, 175, 191n39, 197n63, 209n13
Wyschogrod, Edith, 322n10

yada, 192n44

zeal, 339n142
Zion, 34, 159

MATTHEW LEVERING is the James N. and Mary D. Perry, Jr. Chair of Theology at Mundelein Seminary. He is the author of four previous books with the University of Notre Dame Press, including *Mary's Bodily Assumption* (2014).

www.ingramcontent.com/pod-product-compliance
Lightning Source LLC
Chambersburg PA
CBHW021814300426
44114CB00009BA/166